The Native Peoples
of North America

The Native Peoples
of North America

A HISTORY

Bruce E. Johansen

RUTGERS UNIVERSITY PRESS

NEW BRUNSWICK, NEW JERSEY, AND LONDON

Library of Congress Cataloging-in-Publication Data

Johansen, Bruce E. (Bruce Elliott), 1950–
    The native peoples of North America : a history / Bruce E. Johansen.
        p. cm.
    Includes bibliographical references and index.
    ISBN 978-0-8135-3899-0 (alk. paper)
    1. Indians of North America—Study and teaching.   2. Indians of North America—
History.   3. Indians of North America—Social life and customs.   I. Title.

    E76.6.J65 2005
    970.004'97—dc22

A British Cataloging-in-Publication record for this book is available from
the British Library.

The Native Peoples of North America: A History, Volumes I and II, by Bruce E.
Johansen, was originally published in hardcover by Praeger Publishers, an imprint
of Greenwood Publishing Group, Inc., 88 Post Road West, Westport, CT 06881.
First published in paperback by Rutgers University Press, 2006, by arrangement
with Greenwood Publishing Group, Inc. All rights reserved.

Manufactured in the United States of America

Contents

Preface

 *T*his book is a revival of a rather old tradition—an attempt to survey Native American history in North America. This tradition has been represented admirably in the past by, among others, Brandon (1961), Collier (1947), McNickle (1949), Driver (1969), and Maxwell (1978). The idea of a single historical treatment is being revived by other authors as well, including Robert W. Venables's *American Indian History: Five Centuries of Conflict and Coexistence* (2003) and Steve Talbot's *Contemporary Indian Nations of North America: An Indigenist Perspective* (2004).

A need for such a work exists for the many students at university level who take introductory classes in Native American studies. My own institution, a state university of middling size in the Midwest, offers six to eight sections of this class each semester, with thirty-five to fifty students in each section. The field is interdisciplinary, so content depends on the academic origins of instructors: One may hail from religion, but others are from history, literature, sociology, law, and other fields. Given the lack of general texts, students often are told to read a broad survey of books, such as those by Oswalt (2002), Wilson (1998), Stannard (1992), Garbarino and Sasso (1994), Kehoe (1992), Nabokov (1991), and Wright (1992).

My scope is historical, mainly across the continental United States, with occasional forays into Mexico and Mesoamerica. The cultures are so fascinating that I feel no book of this type could be complete without a description of them. I also occasionally take up subject matter in Canada, mainly concerning contemporary affairs, such as the plight of Pikangikum, one of the most desolate native settlements in North America, as well as Canadian Native peoples' efforts to win compensation for abuses suffered in residential schools.

My wife, Pat Keiffer, asked me once if this book would be "complete." No, I answered, not in the sense that it will encompass all that is known about

Native American history. Such a publication would be too heavy to lift. As with any survey of a much larger body of knowledge, this book is selective and is reflective of work I have done and people with whom I have worked during the past thirty years.

Each attempt to survey this body of knowledge has been different in time and temper. I have sought to bring my account up to date, again being selective. Readers will find an emphasis, for example, on new developments in archeology, which is a surprisingly fluid and lively field. For example, new information has emerged regarding the antiquity of the Olmecs' (and, later, Maya's and Aztecs') writing systems. New information on the Incas' writing system and that of the Iroquois is included as well.

New evidence also is offered here that drought as well as intensifying warfare played important roles in the demise of high civilization among the Maya. New information also has been described in primary literature regarding the antiquity of human occupancy in the Americas going back thirty thousand years or more, mainly in present-day Chile and at other sites in South America. The new finds generally impeach assumptions that all Native Americans migrated to the Americas over the Bering Strait, or that Clovis-style cultures were the earliest peoples in the Americas. New archeological findings (notably regarding the nearly complete skeleton of 9,300-year-old Kennewick Man) bring into question simplistic assumptions about how human beings came to the Americas. Recent studies also have produced new information regarding the founding date of the Haudenosaunee (Iroquois) Confederacy that places this important event at about 1100 C.E., three to four centuries earlier than most academics previously had supposed.

I describe current controversies in Indian country, among them sports mascots, language revival, gambling, repatriation, land claims, and environmental issues, such as the effects of uranium mining on the Navajos. Many contemporary political issues have evolved from earlier events, such as the campaign to revoke Congressional Medals of Honor awarded at Wounded Knee after the massacre there late in 1890. This book also provides in-depth surveys of Native American contributions to general society: political ideas, medicines, foods, women's rights, and so on. This area has been one of my specialties for more than thirty years.

This work also offers analysis of U.S. Census data for 2000, which indicate that Native Americans, once regarded as the "vanishing race," are now the fastest-growing ethnic group in the United States. Some of this is actual increase, and some is the fact that the census now allows people to list more than one ethnic background. Because the census is self-defining, part of the increase may also be "wannabes."

The fact that hundreds of thousands of non-Indians would like to be listed as such at the dawn of the third millennium might have astonished just about anyone living a century earlier. They also might have been astonished to know that many college students today take courses in Native American history—hardly a vanishing race, hardly a vanishing culture, and by no means a vanishing history. Join us on a journey that is wondrous but by no means without profound pain.

In compiling this book, I should acknowledge my colleague Barbara Alice Mann for extracts from her work on the Goschochking (Ohio) massacre of 1782 and the Haudenosaunee origin story. I also acknowledge Donald A. Grinde Jr.; a few sections of what follows are adapted from our *Encyclopedia of Native American Biography* as well as from parts of a prospective textbook manuscript that we developed during the early 1990s but never published, notably parts that he contributed on John Collier's tenure as Indian commissioner, as well as some materials on repatriation. In addition, I need again to thank all the people who keep me going, including wife Pat Keiffer; University of Nebraska at Omaha Communication School Directors Deb Smith-Howell and Jeremy Lipschultz; editor Heather Staines; and the librarians of University of Nebraska at Omaha, who have gotten to know me very well.

FURTHER READING

Brandon, William. *The American Heritage Book of Indians*. New York: Dell, 1961.

Collier, John. *Indians of the Americas*. New York: New American Library, 1947.

Driver, Harold E. *Indians of North America*. 2d ed. Chicago: University of Chicago Press, 1969.

Garbarino, Marvyn S., and Robert F. Sasso. *Native American Heritage*. 3d ed. Long Grove, IL: Waveland Press, 1994.

Kehoe, Alice Beck. *North American Indians: A Comprehensive Account*. 2d ed. Englewood Cliffs, NJ: Prentice-Hall, 1992.

Maxwell, James A., ed. *America's Fascinating Indian Heritage*. Pleasantville, NY: Reader's Digest, 1978.

McNickle, D'Arcy. *They Came Here First: The Epic of the American Indian*. Philadelphia: J. B. Lippincott, 1949.

Nabokov, Peter, ed. *Native American Testimony*. New York: Viking, 1991.

Oswalt, Wendell H. *This Land Was Theirs: A Study of North American Indians*. 7th ed. Boston: McGraw-Hill, 2002.

Stannard, David E. *American Holocaust: The Conquest of the New World*. New York: Oxford University Press, 1992.

Talbot, Steve. *Contemporary Indian Nations of North America: An Indigenist Perspective*. New York: Prentice-Hall, 2004.

Venables, Robert W. *American Indian History: Five Centuries of Conflict and Coexistence*. Santa Fe, NM: Clear Light Publishers, 2003.

Wilson, James. *The Earth Shall Weep: A History of Native America*. Boston: Atlantic Monthly Press, 1998.

Wright, Ronald. *Stolen Continents: The Americas through Indian Eyes Since 1492*. Boston: Houghton-Mifflin, 1992.

Introduction

My sketch of Native American history in North America begins with Native origins, continues with European colonization and its explosive movement westward during the first years of the nineteenth century, and ends with Native peoples' present-day economic and cultural revival.

This account commences with human origins in the Americas—an account, like many to be considered here, which is subject to conjecture. The hundreds of Native peoples who lived in North America before sustained contact with Europeans and other immigrants have their own explanations of how and when they originated. An example is provided by the origin account of the Haudenosaunee (Iroquois) story, by Barbara Alice Mann, of Turtle Island's origins, Skywoman's descent, and the adventures of her two sons.

Chapter 1 next considers origin accounts advanced by Western scientists, principally archeologists. Fifty years ago, Native Americans generally were believed by such academicians to have arrived in the Americas across the Bering Strait within ten thousand years of the present, a neat migration pattern that was said to have filled various parts of the continent with a trail of Clovis spear points. Since then, origin dates have receded; thirty thousand years is becoming respectable now, with speculation reaching further back in time. The Bering Strait is still one possible route but probably not the only one. The first chapter of this book details an irony that has been receiving increasing attention: If the primary migration route was the far north, why are some of the oldest Native remains being found in South America, notably present-day Chile? Another complicating factor has been the recent discovery of Kennewick Man, a nearly complete skeleton dated to more than nine thousand years of age, with features closely resembling no present-day ethnic group.

Development of human societies in North America are followed in this account to the point at which sizable urban areas such as Cahokia (near contemporary St. Louis, MO) served complex trading networks. Some insight is then provided into Native systems of agricultural production and family life that may have greeted the first Europeans, the Vikings, who probably explored small parts of North America about a thousand years ago.

A major issue of conjecture in scholarly circles has revolved around the number of people living in North America before sustained contact with Europeans began following the voyages of Columbus. This subject has sparked intense debate because various population estimates for North and South America differ by at least a factor of ten, from perhaps 12 million to about 120 million. The higher estimates provided by demographic historian Henry F. Dobyns have prompted some of the most intense debate.

Chapter 2 describes the fascinating histories of early Mesoamerican peoples, beginning with the Olmecs, continuing with residents of Mexico's Central Valley, culminating with the Aztecs and the Maya. Special attention is paid to recent discoveries of complex written communication among the Olmecs that probably provided a basis for similar writing systems used by the Maya and Aztecs. Emphasis is provided for recent findings advancing archeologists' understanding of the Mayan language and its revelation of frictions swathed in bloody conflict resulting in widespread war between city-states that probably ended the Maya's classic civilization. Before their decline, the Maya produced considerable written history, a precise calendar reaching to 3114 B.C.E., and a wealth of astronomical observations, some of which even today are among the most accurate in the world. Chapter 2 concludes with the Spanish conquest of Mesoamerica; the Spaniards marveled at the Aztec capital of Tenochtitlan (on the site of today's Mexico City) before their diseases and gold lust destroyed it.

The Spanish soon extended their influence north, west, and east as well, from Florida to California, the primary focus of the narrative at the beginning of chapter 3. This chapter details the expansion of the Spanish Empire and the toll it took on Native peoples, notably the cruelty chronicled by the Catholic priest Bartolome de las Casas, the leading advocate of inquiries into the cruel underside of the Spanish conquest. Las Casas himself chronicled the Spanish brutality against the Native peoples in excruciating detail, as he campaigned to end at least some of it.

Chapter 3 continues the historical narrative of European immigration with the first substantial English colonization on the eastern seaboard of North America, first at Jamestown, in Virginia (1607), then at Plymouth Rock, Massachusetts, in 1620. From a Native point of view, the story is told with some irony as Squanto, who had been to both England and Spain before the Pilgrims set foot in America, greeted them in English. Particular attention is paid to the associations of Roger Williams (dissident Puritan founder of Rhode Island) with Native peoples of the area because these events provide a rare window on intercultural life at the time. Williams was a witness to events, such as the Pequot

War and King Phillip's War, which markedly diminished Native populations and estate in the land that came to be called New England. Williams also was one of few European Americans known as a friend of the native leader Metacom, who was drawn and quartered at the end of the war named after his English name (King Phillip).

Chapter 4 begins with a description of the Iroquois Confederacy's influential role in the seventeenth century, detailing the confederacy's influence in shaping immigrant Europeans' notions of democracy during the next century. The founding of the confederacy is described in detail, with relatively new information regarding its founding date, which is now believed to be 1142 C.E., about four centuries earlier than most dates advanced heretofore by scholars. (The 1142 C.E. date, advanced by Barbara A. Mann and Jerry Fields, is, however, close to some estimates maintained by several Iroquois traditionalists.) This chapter ends with consideration of the Iroquois role in treaty diplomacy and the fur trade, as well as the advent of Handsome Lake's code, a religion that combined traditional and European American religious elements.

By shortly after 1800, European American migration was exploding westward across North America, propelled by the deteriorating economic situation in Europe (especially for the lower-middle classes of the British Isles, a motor of emigration). By midcentury, completion of cross-continental railroad links sped westward movement considerably. Only sixty years separate intensive European American settlement in the Southeast (with the Removal Act of 1830 and the Trail of Tears eight years later) from the Wounded Knee massacre in 1890. The intensity of conflict in the Ohio Valley often has been downplayed in survey histories. The Ohio area was key to the rush westward as several Native alliances tried and eventually failed to stem the advance, beginning with Pontiac, continuing with Little Turtle and Tecumseh, ending with Black Hawk. This period included not only vicious genocidal attacks, such as one at Goschocking, described in chapter 5 by Barbara A. Mann, but also the largest single battlefield defeat of the U.S. Army at the hands of Native Americans during 1791.

In the Southeast, the Cherokees and other "civilized" Native nations prospered for a time in their homelands by building European-style farms and villages until removal forced them westward on the many trails of tears. This narrative includes human history's only single-handed construction of a written language (Sequoyah, in Cherokee), as well as high drama regarding removal in front of John Marshall's U.S. Supreme Court. Marshall found for the Cherokees, but President Andrew Jackson ignored the Court, an impeachable offense under the Constitution. Why wasn't Jackson impeached? Removal had become a states' rights issue; enforcement of the Constitution could have provoked the Civil War during the 1830s instead of the 1860s. In this case, states rights politics trumped the Constitution.

Chapter 5 ends in the middle of the nineteenth century, as a young, muscular United States of America, empowering itself with the national creation myth of "manifest destiny," exploded across North America, east to west, pushing surviving Native Americans westward as well, in one of human history's swiftest demographic movements. Within a generation of the Civilized Tribes' trails of tears, the United States had severed nearly half of Mexico, discovered gold in California, sent Native peoples packing from the site of Seattle, and sent its Navy to Japan to deliver a forceful knock on its door, demanding trade relationships. The speed of U.S. expansion is illustrated by the fact that the Navy's visit to Tokyo occurred during the same decade (the 1850s) that the government negotiated treaties in the Pacific Northwest, not even a generation after the Cherokees' removal.

In Benjamin Franklin's time, general opinion among European immigrants in America held that many centuries might pass before their offspring would expand to fill the width of North America. Before the advent of fossil-fueled industry, railroads, the cotton gin, repeating rifles, and massive immigration from Europe, Africa, and Asia, westward movement proceeded slowly—from the Atlantic's shores to the crest of the eastern mountains, for the most part—during roughly two hundred years. Within a century after Franklin's death in 1790, however, the U.S. government declared the settlement frontier closed, the buffalo were slaughtered, and the last Native military resistance was quelled. After the massacre at Wounded Knee (1890), Native peoples engaged in an often-covert battle to survive, living in what amounted to open-air concentration camps. The fry bread that is so ubiquitous at today's powwows was born of starvation rations: white flour, lard, a frying pan, and an open fire. From there, the twentieth century tells a story of recovery for North America's Native peoples, including the reclamation of land, language, and cultures.

Chapter 6 begins with a description of Northwest Coast Native peoples, who were unique given their hierarchical social structure and ability to build a high civilization without organized agriculture. By the 1850s, barely fifty years after the Lewis and Clark expedition reached the mouth of the Columbia River, European American immigrants were building the city of Seattle on Puget Sound and lobbying the federal government to make their city the terminus of a transcontinental railroad. Chief Sea'th'l, after whom the city was named, was leading his people across Puget Sound, away from the expanding urban area, following his evocative farewell speech.

At about the same time, Anglo-American immigration slammed into California with notable violence as whole Native peoples were exterminated following initiation of a major gold rush that followed the war with Mexico and the area's acquisition by the United States. By the 1870s, European American migration was closing on North America's interior from the east and the west. Chapter 6 ends with the Long March of Chief Joseph's Nez Perce, more than 1,500 miles over some of North America's roughest and most beautiful country, where on October 7, 1877, Chief Joseph and his people surrendered.

By the last decades of the nineteenth century, the U.S. Army, aided by massive slaughter of the buffalo (the basis of the Plains Native economy) as well as waves of smallpox and other diseases, was isolating the last organized Native resistance in the middle of the continent. Chapter 7 describes Native American peoples who began the century as mounted lords of the plains and ended it as prisoners. Sometimes, as at Sand Creek, they were massacred in these camps. The Navajos were forced from their homelands on a journey they still call the "Long Walk," as the U.S. Army pursued the Apaches, led by a number of notable individuals, including the legendary Geronimo. Resistance, as in the Great Sioux Uprising of 1862, was met with brutal repression—in this case, the largest mass hanging in U.S. history at Mankato, Minnesota.

Another kind of resistance, the defeat of George Armstrong Custer and his troops at the Little Bighorn during the summer of 1876, also was met with a broadside of attacks. Yellow Hair, the Boy General, was hardly a model officer. He was disobeying orders at the time, ignoring the reports of his Native scouts regarding the size of the Indian camp, and driving his forces to exhaustion on a risky publicity stunt, but Custer was nonetheless lionized as an ad hoc hero in another century's war on terror.

Even during the cruelest century for Native Americans, local exceptions to the general tenor of conflict occasionally came to light. The Poncas, for example, were forced off their homeland in northern Nebraska during the late 1870s by a clerical error that deeded their land to the Sioux, their traditional enemies. Exiled in Indian Territory (later called Oklahoma), a band of Poncas led by Chief Standing Bear resolved to walk home against the orders of the U.S. Army. Starving, having eaten their horses and their moccasins, the Poncas arrived in Omaha, then a frontier town, as a newspaperman, Thomas Tibbles, took up their case. The people of Omaha rallied behind the Poncas; the Army was taken to federal court, and the Poncas were declared "persons" under U.S. law, the first time this status had been accorded Native Americans. They were eventually permitted to go home.

More characteristically, however, the nineteenth century brought exile and death to Native leaders, notably Crazy Horse and Sitting Bull, as some well-known European Americans, such as *Oz* books' author L. Frank Baum (then a newspaper editor in South Dakota), called for extermination of remaining Native peoples. Chapter 7 ends with the massacre at Wounded Knee and its aftermath as reported by a Native American woman, Susette LaFlesche, Thomas Tibbles's wife.

As the nineteenth century became the twentieth, Native Americans faced recovery from devastating travails that provoked anthropologists and other non-Indians to call them "the vanishing race." They never vanished, however. Instead, survivors coped with a system that sought to assimilate them as an alternative to outright annihilation. As Richard Henry Pratt, who founded the system of boarding schools, put it: "Kill the Indian, Save the Man." Chapter 8 develops the many forms that assimilation took at century's turn, from boarding schools to allotment of property meant to turn Native Americans into individual farmers. All this was presented to survivors of the nineteenth-century holocaust as a favor for their own good, despite the fact that, in some cases, 90 percent of collective land base was taken from them.

Some Native peoples found ways to turn allotment on its head. The Osages, for example, exiled in Indian Territory, found themselves quite by geological accident atop a cache of oil and natural gas at the dawn of the automotive age. In 1906, when allotment came to them, the Osages used its provisions to protect common ownership of their oil and gas, a policy they have since maintained with considerable legal diligence. For most Native peoples, how-ever, allotment was a socioeconomic disaster. The Meriam Report (1928) pointed out just how closely Native poverty could be related to its provisions. During the 1930s, Franklin Roosevelt's Bureau of Indian Affairs, directed by John Collier, reversed the older policies, allowed some additions to Native land base, and implemented limited self-government under the Indian Re-organization Act. By the 1950s, however, established interests were eroding Native American lands again by terminating entire reservations and moving Indian people to urban areas under the "relocation" program.

In the 1960s, a new wave of Native American activism was becoming very direct, personal, and sometimes personally risky for participants. Chapter 9 describes fishing rights protests in the Pacific Northwest that led to a land-mark legal ruling by Judge George H. Boldt, opening to Native peoples access to as many as half the salmon returning to local waters. Alcatraz Island, in San Francisco Bay, was occupied during 1969. Native activists seeking to publi-cize the abrogation of treaties marched across the United States during the late summer and early autumn of 1972, barricading themselves inside the Washington, D.C., headquarters of the Bureau of Indian Affairs. A few months later, activists occupied the village of Wounded Knee on the Pine Ridge Reservation, bringing an avalanche of media attention to the new American Indian Movement. After it ended in May 1973, the Wounded Knee occupation provoked a wave of armed repression at Pine Ridge, during which at least sixty-six people, many of them political activists, were killed by violent means. For a time, the Pine Ridge Reservation had a higher murder rate than Detroit, Michigan, which was reputed at the time to have been the murder capital of the United States. An era of public activism ended during the late 1970s with the pursuit, arrest, trial, and conviction (using questionable evi-dence) of Leonard Peltier, who later became an international symbol of Native political resistance in the Americas.

Chapter 10 presents a summary of ways in which Native American lifeways have influenced general society in America and, through the spread of its ways of life, the entire world. Aside from the usual important items that we use every day (corn and potatoes, for example), Native history may be traced through items and ideas so often utilized today that most people have forgotten their origins. The place names of half the states, for example, have Native American roots. More than two hundred drugs in the U.S. *Pharmacopoeia* were first used by American Indians. Any game that is played with a bouncing ball owes something to Native American sports at some point in its evolution. Before contact with the Americas, Europe had no rubber and thus no rubber balls. The tomatoes in Italian pasta sauces, the "Irish" potato, "Indian" curry, and Jewish potato latkes all at some point in history were borrowed from their first cultivators, American Indians. In addition to material gifts, Sally Roesch Wagner details how much the founding mothers of American feminism, including Elizabeth Cady Stanton and Matilda Joslyn Gage, borrowed from the clan mothers of the Haudanosaunee (Iroquois) Confederacy.

Chapter 11 brings the narrative to the present day with a survey of contemporary reservation economic conditions in South Dakota, a corrective for anyone who thinks that modern-day reservation gambling has made all Native Americans rich. Aside from some of the poorest counties in the United States, Native peoples also occupy some of Canada's most desolate real estate, as characterized here by the village of Pikangikum, where many young people pass the time sniffing gasoline. Alcoholism is still a plague in the cities as well as on rural reservations. Readers will become acquainted in this chapter with the hamlet of Whiteclay, Nebraska, where the major business is selling beer and other alcoholic beverages to Indians of the neighboring Pine Ridge Reservation, where such sales are illegal.

Is gambling the answer? The "new buffalo," as some Native Americans have called it? Some places, such as the Pequots' Foxwoods in Connecticut and some other locales, have been enriched. In other places, such as the New York Oneidas' lands in upstate New York, gambling has provided an enriched upper class the means to hire police to force antigambling traditionalists from their homes. Among the Mohawks at Akwesasne, people have died over the issue. Akwesasne's position on the U.S.–Canadian border also has made smuggling of cigarettes, liquor, other drugs, weapons, and human beings a major industry.

Native America today presents a varied mosaic of life, death, and pervasive struggle. In this book's final chapter, readers will come to know Navajos who mined some of the uranium that powered the nation's nuclear arsenal. Many of them later died painfully, irradiated from the inside out, of lung cancer. Readers also will come to know activists who campaign against the use of Native symbols as sports mascots, something that often has been handled with deft humor, as in the case of the "Fighting Whities," an intramural basketball team in Colorado, which stirred a national debate by adopting an upper middle class European American image as a mascot. Other activists struggle to remove the word *squaw* (which has been associated with references to Native women's vaginas) from place names. Struggles are ongoing to return Native

The Native Peoples
of North America

CHAPTER 1

Early Indigenous North America

AN OVERVIEW

Exploration of indigenous North America's prehistory can be an unexpectedly rocky journey, full of questions raised to challenge assumptions often based on scant evidence. It also can be a journey into a world of wonders, of watching, as best we know on limited evidence, how hundreds of Native cultures evolved over many thousands of years. If human beings were present in the Western Hemisphere for at least 30,000 years before Columbus arrived, as now seems likely, they had been forming and re-forming societies for sixty times the length of time since "old" and "new" worlds began shaping each other in a substantial way with the arrival of Columbus. The most intriguing aspect of this journey is that many of us—even "experts" of various scholarly stripes—are still discovering America. Our knowledge, especially regarding how people lived before the coming of Europeans and other transoceanic immigrants, is still so scanty and subject to so much debate that we should be prepared to be surprised, and sometimes awed, by the peoples and cultures that flourished here.

For the most part, we have very little knowledge that has been related by Native peoples themselves describing how their ancestors lived before roughly 1500 C.E. Some had forms of writing, and they kept some records, but many of these records were misunderstood for what they were and were destroyed by European immigrants. Along with shreds of evidence provided by archaeology, often we have only verbal snapshots left us by immigrants whose main purpose was not preservation and description, but plunder and destruction. Even the best-trained modern experts sometimes have missed clues to the far past of indigenous America because of ethnocentric biases.

The texture of prehistory in the Old World is much more detailed, largely because the peoples who provided them to us still live in substantial numbers. In America, in contrast, we often have but fragments of oral history handed down by obliterated generations who have had to struggle to maintain their traditional ways of life. Native languages—entire "libraries" of native experience—are being lost with the rapidity of rare plant species. For every detail unearthed by scholars, more of America's earliest oral history is dying. Histories of great value have been lost when the people who maintained them through time dwindled to a few, then none. We frequently have tantalizing evidence of civilizations with nearly no voices from the past to explain how people lived, thought, fought, and died.

RECENT SURPRISES IN THE AMAZON VALLEY

Modern archeology regularly provides surprises. For example, researchers working in the Amazon River basin during 2003 discovered a fifteen-square-mile region at the headwaters of the Upper Xingu River that contained at least nineteen villages of 2,500 to 55,000 people each; these villages were spaced at regular intervals of between one and two miles, connected by wide roads, and surrounded by evidence of intense agriculture. This discovery upended long-held assumptions that the rain forest was a pristine wilderness before its first visits by Europeans, as well as assumptions that the environment of the area could not support sophisticated civilizations. For many years, archeologists had argued with considerable conviction that the soil of the Amazon Valley was too poor to support large populations. The ancient residents intensively cultivated cassava, which grows well in poor soil.

These researchers, including some descendants of pre-Columbian Native peoples who lived in the area, found evidence of densely settled, well-organized communities with roads, moats, and bridges. Some of the area's precisely de-signed roads were more than fifty yards wide. The people of the area cleared large areas of the rain forest to plant orchards; they preserved other areas as sources of wood, medicinal plants, and animals.

Michael J. Heckenberger, first author of an article in *Science* (2003), said that the ancestors of the Kuikuro people in the Amazon basin had a "complex and sophisticated" civilization with a population of many thousands before 1492. "These people were not the small mobile bands or simple dispersed popula-tions" that some earlier studies had suggested, he said (according to Recer, 2003). "They were not organized in cities," Heckenberger said. "There was a different pattern of small settlements, but they were all tightly integrated" (Recer, 2003). The extent of the road network is unknown at this time. "Here we present clear evidence of large, regional social formations (circa 1250 to 1650 C.E.) and their substantive influence on the landscape," wrote Heck-enberger and colleagues (2003, 1,710). "This is an incredibly important indi-cator of a complex society," said Susanna Hecht, a geographer at Stanford University's Center for Advanced Study in the Behavioral Sciences; "the extent of population density and landscape domestication is extraordinary" (Stokstad, 2003, 1,645).

According to a 2003 Associated Press account by Paul Recer, Heckenberger said that "the Amazon people moved huge amounts of dirt to build roads and plazas. At one place, there is evidence that they even built a bridge spanning a major river. The people also altered the natural forest, planting and maintaining orchards and agricultural fields, and the effects of this stewardship can still be seen today." Diseases such as smallpox and measles, brought to the New World by European explorers, probably killed most of the population along the Amazon, he said. By the time scientists began studying the indigenous people, the population was sparse and far-flung. As a result, some researchers assumed that the same pattern had been common prior to European exploration. Heckenberger's assertions have been questioned, however, by Betty J. Meggers of the Smithsonian Institution's National Museum of Natural History, who asserted in *Science* (Meggers et al., 2003, 2,067) that this study says little about population density in the Amazon Valley because the site is peripheral to the rain forest.

AMERICAN ORIGINS

Any serious student of Native North America will come to appreciate a diversity of peoples and cultures equal to any area of comparable size in the Old World. In 1492, Native Americans in North and South America spoke an estimated two thousand mutually unintelligible languages: roughly 250 in North America, 350 in present-day Mexico and Central America, and an astonishing 1,400 in South America. This is a greater degree of language diversity than existed in all of the Old World (Sherzer, 1992, 251). We have, however, little tangible evidence of what many of these different peoples may have talked about. Although bones and pottery can be unearthed and carbon dated, ideas are as perishable and mutable as memory in a time when few things were written and fewer writings preserved.

People in every culture on earth maintain accounts that explain how its people and their ways of life came to be. As with the Christian Garden of Eden's Adam and Eve, the Native American peoples of the Americas explained their own origins in their own ways. A condensed version of the Haudenosaunee (Iroquois) origin story follows. This account and many others may be compared with long-held assumptions of Western scholarly inquiry in which nearly all investigators believe that the first people of the Americas arrived from somewhere else. The most common point of origin is still believed to have been northeastern Asia, probably parts of Siberia. As arrival dates have been pushed back, however, the case for a simple, single migration across one land bridge has weakened. As the date when the first Americans are believed to have arrived recedes, the case for several migrations over land (as well as sea voyage arrivals from other continents, such as Africa to present-day Brazil) would seem to become more likely. Origins on the American land itself, maintained by many native peoples, also have a place in today's literature.

⁓

The Haudenosaunee Creation

Barbara Alice Mann

The original ancestors of the Iroquois were the Sky People, denizens of *Karionake*, "The Place in the Sky," commonly called Sky World, a physical place that floated among the stars "on the farther side of the visible sky" ("Mohawk Creation," 32; Hewitt, 1903, 141). Sky World was well populated, with a social order that greatly resembled later Iroquoian society. The people lived in close-knit, matrilineal clans. The Sky People were greatly gifted with *uki-okton* power. In a Mohawk Keeping, it is said that the Sky People "had greatly developed what scientists call E.S.P." ("Mohawk Creation," 1989, 32), a talent later valued by their earthly descendants, especially for tapping into dream knowledge. The geography of Sky World also resembled that of Iroquoia, with trees, crops, and longhouses. All of the flora and fauna later present in physical form on earth had spiritual counterparts (Elder Siblings) preexisting in Sky World. These animal spirit Elders took part in Sky councils and performed creative tasks (Barbeau, 1915, 41–44; Hewitt, 1928, 465).

In the center of Sky World grew a wonderful tree that, running the length of Sky World, held it together from top to bottom. Some say it was a wild cherry tree, and others call it a crabapple tree; still others call it a pilar. The Tuscarora call it a dogwood tree. An Onondaga version named the tree *Ono'ꞌdjă*, or "Tooth," presumably indicating the yellow dogtooth violet. The tree itself was sacred, supplying food that the Sky People might gather. It sprouted from the sides and fell to the ground to be collected, just for the thinking.

Several traditions speak of the conception, birth, childhood, and youth of the girl who was to become Sky Woman, also called *Awenhai* (Fertile Earth), *Ataensic* (Mature Flowers), *Otsitsa* (Corn), and eventually, *Iagentci* (Ancient One, or Grandmother). Sky Woman's mother dallied with a man she did not actually love, enticing him daily by "disentangling" his hair. ("Combing out the hair" was a metaphor for interpreting dreams, part of making them true. It was a spiritual talent.) This unfortunate man, the father of Sky Woman, died before she was born and was "buried" high in the tree of Sky World. His was the first death ever to occur in Sky World, a spirit sign. Sky Woman grew up quickly (another sign of spirit power), in constant mourning for the father she never knew, prompting her grandmother to show her where her father had been buried (Hewitt, 1903, 141–149, 256–265). In another version, the deceased was not a sperm father, but the girl's maternal uncle (Hewitt, 1928, 470). This cultural tidbit seems authentically old because the mother's matrilineal brother, not an out-clan biological father, was traditionally the male authority figure of a longhouse and often was called "Father."

Sky Woman's husband is usually called the Ancient. She was soon with child through the sharing of breath with her husband (Hewitt, 1903, 167).

Skywoman on Turtle's back. (Courtesy of John Kahionhes Fadden.)

In one Seneca version, Sky Woman gave birth to her child in Sky World, but this seems anomalous (ibid., 223). In nearly every other collected version, she was pregnant when she arrived on earth, delivering her daughter there. The Ancient was the presiding officer of Sky World, who lodged in the shade of Tooth.

Dreams were very important to the Sky People. It was necessary not only to understand them, but also to reenact them, thus continually creating reality. One day, the Ancient had a troubling dream, which made him ill. In a Seneca version, he had dreamed that a great "cloud sea" swam around under Tooth, the ocean of a restless and unlit world. Its spirit was calling out to the Sky People for aid in overcoming its extreme loneliness (Converse, 1908, 33).

All of the Elders of the later plants and animals, as well as the heavenly bodies and elements associated with earth, came to peer over the edge at the water world. Deer, Spotted Fawn, Bear, Beaver, the Moving Wind, Daylight, Night, Thick Night, the Sun, Spring Water, Corn, Beans, Squash, Sunflower, Fire Dragon, Meteor, Rattle, Otter, Wolf, Duck, Fresh Water, Medicine, Aurora Borealis, and of course, the Great Turtle, visited the window onto earth (Hewitt, 1903, 173–175). Some add that the Blue Sky, the Air, the Thunderers, the Tree, the Bush, the Grass, the Moon, the Star, and the Sun looked as well (Hewitt, 1928, 473). The hole at the base of Tooth became a regular Sky World tourist destination.

Skywoman Falls to Earth

Having uprooted the tree, the Ancient was thus able to fulfill the second part of his dream, that his wife was to fall through the hole in Sky World, down to the water world below. Occasionally, it is said that she fell because of her own curiosity, having leaned too far over the edge for a better look at earth (Parker, 1913, 6). Some Wyandot Keepings depict the illness as Sky Woman's, not the Ancient's, stating that, to cure her, an aged shaman uprooted the tree, laying Sky Woman as near as possible to its medicinal roots—too near, as it turned out because the soil was unstable, and the sick girl was sucked down into the hole and rolled into the void (Barbeau, 1915, 37).

In yet another variant, this one Mohawk, her husband was considerate, not cruel, and gathered the living bark of Tooth for tea to calm the cravings of his pregnant wife. It was his kind deed that caused the Sky tree to collapse, opening the window onto earth below and occasioning her slip ("Mohawk Creation," 1989, 32). Most Haudenosaunee keep the version of the bad-tempered Ancient, however, attributing Sky Woman's tumble to his jealousy. In several versions, the Ancient was irrationally jealous of the Aurora Borealis, the Fire Dragon, and especially of Sky Woman, who was more gifted with *uki-okton* than he.

Although unable to climb back up the ledge, she did acquire seeds from the munificent Tree. In her right hand, she garnered the Three Sisters: Corn, Beans, and Squash. Some say she also laid hold of Tobacco in her left hand. A Seneca version claimed that the white Fire Dragon or the Blue Panther—an *okton* spirit jealously sought by the Ancient—was at the root hole just as Sky Woman fell. In this version, it was the Blue Panther who gave her Corn, mortar, and pestle (Hewitt, 1903, 224, and 1928, 481; Cornplanter, 1928, 9, 13). Jesse Cornplanter said that it was the Ancient, himself, who threw the Elder plants (corn, beans, squash, sunflower, tobacco) along with the Elder Animals (Deer, Wolf, Bear, Beaver, etc.) down the abyss after her in a final frenzy of rage ([1938] 1992, 10).

In all versions, however, Skywoman slid down, down, down through space and into the atmosphere of Earth. (The suggestion of tradition is that the strong spirit of Sky Woman's father had foreseen all of these events so necessary to the beginning of human life on earth, and that this was why he had urged his daughter on to such an unfortunate marriage, with all of its character-building trials and tribulations.) Sick of the disruption in Sky World, on her fall through the hole in Sky World, the Sky People set Tooth, the Tree of Light, back into its socket (Hewitt, 1928, 480).

Now, the Elder creatures of earth, alerted first by the far-sighted Eagle, saw Sky Woman falling. For the first time, lightning (the Fire Dragon or Meteor Man) streaked across the sky of earth at her side as she hurtled through the atmosphere (Parker, 1912, 6). Sweeping into action, Heron and Loon caught and held the frightened Sky Woman aloft on their interlocking wings while, in an amusing portion of the tradition, the Great Tortoise sent around a moccasin; that is, he called an emergency council of Elder animals to see what was to be done. (For a sprightly Wyandot version of the Elder animals' Creation Council, see Barbeau, 1915, 38–44.) Knowing that she was a Sky Woman, unable to live on their watery planet, the Elder Spirits of earth creatures all quickly agreed that she should not be dropped into the waters to die.

The Origin of Turtle Island

In every version, the great Snapping Turtle offered his carapace, vowing to carry the earth above him forever as he swam. The idea gained ready assent, and the council of earth Elders assembled its divers. Usually, the divers were said to have been Muskrat, Otter, Toad, or Beaver. In some versions, the Muskrat and Otter die in the attempt to bring up dirt in their mouths, with Beaver finally bringing it up on his tail, or Toad in his mouth. A Mohawk version has poor, dead Muskrat floating to the surface, his mouth smeared with the dirt that was to become earth (Hewitt, 1903, 287). A Seneca version says that it was Sky Woman, herself, who arrived with the dirt of Sky World on her hands and under her fingernails, gathered as she frantically clutched at the tree roots during her fall (ibid., 226). A tad of dirt now ready to accept her, the Birds were able to set Sky Woman down on her new abode, Turtle Island. Looking around forlornly, alone and torn from everything she had ever known, Sky Woman wept bitterly (ibid., 225).

Wherever Sky Woman went, every kind of plant sprouted up before her. Now, she planted the Three Sacred Sisters she had brought from Sky World. Some say that she found potatoes here (Hewitt, 1903, 226), although potatoes are usually attributed to the little daughter, soon born to her on Turtle Island. The land was full with the harvest, on which Sky Woman lived. As the land was full of growth, so was Sky Woman. She prepared her birthing hut and delivered herself of an infant daughter. They were at that time, the only two human beings on earth.

The Birth of the Twins: Sapling and Flint

Sky Woman continually refused the Earth Elders as consorts of her daughter until one day the matter passed out of her hands. An engaging man-creature came along, his bark robe tossed rakishly over his shoulder, his black hair pulled up, and his handsome eyes gleaming. He was so gorgeous that the Lynx forgot to ask her mother but lay with him immediately. Some assert that the two did not engage in coitus, but that the young man simply lay an arrow next to her body (Hewitt, 1903, 291–292). In an Onondaga version, Sky Woman consented to, rather than resisted, this final match (Hewitt, 1928, 384–385), but most versions showed Sky Woman was dismayed by the Lynx's unauthorized infatuation.

Young love won out, however, and soon the Lynx was pregnant, a fact that caused her mother to tremble. Sky Woman was fearful of the result of a pregnancy between two such different creatures as a Sky Girl and an earth Man-Being. In the very oldest Keepings of Creation, the Lynx was pregnant not with twins (the common Keeping today), but with quadruplets, analogous to the four sacred messengers of the *Gaiwí:yo* and connected with the Four Winds or cardinal directions (Hewitt, 1928, 468). An interesting, potential echo of this ancient Keeping is found in a Seneca version that told the puzzling story of four children—two male and two female—who were Man-Beings (Hewitt, 1903, 233). The story of the quadruplets, however, is almost completely lost today. The four children of the Lynx were eventually compressed to two, with the personality traits of the four redistributed between them.

As told in modern times, the Lynx overheard twin sons in her womb discussing their plans for the earth life they were about to live. One already knew that he was to create game animals and new trees, but the other was more vague on specifics, merely announcing that he, too, would create in one way or another (Hewitt, 1928, 486). Labor pains overcame the Lynx a few days before her time, and she again overheard her sons holding forth, this time in a discussion over how best to be born because neither precisely knew how to do it. In an Onondaga version, one infant pointed toward the birth canal and said, "I'll go that way," and he did, being first born. The Elder Twin became known as *Tharonhiawakon, Odendonnia, Ioskaha* (Sapling), meaning roughly the Spirit of Life (Hewitt, 1903, 138). Sapling was perfectly formed in the eyes of Sky Woman.

The Younger Twin protested his brother's path. "But this other way is so near," he said, pointing in some versions to the armpit and in others to the navel of his mother. "I shall leave that way," he said, and he did, killing his mother in parturition (Hewitt, 1903, 185). Some Mohawks say that the second son, *Tawiskaro^n* (Flint) was born with a comb of flint on his head, by which means he had cut an exit path through his mother's armpit (ibid., 185). Some Senecas say that he leapt forth from her navel, all covered with warts (ibid., 231).

However it happened, by armpit or caesarean section, when Sky Woman saw that her beloved daughter was dead, she sat on the ground and wept inconsolably. She buried her daughter most tenderly, and from the Lynx's grave sprang all the plants of life: Corn, Beans, and Squash grew from her breasts; potatoes sprang from her toes and tobacco grew from her head (Thomas, 2000). The Lynx had transmuted into Mother Earth, a living entity (Hewitt, 1928, 542). Despite the continued spirit existence of her daughter, Sky Woman's grief almost undid her. It was then that Sky Woman grew suddenly old, becoming known in her turn as the Ancient or Grandmother. Her grief soured into a bitterness of temperament that she had not possessed. She became grumpy and impatient in her old age.

Like Sky Woman and the Lynx before them, the Twins grew rapidly, showing their great spirit power. They soon began to complete the process of creation, although there were many disagreements between the brothers as to what final creation should look like. While Sapling was bringing forth his trademark strawberries, Flint was littering the landscape with brambles and briars. If Sapling created peaceful game animals, Flint responded with a spate of roaring, clawing, dangerous beasts.

Mother Earth. (Courtesy of John Kahionhes Fadden.)

Creation of the Sun, Moon, and Stars

The creation of the sun, moon, and stars is variously attributed to Sky Woman and Sapling. The oldest Wyandot and Onondaga versions give Sky Woman or the Elder Earth animals credit for creating the sun, moon, and stars, especially the Milky Way (Barbeau, 1915, 41). A Seneca version has Sky Woman creating the heavens almost immediately after her arrival on earth (Hewitt, 1903, 226–227). Hewitt also recorded a Mohawk story of Grandmother using dead Lynx's body parts as the material of the heavens (ibid., 295–296), but the Lynx is emphatically Mother Earth in all versions and the Moon is Grandmother, leaving the origin of this version vague and questionable. Yet other versions, following the postmissionary trend of giving Sapling sole credit for creation, showed him hanging the heavens, after the fashion of the Christian god (Hewitt, 1903, 208; 1928, 542–543).

One thing became immediately apparent in nearly every version of Creation: Flint was not nearly as skillful a creator as his brother. This was apparent not only in the animals that each brought forth, but also in their attempts at creating humanity. Some say that whereas Sapling created humankind, Flint in a rival bout of creation only managed to bring forth monkeys (Barbeau, 1915, 51; Hewitt, 1903, 214). Others contend that one day Flint noticed that Sapling had made human beings. Marveling at the feat, he sought to replicate it, going through inferior and unworkable models before he managed a viable version, with the kindly advice of Sapling, who stopped by periodically to check on his little brother's progress.

Flint's first human was mostly made of water and therefore failed to breathe. On his second try, Flint added samples of his own mind, blood, spirit, and breath and finally succeeded in creating a living being, although his creation still lacked luster compared to Sapling's model. It is uncertain just what this creature was intended to have been in the older traditions—perhaps a bear—but postcontact, the Iroquois quickly realized that Flint's water man was the European. By contrast, Sapling had created the True Humans or Native Americans (Hewitt, 1928, 523–525; for a late version of Flint's creation of Europeans, see Parker, 1913, 16–19.)

An older Mohawk version ended the creation story by engaging the brothers in a tit-for-tat spat that escalated into a lethal confrontation. The two lived together in a lean-to, one with a side taller than the other. Flint dwelled at the shorter end and Sapling at the taller. One day, Sapling stoked their shared fire to perilous intensity until it began to chip the chert from Flint's flinty legs. When his complaints did not persuade Sapling to lessen the flames, Flint saw that his brother meant him harm. He ran outside swiftly, looking for a cutting reed and a cattail spear, both of which he knew were harmful to his brother. The fight then spiraled out of control, with the two furiously chasing each other across Turtle Island, leaving huge chasms and water-filled depressions where their feet landed in their hurry. In this version, Sapling killed Flint, whose prone body transmuted into the Rocky Mountains. His spirit dwells to this day inside those mountains (Hewitt, 1903, 328–332).

Flint was not permanently dead, however (Hewitt, 1928, 547). All spirits continue to live, often in renewed bodies (Hewitt, 1903, 218–219). Throughout Iroquoian history, Sapling continued reincarnating, most notably as the Peacemaker, creator of the Haudenosaunee (Iroquois) Confederacy, to aid his favorite creations, human beings; the Lynx became Mother Earth, and Grandmother became the smiling face of the Moon.

≈

NEW DEFINITIONS OF AMERICAN ANTIQUITY

How Old Are North America's First Cultures?

A logical starting place in an exploration of American prehistory might be a question: How long have the first Americans been here? From there, our inquiry broadens to the following: Where did North America's first peoples come from and why? These questions are fraught with debate today, which seems to intensify as we learn more about First Nations' cultures. The Bering Strait theory, an assumption that all of the first Native Americans crossed a land bridge over the Bering Strait following the last major Ice Age, perhaps 10,000 to 11,000 years ago, has taken its lumps recently. Given new knowledge, this theory now seems as simplistic and smug as the folk history that maintains a singular "discovery" of America by Christopher Columbus. The reality may be much more complex.

By 2003, the primacy of the Bering Strait theory had been scorched by the discovery that the Siberian site long thought to be the jumping-off point for the peopling of the Americas (at Ushki, Kamchatka) dated later, by about 4,000 years, than its proponents had thought. Thus, the Siberian site was no older, at 13,000 years, than the most ancient Clovis sites in North America, not to mention the Monte Verde sites in South America. Someone may have migrated to America over the Bering Strait, but they were not the first (Goebel, Waters, and Dikova, 2003, 501; Stone, 2003, 450).

Early in 2004, Russian scientists reported the discovery of a 30,000-year-old site where ancient hunters had lived on the Yana River in Siberia, some three hundred miles north of the Arctic Circle. "Although a direct connection remains tenuous, the Yana . . . site indicates that humans extended deep into the Arctic during colder (Ice Age) times," the authors wrote in a study that appeared in *Science* (Pitulko et al., 2004, 52). The researchers found stone tools, ivory weapons, and the butchered bones of mammoths, bison, bear, lion, and hare, all animals that would have been available to hunters during that Ice Age period. The site was twice as old as any previous Arctic settlement, indicating that "people adapted to this harsh, high-altitude, late Pleistocene environment much earlier than previously thought" (Pitulko et al., 2004, 52).

The researchers determined that artifacts were deposited at the site about 30,000 years before the present. That would be about twice as old as Monte Verde in Chile, the most ancient human life known in the American continents. Donald K. Grayson, a paleoanthropologist at the University of Washington in Seattle, said the discovery is very significant because it is so much earlier than any other proven evidence of people living in the frigid lands of Siberia that were used as one path to the Americas (Recer, 2004). "Until this site was reported, the earliest site in Bering land bridge area was dated at about 11,000 years ago," said Grayson. "Every other site that had been thought to have been early enough to have something to do with peopling of the New World has been shown not to be so" (Recer, 2004).

At the time of the Yana occupation, much of the high latitudes on the earth were in the grip of an ice age that sent glaciers creeping over much of what is now Europe, Canada, and the northern United States. The Yana River area was a dry floodplain without glaciers, however. The area was roamed by mammoths, wild horses, musk oxen, and other animals that provided food for the human hunters who survived the Arctic's climate. "Abundant game means lots of food," said Julie Brigham-Grette of the University of Massachusetts, Amherst, in *Science*. "It was not stark tundra as one might imagine" (Recer, 2004).

Among the artifacts found at the Yana site were weapons that resembled some found at a Clovis, New Mexico, site dated around 11,000 years before the present. Grayson and others said, however, that existing evidence linking those implements to the tool and weapon techniques used by the Clovis people is weak. Similar artifacts also have been found in Europe and western Asia, Grayson said. "The similarities [in the tools and weapons] are not enough to prove they were ancestral to the Clovis people in the New World," said Grayson (Recer, 2004).

Native American Arrival Estimates Recede in Time

We do know that America's indigenous cultures evolved for many thousands of years before permanent European settlements began in North America, but we do not yet know for how long. The academically accepted date for original human origin or arrival has been steadily pushed back in time. By 1900, it was acceptable to assert that America's first human occupants had been here 5,000 years. By 1960, for example, an origin or arrival date preceding 8000 B.C. (almost double the 1900 figure) was considered credible. By 1990, that date was considered conservative.

Today, the date of origin or arrival that one is willing to accept depends on the quality of evidence that is demanded. American archeology now reaches roughly 30,000 to 40,000 years into the past, reminding us again that prehistory holds much yet to be discovered. The fact that accepted dates of human arrival in America have receded so rapidly in the recent past has been part of an evolution of knowledge that reflects fieldwork of increasing intensity and sophistication over time. Undoubtedly, more discoveries will enrich this debate in years to come.

The origin date of humanity in the Americas has been debated for centuries. Often, the earliest European settlers thought that the people they met here had resided in the Americas only a few hundred years before their arrival. Fierce debates raged over whether they had migrated from Asia (a view first put forth in 1589 by the Spanish scholar José de Acosta), or whether they were the remnants of Israel's ten lost tribes. This interpretation was especially popular between 1600 and 1800; William Penn and Cotton Mather, among others, subscribed to it. James Adair popularized the same idea in a landmark study of American Indians ([1775] 1930).

Science's best guess regarding the date of the first human footfalls in the Americas has always been something of a rubber figure, even as defenders of various sites and dates have, at different times, defended their favorite dates and places with dogmatic intensity. Three decades before the Clovis finds rearranged archaeology's American timeline, some scholarly debate centered on the widely accepted biblical timeline, which held that the earth was created by the Christian God in 4004 B.C.E. At the same time, various academic schools of thought contended that Native Americans might have descended from seafaring Egyptians, Phoenicians, Greeks, Romans, Welsh, Chinese, or Japanese or even from the residents of Atlantis, the lost continent of European imagination.

Thomas Jefferson doubted that all the American Indians could have crossed over the Bering land bridge as recently as the last major Ice Age. As a student of Native languages, Jefferson thought that their variety and complexity required a more complex origin story, covering more temporal territory. By 1800, Jefferson was preparing to publish what would have been the most extensive vocabulary of Indian languages in his time. It also was the year Jefferson became president, so his work was delayed until he left office in 1808. Jefferson packed his research papers at the presidential residence and ordered them sent to Monticello. Contained in the cargo were Jefferson's own fifty vocabularies, as well as several others assembled during the Lewis and Clark expedition. Boatmen piloting Jefferson's belongings across the Potomac River ripped them open and, disappointed that they could find nothing salable, dumped the priceless papers into the river (Boyd, 1982, 20:451–452).

The timeline of human occupation in the Americas has become more fluid as new discoveries shatter earlier assumptions. A few researchers now argue that Native Americans have been present here from 100,000 or more years ago. Support for this thesis is said to come from a site at Calico Mountain in Southern California: crude bits of broken rock that may have served as tools for these ancient peoples. One problem is that the artifacts—if that is what they are—are on the surface of an alluvial fan, soil and debris washed from higher hillsides, and not buried in an undisturbed layer that can be safely dated to an earlier time. The chipped stones found at Calico Mountain may be of much more recent vintage. They are also so crude that they may not be human tools at all.

In 1992, a cave site was discovered in New Mexico that was said to have been occupied by human beings 35,000 years ago, moving back (by 23,000 years at one shot) the arguable date of the earliest occupation of that area by human beings. Richard S. MacNeish of the Andover Foundation for Archaeological Research (Honolulu, HI) reported that the Orogrande Cave contained remains of hearths, butchered bones, stone tools, and even a human palm print. As with most findings of such antiquity, experts disputed MacNeish's finds.

One school of thought held that he had mixed up stratigraphic layers and thus misdated his finds ("Peopling the Americas," 1992).

WHY ARE SOME OF THE OLDEST SITES
IN SOUTH AMERICA?

One of the largest credibility problems for the Bering Strait theory may be a growing realization that the oldest human remains are now found, for the most part, in Central and South America, which would have been expected to be the last stop for peoples arriving from the north. In *The Settlement of the Americas* (2000), Thomas D. Dillehay, professor of anthropology at the University of Kentucky, illustrated in rich detail (and in many cases for the first time) the number and complexity of archaeological finds in South America that are undermining long-time support for exclusive diffusion of human cultures in North America from the north. Humanity's prehistory in the Americas, contends Dillehay, is older and more complex than that. Dillehay observed that no major region of South America is without Ice Age sites. In some places, such as the eastern highlands of Brazil, the Andean foothills on the north coast of Peru, and the steppes of southern Chile and Argentina, such sites can be found in profusion (Dillehay, 2000, 89).

Some of these cultures developed sophisticated weapons, including the sling stone and grooved bola stone, both of which can be hurled from a thong or whirled over a hunter's head before release. A number and variety of such weapons have been found in Chilean and Brazilian sites. For scholars seeking projectile points, Dillehay provides a rich variety from across the continent. Some of these points (an example is called the Fishtail Projectile Point) may have diffused from South America to North America.

"Many books have been written about the archaeology of the first North Americans and the process that led to their arrival and dispersion throughout the Americas," wrote Dillehay. "No such book exists for South America" (Dillehay, 2000, xiii). Carrying different assumptions and speaking different languages, North and South American scholars searching for the earliest human origins in the Americas often have failed to communicate with each other. Dillehay's work has removed any excuses for such academic isolation.

Dillehay's book includes a lengthy appendix (2000, 295–321) that lists several hundred significant archaeological finds in South America, several of which pre-date the oldest Clovis sites in North America, first discovered in 1932. Dillehay began his work on one of the best known of these, Monte Verde in southern Chile, during 1976 "after a student at the Southern University of Chile, where I was teaching and doing archaeological research, discovered a large mastodon tooth and other bones" at the site (ibid., xiv). Local men clearing an ox path had found the bones. Monte Verde, an open-air settlement on the banks of a small freshwater creek surrounded by sandy knolls, a narrow bog, and forest, soon became an active archaeological dig.

Artifacts from Monte Verde subsequently were radiocarbon dated as old as 12,500 years before the present (at a minimum), making them the oldest known links to human settlement in the Americas. (To date, no site in North America has been dated earlier than 11,200 years before the present.) Over the years, Dillehay has directed up to eighty professionals at a time excavating Monte Verde.

Dillehay, with scholarly contacts on both continents, is superbly qualified to describe this story's scientific side as well as the political struggle to convince English-speaking North American specialists that Monte Verde was not a fraud because the new range of dates contradicted the assumptions of "stringent Clovis loyalists who had spent their entire careers defending the theory against one pre-Clovis candidate after another" (2000, xvi).

After ten years of research, Dillehay and his colleagues at Monte Verde had found traces of people living at Monte Verde at least 12,500 years ago who practiced a generalized hunting-and-gathering style of life, not just big game hunting (Dillehay, 2000, xvi). "It is now apparent," wrote Dillehay, "that humans were in the Americas much earlier than we previously thought. . . . We are also realizing that the first immigrants probably came from several different places in the Old World and that their genetic heritage and physical appearance were much more diverse than we had thought" (2000, xiv). Previous North American sites are now being pre-dated by several others in addition to Monte Verde, including Meadowcroft Rockshelter in Pennsylvania, Cactus Hill in Virginia, Topper in South Carolina, and several others in eastern Brazil, Venezuela, and Colombia.

"We have enough evidence to be sure that virtually all parts of the continent [South America] were at least traversed, if not occupied, by the end of Pleistocene, around 10,500 B.P. [before the present]," wrote Dillehay (2000, 216). Our knowledge of societies at such an early date is limited by what nature leaves behind. "We are extraordinarily ignorant about certain aspects of the first immigrants to the Americas: their anatomical features, their religious beliefs, when and how they buried their dead, the kinds of languages they spoke," Dillehay wrote. Direct evidence on the physical and genetic makeup of the first Pleistocene Americans, especially South Americans, is scant or entirely missing (ibid., 227).

Dillehay (2000) makes a case that the image of early Americans as principally big game hunters is more a stereotype than a reality, more a reflection of the assumptions of capitalism than a residue of accurate scholarship. He cites Kathleen Gordon, a biological anthropologist:

This preoccupation with hunting as the "master behavior pattern of the human species" . . . has been fueled by many factors: the indisputable evidence of large-scale game hunting in Upper Paleolithic Europe; the visible archaeological record, with its emphasis on stone "weapons" and animal bone fragments, and also (perhaps subliminally) the high value accorded meat and hunting as a leisure activity in Western society. (pp. 28–29)

According to Dillehay (2000), recent excavations in South America indicate that Native Americans may have begun to domesticate plants and form the basis of agriculture that eventually would supply half the world's staple crops as early as 8,000 to 10,000 years ago, earlier than any other present-day evidence. A picture emerges from *The Settlement of the Americas* that human beings not only arrived in the New World earlier than previously thought, but also very quickly thereafter began utilizing all the food sources nature offered them, plant and animal. This picture contradicts the Clovis theory's implicit assumption that ancient Americans lived mostly by hunting big game. Dillehay criticizes defenders of the Clovis theory for being unable (and unwilling) to take seriously any archaeological find that does not occur in a dry location. Different techniques are required in humid sites (such as Monte Verde), wrote Dillehay.

Dillehay did much more than describe archaeological finds in *The Settlement of the Americas* (2000). He also probed the environment in which the earliest American peoples lived. Dillehay's speculations ranged from various aspects of geology to ecology and paleoclimatology. In his own words, Dillehay did his best to reconstruct the complexity of the mutual interaction between society and environment that creates the cultural landscape (ibid., 78).

Dillehay was fascinated by the rapid development of cultures and technologies among the earliest peoples of the New World. He asserted that some of the "first pulses of human civilization," including permanently occupied sites, the appearance of architecture and art, and the use of domesticated plants and animals, developed only five to ten millennia after people first arrived (2000, 275). By contrast, Asia, Africa, and Europe were inhabited for hundreds of thousands of years before the same attributes of culture appeared.

How long ago can a credible archaeologist argue that human beings arrived in the Americas? Dillehay's answer (2000, 283) to that question seems to be 15,000 to 20,000 years ago if one assumes that the primary early migration came from the north and that it reached Monte Verde about 12,500 years ago. Dillehay provided a caveat with this figure, indicating that Monte Verde may place human traces in areas dating 20,000 to 50,000 years before the present. We are reminded again that the date of human origins in the Americas is historically pliable, its boundaries restricted at any time not only by the methods of available science, but also by the dominant cultural and political attitudes of those who decide what is acceptable as general knowledge. If a generally accepted date a century ago was 4004 B.C.E. and now it is 15,000 to 20,000 years, what might science and society tell a curious student a century or two from now?

The archeological record supporting theories of human migration to the Americas is in constant flux. Late in 2002, a 13,000-year-old skull was found in Mexico that may help support theories that some of the New World's first settlers arrived along a Pacific Coast route from Japan instead of across the Bering Strait. This skull was one of the oldest thus far discovered in the

Americas, according to Silvia Gonzalez, a leading world authority on prehistoric humans and mammoths. She said the skull is similar to others found belonging to the now-extinct Pericues people, who populated the southern tip of Mexico's Baja California state, along the Pacific Coast route, until the eighteenth century. "The question is, we have these very ancient individuals, but where did they come from?" said Gonzalez, an earth sciences lecturer at Liverpool's John Moores University in England ("Mexican Skull," 2002).

Within days of the Mexican skull's discovery, news reports described 10,000-year-old human remains found at Boardman State Park on the Oregon Coast at a site roughly 12 miles north of Brookings, excavated the previous August by a team of researchers from Oregon State University led by professors Roberta Hall and Loren Davis. The remains, 2,000 years older than anything previously found in the area, were said to "lend weight to the theory that early inhabitants of the area might have arrived by sea, rather than by land" (Frazier, 2002). According to this account, "The discovery puts their arrival at about the time inland inhabitants arrived, bringing into question the theory that all of the earliest inhabitants crossed the Bering Strait and moved south overland to what is now the United States." The findings are about the same age as those found at a few sites in coastal Alaska, British Columbia, and California.

Dillehay wrote in *Nature* that "more recent archaeological discoveries suggest that there were several different founding populations" (2003, 23); he discussed a study of thirty-three ancient skulls excavated from Mexico that suggests the first Americans' links with southern Asian populations. Writing in the same issue of *Nature*, Gonzalez-José et al. present a comparative study of early historic human skulls from Baja California, Mexico (2003, 62), and their findings lend weight to the view that not all early American populations were directly related to present-day Native Americans.

By late 2004, radiocarbon findings had been presented for a site in present-day South Carolina that may be 50,000 years old, which could rewrite the history of how the Americas were first settled by humans. The new findings were raising considerable controversy among archaeologists. If the dates hold up to scrutiny, they would push back the first date of human occupancy in the Americas by about 25,000 years. "Topper is the oldest radiocarbon-dated site in North America," said Albert Goodyear of the University of South Carolina Institute of Archaeology and Anthropology (Walton and Coren, 2004). Goodyear has been excavating the Topper dig site along the Savannah River since the 1980s. The items that he believes to be 50,000 years of age were found in May 2003.

Theodore Schurr, an anthropology professor at the University of Pennsylvania in Philadelphia and a curator at the school's museum, said that conclusive evidence of stone tools similar to those in Asia and uncontaminated radiocarbon-dating samples are needed to verify that the Topper site is actually 50,000 years old. "If dating is confirmed, then it really does have a significant impact on our previous understanding of New World colonization," he said

(Walton and Coren, 2004). Some scientists expressed skepticism whether Goodyear's findings represented human presence. Stone shards that Goodyear believes to be human may be natural, according to Michael Collins of the Texas Archeological Research Laboratory at the University of Texas at Austin.

KENNEWICK MAN: ARCHAEOLOGY'S RACIAL POLITICS

The discovery during 1996 of a nearly complete human skeleton that came to be called Kennewick Man also threw neat, simple theories of the human oc-cupancy of the Americas into disarray, in large part because the remains seemed not to resemble clearly any present-day ethnic group. Was Kennewick Man European? Norse, perhaps? Was he Asiatic, perhaps Ainu, the indige-nous people of Japan? Was he Native American, from the earth of Turtle Island (North America)? Is Kennewick Man, perhaps, a combination of the worldly elements of his own time, a reminder in our time that human origins in the Americas are much more complex (and much more multicultural) than has been commonly supposed?

Kennewick Man is one anecdote in a long story, one reminder of the in-creasing complexity of our knowledge about human origins in the Americas. The discovery of Kennewick Man is part of an ongoing rewriting of the story of human origins in the Americas. A number of archaeological discoveries (and speculations) during the past generation have effectively jettisoned the neat-and-tidy myth popular in the 1950s that one group of Asiatic people traversed the Bering Strait more or less at one time and populated the continents of the Western Hemisphere in one fell swoop. The racial politics evoked by the dis-covery of Kennewick Man (and other, similarly ancient, remains) have pre-sented us with a number of very diverse opinions, but one thing that nearly all serious observers of human antiquity in the Americas now share is this: Human origins in the Americas are much more diverse, and cover a much greater time span, than the simplistic Bering strait theory allows.

Some present-day Native American peoples do not fit century-old racial classifications. Many Haudenosaunee are light skinned, for example. It takes some imagination to assign a Lakota Sioux and a Maya to a single 10,000-year-old ancestor. Many Native nations adopted people who were not racially sim-ilar to them. The texture of the debate changes when it is viewed through this lens. Kennewick Man could have Asian (or even European) facial features and still be defined as a member of a Native American nation using criteria ac-cepted by many Native peoples.

At the same time that Kennewick Man has thrown some assumptions of mainstream academia into doubt, the skeleton has become a stalking horse for non-Indian academics who have an interest in limiting Native American na-tions' legal rights to newly discovered human remains. Kennewick Man has become the first significant legal test of attempts to limit the Native Ameri-can Graves Protection and Repatriation Act (NAGPRA; 1990) to allow, for example, inspection of remains found on federally owned land, including Kennewick Man, before (or instead of) reburial by Native American peoples.

Assertions that Kennewick Man migrated to America from Europe have made him something of a hero to non-Indians who would like to abrogate treaties and limit Native American sovereignty in our time. Architects of racial fantasies have built an entire racial pedigree for this skeleton on scant evidence and used claims that he was "white" to support a theory that he and his kind were the first human immigrants to the Americas. The more extreme variations of these tales assert that Kennewick man and his kin were slaughtered by the ancestors of present-day Native Americans.

The remains that would come to be called Kennewick Man were stumbled on (literally) by two college students, Will Thomas, 21 years old, and Dave Deacy, 20 years old, on July 28, 1996. The two residents of nearby West Richland, home for the summer, were looking for a spot on the banks of the Columbia River from which to view the annual hydroplane races.

James Chatters of Applied Paleoscience (Richland, WA), who routinely conducted skeletal forensics for Benton County Coroner Floyd Johnson, helped police gather a skeleton that was complete except for its sternum and a few small bones in the hands and feet. Recent flushing from Columbia River Dams, an attempt to preserve salmon runs for commercial and Native fishing, had disturbed the sediments and exposed the human remains, which soon became known as Kennewick Man (Johansen, 1999).

The skeleton seemed to Chatters to have belonged to a man who was old (between 40 and 55 years) by the standards of his time; who was about five feet nine or ten inches, tall for a human being that old; who had led a rough life. He had compound fractures in at least six ribs and damage to his left shoulder, which probably caused his arm to wither. He also had a healed-over skull injury. Kennewick Man, whose dietary staple may have been fish, probably died of injuries sustained after a stone projectile point pierced his thigh and lodged in his pelvis. The projectile probably caused a fatal infection that may have festered for as many as six months. Kennewick Man also suffered from advanced osteoporosis in one of his elbows and minor arthritis in his knees, according to Chatters.

Kennewick Man had a long, narrow skull; a projecting nose; receding cheekbones; a high chin; and a square mandible. The lower bones of the arms and legs were relatively long compared to the upper bones. These traits are not characteristic of modern American Indians in the area, although many of them are common among Caucasoid peoples, said Chatters.

A skeleton can reveal only so much about race, not to mention culture. From a skeleton, no one knows the form and color of eyes, color of skin and hair, whether the lips were thin or broad, and whether the hair was straight, wavy, or curly. No one at present knows what language Kennewick Man spoke or anything about what type of religion, if any, he practiced. In other words, the game of racial classification that so preoccupied much of the popular discourse about Kennewick Man was constructed on a very scant evidence base. On such small foundations, however, castles of imagination have been built.

Anthropologist Grover S. Krantz of Washington State University examined the bones at Chatters's request. The skeleton "cannot be anatomically assigned to any existing tribe in the area, nor even to the western Native American type in general," he wrote to Chatters (Slayman, 1997, 17). "It shows some traits that are more commonly encountered in material from the eastern United States or even of European origin, while certain other diagnostic traits cannot presently be determined" (ibid., 17).

According to many who claim Kennewick Man to be a long-lost Caucasian brother, seven skeletons with similar features have been discovered in North America since 1938. The first such discovery, at Fork Rock Cave, Oregon, was radiocarbon dated to about 9,000 years of age. Spirit Cave Man was caught in the same sort of crossfire as Kennewick Man; the Northern Pauites filed a claim for his remains that was contested by several non-Indian scientists. Researchers also contested the return to the Shoshone-Bannock tribe of a skeleton found near Buhl, Idaho. This set of remains was radiocarbon dated to roughly 10,600 years before the present. Most of the skeletons and associated artifacts were found in the western reaches of North America because the eastern side of the continent is much more humid and acidic, which makes long-term preservation of bones more difficult.

To David Hurst Thomas, writing in *Skull Wars* (2000), the present-day "custody battle" over Kennewick Man's remains tells us less about the world in which he lived than it does about the racial politics of our own time. The central theme of Thomas's book is that the struggle over Kennewick Man

> is not about religion or science. It is about politics. The dispute is about control and power, not philosophy. Who gets to control ancient American history?.... In a nutshell, then, *Skull Wars* explores the curious and often stormy relationship between American Indians and the non-Indians bent on studying them. (p. xxv)

How can an old human skeleton fire such passion of possession? In *Skull Wars* (2000), Thomas, long-time curator of anthropology at the American Museum of Natural History in New York City, describes five centuries of racial politics behind the contemporary debate regarding Kennewick Man's remains. The most intriguing part of the story is that Kennewick Man's remains fully fit no single present-day racial classification. Although some people believe Kennewick Man may have resembled the actor Patrick Stewart, Vine Deloria Jr. made a case in *Skull Wars* that Kennewick Man may have resembled the Sauk-Fox chief Black Hawk as painted in 1833 by John Jarvis. Kennewick Man may be a multicultural reminder that notions of race are present-day human constructs overlaid on a vastly more complicated natural record.

Self-definition, wrote Thomas (2000), walks hand-in-hand with self-determination. The power to name is key to nation building in contemporary

Native America, as well as to the identity politics of the Asatru Assembly and several groups of neo-Nazis who have claimed the remains of Kennewick Man. Thus far, the federal courts at the district and circuit levels have held that the remains should be held by the government and released for study by archaeologists. Federal judges to date have refused all other claims.

PREHISTORIC TIME PERIODS

Academics have designated certain prehistorical periods before sustained Native American contact with Europeans. These periods have had various names at various times and are subject to blurring into one another as we discover more about individual prehistorical cultures in America. In the language of contemporary archaeology, most of the time that human beings are now believed to have occupied North America—possibly as long ago as 40,000 to 8,000 years ago—is classified as the Paleo-Indian Tradition. Before about 8000 B.C.E. (or 10,000 years before the present), the indigenous cultures that existed in North America are generally believed to have been relatively uniform in cultural level and ways of life. Such uniformity may be more in the eye of the beholder than real; at this stage, evidence is scant and often restricted to the sort of hunting projectiles that were used at the time. The oldest (possibly 40,000 to roughly 10,000 years ago) artifacts are classified as from "preprojectile point" cultures. Stones that may have been chipped by human hands were unearthed at the Orogrande Cave in southern New Mexico dating to 38,000 B.C.E. or 40,000 years ago; a bone tool made from the carcass of a caribou has been dated to 25,000 B.C.E. at Old Crow Flats, Yukon Territory.

Before roughly 25,000 years ago, tools (such as chipped stones) were usually quite crude. Several sites in the western parts of the present-day United States have yielded simple materials, such as stone tools and debris from fires, believed by some to have been left behind by people 30,000 to 40,000 years ago. Most of these remains fail many archaeological tests meant to verify that they actually were created by human beings, so they remain, for our time, within the realm of the possible.

By about 25,000 years ago, hunters' technology was improving, with projectile points often made of chert or flint. Human bones found at La Jolla and elsewhere in southern California indicate possible human antiquity in that area from at least 27,000 B.C.E., and possibly as early as roughly 40,000 B.C.E., although the dating methods used in these studies have been subject to debate. A site near Midland in western Texas and the Marmes site in eastern Washington yield an antiquity of 16,500 B.C.E. to 9000 B.C.E. Crude tools and other artifacts of similar age have been found at many other sites. Several sites in Mexico date to roughly 20,000 B.C.E. as well (Kehoe, 1981, 1–11). In the Sandia mountains of New Mexico, archaeologists in 1936 found flint knives, scrapers, and other artifacts that have been dated to between 25,000 and

15,000 B.C.E. From these discoveries, the cultures that evolved in this area at that time have become known as the Sandia phase.

Artifacts are more widespread, more easily identified, and more technologically advanced from 11,000 years ago. Thus, the emphasis on the Folsom, Clovis, and Plano (or Plainview) points (all first found at sites in present-day New Mexico and Texas). Each dates to between 5000 and 10,000 B.C.E. The Clovis points seem to be the oldest, dating to about 12,000 B.C.E., with Folsom points dating to 8000 B.C.E., and Plano points recognizable at 7500 to 4500 B.C.E. Each type of point is used to identify the culture that used it. By the time of the Clovis culture, weapons were becoming much more sophisticated. For example, some hunters used an *atlatl*, a device allowing thrust of a spear with greater speed and accuracy than a hunter could achieve simply by throwing it. With such a device, which combined a spear of older design with a throwing device made from animal skin, hunters could attack game from distances of up to 100 yards. A weapon point of distinctively American design, found in Fort Rock Cave, Oregon, has been radiocarbon dated to 11,000 B.C.E. A site at Debert, in Nova Scotia, has yielded fluted points of a slightly different design, also dating to 8500 B.C.E.

Archeologists have found evidence that by 9000 B.C.E. different cultures were evolving. The Cascade (or Old Cordilleran) style of point, for example, was being used in the Pacific Northwest. Its design differed slightly from the Folsom points used in other areas. Similarly, a distinct culture was evolving at this time in some areas of the Great Basin in Arizona and Utah; today, these peoples usually are called the desert cultures. Even at 5000 to 10,000 B.C.E., the use of a single timeline seems to obscure the differing ways in which cultures developed, but it can be a useful tool given the scarcity of other evidence. Even 5,000 to 7,000 years ago, examples of very distinct cultures arise, such as the copper culture of present-day Wisconsin, in which people forged lance points and other articles from the copper that is common in the region. This was one of the earliest metal-working cultures in the world.

More recently than 5000 B.C.E., individual cultures are best treated on their own in most cases. Generally, a drier and warmer climate, as well as technological advances, allowed many Native cultures to move away from hunting as a sole means of survival. Native peoples began to forage and gather food. This eventually led to domestication of plants and animals, as well as other forms of sedentary agriculture and (in some cases) civilizations with large urban concentrations of population supported by forms of agriculture that present-day scholars are still rediscovering.

As older Native American settlements of greater complexity are found throughout the Americas, we may ask, as Thomas Jefferson did two centuries ago, how peoples assumed to have crossed the Bering Strait so recently could have diffused so rapidly, become so diverse, and (in some cases) built civilizations and spoken languages of such complexity over such a short time. All migrations have causes; there seems to have been no singular reason that propelled great numbers of people across the Bering Strait during one short period and no other. "Migration" may be a misleading term because many of the people who crossed the Bering Strait probably were not consciously moving from one continent to another but were following the animals that gave them sustenance, seeking new land, moving a few miles at a time.

WRITTEN LANGUAGES IN PREHISTORIC AMERICA

A century and a half ago, when American anthropology was born, many academics commonly delineated races as "civilized," "barbarian," and "savage," a system developed by Lewis Henry Morgan, who is widely known as the father of the discipline in the United States. One of the main determinants of civilization was often said to be a culture's development (or lack) of written communication. Until early in this century, many "experts" assumed that America's indigenous peoples had only the slightest inkling of written communication, that their cultures were for the most part singularly oral. Considering such distinctions, many people forgot that in Europe, at the time of Columbus' first voyage, the invention of movable type was within living memory. The number of published books at the time was miniscule, and the practice of writing (and even reading) was isolated generally to people of high economic class and members of religious orders. Barely one in every twenty people in Europe was able to read in 1492. Fewer still had a competent command of written language. For the average person at that time, life and history were mainly oral in Europe.

During the past few decades, deeper study of many ancient cultures in the Americas has revealed that many of them did indeed communicate using written symbols, some of them even phonetic—a system, like the languages of Europe, in which the written symbols may stand for ideas or "words." Such discoveries bring into question the common nomenclature of the periods into which scholars have long divided Native history in the Americas. The word *prehistory* itself implies a lack of written communication, which comprises history in the European sense. Even today, some accounts equate prehistoric with "precontact [with Europe]." Although the indigenous cultures of America may have been prehistoric in the sense that Europeans could not decipher their languages, they did maintain historical records.

Olmec Writing

The earliest form of written communication in the New World may have been a language used by the Olmecs. Several years of research in the Mexican state of Vera Cruz has turned up a number of indications that the Olmecs operated an organized state-level political system that utilized written communication (O. Moore, 2002; M.E.D. Pohl, Pope, and Nagy, 2002, 1,984; Stokstad, 2002, 1,872).

Late in 2002, a team of archeologists led by Mary Pohl of Florida State University described two artifacts containing portions of script found in Olmec ruins that date to about 650 B.C.E., about 400 years earlier than any previously discovered Mayan writing. Fragments of stone plaques and a cylindrical seal bearing glyphs resembling later Mayan writing lend support to the idea that the Olmecs were a "mother culture" pre-dating the writing and calendar systems of both the Maya and the Aztecs (as well as cultures pre-dating the Aztecs in the Valley of Mexico). The cylindrical seal is thought to have been used to imprint clothing with symbols, and the stone plaques were used as a form of jewelry. Both of them may have indicated rank or authority within a hierarchical society.

Other finds included human and animal bones, food-serving vessels, and hollow figurines (O. Moore, 2002). The connection among Olmec writing, their calendar, and kingship is indicated in these communications, dating to 650 B.C.E., "which makes sense, since the Olmecs were the first known peoples in Mesoamerica to have a state-level political structure, and writing is a way to communicate power and influence," said Pohl (O. Moore, 2002).

The new Olmec discoveries depict a bird's beak spewing two diverging lines of symbols that are believed to depict a system of communication that is not purely iconographic, one that must be learned, a hallmark of true writing. Later inscriptions show similar symbols emerging from human mouths (Stokstad, 2002, 1,873). According to M.E.D. Pohl and colleagues, writing in *Science* (2002), the symbols "imply that Mesoamerican writing originated in the La Venta polity" of the Olmec culture near Tabasco, in southern Mexico (p. 1,984).

These discoveries led to speculation that three ancient languages (Mayan, Isthmian, and Oaxacan) could have shared a common origin in the script of the Olmecs. "It was generally accepted that Mayans were among the first Mesoamerican societies to use writing," said John Yellen, an archeologist and program manager for the National Science Foundation. "But this find indicates that the Olmecs' form of written communication led into what became forms of writing for several other cultures" (O. Moore, 2002). Pohl, who led the excavations at San Andres, near La Venta, has worked for years to analyze and fine-tune the estimated dates of the artifacts discovered in the initial dig. "We knew we had found something important," she said. "The motifs were glyph-like but we weren't sure at first what we had until they were viewed more closely" (O. Moore, 2002).

Wampum Belts as Written Language

Indigenous Americans sometimes communicated through pictorial signs and symbols that may be likened in some ways to the hieroglyphs of Egypt. The Iroquois fashioned pictographs into wampum belts that were used to jog memory for oral historians. Replicas of some of these story belts may be examined today, for example, at the Six Nations Indian Museum in Onchiota, New York. The wampum belts that Iroquois diplomats gave and received during meetings with colonial representatives in the seventeenth and eighteenth centuries are adapted on the same model. Like written contracts, they were evidence that certain actions had been taken at a given place and time (B. Mann, 1995, 40–48).

Wampum are strings or arrayed patterns made of seashells and have been used by many American Indians in the Northeast to preserve accounts of history, to conduct diplomacy, and to complete some commercial transactions. Nearly every important treaty negotiated in the eighteenth century was sealed with the presentation of wampum belts. The shells that comprised the belts were harvested and traded to inland peoples by Native American peoples who lived on the coast.

Peace among the formerly antagonistic Iroquois nations was procured and maintained through the Haudenosaunee's Great Law of Peace (*Kaianerekowa*), which was passed from generation to generation by use of wampum belts that outlined a complex system of checks and balances between nations and genders. A complete oral recitation of the Great Law can take several days. The wampum belts, complex designs of purple (or sometimes black) and white shells, were used to prompt the memory of a speaker.

According to the Iroquois Great Law, the blood feud was outlawed and replaced by the Condolence Ceremony. Under the new law, when a person killed someone, the grieving family could forego the option of exacting clan revenge (the taking of the life of the murderer or a member of the murderer's clan). Instead, the bereaved family could accept twenty strings of wampum from the slayer's family (ten for the dead person and ten for the life of the murderer himself). If a woman was killed, the price was thirty wampum strings because women bore life.

Although wampum was used principally in diplomacy, the settlement of disputes, and the recitation of history, it also was used sometimes as currency. In 1612, John Smith of Virginia visited the Susquehannocks in the northern regions of the Chesapeake Bay. He encountered the use of wampum and found hints of the existence of the Iroquois Confederacy. During the course of their meeting, the Susquehannocks implored Smith to defend them against the "Atquanahucke, Massawomecke and other people [that] inhabit the river of Cannida." The Susquehannocks draped "a chaine of white beads (waighing at least 6 or 7 pound) about" Smith's neck while reciting an "oration of love" (Johansen, 1997, 1,353).

The Cherokees used wampum in a ceremony meant to provide for the poor. During a special war dance, each warrior was called on to recount the taking of his first scalp. During the ceremony, anyone with something to spare, according to Henry Timberlake, "a string of wampum, piece of [silver] plate, wire, paint, lead" heaped the goods on a blanket or animal skin placed on the ground (Johansen, 1997, 1,353). Afterward, the collection was divided among the poor of the community, with a share reserved for the musicians who had provided entertainment during the ceremony.

Haudenosaunee (Iroquois) wampum strings. (Courtesy of John Kahionhes Fadden.)

Aztec and Mayan Picture-Writing

The Spanish warmed their hands over fires built from entire Mexica (Aztec) libraries during the early years of the conquest, little realizing what they were burning because Aztec writing did not resemble Spanish. One of the Aztec books that survived this holocaust relates its anguish:

> Broken spears lie in the roads;
> We have torn our hair in our grief
> The houses are roofless now, and their walls
> are red with blood . . .
> —Portilla, 1962, frontispiece

The Aztecs also used a form of pictograph writing that was conceptually similar in some ways to the Iroquois' "story belts." The historical record of Aztec culture was compiled in books and scrolls by priest-scribes. The result was writing that looked something like present-day cartoon strips. Some of these books folded into large screens stacked like an accordion, bound in animal skins. One of these, today called the *Codex Egerton*, recounts the lives of 26 generations of rulers, "symbolized by husbands and wives seated on thrones and passing mysterious presents to one another" (Morison, 1993, 54).

The development of knowledge related to indigenous writing is yet another indication that, after five centuries in the Americas, immigrants from Europe who followed Columbus are still "discovering America." In late 1991, for example, Marilyn M. Goldstein, a professor of art history at the C. W. Post campus of Long Island University in Brookville, New York, announced discovery of a ceramic Mayan vessel bearing rows of glyphs and scenes from mythological events that represented pages from a Mayan book created before the year 900 C.E., at the end of the period in Mayan history that scholars usually refer to as the late classic. This book dated 500 years earlier than similar, earlier finds. Professor Goldstein estimated that, based on the sophistication of these symbols, the Maya probably composed elementary books of this type as early as 300 to 600 C.E.; written symbols have been found on Mayan stone monuments and tombs dating to a century or two before the birth of Christ. The Mayan books could perhaps be compared to the written records kept by monks and others in Europe before the invention of movable type, when literacy was limited to a small fraction of the population. The Mayan vessel, called the Wright codex, was found in a United States private collection.

A Mayan piece, from a book in their language dated to the sixteenth century, idealizes the time before contact with Europeans as a disease-free paradise:

> There was then no sickness;
> They had then no aching bones;
> They had then no high fever;
> They had then no smallpox;
> They had then no burning chest...
> They had then no consumption...
> At that time the course of humanity was orderly,
> The foreigners made it otherwise when they arrived here.
> —Wright, 1992, 14

According to John S. Henderson (1981), the system of symbols that the Maya used for written communication was a

> limited, special-purpose system...that directly represents not [only] units of meaning, but sounds of language. With these signs, they could write any message that could be spoken. With phonetic signs, the Maya carried the elaboration of graphic symbols to a degree unmatched in the Americas. [This was written before more recent discoveries about Inca writing, discussed below.] Maya hieroglyphic writing is just that—a true writing system, capable of expressing an unlimited range of information. (pp. 87–88)

Although Mayan civilization was generally well past its peak when the Spanish arrived, the Maya still possessed several thousand handwritten books that included collections of songs, volumes describing their sciences, biographies, genealogies, accounts of ritual, and other historical material. Spanish religious authorities, who were well aware of the spiritual significance that the Maya vested in these books, destroyed nearly all of them. Today, only four of these ancient volumes are known to have survived the Spanish pillage. In the time of the conquest, possession of native writing could put its holder in peril of his or her life if church authorities learned of them. Diego de Landa, a bishop of Yucatán during the sixteenth century, wrote: "We found a large number of books in these characters [hieroglyphs], and they contained nothing in which there were not to be seen superstition and lies of the devil[;] we burned them all, which they regretted to an amazing degree, and which caused them much affliction" (Tozzer, n.d., 169).

Beginning during the 1970s, scholars translated the Maya's writing for the first time, standing on its head a century or more of archaeological speculation about Mayan society. Until this writing was translated, many archaeologists had thought that the Maya were a relatively peaceful, rural people who lived in a benign theocracy governed by priest-kings. Today, we still know the Maya as people who built complex cities, studied astronomy, and were probably the first in the world to use negative numbers. We now know them also as very violent.

Demarest said that evidence from stone art and texts indicate that "the Maya were one of the most violent state-level societies in the New World, especially after 600 C.E." (Wilford, 1991, 7-L). Sometimes, losing rulers were decapitated with great ceremony. The Maya's writing depicts repeated raids by the elites of adjoining city-states, as well as ritual bloodletting and human sacrifice, all used to build the prestige of ruling families. Linda Schele, a Maya scholar at the University of Texas at Austin, said: "We don't know if early Maya went to war mainly to acquire territory, take booty, control conquered groups for labor, take captives for sacrifice . . . or a combination of these" (1991, 7).

The Maya's written records describe wars that began before 400 C.E. The first recorded Mayan war was fought in the jungles of what is now northern Guatemala in 378 C.E. A stone monument was later erected that gave the date of the conflict and the victorious general, Smoking-frog. Another monument observes that Great Jaguar-paw, the ruler of Tikal, the winning city-state, observed the victory "with a ceremony of bloodletting from his genitals" (Wilford, 1991, 7-L).

In 1990, a treasure trove of Mayan history was uncovered at Dos Pilas, a settlement begun in the seventh century, possibly by emigrants from Tikal, who seemed to have conquered several other Mayan city-states. At Dos Pilas, archaeologists have uncovered a large stairway lined with carved images of warfare, including the torture and execution of captives. The carvings are explained by Mayan writing describing a series of wars in which the army of Dos Pilas subdued the peoples of Tikal in 678 C.E.

During the next century, Dos Pilas grew further by conquest to a size of about two thousand square miles of rain forest, possibly (according to Arthur A. Demarest [1993, 95], an archaeologist at Vanderbilt University), the largest single Mayan kingdom. After its string of conquests, the recorded history indicates that Dos Pilas dissolved into a gaggle of feuding warrior-states. Continual warfare caused the Maya generally to abandon dispersed, undefended settlements that had allowed them to exploit the fragile rain forest ecosystem successfully. Some farmers devastated the forest, trying to produce more food, as others fled to the armed cities. The society's ability to support itself agriculturally declined as warfare intensified, ultimately destroying the civilization.

The written history of Mayan culture (which reached its peak between 200 and 900 C.E.) indicates that it may have declined because increasing militarization (including siege warfare) forced people into urban areas, interrupting agriculture that had fed the cities. Siege warfare also devastated countryside around the urban areas, stripping it of trees (which were used for firewood) and destroying crops. Once soils were laid bare, heavy tropical rains leached them of vital nutrients, further harming agriculture.

Because the Maya are finally telling history to us in their own words, said Demarest, "It's a very exciting time in Maya studies. It's a time for new editions of all the textbooks" (Wilford, 1991, 7-L). According to David Freidel, an archaeologist at Southern Methodist University (Dallas, TX), "No Egyptian tomb's discovery was ever more exhilarating than the decipherment process underway today" (Wilford, 1991, 7-L).

For more on Mayan civilization, including their writing system, see chapter 2.

The Incas' Writing System

Discoveries regarding the writing of the Incas have paralleled those about the Maya. By the 1980s, after more than thirty years of examining ancient Inca textiles, British-born William Burns was piecing together a phonetic writing system that was used in the Andes long before the Spanish conquest. In his book, *Ancient Peru*, Federico Kauffmann Doig wrote that Burns had made "the most revolutionary contribution to the study of the writings of ancient Peru. Given the evidence in [Burns'] work, we should change the idea that ancient Peru did not have an authentic writing system, meaning one with phonetic symbols" (*La Republica*, 1991, 50).

Working as a textile engineer for a Peruvian company, Burns's examination of about four hundred rectangular patterns (called *tocapus*) on Inca textiles convinced him that he was actually dealing with a written language, not random designs. Burns also studied strings of knots in variously colored cords (called *quipus*) that had been previously acknowledged as a system for counting. According to Burns, the Inca *quipus* also utilized the elements of a language that seemed to have been used with some degree of secrecy to describe historical events. Burns also found such a system referenced in the writings of chroniclers who accompanied the Spanish conquistadors. He noted that the Simi Runes (or *Kicwa*, as the Spanish called them), the earliest works describing Peru's aboriginal languages, contained dictionaries with words in them such as *quillcanigui* (to write), *quellca* (paper, letter, or writing) and *quellcascacuna* (the letters). This writing system, which utilized ten consonants and no vowels, could have been used to construct more than 3 million words.

The discovery of phonetic writing among the Incas, together with other work, indicates that human society in the Andes was probably as complex as Egypt's during the time of the Great Pyramids. Ruins have been found of a warehouse believed to be between 3,500 and 3,800 years old that probably contained food stores for very large urban settlements. The building itself was more than 100 yards long and as tall as a present-day three-story building and is divided into dozens of individual compartments. The age of this building places it roughly at the time the Great Pyramids were constructed. In other words, evidence is accumulating that New World civilizations evolved on a timescale rather similar to those of Europe and Asia. In the Andes, archaeologists have been finding evidence of stepped pyramids and very large, U-shaped temples more than ten stories high.

A *New York Times* report described discovery of "bright, multi-colored friezes with jaguar and spider motifs and broad plazas flanked by residential areas" (Stevens, 1989, C-1). Many of the sites have been well preserved by the arid climate of the area, so that "adobe friezes and sculptures that might have been destroyed in another climate are preserved almost intact, with their vivid reds, blues and blacks still showing. Seeds, pollen and animal skeletons are not fossils, but real" (ibid., C-1). Some of these sites dated to 5,000 years ago, at least a thousand years earlier than ruins in Central America, which previously had been thought to be the oldest in the hemisphere. The earliest sites seem to have had economies tied to the sea. Later, for unknown reasons, the settlements moved upward in elevation along more than fifty river valleys along the coast of Peru and sustained themselves on irrigated agriculture that flourished despite the arid, harsh highland climate, providing the basis for the later Incan civilization.

The following elegy was written in Quechua (the Incan language) near the present-day site of Quito, Ecuador, during the conquest. It was titled "Atawallpa Wanuy," meaning "The Death of Atawallpa," the Father Inca to whom the poem refers, at the hands of invading Spanish conquistadors.

> Like a cloud, the wiraqochas,
> the white men,
> Demanding gold,
> Invaded us.
> After seizing
> Our Father Inca;
> After deceiving him,
> They put him to death.
> He with the heart of a puma
> The adroitness of a fox,
> They killed
> As if he were a llama.
> Hail is falling,
> Lightning strikes,
> The sun is sinking;
> It is becoming night.
> And in their terror,

The elders
And the people
Have buried themselves alive.
—Lara, n.d., 193–194

CAHOKIA: AN ANCIENT TRADING CENTER

Archaeology has been, piece by piece, providing us with a picture of human ingenuity in the Americas. Witness, for example, the development of a major trading center that was home to about 30,000 people at the confluence of the Mississippi and Missouri Rivers roughly at the same time that London, England, housed a similar population. Other urban centers in Mesoamerica (see chapter 2) ranked among the largest cities of the world many centuries before sustained contact with Europeans.

Only a few miles from present-day St. Louis, Missouri, one may find the ruins of a ten-story ceremonial mound that covered fifteen acres, two acres more space than the base of Egypt's Great Pyramid. Archaeological inference has it that an ancient ruler called the Great Sun stood on top of that mound and chanted ritually as the sun rose over Cahokia, a six-square-mile city containing 120 mounds, as well as dwellings and places of business. This temple is believed to have been the center of a city that served a trade network reaching from the present-day Dakotas to the Gulf of Mexico, roughly the European distance between Paris and Moscow.

Cahokia was the largest of several population centers that developed in the Mississippi Valley (archaeologists call them the Mississippian culture) around the year 1000, possibly influenced by the civilizations of Mesoamerica through the travels of the *pochtecas*, wide-ranging Mesoamerican traders. The temple mounds of the Mississippians resembled the constructs of the civilizations to the south, as did their social structure, remnants of which survived into the period of European contact among the Natchez.

Cahokia and other ceremonial centers usually were situated at the center of a larger cluster of villages, housing from one hundred to nearly one thousand people each in orderly rows of thatched-roof houses. The people of this hinterland intensively farmed corn and tobacco, as well as several varieties of squash and beans. They also hunted, fished, and gathered other foodstuffs. Doubtless, at least some of the food raised and gathered in these rural hinterlands was taxed for consumption by the elites inside the ceremonial centers.

European immigrants long thought that Natives of America could not have constructed such a city. They attributed the ruins to the lost tribes of Israel, the Phoenicians, the Vikings, or any number of European peoples. This theory held that these obviously enlightened Old World immigrants had been slaughtered by the indolent savages (who must have been very patient as the immigrants somehow constructed a large urban area). The theory finely suited immigrants from Europe, who had convinced themselves that they were putting to good use a continent that the Native peoples were presumed to have left idle.

Native American intelligence built Cahokia, which functioned somewhat as the Aztecs' Tenochtitlan but probably without as a heavy military and political hand on surrounding peoples. The inhabitants of Cahokia also understood basic geometry and astronomy because here (and at other ruins in the eastern United States) the sun lines up with human constructions at the two equinoxes as it does at England's Stonehenge. The city appears to have declined not by conquest but from environmental exhaustion. The people of Cahokia learned that farming a single crop (in this case, corn) on the same land year after year depletes the soil. They also harvested trees for cooking fires and warmth much faster than nature could replace them, altering the topography of their land, the same fate that befell some Mayan urban areas (Weatherford, 1991, 14).

NATIVE AMERICAN AGRICULTURE

Although popular imagination sometimes stereotypes them solely as nomadic hunters, many, if not most, of North America's Native American peoples practiced agriculture, the domestication of plants for human consumption. At least half of the earth's staple vegetable foods, the most important being corn and potatoes, were first cultivated by indigenous peoples in the lands Europeans came to call America; these indigenous people often drew their sustenance from hunting, gathering, *and* agriculture. Agriculture was an established way of life for many Native peoples in North America. At first sight, many immigrating Europeans did not recognize Native American agriculture because it did not resemble their own. Indians did not domesticate draft animals and only rarely plowed their fields. Sometimes, crops were grown in small clearings amid a forest.

Native Americans first cultivated many of the foods taken for granted as everyday nourishment today. The main ingredients of Crackerjacks (peanuts and popcorn), for example, are both indigenous to the Americas, as are all edible beans except horse beans and soybeans, all squashes (including pumpkins), Jerusalem artichokes, the "Irish" potato, the sweet potato, sunflowers, peppers, pineapples, watermelons, cassava, bananas, strawberries, raspberries, gooseberries, and pecans.

Corn was first domesticated in the highlands of Mexico about 7,000 years ago from a wild grass called *teosinte*. The first corn cobs were the size of a human thumbnail. As the use of maize (Indian corn) spread north and south from Mexico, Native peoples domesticated hundreds of varieties and bred them selectively so that the edible kernels grew in size and number.

Corn, the major food source for several agricultural peoples across the continent, enjoyed a special spiritual significance. Often, corn and beans (which grow well together because the beans, a legume, fix nitrogen in their roots) were said to maintain a spiritual union. Some peoples, such as the U'ma'has (Omahas) of the eastern Great Plains, "sang up" their corn through special rituals.

In addition to "singing up the corn," the Pueblos cleaned their storage bins before the harvest so the corn would be happy when they brought it in. The

Pawnees grew ten varieties of corn, including one (called "holy" or "wonderful" corn) that was used only for religious purposes and never eaten. The Mandans had a Corn Priest who officiated at rites during the growing season. Each stage of the corn's growth was associated with particular songs and rituals, and spiritual attention was said to be as important to the corn as proper water, sun, and fertilizer. Among the Zuni, a newborn child was given an ear of corn at birth and endowed with a "corn name." An ear of maize was put in the place of death as the "heart of the deceased" and later used as seed corn to begin the cycle of life anew. To Navajos, corn was as sacred as human life.

Corn is intertwined with the origin stories of many Native American peoples. The Pueblos say that corn was brought to them by Blue Corn Woman and White Corn Maiden, who emerged to the surface of the earth from a great underground kiva, a sacred place. At birth, each infant is given the seed from an ear of corn as a fetish to carry for life as a reminder that the Corn Mothers brought life to the Pueblos. The corn fetish has a practical side as well: Should a harvest completely fail for drought or other reasons, the fetishes may become the seed corn for the next crop.

When colonists arrived in eastern North America, many of the Native American peoples they met farmed corn in large tracts. John Winthrop, governor of the Massachusetts Bay Colony, admired abandoned native cornfields and declared that God had provided the epidemics that killed the people who had tended them as an act of divine providence, clearing the land for the Puritans. Native Americans taught the Puritans which seeds would grow in their territories. Most of the seeds that the Puritans had brought from England did not sprout when planted in the area that the colonists called New England.

Native American agriculture has influenced eating habits around the world so completely that many people forget their culinary origins. Before the voyages of Columbus, Italian food that depends on tomato-based sauces was unknown. The Irish prepared their food without potatoes. Europeans satisfied a sweet tooth without chocolate. Corn was unknown outside the Americas. These crops were produced by experimentation of many Native American cultures over thousands of years. Knowledge of plant life was passed along from generation to generation with other social knowledge, usually by the elder women of a native tribe or nation.

The production of food is woven into Native American spiritual life. Among the Iroquois and many other Native peoples, for example, festivals point to the role of the "Three Sisters" (Corn, Squash, and Beans). The food complex of corn, beans, and squash was transferred northward from Mexico as a set of rituals before it became the basis of an agricultural system. By practicing the rituals, Native Americans in the corn-growing areas of North America became farmers. Corn requires a 160-day, frost-free growing season; the northern limit of corn cultivation also often marks the limit of intensive Native agriculture.

Agriculture among Native American peoples enabled higher population densities than hunting and gathering. According to William Cronon, Native peoples in Maine who did not use widespread agriculture sustained an average density of about 40 people per hundred square miles, and indigenous peoples in southern New England, who raised crops (corn being their major staple), averaged 287 people (seven times as many) on the same amount of land (Cronon, 1983, 42).

Native American agriculture often seemed disorderly to European eyes accustomed to large monocultural fields comprising one crop. Native American fields showed evidence of thought and practice, however. Samuel de Champlain described how Natives planted corn on small hills mixed with beans of several types. "When they grow up, they interlace with the corn, which reaches to the height of five to six feet; and they keep the ground free from weeds," Champlain wrote (Cronon, 1983, 43). John Winthrop, describing Indian fields in Massachusetts within a generation of the Pilgrims' arrival, said that their agriculture "load[ed] the ground with as much as it will beare" (Cronon, 1983, 44). Indian farming methods (usually the responsibility of women, except when growing tobacco) not only kept weeds at a minimum, but also preserved soil moisture.

Many Native peoples offer their thanks to the plants as well as the animals that they consume out of a belief that the essence of life that animates human beings also is present in the entire world, even in the rocks under one's feet. Long before a science of "sustained yield" forestry evolved, Native American peoples along the northwest coast harvested trees in ways that would ensure their continued growth, associating such practices with a belief that trees are sentient beings. Some Native Americans charted farming cycles through complicated relationships with the sun and moon. In addition to domesticating dozens of food plants, they also harvested the wild bounty of the forests for hundreds of herbs and other plants used to restore and maintain health.

Although the Maya are known for their temples in such places as Tikal, Copan, and Palenque, most Maya were commoners (who supported a small elite that maintained the temples) and spent most of their working lives cultivating food, principally corn. Most of the Maya's ceremonial centers were surrounded by earthworks. These artificial ramparts were not discovered by modern archaeologists until they started using satellite images of the land because today the earthworks often are submerged in jungle and thus are very difficult to locate from ground level. The earthworks included complex irrigation channels and raised fields, often hewn from reclaimed swampland. The Maya dredged nutrient-rich soil from the bottoms of the irrigation ditches to fertilize fields that they raised above the flood level of the rainy season. The fields were so rich that they produced several crops a year to feed the people of the urban ceremonial centers.

The discovery of complex agricultural earthworks among the Maya caused scholars to question earlier assumptions that the Maya had practiced slash-and-burn agriculture, which was said to have deforested the land, exhausted and eroded the topsoil, and played a role in the collapse of the "classic" age of the Maya. Today, the collapse of the Maya is usually ascribed not to deforestation caused by agriculture but to ecological damage and social disorganization caused by dense populations and escalating warfare between city-states. Not all of the Maya's earthworks were constructed to aid agriculture. Some ramparts were defensive, and as war became more common and deadly, the Maya's complex agricultural system suffered immensely.

About the same time that Mayan civilization collapsed, the ancestors of today's Pueblos were building a corn-based culture in the Chaco Canyon of present-day New Mexico. The Pueblos of the Rio Grande are cultural and economic inheritors of the Mogollon, Anasazi, and Hohokam communities to the west and southwest of the upper Rio Grande valley. Cultivation of corn was introduced into the area about 3000 B.C.E. About 2000 B.C.E., beans and squash were added. Cotton later became another staple crop.

About 2,000 years ago, irrigation was introduced to supplement dry farming in the same area. The Pueblos used brief, heavy precipitation to advantage by constructing some of their irrigation works at the bases of steep cliffs and collected runoff. The residents of this area constructed roads that often ran for hundreds of miles so that they could share food surpluses. If one pueblo had a bad harvest, others, using the roads, would share what they had. The cultivation of corn in Chaco Canyon supported a civilization that constructed the largest multifamily dwellings in North America before twentieth century high-rise apartments. Such a high degree of agricultural organization supported a culture that dominated the turquoise trade in the area. Turquoise was important as a "liquid asset," a medium of trade. Pueblo centers, such as Pueblo Bonito, became centers of trade, manufacturing, and ceremony.

The vital role of water and irrigation in Pueblo agriculture is illustrated by the fact that the great classic Pueblo civilizations were destroyed by a drought so severe that not even ingenious water management could cope with it. In the thirteenth century C.E., most Pueblo settlements outside the Rio Grande valley had been abandoned after fifty years of nearly rainless drought that destroyed their agricultural base.

Following the Spanish colonization of New Mexico, access to water became a crucial cause of conflict. Land without water is worthless in the arid Southwest. Paradoxically, the Pueblos in 1680 used the waters of the Rio Grande River to defeat the Spanish; they staged their revolt while the river was flooding to keep Spanish reinforcements out.

Irrigation of farmland was *the* key factor in Pueblo agricultural land use. To plan, construct, and maintain elaborate land systems, cooperation between several villages was crucial. Irrigation systems needed routine maintenance that rendered clans inefficient, so nonkinship associations were created to cope with such work. This organizational framework had other community functions, and it revolved primarily around the spiritual life of the Pueblos. The basic rationale for the nonkinship associations was irrigation, however.

Some Native peoples used fire to raze fields for farming and to drive game while hunting. These were not fires left to blaze out of control, however; Navajos who used

Hopi dwelling. (Courtesy of the Nebraska State Historical Society
Photograph Collections.)

range fires customarily detailed half of their hunting party to contain and control
the flames and to keep the blaze on the surface, where the flames would clear old
brush so that new plant life could generate instead of destroying the forest canopy.
When Europeans first laid eyes on North America, it was much more densely
forested than today. In some places, the parklike topography of many eastern forests
was a result of Native American peoples' efforts to manage plant and animal life.

NATIVE AMERICAN FAMILY LIFE

European American immigrants to North America sometimes were con-
founded by ways in which Native American family life differed from their
own. For one thing, women often were (as they continue to be) influential in
family life as well as the political and economic lives of many Native American
peoples. Gender relations that some Europeans thought to be deviant (such as
the *berdache* or homosexual) were accepted in some Native cultures. Many
Native Americans formed and broke marital bonds more quickly and easily
than most European Americans as well. Bonds other than marriage also were
highly significant for many Native Americans. Clan relationships were often

so strong that (even today) relatives that Anglo-Americans call cousins are regarded as brothers and sisters.

Following are capsule descriptions of a few specific Native American family structures and customs. For the most part, practices noted by historical observers are still evident today, along with modifications compelled by association with European American cultures.

The Iroquois

The Iroquois Confederacy is fundamentally a kinship state. The Iroquois are bound together by a clan and chieftain system that is supported by a similar linguistic base. Through the *hearth*, which consists of a mother and her children, women play a profound role in Iroquois political life. Each hearth is part of a wider group called an *otiianer*, and two or more *otiianer* constitute a clan. The word *otiianer* refers to the female heirs to the chieftainship titles of the League, the fifty authorized names for the chiefs of the Iroquois, passed through the female side of the *otiianer*. The *otiianer* women select one of the males within their group to fill a vacated seat in the League.

Such a matrilineal system was headed by a clan mother. All the sons and daughters of a particular clan are related through uterine families. In this system, a husband lives with his wife's family, and their children become members of the mother's clan by right of birth. Through matrilineal descent, the Iroquois form cohesive political groups that have little to do with where people live or from which village the hearths originate.

The oldest daughter of the head of a clan sometimes, on the judgment of the clan, succeeds her mother at the mother's death. All authority springs from the people of the various clans that make up a nation. The women who head these clans appoint the male delegates and deputies who speak for the clans at tribal meetings. After consultation within the clan, issues and questions are formulated and subsequently debated in council.

The Iroquois are linked to each other by their clan system, in which each person has family relations with every other nation of the federation. If a Mohawk of the Turtle Clan had to travel, he or she would be cared for by Turtles in each other nation: the Oneidas, the Onondagas, the Cayugas, and the Senecas.

Iroquois political philosophy is rooted in the concept that all life is unified spiritually with the natural environment and other forces surrounding people. The Iroquois believe that the spiritual power of one person is limited but may be enhanced when combined with other individuals in a hearth, *otiianer*, or clan. Whenever a person dies, by either natural causes or force, through murder or war, this power is diminished. To maintain the strength of the group, families in the past often replaced the dead by adopting captives of war. This practice of keeping clans at full strength through natural increase or adoption ensured the power and durability of the matrilineal system as well as the kinship state.

Childrearing is an important way to instill political philosophy in the youth of the Iroquois. The ideal Iroquois personality demonstrates not only loyalty to the group, but also independence and autonomy. Iroquois people were trained to enter a society in which power is shared between male and female, young and old, more so than in European American society. European society emphasizes dominance and command structures; Iroquois society is more interested in collaborative behavior.

The Wyandots (Hurons)

Native Americans living near the eastern edge of Lake Huron in present-day Ontario called themselves Wyandots. The French called them Hurons, a French reference to the bristles on a boar's head, probably because the first Wyandots they met wore their hair in a style that today is called a Mohawk.

As with the Iroquois, the Wyandot clans—Porcupine, Snake, Deer, Beaver, Hawk, Turtle, Bear, and Wolf—create familial affinity across the boundaries of the four confederated Wyandot nations. Members of each clan can trace their ancestry to a common origin through the female line. In each village, clan members elect a civil chief and a war chief. The titles are carried through the female family line but are bestowed on men, a practice again resembling that of the Iroquois. Although the titles are hereditary in that sense, they do not pass from head to head of a particular family as in most European monarchies.

As among the Iroquois, economic roles among the Wyandots are determined by gender. Women usually tend gardens, gather plants from the forests, and manage the home. Men participate in agriculture mainly by clearing fields for women to work and contribute to subsistence by hunting. Men are the main visible participants in trade and diplomacy, but women contribute trade goods and political advice, usually behind the scenes.

The Apaches

Traditional Apache society is centered around groups of two to six matrilocal extended families, called *gotas*. Members of the *gota* live together, and members of the different households cooperate in the pursuit of game and raising of crops. A *gota* is usually led by a headman, who assumes his status over several years by general consensus of the extended families in the *gota*. The headman in some cases inherits the title of "true chief." He will not retain the position, however, unless he displays leadership. If no qualified headmen are raised through inheritance, a consensus may form in favor of another leader, who will be informally "elected" by members of the *gota*. Headmen are invariably male, but women exercise influence as political advisers. Their society and kinship lineages maintain the Apaches' matrilineal society.

A headman may wield considerable influence, but only if the people in the extended families are willing to follow his advice, which includes detailed lectures on how to hunt, the techniques of agriculture, and who should work with whom. He also coordinates labor for hunting and foraging, advises parties engaged in disputes, and offers advice regarding who should marry whom. At times, the wife of a chief may become, in effect, a subchief. As a chief ages, he is charged not only with maintaining exemplary behavior, but also with identifying young men who may become leaders in the future. He is expected to tutor younger men in the responsibilities of leadership. A chief is also charged with aiding the poor, often by coordinating distribution of donations from more affluent members of the *gota*. If two or more *gotas* engage in conflict, their headmen are charged with resolving the dispute.

Each traditional Apache is a member not only of a *gota*, but also of one of sixty-two matrilineal clans that overlap individual settlements. Members of one's clan (and, in some cases, others identified as being close to it) help each other in survival tasks and usually do not intermarry. Such a system resembles that of many peoples in the eastern woodlands (e.g., Cherokees, Wyandots, and Iroquois).

The Crees

Before challenges from the outside forced them to convene a central council, the Crees, who live in present-day Quebec, had no unified political organization as among the Iroquois and Wyandots (Hurons) to the south. Even the individual bands or hunting parties had little or no organized political structure. Such a lack of structure is sometimes called *atomistic* by scholars; it is the closest that actual Native governance comes to the stereotype of the "noble savage." Instead of a formal council, Cree bands, which were groups of families, informally select a wise elderly man, usually the head of a family, as a source of advice. He exercises informal, limited influence. As with the sachems of the more organized farming and hunting peoples to the south, these informal leaders usually do not relish the exercise of power, probably because most of the people who seek their advice resent any attempt to dictate.

Cree life is marked only rarely by multifamily celebrations or rituals. Social life and social control are usually a function of the extended family. Outside the family, a Cree might appear ambivalent or reticent, usually out of respect for others' autonomy. People who transgress social norms of interpersonal behavior became targets of gossip or sorcery of a type that was used widely across the continent. Although their society is family based, the Crees recognize no clan or other kinship system between different bands. The society thus does not have the interconnections between settlements similar to those offered by the clans of the Iroquois, Wyandots, Cherokees, and others.

Northwest Coast Peoples

Native Americans who live along the northwest coast of North America also do not maintain the strong clan systems that characterize many other Native

American societies. Instead, they have a very class-conscious social system in which family economic status means a great deal.

Northwest coast peoples from the Alaska panhandle to northern California traditionally recognize three social classes that seem as imperishable as the red cedar from which they constructed their lodges: nobility, commoners, and slaves. The nobility includes chiefs and their closest relatives; the eldest son is the family head. He, his family, and a few associates live in the rear right-hand corner of the family longhouse, with people of lower status on each side. These people are said to be "under the arm" of the chief. The next-highest-ranking chief, usually a younger brother of the head chief, invariably occupies the rear left-hand corner of the house with his family. He, too, has a number of people under the arm. The other two corners are traditionally occupied by lesser chiefs' families.

NORSE EXPLORATION OF NORTH AMERICA

Before Columbus's voyages on both sides of the Atlantic, sporadic contacts left a residue of myth transmitted from generation to generation in oral histories. American Indians from Nova Scotia to Mexico told their children about pale-skinned, bearded strangers who had arrived from the direction of the rising sun. Such myths played a large part in Cortes's conquest of the Aztecs, who were expecting the return of men who looked like him. The natives of Haiti told Columbus they expected the return of white men; some Mayan chants speak of visits by bearded strangers. The Lenape (Delaware) told Morovian missionaries that they had long awaited the return of divine visitors from the East. These premonitions, among others, suggest that the peoples of the Old and New Worlds communicated with each other on a sporadic basis centuries before Columbus.

In the realm of what critic Stephen Williams calls "fantastic archaeology" (Williams, 1991), theories establishing European origins for Native American peoples have long historiographic pedigrees. Evidence that meets the strictest standards of professional archaeology is scant in support of any of them.

One exception is the pre-Columbian landfall of the Vikings. Norse sagas (oral histories) and scattered archaeological evidence indicate that, beginning about 1000 C.E., Viking explorers who had earlier settled Iceland and Greenland conducted several expeditions along the East Coast of North America. At three locations—Newfoundland as well as possibly Cape Cod and the James River of Virginia—some evidence exists of small-scale, short-lived Viking settlement. According to the sagas, one Viking (the word is from the Norwegian *viks*, for fjord dweller), Thorfinn Karlsefni, explored 3,000 miles of North American coast in the early eleventh century.

The technical capability of the Vikings to reach North America is not in doubt. They were capable seafarers and built sturdy longships capable of easily reaching Iceland from Norway, a distance much greater than the voyage from Greenland to North America. In 1893, Magnus Andersen, a Norwegian, sailed a reconstructed Viking ship from Norway to Newfoundland.

Vikings may have followed the St. Lawrence River and Great Lakes as far inland as the vicinity of Kensington, Minnesota, where in 1898 a large stone was found inscribed with Norse runic writing that described the ambush and killing of ten men. The runes have been tested as weathered (as would be expected) but authentic. The Norse may have been looking for new sources of furs after the German Hanseatic League captured their trade in Russian furs during 1360 (Kehoe, 2002, 217).

Indisputable proof of Viking landings in North America have been found on the northern tip of Newfoundland. These discoveries began with the explorations of Helge Ingstad, at L'Anse aux Meadows, about 1960. The site has since been excavated and part of it turned into a public park. The evidence there is conclusive—right down to such things as a soapstone spindle whorl, nails, and even the remains of an iron smelter, along with hundreds of other artifacts, many of which have been carbon-14 dated to about 1000 C.E. Most other supposed Viking visits to North America (one in the unlikely venue of Tuscon, Arizona) still reside in the realm of archaeological speculation. According to Frederick Pohl (1972), a science fiction novelist who also has written three books on Norse exploration of North America, eighty-nine locations of Norse landfall have been asserted in North America. Some of these locations are as far apart as present-day Minnesota and New Orleans, Louisiana.

Piecing together evidence found in the Viking sagas, it is likely that about 985 C.E. the Viking sailor Bjarni Herjulfsson sighted land (probably Cape Cod) after several navigational errors led him astray on a voyage to Greenland. He finally reached his destination by sailing northeastward along the North American coast. In Greenland, his story of three land sightings to the southwest excited the imagination of Leif Erickson, who interviewed Bjarni and purchased his ship.

According to the Norse sagas that were told (which have been written and translated into English) after his voyages, Erickson made landfall at three places. He called the first "Helluland," probably Baffin Island; the second was "Markland," possibly Labrador or Newfoundland. The third landing, where Erickson established a small winter settlement, may have been on Cape Cod, near Follins Pond. The sagas tell of their ship being beached and stored, a house being built, and salmon caught that were larger than any the Vikings had ever seen. Although the Viking settlement in Newfoundland lasted several years and left behind many artifacts, the visit to Cape Cod seems to have been more of a temporary stop, leaving little evidence that survived ensuing centuries.

Thorvald Erickson, a brother of Leif, set out on his own voyage of discovery shortly afterward, in 1007 C.E. His plan was to explore the coast north and south from Cape Cod. Along the way, Thorvald's thirty-man crew seized and killed eight American Indians (they called them *Skraelings*, meaning "screamers," after their war-whoops). Thorvald later was killed in revenge for those murders. His crew sailed back to Greenland without him.

A few years later, in 1010 C.E., Thorfinn Karlsefni sailed from Iceland to Leif's settlement on Cape Cod, after which he probably explored the Atlantic Coast southward to the James River of present-day Virginia. The trip took four summers. The first winter was spent along the Hudson River of New York State, where the Vikings were surprised by the depth of snowfall for a place so far south. The second winter was spent along the James River of Virginia. The sagas tell of a voyage up the river to the rapids, far enough upstream to have seen the peaks of the Blue Ridge Mountains. At one point, according to the sagas, Karlsefni's crew was attacked by Native Americans, who used a large hornet's nest as a weapon. In all, the Karlsefni expedition probably logged about 3,000 miles along the coast and adjoining rivers.

Leif Erickson died about 1025 C.E., and his Labrador settlement withered, but not before Karlsefni and Gudrid, his wife, had given birth to a son they called Snorri, the first child believed to have been born in America of European parents. After that, voyages continued from time to time through the thirteenth and fourteenth centuries. King Magnus of Norway and Sweden authorized the Paul Knutson expedition, which sailed in 1355 to explore conditions in Greenland and Vinland. Knowledge of North America was apparently still being recalled in Iceland during 1477, when a young Italian sailor, Cristoforo Colombo, visited and became excited by sailors' gossip of land to the south and west of Greenland.

THE PERILS OF MILKING BUFFALO

Attempts to reconcile new information with old theories can have comical effects in academia. To provide one small but poignant example, a debate arose some years ago among archaeologists regarding the origins of tuberculosis in America. Excavations of Native bones indicated that an epidemic of the disease had begun on Canada's East Coast about the year 1000. Evidence indicated that the disease had spread rapidly down the St. Lawrence Valley, then overland as far as the present-day states of North and South Dakota.

One way to explain this outbreak would have been to acknowledge that Leif Erickson and other Vikings had introduced it. For archaeologists who were not prepared to acknowledge European contact before Columbus, another explanation had to be found. One alternative that was debated for a time had it that Native people had caught a mutated form of tuberculosis from buffalo. How had the buffalo passed the disease? One faction maintained that the Native people had caught it by milking the buffalo. This faction now had to explain why there is no reference in Native oral histories to the use of buffalo milk. Even the notion of "milking" a wild animal seemed a little silly to anyone who had ever contemplated it (Grinde, 1991, 36).

DISPUTES REGARDING NATIVE POPULATION DENSITY

As with theories of Native American origins, questions regarding the number of peoples who lived in the Americas prior to sustained contact with Europeans provoked a lively debate during the last third of the twentieth century. This debate involves two very different ways of looking at historical and archaeological evidence. One side in the population debate restricts itself to strict interpretation of the evidence at hand. Another point of view accepts the probability that observers (usually of European ancestry) recorded and gathered evidence from only a fraction of phenomena that actually occurred in the Americas.

The fact that disease was a major cause of Native depopulation is not at issue; both sides in this debate agree on the importance of disease. Disease ravaged Native Americans to such a degree that many early European immigrants (who at the time had no understanding of how pathogens spread disease) thought they had come to a land that had been emptied for them by their God. The debate is over the *number* of native people who died. There also seems to be little disagreement on indications that the plagues loosed on the Americas by contact with the Old World have not ended, even today. For example, between 1988 and 1990, 15 percent of the Yanomami of Brazil, who had only limited contact with people of European descent until this time, died of malaria, influenza, and even the common cold (Wright, 1992, 14).

Henry F. Dobyns has estimated that about 16 million Native Americans lived in North America north of Mesoamerica, the area populated by the Aztecs and other Central American Native nations, at the time of Columbus's first voyage (1983, 42). Because population densities were much greater in Central America and along the Andes, an estimate of 16 million north of Mesoamerica indicates to Dobyns that 90 to 112 million native people lived in the Americas before the year 1500, making some parts of the New World as densely populated at the time as many areas of Europe and Asia.

Smallpox created such chaos in the Incan empire that Francisco Pizarro was able to seize an empire as large and populous as Spain and Italy combined with a force of only 168 men (C. C. Mann, 2002, 43). By the time imported diseases were done with Native Americans, according to Dobyns, 95 percent of them had died, the worst demographic collapse in recorded human history (ibid., 43). All across America, "Languages, prayers, hopes, habits, and dreams, entire ways of life hissed away like steam" (ibid., 46).

One of the deadliest vectors of disease was pigs brought across the ocean by explorers such as Hernando de Soto to provide members of their expeditions with food on the hoof. The pigs multiplied rapidly and spread European diseases to deer, turkeys, and eventually Native human beings as well. De Soto recorded having seen many well-populated villages; explorers a century later found forests largely bereft of people. According to Charles C. Mann, writing in the *Atlantic Monthly* (2002), "The Coosa city-states, in Western Georgia, and the Caddoan-speaking civilization centered on the Texas-Arkansas border, disintegrated soon after de Soto appeared.... The Caddoan population fell from about 200,000 to about 8,500, a drop of 96 per cent. In the eighteenth century the tally shrank further, to 1,400" (p. 45).

Dobyns's population estimates have risen over time from his initial estimate of 12.5 million in North America north of the Rio Grande (1966, 395). Scholars other than Dobyns agree with his hemispheric estimate of about 100 million (Borah, 1976; Cook and Simpson, 1948). In the meantime, the Smithsonian Institution, under pressure from rising population estimates elsewhere, raised its own estimate of aboriginal population, doubling the population north of the Rio Grande to 2 million from half that number.

Dobyns's estimate of indigenous population at contact represents a radical departure from many earlier estimates, which depended for the most part on actual historical and archaeological evidence of the dead, assuming that Euro-American scholars (and others, such as missionaries) were capable of counting native people who had in some cases been dead for several centuries. Although anthropologists usually date the first attempt at measuring Native populations to Henry Schoolcraft (during the 1850s), Jefferson's *Notes on the State of Virginia* (published in several editions during the 1780s) contained an extensive (if fragmentary) Native American "census." Jefferson did not attempt to count the number of Native people inhabiting all of North America during his time—no one then even knew how large the continent might be, not to mention the number of people inhabiting it. Jefferson prudently settled for estimates of the Native nations bordering the early United States.

The first "systematic" count was compiled during the early twentieth century by James Mooney, who estimated that 1,153,000 people had lived in the land area now occupied by the United States when Columbus made landfall. Mooney calculated the 1907 Native population in the same area at 406,000. Dividing the country into regions, he calculated the percentage of population loss between 1492 and 1900 at between 61 percent (in the North Atlantic states) and 93 percent in California (Mooney, 1910, and Mooney, 1928).

Subsequent to the work of Mooney, the most widely followed population estimates were provided beginning in 1939 by A. L. Kroeber in his *Cultural and Natural Areas of Native North America*. By Kroeber's determination, only about 900,000 native people had occupied North America north of Mexico before sustained European contact. According to Ann F. Ramenofsky (1987, 9), Kroeber did not consider disease a factor in depopulation because he feared that such an emphasis would lead to an overestimation of precontact population sizes. One may speculate whether this was a case of deliberate scientific oversight or simple academic prudence, but the fact was that after nearly a half century of authority for his conservative figures (a time when one could appear "radical" by arguing that perhaps 2 million native people occupied the area now occupied by the United States in 1492), a challenge was likely to arise. Dobyns, who *did* consider disease (some say he overemphasized it), stepped into that role along with others to initiate the present debate.

Defending his pre-Columbian population estimates, Dobyns argued that "absence of evidence does not mean absence of phenomenon," especially when written records are scanty, as in America before or just after sustained

European contact (Dobyns, 1989, 286). Dobyns's position is that European epidemic diseases invaded a relatively disease-free environment in the Americas with amazing rapidity, first in Mesoamerica (via the Spanish), arriving in eastern North America along native trade routes long before English and French settlers arrived. The fact that Cartier observed the deaths of fifty natives in the village of Stadacona in 1535 indicates to Dobyns that many more may have died in other villages that Cartier never saw. Given lack of evidence, conclusions must be drawn from what little remains, according to Dobyns, who extended his ideas to other continents as well: "Lack of Chinese records of influenza does not necessarily mean that the Chinese did not suffer from influenza; an epidemic could have gone unrecorded, or records of it may not have survived" (ibid., 296).

Critics of Dobyns's estimates assert that "there is still little certain knowledge about pre-1500 population levels," and that "on a historiographic level, Dobyns has been accused of misusing a few scraps of documentary evidence we have in an effort to sustain his argument for widespread sixteenth-century epidemics" (Snow and Lanphear, 1989, 299). To the critics of Dobyns, the fact that fifty native people were recorded as dying at Stadacona means just that: Fifty natives died, no more, no fewer. To Dobyns, however, such an argument "minimizes Native American population magnitude and social structural complexity" (1989, 289).

Although Dean Snow and Kim M. Lanphear, both strident critics of Dobyns, maintained that "there were often buffer zones between population concentrations or isolates that would have impeded the spread of diseases" (1989, 299) Dobyns replied that the practice of trade, war, diplomacy, and other demographic movements obliterated such "buffer zones" and aided in the spread of disease (1989, 291). Snow and Lanphear also asserted that the sparseness of native populations in North America itself impeded the spread of disease, a point of view that does not account for the speed with which smallpox and other infections spread once history recorded them as having reached a particular area.

Dobyns not only denied that buffer zones existed, but also maintained that smallpox was the most virulent of several diseases to devastate New World populations. The others, roughly in descending order of deadliness, included measles, influenza, bubonic plague, diphtheria, typhus, cholera, and scarlet fever (1983, 11–24). According to Dobyns (1983):

> The frontier of European / Euro-American settlement in North America was not a zone of interaction between people of European background and vacant land, nor was it a region where initial farm colonization achieved any "higher" use of the land as measured in human population density. It was actually an interethnic frontier of biological, social, and economic interchange between Native Americans and Europeans and/or Euroamericans. (p. 43)

The most important point to Snow and Lanphear (1989), however, was "where one puts the burden of proof in this argument, or, for that matter, in any argument of this kind.... We cannot allow ourselves to be tricked into assuming the burden of disproving assertions for which there is no evidence" (p. 299).

Given the evidence they had in hand, however, even Snow and Lanphear acknowledged (1988) that between 66 and 98 percent of the Native peoples inhabiting areas of the northeastern United States died in epidemics between roughly 1600 and 1650. The Western Abenaki, for example, are said to have declined from 12,000 to 250 (98 percent), the Massachusett (including the Narragansett) from 44,000 to 6,400 (86 percent), the Mohawk from 8,100 to 2,000 (75 percent), and the Eastern Abenaki from 13,800 to 3,000 (78 percent) (p. 24).

Given the number of people killed and the lengthy period during which they have died, the world has probably not again seen such continuous human misery over such a large area. Tenochtitlán, the Aztecs' capital city (which occupied the site of present-day Mexico City), struck Hernan Cortes as a world-class metropolis when he first looked out over it shortly after the year 1500. The Aztec metropolis is estimated to have contained 250,000 people at a time when Rome, Seville, and Paris housed about 150,000 each. Before he destroyed it, Cortes stared at the splendor of the Aztecs' capital and, sounding something like a country bumpkin, he called Tenochtitlán the most beautiful city in the world.

Spanish chronicler Bernal Díaz del Castillo stood atop a great temple in the Aztec capital and described causeways eight paces wide, teeming with thousands of Aztecs, crossing lakes and channels dotted by convoys of canoes. He said that Spanish soldiers who had been to Rome or Constantinople told Díaz that "for convenience, regularity and population, they have never seen the like" (McDowell, 1980, 753). The comparisons of life among the Aztecs with what the Spanish knew of Europe acquire some substance as one realizes that, in 1492, the British Isles were home to only about 5 million people, and Spain's population has been estimated at 8 million (Wright, 1992, 11). Even almost three centuries later, at the time of the American Revolution, the largest cities along the eastern seaboard of the new United States—Boston, New York, and Philadelphia—housed no more than roughly 50,000 people each.

Within a decade of Cortes's first visit, Tenochtitlán was a ruin. Ten years after the Aztec ruler Mochtezuma had hailed Cortes with gifts of flowers and gold (and had paid for such hospitality with his life), epidemics of smallpox and other diseases carried by the conquistadors had killed at least half the Aztecs. One of the Aztec chroniclers who survived wrote the following: "Almost the whole population suffered from racking coughs and painful, burning sores" (Portilla, 1962, 132).

The plague followed the Spanish conquest as it spread in roughly concentric circles from the islands of Hispanola and Cuba to the mainland of present-day Mexico. Bartolomé de las Casas, the Roman Catholic priest who questioned Spanish treatment of the natives, said that when the first visitors found it, Hispanola was a beehive of people. Within one lifetime, the forests were silent. Within thirty years of Cortes's arrival in Mexico, the Native population had fallen from about 25 million to roughly 6 million. After Spanish authorities set limits on money wagers in the New World, soldiers in Panama were said to have made bets with Indian lives instead. Native people who were not killed outright by disease died slowly as slaves under the conquerors' lash.

Las Casas ([1542] 1974), who had arrived in the New World ten years after Columbus, described one form of human servitude, pearl diving: "It is impossible to continue for long diving into the cold water and holding the breath for minutes at a time ... sun rise to sun set, day after day. They die spitting blood ... looking like sea wolves or monsters of another species" (p. 15). Other conquistadors disemboweled native children. According to Las Casas, "They cut them to pieces as if dealing with sheep in a slaughterhouse. They laid bets as to who, with one stroke of a sword, could cut off his head or spill his entrails with a single stroke of the pike" (ibid., 43).

A century later, entering North America, the Puritans often wondered why the lands on which they settled, which otherwise seemed so bountiful, had been emptied of their Native American inhabitants. Four years before the Mayflower landed, a plague of smallpox had swept through Native villages along the coast of the area that the immigrants renamed New England. The disease may have been brought ashore by visiting European fishermen, who had been exploiting the rich coastal banks for many years. John Winthrop admired abandoned Native cornfields and declared that God had emptied the land for his fellow voyagers as an act of divine providence.

As European immigrants spread westward, Native peoples learned to fear the sight of the honeybee. These "English flies" usually colonized areas about a hundred miles in advance of the frontier, and the first sight of them came to be regarded as a harbinger of death. The virulence of the plagues from Europe may be difficult to comprehend in our time. Even in Europe, where immunities had developed to many of the most serious diseases, one in seven people died in many smallpox epidemics. Half the children born in Europe during Columbus's life never reached the age of fifteen years. Life expectancy on both sides of the Atlantic averaged thirty-five years as Europeans made sustained contact with the Americas.

Regardless of the number and density of human population in North America before contact, outside a few specific areas (such as Mayan and Aztec cities, as well as Cahokia), population density was not great enough to devastate the environment on a large scale. Instead, early European observers marveled at the natural bounty of America, of Virginia sturgeon six to nine feet long, of Mississippi catfish that weighed more than 100 pounds, and Massachusetts oysters nine inches across, as well as lobsters that weighed 20 pounds. The immigrants gawked at flights of passenger pigeons that sometimes nearly darkened the sky and speculated that a squirrel could travel from Maine to New Orleans without touching the ground. Bison ranged as far east as Virginia—George Washington observed a few of them and wondered whether they could be crossbred with European cattle.

Regardless of the dispute regarding population size and density before the devastation of European diseases, it is rather widely agreed that Native populations in North America bottomed at about half a million in the early twentieth century (using Mooney's figures), and that they have been increasing since. For the United States, statistics contained in the 1990 census indicated that roughly 2 million people listed themselves as Native American, a figure that nearly doubled in the 2000 U.S. census. Such a measure may not be as precise as it sounds because the census allows people to categorize themselves racially. Also, for the first time, the 2000 census was designed to allow people to report more than one ethnicity, a major source of the numerical increase for Native Americans.

THE ECONOMIC CONSEQUENCES OF DISEASE

When English explorer George Vancouver sailed into Puget Sound in 1793, he met Indian people with pockmarked faces and found human bones and skulls scattered along the beach, grim reminders of an earlier epidemic. Such scenes were repeated coast to coast in North America during the surge of European and European American exploration and settlement.

Epidemics of smallpox, measles, bubonic plague, influenza, typhus, scarlet fever, and many other European diseases sharply curtailed Native Americans' economic productivity, generating hunger and famine. Birth rates fell, and many survivors allayed their losses with alcoholic beverages, further reducing Native societies' vibrancy and economic productivity. Societies that had been constructed on kinship ties dissolved as large parts of many families were wiped out. Survivors faced the world without family elders' help, and traditional Native healing practices were useless against European-imported pathogens. The ravages of disease undermined the traditional authority of Native American healers, who found their practices useless.

Historian Colin Calloway described the widespread impact of epidemics on Native American political, economic, and social institutions (1990):

> The devastating impact of disease cannot be measured only in numerical losses. Epidemics left social and economic chaos in their wake and caused immeasurable spiritual and psychological damage. Killer diseases tore holes in the fabric of Indian societies held together by extensive networks of kinship and reciprocity, disrupted time-honored cycles of hunting, planting, and fishing, discouraged social and ceremonial gatherings, and drained confidence in the old certainties of life and the shamans who mediated with the spirit world. (p. 39)

The arrival of European pathogens affected Native American tribes and nations differently, depending on the economic conduct of their lives. Sedentary groups were hit the hardest, and migratory groups (such as the Cheyennes after about 1800) suffered less intensely, at least at first, because they moved from place to place, leaving their wastes (which drew disease-carrying flies and other insects) behind. Migratory peoples also left behind water that they may have contaminated, usually exchanging it for fresh supplies. The Cheyennes were quite conscious of water contamination and always set up camp so that their horses drank and defecated downstream of human occupants. The Cheyennes consciously fought the spread of disease by breaking camp often and scattering into small family groups so that one infected family would not bring disease to an entire band.

Although the worst of the bubonic plague killed one in three Europeans, continuing waves of epidemics nearly obliterated many Native American societies and economies within a few years of the arrival of Europeans in any given area. Plagues of various pathogens—smallpox, influenza, measles, and others—killed nearly all of the Western Abenakis and at least half the Mohawks. A disease frontier spread across North America about a generation, generally, before European American settlers, traders, and miners reached a given area.

The heritage of suffering brought by imported diseases left its mark on Native America well into the twentieth century. As late as 1955, the annual Native American death rate from gastrointestinal illnesses was 15.4 per 100,000, compared with 3.6 in the United States as a whole. The death rate from tuberculosis was 57.9 per 100,000 in 1955, compared to a nationwide average of 8.4. From alcoholism, the rate was at least 60 per 100,000, compared to a national average of 8.1.

During the last half of the twentieth century, some diseases declined dramatically among Native Americans. The death rate from gastrointestinal diseases fell from 15.4 per 100,000 in 1955 to 4.2 in 1983; the national average in 1983 was 2.8. For tuberculosis, the 1983 rate was 3.3 per annual deaths per 100,000, down from 57.9 in 1955; the national rate fell from 8.4 per 100,000 in 1955 to 0.5 in 1983. For alcoholism, the Native American rate of at least 60 per 100,000 in 1955 declined to about 28 in 1983.

FURTHER READING

Adair, James. *History of the American Indians*. Edited by Samuel Cole Williams. Johnson City, TN: Wataugua Press, [1775] 1930.

Ballantine, Betty, and Ian Ballantine. *The Native Americans: An Illustrated History*. Atlanta, GA: Turner, 1994.

Barbeau, C. M. *Huron and Wyandot Mythology with an Appendix Containing Earlier Published Records*. Anthropological Series, no. 11, Memoir 80. Ottawa: Government Printing Bureau, 1915: 35–51.

Borah, Woodrow. The Historical Demography of Aboriginal and Colonial America: An Attempt at Perspective. In William M. Denevan, ed., *The Native American Population of the Americas in 1492*. Madison: University of Wisconsin Press, 1976: 13–34.

Boyd, Julian P., ed. *The Papers of Thomas Jefferson.* Vol. 20. Princeton, NJ: Princeton University Press, 1982.

Calloway, Colin. *The Western Abenakis of Vermont, 1600–1800: War, Migration, and the Survival of an Indian People.* Norman: University of Oklahoma Press, 1990.

Calloway, Colin. *New Worlds for All: Indians, Europeans, and the Remaking of Early America.* Baltimore: Johns Hopkins University Press, 1997.

Colden, Cadwallader. *The History of the Five Nations of Canada.* New York: Amsterdam, [1765] 1902.

Converse, Harriet Maxwell [Ya-ie-wa-noh]. *Myths and Legends of the New York State Iroquois.* Edited by Arthur Caswell Parker. New York State Museum Bulletin 125. Education Department Bulletin no. 437. Albany: University of the State of New York, 1908: 31–36.

Cook, Sherburne F., and Leslie B. Simpson. The Population of Central Mexico in the Sixteenth Century. In *Ibero-Americana* 31. Berkeley and Los Angeles: University of California Press, 1948.

Corkran, David H. *The Cherokee Frontier: Conflict and Survival, 1740–1762.* Norman: University of Oklahoma Press, 1962.

Cornplanter, Jesse J. *Legends of the Longhouse.* Edited by William G. Spittal. Ohsweken, Ontario, Canada: Iroqrafts, [1938] 1992.

Cronon, William. *Changes in the Land: Indians, Colonists, and the Ecology of New England.* New York: Hill and Wang, 1983.

Deloria, Vine, Jr. *God Is Red.* Golden, CO: North American Press, 1992.

Demarest, Arthur A. The Violent Saga of a Mayan Kingdom. *National Geographic* (February 1993):95–111.

Dillehay, Thomas D. *The Settlement of the Americas: A New Prehistory.* New York: Basic Books, 2000.

Dillehay, Thomas D. Palaeoanthropology: Tracking the First Americans. *Nature* 425 (September 4, 2003):23–24.

Dobyns, Henry F. Estimating Aboriginal American Population. *Current Anthropology* 7(October 1966):395–412.

Dobyns, Henry F. *Their Number Became Thinned.* Knoxville: University of Tennessee Press, 1983.

Dobyns, Henry F. More Methodological Perspectives on Historical Demography. *Ethnohistory* 36:3(Summer 1989):286–289.

Dozier, Edward P. *The Pueblo Indians of North America.* New York: Holt, Rinehart and Winston, 1970.

Fenton, William N., and John Gulick, eds. *Symposium on Cherokee and Iroquois Culture.* Smithsonian Institution Bureau of Ethnology Bulletin 180. Washington, DC: U.S. Government Printing Office, 1961.

Frazier, Joseph B. Humans in Oregon 10,000 Years Ago? Associated Press via seniorstaff@nativenewsonline.org, November 25, 2002.

Goebel, Ted, Michael R. Waters, and Margarita Dikova. The Archaeology of Ushki Lake, Kamchatka, and the Pleistocene Peopling of the Americas. *Science* 301 (July 25, 2003):501–505.

Gonzalez-José, Rolando, Antonio Gonzalez-Martin, Miquel Hernandez, Hector M. Pucciarelli, Marina Sardi, Alfonso Rosales, and Silvina Van der Molen. Craniometric Evidence for Palaeoamerican Survival in Baja California. *Nature* 425(September 4, 2003):62–65.

Grinde, Donald A., Jr. The Reburial of American Indian Remains and Funerary Objects. *Northeast Indian Quarterly* 8:2(Summer 1991):35–38.

Grinde, Donald A., Jr., and Bruce E. Johansen. *Ecocide of Native America: Environmental Destruction of Indian Lands and Peoples.* Santa Fe, NM: Clear Light, 1995.

Heckenberger, Michael J., Afukaka Kuikuro, Urissap Tabata Kuikuro, J. Christian Russell, Morgan Schmidt, Carlos Fausto, and Bruna Franchetto. Amazonia 1492: Pristine Forest or Cultural Parkland? *Science* 301(September 19, 2003):1710–1714.

Henderson, John F. *The World of the Ancient Maya.* Ithaca, NY: Cornell University Press, 1981.

Hewitt, John Napoleon Brinton, ed. Iroquoian Cosmology, First Part. In *Twenty-First Annual Report of the Bureau of American Ethnology to the Secretary of the Smithsonian Institution, 1899–1900.* Washington, DC: U.S. Government Printing Office, 1903: 127–339.

Hewitt, John Napoleon Brinton, ed. Iroquoian Cosmology, Second Part." In *Forty-Third Annual Report of the Bureau of American Ethnology to the Secretary of the Smithsonian Institution, 1925–1926.* Washington, DC: U.S. Government Printing Office, 1928: 453–819.

Hughes, J. Donald. *American Indian Ecology.* El Paso: Texas Western Press, 1983.

Iverson, Peter. Taking Care of the Earth and Sky. In Alvin Josephy, ed., *America in 1492: The World of the Indian Peoples Before the Arrival of Columbus.* New York: Knopf, 1992, 85–118.

Johansen, Bruce E. Wampum. In D.L. Birchfield, ed., *The Encyclopedia of North American Indians.* Vol. 10. New York: Marshall Cavendish, 1997: 1352–1353.

Johansen, Bruce E. Great White Hope? Kennewick Man: The Facts, the Fantasies, and the Stakes. *Native Americas* 16:1(Spring, 1999):36.

Johansen, Bruce E., and Barbara Alice Mann, eds. *Encyclopedia of the Haudenosaunee (Iroquois Confederacy).* Westport, CT: Greenwood Press, 2000.

Kehoe, Alice Beck. *North American Indians: A Comprehensive Account.* Englewood Cliffs, NJ: Prentice-Hall, 1981.

Kehoe, Alice Beck. *America before the European Invasions.* London: Longman, 2002.

Kroeber, A. L. *Cultural and Natural Areas of Native North America.* University of California Publications in American Archeology and Ethnology 38. Berkeley: University of California, 1939.

Lara, Jesus. *La Poesia Quechua.* Cochabamba, Bolivia: Imprenta Universitaria, N.d., 193–194. Cited in Wright, 1992, 31.

La Republica, Lima, Peru. Reprinted in *World Press Review*, September 1991, 50.

Las Casas, Bartolomé de. *The Devastation of the Indies.* New York: Seabury Press, [1542] 1974: 15.

Mann, Barbara A. The Fire at Onondaga: Wampum as Proto-writing. *Akwesasne Notes* New Series 1:1(Spring 1995):40–48.

Mann, Charles C. 1491: America Before Columbus Was More Sophisticated and More Populous than We Have Ever Thought—and a More Livable Place Than Europe. *Atlantic Monthly* March 2002, 41–53.

McDowell, Bart. The Aztecs. *National Geographic* December 1980, 704–752.

McKee, Jesse O., and Jon A. Schlenker. *The Choctaws: Cultural Evolution of a Native American Tribe.* Jackson: University Press of Mississippi, 1980.

Meggers, Betty J., Eduardo S. Brondizio, Michael J. Heckenberger, Carlos Fausto, and Bruna Franchetto. Revisiting Amazonia Circa 1492 [Letter to the Editor]. *Science* 302(December 19, 2003):2067–2070.

Mexican Skull May Explain Indigenous Origins. Reuters, December 5, 2002. Available at http://story.news.yahoo.com/news? tmpl=story&u=/nm/20021205/sc_nm/science_mexico_skull_dc_1.

The Mohawk Creation Story. *Akwesasne Notes* 21.5 (Spring 1989):32–29.

Mooney, J. Population. In F. W. Hodge, ed., *Handbook of American Indians North of Mexico*. Bureau of American Ethnology Bulletin 30(part 2). Washington, DC: U.S. Government Printing Office, 1910: 28–37.

Mooney, James. *The Aboriginal Population of North America North of Mexico*. Edited by J. R. Swanton. Smithsonian Miscellaneous Collections 80(7). Washington, DC: U.S. Government Printing Office,1928.

Moore, John H. *The Cheyennes*. Oxford, U.K.: Blackwell, 1997.

Moore, Oliver. Pre-Mayan Written Language Found in Mexico. *Toronto Globe and Mail*, December 5, 2002. Available at http://www.globeandmail.com/servlet/ArticleNews/front/RTGAM/20021205/w lang1205/Front/homeBN/breakingnews.

Morison, Patricia. Wisdom of the Aztecs, *London Financial Times*. Reprinted in Notes on the Arts, *World Press Review*, January 1993, 54.

Parker, Arthur C. *The Code of Handsome Lake, the Seneca Prophet*. New York State Museum Bulletin 163, Education Department Bulletin No. 530, November 1, 1912. Albany: University of the State of New York, 1913.

Peopling the Americas: A New Site to Debate. *National Geographic* (Geographica), September 1992.

Pitulko, V. V., P. A. Nikolsky, E. Yu. Girya, A. E. Basilyan, V. E. Tumskoy, S. A. Koulakov, S. N. Astakhov, E. Yu. Pavlova, and M. A. Anisimov. The Yana RHS Site: Humans in the Arctic Before the Last Glacial Maximum. *Science* 303(January 2, 2004):52–56.

Pohl, Frederick Julius. *The Viking Settlements of North America*. New York: Potter, 1972.

Pohl, Mary E. D., Kevin O. Pope, and Christopher von Nagy. Olmec Origins of Mesoamerican Writing. *Science* 298(December 6, 2002):1984–1987.

Portilla, Miguel Leon. *The Broken Spears: The Aztec Account of the Conquest of Mexico*. Boston: Beacon Press, 1962.

Ramenofsky, Ann F. *Vectors of Death: The Archeology of European Contact*. Albuquerque: University of New Mexico Press, 1987.

Recer, Paul. Researchers Find Evidence of Sophisticated, Pre-Columbia Civilization in the Amazon Basin." Associated Press, September 19, 2003, in LEXIS.

Recer, Paul. Evidence Found of Arctic Hunters Living in Siberia Near New World 30,000 Years Ago." Associated Press, January 2, 2004, in LEXIS.

Sando, Joe S. *The Pueblo Indians*. San Francisco: Indian Historian Press, 1976.

Schele, Linda. The Owl, Shield, and Flint Blade. *Natural History*, November 1991, 7–11.

Sherzer, Joel. A Richness of Voices. In Alvin Joesphy, ed., *America in 1492: The World of the Indian Peoples Before the Arrival of Columbus*. New York: Knopf, 1992: 251–276.

Slayman, Andrew L. A Battle Over Bones. *Archaeology* 50:1 (January/February 1997):16–23.

Snow, Dean R., and Kim M. Lanphear. European Contact and Indian Depopulation in the Northeast: The Timing of the First Epidemics. *Ethnohistory* 35:1(Winter 1988):16–24.

Snow, Dean R., and Kim M. Lanphear. "More Methodological Perspectives": A Rejoinder to Dobyns. *Ethnohistory* 36:3 (Summer 1989):299–300.

Stannard, David E. *American Holocaust: The Conquest of the New World.* New York: Oxford University Press, 1992.

Stevens, William K. Andean Culture Found to Be as Old as the Great Pyramids. *New York Times,* October 3, 1989, C-1.

Stokstad, Erik. Oldest New World Writing Suggests Olmec Innovation. *Science* 298 (December 6, 2002):1872–1874.

Stokstad, Erik. Amazon Archaeology: "Pristine" Forest Teemed With People. *Science* 301(September 19, 2003):1645–1646.

Stone, Richard. Late Date for Siberian Site Challenges Bering Pathway. *Science* 301(July 25, 2003):450–451.

Stone, Richard. A Surprising Survival Story in the Siberian Arctic. *Science* 303 (January 2, 2004):33.

Thomas, David Hurst. *Skull Wars: Kennewick Man, Archaeology, and the Battle for Native American Identity.* New York: Basic Books/Peter N. Nevraumont, 2000.

Tozzer, Alfred, ed. *Landa's Relacion de las Cosas de Yucatan.* Harvard University Peabody Museum of Archaeology and Ethnology Papers, Vol. 18, p. 169. Cited in Henderson, 1981, 88.

Trigger, Bruce G. *Children of the Aataentsic: A History of the Huron People.* Montreal: McGill-Queen's University Press, 1976.

Wallace, Anthony F. C. *The Death and Rebirth of the Seneca.* New York: Vintage, 1972.

Walton, Marsha, and Michael Coren. Archaeologists Put Humans In North America 50,000 Years Ago. Cable News Network, November 17, 2004. Available at http://www.cnn.com/2004/TECH/science/11/17/carolina.dig/index.html.

Weatherford, Jack. *Native Roots: How the Indians Enriched America.* New York: Crown, 1991.

Wilford, John Noble. Did Warfare Doom the Mayas' Ecology? *New York Times* News Service. In *Miami Herald,* December 22, 1991, 7-L.

Williams, Stephen. *Fantastic Archaeology: The Wild Side of North American Prehistory.* Philadelphia: University of Pennsylvania Press, 1991.

Wright, Ronald. *Stolen Continents: The Americas Through Indian Eyes Since 1492.* Boston: Houghton-Mifflin, 1992.

CHAPTER 2

Mexico and Mesoamerica

BEGINNINGS TO EUROPEAN CONTACT

In present-day Mexico and Central America (*Mesoamerica*, Greek for Middle America), complex civilizations began to organize at about the time that the Roman Empire was expanding across Europe, northern Africa, and Palestine. These civilizations evolved over the centuries in different locations around two centers. One was the highlands of present-day Guatemala into the scrublands of Yucatan, where the Maya flourished. In and around the Valley of Mexico, the second center, a series of city-states had been rising and falling for more than 1,500 years when, in 1519, Cortes met the Aztecs, the last, largest, and grandest civilization of them all.

Both of these centers also formed the nucleus of an agricultural, mercantile, and administrative network, with commercial influence often radiating several hundred miles from the center through a thickly populated agricultural hinterland. The rise of each center was brought about by a well-defined elite purportedly acting under the sponsorship and direction of a pantheon of gods. As archaeologists learn more about the cultures that preceded the Aztecs, a pattern seems to be emerging: More than once, the elites of one center may have escaped popular unrest by moving to other areas and starting the cycle over again. Thus, a similar (but in some ways more technologically advanced) civilization rose in another area as the old city was reclaimed by nature.

URBAN BEGINNINGS IN MESOAMERICA

The Mesoamerican elite tradition probably began with the Olmecs, who constructed towns as centers of politically integrated societies and containing temples, elite residences, stone sculptures, and elaborate tombs. The Olmec civilization, which preceded the Mayan as well as the chain of civilizations that led to the Aztecs in the Valley of Mexico, started organizing complex societies based on the rich wild food resources of the southern Gulf Coast of present-day Mexico shortly after 1500 B.C.E. In the art, rituals, and other lifeways of the Olmecs, one sees the later Mayan, Toltec, and Aztec traditions emerging.

By 1400 B.C.E., the first large Olmec settlement had risen at a site today called San Lorenzo, southwest of the Tuxtla Mountains near Mexico's southern Gulf Coast. The settlement contained large public buildings and stone monuments. Evidence, including the probable number of residential sites, indicates that San Lorenzo was a small city in terms of population but a very large one in terms of economic, political, and religious power across a sizable hinterland (M. D. Coe, 1968).

The elite of San Lorenzo supervised projects involving earth moving of monumental scope, in the hundreds of millions of cubic feet. Thousand of tons of basalt used in construct monuments were quarried in the Tuxtla Mountains. The site also has yielded imported obsidian, mica, and other materials from many hundreds of miles away that were used for jewelry, ritual objects, and other prized possessions. The Olmecs of San Lorenzo also probably imported other items, such as foodstuffs, that left little archaeological evidence. Judging from the number of implements recovered for grinding corn, it was probably the staple food of the common people at San Lorenzo; the people also likely ate turtles and fish; the elite occasionally dined on young puppies raised especially for that purpose.

The Olmecs did not use metal tools, but they did fashion iron ore into shining disks that the elite wore as ornaments. About 1000 B.C.E., San Lorenzo was surpassed in size by another Olmec settlement, La Venta, east of San Lorenzo, near the Gulf Coast. Although La Venta's public and ceremonial areas were larger, its culture was similar to that of San Lorenzo. La Venta reached its peak between 1000 and 750 B.C.E. Other Olmec sites have been identified but, as of this writing, not widely excavated.

The Olmecs did not occupy Mesoamerica alone; other peoples also were establishing organized societies with agricultural bases at about the same time. In the Valley of Oaxaca, for example, a dozen settlements began between 1300 and 1600 B.C.E. Later, at about 750 B.C.E., as La Venta declined, the Oaxacan capitol of Monte Alban included a civic center with large pyramids and surrounded by rich agricultural land. Olmec sculptures also may contain the earliest hints of hieroglyphic writing of a form that later was adopted by the Mayas and Aztecs. (See details on writing systems in chapter 1.)

As the Olmecs' civilization declined after 600 B.C.E., other groups rose and fell at other sites, each enjoying brief authority over an agricultural hinterland. Each in turn organized its society under a religious and military elite, with social classes, rituals, and art forms that continued the tradition that began with the Olmecs and ended with the Aztecs.

More than a century before the birth of Christ, the first true sizable urban areas in North America arose in the Valley of Mexico, at Teotihuacan, northeast of the vast lake on which the Aztecs would later build Tenochtitlán (which translates to place of the prickly-pear cactus). Another urban area arose at Cuicuilco, in the southwestern part of the Valley of Mexico, near the Mexico National University's present-day campus, on the southern side of Mexico City. Cuicuilco probably was the larger city in the beginning, before a volcanic eruption and lava flow ruined its site (and hinterland) and sent much of its population to Teotihuacan, which swelled in size from 20,000 to 30,000 people by about 100 C.E. to as many as 200,000 by 700 C.E. (Maxwell, 1978, 52).

With an estimated population of 200,000, Teotihuacan (meaning place of the gods in Nahuatl, the Aztec language) was one of the largest—if not the largest—urban areas on earth at that time, nearly equal in population to the Aztec capital of Tenochtitlan 700 years later. Cities such as London and Paris did not reach that size until after Europe's Age of Exploration began. Teotihuacan covered twenty square kilometers (or eight square miles) and was thick with ceremonial buildings and more than 2,000 large apartment blocks, some of which functioned as workplaces as well as homes. Some of them specialized in the manufacture of obsidian blades; others manufactured pottery. About 150 ceramic shops have been identified in Teotihuacan, which produced sturdy cooking ware for common people as well as intricately designed vessels for the well-to-do. In other shops, artisans fashioned the elaborate feathered costumes worn by the elite during ceremonial occasions. Artisans carved hundreds of large monuments from basalt blocks, ranging in size up to 40 tons each; these portrayed secular and supernatural rulers and events.

Archaeological evidence indicates well-developed societies with military and religious elites supported by intensive agriculture in an area that was probably much more lush than the capital city of Mexico appears today. During the last 500 years, vegetation has been stripped by overgrazing sheep imported from Europe. In the twentieth century, urban air pollution also has stunted the growth of vegetation in the Valley of Mexico.

Teotihuacan cast a trading net as far as the region today occupied by Guatemala City, where in about 500 C.E. colonists from the Valley of Mexico transformed the Mayan town of Kaminaljuyú into an outpost. The rulers of Teotihuacan had practical motives: The Mayan town lay on the route to their main sources of cocoa and jade. The town also was situated near routes that controlled access to one of North America's richest obsidian mines. No ruler of the time could field an effective army without access to obsidian for weaponry. At about this time, 350 obsidian workshops in Teotihuacan employed thousands of people. Obsidian tools and weapons had become the city's main export.

The Aztecs worked earlier civilizations into their own mythologized history, which maintained that theirs was the last of five epochs during which the universe had been destroyed and reborn. One of the prior epochs was said to have occurred in Teotihuacan; its influence passed to the Aztecs through Tula, the capital of the Toltecs, which reached its height shortly after 1000 C.E. although the Aztecs did not originate in the Valley of Mexico, they were in effect absorbed by the 1,500-year-old urban tradition of the area after they arrived and conquered the descendants of Teotihuacan and other cities. The Aztecs' Great Temple contained an area (two so-called red temples) that affected Teotihuacan-style symbols, including architecture.

According to Aztec myth, the gods met at Teotihuacan to recreate the sun, the moon, and the rest of the universe:

> When it was still night,
> When there was no day,
> When there was no light,
> They met,
> The gods convened,
> There at Teotihuacan
> They said
> They spoke among themselves:
> "Come here, oh Gods!
> Who will take upon himself,
> Who will take charge
> of making days,
> of making light?
> —Leon-Portillo, 1972, 23-24

Richard A. Diehl described Teotihuacan as follows:

A truly cosmopolitan center whose inhabitants included farmers, craftsmen, priests, merchants, warriors, government officials, architects, laborers, and enclaves of resident foreigners. Most of the people lived in single-story rectangular masonry apartment houses sheltering more than 100 residents [each]. (1981, 24)

Teotihuacan was divided into four quadrants by two major causeways, on which fronted most of the important secular and religious buildings of the city. One of these causeways, called the Street of the Dead, ran roughly north to south and was the site of most of these larger buildings. The two avenues intersected at an array of temples, including one dedicated to Quetzalcoatl, the Feathered Serpent who also became an Aztec god. This area also included temples to the sun and the moon (also similar to Aztec cosmology), which were two of the largest pyramidal mounds erected anywhere in the world to that time. The Sun Pyramid measured 200 meters on its sides and 60 meters high. The plazas, parks, and causeways of the ceremonial center comprised a paved area roughly three miles long and two miles wide.

The city of Teotihuacan reached the height of its power about 500 C.E. and declined by roughly 800 C.E., after which other cities competed for power. At about 800 C.E., or just a century before the widespread decline of Mayan culture to the south (see the section "The Maya: Mystery and Speculation" below), Teotihuacan was destroyed by enemies from the outside who set fires in the city. Teotihuacan's sizable population fled in large numbers, leaving only small agricultural communities. One of these, Cholula, was located near modern Puebla, east of the Valley of Mexico. It had been a satellite city of Teotihuacan but survived long after the larger city's demise, well into the Spanish conquest. Xochicalco, in the lowlands near present-day Morelos, collapsed two centuries after Teotihuacan. The best-known urban successor to Teotihuacan was Tula, north of present-day Mexico City and the capital of the Toltecs, whose culture the Aztecs both ransacked and mythologized with tales of how the Toltecs had grown multihued cotton and giant ears of corn.

Tula later was sacked by the invading Aztecs, whose popular history held that the Toltecs had become decadent, drunken into a stupor on *pulque*, a Mexican alcoholic beverage. Before the Toltecs' Tula reached its height in the Valley of Mexico, the Maya spread a diffuse array of city-states to the south. They shared several cultural attributes with their northern neighbors, which indicated copious trade and travel between the two areas.

THE MAYA: MYSTERY AND SPECULATION

To many of the scholars who have studied them, the Maya remain a subject of mystery and speculation. Scholars who had not deciphered their written language once speculated that the Maya at their height had been relatively peaceful—perhaps playing, in imagination, Greeks to the Aztecs' Rome. History displayed in the Maya's own writing now portrays them as very warlike (Demarest, 1993, 95–111).

At the height of their civilization, about 600 to 900 C.E., the Maya dominated most of what is today southern Mexico, Guatemala, and Belize. Their civilization was not an organized empire in the Inca, Roman, or Aztec sense but a collection of independent city-states. The ramparts of fortresslike Tulum looked out over the ragged surf of the Yucatán shore, gateway to a network of trading routes that connected such Mayan cities as Copan, Tikal, Chichén Itzá, and Palenque. Maya cities thrived in natural surroundings of great contrast, from the flat, hot, and humid lowlands of Yucatán, to rain forests further inland, to highland valleys that can be as arid as northern Mexico, and to higher mountains, many volcanic, that are thick with forests.

For fifteen centuries, the Maya made some of the most inhospitable jungles in the world bloom with "the sunbeams of the gods." Corn was the dietary staple of a civilization of substantial monuments that in many respects was a match for any in the Eastern Hemisphere. In more than 100 cities, Mayan artists produced some of the most exquisite art in the world of their time, and Mayan scientists calculated solar and lunar eclipses with an accuracy that would not be exceeded until modern times. The Mayan calendar is a few minutes a year more accurate than the Roman calendar used today but was vastly more complex, requiring a priest trained in its use to establish the date. The Maya also calculated the path of Venus and were the first to develop a

Chichén Itzá scene. (Courtesy of the Library of Congress.)

concept of negative numbers in mathematics. Yet, by the time the first Spanish explorers reached Mesoamerica, Mayan civilization was crumbling, probably from incessant warfare and ecological exhaustion.

Origins of the Maya

The origins of the Maya are not known to contemporary scholars, aside from speculation that aspects of their culture may have been borrowed from the Olmecs, who may have spoken a language related to one or more of the Mayan dialects. Some evidence exists that the Maya may have begun the building of their civilization in Kaminaljuya, which is today part of Guatemala City, before 1100 B.C.E. by the European calendar. In 1936, the Carnegie Institution began excavating the largest "preclassic" Mayan site discovered to that time. These discoveries (and later ones) showed that the Maya were predominantly urban with a complex agricultural infrastructure supporting their cities. These early ruins (dating to roughly 800 to 300 B.C.E.) also showed evidence of hiero-glyphic writing that would later open even more detail of the Mayan worldview and daily life. Scholars unraveling the Maya's writing are discovering that their efforts have been complicated by the fact that Maya scribes apparently liked to play tricks with words: puns, homonyms (two words with the same sound but different meanings), verbal allusions, metaphors, and other wordplay.

From the highlands of Guatemala, the Maya may have moved into the lowlands of Petén and Yucatán (in present-day Mexico) at about the time Christ was born in the Old World. In the Mexican state of Chiapas, Mayan monuments have been found that date to 36 B.C.E.; the precision of this date, and others, is made possible by the Maya's own calendar, which can be matched with ours. The earliest such monuments at Tikal date to about 300 C.E.

A Mayan city known as Dzibilchaltún, excavated by E. Wyllys Andrews IV of Tulane University (New Orleans, LA) beginning in 1956, was occupied con-tinuously between 500 B.C.E. and the time of the Spanish conquest. At its height, this city was probably home to at least 40,000 people, a population roughly equal to that of Alexandria, Egypt, at about the same time (La Fay, 1975, 733–734). Scholars also found evidence of intensive agriculture prac-ticed on terraced fields and platforms raised to escape seasonal flooding. "These features indicate that the Maya practiced permanent and intensive agricul-ture capable of supporting a large population," said Professor B. L. Turner II of the University of Oklahoma (Norman, OK). "If you could have flown over the Petén at the height of the [Mayan] Classic Period, you would have found something akin to central Ohio today" (La Fay, 1975, 733).

The major Mayan urban areas often battled with each other for dominance, even developing their own language dialects and art forms. Slowly, scholars are building a history of Mayan civilization that may someday rival that of Egypt and other Old World civilizations. The description of this history has faced hazards since the first contact; some of the Spanish friars knew how to

A Mayan temple in Tikal. (Courtesy of the Library of Congress.)

read Mayan hieroglyphs but left no guides to later generations. The Spaniard Avendano produced a dictionary and grammar of Mayan language while living among the Yucatec during the eighteenth century, but all copies of it have been lost.

The Maya built a civilization on an epic scale. Tikal, the largest of the Maya's many cities, housing about 100,000 people, rambled over 23 square miles at about the same time that imperial Rome, which was more densely populated, covered only a third as much area. Depictions of early rulers in Uaxactun and Tikal indicate that before the birth of Christ in the Old World, Mayan city-states were raiding each other for captives. Later depictions show warriors holding obsidian-edged clubs and spear throwers. In one depiction, Great Jaguar Paw, a ruler at Tikal, is shown celebrating a military victory with a bloodletting from his genitals. Some of the stellae (rock carvings used to depict historical events) were erected on top of human skeletons. The stellae also contain indications that some of the Mayan cities traded with Teotihuacan in the Valley of Mexico; it is likely that the residents of Mexico traded high-land products (such as obsidian blades) with the lowland Maya for cotton, tropical bird feathers, shells, and other lowland items.

Archaeologists have excavated only a fraction of what the Maya built during their classic period. In the Mexican state of Chiapas, for example, by 1990 archaeologists had unearthed between two and three dozen structures from the thickly wooded hills at Palenque. This collection of buildings make a distinctive site, but they are only a fraction of the structures that stretch for seven miles.

After its founding about 1000 B.C.E., Copán grew into "the most artistically embellished of all the great Maya sites" (Fash and Fash, 1990, 28). To archaeologists, the inscriptions on stellae and altars as well as temple panels, stairways, and portable objects used in everyday life comprise an open history book that allows the life of Copán to emerge. From them, contemporary scholars are reconstructing dynastic lineages as well as the lives of ordinary Maya.

During the height of their civilization, the Maya surrounded themselves with decoration, on their buildings as well as their bodies. The Maya etched tattoos into their bodies and painted them a variety of colors. Priests were painted blue, warriors in black and red, and prisoners in black and white stripes. Some Maya filed their teeth and distended their pierced earlobes, hanging earplugs in them. Many also pierced the septum of their noses and inserted carved jewelry. They flattened their foreheads and worked to make themselves cross-eyed, a standard of beauty. Feathers also conveyed beauty; the Maya wore the plumage of birds bred in aviaries for their most gorgeous plumes. According to William Brandon, "men wore brilliant little obsidian mirrors hanging in their long hair" (1961, 32).

Bishop Diego de Landa's *Relación de Las Cosas de Yucatán* was written in 1556 during the first years of the Spanish conquest with a sense of awe at the civilization of the Maya, remarking on the large number and grand nature of their buildings, at a civilization so exotic that Spaniards at home would think he was fabricating a tall tale.

Today, scholars often find that looters have ransacked newly discovered Mayan sites. The scholars are pursuing knowledge as the looters seek high prices paid in illicit art markets the world over. One such site, uncovered at Rio Usumacinta during 1946, contained multicolored frescoes that described a battle in the middle of the eighth century in detail, from the armed conflict itself to the ritual sacrifice of prisoners afterward. A chronicler described warriors in animal pelts and feathers:

> They came over the hill with the first rays of the rising sun, filling the air with their shouts and war cries, displaying their banners. . . . It was terrible, this descent of the Quiche. They advanced rapidly in columns, down to the edge of the river. The clash was horrible, the screams and shouts. The din of flutes, drums and conch-shell trumpets resounded as the Quiche chiefs vainly sought to save themselves by divine magic. Soon they were hurled back, and many died. A great number were taken prisoner, along with their chiefs. (La Fay, 1975, 735–736)

The Numerical Precision of the Maya

The Maya developed remarkable precision in timekeeping and astronomy because it served their theology; unlike the development of secular science in Europe (which often conflicted with religious beliefs), religion and science were one and the same among the Maya. Their numeric system utilized a

Gregoria Pat, a Maya Indian. (Courtesy of the Library of Congress.)

system of dots and bars and was based on 20 (the sum of fingers and toes) rather than 10 (the sum of fingers), which was used in Europe.

Also, unlike European practice, the Maya generally did not distinguish among past, present, and future; the same word, *kin*, described all three concepts in their language. Time was said to be circular. Events experienced in the past were expected to happen again, in a cycle. A person who knew the past was believed to be able to predict the future. Success in predicting such natural phenomena as eclipses was said to be divine proof of this. Time was seen as one immutable stream, stretching back to a date corresponding to August 11, 3114 B.C.E., the first date on the Maya's "Long count" calendar. After 5,200 years, the Maya's Long Count calendar comes to a close on the winter solstice in 2012. This is not the end of time, however; the Maya tradition has counted three Long Counts before this one and will begin counting again after it.

Mayan religious beliefs and rituals seem similar to those of the Valley of Mexico, which is more than circumstantial. The headdresses of priests and other high officials sometimes included symbols similar to those used in Teotihuacan; traders from the Valley of Mexico ranged into Mayan country very early, and culture traveled with them. As with the Aztecs, Mayan religious life was dominated by a pantheon of gods serving various purposes: Itzamna, the Lord of Life; Ah Kin, the sun god; Ah Puch, who ruled the land of the dead, and Chac, god of rain, among many others. The Maya also worshipped a feathered serpent, Kukulcan, which resembled the Aztecs' Quetzalcoatl.

As with the Aztecs, the Maya believed that their gods required sacrifices of human blood on a regular schedule. Most of this blood was collected from prisoners of war (a motivating factor for many of the intercity raids). Some members of the lower classes were forced to die for the gods, and people of all economic levels sometimes volunteered to feed the gods' appetites with offerings of their blood. Early Spanish records contain accounts of priests drawing thorny ropes through their tongues to draw blood with which to appease the gods; others took blood from their genitals. The sacrifices were accompanied by complex ceremonies, during which priests sometimes slit the chest of a person being sacrificed, emerging with the heart, which often still beat. The Spanish, who seemed to have little qualm with Mayan bloodshed in the name of Christianity's conquest, recoiled in horror at the sight of sacrifices to gods they regarded as pagan; Bernal Díaz del Castillo, the soldier-historian who accompanied Cortes and other explorers during the sixteenth century, described in *Conquest of New Spain, 1517–1521* Mayan priests whose hair was so matted with blood that it could never be combed out.

The Maya pantheon of gods was complex not only because of their large number, but also because their identities were not static; most Mayan deities had four distinct persona, one for each of the four cardinal directions. These multiple persona often embodied contradictions, such as male and female, old and young, good and evil. Sometimes, gods' attributes (and even names) changed from city to city. All of this, along with difficulty in matching gods named in Mayan glyphs with those in postconquest documents, has frustrated experts seeking to assemble a single, definitive inventory of Mayan theological symbols.

Mayan Class Structure

Mayan religion also prescribed a rather strict class structure in which the common people, most of whom were farmers, worked to sustain a small elite that understood astronomy, language, and religious rites. The class structure was so ingrained that when members of the elite traveled, common people often shouldered their litters for miles at a time. In this way, the common people were enlisted in a social structure in which they produced the necessities of life so that the elite could appease the gods and maintain the universe according to Mayan theology. When a baby came into the world, for example, Mayan priests predicted its future using star charts and other records; every moment in time was thought to be governed by the various deities; a child's future was believed to be predetermined.

Mayan custom dictated that people marry within their classes, but outside their families. This was as true for commoners as for the nobility; people in all classes of Mayan society maintained family lineages and married outside them. Between the common farmers and the aristocracy, merchants, artisans, military men, and others occupied the Mayan middle class. Below them were a class of landless serfs who sharecropped the lands of the elite; many of these serfs were freed prisoners of war who had not been sacrificed to the gods. Convicted criminals and people who had failed to pay their debts formed the lowest class of society. The poorest of the poor could be sold into slavery by their relatives; slavery often was the last stop before sacrifice.

Although Mayan society was constructed along well-defined class lines, limited social mobility did exist. Occasionally, a person could ascend in status by marriage or fall because of indiscretions such as chronic indebtedness. The elite seemed to have encouraged the infusion of some new blood into its ranks. For example, several high political offices were designated for commoners who distinguished themselves in battle. A degree of social mobility also was evident in Mayan burial customs, which could be similar for people of all classes. During 1992, archaeologists Arlene and Diane Chase of the University of Central Florida (Orlando), unearthed tombs showing similarities across classes at Caracol, in present-day Belize. The ruins of Caracol cover 55 square miles, and the Chases estimated that its population during the classic Mayan period reached 180,000. In 562 C.E., Caracol defeated Tikal, which had been the preeminent city in the region, in one of an intensifying series of wars that may have been one of many factors, including environmental degradation, that led to the Maya's eventual collapse as a civilization.

Each person in Mayan society was born into a family lineage, which included individuals related through the male side of the family. Inheritance of land, jewelry, and other items of material value also usually was governed by the male line. After marriage, however, a man by custom moved into the home of his bride's family, where he was destined for a period of service of six years or more. Women sometimes owned land in their own right, however, and passed it to their daughters; they also sometimes held high office in civil Mayan society, which was organized into municipal wards, each of which had an administrative officer. The municipal officers of all the wards in a town formed a governing council.

Although the society was fashioned to cater to them, nobles' lives were not without challenge or danger. They often led the intercity wars and often competed in a ritual ball game that also seems to have been tied into Mayan theology. The game shares some attributes of present-day basketball and soccer. Members of two teams tried to put a rubber ball through an elevated stone ring at each end of a ceremonial court. Players were not permitted to touch the ball with their hands (as in soccer). Penalties may have been assessed if the ball touched the ground. Losers at this game sometimes were sacrificed to the gods.

The Unearthing of Tikal and Other Sites

Archaeologists began to unearth a large metropolis at Tikal (in northern Guatemala) during 1956, yielding the tallest group of temple-pyramids in the New World (W. R. Coe, 1975). At Tikal, the Maya built large temples linked by causeways the width of modern freeways, as well as ball courts, a covered marketplace, and thousands of residences. Tikal was well developed by the time of Christ's birth. By its height, 800 years later, Tikal's population was between 30,000 and 60,000. The city's 3,000 structures included six pyramids, seven temple palaces, and several man-made reservoirs, all covering an area at least one mile square. The city is still an impressive sight, even in its decayed state, with remains of the pyramids towering 200 feet into the air and connected by wide causeways. Tikal's location took advantage of a nearby portage between rivers leading to the Gulf of Mexico and Caribbean Sea.

Like most of the other Mayan cities, Tikal declined about 890 C.E. according to the history recorded in its monuments. The religious and scientific elite collapsed, and squatters moved onto the ceremonial plazas amid the temples, living among piles of their own refuse, as the jungle reclaimed the city's outskirts.

The actual spadework at such sites takes large amounts of money and often trails speculation about what the forest still may hold. Like the ancient Egyptians, the rulers of the Maya were very good at immortalizing themselves in stone sculptures and other artifacts with a life of thousands of years. From these inscriptions and monuments, scholars are building a genealogy of rulers at Palenque, the Maya's westernmost major city, which lasted from 500 to nearly 800 C.E. Surprisingly, given the male dominance in most Mesoamerican cultures, at least two of the rulers in this city were women.

The Decline of the Maya

Palenque, like most other Mayan cities, declined abruptly in the ninth century C.E. The Spanish found the Aztecs in their full flower, but the Maya, with a few exceptions, were past their prime. Tulum, for example, still hosted an active trading culture along the Yucatán coast long after much of Mayan civilization had declined. The reasons for this eclipse are not known precisely; various arguments advance a case for the breakdown of trading relations, wars, environmental exhaustion of agriculture near the largest urban centers, earthquakes, hurricanes, and invasions by other peoples.

Disease may have played a role in the Maya's decline even before the Spanish conquest. Medical evidence indicates that the Maya shrunk in stature at the end of the classic period, probably because of malnutrition (La Fay, 1975, 762). The religious and scientific elites may have become overbearing in their demands on the common people, only to have them rise up and destroy the social structure that maintained the elites, according to a theory advanced by Eric Thompson (cited in Gann, 1925), a British scholar. Thompson has speculated that some of the Maya's former rulers may have escaped, joined the Toltecs, then later returned with them to reconquer parts of their former fiefdoms. The history of the Toltecs supports this idea. After most of the Mayan cities fell, the Toltecs are said to have established colonies in the area.

The final glory of Mayan civilization probably played itself out at Uxmal, forty-five miles southwest of present-day Mérida, on the Yucatán peninsula. The Xiu family, which had originated elsewhere, became Mayanized and ruled the city from roughly 1000 c.e. until shortly before the Spanish conquest. Tulum may have been a trading outlet for Uxmal, which means "thrice built," a name that suggests the city had suffered a collapse twice before and then been rebuilt (Williams, 1991, 22).

As scholars learned more about Mayan society, they have discovered that, although a marked general decline occurred in Mayan society at about 900 c.e., it was not uniform. From time to time, new cultural infusions (mainly from the north, including the Valley of Mexico) seemed to cause some centers to rise again. For example, Chichén Itzá saw the rise of a new dynasty that included both Mayan and Toltec elements for roughly two centuries after 1000 c.e. This dynasty dominated most of northern Yucatán at that time. The monumental architecture of Chichén Itzá during this period shows Toltecs and their Mayan allies winning battles and their Mayan adversaries being led to the altar of the gods. After Chichén Itzá declined about 1200 c.e., another center, Mayapan, dominated northern Yucatán. Further inland, the Quiche capital of Utatlán, in the highlands, began to dominate its hinterland at about 1400 c.e., and was in full flower at the time of the Spanish conquest a century and a quarter later.

In some locations, murals that are richly descriptive of the Maya's daily lives were buried under successive renovations of ceremonial centers with great care to ensure that they would survive intact for centuries. The best example of such intentional history comes from Cacaxtla, east of Mexico City, which apparently was a Mayan traders' center between 650 and about 1000 c.e. Spurred by treasure hunters' discoveries in 1975, archaeologists have been uncovering sets of huge murals that still retain much of their original coloration and detail.

The city was renovated eight times, and rebuilt atop its earlier site, which contained the richly hued murals, careful buried against layers of sand that preserved them (Stuart, 1992, 120–136).

The Role of War in the Mayan Decline

By the beginning of the twenty-first century, details of civilization-destroying wars among the Maya became evident as an important cause of their decline. A hurricane during the summer of 2001 uncovered carvings at Dos Pilas indicating that what previously had been described as a series of local wars during the seventh and eighth centuries C.E. really was a "world war" among the Maya between two blocs of allies, centered in Tikal and Calakmul. This picture emerged from explorations made public during 2002 by Arthur Demarest of Vanderbilt University's Institute of Mesoamerican Archeology (Nashville, TN) ("Scholars Rewrite," 2002, 12-A). According to Howard La Fay (1975):

> Gone forever is the image of the Maya as peaceful, rather primitive farmers practicing esoteric religious rites in their jungle fastness. What emerges is a portrait of a vivid, warlike race, numerous beyond any previous estimate, employing sophisticated agricultural techniques. And, like the Vikings half a world away, they traded and raided with zest. (p. 732)

Continual warfare probably also played a role in the environmental destruction of the Copan Valley; the monuments of the ceremonial center provide a chronicle of conflict lasting centuries. At one point, the thirteenth ruler of Copan, a man known to us as 18-Rabbit, was captured by the ruler of another Mayan city and decapitated. The historical evidence contained in inscriptions scattered all around Copan is so detailed that archaeologists can reconstruct not only the names and ruling dates of kings, but also the names or titles of the nine men who usually acted as advisors to the ruler.

According to Jared Diamond, more and more people fought over fewer resources. Maya warfare, already endemic, peaked just before the collapse. That is not surprising when one reflects that at least 5 million people, most of them farmers, were crammed into an area smaller than the state of Colorado. That's a high population by the standards of ancient farming societies, even if it wouldn't strike modern Manhattan-dwellers as crowded (Diamond, 2003, 49; Webster, 2002).

Climate Change and Mayan Decline

In addition to intercity violence, the Maya's final years as a high civilization also were afflicted by three intense droughts that crippled their corn-based agriculture. Recent research indicates that a population in the millions also degraded the environment. "This reinforces the tenuous nature of human civilizations in the face of a capricious Mother Nature," said Tom Pedersen, a University of Victoria (British Colombia) professor who is a recognized world authority on ancient climates (Calamai, 2003).

A research team led by Gerald Haug (who did postdoctoral studies with Pedersen) reconstructed Yucatán rainfall year by year using improved techniques to extract climate information preserved in ocean floor sediments. The scientists were able to read the sediments as if they were tree rings, said Haug, who is now researching ancient climates at a geosciences institute in Potsdam, Germany (Calamai, 2003). The researchers identified three decade-long droughts (around 810, 860, and 910 C.E.) that devastated Mayan society. According to this research, rainfall already had been declining slowly for a century because of changes in large-scale atmospheric circulation patterns. Haug and colleagues (2003) concluded that "a century-scale decline in rainfall put a general strain on resources in the region, which was then exacerbated by abrupt drought events, contributing to the social stresses that led to the Maya demise" (p. 1731).

Intensive harvesting of wood, along with agriculture (which depleted fragile tropical soils), also seems to have caused the abandonment of some Mayan urban centers during the general collapse of Mayan society about 900 C.E. One example of this decline may be found in Copán, once a major Mayan ceremonial center in present-day Honduras. Scholars have discovered that the Copán Valley became overpopulated and overdeveloped. The destruction of the valley's forests (mainly to open new farming fields and to provide cooking fuel) ultimately destroyed the ecological balance of the area, forcing the abandonment of the ceremonial center. Researchers from Pennsylvania State University (University Park) "have demonstrated that that at the end of the [Mayan] Classic Period there was extensive soil loss, massive erosion, a long-term decline in rainfall, and probably a number of highly communicable diseases" (Fash and Fash, 1990, 28).

THE TOLTECS

North of the Valley of Mexico, in the southern reaches of present-day Hidalgo, the Toltecs' capital of Tula emerged as the premier Mesoamerican urban center as most of the Maya centers to the south declined. The urban area and ceremonial center of Tula was situated in a highland river valley that supplied water necessary for the irrigation to support intensive agriculture. Farmers began to occupy the area a few centuries before the birth of Christ; shortly afterward, Chingu, a regional center, rose a few miles north of the site that would later host Tula, probably as part of Teotihuacan's network of commerce. By 600 C.E., however, Chingu was declining as the trade network collapsed.

Documentary and archaeological records indicate that between 800 and 900 C.E., members of elites (as well as some people from the lower classes)

A Toltec princess. (Courtesy of the Library of Congress.)

moved from other cities toward Tula in large numbers, building a new urban center. These records combine history with myth. Some sources indicate that the majority of the Toltecs came from the Gulf Coast or even from northern Mexico. Tula reached a peak population of about 40,000 before the invading Aztecs arrived about 1170 C.E.

One class of priests, craftspeople, and merchants (called the *Nonoalca*) played a particularly pivotal role in making Tula the most influential urban center in Mesoamerica between roughly 900 and 1170 C.E. Various sources indicate that the Nonoalca were multiethnic, and that they spoke several languages (including Nahuatl, the language later used by the Aztecs, Popoloca, Mixtec, Mazatec, and even Maya). Such population movements tend to support the belief that some members of the urban elites and people who provided services for them moved from city to city over the generations and centuries.

At its height, Tula covered 5.4 square miles (Diehl, 1981, 58), including nearly half a square mile of uninhabited swamp (El Salitre), which was used mainly as a source of materials for baskets. This area may have provided Tula its original Toltec name, *Tollan*, which means place of the reeds.

Mesoamerican Urban Population Estimates

Because the number of people who occupied any given prehistoric urban site cannot be counted with a high degree of precision, archeologists have developed systems for obtaining educated guesses. They recognize the imprecision of estimates, so population figures are usually expressed in a range.

Tenochtitlán, the Aztecs' capital, has been estimated (Diehl, 1981, 58) to have had between 175,000 and 300,000 inhabitants at the beginning of the Spanish conquest. David Stannard, a historian of holocausts, wrote in 1992 that an estimate of 350,000 could be regarded as "conventional" (p. 3). Other estimates of the city's population range up to a million people. The range of estimates illustrates two things: first, that demographic history and archeology are not exact sciences; second, even at a consensus estimate of about 300,000, the Aztec capital was at least four times the size of any European urban area when the Spanish arrived in the Valley of Mexico (Gibson, 1964, 337–338).

One common method used to estimate urban populations in Mesoamerica has been to multiply the total occupied area by a density factor of 5,000 people per square kilometer, a figure derived from ethnographic studies of modern rural villages in the same area. This method assumes (perhaps in error) that modern people in that area utilize space in the same ways (vis-à-vis density) as their ancestors. Another method, according to Diehl (1981), is to determine the total number of housing units in an urban area and then multiply that number by the average population that each was believed to have housed. To get an accurate estimate using this method, one must know the total number of housing units, which is not always available. This figure is not known for Tula. Using various methods, the population of Tula, for example, has been estimated at between 18,000 and 55,000, with a compromise figure at 30,000 to 40,000. Because the methodology is not precise and because there are several ways to estimate populations, estimates cited by different authorities often vary widely.

The Design of Tula

The main focus of Toltec archeology has been the urban area's largest buildings, in which ceremonies and affairs of religion and state were carried out: temples, large, colonnaded halls, ball courts, and, most recently, palaces, marketplaces, and storehouses. During the late 1970s and early 1980s, research teams from the University of Missouri at Columbia also made an intensive study of Toltec urban residences. To date, however, archeology has focused almost entirely on the capital, Tula, so very little is known about the network of agricultural villages that surrounded the city and fed its elite. A similar bias is evident in the archeology of other Mesoamerican civilizations, so the concrete results that we see often accentuate the grandeur of the cities and underplay the day-to-day business of feeding a civilization, which leaves fewer artifacts.

The center of Tula featured the usual array of temples and other pyramidlike structures that frequently closely resemble their predecessors in other cities around the valley of Mexico as well as the Maya's cities. Tula was much smaller than Teotihuacan (perhaps one-fifth or fewer population), and its artistic development often pales beside that of the earlier city. Although the Aztecs mythologized the Toltecs in many ways, the capital onto which Cortes' eyes fell in 1519 made Tula look like a provincial outpost. The archeological landscape of Tula is relatively barren in large part because the Aztecs stripped Tula bare of luxuries as they conquered the city. Many artifacts that originated in Tula have been found among the ruins of Tenochtitlan, under contemporary Mexico City. Nevertheless, the Toltecs were capable of producing elaborate friezes (which also often served as a form of written communication), as well as elaborately carved sculptures that served as roof supports for the major temples of Tula.

Private homes at Tula nearly always have been found in groups of three to five, each containing several rooms, all facing into a common interior courtyard. This pattern indicates the presence of extended families who lived together and acted as economic and family units. Each group of houses often was fenced off from other clusters, indicating an interest in privacy. Entrances often were built into halls that turned ninety degrees to ensure the privacy of occupants. The house clusters usually were constructed of stone and earth, with flat roofs resembling those of the later Aztecs. The houses often were used as tombs as well as to attend to the daily needs of the living. Instead of burying their dead in separate tombs or cemeteries, Toltec families often buried the deceased in a pit under the floor of their homes. High-status individuals sometimes were buried under altars in family courtyards. Many of those tombs were looted by the Aztecs.

The houses were well adapted to their highland environment, with thick adobe walls that retained cool air during hot summer afternoons. The same structures also held warmth during cold winter mornings. Drainage pipes were constructed to siphon occasional heavy rains that fell on Tula, and stone foundations helped prevent moisture from leaking into homes through the floors (Diehl, 1981, 90–96).

Like many other major Mesoamerican urban areas, Tula was surrounded by a network of agricultural villages. Although little is known about these villages (compared to knowledge of the urban areas), the Spanish chronicler Bernardino de Sahagún left descriptions of agricultural superlatives attributed to the Toltecs that were probably embellished by Aztec mythology. The Toltecs, for example, were said to have grown cotton in many colors. This is improbable because cotton does not grow well in the highlands.

Toltec Agriculture and City Life

The Spanish chronicler Sahagún wrote that that Toltec ears of corn (their basic food) were of a size that (in Diehl's words) "would have been the talk of the annual Missouri State Fair" (1981, 98), another superlative that probably stretches the truth because early corn was quite small compared to today's varieties. Aside from corn, the people of Tula ate chili sauces, beans, several varieties of squashes, amaranth seeds, wild seeds, fruits, and magueys, sap from the hearts of which could be fermented into the alcoholic brew called *pulque* that the Aztecs said caused the city's drunken downfall. Meat (usually small dogs and turkeys) was rare and usually eaten by most people only on ceremonial occasions.

Agriculture around Tula was made possible by extensive irrigation from a nearby river. The area is laced with ditches and canals, which indicate that water was moved from place to place in large quantities. Some farm fields also were terraced, and many private home clusters also contained intensively cultivated domestic gardens in which people raised vegetables, herbs, and medicinal plants (Diehl, 1981, 98–100). Farmers usually traded their surplus for goods and services in the city; they also had no choice but to pay tax levies utilized to support the urban elite who offered them its protection. Perhaps the heavy hand of tribute played a role in popular uprisings that ended each Mesoamerican empire's era of technological achievement and hierarchical social organization; Cortes could certainly attest to the eagerness with which people who had been subjugated by the Aztecs forged alliances with him. If the Aztecs had been kinder to their subject peoples, Cortes might never have reached Tenochtitlán.

Most of the Valley of Mexico's urban areas (like many Mayan cities) contained ball courts with large spectator areas, indicating the popularity of a ritual game that was played on an enclosed court shaped most often like the capital letter *I*. Although the game was probably first played by the Olmecs, formalized play (indicated by the well-developed courts) came to the Valley of Mexico after the fall of Teotihuacan. Early Spanish chroniclers described the game as being played by two teams; the aim was to get a hard rubber ball into the court of the other team and through stone hoops mounted on the walls of the enclosed court. Players were allowed to move the ball in any way as long as they did not use hands or feet. Spectators at Tula probably engaged in avid betting matches based on the outcome of the game (some were reduced to poverty by their gambling). As with the Maya, the losers sometimes found themselves sacrificed to the gods. In Tula, the skulls of the losers were sometimes displayed on specially made racks, like trophies. As an added attraction at Tula, evidence indicates that the winners were sometimes encouraged to rob losing spectators of their clothing and jewelry.

As with empires of more recent vintage, political power often followed commerce among the Toltecs, as it would with the Aztecs. Traders, who ranged far beyond the areas within which tribute was collected, often traveled in the employ of their home city's military elite, acting as spies, sometimes as double agents. Traders from Tula covered an area that included the entire Yucatán Peninsula and most of the northern reaches of Mayan highland country. In the north, traders sought precious materials, such as turquoise, copper, gold, and silver, in the arid steppes of what is now northern Mexico. Tula seems to have been a manufacturing center for such objects as obsidian cutting tools and other crafts.

A lively debate has arisen among archeologists concerning the quality and quantity of Toltec crafts. Sahagún wrote (probably borrowing from an Aztec account) of the Toltecs' mastery:

> Many of them were scribes, lapidarians, carpenters, stone cutters, masons, feather workers, feather gluers, potters, spinners, weavers. They were very learned. They . . . knew of green stones, fine turquoise, common turquoise. . . . They went on to learn of, to seek out, the mines of silver, gold, copper, tin, mica, lead. . . . They performed works of art, they performed works of skill, [creating] all the wonderful, precious, marvelous things they made. (1950–1969, 10:167)

Some Toltec art portrays men wearing large amounts of jewelry (which may have been copper or gold) around their wrists and upper arms. Tula also bears widespread evidence of having been a center of manufacture for obsidian blades.

Skilled craftspeople gathered in urban centers that had a need for their skills and the means to pay for them; they usually were members of hereditary guilds, distinct ethnically from the cities in which they lived. Often, the craftspeople moved from city to city with the traveling elites. Like craft production, trade in many Mesoamerican civilizations was conducted by a specialized class. Wealth accumulated in trade could improve one's social status to a certain degree in the home city, but if a trader became overly greedy or ostentatious, the envy of fellow residents could cause problems.

Regarding the Toltecs' crafts and commerce, much remains to be discovered. The marketplace at Tula awaits exploration, for example. Some Toltec crafts have been found, including intriguing children's toys with axles and wheels, a discovery that contradicts a former belief that indigenous Americans were ignorant of the wheel. The Toltecs knew of the device but never adapted it to transportation because they had no draft animals. Without large animals, a wheeled conveyance would have been practically useless unless humans pulled it.

At the height of the Toltec culture, continuing into the Aztec period, trade flourished between Mesoamerica and Native nations to the north. Live parrots from the Valley of Mexico were traded with the Pueblos 1,200 miles to the north; other bearers of wares crossed the Gulf of Mexico northward, into eastern North America, spreading goods from as far south as Mayan country through "a grand alliance of prosperous little nations, stretching from the Gulf Coast to Wisconsin, from New York to Kansas and Nebraska" (Brandon, 1961, 50). Many of the people with whom the Mesoamericans traded also sometimes built large earthworks, including temple mounds.

As each major culture rose, expanded, then fell, several smaller cultures sharing some of the same attributes also existed along the fringes of the major administrative states. This was especially true during times of instability, such as those that followed the fall of Teotihuacan. The major center at this time (around 1000 C.E.) was Tula, but other major sites have been found east of the mountains that separate the Valley of Mexico from the Puebla Valley (Cholula), as well as along the Gulf Coast. Tula also competed with Xochicalco, an urban center built on several hilltops near the border of Morelos and Guerrero. This city features well-developed ramparts, indicating warfare in the vicinity, possibly with Toltec forces. Xochicalco controlled access to deposits of jade and other minerals that may have been a source of conflict.

By about 1170 C.E., Tula succumbed to invaders from the north whom they called Chichimecs (Dog People). Lean, hungry, and barbarous, they arrived behind a barrage of bows and arrows and stayed to absorb the culture of the Valley of Mexico. Sources disagree whether the Aztecs, one of the groups of migrants flowing southward, were the first on the scene to pillage Tula. Some of them may have arrived as late as around 1325 C.E. A number of peoples came south, jostling with each other for power, transforming themselves from primitive hunters to "grand patrons of the arts, swooning esthetically over bouquets and manipulating feather fans with a fine aristocratic grace" (Brandon, 1961, 66). Those who did not speak the Aztecs' Nahua language learned it as they began to build a collection of city-states around the lake that would host the crowning glory of the Aztecs.

THE AZTECS (MEXICAS)

The Spanish conquistadors encountered the Aztecs' remarkable civilization in its full flower. A few of them described the Aztec Empire in detail before Spanish guns, avarice, and disease destroyed it. The architectural center of the Aztecs, Tenochtitlán, occupied the contemporary site of another great metropolis, Mexico City.

Much of our archeological knowledge of the Aztecs comes by way of Mexico City public works projects, such as the city's subway, which involved digging into the earth. The most significant remains of the Aztecs' 200-foot high Templo Mayor (Great Temple) were not found until 1978. The first traces of the Great Temple were unearthed during excavations for a sewer line in 1900. In 1913, another public works project uncovered the southwest corner of the temple; in 1967, construction of the Mexico City subway began to unearth sizable numbers of Aztec artifacts. Without such intense (if unintentional) spadework, we would know much less about the capstone civilization that followed more than a millennium of remarkable cities in Mesoamerica.

Archeologists and others, some of whom have deciphered pre-Columbian texts in the Valley of Mexico, are piecing together a fascinating story. Many modern scholars in this area, especially in present-day Mexico, are not using the name "Aztec" as a generalized name for the people who lived in the valley when Cortes arrived. Instead, they refer to "Méxicas," as they called themselves, speakers of the Nahuatl language, a rich quilt of peoples living in cities that rose and fell after the decline of Tula. Several peoples lived in the Valley of Mexico only a few miles from the island that became the Aztecs' "City of the Gods." The people who moved into the valley in the fourteenth century called the place where they lived "México," from which "Mexico" is derived.

As in the Old World, the seat of civilization had passed from people to people over the centuries: from the fertile crescent to Egypt to Greece and Rome in Europe and nearby Africa and Asia; from the Olmec and Maya, to the Toltecs, and to the Mexicas. While Europe endured its Dark Ages, the world of the Mexica flourished. The Aztecs reached their peak as Europe emerged from its own Dark Age during a burst of overseas exploration that began with the voyages of Columbus.

The first Spaniards to witness Tenochtitlán described a city more splendid, and more mysterious, than any their well-traveled eyes ever had seen. While some Spanish conquistadors and priests warmed their hands over fires built from valuable artifacts and records that would have been of immense use to archeologists today, the Franciscan friar Bernadino de Sahagún, born in Spain during 1499, traveled to Mexico and mastered Nahuatl as he began a Franciscan school for sons of surviving Aztec nobles. At the same time, Sahagún prepared a dozen hand-embellished manuscripts (called codices) describing Mexica (Aztec) history, cosmology, legends, and daily life. King Philip II of

Spain refused to permit publication of the codices, which were finally published two and a half centuries later (Sahagún, 1950–1969).

The Méxicas or Aztecs were only the last, largest, and (because of Spanish historians) the best known of many peoples who built civilizations in the Valley of Mexico. Today, archeologists agree that the prehistoric and proto-historic periods of Mexico cover at least 20,000 years. The comparison of this long period with the 300 years of colonial life and the fewer than two centuries of the modern independent (Mexican) nation makes it appropriate to identify the pre-Columbian millennia as "the substratum and root of present-day Mexico" (León Portilla, 1972, 3).

Origins of the Aztecs

The Aztecs probably moved to the Valley of Mexico from the present-day Mexican state of Nayarit, about 450 miles northwest of the site on which they later established Tenochtitlán (Smith, 1984, 153–186). The marshes of the Pacific Coast, not far from Mexicaltitan, fit ancient descriptions of the Aztecs' origin place, Aztlan, "place of the herons," from which they derived "Aztec," meaning "people of the heron place." Professor Wigberto Jiménez-Moreno (1970) believes that the first Aztec village may have been located at Mexicaltitan, on an island in the San Pedro River in Nayarit State. This site has been called the "Venice of Mexico" because during the rainy season its streets flood, and people often convey themselves mainly by boat. Aztec history relates that the people wandered for centuries after leaving Nayarit in search of a permanent home, passing through Tula for a century or longer.

Imagine the amazement of the Aztecs when they found a vast lake in the mountains of central Mexico. On an island in that lake, they built the grandest of early American cities. In its heyday, after their travels returning members of Tenochtitlán's ruling elite were welcomed back into the city with a chant that welcomed them to the court-city, Mexico-Tenochtitlán, in the still water, where the eagle cried, and the serpent hissed, where fish leaped.

Following the decline of the Toltecs, a number of city-states contended for power in the Valley of Mexico before the Aztecs became dominant. Azcapotzalkco, to the west of Lake Texcoco, rose early, followed by the Acolhuas, who ruled the city of Texcoco, to the east of the lake. At one point, they collected tribute from seventy surrounding towns. The Culhuacan also grew in power to the south of Lake Texcoco where it joined Lake Xochimilco. When the Mexicas first came to the valley of Mexico, the Culhuas probably employed them as mercenaries. At one point, the Mexicas decided to "honor" the Culhuan king by slaying his daughter. They asked the king to attend a ceremony "celebrating" the slaying. The king did not appreciate the Aztecs' concept of honor. He enslaved or killed the leaders of the "ceremony" and drove the rest of the Mexicas into exile.

The history of the Aztecs indicates that they were not greeted warmly by peoples who had resided in the Valley of Mexico before them:

> Upon arriving
> when they were following their path
> they were not received anywhere.
> Everywhere, they were reprehended.
> No one knew their face.
> Everywhere they were told:
> "Who are you?
> "Where did you come from?"
> Thus they were unable to settle anywhere;
> they were only cast out,
> everywhere they were persecuted…
> —Sahagún, 1992, 30

According to the Aztecs' chroniclers, their people settled in the Valley of Mexico in a year corresponding to 1325 C.E. on the Christian calendar. From their capital city, the Aztec Empire eventually reached the Gulf of Mexico and into Guatemala, which is a Nahuatl name.

Growth of the Aztec Empire

Eventually, the Aztecs settled on the marshy island where some of their enemies figured that the abundant snake population would torture them. Instead, the Aztecs roasted the snakes and ate them. In the century between 1325 and the early 1400s, the Mexicas negotiated a number of alliances and subjugated other city-states. In the end, they even came to dominate peoples who once had looked down on them. The residents of Texcoco, perhaps the most powerful of these, were besieged, then overwhelmed during 1416. Legend has it that the Aztecs killed Texcoco's king, Ixtlilxochitl, as his son, Nezahualcyotl (Hungry Coyote), escaped to become one of Mexico's most famous legendary figures. Nezahualcyotl hid in the mountains writing poetry, developing a philosophy that centered around the Unknown God, who demanded only prayers instead of human blood. It is said that Hungry Coyote sometimes visited the Aztec-dominated cities in disguise, rallying followers to his faith, as the Aztec minions tried to capture him. At one point he was captured, but a guard released him and was put to death in Hungry Coyote's place.

The rituals of blood sacrifice were so engrained in the culture of the Mexicas and other residents of the valley that Nezahualcoytl, who ruled Texcoco shortly before Columbus' voyages, could not persuade the people to give them up. The priests forcefully talked Nezahualcoytl out of his campaign to stop blood sacrifice, and Nezahualcoytl had to be content with building a new temple, ten stories high, capped by an ornate chapel dedicated to "the

Aztec priest performing a sacrificial offering. (Courtesy of the Library
of Congress.)

Cause of All Causes, the Unknown God," in which offerings were made in
flowers and scented gums instead of blood.

As the Aztecs' empire spread, Tenochtitlán grew on land reclaimed from surrounding swamps. Two aqueducts three miles long were built to carry freshwater
from the mainland; each had two sluices so one could be closed for cleaning
without interrupting the water supply. Tribute and captives flowed into the city
after conquests that spread from the Gulf of Mexico to the Pacific Ocean. West of
the Valley of Mexico, however, the Aztecs' armies were stopped by the bowmen of
the Tarascans. The Aztecs never completely conquered the Tlaxcalans to the east,
although they did surround their city and cut off its commerce. The Aztecs'
hegemony was only rarely administrative; after they pillaged another people's city,
the conquered people usually were left alone to manage their own affairs until the
next call for tribute and captives to satisfy the blood hunger of the Aztecs' gods.

Aztec Warfare and the Power of Ritual

Aztec warfare was as much a pageant as a battle. Wars were fought hand to
hand. Aztecs disarmed their opponents and forced them to surrender or beat
them unconscious. Soldiers made fashion statements as much as war, wearing

headdresses and shirts of yellow parrot feathers and quetzal feathers set off with gold. Soldiers wore jaguar skins and hoods of gold with feather horn adornments. Their shields were decorated with golden disks displaying butterflies and serpents. The armies of the Aztec Empire went to battle with "two-toned drums, conch-shell trumpets, shrill clay whistles, screams full-voiced (. . . to shock and terrify the enemy) calling to the heavens for help and witness" (Brandon, 1961, 67). Priests led the soldiers into battle with trumpet blasts calling on the gods to witness. The priests then waited in the rear with razor-sharp obsidian blades, ready to feed the gods with the still-warm blood of captives' beating hearts.

Like few other peoples in the Americas, the Aztecs were mobilized for war, for expansion, and for expropriation of tribute from less-militaristic peoples. Every Mexica man over the age of 15 years was considered a potential member of the army except those in training for the priesthood or as civil officials. The entire male population was never mobilized at once, however. All young boys were taught the use of basic weapons, such as the spear thrower and bow and arrow. At 15 years of age, most young men in Tenochtitlan were sent to live for a number of months in "houses of youth," where they were taught arts of war, as well as academic subjects. The capital city had 20 "houses of youth," each affiliated with a different *calpulli*, an administrative district.

The Aztecs usually initiated a confrontation with another group of people by sending an emissary to its leaders to exact a set tribute. If the group agreed to submit, the Mexica foreign minister returned with gifts and a schedule of payment, and a peace was established. If no tribute was pledged, the Aztec delegate (or delegates) applied white paint to the prospective enemy's commanding officer, placed feathers on his head, then handed him a sword and shield as a formal declaration of war. The Aztecs did not always follow their own customs, however. Sometimes, they engaged in surprise attacks and pillaging.

After a battle, members of the ruling class often hired musicians to memorialize the occasion in song. A small orchestra usually played for Mochtezuma (the Mexicas' supreme leader at the time of Cortes' arrival) at mealtimes as well. Most Aztec music had overtones not only of war and power, but also of divine rite. All ritual music was performed by members of a specially trained professional caste. A single error, one small departure from established ritual, could result in death because an erring musician was said to have disturbed the gods. The rituals required very well-developed memories, as well as a sense of creative showmanship. The best ritual singers were said to have enjoyed high social prestige (Driver, 1969, 205).

The Aztecs were acutely aware of the power that their capital symbolized in the Mesoamerica of their day. They were not accidental imperialists, as the following Aztec narrative indicates:

> Proud of itself
> Is the city of Mexico—Tenochtitlán

Here no one fears to die in war
This is our glory
This is Your Command
Oh Giver of Life
Have this mind, oh princes
Who would conquer Tenochtitlán?
Who would shake the foundation of heaven?
          —León Portilla, 1969, 87

Symbols played a very important role in the Mexica mind. Their capital was believed to be the center of the universe, and the Great Temple of Tenochtitlán was the center of Aztec spiritual and secular power. Tenochtitlán's two main temples were dedicated to the two gods who influenced the most important events and values in Mexica life: the god of agriculture, rain, and water (*Tlaloc*) and the god of war, tribute, and conquest (*Huitzilopochtli*). The temples dedicated to these two gods displayed an Aztec attitude of dominance over the peoples around them—an attitude that the Spanish replicated when they built their own religious center, a major cathedral, on top of the Great Temple. Eduardo Matos Mochtezuma, a descendant of the Aztec ruler who first met Cortes and general coordinator of the Mexican project that is unearthing the Great Temple, wrote that the great temple was a symbol of the Aztecs' way of thinking, living, and sometimes dying (1988, 15–60).

During the century and a half that the Aztecs dominated Mesoamerica, the Aztecs' Templo Mayor was rebuilt seven times. It became so complex that after the Spanish thought it had been destroyed, several levels still remained to be discovered under the Catholic cathedral that the Spanish built on the same site. The full complexity of the temple was not discovered until the unintentional excavations of twentieth century public works, notably Mexico City's subway, uncovered subterranean levels that had been bypassed by the colonists.

The Blood Sacrifice

The Aztecs were not benign rulers; they dragged thousands of subject peoples back to Tenochtitlan for forced labor and religious sacrifice. The Great Temple was not substantially completed until 1487, a little more than three decades before Cortes' Spanish forces invaded the area. During those three decades, estimates of the number of people sacrificed for religious purposes ranged from 10,000 to 80,000 (McDowell, 1980, 726–727). Bernal Díaz de Castillo wrote that he counted 100,000 skulls of sacrificial victims in the plazas of Tenochtitlán (Wilkerson, 1984, 445–446).

During the periods of ritual killing, four people at a time were sacrificed at the Great Temple from dawn to dusk. The entire city—otherwise a place of magnificent architecture and brilliant colors where fierce warriors often walked the streets celebrating the virtues of flowers in poetry—stank of burning flesh.

At times, the stench was sealed into the valley by the same atmospheric inversions that today capture some of the world's worst air pollution. When the number of prisoners of war available for sacrifice ran low, the Aztecs and neighboring city-states engaged in ritual Wars of the Flowers simply to harvest candidates for sacrifice.

Even as they sacrificed human beings to their gods en masse, the Aztecs seemed to have had no concept of torture solely for the sake of cruelty. Their gods were not conceived as angry as much as they were thought to be hungry. Some of the priests stationed at the foot of the Great Temple even prayed for sacrificial victims: "May he savor the fragrance, the sweetness of death by the obsidian blade" (McDowell, 1980, 729–730). The Aztecs exacted tribute, as well as lives, from vassal peoples; they built a commercial network that brought to the Valley of Mexico all manner of food, rare feathers, precious metals, and other commodities, many of which were traded at a great market at Tlatelolco. Cortes reported having seen up to 60,000 people at a time bartering in this grand bazaar, where disputes were settled on the spot by judges. Among the items for sale in the market were turkeys, which the Aztecs were the first to domesticate. The Spanish took some of the birds home. Turkeys reached England before the first voyages of settlement from Britain. The Pilgrims had turkeys aboard their ships when they arrived in the New World and found similar wild fowl being hunted by Native people.

The imagery of the Aztecs' volatile cosmology resembled the mountainous, volcano-studded land that surrounded them. They believed that the world had been destroyed four times. To create the sun and moon for the fifth epoch, two gods committed suicide by immolating themselves in fire. The Aztec god representing darkness was not a kind personage. The spirit of darkness was described in a poem that survived the conquest:

> He mocks us.
> As he wishes, so he wills.
> He places us in the palm of his hand,
> He rolls us about;
> Like pebbles we roll, we spin . . .
> We make him laugh.
> He mocks us.
> —McDowell, 1980, 729–730

The Mexicas built all their temples, monuments, and homes without using bronze tools. They did use the wheel, but only on children's toys. Instead of using wheeled conveyances to transport building materials, the vassals of the Aztecs carried them or rolled them on beds of logs. All of this also was accomplished without beasts of burden. Scholars have speculated on what the Aztecs might have accomplished had their civilization not been put to the torch by the Spanish. No one really knows; it is known, however, that the rapid growth of the large city was already using up nearby resources of firewood. In 1454, a debilitating famine had swept the area.

Aztec Socioeconomic and Governmental Structures

In Aztec society, each person was born into a social class. At the head of this socioeconomic pyramid was the king (*tlatoani* or *tlacatecuhtli*), a descendant of the Toltec prince Acamapichtli, who in turn was believed to have been descended from Quetzacoatl, an important god of the Toltecs and Aztecs. Aztec history described how the prince had come to Tenochtitlán to found the city's royal line, from unions with 20 wives, probably one from each *calpulli*, or local governing unit.

The Nobles (*pipiltin*) were distinguished by the legal permission afforded them to own land in their own names on reaching adulthood. They also were taught to use glyphs (a form of Mexica writing) along with knowledge of cultural arts and religion. They held the highest judicial, military, civil, and religious posts, but membership in this class did not guarantee a prestigious office. Office also required leadership skills. Nobles who did not have such skills might end up being palace servants or even enduring unemployment. Below the Nobles stood a class of Knights (*caballeros pardos*), who had been raised to their standing, usually from the lower classes, because of valor in warfare.

The commoners or working class (*macehualtin*) were educated to farm communal lands or to practice trades. They could not own land (farms were the common property of the *calpulli*), but they could consume, sell, or exchange what they produced from their labor on the land. A talented member of this class could rise to the higher offices of his *calpulli* and thereby, in practice, outrank a Noble who had no official position. A separate class, a proletariat, owned no land, but also had no masters. Typically, members of this class might work as craftspeople or day laborers. Below the working class, the serfs (*mayeques*) sometimes worked their way upward.

Aztec class structure was sometimes fluid; people could rise and fall on merit or luck. Serfs were assigned to certain plots of land and were paid with a portion of their produce from it. If land was sold, the serfs assigned to it were considered part of the transaction. Besides agricultural work, serfs were expected to render menial services to their masters. Men might haul water or build a house; women might prepare meals. A large number of Mexica serfs had been commoners from conquered nations; some native Aztec commoners even tried to pass as serfs to avoid paying taxes.

The slaves were at the bottom of the hierarchy; they could be assigned to any job by their masters. The master owned only the labor of the slave, not his or her life. A slave could own a residence and could not be traded or sold to another master without consent. The status often was temporary; a slave also was allowed to own the services of another slave.

The Aztecs governed themselves according to a clan-based system that included aspects of consensus and hierarchy. This system did not fit any European category of government. The 20 *calpulli* of the state each elected officials similar to county clerks or aldermen. Each clan also elected a speaker (*tlatoani*), who sat on a supreme state council. From these leaders, four were appointed to executive posts. In Tenochtitlan, one of these four, called *tlacatecuhtli* (chief of men) or *hueytlatoani* (revered speaker), was chosen to be chief executive, a lifetime appointment.

The dual nature of the system considers that some Spanish accounts refer to the government as a "republic," and others called Aztec leaders kings. Elected along kin lines, Aztec leaders enjoyed total authority once they were elevated to office. Ownership of most land (except that owned by members of the elite) rested with the clans. This concept often confused the Spanish, who were accustomed to individual or royal ownership.

Another concept that sometimes confused the Spanish, who came from a male-dominated society, was the influence of Mexica women. The Mexica language referred to a woman as "the owner of a man" (McDowell, 1980, 730–731).

Aztec Cosmology

Mexica cosmology placed the people at the mercy of an array of gods; some researchers have counted as many as 1,600. Most Aztecs believed that the gods could not keep the sun and moon moving (and by implication, continue the cycle of life on earth) without a steady diet of human flesh and blood. The Aztecs waged war to procure prisoners for sacrifice to their gods.

The appetites of the Mexica gods were interpreted according to the so-called Calendar Stone, which is not a calendar at all. The calendar weighs 24 metric tons (of basalt) and measures 3.6 meters (about 12 feet) in diameter with a thickness of 72 centimeters. The stone, which was uncovered in 1790 in Mexico City's Zócalo district, site of Tenochtitlán's main square, is sometimes thought of as a calendar because of the day signs that surround its center. The significance of this enormously complex sculpture was not to mark the passage of time, however, but to help the Aztecs interpret the demands of their gods, whose satisfaction they believed crucial to the continuance of life on earth.

The Stone of the Fifth Sun (so called because the Aztecs believed that they were living in the fifth, and last, epoch of life on earth) detailed how the Aztecs believed the cosmos had begun and would end. According to Aztec cosmology, the fifth epoch had begun in the year they called 13-Reed, or 1011 C.E. Aztec belief held that the fifth epoch would end if the Aztecs' deities were not satiated with an abundant supply of human blood, which required the sacrifices. The history of the Mexica provided precedents in four preceding failed foundings. Earlier generations were said to have been dispersed in the mountains, cross-bred with monkeys, or returned to the earth as turkeys after they refused to please the gods.

The Aztec cosmos was filled with gods for every human activity, from fertility to death. Each community and craft had its deity; some of them were believed to change their characteristics to confuse their enemies. Some of the gods required more than blood to maintain the sun's compass across the sky. They also demanded homage—lavish ritual processions with music, cakes, and costumes. The coming of a vengeful bearded people from the east (the direction of the rising sun) fit the Aztecs' own worldview. Initially, many Mexicas believed the Spanish to be emissaries of their own gods. Some of the gods fused history and myth. Quetzalcoatl, for example, combined the memories of a man who had ruled the Toltecs at Tula with an earlier serpent god; tradition held that he created civilization (agriculture and writing). Quetzalcoatl had been forced out of Tula in disgrace because of public drunkenness, but that he would someday return from the east.

Premonitions of Change

Throughout the decade before the bearded, armor-clothed Europeans whom the Aztecs sometimes called "the people from heaven" arrived, the Aztecs had premonitions that they were about to meet a terrible power greater than their own. The 5,000 priests of Tenochtitlán, who heretofore had been concerned mainly with garnering enough blood to satisfy the appetites of the gods, had religious premonitions that the life of their city was about to be permanently altered. In 1507, a dozen years before Cortes arrived, the New Fire ceremonies were held for the last time. These rituals came at the end of the 52 years that comprised the Aztec temporal cycle. Temples were enlarged or rebuilt, old animosities forgiven, and debts paid.

At about the same time, the people of Tenochtitlán witnessed a number of supernatural events that indicated trouble ahead. The history of the Aztecs says that a temple burst into flame for no apparent reason. At a musicians' school, a ceiling beam sang of impending doom. Lightning struck another temple from a cloudless sky. A sudden flood washed away a number of homes. A terrifying column of flame rose by night in the east, causing a terror-filled populace to panic: "All were frightened; all waited in dread" (Brandon, 1961, 76). The Serpent Woman and Earth Goddess *Cihuacoatl*, who haunted the streets at night telling mothers when their children would die, was said to be heard weeping, night after night, "My beloved sons, whither shall I take you?" (ibid., 76).

The Spanish Marvel at Tenochtitlan

The Spanish soldier Bernal Díaz del Castillo described Tenochtitlán as one of the greatest cities in the world. Although Tenochtitlán's solid temples, residences, and storehouses lent an air of permanence, the city was not old by

Mesoamerican urban standards. Less than two centuries before Díaz saw it, the site had been little more than a small temple surrounded by a few mud-and-thatch huts.

By 1519, however, Díaz found a city of unexpected splendor. He described Tenochtitlán from the top of the Great Temple:

> Here we had a clear prospect of the three causeways by which Mexico [Tenochtitlán] communicated with land, and of the aqueduct of Chapultepec, which supplied the city with the finest water. We were struck with the numbers of canoes, passing to and from the mainland, loaded with provisions and merchandise, and we could now perceive that...the houses stood separate from each other, communicating only by small drawbridges, and by boats, and that they were built with terraced tops. We observed also the temples...of the adjacent cities, built in the form of towers...wonderfully brilliant...and those [Spanish soldiers] who had been at Rome and Constantinople said, that for convenience, regularity, and population, they had never seen the like. (Molina Montes, 1980, 753)

The Spanish compiled a careful chronicle of this amazing new world as their soldiers and pathogens laid waste to it. Friar Sahagún enlisted Aztec eyewitnesses and trained observers (in some ways similar to English bards). He also utilized the Aztecs' hieroglyphic codices. Sahagún himself was fluent in Nahuatl, the Mexicas' language.

Aztec prisoners did the muscle work of building Tenochtitlán's majestic temples and causeways, along which eight horsemen could ride abreast. According to Cortes' accounts, the "excellence" and "grandeur" of the Aztecs' capital outshone anything he had ever seen. "In Spain, there is nothing to compare," he wrote, continuing:

> During the morning, we arrived at a broad causeway, and continued our march from Ixtapalapa, and when we saw so many cities and villages built into the water and other great towns on dry land and that straight and level causeway going towards Mexico [Tenochtitlán], we were amazed, and said that it was like the enchantments they tell of in the legends of Amadis, on account of the great towers and cues [temples], great towers that stood in the water, and all of masonry... [T]here were even some of our soldiers who asked if what they saw was in a dream. It is not to be wondered at that I here write it down in this manner, for there is so much to think over that I do not know how to describe it, seeing things as we did that had never been heard of or seen before. (Del Castillo, 1958, 190–191)

The Aztecs' capital was a cavalcade of color—the architecture was painted turquoise, yellow, red, and green—often annotated with visual history in murals. An observer could have seen the eagle, snake, and cactus that comprise Mexico's modern national symbols on some of the buildings. The Aztecs' history maintained that they had been led to this spot by divine prophecy, to a place where an eagle perched on a cactus extended its wings toward the rays of the sun. The fact that such a city was built in less than two centuries is awesome enough even in modern times. When one reflects on the Aztecs' lack of construction machinery (even the wheel), the scope of the metropolis that grew here becomes even more astonishing. The island on which Tenochtitlán was built contained no construction materials, so virtually everything used to construct it had to be ferried aboard canoes at first. Later, supplies were carried, or rolled on logs using ropes and pulleys, along the causeways that connected the city with the mainland.

Díaz del Castillo marveled at the Mexicas' armaments, and he did not stop at their design. The Aztecs' flint blades cut better than the Spaniards' swords, he admitted:

> Many of them [blades] were richly adorned with gold and precious stones. There were large and small shields, and some *macanas* [clubs], and others like two-handed swords set with some flint blades that cut better than our swords, and lances longer than ours, with a five-foot knife set with many blades. (del Castillo in León Portilla, 1972, 122)

If Tenochtitlán's population was about 300,000, which seems likely, it was the largest Native American city in the hemisphere and the largest urban area of any type in North or South America until after 1800. At the time the United States became independent, its largest cities (Boston, New York, and Philadelphia) housed no more than 50,000 people each. The architects of the Aztec capital faced some problems apart from scarcity of materials and labor. The subsoil of the area was very soft, and buildings, once constructed, tended to sink into it, with some parts of them sinking more quickly than others. Aztec architects tried to combat this problem by building large sections of their temples with light, porous volcanic stone called *tezontle*, which could be quarried in abundance nearby. Slabs of *tezontle* often were cut (with stone, not metal tools) and then assembled so precisely that structures required no mortar. Early Spanish architecture in the Valley of Mexico sometimes utilized the same methods of construction; several of these buildings (such as the National Palace) still stand today in Mexico City (Molina Montes, 1980, 760–761).

The Spanish Conquest of the Aztecs

Cortes and his roughly 400 men forged alliances with many Native peoples, who were more than ready to turn on the domineering Mexicas. Through the adroit use of informants (such as the legendary Malinche) and an uncanny sense of timing that Aztec leaders sometimes thought was supernatural, Cortes's small band of Spanish conquistadors reduced a state that had subjugated millions to ashes within two bloody years. The Spanish also were aided by European diseases (the foremost of which was smallpox) and the Aztecs' own fear of a troublesome future.

The Spaniards' technology was superior but not by enough to swing the balance of power on its own. The Spanish recognized early, for example, that some of the Aztecs' weapons were sharper than theirs. Aztec cotton-padded armor was good enough that some Spanish troops adopted it. Very quickly, the conquistadors set about to turn the Native peoples into their own workforce, usually by compulsion. The rigors of labor, along with conquistador terror and disease, caused the Native population to decline rapidly. Henry Dobyns estimated that the population of Mexico declined from between 30 and 37.5 million people in 1520 to 1.5 million in 1650, a holocaust of a severity unknown in the Old World (1966, 395–449). Even if one argues that Dobyns' figures are too high, cutting them almost in half to 20 million in 1520 would produce a mortality rate in 130 years of 92.5 percent (Driver, 1969, 457).

Cortes began recruiting Indian allies against the Aztecs in Cempoalla, near the Gulf Coast, home to about 30,000 people of the Totonac nation, the first city he visited on his way to Tenochtitlán. The leaders of this city met Cortes on friendly terms and told him of how intensely many of the Aztecs' tributary tribes hated their oppressors. Despite the intensity of this hatred, the people of Cempoalla dared not revolt. However, Cempoalla supplied Cortes with about 400 *tamanes*, or equipment carriers, for the next leg of his journey, to nearby Chiahuitztla.

In that city, Cortes and his men met five Aztec tribute collectors, dressed in finery, whose assistants walked behind them shooing away flies with fans. The Aztecs upbraided the Totonacs for aiding Cortes and demanded twenty young men and women for sacrifice as punishment. Cortes made an emotive speech demanding that the Totonacs throw the tribute collectors into prison. After some frenzied discussion, they did. The following night, Cortes arranged for the escape of two of the tribute collectors, then convinced the Totonacs to transfer the other three to his "care" as well.

With the five captive Aztec tribute collectors in tow, Cortes and his men continued to climb the mountains bordering the Mexican plateau, toward Tenochtitlan. Along the way, Cortes encountered the Tlascalan nation, also enemies of the Aztecs, whose warriors engaged his men in a round of inconclusive fighting before they joined Cortes in his war on the Aztecs. Allied with the Tlascalan warriors, Cortes entered the Valley of Mexico with enough manpower to initiate serious combat.

Cortes then stopped at Cholula, where he was welcomed with open arms. Cortes took advantage of the hospitality to invite leaders of the Cholulan nation to the public square of the city, which the Spanish said contained at least 20,000 buildings within its walls. Once most of the important people in Cholula had assembled to parlay with Cortes, his soldiers and their Tlascalan allies carried out prearranged orders to slaughter the Cholulans. The massacre left thousands of dead. Racing among the carcasses littering the streets, the Spanish then looted Cholula.

The Spanish asserted after the fact that the Mexica ruler Mochtezuma had conspired with a number of Cholulan headmen to exterminate the Spaniards before they reached the capital of the Aztecs. The veracity of this alibi was doubtful because the Spanish used it several times again in Mexico and against the last of the Incan emperors, among others. It was more likely that Cortes sought to paralyze the Aztecs into inaction with a swift and brutal massacre at Cholula. The strategy worked.

Cortes and his allies were received in Tenochtitlán as ambassadors of a mighty foreign country. Mochtezuma housed, fed, and entertained the conquistadors and gave them free access to the city, a period during which Bernal Díaz produced the descriptions that today provide a glimpse through European eyes of the Aztec capital in its full flower. As he had at Cholula, Cortes repaid hospitality with violence: At first, he took Mochtezuma prisoner, then slowly, ruthlessly, undermined his power among the Mexicas. The imprisonment included physical and psychological torture.

Matthew Restall, a professor at Pennsylvania State University, argues that the Aztecs did not perceive the Spaniards as gods (as often has been asserted); he writes that this account was invented decades after the fact by the Catholic Church and its Native allies. The first Native scribes to write the history of the conquest were tutored by Franciscan monks who hoped, in retrospect, to make the Spanish arrival seem providential. Because the scribes hailed from a group unfriendly to the Aztecs, they did not hesitate in their chronicles to disparage their rivals as weak and indecisive (Restall, 2004; Burnham, 2004).

One such incident was described by Benjamin Franklin. In November 1774, following the Boston Tea Party, Franklin scoffed at proposals that Boston ought to negotiate a treaty with Britain while its port was closed and the city itself was occupied by British Army Redcoats. "They will plead at ease, but we must plead in pain," Franklin argued, comparing Boston's position to that of Mochtezuma in the hands of the conquistador Cortes, who demanded "a surrender of his cash." Franklin wrote that the Aztec "Made some objections and desired A TREATY on the reasonableness of the demand. . . . Cortes heated a gridiron red hot, and seated poor Montezuma on it, and consented to TREAT with him as long as he pleased" (Labaree, 1978–, 21:354).

The Spaniards held Mochtezuma captive for several months, while rumors regarding his health spread through the capital. At one point, quite accidentally, Cortes's men discovered a massive amount of gold and silver that belonged to Mochtezuma's father—in effect, the state treasury. While subjugating the ruler personally, the Spanish extracted 162,000 *pesos de oro* (or 19,600 troy ounces) of gold from this cache. At 2002 gold prices, this hoard would have been worth about $8 million (Wright, 1992, 38). Much of what the Spanish purloined comprised many large pieces of intricate artwork that they melted into bullion for convenient shipment back to Spain. Cortes preserved a few of the art pieces intact to impress his sponsors.

Reception of Hernando Cortez by Emperor Mochtezuma. (Courtesy of the Library of Congress.)

After six months in Mexico City, Cortes marched back to the Gulf Coast to meet a new Spanish expedition headed by Panfilo de Narvaez; the expedition had reached Vera Cruz from Cuba, drawn like a bee to honey by reports of Mexican gold. Cortes appointed Pedro de Alvarado, a personal friend, to command the Spanish forces that remained in the Aztec capital.

A few days after Cortes and a contingent of men marched out of Tenochtitlán, the Aztecs prepared to celebrate their annual feast to Huitzilopochtli, the god of war. The festival of song, dance, and human sacrifice was held on the grounds of a monument to Huitzilopochtli, within eyeshot of the Spaniards' quarters, as well as the chambers in which Mochtezuma was held prisoner. Nearly all the royalty of Tenochtitlán gathered, resplendent in their best costumes, decked with gold and silver ornaments, including ceremonial gold and silver swords and other implements of war. Otherwise, the Aztec nobility was unarmed and ready prey for yet another Spanish ambush in the style of Cholula. Alvarado and his cohorts prepared just such a surprise as they surrounded the ceremonial court. Aztecs who tried to escape the massacre were impaled on pikes thrust by Spanish soldiers stationed at the exits. The Spanish then stripped the dead of their gold and silver.

The Florentine Codex described the scene:

> The blood . . . ran like water, like slimy water; the stench of blood filled the air, and the entrails seemed to slither along by themselves. And the Spanish went everywhere, searching the public buildings, thrusting with their weapons. (Sahagún, 1956, 116–117, cited in Wright, 1992, 40)

The Spanish said they feared the Aztecs had secreted their weapons on the ceremonial grounds, requiring that they be killed. The Spaniards' real motive probably was to score an easy hit on the cream of the Aztec nobility and thus collect material rewards.

After months of Spanish torment, Mochtezuma also was killed. The Spanish did their best to argue that he was struck in the head by a rock thrown by an outraged Aztec during a public speech. Díaz even asserted that the Spanish offered to feed Mochtezuma and dress his wounds, but he refused. The ambivalence of his account indicates that Díaz was probably not an eyewitness to the murder. Cortes rather lamely excused himself by asserting that the murder occurred while he was away from Tenochtitlán, on his way back to the capital from the Gulf Coast. The historical record rather irrefutably indicates otherwise. Aztec sources, such as Chimalpahin, a native historian who based his work on the glyphic codices, argued that the Spaniards "throttled him." The Aztecs who relayed their history to Friar Sahagún agreed (Wright, 1992, 42).

Cortes and his comrades soon found the Mexica capital in full revolt against the Spanish, its residents angered by their leader's murder. Publicly, Cortes upbraided Alvarado, but the Aztecs were not consoled. The Spanish then departed Tenochtitlán by night, along one of the causeways that connected the city with the mainland. Seven thousand Spanish and Tlascalan allies surged onto the causeway as the Aztecs attacked them from boats. The battle of Noche Triste became an Aztec folktale, a special comeuppance for many of the Spaniards who drowned because they had tied so much gold to their bodies (Collier, 1947, 64). Having retreated to the mainland, Cortes and his allies awaited reinforcements from Cuba. When they arrived, Cortes began his final march of conquest to Tenochtitlán. In the meantime, most of the Méxicas' former allies had abandoned them.

THE SPANISH SUBJUGATION OF THE MAYA

To the south, Spanish subjugation proceeded much more slowly against the Maya. Generally, when the Spanish won a clear and quick victory over Native peoples in Mesoamerica, they did so with Native allies attacking a centralized authority. Such a situation vis-à-vis the Aztecs and Incas made for a relatively quick conquest. Against the Maya, however, the Spanish had neither allies nor a single head to decapitate. Thus, they stumbled for decades around the hot coastal plains of Yucatán. One ill-fated Spanish expedition after another was repulsed from Maya country. In 1511, a Spanish ship en route from Panama to Santo Domingo sank off the eastern coast of Yucatán, and its entire ragged, starving crew was captured by Natives along the coast. Some of them were eaten in ceremonies; others died in slavery. Only two men, Aguilar and Guerrero, survived, both enslaved to Mayan chiefs. In 1516, an intense epidemic of smallpox hit the Mayan territories, killing people with "great pustules that rotted the body" (Brandon, 1961, 81).

Shortly after he subjugated the Aztecs, Cortes turned his attention to the Maya. At one point, he ransomed Aguilar, but Guerrero refused to leave his Mayan captors, telling Aguilar, according to the chronicler Díaz, who traveled with Cortes:

> I am married and have three children, and the Indians look upon me as a Cacique [chief] and a leader in wartime. You go and God be with you, but I have my face tattooed and my ears pierced, and what would the Spaniards say should they see me in this guise? (Brandon, 1961, 82)

Following destructive wars with each other, the Mayan city-states had been declining for hundreds of years before the Spanish tried to conquer the area. The Maya's slow decline continued long after the Spanish subjugation of the Valley of Mexico. European diseases accelerated the Maya's decline. Mayan intellectuals and their descendants created "living books, copied, recopied and expanded" generation after generation. The pre-Columbian history of the Maya was preserved in these books from memory after the original texts flared on Spanish bonfires (Wright, 1992, 165). From one such book of *Chilam Balam* (meaning spokesman of God, the Jaguar Prophet), written in the

Mayan language using the Spanish alphabet, comes this ironic critique of Christianity:

> With the true God, the true Dios.
> came the beginning of our misery.
> It was the beginning of tribute,
> the beginning of church dues...
> the beginning of strife by trampling on people,
> the beginning of robbery with violence,
> the beginning of forced debts,
> the beginning of debts enforced by false testimony,
> the beginning of individual strife
> —Roys, 1967, 77–79, cited in Wright, 1992, 165–166

The Spanish conquest of the Quiche and the Cakchiquel, the most prominent Maya peoples during the sixteenth century, proceeded quickly, with a brutality that also had marked the Spanish subjugation of the Aztecs. The Cakchiquel's own history, transcribed by the Spanish practically before the conquest had ended, reveals just how brutal it was:

On the day 1 Ganel [February 20, 1524], the Quiches were destroyed by the Spaniards. Their chief, he was called Tunatiuh Avilantaro, conquered all the people.... [The Spaniards] went forward to the city of Gumarcaah [capital of the Quiche, also called Utatlan], where they were received by the kings.... The Quiches paid [The Spanish] tribute. Soon the kings were tortured by Tunatiuh. On the day 4 Qat [March 7, 1524] the kings Ahpop and Ahpop Quamahay were burned by Tunatiuh. The heart of Tunatiuh was without compassion for the people. (Recinos and Goetz, 1953, 119–125)

In another city, the Spanish commander "asked for one of the daughters of the king," who was furnished to him; he followed that demand with another, for money. "He wished for them to give him piles of metal, their vessels and crowns." When the kings did not comply immediately, Tunatiuh was said to have become very angry. He threatened them with death by burning and hanging. Finally, Tunatiuh forced the Maya to flee their own city, and then he chased them: "Ten days after we fled from the city, Tunatiuh began to make war upon us. On the day 4 Camey [September 5, 1524], they began to make us suffer. We scattered ourselves under the trees, under the vines, oh, my sons" (Stannard, 1992, 82).

As the Spanish struggled to subdue the decentralized Maya, the conquest also rolled over Native peoples to the south. In Panama, between 1514 and 1530 as many as 2 million Native people were killed, many after having been taken into slavery. As many as half a million people were taken out of

Nicaragua in chains (most later died); 150,000 were taken from Honduras. Historian David E. Stannard commented:

> Since numbers such as these are so overwhelming, sometimes it is the smaller incident that best tells what it was like—such as the expedition to Nicaragua in 1527 of Lopez de Salcedo, the colonial governor of Honduras. At the start of his trip, Salcedo took with him more than 300 slaves to carry his personal effects. Along the way he killed two-thirds of them, but he also captured 2,000 more from villages that were in his path. By the time he reached his destination in Leon only 100 of the more than 2,300 Indian slaves he had begun with were still alive. All this was necessary to "pacify" the natives. (Stannard, 1992, 82)

During the first half-century of the conquest, the Maya's population fell by 82 percent in the Cuchumatan highlands of Guatemala. On Cozumel Island, off the eastern coast of Mexico's Yucatán Peninsula, 96 percent of the people perished in seventy years. Within sixty years, the Native population of present-day Nicaragua declined by 99 percent, from about 1 million to fewer than 10,000. These are representative figures for the devastation that occurred throughout Mesoamerica during the bloody sixteenth century (Stannard, 1992, 86). The Maya's *Chilam Balam* described it as follows:

> [W]hat the white lords did when they came to our land: "They taught fear and they withered the flowers. So that their flower should live, the maimed and destroyed the flower of others.... Marauders by day, offenders by night, murderers of the world." (Ibid., 86)

Smallpox (as well as other imported diseases) and repeated attempts at Spanish invasion and colonization broke the Maya only slowly. Pedro de Alvarado marched from the Valley of Mexico to Guatemala with 400 Spanish soldiers and as many as 20,000 Native allies, blazing a path of terror through Mayan country, catching women and hanging them. The Spaniards hung babies from their dying mothers' feet. Alvarado, who had recently married a native woman from compliant Tlaxcala, threw unmarried Mayan women to packs of hunting dogs, which tore them to pieces.

Many Maya fought a determined guerilla war that drove the Spanish from Yucatan during 1536. In 1541, after the Spanish forged alliances with some of the Maya and after famine, pestilence, and the ravages of civil war, the Maya finally fell to yet another Spanish invasion. Scattered bands held out for decades longer. The Itza of Lake Petén resisted Spanish domination for more than 100 years after that. For most Maya, however, a way of life ended by 1550 as Spanish priests burned their cherished books. Remarked Bishop Landa of Yucatán: "As they contained nothing but superstition and lies of the devil, we burned them all, which the Indians regretted to an amazing degree" (Recinos and Goetz,

1953, 105). An unnamed Mayan poet wrote: "With rivers of tears we mourned our sacred writings among the delicate flowers of sorrow" (ibid., 105).

The Spanish invented all manner of exotic methods to inflict pain and death—the more excruciating the better. They built a long gibbet, low enough for the toes to touch the ground and prevent strangling, and hanged thirteen Natives at a time in honor of Christ and the twelve Apostles. The Spaniards then tested their blades against the dangling *Indios*, ripping chests open with one blow and exposing entrails. Straw was wrapped around their torn bodies, and they were burned alive. One man caught two children about two years old, pierced their throats with a dagger, then hurled them down a precipice.

One conquistador pastime was indicative of their disregard for Native life. It was called "dogging"—the hunting and maiming of Native people by canines specifically trained to relish the taste of human flesh. According to David E. Stannard, some of the dogs were kept as pets by the conquistadors. Vasco Nuñez de Balboa's favorite was named Leoncico, or Little Lion, a cross between a greyhound and a mastiff. On one occasion, Balboa ordered 40 Indians dogged at once. "Just as the Spanish soldiers seem to have particularly enjoyed testing the sharpness of their yard-long blades on the bodies of Indian children, so their dogs seemed to find the soft bodies of infants especially tasty," wrote Stannard (1992, 83).

Las Casas thundered against the practice of "commending" Indians to *en-comenderos*, which resulted in virtual slavery. He was rebuffed by Spanish authorities, who had a financial interest in this system of legalized slavery. Las Casas, the first priest ordained in the New World, called down a formal curse on the main agent of the bloody terror that eliminated Native people from Cuba, Panfilo de Narvaez. One of the gentle Tainos, offered baptism as he was about to be burned at the stake, refused because he thought he might find himself in the Christians' heaven, populated by even more of the light-skinned people who were torturing him (Las Casas, 1971, 121).

Mayan resistance continued for more than three centuries. In 1848, continuing through 1850, remnants of the Maya launched the Caste War, a coordinated attack on Spanish settlements in Yucatán, the nucleus of the old lowland Mayan cultures. This revolt has been called "without question the most successful Indian revolt in New World history" (Bricker, 1981, 87, cited in Wright, 1992, 255). For a time, the Maya nearly drove the Spanish into the sea, only to see their army dissolve as soldier-farmers returned to their fields for the crucial corn-planting season. The revolt in Quintana Roo was not completely crushed by Mexican troops until 1901.

Five centuries after the Spanish conquest, more than 2 million Maya still live in the homelands that their cities once dominated. Some have become partially assimilated into Western culture; others, such as the Lacandon in the remote forests west of the Rio Usumacinta, still live in relative isolation. In recent years, the population of the Lacandon Maya has dropped to a few hundred people as they have moved deeper and deeper into the lowland forests to escape the pressures of Mexico's twenty-first century society (Duby and Blom, 1969, 7:276–297).

In Guatemala, which had been the Maya's highland nucleus, subjugation that now approaches 500 years goes on in the guise of a bloody and intractable civil war that has been killing an average of 10 people a day for political reasons for more than 30 years. The death toll of 138,000 people includes 100,000 murdered for political reasons and 38,000 more "disappeared." This figure is political murders only; other civilian and military casualties of the war are not included. The war, in a country that is still 60 percent Maya, follows the race and class lines of the original *conquista*—a *meztiso* (or Ladino) landed class brutally holding down a poverty-stricken Mayan majority by every means at its disposal, sometimes (as in 1954) with the political and economic muscle of the United States behind it (Wright, 1992, 266).

FURTHER READING

Borah, Woodrow, and Sherburne Cook. *The Aboriginal Population of Mexico on the Eve of the Spanish Conquest.* Ibero-Americana No. 45. Berkeley: University of California Press, 1963.

Brandon, William. *The American Heritage Book of Indians.* New York: Dell, 1961.

Bricker, Victoria R. *The Indian Christ, the Indian King.* Austin: University of Texas Press, 1981.

Burnham, Philip. Review *Seven Myths of the Spanish Conquest*, by Matthew Restall. *Indian Country Today*, August 5, 2004. Available at http://www.indiancountry.com/ ?1091714398.

Calamai, Peter. Demise of Maya Tied to Droughts: Study Points to Climate Change Culture Depended on Growing Maize. *Toronto Star*, March 14, 2003. Available at http://www.thestar.ca/NASApp/cs/ContentServer?pagename=thestar/Layout/Article_ Type1&c=Article&cid=1035779188042&call_page=TS_Canada&call_pageid= 968332188774&call_pagepath=News/Canada&pubid=968163964505&StarSource= email.

Castillo, Bernardino Díaz del. *Conquest of New Spain.* New York, 1958.

Castillo, Bernal Díaz del. *Historia Verdadera de la Conquista de la Nueva España*, edited by Joaquín Ramírez Cabañas. Mexico City: Editorial Purrua, 1968, 2:273, cited in Leon-Portilla, 1972, 122.

Coe, Michael D. *America's First Civilization.* New York: American Heritage, 1968.

Coe, William R. Resurrecting the Grandeur of Tikal, *National Geographic*, December 1975, 792–799.

Collier, John. *Indians of the Americas.* New York: New American Library, 1947.

Cook, Sherburne F., and Woodrow Borah. *The Indian Population of Central Mexico, 1521–1610.* Ibero-Americana No. 44. Berkeley: University of California Press, 1960.

Demarest, Arthur A. The Violent Saga of a Mayan Kingdom. *National Geographic*, February 1993, 95–111.

Diamond, Jared. The Last Americans: Environmental Collapse and the End of Civilization. *Harper's*, June 2003, 43–51.

Diehl, Richard A. *Tula: The Toltec Capital of Ancient Mexico.* London: Thames and Hudson, 1981.

Dobyns, Henry F. Estimating Aboriginal American Population. *Current Anthropology* 7(1966): 395–449.

Driver, Harold E. *Indians of North America.* 2nd ed. Chicago: University of Chicago Press, 1969.

Duby, Gertrude, and Frans Blom. The Lacandon. In Robert Wauchope, ed., *Handbook of Middle-American Indians.* Vol. 7. Austin: University of Texas Press, 1969.

Fash, William L., Jr., and Barbara W. Fash, Scribes, Warriors and Kings: the Lives of the Copan Maya. *Archaeology,* May–June 1990, 28.

Gann, Thomas. *Mystery Cities: Exploration and Adverture in Lubaantun.* London: Duckworth, 1925.

Gerhard, Peter. *A Guide to the Historical Geography of New Spain.* Princeton, NJ: Princeton University Press, 1972.

Gerhard, Peter. *The North Frontier of New Spain.* Princeton, NJ: Princeton University Press, 1982.

Gibson, Charles. *The Aztecs Under Spanish Rule: A History of the Indians of the Valley of Mexico, 1519–1810.* Palo Alto, CA: Stanford University Press, 1964.

Hassler, Peter. Cutting Through the Myth of Human Sacrifice: The Lies of the Conquistadors. *World Press Review* (reprinted from *Die Zeit,* Hamburg), December 1992, 28–29.

Haug, Gerald H., Detlef Gunter, Larry C. Peterson, Daniel M. Sigman, Konrad A. Hughen, and Beat Aeschlimann. Climate and the Collapse of Maya Civilization. *Science* 299(March 14, 2003):1731–1735.

Henderson, John S. *The World of the Ancient Maya.* Ithaca, NY: Cornell University Press, 1981.

Jiménez-Moreno, Wigberto and Alfonso Garcia-Ruiz. *Historia de México: Una Sintesis.* Mexico City, D. F.: INAH, 1970.

Kelley, David H. *Deciphering the Maya Script.* Austin: University of Texas Press, 1976.

Labaree, Leonard, ed. *The Papers of Benjamin Franklin.* New Haven, CT: Yale University Press, 1950–.

La Fay, Howard. The Maya, The Children of Time. *National Geographic,* December 1975, 729–766.

Las Casas, Bartolomé de. *History of the Indies.* Translated and edited by Andrée Collard. New York: Harper and Row, 1971.

León Portilla, M. *Los Antiguos Mexicanos à Través de sus* Cronicas y Cantares. Mexico City: Fondo de Cultura Economica, 1972.

León Portilla, Miguel. *Pre-Columbian Literatures of Mexico.* Norman: University of Oklahoma Press, 1969.

Lovell, W. George. *Conquest and Survival in Colonial Guatemala: A Historical Geography of the Cuchumatan Highlands, 1500–1821.* Montreal: McGill-Queen's University Press, 1985.

Maxwell, James A., ed. *America's Fascinating Indian Heritage.* Pleasantville, NY: Reader's Digest, 1978.

McDowell, Bart. The Aztecs. *National Geographic,* December 1980, 704–752.

Mochtezuma, Eduardo Matos. Templo Mayor: History and Interpretation. In Johanna Broda, David Carrasco, and Mochtezuma, eds., *The Great Temple of Tenochtitlán: Center and Periphery in the Aztec World.* Berkeley: University of California Press, 1988, 15–60.

Molina Montes, Augusto F. The Building of Tenochtitlán. *National Geographic*, December 1980, 753–766.

Radell, Davis R. The Indian Slave Trade and Population of Nicaragua During the Sixteenth Century. In William E. Denevan, ed., *The Native Population of the Americas*. Madison: University of Wisconsin Press, 1976, 67–76.

Recinos, Adrian, and Delia Goetz, trans. *The Annals of the Cakchiquels*. Norman: University of Oklahoma Press, 1953.

Restall, Matthew. *Seven Myths of the Spanish Conquest*. New York: Oxford University Press, 2004.

Roys, Ralph L. *The Book of Chilam Balam of Chumayel*. Norman: University of Oklahoma Press, 1967, cited in Wright, 1992, 165–166.

Sahagún, Bernardino de. *Historia General de las Cosas de Nueva España*. 4 vols. Edited and translated by Angel Maria Garibay. Mexico City, DF: Porrua, [ca. 1555] 1956.

Sahagún, Bernardino de. Historia de las Cosas de la Nueva España (1905–1907). Cited in Miguel León Portilla, *The Aztec Image of Self and Society: An Introduction to Nahua Culture*. Salt Lake City: University of Utah Press, 1992.

Sahagún, Friar Bernardino de. *Florentine Codex: General History of the Things of New Spain*. Vol. 10. Translated by Arthur J. O. Anderson and Charles Dibble. Santa Fe, NM: School of American Research, 1950–1969.

Scholars Rewrite Mayan History after Hieroglyphics Found. *Omaha World-Herald*, September 20, 2002, 12-A.

Smith, Michael E. The Aztec Migrations of the Nahuatl Chronicles: Myth or History? *Ethnohistory* 31:3(1984):153–186.

Stannard, David E. *American Holocaust: Columbus and the Conquest of the New World*. New York: Oxford University Press, 1992.

Stuart, George E. Riddle of the Glyphs. *National Geographic*, December 1975, 768–791.

Stuart, George E. Etowah: A Southeast Village in 1491. *National Geographic*, October 1991, 54–67.

Stuart, George E. Mural Masterpieces of Ancient Cacaxtla. *National Geographic*, September 1992, 120–136.

Webster, David. *The Fall of the Ancient Maya*. London: Thames and Hudson, 2002.

Wilkerson, Jeffery K. Following the Route of Cortes. *National Geographic*, October 1984, 420–459.

Williams, Stephen. *Fantastic Archaeology: The Wild Side of American Prehistory*. Philadelphia: University of Pennsylvania Press, 1991.

Wright, Ronald. *Stolen Continents: America through Indian Eyes Since 1492*. Boston: Houghton Mifflin, 1992.

CHAPTER 3

Native America Meets Europe

THE COLONIAL ERA

Euuropean immigrants who flowed across North America in successive waves encountered a very large array of Native American peoples. A great variety of Native languages existed in North America at contact, an estimated 500 to 1,000. An even wider variety of languages was spoken in South America (Brandon, 1961, 106). Estimates of the total number of languages at contact on both continents range from 1,000 to 2,000 (Driver, 1969, 25; Beals and Hoijer, 1965, 613). This variety of languages was a result of cultural development spanning many thousands of years that was ended, or arrested, with the advent of immigrating European people and their pathogenic diseases. This chapter briefly sketches the evolution of cultures in parts of the present-day United States, from the Southwest to Southeast. This description is followed by a narrative of contact, first among the Spanish, then the English and French.

THE RISE OF COMPLEX CULTURES

About 5,000 years ago, at the beginning of the epoch that geologists call the Holocene, complex cultures with stable agricultural and trading bases began to form in the area now occupied by the continental United States of America. Although Clovis and Folsom styles of weapons diffused rapidly across North America (indicating trade and other forms of communication), we know little about these cultures other than that they hunted now-extinct forms of large wildlife. We are only beginning to learn from the scanty trail of evidence they left behind how the people of North America's various cultures conducted other aspects of their lives (such as religions). At a half-dozen sites across the United States west of the Rocky Mountains, underground chambers have been found housing caches of items that many believe Clovis era people found valuable, such as their distinctive projectile points. Were these places burial sites? We do not yet know.

At about 3000 B.C.E., not so long after the trail of a complex history begins for the Old World, organized societies began to develop in North America. Perhaps not coincidentally, the Mayan calendar, the most precise measure of time developed in prehistoric America, dates to 3114 B.C.E. North of the Rio Grande, peoples who earlier had subsisted mainly by hunting and gathering began to develop agriculture around 500 B.C.E. Settled societies evolved earliest in two geographic areas: the Southeast (including the Mississippi Valley) and the Southwest. The Southwestern cultures evolved a few hundred years earlier, planting the seeds of the Anasazi (Navajo for ancient ones), who by 1000 C.E. had built communal structures containing up to 650 rooms each across the arid landscape of contemporary Arizona, New Mexico, Colorado, and Utah. In the Southeast, agriculture-based societies evolved into the mound builders of the Mississippian culture. The first Spanish explorers found only the last remnants of both.

CAUTIONS

When surveying the prehistory of North America, one must recognize the fluidity of scholarship and how quickly new knowledge and conjecture may turn recent veracity to dross. Civilization in the Americas is ancient, but much of our knowledge of these civilizations is relatively recent. When studying the condition of societies in the Americas before persistent contact with Europeans, realize that most of our knowledge of these cultures dates from the twentieth century, and that we are still by and large discovering America. Who knows what still waits to be unearthed, deciphered, connected, and revealed.

More good advice comes from Duane Champagne, former editor of the University of California at Los Angeles' *American Indian Culture and Research Journal* and a professor of sociology at the university. Champagne commented on the nature of political consensus and leadership among Native peoples that often confused Europeans, who were accustomed to top-down, command-and-control hierarchies. Although some Native peoples (such as the Aztecs) conformed to this model, many others did not.

When examining Native cultures, both in prehistory and after contact with European colonialism, it is important to distinguish between the types of disagreement between individuals and groups that are routine parts of decision making and change and those that rend the social fabric and make consensus impossible. Champagne, who is a Turtle Mountain Chippewa, wrote the following:

> The literature on Native North Americans tends to regard Indian societies as endemic with internal factionalism. However, what many observers have recorded is largely routine conflict. Since many Indian societies are politically decentralized, with segmentary bands, villages or kinship groups having considerable local political,

social, and economic autonomy, they have considerable difficulty organizing sustained collective action.... While such absence of concerted action may look like factionalism [to an outside observer] the major subgroups are merely exercising their prerogative to make their own political decisions. (1989, 4–5)

"Factionalism," according to Champagne (1989, 4), "should be reserved for conflicts over the rules of social order." The rapid and uncontrolled exposure of a society to outside influences—as occurred across the Americas at the onset of European colonialism—may cause such society-destroying factional splits, most often between those people within the culture who assert that the invasion should be resisted and those who wish to accommodate it. Societal factionalism also may be introduced from within or because of environmental changes. This was the most common cause of major changes in Native North American societies before contact with Europeans.

On contact, historical accounts often display just how ignorant the immigrants were of this consensus model of politics. Leaders of colonial expeditions often asked Natives they met to take them to a clearly identifiable leader with whom they could negotiate for an entire nation. Just as often, the immigrants assumed that Native people they met were leaders who could speak for others, when they could not.

Another problem with much contemporary commentary on Native societies, according to Champagne, is that when change in them is described, it is usually analyzed solely in terms of colonial influence (Champagne, 1989, 4–5). Observers (who usually have been educated within the context of European American society) do not begin their studies with descriptions of the complex indigenous societies that formed and re-formed before contact, but rather as "a mere reflection or reaction to the powerful forces of colonial societies" (ibid., 4–5). Although it is true that European peoples and their cultures have wrought great changes in Native American ways of living during the five-plus centuries since persistent contact began, the Native societies that have absorbed these changes did not adopt them without modification. At the other end of the spectrum, many traditionally trained scholars do not study the ways in which American Indian ways of living, thinking, and organizing societies influenced the many peoples who immigrated to North America from overseas.

Societies indigenous to North America also influenced each other for many thousands of years before continuing contact with Europeans began. The Maya, for example, developed the concept of negative numbers and passed it to the Aztecs, in ways in some ways similar to the Greeks' shaping of Roman knowledge. Native people traded in a wide net across the continent; cultural traits and other types of knowledge were transmitted as well. Because so little of this trade was recorded and because many of the peoples who carried it on do not survive, reconstructing an accurate "prehistory" of North America is one of historical scholarship's greatest challenges. The fact that our interpretations of this period have changed so fundamentally during this century is reflective of how little we still do not know.

AGRICULTURE COMES TO THE SOUTHWEST

A people archeologists call the Mogollon became the first in the present-day United States to adopt agriculture and pottery, around 300 B.C.E. Their pit dwellings and kivas resembled those of other peoples in the present-day U.S. Southwest as well as the early Anasazi. The Mogollon people were a branch of the broader Cochise culture, from which the Anasazi also evolved a few centuries later. They lived in western New Mexico and eastern Arizona (roughly the area occupied by the Navajos today), weaving fine blankets out of cotton, feathers, and wool made from the fur of animals. Some of the modern Hopis and Zunis are descended from the Mogollon peoples.

Another branch of the Cochise, the Hohokam, adopted agriculture as their predominant way of life about 100 C.E. in the Salt and Gila River areas of present-day southern Arizona. To cope with the dry conditions of the area, the Hohokam built massive irrigation works, some of which were still in use when the first Spaniards arrived. The people diverted river water into canals six feet deep and up to thirty feet wide, some of which extended up to ten miles, to nourish the crops that fed the population of their principal settlement, now called Snaketown. This site, close to present-day Phoenix, was occupied for 1,200 consecutive years. The Hohokam also developed a process for etching almost 300 years before it was used in Europe. Hohokam craftspeople worked the surface to be etched with pitch, as they transferred the design with a stylus. They then laced the design with an acid created from the fruit of the saguaro cactus. The Pimas and Papagos, who occupied southern Arizona during early Spanish contact, were descended from the Hohokam people.

THE ANASAZI

Roughly 1000 C.E., the Anasazi, ancestors of today's Hopis and Pueblos, built a network of large stone dwellings atop and into the sides of mesas in the present-day southwestern United States. Their network of villages, centered in Chaco Canyon, covered an area extending from west of Albuquerque (on contemporary maps) westward to Las Vegas, Nevada. Dwellings in these villages housed tens of thousands of people in preplanned complexes as large as 300 rooms each. The settlements were connected by roads as wide as some of today's interstate highways; these roads may have been used to transport food quickly from settlement to settlement to address shortages in a land where rainfall could be scarce and harvests could easily fail. The Anasazi ingeniously utilized what little water they had, but in the end their civilization, which flourished for a little more than a century, collapsed in the face of a severe drought that began about 1150 C.E.

Anglo-American explorers discovered the remains of the Anasazi in 1877, when photographer William Henry Jackson found spectacular ruins of a people who were first called the Basketmakers because their earliest generations used intricately woven baskets even to carry water, while most others used pottery. Only slowly did scholars realize that Chaco Canyon had been the center of a very large civilization. By 2,000 years ago, the people who would build these large settlements were discovering how to grow corn, the basis of a sedentary existence. When the Navajo (Dine) arrived from the north, they called the people they met ancient ones, Anasazi in their language.

Anasazi settlements covered the landscape, giving the area they occupied a population density greater than today, outside of major urban areas. At least 25,000 Anasazi sites have been found in New Mexico, a similar number in Arizona, and thousands more in Utah and Colorado. Archeologists believe that many thousands more will be discovered in the future (Canby, 1982, 563). Many of the canyon walls in an area that European settlers regarded as inhospitable became peppered with cliff dwellings after the Anasazi imported the bow and arrow and discovered the hefted axe about 500 C.E. because they also refined their cultivation of corn, beans, and squash. Even the walls of the Grand Canyon became home to some of the cliff-dwelling Anasazi.

Coaxing food out of the often-dry soil required some ingenuity. The Anasazi learned to mulch soil with gravel to help it retain moisture as they fashioned an irrigation system that took advantage of runoff from drenching summer thunderstorms. As a thunderstorm gathered strength, the Anasazi would leave their other work and rush to the north-facing walls of nearby canyons to channel the runoff into canals leading into their farming fields. In this way, they designed irrigation without access to rivers. Some of these canals were as long as four miles. They required constant, cooperative labor, especially during the summer growing season, when sudden thunderstorms often were the only form of precipitation.

By roughly 700 C.E., Anasazi dwellings began to increase in size and complexity; 300 years later, they built dwellings that could enclose an entire village in one structure, the largest residential housing blocks built in North America until about 1870. These dwellings housed a society in which women usually owned family property, and men oversaw the ceremonial side of life, centered in underground kivas.

Life in this area could be precarious. Crops could fail, and game could disappear for months on end, bringing to the Anasazi haunting memories of droughts and famines past. Archeological reports indicate that many Anasazi died in infancy, and that in old age (by 45 years, on average) many were nearly crippled by arthritis. The Anasazi prospered despite their harsh environment. At 919 C.E., the ceiling beams were cut for Pueblo Bonito, the grandest of all the cliff settlements. Such precision in dating is made possible by measuring the growth rings of the trees used as beams.

By roughly the year 1150, the Anasazi reached their height. When it was completed, Pueblo Bonito contained 650 rooms. Eleven other smaller pueblos surrounded it, many of them connected by roads. Seventy other similar communities lay outside Chaco Canyon; others spread across an area 500 miles east to west and up to 300 miles north to south (Canby, 1982, 564–565, 578). The Anasazis also devised a communication system to complement their roads. One school of thought has it that the various pueblos communicated with fires or mica mirrors reflecting sunlight in coded signals from the tops of mesas (ibid., 585).

After 1150, the Anasazis' civilization quickly collapsed because of severe drought coupled with cooling temperatures. This drought was a drastic, wrenching climatic change that lasted more than a century, reaching its peak between 1276 and 1299, when practically no rain or snow fell in the area. The Chaco River dried up. Agriculture always had been risky in this region, anywhere above 7,000 feet or below 5,500 feet in elevation; the higher elevations were too cold, and lower locations too were hot and dry. With the change in climate, farming became nearly impossible in many locations.

A few Anasazi settlements survived the drought, such as Mesa Verde, one of the latest and most spectacular, but the majority of the pueblos lay in ruins by the time the Spanish arrived. The cliff dwellers at Mesa Verde left a magnificent masonry temple that indicated a massive attempt to appease the gods after the great drought. The construction of religious structures also may have indicated cultural influence from trading with the civilizations of the Valley of Mexico, several hundred miles to the south. The Anasazi also traded buffalo meat with Native peoples of the plains to the east and north. Before the great drought, Pueblo Bonito hosted a large market that may have been a crossroads for traders ranging over thousands of miles. Most of this network died in the dust before 1200 C.E. Scattered remnants are still occupied today. Acoma, for example, is still a functioning community, as is the Hopis' Orabi, which is the oldest continuously occupied community in the present-day United States.

SPANISH EXPLORATION AMONG THE PUEBLOS

The Spanish, who sent several expeditions northward from Mexico beginning in 1540, were the first Europeans to meet Native peoples in the present-day land area comprising the United States of America. Very quickly, learning of the Anasazi, the Spanish explorers realized that Native cultures had been evolving in the area for many centuries before their arrival. The Pueblos, their descendants, built a remarkably intricate culture in their cliff dwellings. Their pottery and jewelry turned Spanish heads. Some of their turquoise necklaces contained thousands of worked stones.

The Pueblos' government was a democratic theocracy; nearly all houses were of roughly equal size. The highest-ranking theocrats were farmers, like the people they led. In some towns, two groups of residents (the Summer

Acoma water carriers. (Courtesy of the Edward S. Curtis Collection,
Library of Congress.)

People and the Winter People) took six-month turns at governing. Ruth Benedict's *Patterns of Culture* (1934, 100) extolled the democratic nature of government among the Zuni Pueblos. They, and the rest of the Pueblos, seemed to
have operated their political system with an innate sense of egalitarianism;
the passage of wealth and power by heredity was almost unknown; a man or

Terraced houses, Acoma Pueblo. (Courtesy of the Library of Congress.)

woman distinguished him- or herself through real achievements in daily life. Although the Pueblos and other southwestern people seem to have borrowed liberally from Mesoamerica in their material cultures, their political system was much more egalitarian than those of the Aztecs and Maya (Driver, 1969, 338–339).

Although archeologists agree that the Acoma Pueblo has been continuously inhabited since at least 1200 C.E., Native elders in the area assert that the site has been occupied for about 2,000 years. Acoma (historically also spelled Akome, Acu, Acuo, Acuco, and Ako) is taken by many elders to mean "a place that always was," as a home, or as an eternal resting place. The Spanish were drawn to the area by rumors of gold (such as the Seven Cities of Cibola and Quivera). Hernando de Alvarado and his companion Fray Juan Padilla, traveling with a small body of soldiers (as part of the Coronado expedition), were the first Europeans to see the Acoma Pueblo.

The Coronado expedition, Spain's initial foray north of the Rio Grande, returned to Mexico in 1542, bereft of gold or other precious cargo. Coronado's failure to find tangible treasure kept Spanish gold seekers out of the area for more than a half century. Spanish missionaries visited the area during 1581 and 1582. The first, led by Fray Agustin Rodriguez, visited Acoma briefly; the account of Hernan Gallegos (1966), a soldier on the expedition, says only that the pueblo was built on a high mesa and contained about 500 houses, each three or four stories high. A second expedition, led by Bernaldino Beltran, brought back reports that Acoma was home to about 6,000 people whose pueblo rose about 250 to 300 feet in the air and who possessed plentiful food stores and enough cotton blankets (called *mantas*) to share with the Spanish. The Spanish noted farm fields two leagues from the pueblo, as well as irrigation works fed from a local river. The members of the expedition also hungrily eyed the mountains, believing that their presence guaranteed riches of gold and silver. Initial contact with the Pueblo people at Acoma was friendly. Many of them juggled and danced to celebrate the Spaniards' arrival; some of the dances were performed with live snakes.

Sustained immigration into New Mexico by the Spanish began in 1598 as about 400 men, women, and children marched northward along the slopes of the Sierra Madre with 7,000 head of stock and 80 wagons. Only at the pueblo of Acoma, on the summit of a steep mesa, did the Spanish meet active resistance. After a short battle, the Spanish invaded the pueblo and imprisoned its men, women, and children. Men who resisted lost one foot and twenty years of their lives to slavery. Women and children older than twelve also were enslaved for twenty years, and children under that age were handed over to the Catholic Church's missionaries for indenture. Two Hopis who were visiting Acoma were sent home missing their right hands as a warning. Fifteen years later, Juan de Oñate, the provincial governor who had been the leader of and chief investor in the original colonization, was stripped of his honors by a Spanish tribunal and was fined for torture and mass enslavement of the Natives. Thus ended the governorship of Oñate, son of one of the richest mine owners in Mexico who had married a great-granddaughter of Mochtezuma. (Four hundred years after his troops chopped off the limbs of their ancestors, Native people in New Mexico removed a foot from a statue of Oñate to memorialize his cruelty.)

Bartolomé de las Casas Decries Spanish Cruelty

Oñate had the miserable fortunate of having gone colonizing with illegal zeal during the late stages of Spanish expansion. The charges levied against Oñate reflected the growing muscle within Spanish government circles, as well as the Catholic Church, of people who sought to check the cruelty and avarice of the conquistadors, several of whom were hauled in front of inquiries into their conduct. In the Americas, the Catholic priest Bartolomé de las Casas avidly encouraged inquiries into the Spanish conquest's many cruelties. Las Casas chronicled Spanish brutality against the Native peoples in excruciating detail. It was Las Casas who laid on Spanish desks and Catholic consciences the history of Latin America's bloody depopulation at the hands of the Spanish. He described how Native people choked to death on mercury fumes in the silver mines as conquistadors bet Native lives in games of cards (Las Casas, 1974).

In large part because of Las Casas's work, a movement arose in Spain for more humane treatment of indigenous peoples. Some of the conquistadors made public statements repudiating their past cruelties. In his will, Hernan Cortes raised the slavery issue. A sharp debate followed within the Catholic Church regarding whether the Natives possessed the spiritual nature (e.g., whether they had souls) suitable to absorb Christian doctrine. Europeans who thought of the Indians as subhuman laughed, asserting that their intelligence was "no more than parrots" (Minge, 1991, 7). During 1552, López de Gómara (1556), known in contemporary Spain as a biographer of Cortes, described Indians as barbarous heathens who fornicated in public (specializing in sodomy), liars, and cannibals who cursed the Old World with syphilis. Gómara asserted that Indians were by nature inferior to Europeans, thereby fit only for slavery in the Spanish New World order.

In the papal bull *Sublimis Deus* (1537), Pope Paul III declared that Indians were to be regarded as fully human, and that their souls were as immortal as those of Europeans. This edict also outlawed slavery of Indians in any form several decades before Oñate sold the Pueblos he had captured. Las Casas's *New Laws for the Indies* (1544) called for gradual elimination of forced labor for Native Americans under Catholic Church sponsorship.

To counter criticism that the conquest had been brutal and cruel, the laws of Spain required a conquistador, at the moment of first contact, to read Native peoples a long statement that explained the story of Adam and Eve, the supremacy of the Pope, and reasons why they should embrace the Catholic faith. This statement was phrased as a contract by which the Native peoples agreed to submit peacefully to the authority of the king of Spain as well as the Church of Rome. If Native people decided not to submit to the Spanish at this point, armed force was brought to bear. By the middle 1500s, the semantics of this statement were refined into a genial proclamation of greeting from the king of Spain to the kings and republics of the "mid-way and western lands." By 1573, the revised New Laws outlawed any mention of conquest. Instead, the role of the explorers was said to be "pacification."

After Oñate's inglorious fall, later governors of New Mexico tried to recoup their investments in the colony, surveying a landscape that was utterly lacking deposits of gold and silver. Unable to wrest wealth from the land themselves, the colonists squeezed the Pueblos more harshly for food and labor. The priests railed against the Indians' devil worship and from time to time whipped some of the Pueblos' most respected elders (sometimes to death) in public displays for their practice of non-Catholic rituals.

The Pueblo Revolt (1680)

Spanish arrogance and cruelty provoked considerable resentment among Native peoples. Fifty years after their first colonization, the Pueblos joined with their ancient enemies the Apaches in an effort to drive the Spanish out. This initial revolt failed, but thirty years later, in 1680, a coalition of Pueblos knit by the war captain Pope raised a furious revolt that killed a quarter of the Spanish immigrants, trashed the hated churches, and sent the surviving Spanish down the trail to El Paso Notre, leaving behind almost everything they owned. The governor summed up the situation: "Today they [the Pueblos] are very happy without religious [missionaries], or Spaniards" (Brandon, 1961, 129).

Pope's policies after the rout of the Spanish proved too zealous for most Pueblos. He took on the airs of a petty tyrant and forbade his people from using anything that the Spanish had imported, including new crops. Most of Pope's edicts regarding crops were ignored. Pope even ordered the execution of some of his reputed enemies, after which the Pueblo Confederacy that had expelled the Spanish broke into two camps, one favoring Pope, the other opposing him. Pope was deposed but was restored to power in 1688, shortly before he died. Four Spanish attempts at reconquest in eight years combined with a plague of European diseases, as well as the Pueblos' existing internal dissension, led to depopulation of the Pueblos' villages after Pope's death. In 1692, the Spanish returned.

THE EASTERN MOUND BUILDERS

The pyramidlike mounds of Cahokia (described in chapter 1) are now known to have been one relatively spectacular and recent example of mound-building cultures that occupied the southeastern quadrant of North America during roughly 4,500 years before Columbus first made landfall.

At Poverty Point, Louisiana, people living in about 1000 B.C.E. constructed earthen mounds on a scale smaller than those of Cahokia 2,000 years later. One such pyramid, at Bayou Macon, fifteen miles west of the Mississippi River, measures 70 feet high and contains 200,000 cubic yards of earth. (The largest pyramid mound at Cahokia fills ten times as much space and rises 100 feet high.) The mounds at Poverty Point are the earliest construction of such size thus far found anywhere in North America. This culture flourished at about the time the Olmecs were becoming organized along the Gulf Coast of Mexico; relationships between the two (possibly via trade across the Gulf of Mexico or by land around it) have been proposed, but not proven. The earthworks at Poverty Point rival those of Mexico's Teotihuacan in size but not in artistic detail. The presence of these and other, smaller mounds indicates a fair-size settlement, as do the thousands of tools left behind. Other remains include small carvings of owls done in great detail and an abundance of goods that were probably imported, some of them from great distances, such as iron, lead ore, and copper.

The Adena culture (named after an estate near Chillicothe, Ohio, where a large mound was excavated in 1902) occupied portions of the Ohio Valley located in contemporary Ohio, Kentucky, and West Virginia. The Adena did not develop organized agriculture but lived in large towns characteristic of later agricultural peoples, supporting themselves by harvesting the rich game of the surrounding forests and by gathering food plants. The Adena did use pottery and copper tools from metal probably imported from the Lake Superior areas. They were the first to construct large earthen mounds in the Mississippi Valley, a custom that continued with the Hopewell and Mississippian cultures for more than a thousand years.

The mounds were symbols of a highly developed religion that probably embraced the Adenans' entire social order. The mounds could not have been constructed without considerable labor organized by a central authority. Most of the mounds served as burial chambers, and considerable time and effort were invested to provide materials to be buried with the dead. One such artifact depicts a man who seems to be dancing and singing, styled into a smoking pipe. He wears a breach cloth with a stylized snake cut across its front and spool-shaped earrings which make him look rather Mesoamerican. Most of the mounds were built in rectangular shapes similar to those of temples in Mesoamerica, but one, the Great Serpent Mound, snaked its way for a quarter mile along a hillside near present-day Cincinnati, Ohio.

THE HOPEWELL CULTURE

In the Hopewell culture, mounds were used as burial sites beginning about 500 B.C.E. According to one estimate, 30 million cubic yards of earth were moved to form all of the Hopewell culture burial mounds, some of which approached the size of Poverty Point's earthworks (Stuart, 1991, 61). Although the precision of this estimate is open to question, it is obvious that a large number of people spent many years building them. They also were highly organized by some sort of central authority, at least at the village level. Artifacts found in the burial mounds indicate a complex, well-developed network of Native settlements centering in present-day Ohio. Archeology in the area indicates that, by 2,000 years ago, the Hopewell peoples were importing obsidian from the Black Hills and alligator teeth from Florida. These and other commodities indicate that a well-developed trading network extended across much of the eastern continent very early.

Unlike the Adena peoples, the Hopewell culture adapted agriculture, principally of maize (Indian corn). Studies of prehistoric climate indicate that warming temperatures allowed the cultivation of corn over larger areas of the Mississippi Valley as the Hopewell Culture reached its height between 200 B.C.E. and 500 C.E. Hopewell people continued to hunt and gather as well; they often located their villages on or near river floodplains to take advantage of mussels, fish, and other aquatic life. The rivers also formed a trading network.

Like many of the Native peoples that Europeans encountered later (such as the League of the Iroquois), the Hopewell peoples may have governed themselves through multiple chieftainships, in some sort of confederation, unlike the more centralized Aztecs. The Hopewell peoples had a trade network large enough to bring them gold, silver, and copper from hundreds of miles away. From these and other materials, they fashioned intricate objects of art. Some of their materials, such as volcanic rock, came from as far away as Wyoming; sheets of mica also found their way to the Hopewell settlements from North Carolina.

The Hopewell was one variant of the Mississippian mound-building cultures that flourished in the southeastern United States shortly after the Anasazi rose in the Southwest. Both show some indications (such as objects of trade, some religious customs, and artistic styles) of contact with the peoples of Mesoamerica. The Hopewell mounds themselves may have been an imitation of Mayan or Aztec architecture. Mound-building cultures developed across much of the Southeast, from portions of Virginia (Thomas Jefferson found a small mound at Monticello, in Virginia) to the Ohio Valley and the area that today comprises the U.S. Deep South. The Spanish explorer de Soto encountered some of the last mound builders in the vicinity of Natchez. As a whole, however, the people who built the mounds had taken up other pursuits by the time immigrants from Europe found them. In the absence of verifiable history, the earliest trans-Appalachian immigrants from Europe attributed the mounds to visitors from Israel, Egypt, or other Old World locales.

About 450 C.E., the climate cooled again, and archeological evidence indicates that the Hopewellian people were forced to spend less time pursuing art and other aspects of high culture and more time gathering enough food to survive longer, snowier winters. Over two centuries, the residents of the towns dominated by giant mounds tried to maintain their cultures in the face of climatic change as raiding neighbors preyed on their fields and food stores. The trading network collapsed because the culture could no longer afford to support large numbers of people who did not directly participate in the production of food. The number of artists and craftspeople who produced trade articles also declined. Chiefs of the villages also may have sustained a loss of authority associated with their inability to command material tribute. The next focus for developing culture in the Southeast would form further south, where corn could still be grown in abundance, even in a relatively cooler, wetter climate.

A LEGACY OF THEOCRACIES

The oral history and mythology of the Cherokees indicate that they (like several other people in the region) once were governed by a theocracy, possibly a remnant of the Temple Mound cultures that had flourished in the area. One version of the Cherokee creation myth holds that their lives originated in seven clans. Each clan appointed a headman, who was subordinate to a head priest and a council of seven, who aided the priest with ceremonies. Villages also included political councils as well as warriors' societies, but both were subordinate to the priests. The people of the villages came to resent the priests' heavy-handed control of their lives and rebelled. After the religious hierarchy was dismantled, the Cherokees maintained their affairs through a network of roughly sixty highly autonomous villages. The principal loyalty of the

Cherokee in precontact times seems to have been to the village, not to a national council.

Like the Cherokees, the Choctaws' oral history indicates that they overthrew a priesthood during the end of the mound builder era, roughly between 900 and 1600 C.E. Following the fall of their theocracy, the Choctaws abandoned the town of Nanih Waiya, a Mississippi culture town with rampart-style defenses surrounding a large mound. Following the collapse of the Choctaw theocracy, the nation was divided into six politico-social divisions called *iksa*, a term that combined kindred group, political chiefdom, and identification with a specific locality. Each *iksa* claimed its own territory. Members of many *iksa* spoke distinct dialects and shared attributes of culture that was theirs alone. Each *iksa* also maintained communal lands for farming. Although men helped clear the fields, women customarily tended them while men hunted and fished. Precontact Choctaw society was probably organized more strongly along kinship lines than the Cherokee. Villages sometimes sent delegations to regional or even national councils as well, but little is known of their powers or how they functioned.

The Chickasaws maintained vestiges of the mound builder culture after the Cherokee and Choctaw abandoned their theocracies. Records from the de Soto expedition, which crossed their homelands in present-day Louisiana and western Tennessee, indicate that the Chickasaw maintained a well-organized agricultural society headed by a chief, who was carried about in a litter and shown great deference. By the time the Chickasaws experienced sustained contact with the British (during the early 1700s) reports indicate that the society had become less hierarchical. Chiefs were regarded as equals of other people unless they showed special talents. A decline in the prestige of leaders may have been a result of the general decline of the mound-building cultures during the first years of steady European contact.

Like the Choctaws, the Chickasaws maintained an integrated kinship system (*iksas*). The nation was divided into two primary kinship groups (called phratries), which also were subdivided into smaller kinship groups down to the family level. Some leading political titles were hereditary, and political organization was to some degree divorced from the kinship system. A national council included civil and military leaders as well as representatives of the various *iksas*. The Chickasaws also utilized more definite notions of social rank than most of the other peoples in the region. At the Green Corn Ceremony, their primary annual meeting and social event, various bands camped in a prescribed pattern indicating each person's rank.

Although Chickasaw political life was more centralized than that of the other peoples in the area, decisions of the national council required unanimous consent. Leaders had little coercive authority. Priests held a special position in this political organization. They could read and interpret signs and omens and pass these messages on to the people, but they did not control the whole system (Champagne, 1989, 38–39).

The Creeks had no myth of an ancient theocracy, indicating that they perhaps migrated to central Georgia and Alabama from the west and did not originate with the Mississippi mound-building peoples. One Creek myth describes how the people migrated from the west searching for "the house of the sun." Reaching the Atlantic, they settled because they could go no farther east.

The Creek world revolved around four principal villages, which later organized into two groups that the English called the red and white towns. This division reflected the cosmology of the Creeks, which they shared with other peoples in the area. The white world was said to be the vault of heaven, the residence of a supreme diety, the home of peace, order, harmony, cleanliness, purity, and wisdom. The red sphere, under the earth, was said to be occupied by monsters and demons that could emerge through caves, rivers, and other breaches in the earth to do harm to human beings who had acted improperly. Red symbolized fertility, change, strife, danger, growth, disorder, and war. The Creeks saw life as the realm between the red and the white in which human beings struggled to achieve a balance between the competing forces. In times of war, red towns governed the Creek Confederacy. In times of peace, governance passed to the white towns. The four major Creek settlements were divided into two red and two white sections (Champagne, 1989, 52).

Primary loyalties among the Creek (as among the Cherokees) were established through the village; each settlement that was large enough to have a ceremonial center also had a myth of having received its ceremonies, laws, and sacred objects from the white world. If people in the village followed these ceremonies, they believed that they would be protected from the evil spirits of the red world, which could bring crop failure, natural calamities, death, and disease. Each village also contained kinship groups divided along red and white lines. As would be expected, the two divisions were delegated authority for civil and military functions; the red groups governed warfare, and the white performed civil government and religious ceremonies (Champagne, 1989, 59).

Like many Mesoamerican peoples, many indigenous Americans who lived in what is now the southeastern United States made an artistic canvas of their bodies. The most esteemed warriors were tattooed with graphic displays of their deeds, until some of them were covered head to foot. In addition, most men donned geometric designs of paint for war, ball games, and other public occasions. In addition to their tattoos and paint, men often wore layers of wooden, shell, copper, stone, or pearl bracelets, necklaces, armbands, and other jewelry.

ETOWAH: A TYPICAL VILLAGE

Etowah, a typical Mississippian village, housed about 3,000 people at a site west of contemporary Atlanta, Georgia, later Cherokee territory. Etowah's principal mound, rather average sized by Mississippian standards, was the height of a six-story building and contained about a million buckets of earth (Stuart, 1991, 60). Thatched-roofed dwellings surrounded the mound, and the whole village was ringed by palisades of spiked logs, indicating a high probability of warfare.

Archeologists have unearthed remains of an Etowahan war chief they called Eagle Warrior. Eagle Warrior wore a heavy necklace of solid shell beads the size of golf balls. From it hung a slender, foot-long pendant crafted from a whole conch shell. Wide bands of shell beadwork encircled his wrists and upper arms. Around his head lay more insignia of the highest status, among them copper-covered wooden coils fastened to a plate of sheet copper cut and embossed in the image of an open bird's wing to form an imposing headdress. Across his chest lay a splendid ceremonial axe, its blade and handle carefully wrought from a single piece of greenstone. The weapon, much too delicate for practical use, served as an emblem of power.

Such chiefs led warriors into battle against other towns, often in the spring. They went into battle almost naked, having painted their faces and upper bodies with red and black ochers that the people of Etowah found nearby. Each warrior carried a club, knife, bow, and arrows. The earliest Spanish explorers found the people of the area exceptionally well trained for war. One of them observed that the warriors he met were "warlike and nimble. . . . Before a Christian can make a single shot [with crossbow or harquebus] . . . an Indian will discharge three or four arrows; and he seldom misses his object" (Stuart, 1991, 64).

Estimates place the occupation of Etowah at about 1200 C.E., with its height of population and cultural development about two centuries later, about 100 to 150 years before the first Spanish explorers traversed the area. The native inhabitants, whose oral history says migrated from the west, found sandy loam soil that was ideal for farming, with a climate with a long growing season, abundant rainfall, and forests jumping with game, including white-tailed deer and many smaller animals. The shoals of rivers near Etowah abounded with mussels, turtles, and fish.

THE NATCHEZ: A LONG-LIVED MOUND PEOPLE

The Natchez are an atypical example of a temple mound people who survived into the period of sustained contact with Europeans. The Natchez were ruled by a man called the Great Sun, whose decisions regarding individuals were absolute and despotic. In decisions regarding the nation, however, he was subject to the consensus of a council of respected elders. Unlike the Pueblos, whose houses were egalitarian, the Natchez gave their ruler a palace. The Great Sun lived in a large house, twenty-five by forty-five feet, built atop a flat-topped earthen mound eight to ten feet high. The Great Sun was an absolute ruler in every sense. A French observer said that when the Great Sun

Gives the leavings [of his meal] to his brothers or any of his relatives, his pushes the dishes to them with his feet. . . . The submissiveness of the savages to their chief, who commands them with the most despotic power, is extreme. . . . If he demands the life of any one of them he comes himself to present his head. (Champagne, 1989, 59–60)

Nearby, on another mound, stood a large building, with two carved birds at either end of its roof: the temple in which reposed the bones of earlier Great Suns. Only the Great Sun (who was also head priest as well as king) and a few assistants could enter the temple.

The sons and daughters of the Great Sun, the younger members of the royal family, were called Little Suns. Below the royal family in status was a class of nobles, and below them was a class of Honored Men. The rest of the people occupied the lower orders, the Stinkards. The term was not used in the presence of Stinkards themselves because they considered it offensive. Into this hierarchical society, the Natchez introduced marriage customs that introduced some (usually downward) class mobility. A Great Sun had to marry from among the Stinkards. The male children of Great Suns became Nobles, who were also obliged to marry Stinkards. The male children of Honored Men became Stinkards. Descent followed the female line, and children of female Suns became Suns themselves. The system was matrilineal, but in the household the man's word was law.

By the time the first English colonists established themselves on the eastern seaboard of North America, Spanish explorers had crossed the Mississippi Valley and regions southeast and southwest of it, fruitlessly seeking gold and other riches. They traveled as far into the Plains as present-day Nebraska, ruining their welcome among a number of Native peoples with their penchant for arrogant plunder. The French also were using the Mississippi River as an aquatic highway, seeking furs. Outside of a few small settlements and a scattering of tiny forts, the Europeans had not become established before the year 1600 C.E. They left trade goods, missionaries, and liquor, as well as disease, the first fingers of the demographic rush that later would swirl across North America during the westward expansion of the United States.

FIRST ENGLISH CONTACT: THE POWHATAN CONFEDERACY

As Shakespeare began staging his most notable plays and England delivered its first colonists to America, the tidewater area of Virginia was home to the numerous and powerful Powhatan Confederacy, which refers to the name the indigenous people gave to the falls of the river that the English named after their King James and that dissects the urban area they later named Richmond. Powhatan, derived from the Algonquian words *pau't-hanne* or *pauwau-atan*, was the name that the English affixed to the leader of the area's Native people. The immigrants believed him to be a king, in the English style, although Powhatan probably was not an absolute ruler.

Powhatan's name among his own people was Wahunsonacock (ca. 1547–1618). He was a remarkable figure who probably had assembled most of the

Powhatan Confederacy during his tenure as leader of one of its bands. The confederacy included about 200 villages organized into several small nation-states when the English encountered it for the first time. Wahunsonacock was about 60 years of age when Jamestown was founded in 1607. Wahunsonacock and other Native people in the area may have met with other Europeans before the Jamestown colonists. The Spanish had established a mission on the York River during 1570 that was destroyed by indigenous warriors. Gangs of pirates also occasionally sought shelter along the Carolina Outer Banks as they waited for the passage of Spanish galleons flush with booty from Mexico, Meso-america, and Peru.

Wahunsonacock's father had been forced northward with his people by the Spanish invasion of Florida. He began the political work that forged an alliance of more than 100 Algonquian-speaking villages containing 9,000 people in Virginia's tidewater country. Wahunsonacock himself strengthened this alliance into a confederacy that included the Pamunkey (his people), Mattaponi, Chickahominy, Nansemond, Potomac, and Rhappahanock. This confederacy stretched from the Potomac River in northern Virginia to Albemarle Sound in North Carolina. Wahunsonacock's main village was located on the York River. He probably had eleven wives, twenty sons, and at least eleven daughters. Pocahontas, who would figure in the founding mythology of the Jamestown Colony, was reputed to have been Wahunsonacock's favorite child.

The Powhatan Confederacy was one example of many Native confederacies that had been assembling and dissolving in eastern North America, perhaps for thousands of years. Most of the villages in the Powhatan Confederacy enjoyed considerable autonomy, although tribute was sometimes paid to the central authority. Individual villages sometimes decided to make war on the English without consulting other members of the confederacy.

In the beginning, as Wahunsonacock sought peace with the English, the colonists were in no demographic position to compete with the Natives. Within the first few years after Jamestown was founded, the peoples of the Powhatan Confederacy could have eradicated the English settlement with ease. Jamestown, in fact, would not have survived in its early years without their help. Of 900 colonists who landed during the first three years (1607–1610), only 150 were alive in 1610. Most of the colonists were not ready for the rugged life of founding a colony; many died of disease, exposure to unanticipated cold weather, and starvation. At one point within a year of their landfall in America, the Jamestown colonists became so hungry that some of them engaged in cannibalism. According to the journals of John Smith, the leader of the colony, one colonist killed his wife and "powdered" (salted) her "and had eaten part of her before it was known; for which he was executed, as he well deserved" (Page, 2003, 159).

General peace persisted during those years, however, because Wahunsonacock as well as the new Virginians wanted it. The owners of the Virginia colony in London decided to treat Wahunsonacock as an independent sovereign and to accept his aid. They even sent him a copper crown. The Powhatans seem to have valued English copper as avidly as the hungry colonists valued the Natives' corn during the early years.

Although Wahunsonacock was deeply suspicious of the English, he fostered an awkward peace between the Jamestown colonists and his people so that they could establish the first permanent English colony in North America. Following the colony's early hardships, some of Wahunsonacock's people, including his son Namontack, provided the English colonists with food and taught them to plant maize (Indian corn).

When John Smith was captured by Wahunsonacock's people during the fall of 1608, he was released unharmed—as legend has it, at the request of Pocahontas. The name *Pocahontas* actually was a nickname that meant frisky or something similar. The name by which the Native woman who befriended the Virginia colonists called herself was Matowake. Captain John Smith wrote of "blessed Pocahontes, the great King's daughter of Virginia, [who] oft saved my life.... She, under God, was the instrument to preserve this colony from death, famine, and utter confusion" (Maxwell, 1978, 76).

In 1610, the Virginians tried unsuccessfully to capture and imprison Wahunsonacock. Reacting to such hostility, Wahunsonacock moved his people farther inland. In spite of this precaution, in 1613 the Virginians took Pocahontas as a hostage. As a result, Wahunsonacock had to ransom her with some English captives. During her captivity, Pocahontas and a young widower, John Rolfe (one of the colony's most prominent men), developed a romantic interest in each other. Pocahontas was about 18 years of age in 1614 when she married Rolfe. The marriage was a political move to ally the colony with Wahunsonacock. On one occasion, Rolfe took Pocahontas to London, where she created a sensation and met the queen. She later contracted a deadly disease, possibly smallpox, and died at about age 21, leaving a son.

During the years following Pocahontas's death, tobacco became the Virginia colony's only export to England, bringing prosperity. The crop exhausted the soil in which it grew after two or three years, so the owners of expanding tobacco plantations expanded onto Native lands. This expansion, along with the death of Wahunsonacock in 1618, caused friction to increase between colonists and Native peoples.

At the time of Powhatan's death (and elevation to the chief's role of Opechancanough, who hated the English), the population of the colony was only 350, but by 1622, with tobacco-induced prosperity, it had grown to four times that. The Native peoples exploded in fury, killing 350 colonists and destroying many homes within a few hours. The colonists then responded in kind, swearing to exterminate the Powhatans and nearly succeeding. Natives were eliminated from the lower James and York Rivers; villages were burned and their inhabitants killed during several expeditions over the next three years. Hostilities continued on and off for several years; in 1641, a surprise attack cost the English hundreds of lives in one day. The attack was coordinated by Opechancanough, who was then more than 90 years of age. He was carried about his official business on a litter. The elderly chief was captured and shot, thus ending the Powhatan Confederacy. The English made peace with its constituent tribes one by one on English terms and assigned them to reservations, which were steadily reduced in size during subsequent years as tobacco farms expanded rapidly, catering to the rapid spread of tobacco addiction in Europe.

THE PILGRIMS' LANDFALL IN NEW ENGLAND

Squanto, who met the Pilgrims on a Plymouth Rock beach speaking English, was kidnapped from his native land (the immigrants later called it New England) about 1605 by English merchants. After Captain George Weymouth anchored off the coast of Massachusetts, he and his sailors captured Squanto and four other New England natives and took them back to England as slaves to impress his financial backers (Richard B. Williams, 2002). Squanto was taken to live with Sir Ferdinando Gorges, owner of the Plymouth Company, who quickly realized Squanto's value to his company's exploits in the New World. Gorges taught Squanto to speak English so that his colonists could trade with the Indians. In 1614, Squanto was returned to America to act as a guide and interpreter and to assist in the mapping of the New England coast. He was kidnapped along with twenty-seven other Indians and taken to Malaga, Spain, to be sold as slaves (ibid.). When local priests learned the fate of the Indians, they took them from the slave traders, Christianized them, and eventually sent them back to America in 1618.

Squanto's travels had not ended. He was recognized by one of Gorges's captains, captured a third time, and sent back to England as a slave. Squanto was later sent to New England once again with Thomas Dermer to finish mapping the coast, after which he was promised his freedom. During 1619, Squanto returned to his homeland once again to find that a large proportion of his people had been wiped out by smallpox. A year later, the Pilgrims met him on the beach, speaking English.

The English immigrants needed help. Half of the 102 people who had arrived on the Mayflower six weeks before the onset of winter (with no provisions for food or shelter) died before the immigrants' first growing season began in America. Those who survived did so by plundering the corn stores of Native American villages emptied by the diseases that had arrived before them. Fishermen from Europe, who occasionally made landfall in the area, probably brought pathogens ashore long before the immigrants' arrival. The English trader Thomas Morton wrote that all along the coast Indians had "died in heapes, as they lay in their houses" (Mann, 2002, 42). Most had died of viral hepatitis, according to research by Bruce D. Spiess, director of clinical research at the Medical College of Virginia (Richmond) (ibid., 43). Roughly 90 percent of the Native peoples in the area had died of disease, but William Bradford, who had no understanding of how disease spread among peoples with no immunity, credited "The good hand of God," which had "favored our beginnings by sweeping away great multitudes of the natives ... that he might make room for us" (ibid., 43).

As the Plymouth Colony was established, Squanto became an invaluable interpreter. He promoted peace between Native peoples and the Pilgrims as he taught the settlers the skills required to survive their second winter. Among other things, Squanto showed the immigrants how to plant corn in hillocks using dead herring as fertilizer. Imported seeds of English wheat, barley, and peas did not grow in American soil. Squanto also taught the immigrants how to design traps to catch fish; he acted as a guide and interpreter.

ROGER WILLIAMS'S ERRAND IN THE WILDERNESS

Like many another Puritan, the preacher Roger Williams originally came to America "longing after the natives' soules" (Chupack, 1969, 63). Within a few months of Williams's arrival in Boston during 1631, he was learning the Algonquian language. He would master the dialects of the Showatuck, Nipmuck, Narragansett, and others. Williams's oratorical flourish and compassion won him esteem with congregations at Plymouth and Salem, as well as among native peoples of the area, all of whom sought his "love and counsel" (Ernst, 1932, 179).

Williams's quick mastery of Native languages did not alarm the soul soldiers of Puritania. What landed him in hot ecclesiastical water was what he learned from the Native peoples as he picked up their languages. Asked by William Bradford (governor of the Plymouth Colony) to compose a paper on the compact that established the Puritan colony in America, Williams declared it invalid. How, he asked, could the Puritans claim the land by "right of discovery" when it was already inhabited? Furthermore, Williams argued that the Puritans had no right to deny the Indians their own religions. Soon, the authorities were fretting over how easily Williams won friends not only among colonists, but also among the Native peoples of the area.

Those friendships would be used to advantage a few years later when Williams founded Providence Plantations, later called Rhode Island. Williams became friendly with Massasoit, a sachem among the Wampanoags (also called Pokanokets), a man described by Bradford in 1621 as "lustie ... in his best years, an able body grave of countenance, spare of speech, strong [and] tall" (Covey, 1966, 125). Williams met Massasoit when the latter was about 30 years of age and, in Williams's words, became "great friends" with the sachem (Brockunier, 1940, 47).

Massasoit (ca. 1580–1661) was among the first Native American leaders to greet English settlers in what would become Puritan New England. Like Powhatan, Massasoit (father of Metacom) initially favored friendly relations with the English colonists when he became the Wampanoags' most influential leader in about 1632. The Wampanoags assisted the Puritans during their first hard winters in the new land and took part in the first Thanksgiving. Massasoit allied with the Pilgrims out of practical necessity; many of his people had died in an epidemic shortly before the whites arrived, and he

Roger Williams. (Courtesy of the Library of Congress.)

sought to forge an alliance with them against the more numerous Narragansetts.

Williams also became close to Canonicus (ca. 1560–1647), an elderly leader of
the Narragansetts. With Canonicus and Massasoit, Williams traveled in the forest
for days at a time, learning what he could of their languages, societies, and

Massasoit on his way to meet the Pilgrims, 1621. (Courtesy of the
Library of Congress.)

opinions, absorbing experiences that, along with his knowledge of European ways, would provide the intellectual groundwork for the model common-wealth Williams sought to establish in Providence Plantations. Canonicus re-garded Williams nearly as a son.

At their height, the Narragansetts, with Canonicus as their leader, held sway over the area from Narragansett Bay on the east to the Pawcatuck River on the west. The Narragansetts were rarely warlike, and their large numbers (about 4,000 men of warrior age in the early seventeenth century) usually prevented other native nations from attacking them.

William Wood, writing in *New England's Prospect*, characterized the Narra-gansetts as "the most numerous people in those parts, and the most rich also, and the most industrious, being a storehouse of all kinds . . . of merchandise" (1977, 80–81). The Narragansetts fashioned wampum in bracelets and pendants for many other Indian nations. They also made smoking pipes "much desired by our English tobacconists for their rarity, strength, handsomeness, and coolness" (ibid., 80–81). According to Wood's account, the Narragansetts had never de-sired "to take part in any martial enterprise. But being incapable of a jeer, they rest secure under the conceit of their popularity, and seek rather to grow rich by industry than famous by deeds of chivalry" (ibid., 80–81). In this fashion, the Narragansetts built a confederacy in which they supervised the affairs of Indian peoples throughout most of present-day Rhode Island and eastern Long Island, about 30,000 Native people in the early seventeenth century (Chapin, 1931, 7).

By 1635, Williams was arguing that the church had no right to compel membership, or contributions, by force of law, the central concept of church-state separation. "Natural men," as Williams called the Native peoples, should not, and could not, be forced "to the exercise of those holy Ordinances of Prayers, Oathes, &c." (Giddings, 1957, 21). By January 1635, the Puritans' more ortho-dox magistrates had decided to exile Williams to England, jailed if possible, and shut up. They opposed exiling Williams in the American wilderness, fearing that he would begin his own settlement, from which his "infections" would leak back into Puritania. A summons was issued for Williams's arrest, but he stalled the authorities by contending he was too ill to withstand an ocean voyage.

At the same time, Williams and his associates were rushing ahead with plans for their new colony, from which the worst fears of the orthodox magistrates would be realized. Williams already had arranged with Canonicus for a tract of land large enough to support a colony. Canonicus would not accept money in payment for the land. "It was not price or money that could have purchased Rhode Island," Williams wrote later. "Rhode Island was purchased by love" (Winslow, 1957, 133). Williams was allowed to remain in Salem until the spring of 1636, provided he refrained from preaching.

About January 15, 1636, a Captain Underhill was dispatched from Boston to arrest Williams and place him on board a ship bound for England. Ar-riving at Williams's home, Underhill and his deputies found that Williams had escaped. No one in the neighborhood would admit to having seen him leave.

Aware of his impending arrest, Williams had set out three days earlier during a blinding blizzard, walking south by west to the lodge of Massasoit at Mount Hope. Walking eighty to ninety miles during the worst of a New England winter, Williams suffered immensely and likely would have died without Indian aid. Nearly half a century later, nearing death, Williams wrote: "I bear to this day in my body the effects of that winter's exposure" (Guild, 1886, 20).

Near the end of his trek, Williams lodged with Canonicus and his family. He then scouted the land that had been set aide for the new colony. Williams's trek took place during a smallpox epidemic that was ravaging native populations in the area. The Plymouth Colony's Governor Bradford described its toll:

> For want of bedding and linen and other helps they [Natives] fall into a lamentable condition as they lie on their hard mats, the pox breaking and mattering and running one into another, their skin cleaving by reason thereof to the mats they lie on. When they turn them, a whole side will flay off at once . . . and they will be all of a gore blood, most fearful to behold. (Stannard, 1992, 108)

Week by week, month by month, Williams's family and friends filtered south from Plymouth and Salem. By spring, they were erecting houses, and fields were being turned. The growing group of immigrants also began to create an experimental government very novel by European (or Puritan) standards of the time. For the first time among English-speaking people in America, they were establishing a political order based on liberty of conscience and other natural rights.

Very quickly, Williams's house became a transcultural meeting place. He lodged as many as fifty Indians at a time—travelers, traders, sachems on their way to or from treaty conferences. If a Puritan needed to contact an Indian or vice versa he more than likely did so with Williams's aid. Among Indian nations at odds with each other, Williams became "a quencher of . . . fires" (Ernst, 1932, 252). When citizens of Portsmouth needed an Indian agent, they approached Williams. The Dutch did the same after 1636. The Narragansetts' council sometimes used Williams's house for its meetings.

When word reached Boston that the Pequots were rallying a Native alliance to drive the Massachusetts Bay settlements into the sea, the Massachusetts Council sent urgent pleas to Williams to use his "utmost and speediest Endeavors" to keep the Narragansetts out of it. Within hours after the appeal arrived in the hands of an Indian runner "scarce acquainting my wife," Williams boarded "a poor Canow & . . . cut through a stormie Wind and with great seas, euery [sic] minute in hazard of life to the Sachim's [Canonicus's] howse" (Ernst, 1932, 252). After traveling thirty miles in the storm, Williams arrived at a Narragansett town larger than most of the English settlements of his day, knowing that the success or failure of the Pequot initiative might rest on whether he could dissuade his friends from joining in the uprising.

Canonicus listened to Williams with his son Mixanno at his side. The younger sachem was assuming the duties of leadership piecemeal as his father aged. The three men decided to seal an alliance, and within a few days, officials from Boston were double-timing through the forest to complete the necessary paperwork. Later, Williams also won alliances with the Mohegan and Massachusetts nations, swinging the balance of power against the Pequots and their allies. The Indians welcomed the Puritan deputies with a feast of white chestnuts and cornmeal with blackberries ("hasty pudding," later a New England tradition); Williams translated for both sides, sealing the alliance.

The Puritan deputies were awed at the size of the Narragansett town, as well as the size of the hall in which they negotiated the alliance. The structure, about fifty feet wide, was likened to a statehouse by the men from Boston. Canonicus, so old that he had to lay on his side during the proceedings, surprised the Puritans with his direct questions and shrewd answers. The treaty was finally sealed much to the relief of the Puritans, who thought the Narragansetts capable of fielding 30,000 fighting men. Although they had only a sixth that number, the Narragansetts still were capable of swinging the balance of power for or against the immigrants, who had been in America only sixteen years at the time.

The outcome of the Pequot War during the summer of 1636 radically altered the demographic balance in New England. Before it, the English colonists were a tiny minority. After it, they were unquestionably dominant. The atrocities of the war stunned Williams's conscience. He had been able to prevent a rout of the English, but at a profound moral cost. He could not prevent the war itself or the cruel retribution the Puritans took on the Pequots and their allies. Williams had put himself in the position of aiding those with whom he shared a birthright, although he disagreed with the rationale of their conquest. All during the war, Williams gleaned intelligence from Narragansett runners and traders, who knew far more about Pequot movements than any European. He was doubtless deeply grieved by their deaths.

Williams was revolted by the Puritans' slaughter of the Pequots. The war reached its climax with the burning of a thatch fort in the Pequot village at Mystic, trapping as many as 600 Indian men, women, and children in a raging inferno. The few who managed to crawl out of this roaring furnace jumped back into it when they faced a wall of Puritan swords. Puritan soldiers and their Indian allies waded through pools of Pequot blood, holding their noses against the stench of burning flesh. The wind-driven fire consumed the entire structure in half an hour. A few Pequot bowmen stood their ground amid the flames until their bows singed; they fell backward into the fire, sizzling to death. Bradford recalled:

> Those that escaped the fire were slain with the sword, some hewed to pieces, others run through with their rapiers, so that they were quickly dispatched and very few escaped. It was conceived that they thus destroyed about 400 at this time. It was a fearful sight to see them thus frying in the fire, and the streams of blood quenching the same, and horrible was the stink and scent thereof. (1967, 296)

Having described the massacre, Bradford then indicated how little guilt the Puritans felt about it. "The victory seemed a sweet sacrifice, and they gave the praise thereof to God, who had wrought so wonderfully for them, thus to enclose their enemies in their hands and give them so speedy a victory" (1967, 296). Although a few Puritans remonstrated, many put the war in the category of God's necessary business, along with all sorts of other things, from smallpox epidemics to late frosts and early freezes.

Williams had collected material for an Indian grammar much of his adult life, but the press of events left him little time to write. However, during a solitary sea voyage in 1643 to England, Williams composed his *Key into the Languages of America* (1643), the first Indian grammar in English, as well as a small collection of Williams's observations among Native Americans. In the *Key*, Williams also began to formulate a critique of European religion and politics that would be a subject of intense debate on both sides of the Atlantic for decades to come.

In the *Key*, Williams makes it obvious that "barbarian" had a more positive connotation to him than the same word would carry three centuries later. Like Peter Martyr before him and Benjamin Franklin after him (among many other observers), Williams used the Indian as counterpoint to European conventions in words very similar to those of Montaigne:

> They [Indians] were hospitable to everybody, whomsoever cometh in when they are eating, they offer them to eat of what they have, though but little enough [is] prepared for themselves. If any provision of fish or flesh comes in, they presently give . . . to eat of what they have. . . . It is a strange truth that a man can generally find more free entertainment and refreshing amongst these Barbarians than amongst the thousands that call themselves Christians. (Rider, 1904, 22)

Some of Williams's American lessons were offered in verse:

> I've known them to leave their house and mat
> To lodge a friend or stranger
> When Jews and Christians oft have sent
>   Jesus Christ to the Manger
> Oft have I heard these Indians say
>   These English will deliver us
> Of all that's ours, our lands and lives
>   In the end, they'll bereave us
>   —Rider, 1904, 44

Williams disputed notions that Europeans were intellectually superior to Native Americans:

> For the temper of the braine [sic] in quick apprehensions and accurate judgements . . . the most high and sovereign God and Creator hath not made them

inferior to Europeans...Nature knows no difference between Europeans and Americans in blood, birth, bodies, &c. God having of one blood made all mankind, Acts 17....The same Sun shines on a Wilderness that doth on a garden. (Rider, 1904, 49, 53, 78)

Williams also wrote: "Boast not, proud English, of thy birth and blood; Thy brother Indian is by birth as good" (Brockunier, 1940, 141).

By implication, the Puritans had no right to take land and resources from Native Americans by "divine right." Williams's statement was the first expression in English, on American soil, of a belief that would power the American Revolution a century and a half later: "All men are created equal, and endowed by their Creator with certain inalienable rights."

In some ways, Williams found what Europeans called "Christian values" better embodied in Native American societies: "There are no beggars amongst them, nor fatherless children unprovided for" (Rider, 1904, 29). The *Key* not only was a grammar but also was a lesson in humility directed at the most pompous and ethnocentric of the English:

> When Indians heare the horrid filths,
> Of Irish, English men
> The horrid Oaths and Murthurs late
> Thus say these Indians then:
> We weare no Cloathes, have many Gods,
> And yet our sinnes are lesse:
> You are Barbarians, Pagans wild,
> Your land's the wildernesse.
> —Rider, 1904, 9

The *Key* became a standard text for English-speaking people wishing to learn the languages of New England's Native peoples. The small book was printed in England and widely distributed there, but not in Boston. Despite diplomatic aid that might have saved the Massachusetts Bay Colony, Williams still was regarded as a dangerous radical by orthodox Puritans. Addressing Christian hypocrisy, using his image of the Indian as counterpoint, Williams minced no words:

> How often have I heard both the English and the Dutch[,] not only the civil, but the most debauched and profane say: "These Heathen Doggs [sic], better kill a thousand of them than we Christians should be endangered or troubled with them; they have spilt our Christian blood, the best way to make riddance of them is to cut them all off and make way for Christians." (Ernst, 1932, 251)

To Williams, the Natives of America were just as godly, even if not as Christian, as Europeans:

He that questions whether God made the World, the Indians will teach him. I must acknowledge I have received in my converse with them many confirmations of these two great points, Heb. II.6, viz: 1. That God is[.] 2. That hee [sic] is a rewarder of all that diligently seek him. (Roger Williams, 1936, 123)

Roger Williams called Indian governmental organizations "monarchies" (as did many Europeans in the earliest colonial days), then contradicted himself by catching the scent of popular opinion in them. In his *Key*, Williams described the workings of Native American polities in ways similar to the structure he was erecting in the new colony: "The sachims . . . will not conclude of ought that concerns all, either Lawes, or Subsidies, or warres, unto which people are averse, or by gentle perswasion cannot be brought" (1963, 1:224).

When some Puritans asked whether a society based on individual choice instead of coerced consent would degenerate into anarchy, Williams found the Indians' example instructive:

Although they have not so much to restraine them (both in respect of knowledge of God and lawes of Men) as the English have, yet a man shall never heare of such crimes amongst them [as] robberies, murthurs, adultries &c., as among the English. (Roger Williams, 1963, 1:225)

Among the colonists of Providence Plantations, as among the Indians he knew, Williams envisioned a society where "all men may walk as their consciences perswade them" (Kennedy, 1950, 42–44). Williams's ideal society also shared with the Indian societies he knew a relatively egalitarian distribution of property, with political rights based on natural law: "All civil liberty is founded in the consent of the People; . . . Natural and civil Right and Privilege due . . . as a Man, a Subject, a Citizen" (Ernst, 1932, 276–277).

Establishing such a utopian society was easier said than done. As Williams watched, some of the early settlers of Providence Plantations established land companies similar to those in other colonies as they tried to hoard land that could be sold at a higher price to future arrivals. The same land earlier had been set aside for newcomers to prevent growth of a landless underclass in the colony. In 1654, in a letter to the town of Providence, Williams showed how isolated he sometimes felt in his quest for a new way of life: "I have been charged with folly for that freedom and liberty that I always have stood for—I say, liberty and equality in both land and government" (Miller, 1953, 221–222).

Williams argued vehemently against assertions that only Christians possessed soul and conscience. If all peoples were religiously equal, Crusades made no sense; this Williams took to be God's word, and like many preachers, he often spoke for himself by invoking deity. To Williams, religion seemed to mean less a professed doctrine than possession of an innate sense of justice and morality, and he saw that capacity in all people, Christian and not. From observing the Indians, he learned that such morality was endowed in human-kind naturally, not by membership in a church or adherence to a doctrine: "It is granted, that nature's light discovers a God, some sins a judgement, as we see in the Indians" (Roger Williams, 1963, 4:441). In his extensive travels with the Narragansetts, Williams sensed "the conscience of good and evil that every savage Indian in the world hath" (ibid., 4:443).

Williams's efforts helped to maintain a shaky peace along the frontiers of New England for nearly two generations after the Pequot War. In 1645, Williams's efforts barely averted another Native uprising against encroaching European American settlements. By the 1660s, however, the aging Williams was watching his lifelong pursuit of peace unravel yet again. This time, he felt more impotent than before: His English ancestry drove him to protect English interests, as wave after wave of colonists provided Native peoples with powerful grievances by usurping their land without permission or compensation. In this matter, Williams had never changed his mind: Neither the Puritans nor any other Europeans had any right, divine or otherwise, to take Indian land. The final years of Williams's life were profoundly painful for a sensitive man who prized peace and harmony above all.

Entering his sixties, Williams's body grew old quickly. In 1663, he complained often of "old pains, lameness, so th't sometimes I have not been able to rise, nor goe, or stand" (Winslow, 1957, 267). Williams found himself using his pastoral staff as more than a ministerial ornament. Massasoit also was aging and becoming disillusioned with the colonists as increasing numbers of European immigrants drove his people from their lands.

On Massasoit's death in 1661, Alexander, one of Massasoit's sons, briefly served as grand sachem of the Wampanoags until his own death. Visiting Boston during 1662, Alexander fell gravely ill and died as Wampanoag warriors rushed him into the wilderness. When Alexander died, the warriors beached their canoes, buried his body in a knoll, and returned home with rumors that he had been a victim of the English. Alexander's death stirred memories of Mixanno, also Massasoit's son, who had been assassinated in 1643. His murder never had been avenged as rumors circulated that the English had plotted the murder and that they were harboring the assailant.

In this context, Metacom, whom the English called King Philip, became grand sachem after Alexander. About 25 years old in 1662, Metacom distrusted nearly all European Americans, with Williams one of the few exceptions. Metacom also was known as a man who did not forgive insults easily. It was once said that he chased a white man named John Gibbs from Mount Hope to Nantucket Island after Gibbs insulted his father. Throughout his childhood, Metacom had watched his people dwindle before the English advance. By 1671, about 40,000 people of European descent lived in New England. The Native population, double that of the Europeans before the Pequot war, was now about 20,000. European farms and pastures were crawling toward Mount Hope, driving away game and creating friction over land that the Indians had used without question for so many generations they had lost count of them. By 1675, the Wampanoags held only a small strip of land at Mount Hope, and settlers wanted it.

Metacom became more embittered by the day. He could see his nation being destroyed before his eyes. English cattle trampled Indian cornfields as encroaching farms forced game animals further into the wilderness. Metacom was summoned to Plymouth to answer questions, and other people in his nation were interrogated by Puritan officials. Traders fleeced Indians, exchanging furs for liquor. The devastation of alcohol and disease and the loss of land destroyed families and tradition. These were Metacom's thoughts as he prepared to go to war against the English.

As rumors of war reached Williams, he again tried to keep the Narragansetts out of it. This time, he failed. Nananawtunu, son of Mixanno, told his close friend Williams that although he opposed going to war, his people could not be restrained. They had decided the time had come to die fighting rather than to expire slowly as a people. Williams's letters of this time were pervaded with sadness as he watched the two groups he knew so well slide toward war.

Shortly after hostilities began in June 1675, Williams met with Metacom, riding with the sachem and his family in a canoe not far from Providence. Williams warned Metacom that he was leading his people to extermination. Williams compared the Wampanoags to a canoe on a stormy sea of English fury. "He answered me in a consenting, considering kind of way," Williams wrote, saying "My canoe is already overturned" (Giddings, 1957, 33).

When Indians painted for war appeared on the heights above Providence, Williams picked up his staff, climbed the bluffs, and told the war parties that if they attacked the town, England would send thousands of armed men to crush them. "Well," one of the sachems leading the attack told Williams, "Let them come. We are ready for them, but as for you, brother Williams, you are a good man. You have been kind to us for many years. Not a hair on your head shall be touched" (Straus, 1894, 220–224).

Williams was not injured, but his house was torched as he met with the Indians on the bluffs above Providence on March 29, 1676. Williams watched flames spread throughout the town. "This house of mine now burning before mine eyes hath lodged kindly some thousands of you these ten years," Williams told the attacking Indians (Swan, 1969, 14). If the colony was to survive, Williams, for the first time in his life, had to become a military commander. With a grave heart, Williams sent his neighbors out to do battle with the sons and daughters of native people who had sheltered him during his winter trek from Massachusetts forty years earlier. As Williams and others watched from inside a hastily erected fort, nearly all of Providence burned. Fields were laid waste and cattle slaughtered or driven into the woods.

Colonists, seething with anger, caught an Indian, and Williams was put in the agonizing position of ordering him killed rather than watching him tortured. The war was irrefutably brutal on both sides as the English fought

PHILLIP alias METACOMET of Pokanoket.

Metacom. (Courtesy of Smithsonian National Anthropological Archives.)

The Landing of Roger Williams

RHODE ISLAND.

The landing of Roger Williams, greeted by Indians, 1636. (Courtesy of the Library of Congress.)

with their backs literally to the sea for a year and a half before going on the offensive. At Northfield, Indians hung two Englishmen on chains, placing hooks under their jaws. At Springfield, colonists arrested an Indian woman, then offered her body to dogs, which tore her to pieces.

By August 1676, the war ended as the Mohawks and Mohegans opted out of their alliance with the Wampanoags, leaving after the English had exterminated the Narragansetts. Nearly all of Metacom's warriors, their families, and friends had been killed or driven into hiding. Metacom himself fled toward Mount Hope, then hid in a swamp. When English soldiers found him, they dragged Metacom out of the mire, then had him drawn and quartered. His head was sent to Plymouth on a giblet, where it was displayed much as criminals' severed heads were shown off on the railings of London Bridge. Metacom's hands were sent to Boston, where a local showman charged admission for a glimpse of one of them. The remainder of Metacom's body was hung from four separate trees.

In terms of deaths in proportion to total population, King Philip's War was among the deadliest in American history. About 1,000 colonists died in the war; many more died of starvation and war-related diseases. Every Native nation bordering the Puritan settlements was reduced to ruin—those whose members, in happier days, had offered the earliest colonists their first Thanksgiving dinner. Many of the survivors were sold into slavery in the West Indies, by

CAPTURE OF THE INDIAN FORTRESS.

Capture of an Indian fortress during King Philip's War, 1675. (Courtesy of the Library of Congress.)

which the colonists served two purposes: removing them from the area and raising money to help pay their enormous war debts. Metacom's son was auctioned off with about 500 other slaves following a brief, but intense, biblical debate over whether a son should be forced to atone for the sins of his father.

Williams died March 15, 1683, in Providence, with the pain of the world bowing his creaking shoulders, likely realizing just how out of step he was with the temper of his time. He was a peacemaker in time of war; a tolerant man in a world full of ideologues; a democrat in a time of ecclesiastical and secular sovereigns; a dissenter wherever self-interest masqueraded as divinity. Williams had planted seeds in American soil that would not fully flower for more than another century. He would have relished the company of Thomas Jefferson, for example, at a time when his ideas were the common currency of political revolution.

HARDER TIMES FOR NATIVE PEOPLES IN THE NORTHEAST

Harder times were to come for the Native peoples of New England. By 1703, Massachusetts was paying £12 sterling for an Indian scalp, an amount worth about $500 today. In 1722, the bounty rose to £100, about $4,000 today, adjusted for inflation. Although the folklore price of Manhattan Island was $24 worth of beads and trinkets, the actual price was 60 Dutch gulden, worth about $10,000 to $15,000 today. The Native peoples of Manhattan probably thought they were accepting a gift to share the land, not selling it, because they did not buy and sell real estate as Europeans did.

The human price of ceding the land was much higher for some Native people in the region. In 1643, the Dutch governor of Manhattan (who was drunk at the time) ordered the massacre of several Wappingers who had fled to the Dutch settlements for protection from the Mohawks. The Dutch lulled the Wappingers with kind treatment for a few days, then slaughtered eighty men, women, and children in their beds. Their heads were severed and taken to Fort Amsterdam on Manhattan Island, where a Dutch dowager stirred considerable attention by playing kickball with them in the street. A Hackensack Indian was tortured in front of a crowd, stripped of his skin piece by piece, then forced to eat it. The Native man tried to sing his death song as he was castrated and dragged through the streets, his raw flesh peeled from head to knees. Still alive, he was trussed to a millstone and beaten to death by Dutch soldiers. The Dutch governor, no bleeding heart, laughed heartily at the scene.

In 1752, General Jeffrey Amherst, commander-in-chief for North America, was reported to have advocated the use of smallpox as a military tactic against the Ottawas, Ojibways, and other Native peoples in the Great Lakes area. "You will be well advised," Amherst told his subordinates, "to infect the Indians with sheets upon which small pox patients have been lying or by any other means which may serve to exterminate this accursed race" (Johansen and Grinde, 1997, 10). Amherst also recommended hunting Indians with trained dogs. An oral history account of the Ottawas, related by Andrew J. Blackbird (1897), nineteenth century Ottawa historian, indicated that smallpox came to them in a box from a white man. They opened the box to find another, smaller one. Inside the second box was a third, even smaller. Inside the last box, the Ottawas found moldy particles, the smallpox "patients."

THE PIVOTAL ROLE OF THE IROQUOIS CONFEDERACY

The Iroquois Confederacy was well known to the British and French colonists of North America because of its pivotal position in diplomacy between the colonists, as well as among other native confederacies. Called the Iroquois by the French and the Five (later Six) Nations by the English, the Haudenosaunee (meaning People of the Longhouse) controlled the only relatively level land passage between the English colonies on the seaboard and the French settlements in the St. Lawrence Valley. The five original nations (Mohawk, Oneida, Onondaga, Cayuga, and Seneca) were joined by the Tuscaroras about 1700 C.E.

Each Iroquois nation has its own council, which sends delegates to a central council, much as each state in the United States has its own legislature, as well as senators and representatives who travel to the central seat of government in Washington, D.C. When representatives of the Iroquois nations meet in Onondaga, they form two groups: the Elder Brothers (Mohawks and Senecas) and the Younger Brothers (Cayugas and Oneidas). The Onondagas are the firekeepers. (In the U.S. Congress, this position is held by the Speaker of the House.) At Onondaga, the site of the struggle with Tadadaho, the Iroquois built a perpetual council fire, The Fire That Never Dies.

The Iroquois Confederacy was founded by the Huron prophet Deganawidah, who is called the Peacemaker in oral discourse among many traditional Haudenosaunee. Deganawidah enlisted the aid of a speaker, Aionwantha (also called Hiawatha) to spread his vision of a united Haundenosaunee Confederacy. Deganawidah needed a spokesman in the oral culture of the Iroquois because he stuttered so badly he could hardly speak, an impediment that Iroquois oral history attributes to a double row of teeth. The confederacy was founded before first European contact in the area, about 1100 C.E. Deganawidah sought to replace blood feuds that had devastated the Iroquois with peaceful modes of decision making. The result was the Great Law of Peace (sometimes called the Great Binding Law).

Peace among the formerly antagonistic nations was procured and maintained through the Haudenosaunee's Great Law of Peace (*Kaianerekowa*), which was passed from generation to generation using wampum, a form of written communication that outlined a complex system of checks and balances between nations and genders.

According to Iroquois oral history, the visionary Hiawatha tried to call councils to eliminate the blood feud, but was thwarted by the evil and twisted wizard Tadadaho, an Onondaga who used magic and spies to rule by fear and intimidation. Failing to defeat the wizard, Hiawatha traveled to Mohawk, Oneida, and Cayuga villages with his message of peace and brotherhood. Everywhere he went, his message was accepted with the proviso that he persuade the formidable Tadadaho and the Onondagas to embrace the covenant of peace.

Just as Hiawatha was despairing, the prophet Deganawidah entered his life. Together, the two men developed a powerful message of peace. Deganawidah's vision gave Hiawatha's oratory substance. Through Deganawidah's vision, the constitution of the Iroquois was formulated. In his vision, Deganawidah saw a giant white pine reaching to the sky and gaining strength from three counter-balancing principles of life. The first axiom was that a stable mind and healthy body should be in balance so that peace between individuals and groups could occur. Second, Deganawidah stated that humane conduct, thought, and speech were a requirement for equity and justice among peoples. He foresaw a society in which physical strength and civil authority would reinforce the power of the clan system.

With such a powerful vision, Deganawidah and Hiawatha were able to subdue the evil Tadadaho and transform his mind. Deganawidah removed evil feelings and thoughts from the head of Tadadaho as he pledged to make reason and the wisdom of peaceful minds prevail. The evil wizard became reborn into a humane person charged with implementing the message of Deganawidah. After Tadadaho had submitted to the redemption, Onondaga became the central fire of the Haudenosaunee, and the Onondagas became the firekeepers of the new confederacy. To this day, the Great Council Fire of the confederacy is maintained in the land of the Onondagas, south of Syracuse, New York.

Each of the five Iroquois nations in Deganawidah's confederacy maintains its own council, whose sachems are nominated by the clan mothers of families holding hereditary rights to office titles. The Grand Council at Onondaga was drawn from the individual national councils.

For each of the Iroquois nations' own councils, sachems are nominated by the clan mothers of families holding hereditary rights to office titles. The Grand Council at Onondaga is drawn from the individual national councils. The Grand Council also may nominate sachems outside the hereditary structure based on merit alone. These sachems, called *pine tree chiefs*, are said to spring from the body of the people as the symbolic Great White Pine springs from the earth.

Rights, duties, and qualifications of sachems are explicitly outlined. Clan mothers may remove (impeach) a sachem found guilty of any of a number of abuses of office, from missing meetings to murder. An erring chief is summoned to face charges by the war chiefs, who act in peacetime as the peoples' eyes and ears in the council, somewhat as the role of the press was envisaged by Jefferson and other founders of the United States. A sachem is given three warnings, then removed from the council if he does not mend his ways. A sachem found guilty of murder not only loses his title, but also deprives his entire family of its right to representation. The women relatives holding the rights to the office are "buried," and the title is transferred to a sister family.

For details on the Iroquois Confederacy's role in the founding of U.S. political institutions, see chapter 4.

GEORGE COPWAY: LONGFELLOW'S HIAWATHA

The name Hiawatha is best known in American popular history through the poetry of Henry Wadsworth Longfellow, who seems to have known little or nothing about the life of the Iroquois cultural hero of the same name. Instead, George Copway (Kahgegwagebow, Stands Fast Chippewa/Ojibway; 1818 to ca. 1863) may have been the model for Longfellow's Hiawatha. Copway was a close friend of Longfellow and was noted among the Ojibways for his physical strength and skill at hunting. Copway also was one of the first Native Americans to write books that were widely read by non-Indians.

Copway was born near the mouth of the Trent River, Ontario, Canada, in 1818. He was raised as a traditional Ojibway; his father was a noted leader and medicine man, but the family often went hungry during Copway's youth. His traditional training included stress on physical strength; Copway once carried 200 pounds of flour and other supplies on his back for a quarter mile without rest. In the spring of 1841, he is said to have run across much of Wisconsin to warn the Ojibways of a Sioux raiding party, traveling 240 miles in four days.

Copway was converted to Methodism in 1830 and attended Ebenezer Academy (Jacksonville, IL) for two years. Copway became a Methodist minister in 1834, after which he translated several religious texts from English into Algonquian and worked with several religious publishers. During 1851, in New York City, Copway started a newspaper about American Indian affairs, *Copway's American Indian*. Only one issue is known to have been published, on July 10, 1851.

Copway wrote *The Life, History and Travels of Kah-Ge-Ga-Gah-Bowh* (1847), which was revised in 1850 as *The Traditional History and Traditional Sketches of the Ojibway Nation*. The same book was reissued again in 1858 as *Indian Life and Indian History*. He also wrote *The Ojibway Conquest* (1850); *The Organization of a New Indian Territory East of the Missouri River* (1850); and *Running Sketches of Men and Places in England, Germany, Belgium, and Scotland* (1851). Copway also toured Europe; in England, he denounced European and American deals for Ojibway ancestral lands as frauds and robberies. Copway died near Pontiac, Michigan, at 45 years of age.

RETHINKING THE IROQUOIS CONFEDERACY'S FOUNDING DATE

The Haudenosaunee (Iroquois) Confederacy is one of the oldest continually operating consensual governments in the world, one that is at least three centuries older than most previous estimates according to research completed during the middle 1990s by Barbara Alice Mann and Jerry Fields of the

University of Toledo, Ohio. Using a combination of documentary sources, solar eclipse data, and Iroquois oral history, Mann and Fields make a case that the Iroquois Confederacy's body of fundamental law was adopted by the Senecas (the last of the five nations to ratify it) August 31, 1142. The ratification council convened at a site that is now a football field in Victor, New York. The site is called Gonandaga by the Seneca.

Mann and Fields concluded that the only eclipse that meets all requisite conditions—an afternoon occurrence over Gonandaga that darkened the sky—is the eclipse of 1142. The duration of darkness would have been a dramatic interval of three-and-a-half minutes, long enough to wait for the sun and long enough to impress everyone with Deganawidah's power to call forth a sign in the sky (B. A. Mann and Fields, 1997, 105). Heretofore, many experts have dated the formation of the confederacy to the year 1451, at the time of another solar eclipse. Mann and Fields contend that the 1451 eclipse was total, but that its shadow fell over Pennsylvania, well to the southwest of the ratifying council's location.

Mann was a doctoral student in English at Ohio's University of Toledo at the time (by 2003, she was a faculty member there); Fields was an astronomer and an expert in the history of solar eclipses. The Senecas' oral history mentions that the Senecas adopted the Iroquois Great Law of Peace shortly after a total eclipse of the sun. Mann and Fields are the first scholars to combine documentary history with oral accounts and precise solar data in an attempt to date the origin of the Iroquois League. Depending on how democracy is defined, their date of 1142 C.E. would rank the Iroquois Confederacy with the government of Iceland and the Swiss cantons as the oldest continuously functioning democracy on earth. All three precedents have been cited as forerunners of the U.S. system of representative democracy.

According to Mann, the Seneca nation was the last of the five Iroquois nations to accept the Great Law of Peace. In an article "A Sign in the Sky: Dating the League of the Haudenosaunee," Mann estimated that the journey of Deganawidah (the Peacemaker) and Hiawatha in support of the Great Law had begun with the Mohawks, at the "eastern door" of the confederacy, about 25 years earlier (B. A. Mann and Fields, 1997).

The argument that the Iroquois League was established substantially before contact with Europeans is supported by oral history accounts. Another traditional method to estimate the founding date is to count the number of people who have held the office of Tadadaho (speaker) of the confederacy. A graphic record is available in the form of a cane that the eighteenth century French observer Lafitau called the Stick of Enlistment and modern-day anthropologist William N. Fenton calls the Condolence Cane.

Mann and Fields used a figure of 145 Tadadahos (from Mohawk oral historian Jake Swamp) and then averaged the tenure of other lifetime appointments, such as popes, European kings and queens, and U.S. Supreme Court justices. Cautioning that different socio-historical institutions are being compared, they figure into their sample 333 monarchs from eight European countries, 95 Supreme Court justices, and 129 popes. Averaging the tenures of all three groups, Mann and Fields found an estimated date that compares roughly to the 1142 date indicated by the eclipse record and the 1090 date calculated from family lineages by Underwood.

Mann and Fields also make their case with archeological evidence. The rise in interpersonal violence that pre-dated the Iroquois League can be tied to a cannibal cult and the existence of villages with palisades, both of which can be dated to the middle of the twelfth century. The spread of the league can be linked to the adoption of corn as a dietary staple among the Haudenosaunee, which also dates between 900 and 1100 C.E., Mann and Fields contend.

Mann and Fields's case has been questioned by David Henige, who also ridiculed Henry Dobyns's population numbers (see chapter 1). In *Numbers from Nowhere* (1998) Henige accuses Dobyns of overemphasizing disease as a cause of death. His critique of Mann and Fields's work (Henige, 1999) contends that they overemphasize a solar eclipse as a method of dating the origin of the confederacy.

As with his critique of Dobyns, Henige develops no extant case of his own. He advances no alternative founding date for the confederacy and no explanation of what the Haudenosaunee account calls a "sign in the sky." Henige does not regard his lack of a case as a shortcoming, however. Henige justifies his vagueness with a quotation from William N. Fenton: "All of these dates I regard as spurious. The whole search for an exact date of the formation of the Iroquois seems to be nonsense" (Henige, 2004, 127). Henige thus is satisfied to perform an intellectual hit-and-run, sowing doubt about new work without advancing the state of knowledge. Henige seems to fall back on an amorphous belief that the Haudenosaunee origin story is a "myth" that cannot be dated. Thus, he renders the entire debate largely a figment of imagination as he reduces the most important events in Haudenosaunee political history to a sort of shimmering make-believe. Having criticized Mann and Fields for falling short of standard cannons for historical evidence, his own case dissolves into pure, unverified speculation.

So, when did the Haudenosaunee "invent" their myth? Henige gives no credit to oral history: "The Iroquois League was not founded on this day [August 31, 1142], or any other day before its first mention in contemporaneous sources" (Henige, 2004, 127). For history to matter, to Henige it must be written, usually by Europeans. Believing this, he can, for example, reduce Hiawatha to an imaginary figure who appears in the record about 1800 or afterward. He does so with an air of scholarly certainty.

Mann also offers another example of what she believes to be the European- and male-centered nature of existing history. Most accounts of the Iroquois League's origins stress the roles played by the Peacemaker Deganawidah and Aionwantha (or Hiawatha), who joined him in a quest to quell the blood feud and establish peace. Mann asserts that most histories largely ignore the role of a third person, a woman, Jingosaseh, who insisted on gender balance in the Iroquois constitution.

Under Haudenosaunee law, clan mothers choose candidates (who are male) as chiefs. The women also maintain ownership of the land and homes and exercise a veto power over any council action that may result in war.

Although a high degree of gender equity existed in Iroquois law, gender roles often were (and remain) very carefully defined, down to the version of history passed down by people of either gender. Men, the vast majority of anthropological informants, tended to play up the role of Deganawidah and Aionwantha, which was written into history. Women, who would have described the role of Jingosaseh, were usually not consulted. Mann points out that Jingosaseh, originally the name of an historical individual, subsequently a title, was a leader of clan mothers. The historic figure Tadadaho, originally Deganawidah's and Aionwantha's main antagonist, became the title of the league's speaker. Occasionally in Iroquois history, a title also may become a personal name; Handsome Lake (a reference to Lake Ontario) was the title to one of the fifty seats on the Iroquois Grand Council before it was the name of the nineteenth century Iroquois prophet. According to Mann, "It is only after the Peacemaker agrees to her terms that she throws her considerable political weight behind him. . . . She was, in short, invaluable as an ally, invincible as a foe. To succeed, the Peacemaker needed her" (Johansen, 1995, 63).

"Jingosaseh is recalled by the Keepers as a co-founder of the League, alongside of Deganawidah and Hiawatha," said Mann. "Her name has been obliterated from the white record because her story was a woman's story and nineteenth-century male ethnographers simply failed to ask women, whose story hers was, about the history of the League" (Johansen, 1995, 63).

The story of how Jingosaseh joined with Deganawidah and Hiawatha is one part of an indigenous American epic that has been compared to the Greeks' Homer, the Mayan *Popul Vu*, and the Tibetan *Book of the Dead*. Although encapsulated versions of the Great Law have been translated into English for more than 100 years, the Great Law of Peace is still being discovered by scholars. As recently as 1992, Syracuse University Press published the most complete available translation of the Iroquois Great Law (Woodbury, Henry, and Webster, 1992). Once every five years, until his death in 1998, the Cayuga Jake Thomas recited the entire epic at the confederacy's central council fire in Onondaga, New York. The recitation usually took him three or four 8-hour days, during which he spoke until his voice cracked. Although numerous other Native confederacies existed along the borders of the British colonies, many of the specific provisions of their governments have been lost.

THE IROQUOIS INFLUENCE ON TREATY DIPLOMACY

Between the mid-seventeenth century and the end of the nineteenth century, the Haudenosaunee negotiated more than a hundred treaties with English (and later United States) representatives. Until about 1800 C.E., most of these treaties were negotiated according to Haudenosaunee protocol. By the mid-eighteenth century, this protocol was well established as the "lingua franca" of diplomacy in eastern North America. According to this protocol, an alliance was adopted and maintained using certain rituals.

Initial contacts between negotiating parties usually were made "at the edge of the forest," on neutral ground, where an agenda and a meeting place and time could be agreed on. Following the "approach to the council fire," the place of negotiation, a Condolence Ceremony was recited to remember those who had died on both sides since the last meeting. A designated party kindled the council fire at the beginning of negotiations and covered it at the end. A council was called for a specific purpose (such as making of peace) and could not be changed once convened. Representatives from both sides spoke in a specified order. No important actions were taken until at least one night had elapsed since the matter's introduction before the council. The passage of time was said to allow the various members of the council to attain unanimity—"one mind"—necessary for consensual solution of a problem.

Wampum belts or strings were exchanged when an important point was made or an agreement reached. Acceptance of a belt was taken to mean agreement on an issue. A belt also might be refused, or thrown aside, to indicate rejection of a proposal. Another metaphor that was used throughout many of the councils was that of the Covenant Chain, a symbol of alliance. If proceedings were going well and consensus was being reached on major issues, the chain (which was often characterized as made of silver) was being "polished" or "shined." If agreement was not being reached, the chain was said to be "rusting."

During treaty negotiations, a speaker was generally allowed to complete a statement without interruption, according to Haudenosaunee protocol, which differs markedly with the cacophony of debate in European forums such as the British House of Commons. Often, European representatives expressed consternation when carefully planned schedules were cast aside so that everyone (warriors as well as their leaders) could express an opinion on an important issue. Many treaties were attended by large parties of Iroquois, each of whom could in theory claim a right to speak.

The host of a treaty council was expected to supply tobacco for the common pipe as well as refreshments (usually alcoholic in nature) to extinguish the sour taste of tobacco smoking. Gifts often were exchanged and great feasts held during the proceedings, which sometimes were attended by entire Haudenosaunee families. A treaty council could last several days even under the most agreeable circumstances. If major obstacles were encountered in negotiations, a council could extend two weeks or longer, sometimes as long as a month.

A main treaty council often was accompanied by several smaller ones during which delegates with common interests met to discuss problems that concerned them. Usually, historical accounts record only the proceedings of the main body, leaving out the many important side conferences, which, in the diplomatic language of the time, were often said to have been held "in the bushes."

Treaty councils were conducted in a ritualistic manner to provide common points of understanding between representatives who otherwise were separated by barriers of language and cultural interpretation. The abilities of a good interpreter who was trusted by both sides (an example was Conrad Weiser in the mid-eighteenth century) could greatly influence the course of negotiations. Whether they knew the Iroquois and Algonquian languages or not, Anglo-American negotiators had to be on speaking terms with the metaphors of Iroquois protocol, such as the council fire, condolence, the tree of peace, and many others.

Haudenosaunee treaty relations, including trading relationships, were characterized in terms of kinship, hospitality, and reciprocity over and above commercial or diplomatic interests. The Dutch in particular seemed to be easily annoyed when they were forced to deal with trade relationships based on anything other than commerce. They, among other Europeans, seemed not to understand that, to the Iroquois, trade was conceived as part of a broader social relationship. The Mohawks seemed to resent the attitude of the Dutch negotiators, who saw negotiations as a commercial transaction. During September 1659, a party of Mohawks complained as follows:

> The Dutch, indeed, say we are brothers and are joined together with chains, but that lasts only as long as we have beavers. After that, we are no longer thought of, but much will depend on it [alliance] when we shall need each other. (Dennis, 1993, 171)

From the first sustained contact with Europeans, shortly after 1600, until the end of the French and Indian War (1763), the Haudenosaunee Confederacy utilized diplomacy to maintain a balance of power in northeastern North America between the colonizing British and French. This use of diplomacy and alliances to play one side against the other reached its height shortly after 1700, during the period that Richard Aquila called the Iroquois Restoration (Aquila, 1983, 16–17).

This period was followed by alliance of most Haudenosaunee with the British and the eventual defeat of the French. By the 1740s, England's developing industrial base had become much better at supplying trade goods to the Haudenosaunee and other Native American peoples; the balance of alliance was shifting. According to Aquila, the Iroquois' power had declined dangerously by about 1700, requiring a concerted effort on the part of the Grand Council to minimize warfare and build peaceful relations with the Haudenosaunee's neighbors. By 1712, the Haudenosaunee's military resources amounted to about 1,800 men. Disease as well as incessant warfare also caused declines in Haudenosaunee populations at about this time; major outbreaks of smallpox swept through Iroquoia in 1696 and 1717. At the same time, sizable numbers of dissenting Haudenosaunee, especially Mohawks, moved to Canada and cast their lots with the French.

Alcohol also was devastating the Iroquois at this time, a fact emphasized by the many requests for restrictions on the liquor trade by Haudenosaunee leaders at treaty councils and other meetings. Aquila wrote as follows:

> Sachems complained that alcohol deprived the Iroquois people of their senses, was ruining their lives . . . and was used by traders to cheat them out of their furs and lands. The Iroquois were not exaggerating. The French priest Lafitau reported in 1718 that when the Iroquois and other Indians became intoxicated they went completely berserk, screaming like madmen and smashing everything in their homes. (1983, 115)

After 1763, the Haudenosaunee were no longer able to play the French and the English against each other. Instead, the Iroquois faced pressure to ally with native peoples to their west against the English. Many Senecas sided with Pontiac against the English in 1763 and 1764.

Today, some members of the Iroquois Grand Council travel the world on their own national passports. The passport states that it has been issued by the Grand Council of the League of the Haudenosaunee, and that "The Haudenosaunee continues as a sovereign people on the soil it has occupied on Turtle Island since time immemorial, and we extend friendship to all who recognize our constitutional government and who desire peaceful relations" (Hill, 1987, 12). The passports were first issued in 1977 to Haudenosaunee delegates who attended a meeting of the United Nations in Switzerland. Since then, the United States, Holland, Canada, Switzerland, France, Belgium, Germany, Denmark, Italy, Libya, Turkey, Australia, Great Britain, New Zealand, Iran, and Colombia have been among the nations that have recognized the Haudenosaunee documents. Even so, it takes a talented travel agent to get a visa on an Iroquois passport because formal diplomatic relations often do not exist between the country recognizing the document and the Haudenosaunee Grand Council.

THE FUR TRADE

Trade and diplomacy were linked as functions of friendly international relations. Many of the rituals were similar. Native American economic relationships often were carried on according to principles of reciprocity involving mutual gift giving. Trade among Native peoples often was conducted as an exchange of gifts. European traders later adopted some of the Native peoples gift-giving practices when they traded in North America.

Notions of reciprocity permeated the daily lives of many Native American peoples. Among the Tlinget, for example, the two major clans (Wolf and Raven) built houses for each other, a process accompanied by feasting and gift giving. Among the Wyandots (Hurons), relations of friendship and material reciprocity were extended beyond the Wyandot Confederacy in the form of trading arrangements. Foreign trade was not merely an economic activity. It was embedded in a network of social relations that were fundamental extensions of the kin relationships within the Huron Confederacy. Like the Iroquois, the Wyandots sometimes formally adopted traders with whom they had frequent and mutually beneficial relations. Traders so adopted often lodged with their friends while visiting; sometimes traders, who were male, took Native American wives.

Across much of North America, Native Americans initially became part of the European cash economy through the fur trade. The type of animal harvested varied (from beaver in the Northeast to deer in the Southeast, bear in the Rocky Mountains, and sea otters along the Alaskan coast, for example), but the economic system was largely the same. The fur trade flourished in most areas until the early to mid-nineteenth century, after which it was curtailed by near extinction of some species as well as changes in European fashions, especially in coats and headgear.

Historian John Fahey described ways in which the fur trade changed Native American societies:

> In little more than a generation, the traditional base of Indian life vanished. The fur traders equipped Indians with better weapons—guns, iron arrowheads, traps, and steel knives—that allowed hunters to deplete game faster; they goaded the Indians to trap fur-bearing animals well beyond their own needs. Some districts became barren because the cycle of reproduction was destroyed. (1986, 44)

During the fur trade, Native American men harvested most of the furs; Native women prepared the skins for market. Native people also provided many goods and services that supported the fur trade, such as corn, maple sugar, wild rice, canoes, and snowshoes. The fur trade brought social as well as economic change to Native American societies. The number of men with more than one wife increased in some Plains cultures, for example, because an individual male hunter could employ more than one woman tanner.

Historian Colin Calloway outlined the mixed blessings of the fur trade:

> [T]he new commercial situation was at best a mixed blessing. The fur trade proved to be a Trojan Horse in Indian North America, unleashing catastrophic forces at the same time as it delivered desired gifts. The trade tied its Indian patrons into the expanding world of European capitalism and threw neighboring customers into desperate competition. Access to hunting grounds and to European traders became major considerations governing the movement and location of Indian bands and the decisions of band chiefs. Tribes clashed in escalating conflicts for pelts, trade, and survival. (1990, 43)

The Haudenosaunee were pivotal in the regional fur trade, as well as in diplomacy. In exchange for furs, the Iroquois took trade goods such as iron needles, copper kettles, and knives. Traders with the Iroquois and other Native peoples soon learned to sell the Indians kettles of thinner metal, using an early form of planned obsolescence because they cost less to manufacture and wore out more quickly, increasing sales (Snow, 1994, 78).

Epidemics, first of measles, then smallpox, reached Haudenosaunee country with the fur trade, peaking in 1634 and 1635. Societies and economies were stressed severely. Mohawk population dropped from 7,740 to 2,830 within a matter of months (Snow, 1994, 99–100). Firearms reached the Haudenosaunee within a generation following the advent of the fur trade. In 1639, the Dutch tried, without success, to outlaw the sale of guns to Indians. By 1648, however, Dutch merchants in Albany were enthusiastic participants in the firearm trade, in part because the use of guns increased Native Americans' productivity as harvesters of beaver and other fur-bearing animals.

By 1640, the Wyandot and many other Native nations in eastern Canada and adjacent areas had become heavily dependent on export of furs, mainly beaver. At the same time, increasing demands for European trade goods were creating new conflicts between various Native peoples and deepening old enmities. According to Fahey:

> The fur trade, without intending it, largely destroyed the Indian way of life by depleting small game and speeding extermination of the buffalo; it mapped the West and estimated the locations and sizes of Native populations; it demonstrated the agricultural promise of large areas previously unknown or discounted as desert. The zenith of the fur trade immediately preceded a period in the United States when white men moved westward to escape crowding on older frontiers, to evade political or military obligations, to hunt gold, or simply to regain lost confidence in individual worth. (1974, 63)

According to David J. Wishart, a historian of the fur trade, "The traders also caused fragmentation by meddling in the power hierarchy of Indian communities. They enriched Indians who were accommodating to their demands and undermined the influence of chiefs who opposed them" (1994, 47). Finally, "and most disastrously," wrote Wishart, "Fur Traders co-opted Indians in the destruction of their own resource base" (ibid., 47). Native people became employees in a worldwide capitalistic enterprise that relaxed traditional inhibitions against overhunting. The beaver often was the first to disappear under intense hunting pressure because of its low reproduction rate.

In the late twentieth century, historians and anthropologists debated how the fur trade changed Native Americans' relationships with animals and the natural world. Calvin Martin, a professor of history at Rutgers University (New Brunswick, NJ), instigated debate with his publication of *Keepers of the Game* (1979), which argued that Native Americans abandoned their environmental ethics because they thought that animals were responsible for epidemic diseases ravishing human populations.

Martin's thesis virtually ignores the fact that Native Americans were being drawn into a capitalistic world economy. Martin also ignores diversity among native cultures, as well as the fact that in many cases epidemic diseases reached Native populations after (not before) the fur trade reached its height. The most important indicators that Martin's thesis lacks validity are Native American oral and written histories. These histories accurately attribute imported diseases to human beings (usually European immigrants) rather than animals that were native to North America. Historian William Cronon commented:

> The fur trade was thus far more complicated than a simple exchange of European metal goods for Indian beaver skins. It revolutionized Indian economies less by its new technology than by its new commercialism, at once utilizing and subverting Indian trade patterns to extend European commercial ones.... The essential lesson for the Indians was that certain things began to have prices that had not had them before.... Formerly, there had been little incentive for Indians to kill more than a fixed number of animals. (1983, 97)

The fur trade eroded native peoples' traditional inhibitions against killing of animals above and beyond their own needs. In New England, beaver populations ceased to be commercially exploitable after 1660, but animals continued to be harvested in areas that had been reached in later years. By the nineteenth century, however, beaver populations had fallen below sustainable levels in most of North America. Fortunately for the beaver, European hat styles changed, sparing surviving stocks in North America from extinction.

THE BEAVER WARS

Beaver Wars has become a historical shorthand reference for the Haudenosaunee campaign against the Wyandots that culminated in their defeat and assimilation by the Haudenosaunee about 1650. Like most wars, this one had more than one provocation. The most prominent reason for the antipathy leading to the war, however, was competition over diminishing stocks of beaver and other fur-bearing animals. The Haudenosaunee cause during this conflict was aided immeasurably by their relatively recent acquisition of European firearms, which the Wyandots for the most part lacked. The Mohawks, situated near trading centers at Albany and Montreal, were among the first to acquire a stock of firearms; one French source estimated that they had close to 300 guns by 1643 (Richter, 1992, 62).

At the beginning of the seventeenth century, the Wyandots, who lived near Georgian Bay on Lake Huron, were a prosperous confederacy of 25,000 to 30,000 people, comparable to the Haudenosaunee. By 1642, the Wyandots had allied with the French and had entered an alliance with the Susquehannocks, south of the Iroquois. In 1642, 1645, and 1647, the Haudenosaunee tried to secure peace with the French, to no avail. After the third try, they decided to break the alliance. The Wyandots had built a confederacy similar in structure to the Haudenosaunee (although more geographically compact).

By 1640, the Wyandots' economy was nearly totally dependent on trade with the French. At the same time, as they were weakened by disease, the Wyandots found themselves facing waves of raids by the Iroquois (principally Mohawks and Senecas), who were seeking to capture the Wyandots' share of the fur trade. The Mohawks had been exposed to European trade goods earlier than the Wyandots and may have been looking for furs to trade. The Wyandots' location at the center of several trade routes also made them an appealing point of attack at a time when demand was rising for beaver pelts, and the available supply of the animals was declining.

For nearly a decade, the Mohawks and Senecas harassed the Wyandots. Fearing Iroquois attacks, the Wyandots curtailed their trade with the French during the 1640s. Between 1647 and 1650, a final Iroquois drive swept over the Wyandots' homeland, provoking the dissolution of their confederacy as well as usurpation of the Wyandots' share of the fur trade by the Senecas and Mohawks.

Iroquois pressure against the Wyandots continued for several years after the conclusion of the Beaver Wars as Wyandot refugees sought new homes throughout the Great Lakes and St. Lawrence Valley. Many of the Wyandot refugees experienced acute hunger, and a sizable number starved during this diaspora. Some Wyandots became so hungry that they ate human excrement; others dug up the bodies of the dead and ate them, a matter of desperation and great shame because cannibalism is directly contrary to Wyandot belief and custom.

Scattered communities of Wyandot gradually revived traditional economies after the hungry years of the 1650s. Many Wyandot settled in or near European communities (including Jesuit missions). Even those who became Christianized and Europeanized continued to live in longhouses during these years. They continued to hunt and trap as much as possible and to practice slash-and-burn agriculture.

A number of Wyandot refugees were adopted after the Beaver Wars by their former enemies, who, true to their own traditions, socialized Wyandot prisoners into the various Haudenosaunee families and clans. The Iroquois also were replenishing their societies, which had been hard hit by European diseases and the casualties of continual war.

RELIGIOUS ADAPTATIONS TO EUROPEAN INVASION

One of the major ways in which the Haudenosaunee adapted to the European invasion was religious. The religion of Handsome Lake, which began as a series of visions in 1799, combined Quaker forms of Christianity with Native traditions. Its influence is still strongly felt among the traditional Iroquois, who often call the Code of Handsome Lake the "Longhouse Religion."

Handsome Lake's personal name was *Ganeodiyo*; Handsome Lake is one of the fifty chieftainship lines of the Iroquois Confederacy, a title bestowed on him by clan mothers. Handsome Lake was a half-brother of the Seneca Chief Cornplanter and an uncle of Red Jacket.

The Code of Handsome Lake is one of several Native American religions that evolved in reaction to European colonization by fusing traditional Native and Western European (usually Christian) elements. These religions combined Native American beliefs and rituals with the introduction of a Christian-style "savior" who was said to be able to recapture for Native Americans the better days they had known before colonization. One well-known example of this fusion was the Ghost Dance Religion, which was begun by the prophet Wovoka, who had been raised with both Native American and Christian influences. Neolin (also known as the Delaware Prophet) also formulated a religion that combined both traditions during the eighteenth century.

Handsome Lake was born at Conawagus, a Seneca village near contemporary Avon, New York, on the Genesee River. He and many other Senecas sided with the British in the French and Indian War and the American Revolution. George Washington and his subcommanders, principally General John Sullivan, were merciless with Native Americans who supported the British. During the late stages of the revolution, many Seneca communities were laid waste by scorched-earth marches that destroyed crops, livestock, and homes.

After that war, many Iroquois and other Native Americans who had supported the British were forced into Canada, principally to lands secured by Joseph Brant at Grand River. Others fled westward to join other Native Americans who were still free. Those who remained in their homelands were forced onto small, impoverished reservations as repeated attempts were made to force them out. By 1794, the Iroquois population bottomed out at about 4,000 people according to Ronald Wright in *Stolen Continents* (1992).

Handsome Lake's revival occurred in an atmosphere of dissension within a fractured Iroquois League. His life course reflected the devastation of his people. Born into a prominent family of the Turtle Clan, Handsome Lake distinguished himself as a leader as a young man before the American Revolution, when Iroquois society was still largely intact. Handsome Lake's decline began after his birthplace was taken by whites, and he was forced to move to the Allegheny Seneca reservation. The Seneca ethnologist Arthur Parker characterized Handsome Lake as "a middle-sized man, slim and unhealthy looking... [who became] a dissolute person and a miserable victim of the drink" (Johansen and Grinde, 1997, 160).

After four years lying ill in a small cabin under the care of a daughter, Handsome Lake began having a series of visions. Later, he used these visions to rally the Iroquois at a time when some of them were selling their entire winter harvest of furs for hard liquor, turning traditional ceremonies into drunken brawls, and, in winter, often dying of exposure in drunken stupors.

By the spring of 1799, Handsome Lake experienced considerable remorse over his alcoholism but did not stop drinking until he was nearly dead. Arthur Parker described him as little more than a shell of yellowed skin and dried bones. During 1799, Handsome Lake also experienced a number of visions in which he was taken on a great journey to the sky. He was shown a number of personages and events, past, present, and future. In one of his visions, Handsome Lake met George Washington, who had died in 1799, and heard him confirm the sovereignty of the Iroquois.

After the series of visions, Handsome Lake stopped drinking alcohol and later committed the Code of Handsome Lake to writing. He persuaded many other Iroquois to stop drinking and to reconstruct their lives. During his lifetime, Handsome Lake achieved some political influence among the Senecas, but his popularity slid because of his ideological rigidity. In 1801 and 1802, he traveled to Washington, D.C., with a delegation of Senecas to meet with President Thomas Jefferson and to resist the reduction of their peoples' landholdings.

The Code of Handsome Lake combines European religious influences with a traditional Iroquois emphasis on family, community, and the centrality of the land to the maintenance of culture. The largest following for Handsome Lake came after his death. Adherents to his code accepted his concepts of social relationships as well as concepts of good and evil that closely resemble Quakerism, which Handsome Lake had studied. The Quaker creed appealed to many Iroquois because they had been persecuted before coming to America and because they had no ornate temples and lived frugally and communally, doing their best to respect their Native American neighbors.

A nationalistic figure in a religious context, Handsome Lake also borrowed heavily from the Iroquois Great Law of Peace, popularizing concepts such as looking into the future for seven generations and regarding the earth as mother. These ideas have since become part of pan-Indian thought across North America and, from there, have been incorporated into late twentieth century popular environmental symbolism. With its combination of Old and New World theologies, the Code of Handsome Lake sought a middle path, a way to reconcile the faiths of Europe and America.

The Code of Handsome Lake is still widely followed in Iroquois country. By the early twenty-first century, roughly a third of the 30,000 Iroquois in New York State attended longhouse ceremonies. Although his code remains popular among many Iroquois, others have accused Handsome Lake of having "sold out" to the Quakers and white religious interests in general. Louis Hall, ideological founder of the Warrior movement in Iroquois Country, regarded the religion of Handsome Lake as a bastardized form of Christianity grafted onto Native traditions. Hall called Handsome Lake's visions "the hallucinations of a drunk" (Johansen, 1993, 160). Opposition to these teachings is one plank in an intellectual platform that allows the Warriors to claim that the Mohawk Nation Council at Akwesasne, and the Iroquois Confederacy Council as well, are enemies of the people, and that the Warriors are the true protectors of "Mohawk sovereignty." Hall, who died in 1993, regarded Handsome Lake's followers as traitors or "Tontos" (Johansen, 1993, 160).

Hall's Warriors split bitterly with followers of Handsome Lake over gambling and other issues, leading to violence at Akwesasne that peaked in 1990 with the deaths of two Mohawks.

FURTHER READING

Aquila, Richard. *The Iroquois Restoration: Iroquois Diplomacy on the Colonial Frontier, 1701–1754*. Detroit: Wayne State University Press, 1983.

Arden, Harvey. The Fire that Never Dies. *National Geographic*, September 1987, 374–403.

Beals, Ralph L., and Harry Hoijer. *An Introduction to Anthropology*. New York: Macmillan, 1965.

Benedict, Ruth. *Patterns of Culture*. Boston: Houghton Mifflin, 1934.

Blackbird, Andrew J. *Complete Both Early and Late History of the Ottawa and Cheppewa* [sic] *Indians of Michigan: A Grammar of Their Language, Personal and Family History of the Author*. Harbor Springs, MI: Babcock and Darling, 1897.

Bolton, Herbet Eugene, ed. *Spanish Exploration in the Southwest, 1542–1706*. New York: Scribner, 1916.

Bolton, Herbet Eugene. *Coronado on the Turquoise Trail*. Albuquerque: University of New Mexico Press, 1949.

Boyd, Julian P., ed. *Indian Treaties Printed by Benjamin Franklin, 1736–1762*. Philadelphia: Historical Society of Pennsylvania, 1938.

Bradford, William. *History of Plymouth Plantation*. Edited by Charles Deane. Boston: Private printing, 1856.

Bradford, William. *History of Plymouth Plantation*. Edited by Samuel Eliot Morison. New York: Modern Library, 1967.

Brandon, William. *The American Heritage Book of Indians*. New York: Dell, 1961.

Brockunier, Samuel H. *The Irrepressible Democrat: Roger Williams*. New York: Ronald Press, 1940.

Brown, Jennifer S. H. *Strangers in Blood: Fur Trade Families in Indian Country*. Vancouver, BC: University of British Columbia Press, 1981.

Caduto, Michael J., and Joseph Brudhac, *Keepers of the Earth: Native American Stories and Environmental Activities for Children*. Golden, CO: Fulcrum, 1988.

Calloway, Colin. *The Western Abenakis of Vermont, 1600–1800: War, Migration, and the Survival of an Indian People*. Norman: University of Oklahoma Press, 1990.

Canby, Thomas Y. The Anasazi: Riddles in the Ruins. *National Geographic*, November 1982, 554–592.

Champagne, Duane. *American Indian Societies: Strategies and Conditions of Political and Cultural Survival*. Cambridge, MA: Cultural Survival, 1989.

Chapin, Howard H. *Sachems of the Narragansetts*. Providence: Rhode Island Historical Society, 1931.

Chittenden, Hiram M. *The American Fur Trade of the Far West*. New York: Press of the Pioneers, 1935.

Chupack, Henry. *Roger Williams*. New York: Twayne, 1969.

Church, Thomas. *Diary of King Philip's War, 1676–77*. Edited by Alan and Mary Simpson. Chester, CT: Pequot Press, 1975.

Colden, Cadwallader. *The History of the Five Nations Depending on the Province of New York in America*. Ithaca, NY: Cornell University Press, [1727, 1747] 1958.

Cook, Sherburne F. Interracial Warfare and Population Decline among the New England Indians. *Ethnohistory* 20:1(Winter 1973):1–24.

Copway, George. *The Life, History, and Travels of Kah-Ge-Ga-Gah-Bowh.* New York: Weed & Parsons, 1847.

Copway, George. *The Ojibway Conquest.* New York: G. P. Putnam, 1850.

Copway, George. *The Organization of a New Indian Territory East of the Missouri River.* New York: S. W. Benedict, 1850.

Copway, George. *The Traditional History and Characteristic Sketches of the Ojibway Nation.* London: Charles Gilpin, 1850.

Copway, George. *Running Sketches of Men and Places in England, Germany, Belgium, and Scotland.* New York: Riker, 1851.

Copway, George. *Indian Life and Indian History.* Boston: Colby, 1858.

Covey, Cyclone. *The Gentle Radical: A Biography of Roger Williams.* New York: Macmillan, 1966.

Cronon, William. *Changes in the Land: Indians, Colonists, and the Ecology of New England.* New York: Hill and Wang, 1983.

Dennis, Matthew. *Cultivating a Landscape of Peace.* Ithaca, NY: Cornell University Press, 1993.

DeVoto, Bernard. *The Course of Empire.* Boston: Houghton-Mifflin, 1952.

Dittert, Alfred E., Jr. The Archaeology of Cebolleta Mesa and Acoma Pueblo: A Preliminary Report Based on Further Investigation. *El Palacio* 59(1952):191–217.

Driver, Harold E. *Indians of North America.* 2nd ed., rev. Chicago: University of Chicago Press, 1969.

Ellis, George W., and John E. Morris. *King Philip's War.* New York: The Grafton Press, 1906.

Gallegos, Hernan. Relacion [diary]. In George P. Hammond and Agapito Rey, *The Rediscovery of New Mexico, 1580–1594.* Albuquerque: University of New Mexcico Press, 1966, 47–144.

Ernst, James. *Roger Williams: New England Firebrand.* New York: Macmillan, 1932.

Fahey, John. *The Flathead Indians.* Norman: University of Oklahoma Press, 1974.

Fahey, John. *The Kalispel Indians.* Norman: University of Oklahoma Press, 1986.

Fenton, William N. *Roll Call of the Iroquois Chiefs.* Washington, DC: Smithsonian Institution, 1950.

Fenton, William N., ed. *Parker on the Iroquois.* Syracuse, NY: Syracuse University Press, 1968.

Giddings, James L. Roger Williams and the Indians [1957]. Typescript, Rhode Island Historical Society.

Green, Michael D. The Expansion of European Colonization to the Mississippi Valley, 1780–1880. In Bruce G. Trigger and Wilcomb E. Washburn, eds., *The Cambridge History of the Native Peoples of the Americas.* Cambridge: Cambridge University Press, 1996: 461–538.

Guild, Reuben Aldridge. *Footprints of Roger Williams.* Providence, RI: Tibbetts and Preston, 1886.

Hale, Horatio. *The Iroquois Book of Rites.* Philadelphia: D. G. Brinton, 1883.

Hamilton, Charles. *Cry of the Thunderbird.* Norman: University of Oklahoma Press, 1972.

Henige, David. *Numbers from Nowhere: The American Indian Contact Population Debate.* Norman: University of Oklahoma Press, 1998.

Henige, David. Can a Myth Be Astronomically Dated? *American Indian Culture and Research Journal* 23:4(1999):127–157.

Hewitt, J. N. B. *Legend of the Founding of the Iroquois League.* Washington, DC: Smithsonian Institution, 1892.

Hewitt, J. N. B. *Iroquois Cosmology.* Washington, DC: Smithsonian Institution, 1903.

Hewitt, J. N. B. *A Constitutional League of Peace in the Stone Age of America.* Washington, DC: Smithsonian Institution, 1918.

Hewitt, J. N. B. Notes on the Creek Indians. In J. R. Swanton, ed., *Bureau of American Ethnology Bulletin No. 123.* Washington, DC: U.S. Government Printing Office, 1939: 124–133.

Hill, Richard. Continuity of Haudenosaunee Government: Political Reality of the Grand Council. *Northeast Indian Quarterly* 4:3(Autumn 1987):10–14.

Hoover, Dwight W. *The Red and the Black.* Chicago: Rand-McNally, 1976: 15.

Jacobs, Wilbur. *Diplomacy and Indian Gifts: Anglo-French Rivalry Among the Ohio and Northwest Frontiers, 1748-1763.* Stanford, CA: Stanford University Press, 1950.

Johansen, Bruce E. *Life and Death in Mohawk Country.* Golden, CO: Fulcrum/North American Press, 1993.

Johansen, Bruce E. Dating the Iroquois Confederacy. *Akwesasne Notes* New Series 1(3/4) (Fall 1995):62–63.

Johansen, Bruce E., and Donald A. Grinde, Jr. *The Encyclopedia of Native American Biography.* New York: Henry Holt, 1997.

Josephy, Alvin, Jr. *The Patriot Chiefs.* New York: Viking, 1961.

Kennedy, John Hopkins. *Jesuit and Savage in New France.* New Haven, CT: Yale University Press, 1950.

Labaree, Benjamin L. *America's Nation-Time: 1607–1789.* Boston: Allyn and Bacon, 1972.

Las Casas, Bartholemé. *The Devastation of the Indies* [1542]. Translated by Herma Briffault. New York: Seabury Press, 1974.

López de Gómara, Francisco. *Historia del Illvstriss[imo] et Valorosiss[ims] Capitano Don Ferdinando Cortes Marchese della Valle.* Trans. Agustino de Cravaliz. Rome: Valerio & Luigi Dorici Fratelli, 1556.

Mann, Barbara A., and Jerry L. Fields. A Sign in the Sky: Dating the League of the Haudenosaunee. *American Indian Culture and Research Journal* 21:2(1997): 105–163.

Mann, Charles C. 1491: America Before Columbus Was More Sophisticated and More Populous than We Have Ever Thought—and a More Livable Place than Europe. *The Atlantic Monthly* March 2002, 41–53.

Martin, Calvin. *Keepers of the Game.* Berkeley: University of California Press, 1979.

Mather, Increase. *A Brief History of the War with the Indians in New England.* London: Richard Chiswell, 1676.

Maxwell, James A., ed. *America's Fascinating Indian Heritage.* Pleasantville, NY: Reader's Digest, 1978.

McManus, John C. An Economic Analysis of Indian Behavior in the North American Fur Trade. *Journal of Economic History* 32(1972):36–53.

Miller, Perry. *Roger Williams: His Contribution to the American* Tradition. Indianapolis: Bobbs-Merrill, 1953.

Minge, Ward Alan. *Acoma: Pueblo in the Sky.* Albuquerque: University of New Mexico Press, 1991.

Morgan, Lewis Henry. *League of the Ho-de-no-sau-nee, or Iroquois.* New York: Corinth Books, [1851] 1962.

Page, Jake. *In the Hands of the Great Spirit: The 20,000 Year History of the American Indian.* New York: Free Press, 2003.

Parrington, Vernon Louis. *Main Currents in American Thought.* New York: Harcourt, Brace, 1927.

Phillips, Paul C. *The Fur Trade.* 2 vols. Norman: University of Oklahoma Press, 1961.

Reaman, G. Elmore. *The Trail of the Iroquois Indians: How the Iroquois Nation Saved Canada for the British Empire.* London: Frederick Muller, 1967.

Richter, Daniel K. *The Ordeal of the Longhouse: The Peoples of the Iroquois League in the Era of European Colonization.* Chapel Hill, NC: University of North Carolina Press, 1992.

Rider, Sidney S. *The Lands of Rhode Island as They Were Known to Caunonicus and Mian-tunnomu When Roger Williams Came in 1636.* Providence, RI: private printing, 1904.

Saum, Lewis. *The Fur Trader and the Indian.* Seattle: University of Washington Press, 1965.

Segal, Charles M., and Stineback, David C. *Puritans, Indians, and Manifest Destiny.* New York: Putnam, 1977.

Siegel, Beatrice. *Fur Trappers and Traders.* New York: Walker, 1981.

Slotkin, Richard, and James K. Folsom, eds. *So Dreadful a Judgement: Puritan Responses to King Philip's War 1676–1677.* Middleton, CT: Wesleyan University Press, 1978.

Snow, Dean. *The Iroquois.* London: Blackwell, 1994.

Spicer, Edward H. *Cycles of Conquest.* Tucson: University of Arizona Press, 1962.

Stannard, David E. *American Holocaust: Columbus and the Conquest of the New World.* New York: Oxford University Press, 1992.

Stuart, George E. Etowah: A Southeast Village in 1491. *National Geographic,* October 1991, 54–67.

Straus, Oscar S. *Roger Williams: Pioneer of Religious Liberty.* New York: Century, 1894.

Swan, Bradford F. New Light on Roger Williams and the Indians. *Providence Sunday Journal Magazine,* November 23, 1969, 14.

Tehanetorens [Ray Fadden]. *Tales of the Iroquois.* Rooseveltown, NY: Akwesasne Notes, 1976.

Tehanetorens [Ray Fadden]. *Basic Call to Consciousness.* Rooseveltown, NY: Akwesasne Notes, 1986.

Tehanetorens [Ray Fadden]. *Wampum Belt.* Onchiota, NY: Six Nations Museum, n.d.

Trelease, Allen W. *Indian Affairs in Colonial New York: The Seventeenth Century.* Ithaca, NY: Cornell University Press, 1960.

Trigger, Bruce G. *Children of the Aataentsic: A History of the Huron People.* Montreal: McGill-Queen's University Press, 1976.

Van Kirk, Sylvia. *Many Tender Ties: Women in Fur Trade Society, 1670–1870.* Norman: University of Oklahoma Press, 1983.

Vaughan, Alden T. *New England Frontier: Puritans and Indians, 1620–1675.* Boston: Little, Brown, 1965.

Wallace, Anthony F. C. *The Death and Rebirth of the Seneca.* New York: Random House, 1969.

Wallace, Paul A. W. *The White Roots of Peace.* Santa Fe, NM: Clear Light Publishers, 1994.

White Roots of Peace. *The Great Law of Peace of the Longhouse People.* Rooseveltown, NY: White Roots of Peace, 1971.

Williams, Richard B. The True Story of Thanksgiving. November 19, 2002. Available at IndigenousNewsNetwork@topica.com.

Williams, Roger. *A Key Into the Languages of America.* London: Gregory Dexter, 1643; Providence, RI: Tercentenary Committee, 1936.

Williams, Roger. *The Complete Writings of Roger Williams.* Vol. 1. New York: Russell and Russell, 1963.

Wilson, Edmund. *Apologies to the Iroquois.* New York: Farrar, Strauss, and Cudahy, 1960.

Winslow, Elizabeth Ola. *Master Roger Williams.* New York: Macmillan, 1957.

Wishart, David J. *The Fur Trade and the American West, 1807–1840.* Lincoln: University of Nebraska Press, 1979.

Wishart, David J. *An Unspeakable Sadness: The Dispossession of the Nebraska Indians.* Lincoln: University of Nebraska Press, 1994.

Wood, William. *New England's Prospect.* Amherst: University of Massachusetts Press, 1977.

Woodbury, Hanni, Reg Henry, and Harry Webster, comps. *Concerning the League: The Iroquois League Tradition as Dictated in Onondaga by John Arthur Gibson.* Algonquian and Iroquoian Linguistics Memoir No. 9. Winnipeg, Manitoba: University of Manitoba Press, 1992.

Wright, Ronald. *Stolen Continents.* Boston: Houghton-Mifflin, 1992.

CHAPTER 4

The Transfer of Ideas

NATIVE CONFEDERACIES AND THE EVOLUTION OF DEMOCRACY

Europe did not discover America, but America was quite a discovery for Europe. For roughly three centuries before the American Revolution, the ideas that made the American Revolution possible were being discovered, nurtured, and embellished in the growing English and French colonies of North America. America provided a counterpoint for European convention and assumption. It became, for Europeans in America, at once a dream and a reality, a fact and a fantasy, the real and the ideal. To appreciate the way in which European eyes opened on the "New World," we must take the phrase literally, with the excitement evoked in our own time by travel to the moon and planets. There was one electrifying difference: the voyagers of that time knew that their New World was inhabited. They had only to look and learn, to drink in the bewildering newness and enchanting novelty of seeing it all for the first time.

THE TRANSATLANTIC IDEOLOGICAL INCUBUS

Coming from societies based on hierarchy, early European explorers and immigrants came to America seeking kings, queens, and princes. What they sought they believed they had found, for a time. Quickly, however, they began to sense a difference: The people they were calling kings had few trappings that distinguished them from the people they "ruled" in most native societies. They only rarely sat at the top of a class hierarchy with the pomp of European rulers. More important, Indian kings usually did not rule. Rather, they led by mechanisms of consensus and public opinion that Europeans often found admirable.

COLONISTS' PERCEPTIONS OF NATIVE POLITIES

European colonists' lives were pervaded by contact with Native American peoples to a degree that we today sometimes find difficult to comprehend. Especially in its early years, colonization was limited to a few isolated pockets of land, widely dispersed, on a thin ribbon along the eastern seaboard. In the mid-eighteenth century, the frontier ran from a few miles west of Boston, through Albany, to Lancaster, Pennsylvania, or roughly to the western edges of today's eastern seaboard urban areas. The new Americans looked inland across a continent they already knew to be many times the size of England, France, and Holland combined. They did not know with any certainty just how far their new homeland extended. Maps of the time did not comprehend accurately the distances between the Atlantic and Pacific Oceans. A few Spanish and French trappers and explorers had left their footprints in this vast expanse of land, but at that time at least 90 percent of North America was still the homeland of many hundreds of Native peoples.

The people of that time were conditioned by their perceptions of time and space, just as we are. In a time when the fastest method of communication and transportation was by wind-powered sail, it took six weeks for King George III to learn that the thirteen newly united colonies had posted the Declaration of Independence. Overland, on a fresh horse traveling the trails worn by Native peoples, a person could cover as much ground in a day as a late-twentieth century automobile covers in 20 minutes or a jet aircraft in three minutes. In our day, news travels around the world in a fraction of a second.

Although hostile encounters between European immigrants and Native peoples took uncounted lives during those early years, day-to-day life was usually peaceful. History, like the daily news, tends to accentuate conflict, so we are left with a record that overstates the role that war actually played in history. In fact, on a daily basis the immigrants and Native peoples traded, socialized, and concluded treaties more often than they went to war. Enlightened eyes looked westward with a degree of curiosity, respect, and even awe, drinking in the ways of peoples who knew America better than they did. In the written perceptions of the immigrants, there is a pervasive sense that the native peoples held the keys to ways of ordering society that Europeans were only beginning to understand.

Increasingly, Native societies in America came to serve the transplanted Europeans, including some of the United States' most influential founders, as a counterpoint to the European order. They found in the Native polities the values that the seminal documents of the time celebrated: life, liberty, happiness, a model of government by consensus, with citizens enjoying rights due them as human beings. The fact that native peoples in America were able to govern themselves in this way provided advocates of alternatives to monarchy with practical ammunition for a philosophy of government based on the rights of the individual, which they believed had worked, did work, and would work for them, in America.

This is not to say they sought to replicate Native polities among societies in America descended from Europeans. The new Americans were too practical to believe that a society steeped in European cultural traditions could be turned on its head so swiftly and easily. They chose instead to borrow, to shape what they had with what they saw before them, to create a new order that included aspects of both worlds. They may be faulted in our time for failing to borrow certain aspects of Native American societies, such as important political and social roles for women.

NATIVE AMERICAN CONFEDERACIES

All along the Atlantic Seaboard, Native American nations had formed confederacies by the time they encountered European immigrants, from the Creeks, which Hector St. John de Crevecoeur called a "federated republic" (Crevecoeur, [1801] 1964, 461), to the Cherokees and Choctaws, to the Iroquois and the Wyandots (Hurons) in the St. Lawrence Valley, as well as the Penacook federation of New England, among many others. The Illinois Confederacy; the "Three Fires" of the Chippewa, Ottawa, and Pottawatomi; the Wapenaki Confederacy, the Powhatan Confederacies; and the tripartite Miami also were members of confederations.

Each of these Native confederacies developed its own variation on a common theme of counselor democracy. Most were remarkably similar in broad outline. By the late eighteenth century, as resentment against England's taxation flared into open rebellion along the Atlantic seaboard, the colonists displayed widespread knowledge of Native governmental systems. Thomas Jefferson, Benjamin Franklin, and others the length of the coast observed governmental systems that shared many similarities.

Colonists arriving in eastern North America encountered variations of a confederacy model, usually operating by methods of consensus that were unfamiliar to people who had been living in societies usually governed by queens, princes, and kings. The best known of these consensual governments was the Haudenosaunee (Iroquois Confederacy), which occupied a prominent position in the diplomacy of the early colonies.

THE IMPORTANCE OF THE IROQUOIS CONFEDERACY

Observations of Indian governments showed a remarkable similarity all along the seaboard. Everywhere they looked, immigrant observers found confederacies of Native nations loosely governed by the kind of respect for individual liberty that European savants had established only in theory or as relics of a distant European golden age. Indian languages, customs, and material artifacts varied widely, but their form of government, perhaps best characterized as counselor democracy, seemed to be nearly everywhere.

The ideas and political systems of the Iroquois and other confederations were so appealing that 300 years ago while he was still in England, William Penn described the functioning of the Iroquois Confederacy in glowing terms:

> Every King hath his council, and that consists of all the old and wise men of his nation . . . nothing is undertaken, be it war, peace, the selling of land or traffick [*sic*], without advising with them; and which is more, with the youngmen also. . . . The kings move by the breath of their people. It is the Indian custom to deliberate. . . . I have never seen more natural sagacity. ("William Penn to the Society," 1982, 2:452–453)

Penn described the Native confederacies of eastern North America as political societies with sachemships inherited through the female side. Penn also was familiar with the Condolence Ceremony of the Iroquois, which was crucial for an understanding of their confederacy. He stated that when someone kills a "woman they pay double [the wampum]" because ". . . she breeds children which men cannot" ("William Penn to the Society," 1982, 454). In 1697, after lengthy personal exposure to American Indian forms of government, Penn proposed a Plan for a Union of the Colonies in America ("Mr. Penn's Plan," 1853, 4:296–297).

The Iroquois' system was the best known to the colonists in large part because of the Haudenosaunee's pivotal position in diplomacy not only between the English and French, but also among other Native confederacies. Called the Iroquois by the French and the Five (later Six) Nations by the English, the Haudenosaunee controlled the only relatively level land pass between the English colonies on the seaboard and the French settlements in the St. Lawrence Valley, later the route of the Erie Canal.

Without authority to command, Iroquois and other Native American political leaders honed their persuasive abilities, especially their speaking skills. In his *History of the Five Nations* ([1727] 1958), Cadwallader Colden attributed the Iroquois' skill at oratory to the republican nature of their government. Colden described the intense study that the Iroquois applied to the arts of oral persuasion, to acquisition of grace and manner before councils of their peers. Franklin compared the decorum of Native American councils to the rowdy nature of debate in British public forums, including the House of Commons. This difference in debating customs persists to our day.

Each Iroquois nation has its own council, which sends delegates to a central council, much as each state in the United States has its own legislature, as well as senators and representatives who travel to the central seat of government in Washington, D.C. When representatives of the Iroquois nations meet at Onondaga, they form two groups: the Elder Brothers (Mohawks and Senecas) and the Younger Brothers (Cayugas and Oneidas). The Onondagas are the firekeepers. (In the U.S. Congress, a similar position is held by the Speaker of the House.)

The Iroquois built certain ways of doing business into their Great Law to prevent anger and frayed tempers. For example, an important measure may not be decided the same day it is introduced to allow time for passions to cool. Important decisions must take at least two days to allow leaders to "sleep on it" and not to react too quickly. The Great Law may be amended just as one adds beams to the rafters of an Iroquois longhouse. The Great Tree of Peace is regarded as a living organization. Its roots and branches are said to grow in order to incorporate other peoples.

The Iroquois also are linked to each other by their clan system, which ties each person to family members in every other nation of the federation. If a Mohawk of the Turtle Clan has to travel, the Mohawk will be hosted by Turtles in each other Iroquois nation.

A leader is instructed to be a mentor for the people at all times. Political leaders must strive to maintain peace within the league. A chief may be *de-horned* (impeached) if he engages in violent behavior of any kind. Even the brandishing of a weapon may bring sanction. The traditional headdress of an Iroquois leader (an emblem of office) includes deer antlers, which are said to have been "knocked off" if the sachem has been impeached. Chiefs of the Iroquois League are instructed to take criticism honestly and that their skins should be seven spans thick to absorb the criticism of the people they represent in public councils. Political leaders also are instructed to think of the coming generations in all of their actions.

Sachems are not allowed to name their own successors or carry their titles to the grave. The Great Law provides a ceremony to remove the antlers of authority from a dying chief. The Great Law also provides for the removal from office of sachems who can no longer adequately function in office, a measure remarkably similar to a constitutional amendment adopted in the United States during the late 20th century providing for the removal of an incapacitated president. The Great Law of Peace also includes provisions guaranteeing freedom of religion and the right of redress before the Grand Council. It also forbids unauthorized entry of homes, one of several measures that sound familiar to U.S. citizens through the Bill of Rights.

In some ways, the Grand Council operates like the U.S. House of Representatives and Senate, with their conference committees. As it was designed by Deganawidah, the Peacemaker (founder of the confederacy with his spokesman Hiawatha), debating protocol begins with the Elder Brothers, the Mohawks and Senecas. After debate by the Keepers of the Eastern Door (Mohawks) and the Keepers of the Western Door (Senecas), the question is then thrown across the fire to the Oneida and Cayuga statesmen (the Younger Brothers) for discussion in much the same manner. Once consensus is achieved among the Oneidas and the Cayugas, the discussion is then given back to the Senecas and Mohawks for confirmation. Next, the question is laid before the Onondagas for their decision.

Peacemaker in Stone Canoe. (Courtesy of John Kahionhes Fadden.)

At this stage, the Onondagas have a power similar to judicial review; they may raise objections to the proposed measure if it is believed inconsistent with the Great Law. Essentially, the legislature can rewrite the proposed law on the spot so that it can be in accord with the constitution of the Iroquois. When the Onondagas reach consensus, Tadadaho asks Honowireton (an Onondaga sachem who presides over debates between the delegations) to confirm the decision. Finally, Honowireton or Tadadaho gives the decision of the Onondagas to the Mohawks and the Senecas so that the policy may be announced to the Grand Council as its will.

BENJAMIN FRANKLIN AND THE LANCASTER TREATY COUNCIL (1744)

If the U.S. government's structure closely resembles that of the Iroquois Confederacy in some respects, how did the founders observe the Native model? The historical trail begins in 1744, as Pennsylvania officials met with Iroquois sachems in council at Lancaster. Canassatego, an Onondaga sachem, advised the Pennsylvania officials on Iroquois concepts of unity. Canassatego and other Iroquois sachems were advocating unified British management of trade at the time. Although the Iroquois preferred English manufactured products to those produced in France, the fact that each colony maintained its own trading practices and policies created confusion and conflict:

> Our wise forefathers established Union and Amity between the Five Nations. This has made us formidable; this has given us great Weight and Authority with our neighboring Nations. We are a powerful Confederacy; and by your observing the same methods, our wise forefathers have taken, you will acquire such Strength and power. Therefore whatever befalls you, never fall out with one another. (Van Doren and Boyd, 1938, 75)

Richard Peters provided the following word portrait of Canassatego at Lancaster: "a tall, well-made man," with "a very full chest and brawny limbs, a manly countenance, with a good-natired [sic] smile. He was about 60 years of age, very active, strong, and had a surprising liveliness in his speech" (Boyd, [1942] 1981, 244–245). Dressed in a scarlet camblet coat and a fine, gold-laced hat, Canassatego is described by Peters as possessing a captivating presence that turned heads whenever he walked into a room.

Benjamin Franklin probably first learned of Canassatego's 1744 advice to the colonies as he set his words in type. Franklin's press issued Indian treaties in small booklets that enjoyed a lively sale throughout the colonies. Beginning in 1736, Franklin published Indian treaty accounts on a regular basis until the early 1760s, when his defense of Indians under assault by frontier settlers cost him his seat in the Pennsylvania Assembly. Franklin subsequently served the colonial government in England.

Using Iroquois examples of unity, Franklin sought to shame the reluctant colonists into some form of union in 1751:

> It would be a strange thing...if Six Nations of ignorant savages should be capable of forming such an union and be able to execute it in such a manner that it has subsisted for ages and appears indissoluble, and yet that a like union should be impractical for ten or a dozen English colonies, to whom it is more necessary and must be more advantageous, and who cannot be supposed to want an equal understanding of their interest." (Smyth, 1905–1907, 3:42)

Canassatego. (Courtesy of John Kahionhes Fadden.)

As he often did, Franklin put a backward spin on the phrase "ignorant savages." He showed that the original peoples of America had much to teach the immigrants. In October 1753, Franklin began a distinguished diplomatic career that would later make him the premier U.S. envoy in Europe by attending a treaty council at Carlisle, Pennsylvania. During the same year, Franklin also recognized the enormous appeal of American Indian ways to the American people. He wrote that American Indian children reared in Anglo-American society returned to their people when they took but "one ramble with them." Furthermore, Franklin asserted that when "White persons of either sex have been taken prisoners young by Indians, and lived a while among them, tho' ransomed by their friends . . . [they] take the first good opportunity of escaping again into the woods, from whence there is no reclaiming them" (Labaree, 1961, 4:481).

During the Carlisle treaty council with the Iroquois and the Ohio Indians, Franklin saw the rich imagery and ideas of the Iroquois at close hand. On October 1, 1753, he watched an Oneida chief, Scarrooyady, and a Mohawk, Cayanguileguoa, condole the Ohio Indians for their losses against the French. Franklin listened while Scarrooyady spoke of the origins of the Iroquois Great Law to the Ohio Indians:

> We must let you know, that there was friendship established by our and your Grandfathers, and a mutual Council fire was kindled. In this friendship all those then under the ground, who had not obtained eyes or faces (that is, those unborn) were included; and it was then mutually promised to tell the same to their children and children's children. (Van Doren, 1938, 197–198.)

The following day, Franklin and the other treaty commissioners echoed earlier admonitions of the Iroquois when they stated the following:

> We would therefore hereby place before you the necessity of preserving your faith entire to one another, as well as to this government. Do not separate; Do not part on any score. Let no differences nor jealousies subsist a moment between Nation and Nation, but join together as one man. (Van Doren, 1938, 131)

In replying to these remarks, Scarrooyady took for granted the treaty commissioners' knowledge of the Iroquois Confederacy's structure when he requested that "You will please to lay all our present transactions before the council at Onondago, that they may know we do nothing in the dark" (Van Doren, 1938, 131).

ANGLO-IROQUOIS SYNTHESIS IN THE ALBANY PLAN OF UNION

On the eve of the Albany Conference in 1754, Franklin already was persuaded that the words of Canassatego (who had died in 1750) were good counsel. He was not alone in these sentiments. James DeLancey, acting governor of New York, sent a special invitation to Tiyanoga (ca. 1680–1755), a Mohawk sachem the English called Hendrick, to attend the Albany Conference, where he provided insights into the structure of the League of the Iroquois for the assembled colonial delegates. The Albany Plan of Union proposed a federal union of the colonies but retained colony autonomy except for matters of mutual concern, such as diplomacy and defense; this structure was very similar to the Iroquois Confederacy that Canassatego had urged the colonists to emulate ten years earlier. Although the Albany Plan was not approved by the colonies or the Crown, it became a model on which the Articles of Confederation later was based.

Tiyanoga was a major figure in colonial affairs between 1710, when he was one of four Mohawks invited to England by Queen Anne, and 1755, when he

Benjamin Franklin. (Courtesy of the Library of Congress.)

died in battle with the French as an ally of the British. A member of the Wolf Clan, Tiyanoga knew both Iroquois and English cultures well. He converted to Christianity and became a preacher of its tenets sometime after 1700. In England, he was painted by John Verelst and called the Emperor of the Five Nations. Hendrick was perhaps the most important individual link in a chain of alliance that saved the New York frontier and probably New England from

Hendrick (Tiyanoga) ca. 1710. (Courtesy of Smithsonian
National Anthropological Archives.)

the French in the initial stages of the Seven Years' War, which was called the
French and Indian War (1754–1763) in North America. Tiyanoga died at the
Battle of Lake George in the late summer of 1755 as Sir William Johnson
defeated Baron Dieskau. The elderly Mohawk was shot from his horse and
bayoneted to death while on a scouting party September 8.

A lifelong friend of Sir William Johnson, Tiyanoga appeared often at Johnson Hall, near Albany, and had copious opportunities to rub elbows with visiting English. Sometimes, he arrived in war paint, fresh from battle. Thomas Pownall, a shrewd observer of colonial Indian affairs, described Hendrick as "a bold artful, intriguing Fellow and has learnt no small share of European Politics, [who] obstructs and opposes all [business] where he has not been talked to first" (Jacobs, 1966, 77).

Well known as a man of distinction in his manners and dress, Hendrick visited England again in 1740. At that time, King George presented him with an ornate green coat of satin, fringed in gold, which Hendrick was fond of wearing in combination with his traditional Mohawk ceremonial clothing. Crevecoeur, himself an adopted Iroquois who had sat in on sessions of the Grand Council at Onondaga, described Hendrick in late middle age, preparing for dinner at the Johnson estate, within a few years of the Albany Congress:

> [He] wished to appear at his very best. . . . His head was shaved, with the exception of a little tuft of hair in the back, who which he attached a piece of silver. To the cartilage of his ears . . . he attached a little brass wire twisted into very tight spirals. A girondole was hung from his nose. Wearing a wide silver neckpiece, a crimson vest and a blue cloak adorned with sparkling gold, Hendrick, as was his custom, shunned European breeches for a loincloth fringed with glass beads. On his feet, Hendrick wore moccasins of tanned elk, embroidered with porcupine quills, fringed with tiny silver bells. (1926, 170)

By the time Hendrick was invited to address colonial delegates at the Albany Congress, he was well known on both sides of the Atlantic among Iroquois and Europeans alike. At the Albany Congress, Hendrick repeated the advice Canassatego had given colonial delegates at Lancaster a decade earlier, this time at a conference devoted not only to diplomacy, but also to drawing up a plan for the type of colonial union that both the Iroquois and Franklin had advocated. The same day, the colonial delegates were in the early stages of debate over the plan of union.

At the Albany Congress, Hendrick admonished the Americans to use Iroquois-style unity and to bring "as many into this covenant chain as you possibly can" (O'Callaghan, 1855, 6:869). With this admonition and his knowledge of the imagery and concepts of the Iroquois Great Law at hand, Franklin met with colonial and Iroquois delegates to create a plan of unity that combined the Iroquois and English systems. Franklin said that the debates over the Albany Plan "went on daily with the Indian business" (Bigelow, 1868, 295). During these discussions, Hendrick openly criticized the colonists and hinted that the Iroquois would not ally with the English colonies unless a suitable form of unity was established among them. Hendrick asserted on July 9, 1754, that "we wish [that] this . . . [tree] of friendship may grow up to a great height and then we shall be a powerful people" (O'Callaghan, 1855, 6:869–884).

DeLancey replied to Hendrick's speech using Iroquois metaphors: "I hope that by this present Union, we shall grow up to a great height and then we shall be as powerful and famous as you were of old" (O'Callagahan, 1855, 6:884).

Hendrick followed that admonition with an analysis of Iroquois and colonial unity, when he said, "We the United Nations shall rejoice of our strength...and...we have now made so strong a Confederacy" (Colonial Records of Pennsylvania, 1851, 98). Benjamin Franklin was commissioned to compose the final draft of the Albany Plan the same day.

Franklin's Albany Plan of Union included a Grand Council and a Speaker and called for a "general government...under which...each colony may retain its present constitution" (Labaree, 1962, 5:387–392). The plan also included an English-style chief administrator. Although representation on the Iroquois Grand Council was determined by custom, the number of delegates that each colony would have had on Franklin's council was to be determined by each colony's proportional tax revenues. In 1943, after editing Franklin's Indian treaties, Julian P. Boyd stated that Benjamin Franklin in 1754 "proposed a plan for union of the colonies and he found his materials in the great confederacy of the Iroquois." Boyd also believed that the ability of the Iroquois to unite peoples over a large geographic expanse made their form of government "worthy of copying" (Boyd, 1942, 239, 246).

THE BOSTON TEA PARTY'S "MOHAWKS"

Few events of the revolutionary era have been engraved on America's popular memory like the Boston Tea Party. Nearly everyone, regardless of sophistication in matters American and revolutionary, knows that the patriots who dumped tea in Boston Harbor dressed as American Indians—Mohawks, specifically. Regarding why the tea dumpers chose this particular form of disguise, we are historiographically less fortunate. Judging by the dearth of commentary on the matter, one might conclude that it was chosen out of sheer convenience, as if Paul Revere and a gaggle of late-eighteenth century "party animals" had stopped by a costume shop on their way to the wharf and found the Mohawk model was the only one available in quantity on short notice.

Boston's patriots were hardly so indiscriminate. The Tea Party was a form of symbolic protest—one step beyond random violence, one step short of organized, armed rebellion. The tea dumpers chose their symbols with utmost care. As the imported tea symbolized British tyranny and taxation, so the image of the Indian, and the Mohawk disguise, represented its antithesis: a "trademark" of an emerging American identity and a voice for liberty in a new land. The image of the Indian was figured into the tea dumpers' disguises not only in Boston, but also in cities the length of the Atlantic seaboard. The tea parties were not spur-of-the-moment pranks, but the culmination of a decade of colonial frustration with

British authority. Likewise, the Mohawk symbol was not picked at random. It was used as a revolutionary symbol, counterpoised to the tea tax.

The image of the Indian (particularly the Mohawk) also appears at about the same time, in the same context, in revolutionary songs, slogans, and engravings. Paul Revere, whose "midnight rides" became legendary through the poems of Henry Wadsworth Longfellow, played a crucial role in forging this sense of identity, contributing to the revolutionary cause a set of remarkable engravings that cast an American Indian woman as America's first national symbol, long before Brother Jonathan or Uncle Sam.

The colonists used the American Indian as a national symbol in their earliest protests of war taxes. In an engraving titled "The Great Financier, or British Economy for the Years 1763, 1764 and 1765," George Grenville, first Lord of the Admiralty, held a balance, while a subordinate loaded it with rubbish. Lord William Pitt, the prime minister, leaned on a crutch at one side as an Indian, representing the colonies, and groaned, on one knee, under the burden of royal taxes. In this early engraving, America was shown enduring the load, but within a dozen years, the same symbol assumed a more aggressive stance, pointing arrows on taut bows at the hearts of their oppressors, a prelude to armed insurrection by the colonists themselves.

Before the tea parties, the Sons of Liberty, of which Paul Revere was one of the earliest members, advertised its intentions in handbills. One was titled "Mohawk Tea Proclamation," purportedly the work of "Abrant Kanakartophqua, chief sachem of the Mohawks, King of the Six Nations and Lord of all Their Castles." The broadside asserted that tea is "an Indian plant . . . and of right belongs to Indians of every land and tribe." It urged "Indians" to abstain from the "ruinous Liquor Rum, which they [the British] have poured down our throats, to steal away our Brains." The "Mohawk Tea Proclamation" concluded that British tea should be "poured into the Lakes," and that any true American should be able to break addictions to European beverages in favor of pure, cold American water (Goss, 1972, 123–124).

While they emptied British tea into Boston Harbor, those posing as Mohawks sang the following:

> Rally Mohawks, and bring your axes
> And tell King George we'll pay no taxes
> on his foreign tea;
> His threats are vain, and vain to think
> To force our girls and wives to drink
> his vile Bohea!
> Then rally, boys, and hasten on
> To meet our chiefs at the Green Dragon!
> Our Warren's here, and bold Revere
> With hands to do and words to cheer,
> for liberty and laws;

Our country's "braves" and firm defenders
Shall ne'er be left by true North Enders
   fighting freedom's cause!
Then rally, boys, and hasten on
To meet our chiefs at the Green Dragon
   —Goss, 1972, 123–124

Between the Boston Tea Party and his most famous midnight ride on April 18, 1775, Paul Revere created a remarkable series of engravings akin to modern political cartoons. The engravings were meant to galvanize public opinion against the British. Many of them used the Indian (usually a woman) as a symbol of independent American identity, much as the Mohawk disguise had been used in the Tea Party, which Revere also helped to plan and execute.

Revere's engravings that used an Indian woman as a patriotic symbol often were sharply political. One of them, "The Able Doctor, or America Swallowing the Bitter Draught," portrayed an Indian woman (symbolic of America being held down by British officials) forced to drink "the vile Bohea." Lord Mansfield, in a wig and judicial robe, held America down as Lord North, with the Port Act in his pocket, poured tea down her throat. Lord Sandwich occupied his time peering under "America's" skirt as Lord Bute stood by with a sword inscribed "Military Law." The bystanders (Spain and France) considered aid for the colonies. In the background, Boston's skyline is labeled "cannonaded." A petition of grievances was shredded in the foreground, symbolic of the British government's failure to provide justice for America (Grinde and Johansen, 1991, 128).

Revere was not the only artist to use Native images as symbols of liberty during the revolutionary period. About the same time that Revere contributed political engravings to the *Royal American Magazine*, another artist was using the same ideas in Philadelphia. This engraving is believed to have been the work of Henry Dawkins. Again, patriots are represented as Indians. Instead of shouldering Britain's burdens as they had a dozen years earlier, these Indians, drawn on the eve of the Declaration of Independence, aimed their arrows across the Atlantic Ocean straight at Lord North's heart. British officials lined the English shore, discussing the tea crisis and related events. On the North American side, Tories did the same, dressed in European garb, unlike the newly aggressive "Indians" (Grinde and Johansen, 1991, 132).

An anonymous engraving created at the beginning of the Revolutionary War in 1776 pitted "The Female Combatants"—an Englishwoman under an enormous beehive hairdo—against America, an Indian woman. The English woman said: "I'll force you to Obedience, you Rebellious Slut," to which America replied: "Liberty, Liberty forever, Mother, while I exist" (Grinde and Johansen, 1991, 134).

THE IROQUOIS AND THE DEBATE OVER INDEPENDENCE

After the Albany Plan failed to receive colonial approval, British attempts to raise taxes following the war with France spurred talk of colonial union again. During the Stamp Act crisis, the New York City Sons of Liberty sent wampum belts to the Iroquois asking them to intercept British troops moving down the Hudson to occupy New York City. After this appeal, the Sons of Liberty put up a "pine post... called... the Tree of Liberty" where they conducted their daily exercises (*Journals*, 1868, 14:357, 367–368).

As symbolic protest turned to armed rebellion against England, delegates of the Continental Congress met with Iroquois leaders at several points along the frontier to procure their alliance in the coming war for independence. At Cartwright's Tavern in German Flats, near Albany, New York, on August 25, 1775, treaty commissioners met with the sachems and warriors of the Six Nations. The commissioners (acting on instructions from John Hancock and the Second Continental Congress) told the sachems that they were heeding the advice Iroquois forefathers had given to the colonial Americans at Lancaster, Pennsylvania, in 1744, as they quoted Canassatego's words:

> Brethren, We the Six Nations heartily recommend Union and a good agreement between you our Brethren, never disagree but preserve a strict Friendship for one another and thereby you as well as we will become stronger. Our Wise Forefathers established Union and Amity between the Five Nations....We are a powerful Confederacy, and if you observe the same methods... you will acquire fresh strength and power. (*Proceedings*, 1775, no page).

After quoting Canassatego, the Americans said their forefathers had rejoiced to hear his words and that they had

> sunken deep into their Hearts, the Advice was good, it was Kind. They said to one another, the Six Nations are a wise people, let us hearken to their Council and teach our children to follow it. Our old Men have done so. They have frequently taken a single Arrow and said, Children, see how easy it is broken, then they have tied twelve together with strong Cords—And our strongest Men could not break them—See said they—this is what the Six Nations mean. Divided a single Man may destroy you—United, you are a match for the whole World. (*Proceedings*, 1775, no page)

The delegates of the Continental Congress then thanked the "great God that we are all united, that we have a strong Confederacy composed of twelve Provinces." The delegates also pointed out that they have "lighted a Great Council Fire at Philadelphia and have sent Sixty five Counselors to speak and act in the name of the whole." The treaty commissioners also invited the Iroquois to visit and observe our "Great Council Fire at Philadelphia" (*Proceedings*, 1775, no page).

NATIVE AMERICAN POLITICAL SYSTEMS AND THE THOUGHTS OF FRANKLIN, JEFFERSON, AND PAINE

As Americans, and as revolutionaries who believed in the universal moral sense of all peoples, Benjamin Franklin, Thomas Jefferson, and Thomas Paine bristled at suggestions that nature had dealt the New World an inferior hand. Under the guise of science, so-called degeneracy theories had gained some currency in Europe during the late eighteenth century. This particular school of pseudoscience was pressed into service as a justification for colonialism in much the same way that craniology (which linked intelligence to the volume of a race's skulls) would be a century later.

Jefferson wrote *Notes on the State of Virginia* ([1784] 1955) partially to refute assertions of France's Comte de Buffon, among others, that the very soil, water, and air of the New World caused plants and animals (including human beings) to grow less robustly and enjoy less sexual ardor than their Old World counterparts. The ongoing debate over the innate intelligence of American Indians also was factored into this debate, with France's Count de Buffon and compatriots asserting inferiority. Franklin and Jefferson took the lead in countering the degeneracy theorists, maintaining that Native peoples of America enjoyed mental abilities equal to those of Europeans. In *Notes on Virginia*, Jefferson used the eloquent speech of Logan (delivered after whites had massacred his family) as evidence that American Indians were not lacking intelligence and compassion.

While serving as ambassador to France, Jefferson was fond of describing a dinner attended by Franklin, a few other Americans, and French degeneracy theory advocates while Franklin was representing the new United States there. Franklin listened to Abbe Raynal, a well-known proponent of American degeneracy, describe how even Europeans would be stunted by exposure to the New World. Franklin listened quietly, then simply asked the French to test their theory "by the fact before us. Let both parties rise," Franklin challenged, "and we shall see on which side nature has degenerated." The table became a metaphorical Atlantic Ocean. The Americans, on their feet, towered over the French. "[The] Abbe, himself particularly, was a mere shrimp," Jefferson smirked (Boorstin, 1948, 307).

In a letter to John Adams, Jefferson pointed out that, as a child and as a student, he was in frequent contact with Native Americans:

Concerning Indians, in the early part of my life, I was very familiar, and acquired impressions of attachment and commiseration for them which have never been obliterated. Before the Revolution, they were in the habit of coming often and in great numbers to the seat of government, *where I was very much with them.* I knew much the great Ontassete, the warrior and orator of the Cherokees; he was always the guest of my father, on his journey's to and from Williamsburg. (Bergh, 1903–1904, 11:160, emphasis added)

Thomas Jefferson. (Courtesy of the Library of Congress.)

A few months before the Constitutional Convention, Jefferson wrote John Madison about the virtues of American Indian government. "Societies . . . as among our Indians . . . [may be] . . . best. But I believe [them] . . . inconsistent with any great degree of population" (Boyd, 1950, 11:92–93).

While Jefferson, Franklin, and Paine were too pragmatic to believe they could copy the "natural state," ideas based on their observations of Native societies were woven into the fabric of the American Revolution early and prominently. Jefferson wrote: "The only condition on earth to be compared with ours, in my opinion, is that of the Indian, where they have still less law than we" (Commager, 1975, 119). When Paine wrote that "government, like dress, is the badge of lost innocence" (1892, 1) and Jefferson said that the best government governs least, they were recapitulating their observations of Native American societies either directly or through the eyes of European philosophers such as Locke and Rousseau. Franklin used his image of Indians and their societies to critique European society:

The Care and Labour of providing for Artificial and fashionable Wants, the sight of so many Rich wallowing in superfluous plenty, while so many are kept poor and distress'd for want; the Insolence of Office ... [and] restraints of Custom, all contrive to disgust them [Indians] with what we call civil Society. (Labaree, 1973, 17:381)

As primary author of the Declaration of Independence and Bill of Rights, Jefferson often wove his perceptions of Native American polities into his conceptions of life, liberty, and happiness. Conversely, Jefferson described the class structure of Europe as hammers pounding anvils, horses mounting riders, and wolves gouging sheep. As a student of government, Jefferson found little ground less fertile than the Europe of his day. The political landscape of England was, to Jefferson, full of things to change, not to emulate.

Jefferson characterized the Native societies he knew in his *Notes on Virginia*. This wording was inserted into the 1787 edition, as the Constitutional Convention was meeting. Native Americans, wrote Jefferson, had never

submitted themselves to any laws, any coercive power and shadow of government. Their only controls are their manners, and the moral sense of right and wrong.... An offence against these is punished by contempt, by exclusion from society, or, where the cause is serious, as that of murder, by the individuals whom it concerns. Imperfect as this species of control may seem, crimes are very rare among them. ([1784] 1955, 93)

The lesson here seemed clear to Jefferson:

Insomuch that it were made a question, whether no law, as among the savage Americans, or too much law, as among the civilized Europeans, submits man to the greater evil, one who has seen both conditions of existence would pronounce it to be the last. (Ford, 1892, 3:195n)

Writing to Edward Carrington during 1787, Jefferson associated freedom of expression with happiness, citing American Indian societies as an example:

The basis of our government being the opinion of the people, our very first object should be to keep that right; and were it left to me to decide whether we should have a government without newspapers or newspapers without a government, I should not hesitate for a moment to prefer the latter.... I am convinced that those societies [as the Indians] which live without government enjoy in their general mass an infinitely greater degree of happiness than those who live under European governments. (Boyd, 1950, 11:49)

To Jefferson, "without government" could not have meant without social order. He, Franklin, and Paine all knew Native American societies too well to argue that their members functioned without social cohesion, in the classic

Noble Savage image, as autonomous wild men of the woods. It was clear that the Iroquois, for example, did not organize a confederacy with alliances spreading over much of northeastern North America without government. They did it, however, with a non-European conception of government, one of which Jefferson, Paine, and Franklin were appreciative students who sought to factor "natural law" and "natural rights" into their designs for the United States during the revolutionary era.

Franklin's Articles of Confederation (1775) resembled the political structure of the Iroquois and other native nations that bordered the thirteen colonies. This resemblance included the language Franklin used when he called the proposed confederacy "a firm league of friendship." The new states retained powers similar to those of the individual tribes and nations within many native confederacies; local problems were to be solved by the local unit of government best suited to their nature, size, and scope; national problems, such as diplomacy and defense, were to be handled by the national government. This notion of "federalism" was very novel to European eyes at that time.

THE TAMMANY SOCIETY'S INFLUENCE

By 1786, the Tammany Society had become a major factor in American politics in its birthplace, Philadelphia, as well as in many other cities along the eastern seaboard. In April 1786, the Tammany Society welcomed Cornplanter and five other Seneca leaders to Philadelphia. In an impressive ceremony, Tammany Society leaders escorted the Senecas from their lodgings at the Indian Queen Tavern to Tammany's wigwam on the banks of the Schuylkill River for a conference on governmental unity.

A few days after his address to the Tammany Society, Cornplanter and the Senecas traveled to New York City to address the national government. Echoing his concern for the nature of American government and unity, Cornplanter stated the following:

> Brothers of the Thirteen Fires, I am glad to see you. It gives me pleasure to see you meet in council to consult about public affairs. May the Great Spirit above direct you in such measures as are good. I wish to put the chunks together to make the Thirteen Fires burn brighter. (*Virginia Gazette*, 1786, no page)

DISCUSSION OF NATIVE GOVERNANCE IN JOHN ADAMS'S DEFENCE OF THE CONSTITUTIONS

Sensing the need for an analysis of American and world governments, John Adams wrote his *Defence of the Constitutions ... of the United States* in 1786 and published it in 1787 on the eve of the Constitutional Convention. The *Defence* has been called "the finest fruit of the American Enlightenment" (Wood, 1969, 568). Adams saw two conflicting views on the nature of government in America on that eve. He recognized in Franklin's admonitions of a unicameral legislature (as in the Pennsylvania Constitution of 1776) a sense of serenity of character because the Pennsylvania Constitution placed a great deal of faith in one house as the best way to express the will of the people. However, Adams believed in a kind of intellectual perpetual motion in which balancing the interests of the aristocracy and the common people through a divided or "complex" government seemed the best course to avoid anarchy and tyranny.

The *Defence*, which was used extensively at the Constitutional Convention, examined the strengths and weaknesses of ancient and modern forms of government, including an analysis of American Indian traditions. Rather than having faith, as Franklin did, in the voice of the people, Adams was more pessimistic about human nature and all orders of society in his *Defence*. He believed that separation of powers in government was crucial to maintain a republic. Adams remarked that in Native American governments, the "real sovereignty resided in the body of the people." Adams also observed that personal liberty was so important to the Mohawks that in their society they have "complete individual independence" (Charles F. Adams, 1851, 4:511).

Drawing on his knowledge and experience with American Indians, Adams's *Defence* urged the founders at the Constitutional Convention to investigate "the government of . . . modern Indians" because the separation of powers in their three branches of government is marked with a precision "that excludes all controversy" (Charles F. Adams, 1851, 4:296, 4:298, 511, 566–567). Adams wrote that a Native American sachem is elected for life and lesser "sachems are his ordinary council." In this ordinary council, all "national affairs are deliberated and resolved" except declaring war when the "sachems call a national assembly round a great council fire." At this council, the sachems "communicate to the people their resolution, and sacrifice an animal." No doubt, the animal sacrifice is a reference to the White Dog Ceremony of the Iroquois. Adams further described Iroquois custom when he stated that "The people who approve the war . . . throw the hatchet into a tree" and then "join in the subsequent war songs and dances." Adams also exhibited an understanding of the voluntary nature of Iroquois warfare when he asserted that those who do disapprove of the decision to go to war "take no part in the sacrifice, but retire" (ibid., 4:511, 566–567).

Adams' *Defence* was not an unabashed endorsement of Native American models for government. Instead, Adams was refuting the arguments of Franklin, who advocated a one-house legislature resembling the Iroquois Grand Council that had been used in the Albany Plan and Articles of Confederation. Adams did not trust the consensus model that seemed to work for the Iroquois. Adams believed that without the checks and balances built into two houses, the system would succumb to special interests and dissolve into anarchy or despotism. When Adams described the Mohawks' independence, he exercised criticism; Franklin wrote about Indian governments in a much more benign way.

Adams sought to erect checks on the caprice of the unthinking heart. Thus, he cited the Iroquois Grand Council (the fifty families) as a negative example, ignoring the fact (as Franklin had written to his printing partner James Parker in 1751) that it "has subsisted for ages" (Smyth, 1905–1907, 3:42). Franklin was more of a utopian: He still sought a government based on the best in human nature, calling its citizens to rise to it. He did not fear unrestrained freedom as did Adams. During the convention, Franklin, according to James Madison's notes, argued that "We shd. not depress the virtue & public spirit of our common people.... He did not think the elected had any right in any case to narrow the privileges of the electors" (Grinde and Johansen, 1991, 204). A consensus in the United States, having tasted revolution and near-anarchy under the Articles of Confederation, seemed ready in 1787 to agree with Adams, whose advocacy of two houses prevailed over Franklin's uni-cameral model. Still, the example of Native liberty exerted a telling pull on the national soul, and conceptions of Native America played an important role in these debates. The fact that Adams repeatedly called on Native imagery even in opposition to its use is evidence of how widely these ideas were discussed.

FURTHER READING

Adams, Charles F. *Works of John Adams*. Boston: Little-Brown, 1851.

Adams, John. *Defence of the Constitutions . . . of the United States*. Philadelphia: Hall and Sellers, 1787.

Bergh, Albert E., ed. *The Writings of Thomas Jefferson*. Vol. 11. Washington, DC: Jefferson Memorial Association, 1904.

Bigelow, John, ed. *Autobiography of Benjamin Franklin*. Philadelphia: J. B. Lippincott, 1868.

Boorstin, Daniel J. *The Lost World of Thomas Jefferson*. New York: Henry Holt, 1948.

Boyd, Julian P., ed. *The Papers of Thomas Jefferson*. Vol. 11. Princeton, NJ: Princeton University Press, 1955.

Boyd, Julian. Dr. Franklin, Friend of the Indian. In Ray Lokken Jr., ed. *Meet Dr. Franklin*. Philadelphia: Franklin Institute, 1981.

Butterfield, Lyman H., ed. *The Diary and Autobiography of John Adams*. Cambridge, MA: Harvard University Press, 1961.

Colden, Cadwallader. *The History of the Five Nations Depending on the Province of New York in America*. Ithaca, NY: Cornell University Press, [1727, 1747] 1958.

Colonial Records of Pennsylvania. Vol. 6. Harrisburg, PA: Theo. Penn & Co., 1851.

Commager, Henry Steele. *Jefferson, Nationalism and the Enlightenment*. New York: Braziller, 1975.

Crevecoeur, Hector St. Jean de. *Letters from an American Farmer*. New York: Dutton, 1926.

Crevecoeur, Hector St. John de. *Journey into Northern Pennsylvania and the State of New York* [in French]. Ann Arbor: University of Michigan Press, [1801] 1964.

Ford, Paul L., ed. *The Writings of Thomas Jefferson*. Vol. 3. New York: Putnam, 1892–1899.

Goss, Eldridge Henry. *The Life of Colonel Paul Revere*. Boston: Hall/Gregg Press, 1972.

Grinde, Donald A., Jr., and Bruce E. Johansen. *Exemplar of Liberty: Native America and the Evolution of Democracy*. Los Angeles: UCLA American Indian Studies Center, 1991.

Howard, Helen A. Hiawatha: Co-founder of an Indian United Nations. *Journal of the West* 10:3(1971):428–438.

Jacobs, Wilbur R. *Wilderness Politics and Indian Gifts*. Lincoln: University of Nebraska Press, 1966.

Jefferson, Thomas. *Notes on the State of Virginia*. Edited by Willam Peden. Chapel Hill: University of North Carolina Press, [1784] 1955.

Johansen, Bruce E. *Forgotten Founders: How the Iroquois Helped Shape Democracy*. Boston: Harvard Common Press, [1982] 1987.

Journals of Captain John Montresor, 1757–1778, 2nd set, Vol. 14. April 4, 1766, Collections of the New York Historical Society. New York: Printed for the Society, 1868–1949.

Labaree, Leonard W., ed. *The Papers of Benjamin Franklin*. Vol. 4. New Haven, CT: Yale University Press, 1961.

Mr. Penn's Plan for a Union of the Colonies in America, February 8, 1697. In E. B. O'Callaghan, ed., *Documents Relative to the Colonial History of New York*. Vol. 4. Albany: Weed, Parsons, 1853–1887.

O'Callagahan, E. B., ed. *Documentary History of the State of New York*. Vol. 1. Albany: Weed, Parsons, 1849.

O'Callaghan, E. B., ed. *Documents Relative to the Colonial History of New York*. Vols. 4, 6. Albany: Weed, Parsons, 1853–1887.

Paine, Thomas. *The Political Writings of Thomas Paine*. New York: Peter Eckler, 1892.

Proceedings of the Commissioners Appointed by the Continental Congress to Negotiate a Treaty with the Six Nations, 1775. Papers of the Continental Congress, 1774–89, National Archives (M247, Roll 144, Item No. 134). See "Treaty Council at German Flats, New York, August 15, 1775," unpaginated.

Smyth, Albert H., ed. *The Writings of Benjamin Franklin*. Vol. 3. New York: Macmillan, 1905–1907.

Van Doren, Carl, and Julian P. Boyd, eds. *Indian Treaties Printed by Benjamin Franklin 1736–1762*. Philadelphia: Historical Society of Pennsylvania, 1938.

Virginia Gazette, May 24, 1786, no page. Cited in Grinde and Johansen, 1991, 184.

Wallace, Paul A. W. *The White Roots of Peace*. Philadelphia: University of Pennsylvania Press, 1946.

William Penn to the Society of Free Traders, August 16, 1683. In Richard S. and Mary M. Dunn, eds., *The Papers of William Penn*. Vol. 2. Philadelphia: University of Pennsylvania Press, 1982.

Wood, Gordon S. *The Creation of the American Republic*. Chapel Hill: University of North Carolina, 1969.

CHAPTER 5

The Explosion Westward

THE ACCELERATING SPEED OF FRONTIER MOVEMENT

By 300 years after Columbus' first voyage, most of America north of the Rio Grande in 1792 was under claim by the new United States, Britain, France, and Spain. Most of the same area was still primarily occupied by Native American peoples. The edicts of European treaty making said that the United States extended westward to the east bank of the Mississippi River. In another decade, its European-issued title would extend, via the Louisiana Purchase, to the Rocky Mountains.

In reality, however, only the eastern seaboard was thickly settled by descendants of Europeans in 1792. The territory to the west was home to sparse settlements, a few mountain men, some traders, and a few soldiers in a few small forts. The main day-to-day U.S. diplomatic activity in 1792 was maintaining relationships with the many Native nations that still lived on lands they knew as theirs. At the same time, a thin ribbon of French trading and military activity followed the St. Lawrence River to the Great Lakes, then followed the Mississippi to New Orleans. Most of the present-day western United States south of the Oregon and Wyoming borders was claimed by a disintegrating Spanish Empire, which was no longer able to sustain its far-flung mission, military, and mining outposts.

Three centuries into America's discovery by Europe, many Native American peoples had yet to be touched significantly by European American migration. Others had adopted European animals (such as the horse), guns, and other trade goods. A majority still swore no allegiance to any European power or the United States of America. Within the space of one century, however, the frontier would leap from the East Coast to the West Coast, meanwhile also occupying the inland west and Great Plains. By 1892, very few of North America's surviving Native peoples would be able to say that they lived independently as their great-grandfathers and great-grandmothers had barely two or three generations earlier.

In one century, sped by a massive increase in immigration from Europe and technological change (most notably the arrival of transcontinental railroads) as well as the ravages of imported diseases, Native American free space in the contemporary United States (south of Alaska) shrank to nearly nothing. By the time of the massacre at Wounded Knee at the end of 1890, North Americas' Native peoples would be living mainly on reservations controlled by the U.S. government or in its rapidly growing cities. North America was about to witness the most rapid surge of humanity in the history of the human race. By the turn of the century, the non-Indian population of the U.S. portions of the Mississippi Valley had risen to 377,000. By 1830, the non-Indian population of the same area was roughly 900,000.

During the first two centuries of English-dominated settlement along the Atlantic seaboard, the settlement frontier barely reached the foothills of the Appalachian Mountains. Following the turn of the century, however, a tide of humanity spilled across the mountains into the rich bottomlands of the Mississippi, the fertile valley of the Ohio, northward, and westward. From 1830 to 1890, three human generations, the Anglo-American frontier advanced from the woods of Georgia with passage of the Removal Act, to California with the gold rush of 1849, and inland again to the prairies of South Dakota. In 1890, the U.S. census declared the frontier closed. Benjamin Franklin once conjectured that North America would not fill with the offspring of Europe for at least a thousand years, a risky prediction because he did not even exactly know the size of the continent. He missed the date the continent would fill with the progeny of Europe by roughly 900 years.

The nineteenth century is usually justly and correctly characterized as a time of exploding westward movement by European Americans. The same century, however, also provided many examples of shaping of the immigrants by Native American peoples and their culture. American feminism's founding mothers drew from the Iroquois matrilineal society as Frederick Engels's esteemed American Native peoples as examples of a possible future society without economic classes (see chapter 10). The poet Walt Whitman, writing to the Santa Fe City Council during 1883, advised:

> As to our aboriginal or Indian population . . . I know it seems to be agreed that they must gradually dwindle as time rolls on, and in a few generations more leave only a reminiscence, a blank. But I am not at all clear about that. As America . . . develops, adapts, entwines, faithfully identifies its own—are we to see it cheerfully accepting using all the contributions of foreign lands from the whole outside globe—and then rejecting the only ones distinctively its own? (Moquin, 1973, 5–6)

SACAJAWEA GUIDES LEWIS AND CLARK

The nineteenth century opened with the U.S. purchase of the Louisiana Territory from France, which quickly nearly doubled the country's size, at least on paper. A few months later, President Jefferson sent Meriwether Lewis and William Clark to survey that area and to reach the Pacific Ocean. They were led much of the way by Sacajawea (Bird Woman, Shoshoni, born ca. 1784; death dates vary widely). For nineteen months, Sacajawea guided Lewis and Clark over the Rocky Mountains toward the Pacific Coast near present-day Astoria, Oregon. Without her, the expedition probably would have halted for lack of direction. She also guaranteed friendly relations with Native peoples along the way.

Little was known of Sacajawea by whites other than Lewis and Clark until 1811, when she and her French-Canadian husband Toussaint Charbonneau traveled to St. Louis, site of Clark's office as a regional superintendent of Indian affairs. Sacajawea and her husband were visiting St. Louis to accept an offer by Clark to educate their son "Pomp," of whom Clark had become fond during the expedition. Clark's papers noted that Sacajawea died shortly after that visit, but some argue that Sacajawea returned to the Shoshonis and lived to be almost 100 years old. The source of the confusion seems to be the fact that Charbonneau (unknown to Clark) had two Shoshoni wives. An argument has been made that the wife who died was not Sacajawea, but Otter Woman, his other wife. Various historians cite accounts of Sacajawea into old age; others assert that Clark knew Sacajawea well enough not to mistake her for another woman.

ATTEMPTS AT NATIVE CONFEDERATION IN THE "OLD NORTHWEST"

As Euro-American immigration began to explode across the Appalachians into the Ohio Valley and Great Lakes shortly after 1790, Native resistance expressed itself in attempts at confederation along lines of mutual interest. Movements of this kind occupied the better part of a century, from Pontiac (during the eighteenth century), to Black Hawk during the 1830s, with the legendary Little Turtle and Tecumseh in between.

Frank Waters characterized Pontiac (Ponteach, Ottawa, ca. 1720–1769) as "a man of steel pounded between a British hammer and a French anvil" (Waters, 1993, 35). Pontiac, after whom General Motors named a long-lived automobile model, tried to erect a Native confederacy that would block Euro-American immigration into the "Old Northwest." Pontiac was a man of medium build and dark complexion who highly valued personal fidelity. If Pontiac owed a debt, he would scratch a promissory note on birch bark with his sign, the otter. The notes always were redeemed. He was an early ally of the French in 1755, at Fort Duquesne, now the site of Pittsburgh, along with an allied force of Ottawas, Ojibwas, Hurons, and Delawares. Pontiac also played a major role in the French defeat of English General Braddock in 1755 during the opening battles of what came to be known as the French and Indian War.

Pontiac was probably born along the Maumee River in northern Ohio of an Ottawa father and a Chippewa mother. He married Kantuckeegan and had two sons, Otussa and Shegenaba. Pontiac held no hereditary chieftainship among the Ottawas, but by about 1760 his oratorical skills and courage as a warrior had raised him to leadership. By 1763, Pontiac also had formed military alliances with eighteen other Native peoples from the Mississippi River to Lake Ontario.

After the British defeat of the French in 1763, Pontiac found himself faced on the southern shore of Lake Erie with an English force that included Robert Rogers's legendary Rangers, who were self-trained as forest warriors. Rogers told Pontiac that the land his people occupied was now under British ownership, having been ceded by France, and that Rogers's Rangers were taking possession of French forts. Pontiac said that although the French might have surrendered, his people had not. After four days of negotiations, Rogers agreed with Pontiac's point of view. Rogers was allowed to continue to the former French fort on the present-day site of Detroit. Power was transferred as hundreds of Indians watched. Rogers and Pontiac became friends.

Pontiac now looked forward to peaceful trade with the British, but Rogers left the area, and fur traders began swindling the Indians, getting many of them addicted to cheap liquor. Pontiac sent a belt of red wampum, signifying the taking up of arms as far eastward as the Iroquois Confederacy, then southward along the Mississippi. He appealed for alliance, telling assembled chiefs of each nation he visited that if they did not unify and resist colonization, English immigrants would flood their lands, like waves of an endless sea.

By the spring of 1763, a general uprising was being planned by the combined forces of the Ottawa, Wyandot (Huron), Delaware, Seneca, and Shawnee. According to plans, on May 9 each constituent of the alliance was to attack the closest English fort. Pontiac's plan was betrayed to the commander of the British fort at Detroit by an Ojibwa woman named Catherine, to whom the officer had made love. Pontiac laid siege to the fort at Detroit as other members of the alliance carried out their respective roles, but an appeal to the French for assistance was ignored. After a siege that lasted through the winter and into the spring of 1764, the fort received outside reinforcements, tipping the balance against Pontiac after fifteen months.

After the rebellion, European American immigrants swarmed into the Ohio Valley in increasing numbers. Pontiac now counseled peace. The younger warriors were said to have "shamed" him and possibly beat him in their frustration. With a small band of family and friends, Pontiac was forced to leave his home village and move to Illinois. On April 20, 1769, Pontiac was murdered in Cahokia. According to one account, he was stabbed by a Peoria Indian who may have been bribed with a barrel of whiskey by an English trader named Williamson.

~

The Goschochking (Ohio) Genocide, March 8, 1782

Barbara A. Mann

Goschochking (Gnadenhütten) was the site of the most brutal of the many genocides against Native American peoples in Ohio during the eighteenth and nineteenth centuries. It was conducted in 1782 by the Pennsylvania militia, 160 strong, commanded by Colonel David Williamson, who was acting under the authority of General George Washington.

The militia murdered 96 League Delaware-Mahicans in Gnadenhütten, a Moravian "praying town" within the territory of Goschochking, the Delaware capitol in Ohio. Another 30 Delaware-Mahicans taken prisoner during Williamson's hasty retreat to Fort Pitt were murdered along the way to silence everyone with any knowledge of the war crime. Despite the militia's attempt to eliminate all witnesses, some escaped: a young man who witnessed the opening fire and two adolescent boys who fled Gnadenhütten in the midst of the murders.

The Revolutionary War was fought on two fronts, along the Atlantic seacoast and on the league lands. To break the back of the league, General George Washington devised a plan to starve it out, ordering the destruction of New York's rich farmlands in 1779, following that up in 1781 (as soon as he could penetrate Ohio) by ordering his commander at Fort Pitt, Colonel Daniel Brodhead, to destroy Goschochking, a task he finally accomplished in 1782. Goschochking was actually a trio of League-Delaware towns (one for each Delaware clan). It lay along the Muskingum River, which had bottomlands that were quite fertile. For two years after the ravaging of the league's breadbaskets in New York, Goschochking had been sharing its harvests with the hungry leaguers of New York.

As part of his campaign, Brodhead was ordered to kill the league Delaware-Mahicans entirely. Learning of this plan, the league ordered the hasty removal of the Delaware-Mahicans from the Muskingum valley to the league Wyandot capitol at Upper Sandusky, in well-defended territory. Accordingly, from September 2–4, 1781, the Wyandots under Katepakomen (Simon Girty) and the Delaware under Hopocan (Captain Pipe) secretly escorted the entire Delaware-Mahican nation to safety, thwarting the planned genocide for the time being.

The removal to Upper Sandusky was accomplished over the objections of the tiny faction of Delaware-Mahicans who had converted to the Moravian sect of Christianity. They believed themselves to be safe from the Americans because they were Christians and because the Moravian missionary John Heckewelder was an important spy against the league for General Washington. The league had better information, however, and knew that the Moravian Delaware-Mahicans were meant to have been killed along with all the rest.

The winter in Upper Sandusky was hungry, although safe from attack, because the Wyandot also had been dependent on the Muskingum harvest. Unable to transport their harvest—a rich one in 1781—during their hasty withdrawal from Goschochking, the Delaware-Mahicans had buried it to prevent the American forces from looting. Thus, when Brodhead finally attacked Goschochking, he found both the people and the harvest gone. Burning the deserted towns, he returned to Fort Pitt empty-handed.

By midwinter, the league peoples had been reduced to walking skeletons, many dying during 1781 and 1782 from starvation. Dangerous though it was for league peoples to venture back to Goschochking, now easily struck by forces out of Fort Pitt, the league had no choice. The famine had reached crisis proportions, so the buried food had to be recovered. Still believing themselves safe as neutrals, the Christianized Delaware-Mahicans elected to return to the Muskingum fields as the bulk of the workers recovering the buried harvest. To reinforce the fact that they were a work crew and not a war party, the majority of those going were women and children. Accordingly, 140 Delaware-Mahicans left Upper Sandusky on March 3, 1781, heading back to Goschochking. Heckewelder promptly sent intelligence to Fort Pitt of their movements.

The Revolutionary Army's members, who also were starving (an unintended result of destroying the league fields), had every intention of resupplying themselves by finding and plundering the Muskingum harvest. In a March 8, 1782, memorandum to General William Irvine, the new commander at Fort Pitt, Washington said that he had taken care of the provisioning problem, indicating that Williamson and the Pennsylvania militia had been dispatched to Goschochking anew under his orders (Mann, 1997, 166).

Arriving at Goschochking on March 8, the militia first murdered Shebosh, a leader, an act witnessed by a youth Heckewelder called Jacob. Seeing what was afoot, Jacob instantly fled, his personal terror preventing him from warning anyone else. Next seeking out the bulk of the harvesters at Goschochking, Williamson and his men pretended that they had been piously sent to aid fellow Christians to retrieve their harvest. The militia had also brought along children to play with the Native children, to help lull the harvesters into a sense of well-being. Seeing both the piety of the militia and the presence of settler children as proof that they were indeed safe as Christians, the Delaware-Mahicans even helped Williamson locate all but one of the work crews.

Once the harvest was unearthed, however, the militia dropped its pretense, brutally taking the Delaware-Mahicans prisoner, shooting two young children. The militia then confined its prisoners in two huts at Gnadenhütten, the men and boys in one, the women and small children in the other. Williamson charged them with being a party of "Warriors" sent to attack the militia. They also charged the Delaware-Mahicans with horse theft. Both were capital crimes of which they were promptly convicted by Williamson's kangaroo court. The harvesters were sentenced to death.

The militia voted to club and scalp the Natives and then set the huts on fire to cover up the evidence of its crimes. Because of the heroics of the women, two children were hidden in a root cellar below the floorboards of the women's prison, but only one boy thereafter avoided death by smoke inhalation, escaping through a narrow vent to the outside. Unnamed by Heckewelder (because he was not a Christian convert), the boy later recalled that, as he lay on his back in the crawl space, the blood from the murdered women fell so profusely through the floorboards that he feared being drowned in it.

In the men's hut, an adolescent boy (called Thomas by the missionaries) escaped by lying among the stacked bodies, playing dead, and then stealing out inches behind the armed guards, just before the hut was set afire. These two eyewitnesses to the crimes made it back to Upper Sandusky, their stories recorded by a remorseful Heckewelder in "Captivity and Murder" (1971) and again in his *Narrative* ([1818] 1971). On the way back to Fort Pitt, the militia took thirty more league Delawares captive, murdering them all along the way. No one escaped this second massacre (P. A. W. Wallace, 1958, 197; Butterfield, 1890, 30).

When Katepakomen unmasked Heckewelder's treachery in a fraught public scene at Upper Sandusky, Weshkahattees, a young Delaware, raced to Goschochking to rescue his relatives, arriving March 8. At Welhik-Tuppeek (a field), he found a small group of harvesters not discovered by Williamson. As the militia celebrated its kill into the evening, Weshkahattees stole into Gnadenhütten, floating away a canoe from under the eyes of the armed guards, and in several trips silently ferried the survivors across the Muskingum, "west of death." With children and old folks on their backs, the party ran all the way back to Upper Sandusky, a night-long journey. On unloading the morning of March 9, they discovered that during their desperate flight, one child had died of hunger on its mother's back (Mann, 1997, 180–181).

The militia stole not only the harvest, but also 80 pack animals, furs, equipment, and the personal possessions of their victims (Marsh, 1967, 10; Mann, 1997, 222). Plundered items later sold by militiamen for personal profit at Pittsburgh also included "souvenir" shaving strops made from the skins of Delaware-Mahicans (Heckewelder [1820, 1876] 1971, 342), indicating the fate of the thirty who had been murdered on the way back to Fort Pitt.

In a deceitful report printed in the *Philadelphia Gazette*, Williamson boasted of the genocide as a great victory in battle, presenting the harvesters as warriors and their goods, as "provisions to supply their war parties" ("Notice," 1782). Aware of the truth, Heckewelder spent the rest of his life atoning for what he had done. He went on a campaign to set the record straight, later recording that he was "ashamed of being a *white man*" (italics in the original; Heckewelder, [1820, 1876] 1971, 76). Heckewelder's most faithful reader, James Fenimore Cooper, later immortalized the phrase "the last of the Mohicans," coined by settlers after the genocide. Though dramatic, it wrongly leaves the impression that all Delaware-Mahicans had perished on March 8, 1782.

After the details of the crime became clear to them, John Bull, the Euro-father of Shebosh, and the Moravians David Zeisberger and John Heckewelder raised a mighty ruckus, calling for justice. A half-hearted inquiry into the matter by Revolutionary officials allowed the Pennsylvania militia to stonewall the investigation (Mann, 1997, 227). No one was ever indicted. In fact, Williamson became a public figure and mayor of Catfish, Pennsylvania (ibid., 220). Washington was pleased enough with him to send him back into Ohio two months later under Colonel William

Little Turtle (Michikinikwa). (Courtesy of Smithsonian National Anthropological Archives.)

Crawford for an unsuccessful follow-up attack on the Delawares during May 1782.

LITTLE TURTLE'S WAR: A NEW ATTEMPT AT NATIVE CONFEDERATION IN THE OHIO VALLEY

A confederation comprising elements of the Shawnees, Delawares, Wyandots, Miamis, and Ottawas told the United States in 1790 that settlers were not to transgress beyond the Ohio River. Thousands of settlers were surging into the area, ignoring governmental edicts from both sides. The settlers, who were squatters in the Indians' eyes, sought military help after members of the Native confederacy began attacking their settlements. Military expeditions were sent into the Ohio country during 1790 and 1792, but the Native confederacy remained unbowed and unmoved. This resistance stiffened after allied Native American forces led by Little Turtle, whose Native name was Michikinikwa (1752–1812), during 1791 inflicted on the U.S. Army, under General Arthur St. Clair, its worst defeat of the Indian wars, measured by the number of troops killed in one battle. The victory was short-lived, however; in 1794, "Mad Anthony" Wayne's forces defeated Little Turtle and his allies at the Battle of Fallen Timbers. On August 3, 1795, by signing the Treaty of Greenville the Indians gave up most of their hunting grounds west of the Ohio River following the defeat.

Little Turtle was known as a master of battlefield strategy. Born as the son of a Miami chief and a Mohican mother, Little Turtle became a war chief of the Miamis because of his extraordinary personal abilities; under ordinary circumstances, the matriarchal nature of the culture would have prohibited a leadership role for him. In 1787, the hunting grounds of the Miamis and their allies had been guaranteed "in perpetuity" by the U.S. Congress. The act did not stop an invasion of immigrants from the east. By the early 1790s, Little Turtle had cemented an alliance that foreshadowed later efforts by Tecumseh, who assembled an alliance of several Native nations a generation later.

Little Turtle's principal allies in this effort were the Shawnee Blue Jacket (Weyapiersenwah) and the Delaware Buckongahelos. This alliance first defeated a 1,000-man force under Josiah Harmar during October 1790. Harmar dispatched an advance force of 180 men, who were drawn into a trap and annihilated. Harmar then dispatched 360 more men to "punish the Indians." They also were drawn into a similar trap, in which about a hundred of them were killed. The remainder of Harmar's force then retreated to Fort Washington, on the present-day site of Cincinnati.

Harmer's defeat stunned the Army, whose commanders knew that the Old Northwest would remain closed to immigrants as long as Little Turtle's alliance held. General Arthur St. Clair, who had served as president of the Continental Congress during the mid-1780s, gathered an army of 2,000 men during the summer of 1791, then marched into the Ohio country. About a quarter of the men deserted en route. To keep the others happy, St. Clair permitted about 200 soldiers' wives to travel with the army. Despite Harmar's defeat, they seemed to have little inkling of what lay in waiting for them.

On November 4, 1791, the Miami/Mohican Little Turtle was one of the principal chiefs among a coalition of Shawnees, Miamis, Delawares, Potawatomis, Ottawas, Chippewas, and Wyandots in the Old Northwest (Ohio country) who defeated St. Clair's army of 1,400 soldiers. Near St. Mary's Creek, a tributary of the Wabash River, about 1,200 warriors rallied by Little Turtle and aided by an element of surprise lured St. Clair's forces into the same sort of trap that had defeated Harmar's smaller force. Thirty-eight officers and 598 enlisted men died in the battle; 242 others were wounded, many of whom later died. Fifty-six wives also lost their lives, bringing the total death toll to about 950, a death toll higher than any inflicted on the United States by the British in any single battle of the American Revolution. The death toll was four times the number sustained by General George Armstrong Custer at the Little Big Horn in 1876. After the battle, St. Clair resigned his commission in disgrace.

Dealing from strength, Little Turtle's alliance refused to surrender land to the United States. In 1794, however, Mad Anthony Wayne was dispatched with a fresh army that revisited the scene of St. Clair's debacle. According to Wayne, "Five hundred skull bones lay in the space of 350 yards. From thence, five miles on, the woods were strewn with skeletons, knapsacks, and other debris" (Johansen and Grinde, 1997, 216). Little Turtle had more respect for Wayne than for Harmar or St. Clair, calling him "the chief who never sleeps" (ibid., 216). Aware that Wayne was unlikely to be defeated by his surprise tactics, Little Turtle proposed that the Indian alliance talk peace. A majority of the warriors rebuffed Little Turtle, so he relinquished his command to Blue Jacket, a Shawnee. The Native coalition under Blue Jacket's leadership was defeated by Wayne at the Battle of Fallen Timbers. Afterward, Blue Jacket signed the Treaty of Greenville (1795) and the Treaty of Fort Industry (1805), ceding millions of acres of Native land.

Little Turtle in 1802 addressed the legislatures of Ohio and Kentucky, urging members to pass laws forbidding the ingress of traders who supplied Indians with whiskey. He said that whiskey traders had "stripped the poor Indian of skins, guns, blankets, everything—while his squaw and the children dependent on him lay starving and shivering in his wigwam" (Johansen and Grinde, 1997, 217). Neither state did anything to stop the flow of whiskey, some of which was adulterated with other substances, from chili peppers to arsenic.

Little Turtle died July 14, 1812, at his lodge near the junction of the St. Joseph River and St. Mary Creek. He was buried with full military honors by Army officers who knew his genius. William Henry Harrison, who had been an aide to Wayne and who later defeated Tecumseh in the same general area, paid Little Turtle this tribute: "'A safe leader is better than a bold one.' This maxim was a great favorite of [the Roman] Caesar Augustus . . . who . . . was, I believe, inferior to the warrior Little Turtle" (Johansen and Grinde, 1997, 217).

For almost two centuries, local historians placed the site of the battle of Fallen Timbers along the Maumee River floodplain near U.S. Highway 24, near present-day Toledo, Ohio. A monument was erected at the site, even as Native Americans contended that the battle had really occurred a mile away in what is today a soybean field. In 1995, to settle the issue, G. Michael Pratt, an anthropology professor at Heidelberg College, Tiffin, Ohio, organized an archeological dig in the soybean field. He organized teams that included as many as 150 people who excavated the site, which yielded large numbers of battlefield artifacts, indicating conclusively that the Native American account of the site was correct.

TECUMSEH'S ALLIANCE

Native resistance surged again shortly after the turn of the century under the aegis of the Shawnee Tecumseh (ca. 1768–1813), which translates as Crouching Tiger. Tecumseh, a major military leader and alliance builder, sought to stop Euro-American expansion into the Ohio valley area early in the nineteenth century, after alliances led by Pontiac and Little Turtle had failed. Tecumseh assembled an alliance that posed the last major obstacle to Anglo-American expansion across the Ohio valley westward.

Tecumseh was born about 1768 near present-day Oldtown, Ohio. He fought, as a young warrior, the battle of Fallen Timbers. Tecumseh's influence grew rapidly as he came of age not only because of his acumen as a statesman and a warrior, but also because he forbade torture of prisoners. Immigrants and Tecumseh's Native American allies trusted Tecumseh implicitly.

Tecumseh was raised from birth to make war on the encroaching European Americans by his mother, Methoataske, whose husband, the Shawnee Puckeshinwa, had been killed in cold blood by immigrants when Tecumseh was a boy. Tecumseh and his mother found him dying. As he watched his father die, Tecumseh vowed to become like "a fire spreading over the hill and valley, consuming the race of dark souls" (Johansen and Grinde, 1997, 383). A few years later, Tecumseh's hatred for the immigrants was compounded by the murder of Cornstalk, a Shawnee chief who had been his mentor.

By the turn of the century, as the number of non-Indian immigrants grew, Tecumseh began to assemble the Shawnees, Delawares, Ottawas, Ojibwas, Kickapoos, and Wyandots into a confederation with the aim of establishing a permanent Native American confederation that would act as a buffer zone between the United States to the east and English Canada to the north. One observer recalled Tecumseh as a commanding speaker. His voice was said to have "resounded over the multitude . . . his words like a succession of thunderbolts" (Johansen and Grinde, 1997, 384).

Rallying Native allies with an appeal for alliance about 1805, Tecumseh urged all Indians in the area to unite as brothers, as sons of one Mother Earth. He scoffed at the idea of selling the land. Why not sell the air? he asked. Sale of land, to Tecumseh, was contrary to the ways of nature. He tried to unite the southern tribes by appealing to history:

Where today are the Pequot? Where are the Narraganset, the Mohican, the Pocanet, and other powerful tribes of our people? They have vanished before the avarice and oppression of the white man, as snow before the summer sun. . . . Will

Tecumseh. (Courtesy of Smithsonian National Anthropological Archives.)

we let ourselves be destroyed in our turn, without an effort worthy of our race? Shall we, without a struggle, give up our homes, our lands, bequeathed to us by the Great Spirit? The graves of our dead and everything that is dear and sacred to us? . . . I know you will say with me, never! Never! (Armstrong, 1984, 45)

Tecumseh told representatives of southern Native nations that they faced extinction:

> Our broad domains are fast escaping from our grasp. Every year our white intruders become more greedy, exacting, oppressive, and overbearing. ... Before the palefaces came among us, we enjoyed the happiness of unbounded freedom, and were acquainted with neither riches, wants, nor oppression. How is it now? Wants and oppression are our lot. ... Dare we move without asking, by your leave. Are we not being stripped, day by day, of the little that remains of our ancient liberty? Do they not even kick and strike us as they do their black-faces? How long will it be before they will tie us to a post and whip us, and make us work for them. ... Shall we wait for that moment or shall we die fighting before submitting to such ignominy? (Johansen and Grinde, 1997, 384)

Territorial Governor (and Army general) William Henry Harrison (who later popularized his battle with Tecumseh at Tippecanoe in his successful campaign for the presidency with the campaign slogan "Tippecanoe and Tyler Too") tried to undermine the growing strength of Tecumseh's Native alliance by negotiating treaties with individual Native nations. Because only a portion of each tribe or nation's warriors elected to follow Tecumseh, Harrison found it easy enough to find "treaty Indians" among those who did not elect to fight. By 1811, Harrison had negotiated at least fifteen treaties, all of which Tecumseh repudiated.

Harrison's wariness of Tecumseh's power sprung from a deep respect for him:

> The implicit obedience and respect which the followers of Tecumseh pay to him is really astonishing and more than any other circumstance bespeaks him [as] one of those uncommon geniuses, which spring up occasionally to produce revolutions and to overturn the established order of things. ... If it were not for the vicinity of the United States, he would, perhaps, be the founder of an Empire that would rival in glory Mexico or Peru. No difficulties deter him. (Hamilton, 1972, 159)

Tecumseh was particularly galled by Harrison's choice as his territorial capital the village of Chillicothe, the same site (with the same name) as the Shawnees' former principal settlement. The name itself is anglicized Shawnee for principal town. At one treaty council, Tecumseh found himself seated next to Harrison on a bench. Tecumseh slowly but aggressively pushed Harrison off the edge of the bench, then told him that this was what the immigrants were doing to his people. They were being slowly squeezed off their lands. During his last conference with Tecumseh, Harrison bid the chief to take a chair. "Your father requests you take a chair," an interpreter told Tecumseh, to which he replied, defiantly: "My father! The sun is my father and the Earth

William Henry Harrison. (Courtesy of the Nebraska State
Historical Society.)

is my mother. I will repose upon her bosom" (Gill, 1987, 14). Tecumseh then
sat, cross-legged, on the ground.

Tecumseh also was angry over Harrison's treaty of September 30, 1809,
with the Delawares, Potawatomies, Miamis, Kickapoos, Wea, and Eel River
peoples. For $8,200 in cash and $2,350 in annuities, Harrison had laid claim
for the United States to roughly 3 million acres of rich hunting land along the
Wabash River in the heart of the area in which Tecumseh wished to build his
Native confederacy. When Tecumseh and his brother, also a Shawnee war
chief, complained to Harrison that the treaty terms were unfair, Harrison at

first rebuked Tecumseh by saying that the Shawnees had not even been part of the treaty. The implicit refusal to recognize Tecumseh's alliance angered the Indians even more. Realizing that Tecumseh's influence made it politic, Harrison agreed to meet with him. At an August 12, 1810, meeting, each side drew up several hundred battle-ready warriors and soldiers. Harrison agreed to relay Tecumseh's complaints to the president, and Tecumseh said that his warriors would join the Americans against the British if Harrison would annul the treaty.

Nothing came of Harrison's promises, and during 1811, bands of warriors allied with Tecumseh began ranging out of the settlement of Tippecanoe to terrorize nearby farmsteads and small backwoods settlements. Harrison said he would wipe out Tippecanoe if the raids did not stop; Tecumseh said they would stop when the land signed away under the 1810 treaty was returned. Tecumseh then journeyed southward to bring the Creeks, Chickasaws, and Choctaws into his alliance. Tecumseh carried the message that he had used to recruit other allies:

> Brothers—When the white men first set foot on our grounds, they were hungry. They had no place on which to spread their blankets, or to kindle their fires. They were feeble; they could do nothing for themselves. Our fathers commiserated with their distress, and shared freely with them whatever the Great Spirit had given his red children. They gave them food when hungry, medicine when sick, spread skins for them to sleep on, and gave them ground so that they might hunt and raise corn. Brothers—the white people are like poisonous serpents: when chilled, they are feeble, and harmless, but invigorate them with warmth, and they sting their benefactors to death. (Johansen and Grinde, 1997, 385–386)

Tecumseh failed, for the most part, to acquire new allies. While Tecumseh was traveling, the command of the existing alliance fell to Tecumseh's brother Tenskwatawa, who was called the Prophet. On September 26, 1811, Harrison decamped at Vincennes with more than 900 men, two-thirds of them Indian allies. He built a fort and named it after himself on the present-day site of Terre Haute, Indiana. Harrison then sent two Miamis to the Prophet to demand the return of property Harrison alleged had been stolen in the raids, along with the surrender of Indians he accused of murder. The Miamis did not return to Harrison's camp. The governor's army marched to within sight of Tippecanoe and met with Tenskwatawa, who invited them to make camp, relax, and negotiate. Harrison's forces did stop, but set up in battle configurations as the Prophet's warriors readied an attack.

Within two hours of pitched battle, Harrison's forces routed the Indians, then burned the village of Tippecanoe as Tenskwatawa's forces scattered into the woods. Returning to the devastation from his travels, Tecumseh fled to British Canada, where, during the War of 1812, he was put in command of a force of whites and Indians as a British brigadier general. Harrison's forces met Tecumseh at the Battle of the Thames in Kentucky. Tecumseh was killed during that battle on October 5, 1813. After it, some of the Kentucky militia who had taken part found a body they thought was Tecumseh's and cut strips from it for souvenirs. His warriors, who had dispersed in panic when Tecumseh died, said later that they had taken his body with them. Having committed 20,000 men and $5 million to the cause, the United States had effectively terminated armed Indian resistance in the Ohio Valley and surrounding areas.

BLACK HAWK'S ALLIANCE

A member of the Thunder Clan of the Sauk Nation, Black Hawk (Makataimeshekiakiak, Sauk, ca. 1770–1838) won renown as a warrior from the time he carried home his first scalp at the age of 15 to his leadership of a Native rebellion that bears his name in the early 1830s.

Black Hawk was capable of murderous hatred as well as the most intense personal compassion. In one battle with the Osages, he personally killed nine people, but on another raid, against the Cherokees, he found only four people, three men and a woman. He took the woman captive and then freed the three men, figuring it was dishonorable to kill so few. During the siege of an American fort during the War of 1812, when he was allied with the British, Black Hawk found two white boys hiding in a bush. "I thought of my own children," he said later, "and passed on without noticing them" (Johansen and Grinde, 1997, 38). During the same war, Black Hawk learned that some of his Indian allies, who were aiding the British, were torturing white American prisoners. He halted the practice and poured his scorn on Colonel Henry Procter, the British commander, for permitting it. "Go and put on petticoats," Black Hawk stormed. "I conquer to save, and you to murder!" (ibid., 38).

About 1820, the Fox and Sauk divided over whether to resist European American expansion into their country in what is now southern Illinois. Keokuk and a number of his supporters decided to accommodate the expansion as they moved into Iowa. Black Hawk and his supporters remained at their principal village, Saukenuk, at the confluence of the Rock and Mississippi Rivers, the site of present-day Rock Island. The land provided abundant crops, and the river was a rich source of fish. Black Hawk consulted with the spiritual leaders White Cloud and Neapope, who advised him to seek allies in defense of the land.

In the meantime, George Davenport, Indian agent in the area, had purchased the site on which Saukenuk was built, including Black Hawk's own lodge and his people's graveyard. Anglo-American immigrants began to take land around the village. Illinois Governor John Reynolds ordered the state militia to march on Saukenuk. Black Hawk and his band moved west across the Mississippi but pledged to return.

Black Hawk recalled the following:

> Upon our return to Saukenuk from our winter hunting grounds last spring, we
> found the palefaces in our lodges, and that they had torn down our fences and were
> plowing our corn lands and getting ready to plant their corn upon the lands which
> the Sauks have ... cultivated for so many winters that our memory cannot go back
> to them.... They are now running their plows through our graveyards, turning
> up the bones and ashes of our sacred dead, whose spirits are calling on us from the
> land of dreams for vengeance on the despoilers. (Johansen and Grinde, 1997, 39)

In 1832, Black Hawk's band recrossed the Mississippi and sought Winnebago
support. Contrary to the promises of Neapope and White Cloud, only a few
Winnebagos joined. Black Hawk, his warriors, and their homeless families then
attacked frontier settlements in the area. In response, Governor Reynolds
called out the militia again, assembling freshly recruited companies in the area.
One of the new recruits was Abraham Lincoln, a young man at the time.
Lincoln's unit was later disbanded after its members took a vote over whether to
fight Black Hawk. The vote was a tie. Lincoln later reenlisted but saw no
fighting.

Regular Army troops were brought in to pursue Black Hawk's band, whose
members had been forced to subsist on roots in the swamplands near the
Mississippi. Several Army and militia units caught Black Hawk and his people, their backs to the river, where the Indians hoisted a flag of truce. General
Winfield Scott and other officers ignored the appeal for a truce and engaged in
a one-sided slaughter that became known as the Battle of Black Ax. General
Scott later apologized for the large number of women and children killed by
his men. He complained that they could not be distinguished from warriors in
the heat of battle.

Black Hawk, Neapope, and other survivors of the battle fled north to a
Winnebago village, where they were betrayed for a bribe of twenty horses and
$100. Black Hawk was defiant in surrender:

> You know the cause of our making war. It is known to all white men. The white
> men despise the Indians, and drive them from their homes. They smile in the face
> of the poor Indian, to cheat him; they shake him by the hand, to gain his
> confidence; they make him drunk, to deceive him. [Black Hawk continued, saying
> that he had] Done nothing for which an Indian ought to be ashamed. He has fought
> for his countrymen ... against white men who came, year after year, to cheat them
> and take away their lands. You know the cause of our making war. It is known to all
> white men. They ought to be ashamed of it. (Rosenstiel, 1983, 118)

After his arrest, Black Hawk was led away in chains by Jefferson Davis, who
later would become president of the Confederate States of America. After
several months in prison, Black Hawk was taken on a tour of several eastern
cities. As part of this tour, he met with President Andrew Jackson at the White

House. Jackson gave Black Hawk a military uniform and a sword, but the aging chief was not mollified. He told Jackson that he had made war to avenge injustice against his people. Behind Black Hawk's back, Jackson recognized Keokuk as principal chief of the Sauks and Foxes. The news came to Black Hawk and Keokuk as they stood together with Army officers. Angry and frustrated, Black Hawk removed a breechclout from his loins and slapped Keokuk across the face with it.

Black Hawk's body was still lean and firm at the age of 60, his "hawk-like face with its long nose, luminous dark eyes, and firm mouth.... All the hair above his high forehead had been shaved off except for a scalp lock, and by this one knew he was a warrior" (Waters, 1993, 69). Eventually, Black Hawk settled on land governed by Keokuk, near Iowaville on the Des Moines River. Shortly before his death in 1838, Black Hawk acknowledged his defeat without lingering bitterness, telling a Fourth of July gathering near Fort Madison the following:

> A few winters ago, I was fighting against you. I did wrong, perhaps, but that is past; it is buried; let it be forgotten. Rock River is a beautiful country. I liked my towns, my cornfields, and the home of my people. I fought for it. It is now yours. Keep it as we did; it will produce you good crops. (Johansen and Grinde, 1997, 40)

GENERAL JACKSON SUBDUES WILLIAM WEATHERFORD AND THE CREEKS

While Tecumseh was losing the Battle of Tippecanoe in absentia, he was building his alliance of Indian nations in the South among the Creeks and other Native nations. His eloquence inspired one man among the Creeks, William Weatherford (who was only one-eighth Indian). Weatherford raised a 1,000-man army whose members expressed the Creeks' frustration at the continuing usurpation of their land by Anglo-American immigrants by attacking roughly 500 whites, mixed bloods, and black slaves. This group had taken refuge at the fortified home of Samuel Mims, a Creek of mixed blood, along the Alabama River near the Florida border. On August 30, 1813, at noon, Weatherford's men sprang from the tall grass around the Mims stockade, rising like waves of heat on an exceptionally hot and humid day. Using arrows against the defenders' guns, the Creeks rampaged into the stockade, killing more than 400 people by sundown. When the Creek warriors began to withdraw after an initial assault on Mims's fortified house, Weatherford spurred them on by setting buildings on fire with flame-tipped arrows. Many of the victims were hacked to death.

The brutality of Weatherford's massacre brought calls for extermination of the Creeks from swelling numbers of Anglo-American immigrants across the South. The U.S. Army officer assigned to march against them was Andrew Jackson, whose name would scorch the memories of Native peoples in the South for years to come. First, Jackson made his name as an Indian fighter, and then, after he was elected president of the United States, as the premier architect of the "removal" of Native peoples to Indian Territory (now Oklahoma). Every bit as brash as Weatherford (who announced that he would kill any Indians who did not cooperate with him), Jackson blazed a trail of fire and blood through the South, refusing to retreat even when his superiors ordered him to relent. In a battlefield confrontation with Weatherford's Creeks, Jackson imprisoned assistants who advised retreat.

During December 1813, Weatherford narrowly escaped capture by Jackson's troops. On March 27, 1814, Jackson, leading 2,000 men, attacked Weatherford's force of 900, which was holed up in a stronghold at Horseshoe Bend in an area isolated by rivers on three sides and a high log rampart on the fourth. Jackson sent men to seize a fleet of canoes that Weatherford had been keeping for escape. Jackson sent his men into the Creek encampment by announcing that any officer or soldier who fled the enemy without being compelled to do so by superior force would be put to death.

The Creeks under Weatherford fought bitterly, but their clubs and tomahawks could not match the Army's bayonets. One of the first soldiers to invade the Creek camp was Ensign Sam Houston, who later would become a hero among Anglo-Americans in Texas. As Jackson's troops swarmed over the Creek camp, many of the Native people ran for their lives. Those who leaped into the river were picked off by Army sharpshooters. Jackson had restrained his initial attack while women and children were ferried across the river to a place that was supposed to spare them the worst of the battle. Several of them died anyway as the frenzy of battle spilled across the landscape. When the battle was over, Jackson's forces had sustained 49 killed and 157 wounded; Cherokees who had fought at his side sustained 18 killed and 36 wounded. Of the Creeks' 900-man force, about 750 were killed. Weatherford himself was not among the dead. Not expecting Jackson to attack so quickly, he had been elsewhere that day. A few days after the battle, Weatherford surrendered to Jackson personally, at the general's tent. By that time, word of Jackson's victory had spread eastward. The general was beginning to build the popular reputation that later would elect him president of the United States.

During July 1814, General Jackson returned to Horseshoe Bend for what was officially being called a treaty conference with the defeated Creeks. The location was symbolic; Jackson relished rubbing in defeat on his enemies. The general, who never made a point of studying the cultures of the Indians he subjugated, probably did not know he was compounding the Creeks' humiliation by holding the "treaty" on ground they regarded as sacred. This meeting contained none of the diplomatic equity that characterized eighteenth century frontier diplomacy. The Creeks were summoned to this parley on pain of death by Jackson, who demanded 23 million acres—60 percent of the area that would later become Alabama as well as nearly a quarter of Georgia. This was half the land previously under Creek control. When the Creek chiefs asked for time to seek concessions and to think the matter over,

Andrew Jackson. (Courtesy of the Nebraska State Historical Society.)

Jackson demanded an answer and hinted strongly that a negative reaction would be construed as a hostile act inviting retaliation by the U.S. Army. As he refused all concessions, Jackson watched the Creeks starve as they picked at grains of corn that the soldiers had fed their horses.

STALEMATE WITH THE SEMINOLES

Having subdued the Creeks, General Jackson next received orders to quell a disturbance that the War Department politely called "troubles" in Georgia, principally among the Seminoles. During 1818, Jackson's troops chased them into Florida, which was still under Spanish jurisdiction (the area was ceded to the United States in 1821). Having seized several Spanish forts along the way, Jackson then withdrew and endured a debate over his extranational expedition in Congress. Jackson also reaped popular acclaim from expansion-minded Americans, in the meantime building his reputation for a future presidential campaign.

The Seminoles, many of whom were descended from Creeks, had elected to ally themselves with the Spanish rather than the United States, an act of virtual treason in General Jackson's eyes. In addition, the Seminoles were giving shelter to escaped slaves. The pretext of Jackson's raid thus was recovery of stolen human property. After Florida was purchased from Spain by the United States, slave-hunting vigilantes invaded the area en masse, killing Seminoles as well as blacks.

Later, during the 1830s, when President Jackson proposed to remove the Seminoles to Indian Territory, they refused. Moving deep into the swamps of southern Florida (an area that ironically was being used as a removal destination for other Native peoples), the Seminoles fought U.S. Army troops to a bloody stalemate during seven years of warfare. They were never defeated and never moved from their new homeland.

Osceola (ca. 1803–1838), whose name was derived from *asi-yahola*, meaning Black Drink Crier, was the best-known leader of the Seminoles during their pursuit by the U.S. Army. He was born on the Talapoosa River near the border of Alabama and Georgia. His mother was Polly Copinger, a Creek woman, and she married William Powell, a white man. As a result of his mother's marriage to Powell, Osceola was sometimes called Bill Powell, but he considered Powell his stepfather and asserted that he was a full-blood. During his boyhood, Osceola moved with his mother to Florida and took up residence along the Apalachicola River about 1814. As a young man, he is believed to be a veteran of the First Seminole War of 1817–1918. Some reports during the war asserted that he was captured along the Enconfino River by troops under General Andrew Jackson in 1818 and then released because of his age.

In 1823, Seminole leaders agreed to the Treaty of Mounltrie Creek, which ceded land and created reservations for the Seminoles. Later, as a result of

U.S. removal policies, the Treaty of Payne's Landing of 1832 required all Seminoles to leave Florida for Indian Territory within three years. According to the treaty, Seminoles with African American blood were to be sold into slavery. In 1833, seven Seminole chiefs, including Charley Emathla and Foke Luste Hajo, endorsed the Treaty of Fort Gibson, which created a homeland in Oklahoma near the Creeks. However, most Seminoles did not comply with the requirements of the treaty. At this time, Osceola became a noted leader because he urged Seminoles to remain in Florida.

At Fort King during April 1835, Wiley Thompson, an Indian agent, dictated a new treaty with the Seminoles requiring their removal to Oklahoma. Several chiefs declined to endorse the treaty or to deal with white officials. Seminole oral history maintains that Osceola angrily slashed the treaty with his knife. Subsequently, Osceola was seized and jailed. Although Osceola continued to protest, in the end he agreed to the terms of the treaty. But after his release, he slipped into the marshes, and many Seminole people followed him into the swamps.

During preparations for removal, Osceola's forces ambushed Emathla. Osceola allegedly threw money that the whites had given Emathla onto his dead body. Osceola then attacked and killed Wiley Thompson on December 28, 1835. On the same day, Alligator, Micanopy, and Jumper led about 300 men in an attack on Major Francis Langthorne Dade's detachment of 108 soldiers. All except 3 soldiers were killed. On New Year's Eve 1835, Osceola's men won a battle against General Duncan Lamont Clinch's force of 800 men on the Withlacoochee River. There were 4 infantrymen killed, and only 3 Indians died. Osceola was injured but eluded capture.

While waging a guerilla war for two years, Osceola devastated the countryside. So that they could fight alongside the men, some Seminole women killed their own children. The war degenerated into a deadly search-and-destroy mission in the Everglades.

Finally, Micanopy and other rebel chiefs stopped fighting in the spring of 1837. Osceola forced Micanopy to flee with him into the swamps; however, Micanopy stopped fighting again later in the year.

Attempts to remove the Seminoles by force cost the lives of 1,500 U.S. soldiers. During October 1837, General Thomas S. Jesup summoned the Seminole chief Osceola to parlay under a flag of truce at Fort Augustine. Jesup surrounded the conference site with troops and took Osceola prisoner. Betraying the flag of truce, Jesup bound Osceola and incarcerated him at Fort Moultrie outside Charleston, South Carolina.

Once they were captured, many of the Seminoles eventually moved west to Indian Territory, but a few bands remained in the Everglades. The removal of the Seminoles was one of the most expensive Indian campaigns that the U.S. Army ever has waged. In addition to the 1,500 soldiers killed (1 for every 2 Seminoles eventually removed to Indian Territory), the government spent an average of $6,500 for each Native person transferred to Indian territory. At a time when the average job paid less than $1,000 a year, this amount represented a small fortune.

Varying accounts exist of Osceola's demise: Poisoning, malaria, or abuse in prison may have been the causes, but the whites were excoriated for their treachery and his tragic death. On January 30, 1838, Osceola died at Fort Moultrie in full battle regalia. Even in death, Osceola did not escape white exploitation. Dr. Frederick Weedon, the military surgeon, kept his head in a medical museum until it was destroyed by a fire in 1866. In spite of the death of their renowned leader, many Seminoles continued to resist removal to Oklahoma for many years, using the Florida swamps as a base for their operations.

THE ROAD TO THE TRAILS OF TEARS

With nearly a million U.S. citizens in the Mississippi valley by 1828, the area was acquiring political leverage, which expressed itself in widespread support for Andrew Jackson's election to the presidency. Eli Whitney's invention of the cotton gin in 1793 had opened the technological door to a whole new age of agriculture in the lands that the Cherokee, Choctaw, Chickasaw, Creek, and Seminole (the Five Civilized Tribes), among others, occupied. Lands that had been occupied by Native peoples in 1800 were planted in cotton, harvested by African slaves two generations later. As a politician, luck smiled on President Jackson, who arrived just in time to ride a wave of economic development across the South built on the economy of slavery, which demanded removal of the Native peoples. At times, Native Americans were exported as slaves; one author estimated that 30,000 to 50,000 Indians were shipped out of Charleston, South Carolina, in this fashion, and smaller numbers were sold through Boston and Salem, Massachusetts, as well as New Orleans (Gallay, 2003, 3-B).

Before 1800, Euro-American immigration in the South had been limited mainly to the pine barrens of coastal Georgia, on land that was practically useless for farming before the advent of modern commercial fertilizers. The immigrants, seeing the value of the developing cotton culture, cast a covetous eye on the fertile inland valleys that were occupied by the Five Civilized Tribes, who had utilized them for hundreds of years. As waves of land speculators and other immigrants moved in to evict them, the Creeks, Cherokees, Choctaws, Chickasaws, and others were doing exactly what the Jeffersonians thought they should: building farms and towns in the European manner. The civilized tribes were well on their way to becoming some of the most prosperous farmers in the South.

Whether in purposeful contravention of the treaties or because he thought he had the right to annul them personally, Jackson within a decade cooperated with the land-industry business to move tens of thousands of Native peoples from their homelands. Jackson, who as a general told his troops to root out Indians from their "dens" and kill Indian women and their "whelps," struck only a slightly more erudite tone as president in his second annual message to Congress. He reflected on the fact that some European Americans were growing "melancholy" over the fact that the Indians were being driven to their "tomb." These critics must understand, Jackson said, that "true philanthropy reconciles the mind to these vicissitudes as it does to the extinction of one generation to make way for another" (Stannard, 1992, 240).

Jackson's policy—to move the Indians out of territory that could be used by immigrating Anglo-Americans—became the national standard during his eight years as president. Alabama already had been created in 1819 from Creek and Cherokee territory; Mississippi was created in 1817 from Choctaw and Chickasaw country. These two states, along with Georgia, passed laws outlawing indigenous governments, subjecting their peoples to state jurisdiction, after which open season was declared on remaining Native lands. All of this violated treaties negotiated earlier. President Jackson told the Indians that he was unable to stand by the treaties, very likely because of the pressures caused by states' rights, an emerging issue in the decades before the Civil War. Instead, Jackson proposed that the Indians be moved westward. At first, the moving of whole tribes was proposed as a voluntary act. In the meantime, land speculators and squatters closed a deadly vise of lands that had been home to the newly civilized tribes for thousands of years.

In 1829, small amounts of gold were discovered on Cherokee land in the mountains of northern Georgia. The state legislature quickly passed a law forbidding the Cherokee to prospect or mine gold on their own land as more than 3,000 invaders surged onto Cherokee territory, wrecking the farmsteads and villages that they had so carefully built. When the Cherokee Nation indicted whites for destruction of Native life and property, Georgia courts, having asserted their jurisdiction over Cherokee lands and lives, dismissed all Cherokee testimony as incompetent.

Because Native peoples no longer enjoyed federal protection from predatory state interests promised in treaties, Indian lands were thrown open to anyone, including dealers in alcohol, who had a heyday exchanging land and anything else they could get their hands on for strong whiskey and rum. Actions could be brought against Indians in state courts, so their lands and other belongings often were taken for debt. State laws were enacted barring courts from accepting an Indian's testimony against white men in court. Thus, no legal claim by a white man, no matter how baseless, could be contested by any Native person.

By about 1830, white squatters were swarming onto the lands of the civilized tribes. Many Native people were dispossessed by force even before the removals began. They had the choice of two untenable options: move, usually to Indian Territory (later Oklahoma) or be pushed off their lands anyway. When a well-known Chickasaw leader, Emubby, was killed by a European American named Jones, the incident made the papers only because Emubby had served several campaigns with General Jackson. Before their removal westward, the Creeks were driven into the forests and swamps by non-Indian squatters. Their homes were taken, and many starved.

A newspaper of the time described their destitution:

> To see a whole people destitute of food—the incessant cry of the emaciated creatures being bread! bread! is beyond description distressing. The existence of many of the Indians is prolonged by eating roots and the bark of trees.... [N]othing that can afford nourishment is rejected, however offensive it may be.... They beg their food from door to door.... It is really painful to see the wretched creatures wandering about the streets, haggard and naked." (Brandon, 1964, 227)

Removals began with 4,000 Choctaws in 1831, bound for western Arkansas. The winter was harsh, but during the next few years it often was even worse. The cruelty of the removals was compounded by governmental mismanagement and by Indian agents, who kept for themselves much of the money that the government had appropriated to feed native people while they were being moved. In the summer of 1831, cholera spread through areas of the South, returning each summer until 1836. Only the Chickasaws managed to transport much of what they owned westward (agents complained about the bulk of their livestock and baggage). The rest of the people suffered cruelly, complaining that they had been driven off their own lands like wild wolves, with their women and children's shoeless feet bleeding from the long marches over rough terrain. Indian agents infamous for their penny pinching sometimes hired rotten boats to transport Indians across rivers. Many of the boats sank, with the loss of uncounted lives. Dead Indians did not cost anything to feed.

Alexis de Tocqueville, author of *Democracy in America*, witnessed portions of the early removals and wrote:

> At the end of the year 1831, whilst I was on the left bank of the Mississippi, at a place named by the Europeans Memphis, there arrived a numerous band of Choctaws. These savages had left their country, and were endeavoring to gain the right bank of the Mississippi, where they hoped to find an asylum that had been promised them by the American government. It was in the middle of the winter, and the cold was unusually severe; the snow had frozen hard upon the ground, and the river was drifting huge masses of ice. The Indians had their families with them; and they brought in their train the wounded and the sick, with children newly born, and old men upon the verge of death. They possessed neither tents nor wagons, but only their arms and some provisions. I saw them embark to pass the mighty river, and never will that solemn spectacle fade from my remembrance. No cry, no sob was heard amongst the assembled crowd; all were silent.... The Indians had all stepped into the bark which was to carry them across, but their dogs remained upon the bank. As soon as these animals perceived that their masters were finally leaving the shore, they set up a dismal howl and, plunging all together into the icy waters of the Mississippi, swam after the boat. (Tocqueville, 1898, 435–436, 448)

THE ORIGINS OF REMOVAL LEGISLATION

Provisions for "removal"—the relocation of entire Native nations from areas about to be annexed by non-Indians—were first laid down in a 1817 treaty between the United States and the Cherokee Nation (7 Stat. 156). By 1830, the federal government had passed general removal legislation aimed at the Five Civilized Tribes because of the intensive efforts they had made in adopting ways of life and political institutions resembling those of European Americans. Many other Native American nations (such as the Osage and Poncas) also were removed to Indian Territory during the nineteenth century. By 1883, twenty-five Indian reservations occupied by a total of thirty-seven nations had been established in Indian Country.

As president, Andrew Jackson thought that Indian treaties were anachronisms. "An absurdity," he called them, "Not to be reconciled with the principles of our government" (Johansen, 2000, 88). As Jackson elaborated, before his election to the presidency, in a letter to President James Monroe (another advocate of Indian removal) in 1817:

> The Indians are the subjects of the United States, inhabiting its territory and acknowledging its sovereignty. Then is it not absurd for the sovereign to negotiate by treaty with the subject? I have always thought, that Congress had as much right to regulate by acts of legislation, all Indian concerns as they had of territories, are citizens of the United States and entitled to all the rights thereof, the Indians are subjects and entitled to their protection and fostering care. (McNickle, 1949, 193)

The confusions of convoluted grammar aside, it is not easy to decipher what General Jackson is saying. Is he declaring the Indians to be citizens? Legally, that was not the case until a century later. Is he personally annulling the treaties, which had been signed by parties who regarded each other as diplomatic peers barely two generations earlier? Whatever the nature of his rhetoric, the ensuing decades made clear, especially for the Native peoples of the South, just what Jackson meant by "protection and fostering care."

The private rationale for removal was expressed by Henry Clay (like Jackson, a political product of the trans-Appalachian west). Clay's recitation, preserved in the *Memoirs* of John Quincy Adams, came at the end of a meeting of Adams's cabinet on December 22, 1825, during which the entire agenda was taken up by the conflict between the Creeks and Georgia. Clay was responding to a suggestion that the United States stop making treaties with the Indians and treat them as citizens. According to Adams, Clay said the following:

> It is impossible to civilize Indians. . . . There never was a full-blooded Indian who took to civilization. It was not in their nature. He said they are destined to extinction and, although he would never use or countenance inhumanity towards

them, he did not think them, as a race, worth preserving. He considered them as essentially inferior to the Anglo-Saxon race, which were now taking their place on this continent. They were not an improvable breed, and their disappearance from the human family will be no great harm to the world. (Drinnon, 1990, 179–180)

Clay's point of view was popular among Anglo-Americans in need of a rationale for relieving Native Americans of their land. The fact that the civilized tribes had become, in some respects, as Europeanized as the immigrants seemed not to matter. Removal was less an ideological statement than a convenient method to transfer land from one group of people to another. During the 1820s, before their forceful removal from their homelands, the Cherokees developed prosperous villages and a system of government modeled after that of the United States. The Cherokees owned 22,0000 cattle, 2,000 spinning wheels, 700 looms, 31 grist mills, 10 saw mills, 8 cotton gins, and 1,300 slaves. The Cherokees also had a written constitution that emulated that of the United States; a written language, developed by Sequoyah; and a bilingual newspaper, the *Cherokee Phoenix*.

Passage of the Removal Act of 1830 climaxed a years-long struggle. The Creeks, for example, had become concerned about non-Indian usurpation of their lands as early as 1818, when the Muscogee (Creek) Nation passed a law against the sale of any Native American land without council approval and under penalty of death for the transgressing party. The edict was enforced. In 1825, federal treaty commissioners bribed William McIntosh, leader of the Creek Lower Towns, to sign a land-cession agreement, the Treaty of Indian Springs, with a few of his close associates. The National Council declared McIntosh to be a traitor and on May 1, 1825, sent a delegation to torch his house. When McIntosh appeared at the door of his burning home, his body was riddled with bullets.

Removals for specific Native nations usually were negotiated by treaties (frequently under duress) in which specific nations surrendered what remained to them of their aboriginal homelands in exchange for lands west of the Mississippi River. Although some small bands (and a few members of larger nations) had been moving westward since the War of 1812, the Removal Act forced the wholesale removal of entire Native nations, notably the Five Civilized Tribes on the several trails of tears.

As the federal government prepared to remove entire nations of Native people west of the Mississippi River, little thought was given to the fact that Indians, European Americans, and Afro-Americans had been intermarrying among Native peoples for nearly a century. Many of the families forced to abandon their homes were nearly as European American genetically as their nonreservation neighbors. John Ross, the Cherokee best known as an opponent of removal, was only one-eighth Cherokee, for example. He lived in a plantation house and owned slaves.

Sequoyah. (Courtesy of the Library of Congress.)

These complications meant little to President Andrew Jackson, who had earned his national reputation as a general in the U.S. Army, which had the primary business of subjugating Indians. When he ran for president, Jackson sought frontier votes by favoring removal. Once in office, Jackson considered the Removal Act of 1830 to be the fulfillment of a campaign promise. Others felt less sanguine; even with extensive lobbying from the White House, the House of Representatives passed the Removal Act by only six votes (103 to 97). Representative William Ellsworth of Connecticut opposed the Removal Act in a passionate speech delivered on the House floor, when he said, in part:

> We must be just and faithful to our treaties. There is no occasion for collision. We shall not stand justified before the world in taking any step which shall lead to oppression. The eyes of the world, as well as of this nation, are upon us. I conjure this House not to stain the page of our history with national shame, cruelty, and perfidy. (Johansen, 1998, 275)

John Ross. (Courtesy of the Nebraska State Historical Society.)

John Ross (1790–1866; called Coowescoowe, meaning the Egret, among the Cherokee) was more than an opponent of the Removal Act. He also was the founder of a constitutional government among the Cherokees. Ross was the third of nine children. His father was Daniel Ross, a Scot, and his mother, Mary (Molly) McDonald, was a Scot-Cherokee. As a youth, he was called Tsan-usdi or Little John. Ross was educated at home by white tutors and then sent to Kingston Academy in Tennessee. In 1813, he married Quatie, Elizabeth Brown Henley, a full-blooded Cherokee. They had five children.

By 1811, at age 21, Ross was a member of the Standing Committee of the Cherokee Council. During 1813 and 1814, he served as an adjutant in a Cherokee regiment under the command of General Andrew Jackson and saw action with other Cherokees at Horseshoe Bend in 1813 against the Red Sticks commanded by William Weatherford. Ross led a contingent of Cherokee warriors in a diversionary tactic and thus was an important factor in Jackson's success in that battle.

In 1814, Ross established a ferry service and trading post at Ross's Landing. In 1817, he became a member of the Cherokee National Council and served as its president from 1819 to 1826. In 1820, a republican form of government was instituted by the Cherokee, similar in structure to the United States. As an advocate of education and mission work, Ross proposed that the Cherokee Nation become a state in the union with its own constitution.

When New Echota became the Cherokee national capital in 1826, Ross moved there with his family. In 1827, he became president of the Cherokee constitutional convention. From 1828 to 1839, Ross served as principal chief of the Cherokee Nation under the new constitution he had helped to draft.

Although Ross continued to resist removal policies as principal chief of the Cherokees, a dispirited minority of Cherokee leaders called the Treaty Party, including Major Ridge, John Ridge, Elias Boudinot, and Stand Watie, in 1835 consented to removal by signing the Treaty of New Echota. Ross and a majority of Cherokees sought to have the treaty reversed and sent a letter to Congress in 1836 asking for an investigation into its legality.

SEQUOYAH:
THE ONLY PERSON TO SINGLY INVENT A
WRITTEN LANGUAGE

One spectacular example of the Cherokee penchant for European-style civilization was Sequoyah (1776–1843), who invented the Cherokee alphabet in 1821 after twelve years of work. Sequoyah, a warrior who had been crippled in a hunting accident, became known in the history of letters as the only person in human history to single-handedly invent an entire written language.

Sequoyah was born in Taskigi near Fort Loudon, Tennessee, of a Cherokee mother named Wurtee and (some say) the Revolutionary War soldier and trader Nathaniel Gist. Sequoyah's name was anglicized from *sikwaji* or *sogwili*, meaning sparrow or principal bird in Cherokee; he also was known variously as George Gist, George Guess, and George Guest. As a boy of 12 living with his mother near Willstown, Alabama, Sequoyah learned to tend dairy cattle and make cheese. He also broke horses, planted corn, and gained skills in hunting and trading furs.

With a quick mind and an active imagination, Sequoyah was intrigued by the "talking leaves," the written language of the immigrants. Perhaps out of frustration with his disability and its effects on his hunting, Sequoyah developed a drinking habit as a young man. Realizing what alcohol was doing to him, he turned away from the habit and sought a new way of life. As a result, Sequoyah became an excellent silversmith. In 1815, he married Sarah (Sally), a Cherokee woman. They subsequently had several children.

By 1809, Sequoyah had started to work on a written version of the Cherokee language using pictorial symbols, but he abandoned this method as untenable after he had created more than 1,000 symbols. Next, Sequoyah reduced the Cherokee language initially to 200, then finally to 86 characters that represented all the syllables or sounds in the language. He derived the resulting syllabary in part from English, Greek, and Hebrew characters in mission school books. Some Cherokee were mystified by Sequoyah's work and accused him of witchcraft. At one point, his home was burned down and his notes lost.

Undaunted by allegations of witchcraft, Sequoyah in 1821 completed his writing system. The same year, before an assembly of Cherokee leaders, he proved the viability of his system by writing messages to his six-year-old daughter that she understood and answered independently. The Cherokee tribal council formally adopted Sequoyah's syllabary soon after this demonstration. Within a few months, several thousand Cherokees had learned Sequoyah's writing system. By 1824, white missionaries had translated parts of the Bible into Cherokee. In 1828, the Cherokee Tribal Council started a weekly newspaper called the *Cherokee Phoenix and Indian Advocate*, which was bilingual in English and Cherokee. The newspaper was published until it was suppressed in 1835 by the state of Georgia for advocating Cherokee rights to their lands in Georgia.

In 1829, Sequoyah moved with his wife and children to Indian Territory in what would become Sequoya County, Oklahoma. He also helped to unite uneasy eastern and western Cherokee factions in 1839. In 1841, the Cherokee National Council granted him a pension; Sequoyah became the first member of any Indian tribe to be rewarded in this manner.

In 1842, Sequoyah launched an expedition to find a group of Cherokees who had gone west during the American Revolution. The trip through Texas took a toll on Sequoyah's failing health. Suffering from dysentery, he died in August 1843 near San Fernando, Tamaulipas, Mexico, and he was buried there along with his treasured papers in an as-yet-undiscovered grave. Later, Oklahoma memorialized Sequoyah by placing his statue in the U.S. capitol's Statuary Hall. His homestead also was designated as an Oklahoma State historical site. As a testimony to his remarkable genius, Stephen Endilicher, the Hungarian botanist, named a species of giant California coastal redwood trees after him.

CHIEF JUSTICE JOHN MARSHALL'S CHEROKEE RULINGS

The assertion of states' rights vis-à-vis Native American territorial sovereignty provided the legal grist for a 1832 Supreme Court decision written by Chief Justice John Marshall (1755–1835); it has defined the relationship of Native American and states' rights for more than a century and a half.

Marshall's opinions outlining Native Americans' status in the U.S. legal system occurred as he defined the Supreme Court's place within U.S. politics.

When Marshall became chief justice during 1801, the Supreme Court was little more than a clause in the Constitution. For 35 years as chief justice, Marshall played a major role in defining the Court as an institution. According to author Jean Edward Smith (1996), if George Washington founded the United States, John Marshall legally defined it.

Chief Justice Marshall had long-running political differences with President Jackson, and he agonized over the conflicts between states' rights and Native sovereignty. In 1831, in *Cherokee Nation v. United States* [5 Peters 1 (1831)], Marshall held that the Cherokees had no standing at court to appeal the state of Georgia's seizure of their lands. This situation troubled Marshall so deeply that he said at one point that he thought of resigning from the Supreme Court because of it. A year later, in *Worcester v. Georgia* [31 U.S. (6 Pet.) 515 (1832)], Marshall held unconstitutional the imprisonment by Georgia of a missionary (Samuel Worcester) who had worked with the Cherokees. The specific issue was the refusal of Worcester, while resident on Cherokee land, to swear loyalty to the state of Georgia in conformance with a state law.

The case began when three white missionaries living on Cherokee territory refused to swear an oath of allegiance to the state of Georgia. They were arrested, chained to a wagon, and forced to walk more than 20 miles to jail. Two Methodist preachers who objected to the cruelty that accompanied the arrests also were chained and taken to jail. The three missionaries were tried, convicted, and sentenced to four years of hard labor at the Georgia state penitentiary. Two of them later swore allegiance and were released; one (Worcester) did not. When the case reached the Supreme Court (as *Worcester v. Georgia*), Justice Marshall wrote that Native nations had a degree of sovereignty that denied Georgia the right to compel an oath of loyalty.

Historians disagree over whether President Jackson actually said, "John Marshall has made his decision, now let him enforce it." Whether Jackson expressed himself in those words may be moot; his implementation of removal flew in the face of the law as interpreted by Marshall in *Worcester v. Georgia*. Marshall wrote that the Cherokees had

> always been considered as distinct, independent political communities, retaining their original natural rights . . . and the settled doctrine of the law of nations, that a weaker power does not surrender its independence—its right to self-government— by associating with a stronger, and taking its protection. . . . The Cherokee nation, then, is a distinct community, occupying its own territory, with boundaries accurately described, in which the laws of Georgia can have no force, and which the citizens of Georgia have no right to enter, but with the assent of the Cherokees, or in conformity with treaties, and with the acts of Congress. (*Worcester v. Georgia*, 1832)

Marshall reasoned in *Worcester v. Georgia* that the Constitution, by declaring treaties to be the supreme law of the land, had adopted and sanctified

On the Trail of Tears. (Courtesy of John Kahionhes Fadden.)

previous treaties with the Indian nations. The words *treaty* and *nation* are "words of our own language," wrote Marshall, "selected in our diplomatic and legislative proceedings, by ourselves, having each a definite and well-understood meaning. We have applied them to Indians, as we have applied them to the other nations of the earth; they are applied to all in the same sense" (*Worcester v. Georgia*, 1832). Marshall defined Indian nations not as totally sovereign or as colonies but as "domestic dependent nations."

Marshall's opinion was ignored by Jackson, an action that comprised contempt of the Supreme Court, an impeachable offense under the U.S. Constitution. The Congress, fearing that a confrontation over states' rights could provoke civil war, took no action against Jackson. After almost six years of delays, the Trail of Tears was initiated in 1838.

Although Marshall's opinion was ignored by President Jackson, it has shaped the relationship of the United States to Native American nations within its borders to the present day. The 1934 Indian Reorganization Act and legislative efforts promoting self-determination after the 1960s were based on Marshall's opinion that the rights of discovery did not extinguish the original inhabitants' claims to possession and use of their lands.

Although Ross continued to protest removal for several more years, the state of Georgia coerced Cherokees to sell lands for a fraction of their value. Marauding immigrants plundered Cherokee homes and possessions as they destroyed the *Cherokee Phoenix's* printing press because it had opposed removal. The U.S. Army forced Cherokee families into internment camps to prepare for the arduous trek westward. As a result of unhealthy and crowded conditions in these hastily constructed stockades, many Cherokees died even before their Trail of Tears began. Although failing in his efforts to stop removal, Ross managed to gain additional federal funds for his people.

Before they were exiled from their homelands by force of arms, the Cherokee released a "memorial" expressing their feelings:

> The title of the Cherokee people to their lands is the most ancient, pure, and absolute known to man; its date is beyond the reach of human record; its validity confirmed by possession and enjoyment antecedent to all pretense of claim by any portion of the human race.
>
> The free consent of the Cherokee people is indispensable to a valid transfer of the Cherokee title. The Cherokee people have neither by themselves nor their representatives given such consent. It follows that the original title and ownership of lands still rests with the Cherokee Nation, unimpaired and absolute. The Cherokee people have existed as a distinct national community for a period extending into antiquity beyond the dates and records and memory of man. These attributes have never been relinquished by the Cherokee people, and cannot be dissolved by the expulsion of the Nation from its territory by the power of the United States Government. (O'Brien, 1989, 57)

In preparation for the Cherokees' removal, John Ross was evicted from his mansion and was living in a dirt-floored cabin. When John Howard Payne, author of the song "Home Sweet Home," came to visit him at the cabin, just across the Georgia State line in Tennessee, the Georgia State Guard crossed the state line and kidnapped both men. Realizing that the federal government did not intend to protect the Cherokees, Ross and others reluctantly signed the Treaty of New Echota in 1835 and prepared, with heavy hearts, to leave their homes.

The Cherokees displacement involved the most human suffering, and their phrase for the long, brutal march (*nuna-daa-ut-sun'y*, the trail where they cried) gave the march its enduring name. At least one-fourth of the Cherokees who were removed died along the way. According to one scholar who studied Cherokee mortality on the Trail of Tears, the conventional estimate of 4,000 dead is too low. The losses among the Cherokee alone may have reached 8,000 people. In 1838 and 1839, the U.S. Army removed the Cherokees by force, except for a few hundred who escaped to the mountains.

The many trails of tears during the 1830s and early 1840s resulted in immense suffering among the estimated 50,000 to 100,000 Native people who were forced to move. Between one-third and one-fourth of those who were removed died on the marches or shortly thereafter of exposure, disease, and starvation. Ross' wife, Quatie, was among the victims of this forced emigration.

Many Cherokees died after they arrived in Indian Territory as epidemics and food shortages plagued the new settlements.

James Mooney described how the Cherokees were forced from their homes:

> Squads of troops were sent to search out with rifle and bayonet every small cabin hidden away in the coves or by the sides of mountain streams.... Families at dinner were startled by the sudden gleam of bayonets in the doorway and rose up to be driven with blows and oaths along the trail that led to the stockade. Men were seized in their fields or going along the road, women were taken from their wheels, and children from their play. (Van Every, 1966, 242)

A U.S. Army private who witnessed the Cherokee removal wrote as follows:

> I saw the helpless Cherokee arrested and dragged from their homes, and driven by bayonet into the stockades. And in the chill of a drizzling rain on an October morning I saw them loaded like cattle or sheep into wagons and started toward the west.... Chief Ross led in prayer, and when the bugle sounded and wagons started rolling many of the children ... waved their little hands goodbye to their mountain homes. (Worcester, 1975, 67)

Despite the cruelty of the marches they were forced to undertake and the death and disease that dogged their every step, the surviving members of the peoples who were removed to Indian Territory quickly set about rebuilding their communities. Much as they had in the southeast, the Creeks, Cherokees, and others built prosperous farms and towns, passed laws, and set about organizing themselves once again. Within three generations, however, this land that in the 1830s had been set aside as Indian Territory was being sought by non-Indians for its oil and because the frontier had closed everywhere else. At the turn of the century, as a rush for "black gold" inundated Oklahoma, the Allotment Act (1887) was breaking up the Native estate much as Georgia's state laws had done a little more than a half century earlier. There would be no trail of tears this time, however; there was no empty land left to occupy.

FURTHER READING

Armstrong, Virginia Irving. *I Have Spoken: American History Through the Voices of the Indians*. Athens, OH: Swallow Press, 1984.

Baker, Leonard. *John Marshall: A Life in Law*. New York: Macmillan, 1974.

Beckhard, Arthur J. *Black Hawk*. New York: Julian Messner, 1957.

Brandon, William. *The American Heritage Book of Indians*. New York: Dell, 1964.

Bryant, Martha F. *Sacajawea: A Native American Heroine*. New York: Council for Indian Education, 1989.

Butterfield, Consul Wilshire. *History of the Girtys, Being a Concise Account of the Girty Brothers—Thomas, Simon, James and George, and of Their Half-Brother, John Turner— Also of the Part Taken by Them in Lord Dunmore's War, in the Western Border War of the Revolution, and in the Indian War of 1790-1795.* Cincinnati: Robert Clark, 1890.

Carter, Harvey Lewis. *The Life and Times of Little Turtle: First Sagamore of the Wabash.* Urbana: University of Illinois Press, 1987.

Cherokee Nation v. Georgia 5 Peters 1 (1831).

Cole, Donald B. *Presidency of Andrew Jackson.* Lawrence: University Press of Kansas, 1993.

Collier, John. *Indians of the Americas.* New York: New American Library, 1947.

Deardorff, Merle H. *The Religion of Handsome Lake: Its Origins and Development.* American Bureau of Ethnology Bulletin No. 149. Washington, DC: BAE, 1951.

Deloria, Vine, ed. *American Indian Policy in the Twentieth Century.* Norman: University of Oklahoma Press, 1985.

Drinnon, Richard. *Facing West: Indian Hating and Empire Building.* New York: Schoken Books, 1990.

Eckert, Allan W. *A Sorrow in Our Heart: The Life of Tecumseh.* New York: Bantam, 1992.

Edmonds, Della, and Margot Edmonds. *Sacajawea of the Lewis and Clark Expedition.* Berkeley: University of California Press, 1979.

Eggleston, Edward, and Lillie Eggleston-Seelye. *Tecumseh and the Shawnee Prophet.* New York: Dodd, Mead & Co., 1878.

Edmunds, R. David. *The Shawnee Prophet.* Lincoln: University of Nebraska Press, 1983.

Edmunds, R. David. *Tecumseh and the Quest for Indian Leadership.* Boston: Little-Brown, 1984.

Frazier, Neta L. *Sacajawea: The Girl Nobody Knows.* New York: McKay, 1967.

Gallay, Alan. Indian Slave Trade Thrived in Early America. *Daytona Beach News-Journal*, August 3, 2003, 3-B.

Gill, Sam. *Mother Earth: An American Story.* Chicago: University of Chicago Press, 1987.

Griffith, Benjamin W., Jr. *McIntosh and Weatherford: Creek Indian Leaders.* Tuscaloosa: University of Alabama Press, 1988.

Hagan, William T. *The Sac and Fox Indians.* Norman: University of Oklahoma Press, 1958.

Hamilton, Charles, ed. *Cry of the Thunderbird.* Norman: University of Oklahoma Press, 1972.

Harold, Howard. *Sacajawea.* Norman: University of Oklahoma Press, 1971.

Hays, Wilma P. *Pontiac: Lion in the Forest.* Boston: Houghton-Mifflin, 1965.

Heckewelder, John. *History, Manners, and Customs of the Indian Nations Who Once Inhabited Pennsylvania and the Neighboring States.* The First American Frontier Series. New York: Arno Press and *The New York Times*, [1820] 1971.

Heckewelder, John. *Narrative of the Mission of the United Brethren among the Delaware and Mohegan Indians from Its Commencement, in the Year 1740, to the Close of the Year 1808.* New York: Arno Press, [1818] 1971.

Hobson, Charles F. *The Great Chief Justice: John Marshall and the Rule of Law.* Lawrence: University Press of Kansas, 1996.

Howells, William D. Gnadenhütten. In *Three Villages.* Boston: James R. Osgood and Company, 1884.

Jackson, Donald, ed. *Black Hawk: An Autobiography.* Urbana: University of Illinois Press, 1964.

Johansen, Bruce E., ed. *Encyclopedia of Native American Legal Tradition*. Westport, CT: Greenwood Press, 1998.

Johansen, Bruce E. *Shapers of the Great Debate on Native Americans: Land, Spirit, and Power*. Westport, CT: Greenwood Press, 2000.

Johansen, Bruce E., and Donald A. Grinde, Jr. *The Encyclopedia of Native American Biography*. New York: Holt, 1997.

Johnson v. MacIntosh 8 Wheaton 543 (1823).

Jones, Louis Thomas. *Aboriginal American Oratory*. Los Angeles: Southwest Museum, 1965.

Josephy, Alvin, Jr. *The Patriot Chiefs*. New York: Viking, 1961.

Mann, Barbara A. "The Last of the Mohicans" and " 'The Indian-haters.' " Forbidden Ground: Racial Politics and Hidden Identity in James Fenimore Cooper's Leather-Stocking Tales. Ph.D. dissertation, University of Toledo, 1997: 168–182, 219–229.

Marsh, Thelma R. *Lest We Forget: A Brief Sketch of Wyandot County's History*. Upper Sandusky, OH: Wyandot County Historical Society, 1967.

McNickle, D'Arcy. *They Came Here First: The Epic of the American Indian*. Philadelphia: Lippincott, 1949.

McNickle, D'Arcy. *Native American Tribalism*. New York: Oxford University Press, 1973.

Moquin, Wayne. *Great Documents in American Indian History*. New York: Praeger, 1973.

Moulton, Gary. *John Ross: Cherokee Chief*. Athens: University of Georgia Press, 1978.

Moulton, Gary, ed. *The Journals of the Lewis and Clark Expedition*. 11 vols. Lincoln: University of Nebraska Press, 2001.

Nabokov, Peter. *Native Testimony*. New York: Viking, 1991.

Nebard, Grace R. *Sacajawea*. Glendale, CA: Arthur H. Clark, 1932.

Notice. *Philadelphia Gazette*, 2705, April 1782, 2.

O'Brien, Sharon. *American Indian Tribal Governments*. Norman: University of Oklahoma Press, 1989.

Oskinson, John M. *Tecumseh and His Times*. New York: J. P. Putnam, 1938.

Parker, Arthur. *The Code of Handsome Lake, the Seneca Prophet*. New York State Museum Bulletin No. 163. Albany, 1913.

Parker, Arthur. *Parker on the Iroquois*. Edited by William Fenton. Syracuse, NY: Syracuse University Press, 1968.

Parkman, Francis. *History of the Conspiracy of Pontiac*. Boston: Little, Brown, 1868.

Peckham, Howard H. *Pontiac and the Indian Uprising*. Chicago: University of Chicago Press, 1947.

Porter, C. Fayne. *Our Indian Heritage: Profiles of Twelve Great Leaders*. Philadelphia: Chilton, 1964.

Rogers, Robert. *A Concise Account of North America*. London: J. Millan, 1765.

Rogin, Michael Paul. *Fathers and Children: Andrew Jackson and the Subjugation of the American Indian*. New York: Knopf, 1975.

Rosenstiel, Annette. *Red and White: Indian Views of the White Man, 1492–1982*. New York: Universe Books, 1983.

Satz, Ronald N. *American Indian Policy in the Jacksonian Era*. Lincoln: University of Nebraska Press, 1975.

Seymour, Flora W. *Sacajawea: American Pathfinder*. New York: Macmillan, 1991.

Smith, Jean Edward. *John Marshall: Definer of a Nation*. New York: Holt, 1996.

Stannard, David. *American Holocaust: Columbus and the Conquest of the New World*. New York: Oxford University Press, 1992.

Tebbel, John, and Keith Jennison. *The American Indian Wars*. New York: Bonanza Books, 1960.

Thwaites, Reuben Gold. *The Original Journals of Lewis and Clark*. New York: Dodd, Mead & Co., 1904–1905.

Tocqueville, Alexis de. *Democracy in America*. Translated by Henry Reeve. New York: Century, 1898.

Tucker, Glenn. *Tecumseh: Vision of Glory*. Indianapolis: Bobbs-Merrill, 1956.

Vanderworth, W. C. *Indian Oratory*. Norman: University of Oklahoma Press, 1971.

Van Every, Dale. *Disinherited: The Lost Birthright of the American Indian*. New York: Morrow, 1966.

Wallace, Anthony F. C. *The Death and Rebirth of the Seneca*. New York: Knopf, 1970.

Wallace, Paul A. W., ed. Captivity and Murder. In *Thirty Thousand Miles with John Heckewelder*. Pittsburgh: University of Pittsburgh Press, 1958: 170–207.

Washburn, Wilcomb E., ed. *The American Indian and the United States: A Documentary History*. New York: Random House, 1973.

Waters, Frank. *Brave Are My People: Indian Heroes Not Forgotten*. Santa Fe: Clear Light, 1993.

Wheaton, Henry. *Elements of International Law*. Boston: Dana, 1866.

Wilkinson, Charles F. *American Indians, Time, and the Law: Native Societies in a Modern Constitutional Democracy*. New Haven, CT: Yale University Press, 1987.

Worcester, Donald, ed. *Forked Tongues and Broken Treaties*. Caldwell, ID: Caxton, 1975.

Worcester v. Georgia 31 U.S. (6 Pet.) 515 (1832).

Wright, Ronald. *Stolen Continents: The Americas through Indian Eyes Since 1492*. Boston: Houghton-Mifflin, 1992.

Young, Calvin. M. *Little Turtle*. Fort Wayne, IN: Public Library of Fort Wayne and Allen County, 1956.

CHAPTER 6

~

The Northwest Coast and California

The peoples of the Northwest Coast of North America have proved themselves to be exceptional on several counts. For example, they produced a genuinely high culture (ranking with that of the Pueblos of the Southwest or the temple mound people of the Southeast) without benefit of agriculture, a very rare event in the history of humankind. Instead of pottery and agriculture, the Northwest Coast peoples, extending along the coast from the Alaska Panhandle to coastal Oregon and northern California, created exquisite baskets and wooden bowls that they filled with the bounty of the forests and the sea. The Saskatoon berry, which they harvest, for example, contains three times as much iron as prunes and raisins. The bounty of the ocean and forests was so abundant and so skillfully exploited by the Northwest Coast peoples that most were able during the summer to lay up enough food (much of it dried) to last the winter. The major sources of protein for the Northwest Coast peoples were fish and sea mammals. Among the Makah, the word for "fish" is the same as the word for "food."

The social and economic lifeways of Northwest Coast peoples evolved very differently compared to those of Native peoples across the rest of North America. Although many other American Indian peoples were democratic in their political orientation, the Northwest Coast peoples maintained a very strict caste system. They also maintained an economy that was not communal, like those of many other Native peoples in North America. In a Northwest Coast village, everyone had a class, and everything had an owner.

Economic, political, and ceremonial power were highly prized and unequally distributed among the Northwest Coast peoples. Like few other Native peoples, they paid intense attention to private property. Such wealth was inherited. A chief might own a lodge, salvage rights in nearby forests, and even fishing rights along a portion of coastline for miles offshore. Chiefs also

Wilson Parker, a Makah whaler, carrying sealskin floats and
a harpoon. Photographed by E. S. Curtis. (Courtesy of the
Edward S. Curtis Collection, Library of Congress.)

owned salmon spawning streams and the right to fish in them. A chief also
might own important ceremonial property, such as dances and songs, as well
as the right to present certain rituals. Lesser chiefs owned less-valuable resources. All land that had an economic use was owned by some member of the
nobility. A chief could create power networks under his aegis by allowing
lesser chiefs' families or commoners access to his lands and waters, usually for
a second harvest.

An elderly Makah woman carrying faggots at Neah Bay, Washington. (Courtesy of the Library of Congress.)

Ownership extended to human beings. Slavery in Northwest Coast cultures was not an imitation of Anglo-American cultures before the U.S. Civil War; it pre-dated European contact. In the richest villages, slaves made up roughly a third of the population; the richest chiefs might own fifty slaves of both sexes. Slaves had no rights and owned nothing except their ability to work. Some male slaves, at least among the Makah, were initiated into the Klukwali (or wolf) Society; during its ceremonies, they participated as equals with nobles and commoners. Members of this secret society also could lodge complaints against each other and discuss grievances regardless of social rank or class, thus bringing some degree of accountability and equality to an otherwise very stratified society.

Slave labor became so important in Tlinget society that upper-class women did little or no work. At puberty, an upper-class Tlinget woman was sent into seclusion for from four months to a year. The longer the period of seclusion, the higher the person's rank and the greater the necessity of having slaves to meet everyday needs. A woman in seclusion was not allowed to engage in any economically productive activity.

Slaves were important commodities in the social economy of the Tlinget. Slaves might be killed or freed to give family and clan "crests" ceremonial value. Slaves were more often freed than killed, however; freed slaves (often captives from other villages) could then assume important positions in Tlinget society, sometimes because of their talents as carvers, dancers, or sorcerers. A skilled slave had some leverage in Tlinget society, and several families might vie for his services.

Native peoples living around Puget Sound were prime targets of their slave-raiding neighbors to the north, with the Makahs (some of whom held slaves themselves) notable as middlemen in the coastal slave trade. Occasionally, the Puget Sound tribes struck back. Chief Sea'th'l (Seattle) gained influence among his people, the Duwamish (who lived on the site of the present-day city of Seattle), in 1810 by leading warriors against tribes in the foothills of the Cascades who had taken some of his people as slaves.

OZETTE: A VILLAGE PRESERVED BY A NATURAL DISASTER

Ozette, on the Pacific coast of present-day Washington State, was one of several hundred Northwest Coast native villages. For archeologists, however, it is a special place. During the fifteenth century, a mudslide sealed the village almost airtight, preserving wooden houses, canoes, and other artifacts that would have decayed if they had been exposed to open air. The Northwest Coast peoples used wood for nearly every article they made, from canoes (which were hollowed out of huge logs) to eating utensils. Most of these implements were carved and painted with exquisite abstract designs depicting cosmology and the natural world. Five hundred years later, in 1966, a team from Washington State University found Ozette (Pascua, 1991, 38–53).

Related families lived together in plank houses flanked by gables, behind house posts carved and painted with family crests. Thus, totem poles are not religious icons, but family heralds, similar in some ways to European coats of arms. The word *totem* (meaning clan) was applied to the poles by European Americans; it stems from central Algonquian and is unrelated to any Northwest Coast language.

The Northwest Coast peoples also traded with their neighbors. The region drained by the Columbia River was a Native crossroads, a network of trade routes, that extended mainly north to south and vice versa along the entire coast; the language of the Chinook was reduced to an elementary form as a trading medium that spread from Alaska to California. Ironically, the Chinook people merged with the Chehalis in the mid-eighteenth century, and quit using their own language, which survived for many years afterward only in the abbreviated form used for trading. One of the words in this trade jargon, *hootchenoo*, became "hooch," slang for alcoholic beverages in American English.

THE POLITICAL AND CEREMONIAL
ECONOMY OF THE POTLATCH

Because the chiefs controlled access to food, shelter, and even spiritual sustenance, the societies of the Northwest Coast peoples were more hierarchical than even the Aztecs or the monarchical societies of Europe during the period of first contacts with Native America. No councils of chiefs existed to exercise restraint on them. Customs did exercise restraint on unbridled power, however. A good chief gathered power by being generous to those "under the arm." The ceremonial potlatch was an expression of this ethic: On one level, it was a display of wealth by the chief or chiefs hosting it; on another level, the intricate gift-giving of the ritual bespoke an inherent desire to distribute the bounteous wealth of Northwest Coast Native American societies. The potlatch thus consolidated the power and authority of its hosts by reminding lesser nobles and commoners that the high chiefs controlled every aspect of village life.

The mild, rainy winters of the Northwest Coast are a time of elaborate socializing and ceremonies. The potlatch often became a festival of wealth squandering between rival chiefs. Everything about the potlatch bespoke ostentation. Guests arrived in ornately carved canoes, flanked by assistants, all dressed in their best clothes. Once at the potlatch, which might have been planned for years, guests were expected to feast until they became ill from overindulgence. Competing chiefs wore headgear topped with special rings that indicated the number of potlatches they had held. In a social and economic context, the potlatch indicated the value the Northwest Coast peoples placed on status. The ostentation of the ritual also bespoke a society of surplus—one so successful at adapting to its environment that its members virtually had resources to burn or otherwise consume with reckless disregard for necessity.

Northwest Coast ceremonies, including the potlatch, were not usually concerned so much with the economic motives of getting and giving as with enhancing social status, honoring ancestors, and sealing personal relationships. According to Duane Champagne, the potlatch "should be understood from within its own cultural and institutional framework, and not be too easily compared with self-interested materialism" (1989, 110). Similarly, the emphasis on rank in Northwest Coast societies was not simply an imitation of Western hierarchical societies. Instead, the Tlinget concept of rank was integrated into that peoples' belief that proper behavior in the present (such as contributing to potlatches, fulfilling one's clan obligations, and submitting to the collective will of the house group) could cause a person to be reborn into a more aristocratic lineage.

The word *potlatch* is anglicized from *patshatl*, meaning "giving." Such giving could take many forms. At a "grease feast," for example, precious oil sometimes was splashed on fires until erupting flames burned members of competing households. Sometimes, the spattering oil set their cedar clothing aflame.

As a potlatch continued, the value of gifts usually rose steadily. After the rival chiefs had given away valuable cedar boxes and other expensive items, one chief might up the ante by sacrificing a slave with a special club called a slave killer. The giving chief might then hurl the scalp of the slain slave at his rival. Slaves also could be freed at potlatches. Another act of potlatch one-upmanship was the giving and destruction of large copper plates that served

Kaw-Claa, Tlinget Native woman in full potlach dancing costume. (Courtesy of the Library of Congress.)

as currency of very high denomination, in the thousands of dollars if converted into U.S. currency.

Like most other aspects of life among Northwest Coast peoples, the potlatch was carried out with rigid, time-honored formality. Part of the ritual was rehearsed insults in which one chief often dared the other to give away ever more precious objects, such as the fabled canoes that were carved out of huge tree trunks and used to hunt whales. Some of the insults were very personal. The Kwakiutl may have been adopting a European custom from the Hudson's Bay Company when they complicated the potlatch by demanding 100 percent interest on gifts, a postcontact wrinkle in the ritual in which the act of giving now incurred a debt at twice the value of the original gift.

The Northwest Coast peoples hosted a number of other ceremonies and rituals in addition to the potlatch. Some of these rituals were associated with secret societies (exclusive groups of genetically unrelated individuals sometimes called sodalities by anthropologists). Perhaps the most important such ritual among the Kwakiutl-speaking peoples of the British Columbia coast was the cannibal dance, in which an individual, seized by an emotional frenzy, pretended to consume the flesh of another person. Illusions and fakery enjoyed a high degree of prestige among the Northwest Coast peoples, and a small bear might be cooked in such a way that it resembled a human being to be consumed during the cannibal dance. The person doing the cannibal dance might enliven the atmosphere by seizing bits of skin and flesh from members of the audience.

FIRST EUROPEAN CONTACTS

At the time of the American Revolution, English-speaking people on the Atlantic coast had only the slightest knowledge of the Northwest Coast peoples. The first, brief, European contact with them occurred when Vitus Bering, a Dane, sailed from Siberia in search of the strait that now bears his name. A few years after that, Juan de Fuca sailed through the strait between the Olympic Peninsula and Vancouver Island, where he left his name. Bering made only the slightest contact with Native peoples (on Kayak Island) before his ship, the St. Peter, was wrecked on an island between Siberia and Alaska during his return trip. Bering died on that island, but most of his crew survived, eating the flesh of sea otters as they rebuilt the ship. The crew took some of the otters' sleek pelts home with them to Europe. Within a few years, those otter skins ignited a commercial stampede to the Northwest Coast in search of the biggest fur discovery since the beaver.

During 1792, exploring the Pacific Northwest, British navigator George Vancouver found the bones of smallpox victims scattered on the beaches in great numbers. The survivors, noted Peter Puget, a sailor in Vancouver's party, were "most terribly pitted . . . indeed many had lost their eyes" (Mann, 2002, 44). In *Pox Americana* (2001), historian Elizabeth Fenn asserted that the deaths along the Pacific coast were part of a continent-wide pandemic that was almost two decades old, having begun near Boston during 1774, sweeping from Alaska to Mexico.

Employees of the Hudson's Bay Company entered the otter hunt early, as English envoys among the coastal peoples. The company, the premiere vehicle for English trade across the entire north country, was initiated during 1670 to counter the trading acumen of the French *coureurs de bois*, especially in competition for the best of *oiled beaver*, the term for a skin that had been worn with the skin side in, usually by an Indian, for several months to give it a luxurious, subtle texture and shine. In 1796, the Hudson's Bay Company split into two rival factions that engaged in a vicious trade war in which both companies wooed the Indians with 195,000 gallons of liquor in two years. The two factions then merged again until 1821.

In the meantime, whales, caribou, and other sea and land animals that had sustained Native peoples for many thousands of years were hunted nearly to extinction by immigrants in some areas of the Northwest. Freebooting Russian *promyshleniki* killed whatever they could find, from giant (six feet claw to claw) Bering Sea king crabs to beached seals. The freebooters also slaughtered the native Aleuts, whom they described as artistic, mild, polite, and hospitable. The Russians' words seemed to echo those of Columbus nearly three centuries earlier, as he spoke of the Indians' hospitality and then of how easily they might be enslaved. By 1799, when the Russian-American Company (a monopoly granted by the Russian czar) brought the slaughter under control, 90 percent of the Aleuts had been killed. By 1824, the Greek Orthodox Church was recruiting the souls of the few Aleuts who remained. The Aleuts, recalling the violent nature of the Russians they had so regrettably encountered in earlier years, had great respect for any holy man who could save their souls.

Among the Native peoples of the Northwest Coast, the Russians became known as the most ruthless of colonizers. Their demands for tribute in furs were met by armed resistance by the Tlingit, to whom the Russians' British and American colonial competitors happily supplied firearms, even cannons. In 1802, Tlingit war parties, long practiced in internecine warfare up and down the coast, struck at Russian settlements. A large force of Tlingit descended on the Russian colony of New Archangel on Sitka Island, burned most of the structures in the town, and made off with 4,000 sea otter pelts as they killed 20 Russians and 120 vassal Aleuts. The Tlingits held the position for two years, until Russian warships shelled it in 1804. The next year, the Tlingits resumed their insurgency, attacking the Russian settlement of Yakutat, killing twenty-two Russians and many Aleuts. In 1806, roughly 2,000 Native warriors assembled near Sitka in 400 boats. The Russians, warned of the attack, decided to throw a large feast, which defused the planned assault. Nevertheless, the Russian settlements faced regular guerilla raids by smaller native bands for years after that.

A search for a reliable food supply to provision their growing settlements brought the Russians to the California coast shortly after 1800, where they imitated the Spanish missions by establishing farming settlements that used coerced Native labor. Landing at Bodega Bay in 1812, ninety-five Russians and eighty Aleuts founded Fort Ross. The location was appealing because rocky islands offshore allowed the Russians to hunt sea otters for their prized pelts. At the fort, the Russians established vineyards, orchards, and fields of grain. The Russians ordered the fields tended by labor drafted from local Pomo Indians. As the demand for labor rose from fewer than 100 people to more than 250, the Pomos rebelled, burning fields, killing stock, and running from

A Pomo family. (Courtesy of the Library of Congress.)

Russian conscription squads. In the meantime, diseases introduced by the Russians were killing Pomos in larger numbers than slave labor.

Among the Inuit of the Canadian North, trade brought the "summer drunk," during which men, having been paid for their furs, spent the short summer returning their money to the traders in exchange for hard liquor. In the traditional way of life, summer had been a time of hunting and gathering, storing provisions for the long, hard winter. Coming off their summer drunks with empty larders, the Inuit men and their families died en masse during the winter. (In their language, *Inuit* means "real people." The term *Eskimo*, which is Algonquian for "eater of raw meat," has no indigenous meaning.) During 1888, a revenue ship docked at St. Lawrence Island, at the southern aperture of the Bering Strait, to find the entire population of three settlements, 400 people of both sexes and all ages, dead of starvation. Hunters who spent their summers trying to lay up game for winter found that meat animals were getting harder to find every year.

NATIVE AMERICANS AND SLAVERY

The Russians were hardly alone as they enslaved Native Americans. Early Spanish explorers arrived in America planning to take slaves. When De Soto's expedition arrived in Florida, they brought leg irons and metal collars linked with chains for the express purpose of conveying Indian slaves along their line of march. After the Pequot War, in 1675, Massachusetts colonists sold their prisoners into slavery in the West Indies. The Spanish at about the same time were shipping their Native American prisoners of war to Cuba as slaves. The Apaches greatly enhanced their diets by raiding Spanish settlements and missions for cattle, mules, and horses. The Spanish retaliated by capturing Apaches and selling them as slaves. Most of the slaves were compelled to work in Spanish mines. Any Apache was game for enslavement, even those who had come to trade or who had converted to Christianity.

During early English colonial history, several hundred Native Americans were listed as slaves. In 1704, South Carolinians under Colonel James Moore united with Indian allies to invade northern Florida, which was under Spanish control at the time, razing fourteen missions and capturing about 1,000 people, who were taken home as slaves. In 1708, about 1,400 slaves of Native American descent were listed in South Carolina, a quarter of the total slaves in the colony. In 1726, Louisiana, under French control, listed 229 Indian slaves and 1,540 blacks. The Pawnees were captured so often that the word *Panis* became a synonym for "slave" in the language of the French colonies.

Early in the nineteenth century, as Mexico became independent, Navajos, Utes, and Comanches, sometimes working with Mexicans, staged many raids in Hopi country for scalps (to exchange for money) and slaves, to be sold in markets at Santa Fe and Chihuahua. Children were targeted most frequently by the raiders.

The slave trade sometimes became entwined with trade in horses. As noted, Northwest Coast peoples held slaves, so some European Americans were taken and sold as well. Having acquired horses in the early nineteenth century, the Klamaths raided Shasta and Pit River Indian villages in northern California, acquiring slaves who were traded at The Dalles, in present-day Oregon (site of a regional slave market), for more horses and trade goods. With the advent of the fur trade, Russians (and even some Japanese fishermen) sometimes were taken captive for sale and barter at The Dalles.

The trading markets of The Dalles were part of a commercial network maintained by the Chinooks along the lower Columbia River. Native peoples from as far away as Hawaii sometimes changed hands in The Dalles slave markets, where canoes and blankets, as well as horses, also were exchanged. Some of the treaties signed by Isaac Stevens in Washington Territory contained legal prohibitions of slave-taking by Native Americans, an indication that the practice was economically significant at the time. After the Civil War, agents of the U.S. government actively tried to suppress the Native American slave trade, causing prices to rise. During 1830, the going rate for a young, healthy, male slave in The Dalles' market was about ten blankets. Within a few decades, the Haida were paying up to 200 blankets per slave.

On balance, however, many more Native Americans were enslaved by Europeans than vice-versa. Los Angeles maintained a thriving slave market in the shell of an old mission, to which Indians were delivered after they had been arrested for drunkenness. The *aguardiente* sold to the Indians was very powerful alcohol; it was sometimes mixed with corrosive acids. This addictive poison was sometimes called *forty rod*, the estimated distance that an Indian might stagger before dying after drinking it. Indians were said to go insane from it following wild drunks. Thousands of Indians may have died in this way. The death toll from alcohol and murder was never tallied. Anyone with a need for cheap labor could bail Indians out for a day at $2 or $3 a head, renting them from the drunk tank as slave labor.

Into the 1860s, Native Americans who had been picked up for drinking by the Los Angeles police were "sold" to local farmers and ranchers as day labor. In 1850 and 1860, the newly established state of California enacted laws that allowed for Indian "apprenticeship," a state-approved grant of a form of near-slavery by which a property owner could obtain the labor of as many Native young people as he wished, on stipulation that he feed and clothe them and treat them "humanely." The measure was promoted as a means of teaching the Indians "civilized" habits. A debate rose over the terms of the laws, which in effect made several thousand Indian young people indentured servants at the same time that California had been admitted to the United States as a "free" state. In the 1850s, the going sales price for an adult Indian was about $50. The indenture law was repealed in 1863 (as part of the nationwide Civil War debate over slavery), but illegal kidnappings and sales of Indians continued through at least the 1870s, although in smaller numbers. Travel literature sometimes drew the attention of potential immigrants to the advantages of free Indian labor that was not available in other states.

The Aztecs also held slaves, but their society invoked some social sanctions against mistreatment of domestic servants. Slaves were said to be under the protection of their own god, Tezcatlipoca, who, it was believed, could ruin the lives of rich people who mistreated them. It was said that Tezcatlipoca could cause mistreated slaves to be freed and their cruel masters to lose their wealth. Aztec society not only was stratified, but also offered people some degree of social mobility, both upward and downward. Not infrequently, an affluent individual might fall into slavery for debt. Gamblers sometimes put their personal liberty up for sale when they had lost all else (Soustelle, 1961, 159). When the Spanish conquered Tenochtitlán, they incorporated some of the Aztecs' slavery system into their own economy. According to the Spanish chronicler Bernadino de Sahagún, "In the first years there was such haste to make slaves that they poured into Mexico City from all directions, and throughout the Indies they were taken like sheep in flocks to be branded" (de Zorita, 1963, 207).

The Spanish god did not reproach them for mistreating slaves, so Native Americans often were worked to death in the mines or as personal porters who were compelled to carry Spanish household goods and merchandise on their backs, as many as a thousand porters at a time, for hundreds of miles. According to official edict, Indian labor was "voluntary." According to Sahagún, "In actual fact, the Indians never go voluntarily." Women and children were pressed into the porters' brigades along with men, "loaded down with [Spaniards'] household furnishings, beds, chairs, tables, and all the other appointments for their household and kitchen service. Thus weighted down ... they returned to their homes half dead, or died along the way" (de Zorita, 1963, 208). Indians in New Spain, according to Sahagún, "have also been laid low by the labor of making sheep, cattle, and pig farms, fencing those farms, of putting up farm buildings, and by their labor on roads, bridges, watercourses, stone walls, and sugar mills," as well as mines (ibid., 209). On top of all this labor, Indian villages were compelled to pay tribute to the Spanish, at central collection sites. Sahagún believed that the labor the Spanish imposed on the Indians destroyed them: "So the Indian returns home worn out from his toil, minus his pay and his mantle, not to speak of the food that he had brought with him," he wrote, continuing: "He returns home famished, unhappy, distraught, and shattered in health. For these reasons, pestilence always rages among the Indians" (ibid., 215).

EXTERMINATION OF THE CALIFORNIA NATIVES

The Spanish mission system was a form of slavery in all but name. Women in some of the missions around San Francisco Bay aborted their children rather than allow them to grow up under the subjugation of the missions. Captive Apaches, Navajos, Comanches, Utes, Pawnees, and Wichitas served as muleteers, household servants, day laborers, shepherds, silversmiths, blacksmiths, masons, and weavers. California Indians, who lived in hundreds of independent groups, were generally unable to mount organized resistance to the Spanish mission system, but they went into service of the Catholic Church without enthusiasm. So testified numerous friars, who nonetheless impressed Indian labor to cultivate bountiful crops and create a rich variety of salable crafts.

The Spanish empire and its mission system in California came to a very sudden end between 1811 and 1825, after 300 years of virtual slavery for thousands of Native American peoples. During the decade and a half after 1811, most of Spain's colonies in the New World achieved their independence. Mexico became an independent kingdom in 1821 and a republic in 1824. California, at first a province of Mexico, secularized its wealthiest missions in 1834. In theory, the land that had comprised the missions was to be returned to the Indians who had worked on them, making them self-sustaining peoples. Instead, most of the land became part of private ranches, and most of the Indians were driven away. By the time the mission lands and other property had been distributed to California's new Hispanic upper class, the United States conquered the area between 1846 and 1848.

Like most of Mexico's northern half, California became a territory of the westward-expanding United States. In 1848, gold was discovered; within a year, California was flooded by gold-rushing "Forty-niners." In 1848, before California became a state, its non-Indian population was about 15,000. By 1850, the population had increased to 93,000 according to the federal census. At least 100,000 Indians had lived in the area before the gold rush; the best estimate in 1856 was 40,000. The Native American population of the area fell to fewer than 30,000 in 1864 and 19,000 in 1906 as the immigrant population continued to swell.

With the discovery of gold in present-day Nevada, the Paiutes, who had lived in the Great Basin at least 10,000 years, were forced to face a tidal wave of European American settlement. The gold-seekers surged into Virginia City and other quickly erected commercial centers so fast that some of the Paiutes, who had no warring tradition and no capacity for armed resistance, tried to get away as quickly as they could. Some Paiutes buried their children up to the necks in the desert sand and piled clumps of brush over their heads. The Paiutes had hoped to retrieve the children later, but most of them were never able to return to a land suddenly awash with a flood of miners and land speculators.

Stands of pinon trees, with nuts that had been a staple in the Paiutes' diet, were cut in huge swaths for firewood, and cattle, sheep, and horses denuded the dryland prairie. Cholera quickly killed 2,000 Paiutes. A few of the survivors, skirting starvation, joined with Shoshonis and Utes in occasional petty theft from white settlements. During the 1860s, the Paiutes were subjugated by military force and vigilantes. Within a generation, the only means of survival open to a Basin Indian was menial work as a housekeeper or field hand. By 1874, 10,000 years of a people's life in the Great Basin were nearly wiped clean from humankind's memory.

For several decades, the new immigrants in California and Nevada took part in what may have been the largest unprovoked slaughter of Native peoples during the bloody nineteenth century. In one massacre, thirty Indians were butchered in retaliation for the wounding by a Native man of a single steer. The Indians were not able to organize a mass resistance, but every hint of trouble was met by hastily organized "volunteer" Indian fighters, who later billed the federal government for their services on the theory that they were doing the work of the U.S. Army. During the 1850s, the federal government reimbursed California almost $1 million (several million dollars today) for freelance Indian hunting. The victims of the volunteers, who had none of the scruples displayed by some regular Army officers, were mainly (but hardly exclusively) Native American men.

The earliest gold rush was led by single men. Although they did not kill Native women as frequently as men, women suffered rape and assault. Venereal diseases from prostitution ravaged the native women of California. Even the immigrants' newspapers protested frequent gang rapes of native women by miners. Between 3,000 and 4,000 Indian children were stolen to be sold as servants or slaves between 1852 and 1867, not including women forced into having sex or adults taken into slavery (often to redeem debts) for field labor.

A few Natives fought back. One was a Modoc called Captain Jack by the immigrants (his native name was Kintpuash), leader of a renegade band that rebelled against intolerable reservation conditions by escaping to the northern California lava beds of their homeland. With about sixty compatriots, Captain Jack kept as many as a thousand soldiers at bay for seven months in the rugged country. After they kidnapped several children, Captain Jack and his allies were regarded as terrorists by farmers in the Yureka area of northern California.

Troops arrived in 1872 to force Captain Jack and his men back to their as-signed reservation. Before the Army hanged him and three of his close friends, Captain Jack led a campaign through the lava beds of northern California that took the lives of more than 100 soldiers. At a peace conference, Captain Jack shot General E. R. S. Canby, the leader of the non-Indian treaty commissioners, to death. After the killing of Canby, the Army shelled the lava beds with field guns to drive Captain Jack and his band out. Captain Jack wore Canby's uniform until the day he was hanged.

MARTIAL LAW IN WASHINGTON TERRITORY

Beginning in 1843, continuing until the middle 1850s, Washington Territory Governor Isaac Stevens "negotiated" at least 50 heavy-handed treaties with the Natives of the Pacific Northwest. Most of his effort was concentrated east of the Cascades, in the areas that today comprise eastern Washington, eastern Oregon, and Idaho. The Native peoples felt insulted by most of the treaties, by which they were cajoled and threatened into signing away 157 million acres.

The 1855 Walla Walla Treaty galled them the most. The Yakimas, claim-ing that Stevens had bought off their leaders, recruited allies from several other tribes and waged an armed guerilla war with the U.S. Army that spread over the mountains to the Pacific coast. The Army brought the rebellion under control after three years of occasionally bloody fighting. During the rebellion, Dr. Marcus Whitman (whom, it was said, had come to the Walla Walla area to civilize the Indians with a Bible in one hand and a whip in the other) was murdered, along with his wife and twelve other immigrant European Amer-icans. A freelance posse formed immediately and hung five captured Cayuse in retribution.

Although settlement of the coastal Northwest began at the same time as California, accelerating about 1850, most of the people who traversed the continent along the Oregon Trail were not looking for gold or other quick riches. Most sought farms (some planned utopian communes), and they found alliances with the Native peoples of the area to be in their interests. Some even aided Indians who were dissatisfied with the terms of a series of treaties negotiated by Governor Stevens. When his white opponents sought the protection of local courts, Stevens called up a militia of a thousand men, declared martial law, closed the courts, and arrested the chief justice of the territory—a rare example of government by fiat in the face of settlers' resistance to ill treatment of Indians. By that time, European American immigrants were flooding the area around Puget Sound as the Duwamish (led by chief Sea'th'l) abandoned their homelands peacefully as the urban area approached.

A brief but bloody native uprising followed, ending with the hanging of Chief Leschi, the leader of the Native people opposing the treaties, in 1858. Chief Leschi was hanged for killing Colonel A. Benton Moses of the territorial militia during the region's Indian war of 1855. After the chief's first trial ended with a hung jury, the judge in the second trial refused to instruct jurors that killing an enemy soldier in war was not considered murder. Chief Leschi was convicted and sentenced to death. On appeal, the territorial Supreme Court refused to consider new evidence showing that Chief Leschi had been miles away when Colonel Moses was killed.

During December 2004, Chief Leschi was exonerated by a historical court, nearly a century and a half after he was hanged. The unanimous verdict by a seven-judge panel was not legally binding, but it drew cheers from several hundred people who gathered at the Washington State history museum to hear the decision. The historical court was led by the chief justice of the State Supreme Court, Gerry L. Alexander. It ruled that if Chief Leschi did in fact kill Colonel Moses, a murder charge was not justified because they were lawful combatants in a time of war. "I'm just happy; this is really about the future," said Cynthia Iyall, a descendant of Chief Leschi's sister and chairwoman of the Committee to Exonerate Chief Leschi. "This is for all the kids: they need to know who that man was and what truthfully happened to him" ("Indian Chief," 2004).

The historical trial's verdict thus came to agree with the U.S. Army, which refused to execute Chief Leschi at the time because military leaders believed the rules of war should have prevented him from being charged with murder. Instead, civilian Pierce County authorities oversaw his execution on February 19, 1858. Leschi's hangman, Charles Grainger, later said, "I felt then I was hanging an innocent man, and I believe it yet" ("Indian Chief," 2004). Chief Leschi's name is remembered in the region. His name appears on schools, monuments, a park, and a Seattle neighborhood.

Chief Sea'th'l (Seattle) and Angeline with views of Mt. Rainier and Seattle.
(Courtesy of the Library of Congress.)

Sea'th'l's Haunting "Farewell Speech"

Sea'th'l (Duwamish/Suquamish, ca. 1788–1866) probably was born on Blake Island in Puget Sound. He was a principal chief of the Duwamish, whose original homeland is today an industrial area immediately south of downtown Seattle. Sea'th'l was described in 1833 by William Fraser Tolmie, a Hudson's Bay Company surgeon, as "a brawney Suquamish with a Roman countenance and black curley [sic] hair, the handsomest Indian I have ever seen" (Johansen and Grinde, 1997, 341). David Denny, one of the first white settlers of Seattle, said that Sea'th'l's voice could be heard a half-mile away when he spoke, and that he led his people by force of his considerable intellect.

Son of the Duwamish chief Schweabe, Sea'th'l was about seven years of age when George Vancouver sailed the *Discovery* into Puget Sound and met briefly with the Duwamish and their allies, the Suquamish. Sea'th'l later aided his father and other Duwamish in the construction of the Old Man House, a community longhouse 1,000 feet long that housed 40 families. The Duwamish and the Suquamish formed an alliance that ringed central Puget Sound. Sea'th'l took a wife, La-da-ila, and he became chief of the Duwamish-Suquamish alliance at the age of 22. La-da-ila had died by 1833, when the Hudson's Bay Company established a trading post at Nisqually, in southern Puget Sound. In 1841, the first "Bostons," as the Duwamish called whites (they had arrived from Boston), sailed into Central Puget Sound in Sea'th'l's territory. Ten years later, the schooner *Exact* delivered the first settlers in what later became the city of Seattle.

From the beginning, Sea'th'l resolved to cooperate with the settlers, but when they proposed naming their city after him, he protested that his spirit would be disturbed if his name was mentioned after he died. The settlers retained the name anyway, in an anglicized form. Sea'th'l, who had been a Catholic since the 1830s when he was converted by missionaries, adopted the biblical name Noah at his baptism and began regular morning and evening prayers among his people.

Sea'th'l and his band moved westward across Puget Sound after signing the Treaty of Point Elliot with Washington Territorial Governor Isaac Stevens during 1854. As his people prepared to move, Sea'th'l delivered a haunting farewell speech that has come to be recognized as one of history's great pieces of Native American oratory. The speech was given in Salish and translated by Dr. Henry Smith, who published it in 1887, which was 33 years after the original oration. Given the amount of time between the speech and its publication, the fact that Sea'th'l was not speaking English (Smith heard a translation), and numerous modern embellishments of the original printed text, modern versions sometimes are unreliable.

Environmental conservation was not a subject of general debate and controversy in the mid-nineteenth century, as Euro-American settlement sped across the land mass of the United States. Yet, from time to time, the records of the settlers contain warnings by Native leaders whose peoples they were displacing describing how European-bred attitudes toward nature were ruining the land, air, and water. Perhaps the most famous warning of this type came from Chief Sea'th'l's farewell speech.

> Our dead never forget the beautiful world that gave them being. They still love its verdant valleys, its murmuring rivers, its magnificent mountains, sequestered vales and verdant-lined lakes and bays. . . . Every part of this soil is sacred in the estimation of my people. Every hillside, every valley, every plain and grove has been hallowed by some sad or happy event in days long vanished. Even the rocks, which seem to be dumb and dead as they swelter in the sun along the silent shore, thrill with memories of stirring events connected with the lives of my people. (Vanderwerth, 1971, 120–121)

In the development of environmental philosophy, Chief Sea'th'l's words are often cited in the late twentieth century as evidence that many Native Americans practiced a stewardship ethic toward the earth long before such attitudes became popular in non-Indian society. The debate ranges from acceptance of several versions of Sea'th'l's speech to a belief that the original translator, Dr. Henry Smith, as well as many people who followed him, put the ecological concepts into the chief's mouth.

Regardless of the exact wording of Sea'th'l's speech, it did contain environmental themes. Sea'th'l was not telling the immigrants what they wanted to hear because they displayed no such ideological bent. The farewell speech, as recorded, also touched on fundamental differences between cultures:

> The white man's god cannot love his red children[,] or he would protect them. . . . We are two distinct races with separate origins and separate destinies. . . . To us, the ashes of our ancestors are sacred and their resting place is hallowed ground. You wander far from the graves of your ancestors, seemingly without regret. Your religion was written on tables of stone by the iron fingers of your God so that you cannot forget it. The Red Man could never comprehend nor remember it. Our religion is the tradition of our ancestors—the dreams of our old men, given to them in the solemn hours of the night by the Great Spirit, and the visions of our sachems; and it is written in the hearts of our people. Your dead cease to love you and the land of their nativity as soon as they pass the portals of the tomb and wander away among the stars. They are soon forgotten and never return. Our dead never forget the world that gave them being. (Furtwangler, 1997, 14–15)

> It matters little where we pass the remnants of our days. They will not be many. A few more moons, a few more winters—and not one of the descendants of the mighty hosts that once moved over this broad land . . . will remain to mourn over the graves of a people once more powerful and hopeful than yours. But why should we repine? Why should I murmur at the fate of my people? Tribes are made up of individuals and are no better than they. Men come and go like waves of the sea. A tear, a *tahmanawis* [a mourning ceremony], a dirge, and they are gone from our longing eyes forever. Even the white men, whose God walked and talked with him, is not exempt from the common destiny. We *may* be brothers after all. We shall see. (emphasis in original; Smith, 1887, n.p.)

In the mid-1850s, when the Yakima War spilled over the Cascades into Seattle under Chief Leschi, Sea'th'l and his people looked on from their retreat on the western shores of Puget Sound. He died there in 1866.

Whites Arrested for Aiding "Renegade" Indians

During the hostilities with Chief Leschi and his allies, Governor Stevens's militia also arrested several settlers suspected of aiding "renegade" Indians. Lion A. Smith, Charles Wren, Henry Smith, John McLeod, Henry Murray, and another man asserted that they were taken from their land claims in Pierce County "without process of law, and without any complaint or affidavit being lodged against them" ("A Brief Notice," 1856, 385). The men were escorted against their will to Fort Steilacoom (near Tacoma), where they were held, at Stevens's request, on charges of treason.

Following complaints by attorneys for the men, Stevens issued a martial law declaration suspending civil liberties in Pierce County, accusing the arrested settlers of giving "aid and comfort to the enemy" ("A Brief Notice," 1856, 386). A few days later, Stevens ordered the men back to Olympia, out of Pierce County, because a judge there had issued a writ of habeas corpus on their behalf. Later, the case was taken up in the court of Honorable Edward Lander, chief justice of the territory. When Judge Lander convened court to hear the case, a column of militiamen filed into his courtroom and arrested him, leading the judge and the clerk of the court from the bench. The arrests occurred on May 6; by May 9, the judge was released. A few days later, Stevens extended martial law to Thurston County, including Olympia, the territorial capital.

A legal ballet ensued in which Governor Stevens refused to honor the writ of habeas corpus. Members of the militia stood outside the house in which Chief Justice Lander was holding court. "The marshal, being ordered to keep the room clear of armed men, was compelled to lock the door. . . . The counsel engaged inside could distinctly hear the men [outside] cocking their rifles," said a contemporary statement. An officer of the militia called on Judge Lander to surrender once again. He refused. Finally, the armed men barged into the courtroom, seized the judge and clerk, and transported them to the office of Governor Stevens. An observer said the judge was "kidnapped" ("A Brief Notice," 1856, 389). The judge was told that he would be freed if he stopped issuing orders contrary to the decree of martial law. The judge flatly refused. Stevens had violated his oath of office by refusing to respect a writ of habeas corpus, an act that the U.S. Constitution says may be suspended only by Congress.

CHIEF JOSEPH LEADS THE NEZ PERCE LONG MARCH

The Nez Perce became steadfast U.S. allies as immigrants moved into the Pacific Northwest in the face of opposition from Great Britain. They even rescued a body of U.S. troops in 1858. Nevertheless, during the same year, the United States signed a treaty with Nez Perce "treaty commissioners" who did not represent the nation. The treaty ceded the Nez Perce's Wallowa Valley to the United States, opening it for settlement. Chief Joseph (father of Young Joseph, whose long march with his people subsequently became legendary) protested that the treaty was illegal, a violation of another signed only three years earlier.

Joseph the Elder died in 1871, passing the leadership of his Nez Perce band to Hinmaton Yalatik, Thunder Rolling Over the Mountains (1841–1904), whom English speakers at first called Young Joseph and later Chief Joseph. Like his father, Young Joseph refused to surrender to reservation life.

Chief Joseph, Younger. (Courtesy of Smithsonian National
Anthropological Archives.)

The Nez Perce in Joseph's band stayed in the valley, tending their large herds
of prized horses, as European American immigrants moved in around them,
sparking several violent incidents.

As Young Joseph assumed leadership of his Nez Perce band, government
emissaries continued to press the Nez Perce to move to a reservation where they
would be allocated far too little land to run the blue Appaloosas that the Nez
Perce used for hunting and war. Under pressure from the United States, during
1871 Joseph and his band signed the last treaty negotiated by any Native nation

with the United States. Under the terms of the treaty, the Nez Perce agreed to move to Lapwai, Idaho. As the logistics of the move were being worked out, settlers stole hundreds of the Nez Perce's horses. A renegade band of young Nez Perce led by young Wahlitis, whose father had been murdered by whites two years earlier, retaliated by killing eighteen settlers. The Army was brought in to arrest the "hostiles." Instead of surrendering, the entire band of about 500 men, women, and children decamped and marched into the mountains.

During the next several months, the vastly outnumbered Nez Perce led U.S. Army troops on a 1,500-mile trek through some of the most rugged country on the continent, north into Canada, then south again. Joseph, with at most 200 warriors, fought more than a dozen engagements with four U.S. Army columns, evading capture every time. On one occasion, in a night raid, the Nez Perce made off with the pursuing Army's pack animals. At other times, the Nez Perce so skillfully evaded Army pincer movements that the two closing columns ran into each other without capturing a single hostile. The Army did inflict casualties on the Nez Perce at other times. Eighty-nine were killed in one battle, fifty of them women and children. Despite the deaths, the Nez Perce continued.

Chief Joseph instructed his warriors not to take scalps. The Nez Perce earned praise for their military acumen from General William Tecumseh Sherman, who said the Indians went to great lengths to avoid killing innocent settlers. General Nelson A. Miles, whose troops brought the Nez Perce's long march to an end, seconded Sherman's opinion: "In this skillful campaign, they have spared hundreds of lives and thousands of dollars worth of property that they might have destroyed" (Johansen and Grinde, 1997, 189).

Through the Bitterroot Mountains and the present-day Yellowstone National Park, to the headwaters of the Missouri, then to the Bear Paw Mountains, Joseph's band fought a rear-guard action with unquestioned brilliance. At one point, the Indians were harbored briefly in Canada by Sitting Bull's Lakota, who also had been exiled from their homelands. Exhausted, the Nez Perce surrendered October 5, 1877, at Eagle Creek, roughly 30 miles south of the Canadian border. Many of the Nez Perce were starving. Several also were maimed and blind. Joseph handed his rifle to General Miles, and said he was

> tired of fighting. . . . My people ask me for food, and I have none to give. It is cold, and we have no blankets, no wood. My people are starving to death. Where is my little daughter? I do not know. Perhaps, even now, she is freezing to death. Hear me, my chiefs. I have fought, but from where the sun now stands, Joseph will fight no more forever. (Johansen and Grinde, 1997, 189)

Chief Joseph then drew his blanket over his face and walked into the Army camp, a prisoner. Of roughly 650 Nez Perce who had begun the long march, only about 400 remained at its end.

At roughly the same time, a band of 297 Cheyennes, unhappy with life on an assigned reservation near Fort Reno, Oklahoma, walked a thousand miles back to their homelands along the eastern slopes of the Rockies, to the northwest. After an extremely arduous journey, about a hundred of them were captured and imprisoned at Fort Robinson, Nebraska. The Cheyennes refused to march south again in the middle of winter, and officers at the fort decided to deny the native people food until they changed their minds. Instead of changing, the captive Cheyenne burst out of the barracks, killing several soldiers. They were eventually recaptured, along with the rest of the band, and dispersed to several reservations against their wills. Meanwhile, a large number of the men, women, and children died of exposure and starvation. The march of the Cheyennes was described in Mari Sandoz's historical novel *Cheyenne Autumn*, which in turn provided the material for John Ford's 1964 movie of the same name. It was the only motion picture that Ford, the famous director of westerns, made from a Native point of view.

In 1879, Chief Joseph appealed to Congress (speaking in person to a full chamber) to let his people return home. "It has always been the pride of the Nez Perce that they were the friends of the white men," he began, recounting how the Indians helped support the first few immigrants. "There was room enough for all to live in peace, and they [Joseph's ancestors] were learning many things from the white men that appeared to be good.... Soon [we] found that the white men were growing rich very fast, and were greedy to possess everything the Indian had." He recalled how his father had refused to sign a treaty with Washington territorial governor Isaac Stevens: "I will not sign your paper.... You go where you please, so do I; you are not a child; I am no child; I can think for myself.... Take away your paper. I will not sign it." (Nabokov, 1991, 130–131). Joseph said that the Nez Perce had given too much, and that they had only gone to war when the immigrants forced them off their cherished homeland.

The War Department refused Chief Joseph's request to let his people resettle in their homeland. Instead, they were imprisoned at Fort Leavenworth, Kansas, where many who had survived the Long March died of malaria. In 1885, the 268 surviving Nez Perce were marched to Indian Territory (later Oklahoma), where more died.

Later in 1885, roughly seven score survivors were finally allowed to return to the Northwest, some to Lapwai, Idaho, and others to the Colville reservation in eastern Washington. The Nez Perce were provided no supplies as they arrived at the onset of winter. They experienced profound suffering. Lieutenant Wood, who had witnessed Chief Joseph's surrender speech and later wrote a narrative of the Nez Perce's long march, said: "I think that, in his long career, Joseph cannot accuse the Government of the United States of one single act of justice" (Johansen and Grinde, 1997, 190). Joseph died at Colville in 1904, his heart still yearning to go home to the land where he had buried his father.

A VISE CLOSES ON THE PLAINS

By the last third of the nineteenth century, the settlement frontier was closing in on the plains and steppes of North America, the continent that Benjamin Franklin once had speculated would not be occupied by settlers for a thousand years. The development of transportation technology (notably the railroad) had complemented the lure of land and gold, among other resources, to push Native peoples into isolated pockets of resistance. For most Native peoples in North America, this was a time of profound cultural change, often accompanied by acute suffering, especially from European diseases. A long decline of Native populations followed a brief flash of prosperity that had come with the advent of widespread trade with Euro-Americans. The settlement frontier soon would close in 1890 in Wounded Knee, a small hamlet on the windswept plains of South Dakota.

FURTHER READING

Anderson, Eva Greenslit. *The Life Story of Chief Seattle*. Caldwell, ID: Caxton Publishers, 1950.

Baily, L. R. *Indian Slave Trade in the Southwest*. Los Angeles: Westernlore Press, 1973.

Beal, Merrill D. *I Will Fight No More Forever*. Seattle: University of Washington Press, 1963.

"A Brief Notice of the Recent Outrages Committed by Isaac Stevens . . . May 17, 1856." Cited in W. H. Wallace, "Martial Law in the Washington Territory," *The Annals of America*, 1856, 384–389.

Calloway, Colin. *New Worlds for All: Indians, Europeans, and the Remaking of Early America*. Baltimore: Johns Hopkins University Press, 1997.

Chalmers, Harvey. *The Last Stand of the Nez Perce*. New York: Twayne, 1962.

Champagne, Duane. *American Indian Societies: Strategies and Conditions of Political and Cultural Survival*. Cambridge, MA: Cultural Survival, 1989.

Davis, Russell, and Brant Ashabranner. *Chief Joseph: War Chief of the Nez Perce*. New York: McGraw-Hill, 1962.

DeVoto, Bernard. *Across the Wide Missouri*. Cambridge, MA: Harvard University Press, 1947.

De Zorita, Alonso. *Life and Labor in Ancient Mexico*. Translated by Benjamin Keen. New Brunswick, NJ: Rutgers University Press, 1963.

Drucker, Philip. *Indians of the Northwest Coast*. New York: McGraw-Hill, 1955.

Fee, Chester. *Chief Joseph: The Biography of a Great Indian*. New York: Wilson Erickson, 1936.

Fenn, Elizabeth. *Pox Americana: The Great Smallpox Epidemic of 1775–82*. New York: Hill & Wang, 2001.

Furtwangler, Albert. *Answering Chief Seattle*. Seattle: University of Washington Press, 1997.

Gibson, Arrell Morgan. *The American Indian: Prehistory to Present*. Lexington, MA: Heath, 1980.

Gunther, Erna. *Indian Life on the Northwest Coast of North America*. Chicago: University of Chicago Press, 1972.

Howard, Helen A., and Dan L. McGrath. *War Chief Joseph*. Caldwell, ID: Caxton, 1952.

Howard, Oliver O. *Nez Perce Joseph*. Boston: Lea & Shepherd, 1881.

Indian Chief Hanged in 1858 Is Cleared. *New York Times*, December 12, 2004. Available at http://query.nytimes.com/mem/tnt.html?oref=login&tntget=2004/12/12/national/12chief.html&tntemail1.

Johansen, Bruce E., and Donald A. Grinde, Jr. *The Encyclopedia of Native American Biography*. New York: Henry Holt, 1997.

Joseph, Chief [In-mut-too-yah-lat-lat]. An Indian's View of Indian Affairs. *North American Review* 128(April 1879):415–433.

Josephy, Alvin, Jr. *The Patriot Chiefs*. New York: Viking, 1961.

Josephy, Alvin M. *The Nez Perce Indians and the Opening of the Northwest*. New Haven, CT: Yale University Press, 1965.

Lavender, David. *Let Me Be Free*. San Francisco: HarperCollins, 1992.

Mann, Charles C. 1491: America before Columbus was More Sophisticated and More Populous than We Have Ever Thought—and a More Livable Place Than Europe. *The Atlantic Monthly*, March 2002, 41–53.

Maxwell, James A. *America's Fascinating Indian Heritage*. Pleasantville, NY: Reader's Digest, 1978.

McNickle, D'Arcy. *They Came Here First: The Epic of the American Indian*. New York: Harper and Row Perennial Library, 1975.

Moore, John H. How Giveaways and Pow-wows Redistribute the Means of Subsistence. In John H. Moore, ed., *The Political Economy of North American Indians*. Norman: University of Oklahoma Press, 1993: 240–269.

Nabokov, Peter, ed. *Native American Testimony*. New York: Viking, 1991.

Oberg, Kalervo. *The Social Economy of the Tlinget Indians*. Seattle: University of Washington Press, 1973.

Olexer, Barbara. *The Enslavement of the American Indian*. Monroe, NY: Library Research Associates, 1982.

Pascua, Maria Parker. Ozette: A Makah Village in 1491. *National Geographic*, October 1991, 38–53.

Ruby, Robert H., and John A Brown. *Indian Slavery in the Pacific Northwest*. Spokane: Arthur H. Clark, 1993.

Sahagún, Bernardino de. *General History of the Things of New Spain: Florentine Codex*. Book 12, *Conquest of Mexico*. Translated by A. J. O. Anderson and C. E. Dibble. Salt Lake City: University of Utah Press, and Santa Fe, NM: School of American Research, 1950.

Smith, Henry A. Early Reminiscences. Number Ten. Scraps from a Diary. Chief Seattle—a Gentleman by Instinct—His Native Eloquence, etc., etc. *Seattle Star*, October 29, 1887, n.p.

Snell, William Robert. Indian Slavery in Colonial South Carolina, 1671–1795. Ph.D. dissertation, University of Alabama, 1972.

Soustelle, Jacques. *Daily Life of the Aztecs on the Eve of the Spanish Conquest*. Translated by Patrick O'Brian. Palo Alto, CA: Stanford University Press, 1961.

Tebbel, John, and Keith Jennison. *The American Indian Wars*. New York: Bonzaza Books, 1960.

Vanderwerth, W. C., ed. *Indian Oratory: Famous Speeches by Noted Indian Chieftains.* Norman: University of Oklahoma Press, 1971.

Waters, Frank. *Brave Are My People: Indian Heroes Not Forgotten.* Santa Fe: Clear Light, 1992.

Weeks, Philip. *Farewell, My Nation: The American Indian and the United States, 1820–1890.* Arlington Heights, IL: Harlan Davidson, 1990.

Wood, H. Clay. *The Status of Young Joseph and His Band of Nez Perce Indians.* Portland, OR: Assistant Adjutant General's Office, Department of the Columbia, 1876.

CHAPTER 7

⁓

The Frontier Closes on the Southwest and Great Plains

By the 1850s, the demographic fingers of European American immigration extended into the North American continent from both coasts. The last great series of "Indian wars" began on the plains and prairies and in the American Southwest. At the time, an estimated 200,000 of 300,000 Native people were living in the center of the continent. Some (such as the Mandan) had lived in the area for centuries; others, including the Lakota (Sioux) were recent immigrants, crowded westward by surges of European American movement from the east. Still others, notably the Five Civilized Tribes, formerly of the South, had been removed from their homelands to the southern plains on the trails of tears.

European American immigration accelerated with the laying of rails across the continent. Although the earliest European American immigrants had traversed the open country in ox-drawn covered wagons, averaging 20 miles a day (the speed of a brisk walk), by 1870 the railroads conveyed them across the continent at nearly the speed of modern automobiles on interstate highways. Many of the Plains Indian wars began as disputes over whether, and where, railroads ought to run.

ECONOMIC IMPACT OF THE HORSE

Before arrival of the horse from the Spanish colonies to the south, beginning about 1600, the economic life of Plains peoples was simple, even stark. Peoples' belongings were restricted to the bulk that they could move on an A-shaped travois pulled by a dog or a human being. Not surprisingly, horses were first greeted as a larger, stronger kind of dog. Native peoples who acquired horses usually affixed travois to them before learning to ride. A number of Native peoples gave horses names based on their earlier nouns for dogs: the Assiniboin called them *sho-a-thin-ga* and *thongatch-shonga*, both meaning "great dog." The Gros Venture called horses *it-shou-ma-shunga*, meaning "red dog." The Black-feet called them *ponokamita*, for elk dog. The Cree called horses *mistatim*, meaning "big dog." The Comanche, whose horsemanship became legendary, gave horses names that translated as medicine dogs, good dogs, or mystery dogs. The Lakota, who used horses to extend the range of their buffalo hunts, called their wonderful newly domesticated beasts *honk-a-wakan*, meaning "mystery dog" or "amazing dog" (Roe, 1955, 61). The Lakota had such a high regard for the horse that they sometimes also called it sacred dog (Johnson, 1984, 67).

Ethnohistorian Dean Snow described the diffusion of the horse through the Plains:

> The Shoshones adopted Spanish horses quickly, taking them north and east, introducing them to the Indian societies of the Great Plains. Algonquians such as the Blackfeet, Gros Ventres, and Arapahos, as well as some Crees and Ojibways, abandoned forest hunting and gathering to become mounted nomadic hunters on the Great Plains.... Later, the horticultural Cheyennes (Algonquians) entered the Plains as well, quickly becoming the quintessential American Indian nation in the eyes of many. (1996, 193)

Horses diffused northward after Spanish settlement began in New Mexico after 1600 C.E., but as early as the 1500s some horses escaped Spanish herds and bred wild in New Mexico and Texas. These "Indian ponies" averaged less than 1000 pounds in weight, smaller than modern-day riding horses; these agile, fast horses were interbred with larger animals acquired from Spanish (and later Anglo-American) herds.

The Pawnees, who were strategically located on the plains of latter-day Nebraska, later built a trade in horses that nearly spanned the continent. Patrick Henry bought a "Santa Fe" horse through a chain of merchants who included the Pawnees during the 1750s. The Pawnees especially became known as horse traders on the Plains. These horses probably were traded to the Pawnees by native horse merchants who tapped supplies in Mexico (Wissler, 1914, 2, 10).

Horses may have been introduced to some Native American peoples as long ago as the Coronado expedition of the early 1540s, but the Native American horse culture probably sprang from the herds the Spanish built at Santa Fe following the Oñate expedition a half-century later. During the seventeenth and early eighteenth centuries, horses spread rapidly among Native American peoples from the Apaches in present-day New Mexico (on one occasion, Apaches stole nearly every horse at the Santa Fe garrison).

The horse turned a subsistence lifestyle on the harsh high plains of North America into a festival of ornamentation, and a brief period of prosperity for many Native peoples before disease and settlement frontiers reached them, killing a large majority of Native peoples there. Maximilian described the Sioux in 1833: "Many of the Sioux are rich, and have twenty or more horses, which they obtained originally from the Spanish" (Roe, 1955, 90). Many Native nations on the Plains and in the adjacent Rocky Mountains became rich in horses. The various divisions of the Lakota, Nakota, and Dakota; the Crow; and the Nez Perce are only a few examples of many.

Horses became such an essential part of many North American Indian cultures that the Apaches, for example, incorporated them into their oral history as gifts of the gods. The horse completely changed the lifestyles of some Plains Indian nations, who adapted their use to the hunting of buffalo and other animals. The image of the warrior Sioux on horseback firing his rifle at buffalo or calvarymen, which became fixed in many twentieth century non-Indian minds as the sine qua non of "Indianness" actually was a product of European trade and technology. The horses came from the Spanish to the south, and the guns and trade beads on buckskin arrived with the French and English. Guns aided hunting and raised the level of violence in wars that once had been mainly ceremonial. Trade also brought to the Native peoples of the Plains the "traditional" flowing-feather headdresses that now adorn so many generic Indians from coast to coast. In addition, the same metamorphosis transformed the Cheyenne, who also moved westward in advance of the Euro-American frontier, to the high plains of Wyoming and Montana and southward.

The horse extended Native peoples' ranges, as well as control over their environments. A Native group on foot was limited to a few miles a day; with horses, a camp could be moved 30 miles or more in the same period. A small party of warriors on horseback could cover a hundred miles of rough country in a day or two. By 1659, Spanish reports indicated that the Apaches were stealing horses from them despite their best efforts to keep the valuable animals out of Indian hands. At roughly the same time, the Apaches and Pueblos traded for horses; by shortly before 1700 C.E., the Utes and Comanches had acquired mounts. After that, Native peoples' use of horses diffused across the continent. By 1750, the horse frontier had reached a line stretching roughly from present-day eastern Texas, northward through eastern Kansas and Nebraska, then northwest through Wyoming, Montana, Idaho, and Washington.

Native Americans explored different ways of training horses. Unlike the English and Spanish, the Cheyennes, for example, did not usually "break" their horses. Instead, they "gentled" them. Boys who tended horses stroked them, talked to them, and played with them. An owner of a horse might sing to it or smoke a pipe and blow smoke in its face. At age 18 months, the horse would begin more intense training, but was still sung to, smoked over, and stroked with eagle-wing fans. Gradually, the horse was habituated to carrying a human being, saddle, and bridle. Horses were trained specifically for war or hunting.

The horse shaped economic behavior in many ways. One was the productivity of raiding, which acquired considerable status. By the early nineteenth century, raiding on horseback was the Apaches' major economic activity; the greatest fame a Crow could earn came when he was able to snatch a tethered horse from under the nose of an enemy. "What must certainly be considered a really remarkable feature in the Plains Indian horse culture is the almost phenomenal rapidity with which they mastered their early fears and developed into one of the two or three foremost equestrian peoples on earth," commented historian Frank Gilbert Roe (1955, 56).

The horse also changed some peoples' housing styles from fixed lodges to mobile tipis and allowed the size of the average tipi to increase because a horse could haul a tipi as large as 18 to 20 feet in diameter, much larger than a dog or a human being could carry. Some tipis weighed as much as 500 pounds and required three horses. The horse reduced economies of scale in hunting, especially of buffalo, making hunting parties smaller. The increased mobility brought by horses energized trade, as well as intertribal conflict, because ease of transport brought more contact between diverse peoples, friendly and not (Anderson, 1995, 59–61).

When they provided the major form of land transportation in North America, horses were invested with considerable financial value. Cortés personally kept track of the Spaniards' stable as the Aztecs were conquered: "When anything happened to a horse, he does not fail to notice it," a Spanish observer said of Cortés (Roe, 1955, 35). Once Spanish colonization of New Mexico began about 1600 C.E., the immigrants were conscious of their monopoly on the horse as they sought to outlaw use of the animals by Native peoples.

THE ROLE OF DISEASE ON THE PLAINS

The U.S. Army killed fewer Native people during the conquest of the American West in the nineteenth century than freelance Indian fighters (who often were reimbursed by the federal government) or imported diseases. Between 1789 and 1898, the Army was responsible for killing about 4,000 Native people, probably less than 1 percent of those who died because of imported influences.

Disease was by far the biggest killer of Native people along the frontier. Euro-American settlement brought a host of ailments for which the Native people had no immunity and no cure. Some of these diseases were not usually fatal to whites, even in the nineteenth century: whooping cough, measles, scarlet fever. These "minor" maladies killed Indians by the thousands. The diseases that killed some European Americans, such as cholera and smallpox, nearly extinguished large numbers of Indians. Often, the disease frontier preceded sustained Euro-American immigration. European diseases often arrived in Native communities with the English honeybees, which traveled more quickly than the immigrants themselves.

All along the expanding frontier, initial contact with European Americans initially caused drastic population declines among Native groups, mainly because of diseases. After this initial decline and before the Indian peoples were subjugated in a series of wars that accompanied the settlement frontier, many Native tribes and nations recouped population because of trade and general prosperity brought by the fur trade. Jeanne Kay has made a case that during the late eighteenth and early nineteenth centuries, the Fox, Sauk, Menominee, and Winnebago experienced "significant population increases"— some on the order of five to eight times the number of people who survived the initial epidemics (Kay, 1984, 265).

Native settlement patterns sometimes defined whether groups lived or died in large numbers. The Lakota may have enjoyed a brief flash of prosperity during the early contact period not only because of trading patterns and their ability to adopt to European imports such as the horse, but also because they were favored by vectors of disease; their villages were relatively small and widely scattered, offering some insulation from the waves of smallpox and other diseases. The same diseases ravaged other Plains peoples who practiced agriculture and lived in larger, more permanent towns. This seemed to be true across the continent. In the Northwest, two-thirds of the Makah, who lived in villages along the coast, were killed by smallpox, measles, and other diseases shortly after intensive settlement of the area began in the 1850s (Pascua, 1991, 40).

Richard White wrote of how "winter counts," pictorial histories of bands or tribes, often drawn on hides, provided records of epidemics.

The Brule winter counts record smallpox in 1779–1780, 1780–1781 and 1801–1802 (the epidemics were dated slightly differently in other winter counts), but their loses were slight when compared to those of the Arikaras, Hidatsas, and Mandans. In 1795, Truteau reported that the Arikaras had been reduced "from 32 populous villages" to two and from 4,000 warriors to 500—a loss of population which, in turn, caused severe social and economic disruption. The smallpox reached the Mandan and Hidatsa villages in 1781, inflicting loses proportionate to those of the Arikaras. (1978, 325)

The Pawnees and Omahas also were ravaged by disease during the early nineteenth century. In 1806, Zebulon Pike counted roughly 4,000 Pawnees (1,973 men and 2,170 women); in 1859, agent William Dennison listed 820 men and 1,505 women. Both figures were low (the counters missed many people), but the proportions probably were roughly correct. The Pawnees' population had been cut nearly in half during one horrible winter, in 1831, when smallpox ravaged their villages. People under the age of 30, lacking immunity from earlier epidemics, died in very large numbers. The population of the Pawnees, a sedentary, corn-growing people, fell from about 25,000 before the epidemic to 12,500 afterward. "Not one under 33 years of age escaped this monstrous disease, it having been the length of time since it visited them before," wrote John Dougherty, who was present at several of the villages during the epidemic (Johnson, 1984, 13). The loss of so many young people crippled the Pawnee for almost a century. Smallpox ravaged the area again in 1837–1838, and cholera surged through Pawnee country in 1849. The population of the Pawnees continued to decline and did not begin to rise again until after 1920.

The disproportionate loss of men was caused by war with the Sioux. In 1843, Sioux warriors destroyed a Pawnee village and inflicted sixty-seven deaths. The Pawnees were forced to retreat to the Platte River, where hostile whites awaited them. By 1850, the Omahas, Otos, and Poncas had given up attempts to hunt on the western plains because of the area's domination by growing bands of Sioux. By 1873, the Sioux harassment of the Pawnees became so intense that the latter asked federal Indian agents to remove them to the Indian Territory (White, 1978, 13).

Roughly 1,500 of 1,600 Mandans were killed by a series of smallpox epidemics after Lewis and Clark encountered them but before immigration started in the western Dakotas, their homeland. Half the Blackfeet died before the settlement frontier reached their country. More than half the Kiowas and Comanches, also high plains peoples, died of cholera. From the coasts of Oregon, Washington, and California, inland to the Pawnee territory along the Platte River—more than 1,500 miles—a half-dozen diseases raged during the middle of the nineteenth century. Henry Schoolcraft, who served as an Indian agent among the Mandans at this time, said at one point that their surviving population shrank to thirteen people. Wolves roamed abandoned Pawnee villages from lodge to lodge, ripping flesh off human carcasses.

THE ECONOMIC ROLE OF THE BUFFALO

The buffalo was the basis of the Plains Native economy. When European American settlement began to encroach on the area early in the nineteenth century, an estimated 30 million buffalo lived in a large area from present-day Texas in the south to northern Alberta. Buffalo ranged from present-day New York State to Alabama and Mississippi, to Idaho and eastern Oregon. Within three-quarters of a century, competition from European Americans, including deliberate slaughter, reduced the buffalo population to about 100,000 animals. By 1995, a concerted effort to replenish buffalo herds had raised the population to about 200,000.

The Native peoples there had learned to make dozens of products essential to their lives from this one animal. They ate meat and marrow, tongue, intestines, and other innards. They drank buffalo blood and preserved its fat and marrow, among other parts, in jerky, the original trail food. From the tanned hide of the buffalo, Plains people fashioned tipi covers, moccasin tops, shirts, dresses, leggings, breechcloths, robes, bedding, belts, caps, mittens, bags, pouches, dolls, and items for trade. From raw buffalo hides, Plains peoples made containers, sheaths, soles for moccasins, shields, rattles, drums, saddles, bridles and other horse tack, lariats, masks, bindings, snowshoes, and bodily ornaments. The horns were raw material for cups, spoons, ladles, powder flasks, toys, parts of head-dresses, and rattles, as well as knives, arrowheads, shovels, hoes, runners for sleds, war clubs, and tool handles. The hair of the animal provided parts of headdresses, stuffing and padding, and ornaments. Hooves were used to manufacture glue. The bladder supplied pouches, buckets, cups, water basins, and cooking vessels; the chips provided fuel (Johnson, 1984, 60–61).

Native acquisition of the horse had an immense impact both on the hunting of buffalo and on the economic behavior and social structure of Native societies. A large number of Native societies transformed themselves into roving buffalo-hunting bands. Elite societies of young men skilled at buffalo hunting emerged, forming the basis of the Plains warrior societies, who pursued the animals. A male buffalo can weigh a ton and can charge at 30 miles an hour.

Most Native peoples worked nature into their rituals and customs because their lives depended on the bounty of the land around them. Where a single animal formed the basis of a Native economy (such as the salmon of the Pacific Northwest or the buffalo on the plains), strict cultural sanctions came into play against killing of such animals in numbers that would exceed their natural replacement rate. On the plains, the military societies of the Cheyenne, Lakota, and other peoples enforced rules against hunting buffalo out of season and against taking more animals than a people could use. Many Plains societies had special police who maintained discipline before and during communal buffalo hunts. An individual who began the hunt early could be severely punished.

Before they acquired horses, Native bands sometimes hunted Buffalo by herding them over "jumps," cliffs that were nearly invisible to the stampeding animals until they were pushed over the edge by animals behind them. Following such a stampede, the hunters and their wives worked quickly to preserve the meat, often by drying it in the sun to make jerky. In the heat of summer, when buffaloes were usually hunted, undressed meat could spoil within a day.

THE SLAUGHTER OF THE BUFFALO

Before 1870, large buffalo herds still roamed the southern plains, and many thousands of Native people still lived as they preferred, with the buffalo at the base of their economies. The slaughter of the vast buffalo herds that roamed the plains and prairies until the 1840s reached a million animals a year during the 1870s. Along their newly opened tracks, the railroads ran special excursions from which self-styled sportsmen shot buffalo from the comfort of their seats. General Phil Sheridan remarked that buffalo hunters had done more in two years to defeat the Indians than the entire regular Army had been able to do in the previous thirty years. "I would not seriously regret the total disappearance of the buffalo from our western prairies, in its effect upon the Indians, regarding it rather as a means of hastening their dependence upon the products of the soil" (Morris, 1992, 343). At one point, Sheridan suggested rewarding buffalo poachers by giving them medals with an engraving of a dead buffalo on one side and a discouraged-looking Indian on the other.

The buffalo herds of the central plains had been finished off during the 1860s with a technological boost from a new line of high-powered hunting rifle. Hunters of the dwindling herds were followed by skinners, who (depending on market conditions) might strip the hides or just remove the slain buffaloes' tongues. No one ever counted the number of buffalo that fell. The death toll was probably at least 20 million.

By the 1870s, European Americans were killing more buffalo than the Native Americans. Of 1.2 million buffalo skins shipped east on the railroads in 1872 and 1873, about 350,000 (28 percent) were supplied by Indians. By that time, the plains were swarming with unemployed railroad workers, would-be farmers whose homesteads would not sustain their families, and hopeful miners caught between gold rushes. By the time buffalo populations were reduced to levels that would no longer sustain the trade during the 1880s, there were an estimated 5,000 non-Indian hunters chasing them.

By the early 1880s, the U.S. Army's version of total war against the Plains Indians had reached its goal: The buffalo were nearly extinct. Ten years earlier, some of the Plains Indians still had an ample supply of food; by the early 1880s, they were reduced, as General Sheridan had intended, to the condition of paupers, without food, shelter, clothing, or any of those necessities of life that came from the buffalo.

CHANGES IN THE NATURE OF PLAINS WARFARE

A major aim of Plains warfare during prosperous times was acquisition of goods, often an enemy's best horses. In its essence, Plains Native warfare before full-scale white contact was an elaborate ritual that called for splendid dressing and skilled fighting that only rarely did a great deal of human damage. The main aim (other than making off with horses) was "counting coup" (*coup* is French for "a blow")—touching, but not injuring, an enemy in battle. Scalps were not regarded as trophies by most Lakota (the Tetons were an exception). Plains war was more than a game or a ritual, however. Skirmishes did take place. Warriors were killed and seriously injured, although not on the scale of European set-piece warfare.

The scale and violence of intertribal warfare increased with the advent of horses, guns, and bids for alliance by Euro-Americans. The systematic destruction of the buffalo herds by non-Native hunters sharpened competition for remaining animals between some Native groups. This competition resulted in additional warfare, raising the death toll for societies that also were suffering epidemics of disease. All of these factors, along with the crowding caused by immigration sped by the advent of the railroad (after the middle 1860s), provoked further Native societal deterioration.

In 1849, the United States established two forts on the Platte River. Two years later, the largest gathering of Plains Native peoples in memory took place at Fort Laramie. Between 8,000 and 12,000 people—Lakota, Cheyenne, Assiniboins, Crows, Shoshonis, and others—negotiated a treaty with representatives of the United States that allowed unhindered crossing for wagon trains heading to California and the Oregon Territory. The United States promised to keep troops on the plains to protect Native peoples against aggression by European American immigrants.

The Plains wars began two years later with provocations that sound absurd, considering the intensity of retribution later exacted against Native peoples. In one case, an Indian killed an immigrant's stray cow. This incident occurred ten miles from Fort Laramie during 1854. The cow-napping was reported by a white transient at Ft. Laramie; the transient asserted that neighboring Indians owed him $25 for the cow. A spokesman from the Minneconjou Sioux camp offered $10. An argument developed, and a $15 disagreement prompted the arrival of a hotheaded junior officer with thirty-two men and a battery of large field guns. The officer ordered a Native elder shot on the spot. The Sioux then retaliated by killing the officer and all the soldiers. The following summer, 1,300 troops marched against the recalcitrant Plains tribes from Fort Leavenworth, Kansas, killing 86 Natives. After that, battles became steadily more frequent and brutal, a set of circumstances made worse by the immigration of several thousand non-Native people after gold was discovered near Denver during 1858.

THE FRONTIER CLOSES IN THE SOUTHWEST

The Apaches and Navajos migrated from the area today called the Yukon (home of the Athapascan peoples) several centuries before the Spanish invaded their new home in present-day Arizona, Utah, and New Mexico. The word *Apache* is Zuni for "enemy." The Navajos, originally a band of Apaches, settled in an abandoned pueblo the Spanish called Navaho. The Spanish called them Apaches de Navaho. After that, the Navajos moved to the homeland that is familiar as Navajo country today, increasing in numbers. By the late nineteenth century, the Navajos were one of the largest Native groups in the region. Pursuing a quiet ranching life from their widely dispersed hogans (traditional Navajo residences), living "the Right Way," as they say, the Navajos also have become one of the most populous of Native peoples in the present-day United States.

The Navajos adopted sheep herding, weaving, and silversmithing from the Spanish and became expert at all of them. From the Pueblos they adopted kivas, sand paintings, and several religious rituals. By the time the U.S. frontier reached them, the Navajos had been totally made over into a new people by both Spanish and regional Native influences. They had little organized political or tribal life, at least at first, because they were so widely dispersed in solitary hogans or very small settlements. With the Hopis, the Navajos stood their ground on land that very few non-Indians coveted until coal and uranium were discovered there during the early twentieth century.

The Hopis never left their traditional mountain homes, preserving their way of life as well as their name (from Hopitou, "the peaceful ones") as tides of Spanish and Anglo-American settlement ebbed and flowed around them. Likewise, until recent times, many Navajos had never even heard the name the Spanish gave them. Because the Navajos' language contains no sound for the letter "v," many native-speaking Navajos cannot pronounce it. The Navajos' own name is Dine, which means, "the people." Indicative of their origins, the name is very similar to Dene, the term by which some Native groups in the Canadian Northwest refer to themselves today.

Although the Navajos and Hopi sought as best they could to distance themselves from the invading colonists (Spanish and English), the Apaches, rarely by choice, found themselves embroiled in nettlesome relationships with both groups of colonizers. The Apaches had long experience with Europeans, the first being the Spanish, who made a habit of drawing up ambitious plans (which never succeeded) to exterminate them. After Mexican independence, the northern states offered bounties for Apache scalps. As late as 1866, U.S. officials in Arizona were paying as much as $230 per Apache scalp, an amount worth several thousand dollars today. In 1837, scalp bounty fever ran through Anglo-American trappers in the area. A number of trappers invited a group of Mimbres Apaches to a social gathering at the Santa Rita copper mines, then quickly slaughtered all of them and cashed in their scalps. Until that time, the Mimbres had not been troublesome to Anglo-Americans in the area; afterward, surviving members of the victimized families haunted the mines like vengeful ghosts.

Such murders galled the Apaches, but what inflamed them even more was abduction of their women and children, who were sold into slavery or prostitution. This practice began under the Spanish but continued under the Anglo-Americans despite antislavery legislation. By 1821, all forms of involuntary servitude had been officially outlawed in newly independent Mexico; in the United States, the Civil War was fought over this issue, among others. Nevertheless, in 1866, after that war ended, between 2,000 and 10,000 Apaches were enslaved to whites. Other Apaches also were being held as slaves in the Mexican states of Sonora and Chihuahua.

THE NAVAJOS' LONG WALK

Kit Carson, who was dispatched from Fort Defiance, Arizona, to subdue the Navajos, disdained killing women and children or taking slaves, but he showed no remorse when it came to burning Navajo villages, razing their fields, and scattering their flocks. Men who elected to remain free of U.S. government control were killed by Carson's forces. Women and children (as well as men who surrendered) were promised new lands and food. Carson wore down the Navajos over months of pursuit.

A final confrontation took place as Carson and his men backed a substantial majority of the surviving Navajos into their sacred Canyon de Chelly, a gorge between towering cliffs and mesas. The Navajos were rounded up and bound with ropes. The first group of imprisoned Navajos departed on March 6, 1864, on a 300-mile forced march from Fort Defiance to Fort Sumner in Bosque Redondo, 185 miles southeast of Santa Fe. About 2,400 people departed; only the very young, the very old, and the infirm were allowed to ride. The weather was very cold, even for early March, and many of the Navajos (no one recorded the total number) died along the way. The series of forced marches continued until December 1864.

About 80 percent of an estimated 10,000 Navajos were forced onto a march that they called the Long Walk. At Fort Sumner, government agents tried to remake the Navajos in the white man's image as literate, Christian yeoman farmers, but most Navajos refused to cooperate. They were sharing 40 square miles of arid land with another tribe, and the alkaline waters of the Pecos River sickened them. There was no way to gather wild plants or to hunt, and government agents never issued them any housing materials or shelter. Many of the Navajos had to burrow into the ground to escape the elements. In 1868, the government gave up its intensive indoctrination and allowed the Navajos to return to their homelands.

Before they became reestablished, the Navajos survived several years as hunters and gatherers. Even after the government issued stock to them, the people found themselves facing frequent drought. As circumstances allowed, they took up old agricultural ways, tending small flocks of sheep, goats, and other animals issued them by the government.

WAR AGAINST THE APACHES

The Apaches' reputation as homeless raiders was a product of attacks against them as the frontier warfare invaded their homelands. Before they were driven from them, Apaches often lived in humble rancherias and practiced agriculture in areas where moisture and soil conditions permitted. Starting in 1864, a number of Army expeditions killed several hundred Apaches. General Edward Ord, while commanding the Army's Department of California, encouraged his troops to capture and root out the Apache by every means, to hunt them, he said, as they would wild animals.

Cochise (also known as Hardwood, Chiricahua Apache, ca. 1823–1874), a major leader in the Apache Wars of the 1870s, was the son of an Apache chief who became the leader of his father's band after his death. Everyone who dealt with Cochise held him in high regard. He was a powerfully built man who carried himself with dignity. In peaceful situations, Cochise was mild mannered, but during war he was capable of ferocity, great courage, and cruelty. Ultimately, he understood that a lasting peace was the only way to ensure the survival of his people in the Southwest.

During the 1860s, Cochise waged a formidable campaign to retain the traditional homelands of the Apaches. In 1861, Cochise was summoned to see Lieutenant George N. Bascom at Apache Pass because a rancher had accused Cochise of stealing cattle and kidnapping Mickey Free, a white settler's child. Cochise arrived under a flag of truce along with members of his family, including a son, Naiche, to meet with Bascom. Bascom accused Cochise of the earlier raid. Although Cochise denied any wrongdoing, Bascom attempted to arrest him. A fight ensued, and Cochise was badly wounded. He then slashed his way through the tent with a knife and managed to escape. One Apache was killed, and Bascom took the others hostage. During the next few days, Cochise took a number of whites as prisoners, offering them in exchange for the Apache captives. When Cochise's negotiations with Bascom broke down, both sides killed their hostages.

The Bascom fiasco started the Apache Wars. Soon, the Mimbreno Apaches under Cochise's father-in-law, the leader Apache Mangas Coloradas, joined the Chiricahuas and the White Mountain (Coyotero) Apaches in war against the invading Anglo-Americans. Mangas Coloradas had been well known since the early 1850s, when American miners captured him and cut his back to ribbons with a whip. During the Apache Wars, Cochise and Mangas Coloradas led raiding parties that wreaked havoc along the Arizona frontier during the early years of the Civil War, when many of the U.S. Army's troops had been recalled to battles in the east. They drove most settlers out of the area for a time. The only sizable U.S. settlement in the territory during the Apache uprising was Tucson, where the population dwindled to about 200 people.

As the Civil War wound down, garrisons were replenished in the area. Volunteer Indian fighters organized and billed the War Department for their services. Some of the volunteers had arrived from California and were men who had recently taken part in the wholesale slaughter of many peaceful, unorganized Native bands. Any tactic sufficed for the War Department as long as it killed Indians. Many times, vigilantes invited Indians to fake "treaty conferences," at which they were gunned down. Red Sleeves was killed at such an event in 1863. After killing Mangas Coloradas, soldiers cut off his head and boiled it, deliberately offending an Apache belief that a person goes to the afterlife in his or her bodily condition at death.

During the early Civil War years, Apache depredations sought to drive both Mexicans and Anglo-Americans from Arizona. During July 1862, there were 3,000 California volunteers under Colonel James H. Carleton sent to remedy the situation. Meanwhile, Mangas Coloradas and Cochise set a trap for the newly arrived troops. At Apache Pass, with about 500 men behind fortifications, the Apaches held off the California forces until Carleton utilized howitzers against them. The Apaches then retreated to Mexico with a wounded Mangas Coloradas; Cochise sought out a Mexican surgeon, who healed his father-in-law's wounds. For more than a decade, Cochise and about 200 warriors raided Anglo-American settlements along the Butterfield Trail and adjacent areas from his "stronghold" in the Dragoon Mountains of southern Arizona. He resisted all efforts to exterminate him and his men.

In 1871, Colonel George Crook took command of the Army's Department of Arizona. Realizing the futility of warfare aimed at annihilating the Apaches, Crook developed a group of highly effective Indian scouts who pursued Cochise and his supporters in the rugged terrain of southern Arizona. At one point, General Crook arranged Cochise's surrender, but when Cochise heard plans that his band would be sent to a reservation near Fort Tularosa, New Mexico (and not set free), he renounced the agreement. As a result, General Oliver O. Howard was dispatched by President U. S. Grant to meet with Cochise. After eleven days of deliberations during the fall of 1872, Howard granted Cochise's request for a reservation along Apache Pass. Shortly after this meeting, Cochise's 200 men surrendered, and Cochise promised to keep order along the pass. He remained peaceful until his death in 1874.

Also during 1871, American, Mexican, and Papago Indian residents of Tucson slaughtered eighty-five Natives who had put themselves under protection of the Army at Camp Grant. The Army tried to stop the massacre but arrived too late. The camp was razed, the dead bodies of twenty-one women and children were scattered across the ground, and some of their brains were beaten out with stones. Two of the women were raped during the massacre, and nearly all of the dead were mutilated. One ten-month-old infant was shot twice, and one of his legs was nearly hacked off.

The first phase of the war against the Apaches took ten years and cost about 1,000 Anglo-American lives, as well as those of uncounted Native people. The dying did not end in 1871, although some of the excessively brutal episodes did after a nationwide outcry over the massacre at Camp Grant and associated depredations. As whites flowed back into the area, opening old mines, farms, and commercial centers, vigilantes chased Apache bands into the rugged mountains, preying on what was left of their rancherias. The Apaches retaliated by making life very difficult for prospectors and settlers. Knowledge that Apaches might be in the area chilled the blood of just about every non-Indian in the territory as rumors spread that Apaches tormented their captives by such methods as tying them, feet up, over crackling fires as flames slowly roasted their brains. True or not, the rumors only enhanced the Anglo-American immigrants' beliefs that their own murderous retaliation was justified. General George Crook negotiated peace with many of the bands and rounded up those who would not agree to cease raiding. He also enlisted a number of Apache scouts.

Taza, Cochise's oldest son, who became chief after his death, attempted to continue the peace agreement. When Taza died, however, Naiche (another of Cochise's sons) joined forces with Geronimo. After Cochise's death in 1874, the number of Chiricahua raids in Mexico increased despite efforts by agent Thomas J. Jeffords. Apache war parties crossed into Mexico, then returned to use the reservation at Apache Pass on the Butterfield Trail as a safe haven. After an altercation involving the killing of two stagecoach attendants, the reservation was dissolved by the U.S. government. Subsequently, John P. Clum, Indian agent to the Chiricahuas, moved residents of Apache Pass north to the San Carlos Reservation in Arizona, where they joined 4,000 other Apaches from other bands.

GERONIMO'S WAR: THE APACHES' FINAL REBELLION

During the late 1870s, the Indian Bureau made a practice of moving Apache bands from one reservation to another without asking their consent. Resentment regarding this practice provoked the last great Apache uprising, led by the legendary Geronimo.

The man the Spanish would call Geronimo (Goyathlay, Chiricahua Apache, ca. 1830–1909) was born along the upper Gila River, very likely on the Arizona side of the New Mexico-Arizona border. Taklishim, his father, was a Chiricahua, as was his mother Juana, although she had been a captive among the Mexicans during childhood. After he was born among the Bedonkohe Apaches about 1830, the man who would lead the Apaches' final rebellion was named Goyathlay, "One Who Yawns."

In his youth, Geronimo served under Cochise and Mangas Coloradas. Although Geronimo was not a hereditary chief, his repute among the Apaches increased because of his bravery and prowess in battle. In 1858, Mexicans killed his wife, mother, and three children, provoking Geronimo to mount campaigns against the Mexicans for revenge. Given the ferocity of the avenging raids that followed, it is said that the Spanish invoked St. Jerome (Geronimo in Spanish, the Catholic saint of lost causes) whenever they crossed paths with him.

In the 1860s, Geronimo married into the Chiricahua Apaches and began a new life as medicine man, warrior, leader, and avenger of his family. During ensuing years, the Army and mercenaries waged a bitter war of attrition against Apaches who remained off assigned reservations, including Geronimo and his band. Part of the problem was the departure of the conciliatory General George Crook and his replacement by General Nelson A. Miles. Miles sent Crook's Apache scouts to talk Geronimo into surrendering with promises of humane treatment.

Geronimo and his band then escaped, fleeing into Mexico, taking refuge in the Sierra Madre. Geronimo's band merged with Juh's Nednhi band, carrying out raids on the American side of the river. Following these raids, in April 1877, Geronimo was captured and transported to the San Carlos Reservation. Victorio, a Mimbreno, was relocated along with his Warm Springs band at that time as well. Victorio fled San Carlos in the fall of 1877, resisting U.S. control until his death in 1880. During the late 1870s, Geronimo remained at San Carlos, although he went raiding in Mexico once with Juh, withdrawing quickly to San Carlos because of retaliation by Mexican troops.

Geronimo. (Courtesy of the Nebraska State Historical Society.)

The U.S. Army decided on August 30, 1881, to arrest Nakaidoklini, a White Mountain Apache prophet. He was seized for espousing a new vision that postulated the resurrection of dead warriors to overwhelm the whites. The U.S. Army killed Nakaidoklini at a battle near Cibecue Creek. Subsequently, some of Nakaidoklini's group attacked Fort Apache unsuccessfully as military reinforcements were summoned against the rebellious Apaches to forestall further chaos. In September 1881, after the battle at Cibecue Creek, Geronimo, Juh, Naiche, hereditary chief Chato, and seventy-four followers left

San Carlos for Mexico. Returning in April 1882 to raid the reservation, Geronimo and others slew the chief of police and forced Loco and his band of Mimbrenos to follow them into Mexico, uniting them with Nana's more war-like Mimbrenos.

At the end of 1882, General George Crook was ordered to the Southwest to subdue the Apaches. Believing in the virtues of mobility, Crook quickly developed a number of mounted units with Apache scouts who could track fellow Apaches effectively. Crook, in May 1883, led units into the Sierra Madre of Mexico, with Mexican government permission, led by Captain Emmet Crawford and Lieutenant Charles Gatewood. Because of desert conditions, they used mules instead of horses. On May 25, 1883, the U.S. military struck Chato's camp. As a result, some Apache leaders agreed to return to the reservation. It was a year before all bands complied. Although Juh had died earlier in an accident, Nana, Naiche, Loco, and Chato slowly returned to San Carlos with their bands. Geronimo returned to the reservation as one of the Apaches' most revered war chiefs in March 1884.

A year later, Geronimo, Nana, Naiche, and about 150 others abandoned reservation life and headed for Mexico again. Crook's men trailed them until the fleeing Apaches agreed to talk at Canyon de los Embudos on March 25, 1886. Crook insisted that the Apaches submit to unconditional surrender and imprisonment in the east for two years. Geronimo initially agreed to the Army's terms. While being escorted to Fort Bowie, however, Naiche, Geronimo, and twenty-four followers escaped. To capture the escaped Apaches, the U.S. Army placed 5,000 soldiers in the field with Apache scouts. While leading a unit into Mexico, Captain Henry Ware Lawton skirmished with the Apaches on July 15, 1886. However, Geronimo was able to escape the grip of the Army. After avoiding the Army for another month, Geronimo agreed to surrender, but only to Miles personally. At Skeleton Canyon, sixty-five miles south of Apache Pass, Geronimo and the remaining members of his group surrendered for the last time.

Following their surrender, Geronimo and his band were shuttled off to Florida in chains, via railroad, where the warriors were housed in one prison camp, and their families (along with some "peaceful" Apaches) in another. Later, the families were reunited at another camp in Alabama. Tuberculosis, the damp climate, "swamp fevers," and other diseases killed at least a quarter of the Apaches in the camps. The scouts had agreed to talk Geronimo into surrendering on a promise that, once captured, Apache warriors would not be separated from their families. The breaking of this latest promise only deepened Geromino's bitterness toward the invading Euro-Americans.

The Aravaipas-Pinal band returned to Arizona, but Geronimo's and Naiche's Chiricahuas were not allowed to return to their homelands. Eventually, Geronimo and his followers accepted the Comanches' and Kiowas' offer to share their reservation in the Indian Territory. In 1894, the remaining incarcerated Apaches were relocated to Fort Sill in western Oklahoma. At Fort

Sill, Geronimo played baseball and became a member of the Dutch Reformed Church. He also collaborated with S. M. Barrett on the publication of his memoirs, *Geronimo's Story of His Life*, published in 1906. Geronimo also tried farming and sold souvenirs, including photos of himself, at expositions and fairs. He took occasional engagements with Buffalo Bill's (originally Pawnee Bill's) Wild West Show. Geronimo rode in President Teddy Roosevelt's inaugural parade at his request in 1905. Geronimo died of pneumonia on February 17, 1909, at Fort Sill, never having been allowed to return to his beloved homeland.

OFFICIALLY SANCTIONED INDIAN EXTERMINATION IN TEXAS

Mexico, seeking to contain increasing Anglo-American settlement of the area that was later called Texas during the 1820s, forbade further colonization and strengthened central authority over the province. The Mexicans outlawed slavery, causing the Anglos to rebel in 1835 and to declare their own republic in 1836. The Texans applied for entry to the United States, but admission was put off several years by pressures from northern states, representatives of which argued that addition of the Lone Star Republic would provide the South with a powerful new ally.

Sam Houston, the first president of the independent republic of Texas, moved swiftly to make peace with the numerous bands of Native peoples who occupied the area—Comanches, Lipan Apaches, Kiowas, Wichitas, Wacos, and Caddos, among others. In 1838, however, Mirabeau Lamar defeated Houston for the presidency on a campaign platform that included a legalized war of extermination against Texas Natives. After four years of bloody warfare against Native peoples, Texans again elected Houston on a peace platform. The hero of the Texas revolution tried to arrange an Indian territory in the western part of the state, even sending Texas Rangers to keep settlers out of it for a time. During the next decade, however, increasing numbers of immigrants squatted on Indian lands anyway, and the Rangers proved as ineffective at stopping the migration as the British Army had been at enforcing the Proclamation of 1763, which had been meant to halt European settlement at the crest of the Appalachians.

In 1845, Texas became a state that retained title to all open land within its borders. There was no federal land in Texas and, many Texans maintained, no federal jurisdiction over relations with the Indians. Federal agents negotiated a number of treaties with Natives in Texas, only to watch the state and the rapidly increasing number of Anglo-American immigrants ignore them. The Indian wars in Texas resumed and reached such a pitch by 1859 that the federal government, unable to control the aggressiveness of Anglo-American immigration, legally sanctioned the removal of all Indians in Texas, most of them to Indian Territory (later Oklahoma) to the north.

Those Native peoples who could be persuaded by the federal agents moved to the Indian Territory; those who would not leave Texan territory largely migrated to its less-densely populated western steppes. Both groups developed a generally bitter enmity with the Anglo-American settlers concentrated in eastern Texas, establishing de facto (at least for a time) the line of demarcation that Sam Houston had sought. By the 1870s, however, the last of the great buffalo herds was shrinking, and discontent was rising among the Kiowas and Comanches, many of whom pledged to ride with young firebrand war chiefs on numerous raids into settled areas. The names Satanta, Big Tree, Satank, Eagle Heart, and others were seared into the memories of homesteaders from the southern rim of Indian Territory to the arid high plains of the Texas Panhandle. The Kiowas and Comanches also drew Southern Cheyenne war parties into these raids.

During the summer of 1871, General Sherman ordered the arrest of Satanta and Big Tree, asserting that they had bragged openly to informants about robbing and killing white people. Both were taken to the Texas state penitentiary. Humanitarian groups protested the imprisonment as unjust, and while the Kiowas' lesser-known chiefs continued raids in the absence of their two most influential leaders, the government decided to release Big Tree and Satanta. All the time, Indian anger was rising on the reservations of Indian Territory because of immigrant horse thieves (probably roaming from Kansas), a lack of promised government rations, and the unwillingness of the reservation's poor land to yield to the plows with which the government so earnestly hoped to turn the Natives into Jeffersonian yeomen.

Slowly, the raids diminished as the ravages of alcohol eroded the Indians' ability to fight back. During the remainder of the 1870s, a series of military campaigns subjugated the surviving Kiowas, Comanches, Cheyenne, and others. It was a slow, arduous war of attrition. Some of the Natives died in Texas prisons, including Satanta, who had been sentenced to life. Satanta was so discouraged by the prospect of a lifetime in confinement that he jumped to his death from a prison window on March 11, 1878.

THE ARMY CLOSES ITS VISE ON THE GREAT PLAINS

During the years between 1860 and 1890, when the massacre at Wounded Knee heralded the closure of the frontier, the last great wave of Indian wars was spurred by more than prospects of land and gold. This wave of conquest also occurred under the aegis of an ideology based on Darwinistic principles in biology that stressed the "survival of the fittest." This doctrine, called social Darwinism, had been called into service to justify manifest destiny, the belief that the laws of nature (as well as the laws of the Christian God) had sanctioned the westward explosion of settlement. Darwin's work itself was hardly bereft of politics. His *Origin of Species* (1859) was first published with a now-forgotten subtitle: *The Preservation of Favored Races in the Struggle for Life.* In the *Voyage of the Beagle* (1839), Darwin wrote: "at some future period, not very distant when measured by centuries, the civilised races of man will almost certainly exterminate, and replace, the savage races throughout the world" (1962, 433–434). It was in this frame of mind that many of the pioneers (the word is archaic French for foot soldier) met the Great Sioux Nation and dozens of other Plains peoples.

The Native people who were so transformed as the frontiers closed around them have been called the Sioux (an archaic French word meaning snake or enemy). Their own name was Lakota, Dakota, and Nakota (allies). They sometimes called themselves *Ochheti shakowin* (the seven council fires, a confederacy). The Lakota moved to the plains from the Great Lakes area as the frontier expanded westward.

THE GREAT SIOUX UPRISING OF 1862

By the mid-nineteenth century, the Bureau of Indian Affairs, which had been transferred from the War Department to the Interior Department in 1849, was readying its version of the welfare state for subjugated Plains Native peoples. One by one, Native peoples were defeated, forced into camps, and promised supplies that often did not arrive. Despite occasional exposés in the press, "Indian rings" made graft a fine art in the bureaucracy, siphoning goods and money meant to purchase supplies for reservation-bound peoples. The Indians, now cut off from their traditional hunting economy, had no other means of survival. Some reservation-bound Indians ate their horses, many of which also were starving. When they had finished with the emaciated horses, the Indians ate the bark of trees and their moccasins. After that, they starved, sometimes hundreds at a time.

The Minnesota Sioux (Santee) signed a treaty in 1851 and moved onto reservations. By the early 1860s, with the outbreak of the Civil War, the U.S. government fell so far behind on providing promised food supplies and payment of annuities that many Santees were starving. By August 1862, the situation was so desperate that Santees from the Upper Agency (the northern part of the reservation) broke into a government warehouse and took enough pork and flour to feed their families. Santees under the jurisdiction of the Lower Agency, who also were starving, requested emergency rations. Indian agent Thomas Galbraith flatly refused to supply the food, telling the Santees to "eat grass or their own dung" (Weeks, 1990, 92). The desperation of hunger, combined with Galbraith's insult, provoked a revolt that came to be known as the Great Sioux Uprising of 1862. This uprising ended with the largest mass hanging in U.S. history.

Little Crow, then about sixty years old, led the uprising, which began during the early hours of August 18, 1862, with strikes on outlying farms. The Indians quickly killed several hundred immigrants. Individuals with whom the Indians had specific grievances (such as the Indian trader Andrew Myrick) were found slain, with grass stuffed in their mouths, recalling Galbraith's remark. After three days of intensive raiding, reinforcements joined troops in the area, driving the Santee back slowly, under orders from President Lincoln to quell the uprising at any cost. "Necessity knows no law," Lincoln reportedly told Army commanders in the area (Weeks, 1990, 94). Colonel Henry Hopkins Sibley of the Third Minnesota Volunteer Regiment issued orders to "destroy everything they own and drive them out into the Plains.... They are to be treated as maniacs or wild beasts" (ibid., 94).

The Santees killed more than 700 settlers and 100 soldiers before the Army drove them westward into the plains. A large number of Santees who had not taken a direct role in the uprising stayed in Minnesota. They expected to be treated as neutrals, but the immigrants' thirst for revenge fell on them. After the uprising was quelled, a military court condemned 303 of 392 imprisoned Santees to death by hanging. President Lincoln demanded a review of the sentences and cut the number to be executed to 38. Lincoln asserted that each of the accused had taken part in the massacre, raped women, or both. The 38 Santees died on a single scaffold at Fort Mankato on December 26, 1862, the largest mass hanging in U.S. history. William J. Dudley, who lost two children to the Santees' scalping knives during the massacre, cut the rope that hung the Santees.

The bodies of the executed men were removed from their mass grave after nightfall by medical doctors, who used them as laboratory specimens. Army units trailed the Santees who had escaped Minnesota to the Badlands of South Dakota. On August 4, 1864, Sibley's forces killed more than 500 Santee warriors in a single day. A dwindling number of survivors moved westward and took shelter with the Cheyennes. They forged parts of an alliance that General George A. Custer would face at the Little Big Horn a dozen years later.

Little Crow escaped Sibley's raids. He later was shot by a farmer (some say the farmer's son made the shot) as he foraged for berries in a nearby field. The farmer did not know until later that he had shot the man who started the Great Sioux Uprising. The Minnesota legislature voted the farmer a $500 honorarium. On May 4 and 5, 1863, two steam boats were boarded by 1,300 neutral Santees, most of them women and children, going into exile from their homelands. Settlers on shore threw rocks at them.

THE SAND CREEK MASSACRE (1864)

During the spring of 1864, Reverend J. M. Chivington, an officer with the Colorado volunteers (militia), reported that Cheyennes had stolen a number of cattle. The report may have been faked as an excuse to retaliate, which he did, attacking Cheyenne camps and indiscriminately killing women and children as well as warriors. The governor of Colorado persuaded the Cheyennes to settle peacefully at Sand Creek. Shortly thereafter, again acting on his own volition, Chivington raised between 600 and 1,000 men, mostly volunteers seething to

Mankato hanging, 1862. (Courtesy of the Nebraska State Historical Society.)

drive the Indians out, and mounted a surprise attack on the village. Chivington shouted: "Kill and scalp all the big and little; nits make for lice" (Virtual Truth Commission, 1998).

The Southern Cheyennes had lived peacefully during their early years of contact with immigrants in and around the new city of Denver. A village of Arapahoes camped in the heart of Denver around 1860. In 1861, Arapaho and Southern Cheyenne "treaty chiefs" were pressured into signing an agreement with the federal government without consulting their nations as a whole. Resentment rose among the Indians as more settlers and gold seekers moved in, further encroaching on their hunting lands.

As Black Kettle (Moketavato, ca. 1800–1868), the ranking chief in the village, hoisted a white flag and the stars and stripes, Chivington's men tore the Indians apart with sadistic enthusiasm. Black Kettle's wife was shot nine times but somehow survived. Black Kettle himself survived the Sand Creek massacre, only to be killed by George Armstrong Custer's Seventh Calvary four years later in the Washita massacre.

Another leader of the encampment at Sand Creek, White Antelope, stood in front of his lodge and sang his death song: Nothing, he sang, lives long, except the earth and the mountains. The elderly White Antelope was shot as he sang, along with at least 300 other Native men, women, and children. Chivington's detachment never accurately counted the casualties. The volunteers severed several Indians' limbs and heads, took them to Denver, and charged admission at a theater for a glimpse of the bloody body parts.

David Hurst Thomas described the aftermath of the Sand Creek massacre (1864): "One trooper cut off White Antelope's testicles, bragging that he needed a new tobacco pouch. . . . Returning to Denver, the Sand Creek heroes paraded through the streets, to the cheers of throngs. Theatergoers applauded an intermission display of Cheyenne scalps and women's pubic hair, strung triumphantly across the stage" (2000, 53). Shortly after the massacre, according to Thomas's account, several of the victims were packed into crates "[a]fter the corpses were beheaded, [and] the skulls and bones were defleshed" for shipment to the newly established Army Medical Museum in Washington, D.C. (ibid., 53). Some of these remains later became part of the Smithsonian Institution's collections. Army doctors often cut first and asked questions later, if at all. On another occasion, "Upon the death of a young Yankton Sioux woman—a 'squaw having remarkable beauty'—a post surgeon in the Dakotas dug up her grave, severed her head, and dispatched it to Washington [D.C.] as 'a fine specimen'" (ibid., 57).

The behavior of Chivington and the Colorado volunteers was so reprehensible to Kit Carson that he called Chivington's men cowardly dogs. The surviving Cheyennes retaliated with fire and fury, killing uncounted immigrants during the next three years. Four years after Chivington's attack, a federal commission concluded that he and his men had acted with a degree of barbarism that even the most brutal of Indians could not match.

Following the Sand Creek massacre, Black Kettle labored without success to restore the peace. Survivors of the massacre camped near the Washita River in Oklahoma. During the winter of 1868, they were attacked again by troops with orders to raze the village, hang all the men, and take women and children captive. The leader of this attack was George Armstrong Custer, the brash "boy general" whose enthusiasm for a big victory later would cost him his scalp at the Little Big Horn. Custer, the U.S. Army's youngest general, a rank that he held on a brevet (temporary) basis, won a number of battlefield promotions during the Civil War. Custer's attack on the Southern Cheyennes' camp at Washita during 1868 was his first experience in the Indian wars. Between 40 and 110 Indians were killed, including Black Kettle. During the attack, Arapahoes, Comanches, and Kiowas came to the rescue of the Cheyennes, forcing Custer and his troops to withdraw prematurely.

RED CLOUD FORCES THE U.S. ARMY TO RETREAT DURING THE LATE 1860s

When Red Cloud (Makhpiya-luta, Oglala Lakota, ca. 1820–1909, whose name refers to an unusual formation of crimson clouds that hovered over the

Red Horse's depiction of the Custer battle, 1876. (Courtesy of
Smithsonian National Anthropological Archives.)

western horizon) was born about 1820 near the forks of the Platte River in
present-day Nebraska, only a few European Americans lived in that area. By
the time he died, in 1909, Red Cloud's people had been pushed onto a tiny
fraction of their former lands, imprisoned in concentration camp conditions,
famished, and impoverished. Born into the heyday of the Plains horse culture,
Red Cloud died in the era of the "vanishing race."

As a young man, Red Cloud learned to fight and hunt, as did most other
Oglala Lakota boys. Very quickly, he proved himself adept at both. Red Cloud
was especially known as a fierce warrior who was always ready to personally
take an enemy's scalp. Red Cloud also had five children and possibly as many
as six wives. Red Cloud became a major leader of the Oglala Lakota during the
late phases of the Plains Indian wars. At one point, during the 1860s, Red
Cloud and his allies forced the United States to concede considerable territory
in and around the Black Hills, borders of which were outlined in the Fort
Laramie Treaty of 1868.

In 1865, the Lakota refused to sign a treaty permitting passage across their
lands from Ft. Laramie, along the Powder River, to the gold fields of Montana.
They dominated the northern plains as the energies of the U.S. Army were
being directed toward fighting the Civil War. When U.S. Army troops built
forts without Lakota permission, war parties cut off food supplies to Fort
Phil Kearney in northern Wyoming and laid siege to the outpost for two

years. During this offensive, in December 1866, Captain William J. Fetterman bragged that he could ride with eighty men across the whole of Sioux country. He set out with eighty-one men and high ambitions only to be led into a deadly ambush by Crazy Horse, a son-in-law of Red Cloud, and a dozen warriors.

In 1868, with the wagon road still closed, the government signed a treaty at Fort Laramie that caused its forts to be dismantled. The Powder River country and the Black Hills were reserved for the Lakotas forever, or so the treaty said. Red Cloud advised trading with the immigrants, but otherwise avoiding them. Red Cloud's valor as a warrior was legendary. He counted more than eighty coups and once returned from battle against a contingent of Crows with an arrow through his body.

Once Red Cloud was asked by a trader at Wolf Point why he continued to pursue diminishing herds of buffalo rather than settle on a reservation despite cold and near starvation:

> Because I am a red man. If the Great Spirit had desired me to be a white man, he would have made me so in the first place. He put in your heart certain wishes and plans, in my heart he put other and different desires. Each man is good in his sight. It is not necessary for eagles to be crows. Now we are poor but we are free. No white man controls our footsteps. If we must die, we die defending our rights. (Johansen and Grinde, 1997, 313)

During the 1870s and 1880s, Red Cloud fought the Army and the reservation system, but at the same time he provided aid to Yale professor Othniel C. March, who was searching the area for dinosaur bones. In exchange, March said he would take Lakota allegations of mistreatment "to the highest levels" of government (Milner, 1990, 387). March and his crew excavated two tons of bones during the midst of the war for the Black Hills. March investigated Red Cloud's complaints of rotten food and unmet promises. The Yale professor also documented massive profiteering by Indian rings in the Grant administration, sparking a congressional investigation and several newspaper exposés. At one point, March confronted Grant personally. March and Red Cloud became friends for the rest of their lives, into the twentieth century. Red Cloud said that he appreciated the fact that March, unlike many whites who dealt with Indians, did not forget his promises after he got what he wanted.

Red Cloud's biographer George E. Hyde characterized him in old age as "wrinkled, stooped, and almost blind" (1967, 336). Red Cloud was sometimes given to ironic bitterness over what had become of him and his people: "I, who used to control 5,000 warriors, must tell Washington when I am hungry. I must beg for that which I own" (ibid., 336). Red Cloud spent his final years in retirement, having little to do with his people's affairs. He died December 10, 1909.

GEORGE ARMSTRONG CUSTER'S LAST INDIAN WAR

Best known as the loser of the Battle of the Little Big Horn (1876), George Armstrong Custer (1839–1876) had earned the enmity of Native Americans for his participation in earlier campaigns against them, as well as for leading an Army expedition into the Lakota's sacred *Paha Sapa* (Black Hills) in 1874.

Six years after his men killed the Southern Cheyenne Black Kettle, Custer headed an Army column that marched into the Lakota Sioux's sacred *Paha Sapa*, despite legal reservation of the area to the Sioux in the 1868 Fort Laramie Treaty. The expedition was less a military invasion than a geological assay; Custer brought with him a sixteen-piece brass band, as well as civilians to catalogue the area's flora and fauna, most notably its rich deposits of gold.

As he returned to Fort Abraham Lincoln in September 1874, Custer telegraphed news to Chicago and Denver that the whole area was thickly veined with gold, as he put it for maximum emphasis, from the grass roots downward. The news soon sparked a stampede of fortune seekers into the *Paha Sapa*. The power of the stampede was slackened only slightly by Lakota warriors who murdered a small number of miners. The miners ignored several federal edicts directing them away from land that belonged to the Lakota by treaty. Commanding officers faced a problem that often had perplexed the U.S. Army during the years of westward expansion: How strenuously did soldiers dare to enforce unpopular laws against citizens of their own country? Most soldiers escorted miners out of the Black Hills, leaving them free to return via different routes.

The invasion of the Black Hills changed the demographic balance in the entire surrounding area. In 1870, fewer than 5,000 whites had lived in the Dakota Territory. By 1880, the non-Indian population had grown to 134,000, with 17,000 of these individuals digging gold in the Black Hills.

Crazy Horse (Tashunka Witco, Oglala Lakota, ca. 1842–1877), who had led the decoy mission that had ambushed the bragging Fetterman, was among the best-known Lakota war leaders during the time that the Black Hills gold rush began. Crazy Horse had a reputation that spanned the Plains for sometimes-shrewd and often-reckless bravery. Crazy Horse, a daring military strategist, was a major leader of the Lakota during the last half of the nineteenth century, during the final phases of the Plains Indian wars. Alone among the Native leaders of the Plains wars, he never signed a treaty with the United States. Crazy Horse repudiated the idea of living on a reservation until his violent death at age 35. He never wore European-style clothing, and his photograph was never taken. To the Oglala Lakota and to many other Native people generally, his memory has become the essence of resistance to European colonization. Alvin Josephy Jr. wrote that "To the Sioux, he is the greatest of all their leaders" (1961, 259). Crazy Horse was of average height, with a complexion that was lighter than most other Lakota. He was known to wander away from his village after a battle with the detachment of a poet.

Crazy Horse is an old name among the Oglalas, having been handed down generation to generation. For several centuries, Crazy Horse's ancestors kept historical records for the Oglalas on buckskin, a method of historical record keeping related to the "winter counts" of other Sioux tribes. Crazy Horse married a Cheyenne and thus cemented the alliance that functioned during the final phases of the Plains Indian wars.

Crazy Horse was born about 1842 on what would later become the site of Rapid City, South Dakota. His father was a Lakota holy man, and his mother was Brule Sioux. As a youth, Crazy Horse was called the Light-haired One or Curly. He received the name Crazy Horse from his father after a battle with the Arapahos in 1858, at about sixteen years of age. From an early age, Crazy Horse was a master of the psychological aspects of Plains warfare. He often rode into war naked, except for a breechclout around his loins, "his body painted with white hail spots, and a red lightning streak down one cheek.... His battle cry was 'It's a good day to die!'" (Waters, 1992, 152). Crazy Horse was never seriously injured in battle, and he made a point of never scalping anyone he killed. After attaining "shirt wearer" rank in 1865, he attended leadership meetings, but rarely spoke. Introverted and eccentric, Crazy Horse was shot in the face and relieved of the shirt of rank in 1870 following an attempt to steal another man's wife.

During mid-1870s, the U.S. Army had ordered all Plains Indians onto assigned reservations. Several Sioux and Cheyenne bands roamed in their accustomed patterns between summer and winter camps despite the Army orders. In December 1875, the government's Indian Bureau, alarmed that the Sioux were not staying on their reservation, sent out orders that all "roving bands" must return to stations assigned them within two months. The winter was severe, and so many of the Sioux, including Crazy Horse's and Sitting Bull's bands, ignored the order so that they could replenish their depleted stores of buffalo meat and other game. When the government's orders were not obeyed, the Army sent General Crook to attack the Natives' winter camps.

General George Crook set out with ten cavalry units and two infantry companies, one of the largest forces the Army ever sent into the field against Indians. Having spotted Crazy Horse's camp, Crook dispatched Colonel J. J. Reynolds and 450 men to round them up. Reynolds's detachment took the Sioux almost completely by surprise—the warriors had just enough warning to scatter into the nearby woods as Reynolds ordered the burning of their village and the capture of their ponies. Crazy Horse then emerged from the woods, leading a frenzied charge that not only drove Reynolds out of the razed village with heavy losses, but also reclaimed the ponies. Crazy Horse did not stop there. His force chased Reynolds's retreating force back to Crook's camp, where warriors stole the cattle that fed them. Without meat animals, caught in a bleak, cold Plains winter, Crook was forced to retreat to Fort Fetterman.

By 1876, several allied peoples, Lakota, Cheyenne, and others, were camped at the Little Big Horn when they were presented with an unexpected opportunity to avenge Custer's invasion of the Black Hills. Their camp, perhaps as many as 5,000 people, including about 2,000 warriors, followed the Little Bighorn River for about three miles. The Seventh Calvary, under Custer, had expected only about a thousand because he had ignored reports of his Crow scouts. Even after Custer discovered that the camp was twice the size that he had expected, Custer decided to attack the Indians on their home ground. That decision resulted in the deaths of Custer and his entire force of about 225 men, who were exhausted from having marched most of the previous night.

The Seventh Calvary rode into a battle that the Lakota chief Kill Eagle likened to a hurricane or bees swarming out of a hive. Riding horses exhausted after a 350-mile night ride, completely surrounded, and cut off from reinforcements stationed only nine miles away, Custer's force was cut to ribbons during one furious, bloody hour on a battleground that nearly disappeared under a huge cloud of dust. The Lakota religious leader Black Elk (Hchaka Sapa, Oglala Lakota, 1863–1950) was heartened by the outcome: "I was not sorry at all. I was a happy boy. Those *wasi'chus* [takers of the fat, or greedy ones, e.g., white men in Lakota] had come to kill our mothers and fathers and us, and it was our country" (Weeks, 1990, 185). The battle provoked momentary joy among the Lakota and Cheyennes, who for decades had watched their hunting ranges curtailed by what Black Elk called "the gnawing flood of the *wasi'chu*" (Gibson, 1980, 426).

Black Elk came of age during the late nineteenth century, as European settlement reached his homeland. His views of Native life at that time reached large audiences in the twentieth century through the books of John Neihardt; the best known of these books is *Black Elk Speaks* (Black Elk, [1932] 1972). Black Elk was eleven years old during the summer of 1874 when, by his account (published in *Black Elk Speaks*), an expedition under the command of Custer invaded the *Paha Sapa*. In the words of Black Elk, the Lakota and Cheyennes painted their faces black—went to war—to regain the Black Hills. In *Black Elk Speaks*, Black Elk told Neihardt that he had been a young warrior at the battle of the Little Big Horn, and that he had witnessed the battle. Young Black Elk tried to take the first scalp at that battle. The soldier under Black Elk's hatchet proved to have an unusually tough scalp, so Black Elk shot him instead.

News of Custer's defeat spoiled the U.S. centennial celebrations of July 1876. After the battle, the aging Lewis Henry Morgan, who had founded American anthropology four decades earlier with his landmark work on the Iroquois, *The League of the Haundenosaunee* ([1851] 1962), wrote in *The Nation* that the Lakota and Cheyenne who had defeated Custer's troops were only defending their birthright (Hoover, 1976, 157, 277). Morgan's point of view was not popular among non-Indians, however. Retaliation against the Lakota, Cheyenne, and others followed, by progressively larger Army units, drawn into the last "untamed" section of the continental United States.

Black Elk, *left*, about 19 years of age, on tour in Europe.
(Courtesy of the Smithsonian National Anthropological Archives.)

After the battle of the Little Big Horn, Indians who remained free of reservations were hounded relentlessly by reinforced U.S. Army troops. The Sioux who had defeated Custer were pushed onto the Great Sioux Reservation, band by band. Crazy Horse and his contingent of 800 Oglalas, 145 lodges with 1,700 ponies, were among the last to surrender. On May 5, 1877, the Oglalas formed a parade two miles long as they marched into Red Cloud Agency, where they surrendered their horses and guns. Red Cloud met the Oglalas en route and guided them to Fort Robinson, near the agency.

Shortly after the surrender, Crazy Horse's wife Black Shawl became sick with tuberculosis. He asked permission to take her to Spotted Tail's people at the Brule Agency, forty miles away, but was denied. Crazy Horse then departed Fort Robinson anyway. Several dozen soldiers chased Crazy Horse to the Brule Agency but failed to catch him. Instead, the Brule Indian agent and Spotted Tail himself convinced Crazy Horse to return to Ft. Robinson.

Crazy Horse began to return; fifteen miles from the Brule Agency, he was surrounded by forty of Spotted Tail's government-employed scouts. Crazy Horse was taken prisoner and escorted back to Ft. Robinson. Rumor had it that Crazy Horse would be killed or taken in chains to Fort Augustine, Florida, to be imprisoned for life. At Fort Robinson on September 5, 1877, Crazy Horse was led toward a stockade. He rebelled at the sight of the prison and tried to escape. Little Big Man and several other Indians grabbed Crazy Horse as Private William Gentles ran his bayonet through his body. Crazy Horse was about thirty-five years of age at the time.

On his deathbed, Crazy Horse recalled why he had fought:

I was not hostile to the white man.... We had buffalo for food, and their hides for clothing and our tipis. We preferred hunting to a life of idleness on the reservations, where we were driven against our will. At times, we did not get enough to eat, and we were not allowed to leave the reservation to hunt. We preferred our own way of living. We were no expense to the government then. All we wanted was peace, to be left alone.... They tried to confine me, I tried to escape, and a soldier ran his bayonet through me. I have spoken. (Johansen and Grinde, 1997, 88–89)

After Crazy Horse's assassination, about 240 Lakota lodges occupied by people who had supported him migrated to Canada, where they joined Sitting Bull's people. With the "Crazy Horse band," Sitting Bull's camp grew to about 800 lodges.

SITTING BULL'S EXILE IN CANADA

Tatanka Yotanka (ca. 1830–1890), or Sitting Buffalo (or, as he was more widely known, Sitting Bull), was the Lakota's best-known political leader

Sitting Bull. (Courtesy of the Nebraska State Historical Society.)

during the late nineteenth century. He was a Hunkpapa Teton Sioux, a seer of visions and an esteemed statesman as well as a warrior.

Sitting Bull, whose Lakota name portrays a large bull buffalo at rest, was one of the principal war chiefs who negotiated the Fort Laramie Treaty of 1868, which forced the United States to abandon several forts and to respect the Lakota's claim to their sacred *Paha Sapa*, "the heart of everything that is."

Sitting Bull was known among the Lakota as an outstanding warrior as a young man; in later years, he was best known as a spiritual leader—a visionary and a dreamer. Before the Battle of the Little Big Horn, Sitting Bull experienced a vision that portended a native victory. After the battle, the Army forced Sitting Bull and his people into exile in Canada.

Captain Edmund Fechet, who observed Sitting Bull's influence after he surrendered to reservation life during the 1880s, later wrote: "Since the days of Pontiac, Tecumseh, and Red Jacket, no Indian has had the power of drawing to himself so large a following . . . and molding it and wielding it against the authority of the United States" (Johansen and Grinde, 1997, 352).

Born at a site the Hunkpapas called Many Caches along the Grand River in Dakota Country, Sitting Bull's first childhood name was Slow. He apparently resented the stigma and worked to prove himself from a very early age. At ten, he killed a buffalo. At age fourteen, he counted coup on an enemy and received his adult name. Sitting Bull, as a teenager, also showed promise as a medicine man by undertaking an early vision quest. Shortly after that, he was initiated into the Strong Heart warrior society. Sitting Bull assumed leadership in the society during 1856, after he killed a Crow in combat and sustained a bullet wound that forced him to limp for the rest of his life. From early in his life, Sitting Bull was conscious of his leadership role in battle as well as the buffalo hunt. White Bull, a Hunkpapa Sioux leader, remarked: "Wherever he was, and whatever he did, his name was great everywhere" (Johansen and Grinde, 1997, 353). Sitting Bull's enemies held his name in such awe that Hunkpapa warriors could intimidate enemies by shouting "*Tatanka-Iyotanka tahoksila*," meaning "We are Sitting Bull's Boys." Sitting Bull grew to be both a great warrior and *wichasha wakan*—a man of mystery, a "medicine man."

Sitting Bull was reluctant to engage the U.S. Army in war until the Hunkpapas' land was invaded. After that happened, he allied with other Sioux bands, as well as Cheyennes, to try to stem the flood. Sitting Bull and his allies closely watched the invasion of the Black Hills by Custer in 1874 and played a key role in rallying the Lakota and Cheyennes to defeat Custer in 1876 at the Little Big Horn. Sitting Bull's dreams foreshadowed the defeat of Custer. In June 1876, a large Sun Dance was held on the west bank of the Rosebud River. Sitting Bull performed the dance 36 hours straight, after which he had a vision that U.S. Army soldiers without ears were falling into a Sioux village upside down. The lack of ears signified ignorance of the truth, and the upside-down positioning indicated that they would die. Sitting Bull said of the battle: "Let no man say that this was a massacre. They came to kill us and got killed themselves" (Johansen and Grinde, 1997, 353).

Later in the 1870s, Sitting Bull and about 200 other Lakota escaped the Great Sioux Reservation and took refuge in Canada. In Canada, Sitting Bull was afforded the deference due a visiting head of state. He received visitors from around the world. In 1881, Sitting Bull and his band returned to the

United States and surrendered. By this time, his once-vast following had dwindled to 44 men and 143 women and children. Sitting Bull was taken to the Standing Rock Agency, where he ridiculed efforts to sell Indian land: "Take a scale and sell it by the pound!" he is said to have shouted in derision (Johansen and Grinde, 1997, 354). On the Great Sioux Reservation, millions of acres were being sold to non-Indians, and epidemics were spreading. Sitting Bull staunchly opposed any form of allotment, and although he adopted farming and sent his children to reservation schools, Sitting Bull maintained until his death that "I would rather die an Indian than live as a white man" (ibid., 354).

THE TRAVAIL OF STANDING BEAR'S PONCAS: 1877–1879

The Ponca Standing Bear (ca. 1830-1902) gained national notoriety in the late 1870s, during a time of forced removal for the Ponca and other native peoples on the Great Plains. Standing Bear and his companions soon became engaged in the first court case to result in a declaration that American Indians should be treated as human beings under the law of habeas corpus. Thus, under U.S. law, the Army could not relocate Standing Bear's party by force without cause.

Before they were forcibly removed from their homeland along the Niobrara River, along the northern border of present-day Nebraska, the Poncas had gone to great lengths to maintain friendly relationships with the United States. In 1858, they ceded part of their homeland along the Niobrara in exchange for a homeland in the same area that was said, at the time, to be theirs in perpetuity. Ten years later, the United States, in a classic example of sloppy bureaucracy, signed the Poncas' land over to the Sioux, their traditional enemies, in the Laramie Treaty of 1868.

During 1877, federal troops removed 723 Poncas from three villages along the Niobrara River to Indian Territory. The tribe was moved at bayonet point after eight of their leaders had inspected and refused to accept the arid land that the government wanted the Poncas to occupy in Oklahoma. During their march to Indian Territory, several of the Poncas died of starvation and disease.

A year after their removal, a third of the Poncas had died. One of the dead was a son of Standing Bear. Following that death, Standing Bear, determined to bury the bones of his son in the lands of his ancestors, escaped northward, toward the Niobrara, with thirty other Poncas. Standing Bear recalled: "It was winter. We started for home on foot. We barely lived [un]til morning, it was so cold. We had nothing but our blankets. We took the ears of corn that had dried in the fields; we ate it raw. The soles of our moccasins wore out. We went barefoot in the snow" (Massey and the Omaha Indian Center, 1979, n.p.). After two months of walking, including a ten-day stop among the Otoes, the group led by Standing Bear took shelter on land owned by the Omahas.

Standing Bear, Ponca chief. (Courtesy of the Nebraska State Historical Society.)

They had run out of food, eaten their horses, and finally consumed their moccasins. Their bare, bloody feet left tracks in the snow.

During March 1879, troops under General George Crook arrested Standing Bear and his party and conveyed them to Fort Omaha, just north of the growing frontier city of the same name. Once he had arrived at the fort, which was serving as his headquarters, Crook called Omaha newspaperman Thomas Tibbles, whose dispatches were wired to larger newspapers on the East Coast, causing a storm of protest letters to Congress on the Poncas' behalf.

Crook already had announced his disgust at how Standing Bear's party was being treated: "An Irishman, German, Chinaman, Turk, or Tarter will be protected in life and property" under the laws of the United States, General Crook had said, "But the Indian can command respect for his rights only so long as he inspires terror for his rifle" (Mathes, 1989, 46).

Tibbles, who was thirty-nine years of age at the time, described himself as the "ebullient, volatile assistant editor of the Omaha *Daily Herald*" when he first met Standing Bear (Tibbles, [1880] 1972, xii). Before taking a job at the Omaha *Herald*, Tibbles had been an outspoken abolitionist, a scout in the Civil War, and a circuit-riding preacher.

The day that General Crook brought the Poncas to town, Tibbles put the Sunday newspaper to bed at 4:30 A.M., slept for two and a half hours, then rose at 7 A.M. and walked five miles north from the newspaper's downtown offices to Fort Omaha. After he interviewed members of Standing Bear's group, Tibbles then made his way south again, running part of the way, stopping at every church he could find, asking pastors if he could address their congregations about the travail of the Poncas. At a Congregational church, the pastor, Reverend Mr. Sherill, allowed Tibbles to speak between the opening hymns. After hearing Tibbles's account, two churches passed resolutions to the Interior Department and Secretary Carl Schurz on the Poncas' behalf. By the next day, Tibbles was preparing wire dispatches for newspapers in Chicago, New York, and other cities as he searched for attorneys who would represent Standing Bear and his people in Omaha federal district court.

Omaha citizens obtained a writ of habeas corpus and brought the Army into the federal court of Judge Elmer Dundy, who ruled during 1879 that an Indian is a person within the meaning of the law, and no law gave the Army authority to forcibly remove them from their lands. After initially refusing to let Standing Bear speak during the trial on April 30, 1879, Judge Dundy relented. Standing Bear spoke in Ponca through an interpreter. Another translation was provided later by Tibbles. Standing Bear spoke with the passion of a man who had lost a brother, a sister, two daughters, and two sons during the Poncas' diaspora.

Standing Bear raised one of his hands and said: "This hand is not the same color as yours, but if I pierce it, I shall feel pain. If you pierce your hand you will also feel pain. The blood that will flow from mine will be the same color as yours. I am a man. The same God made both of us" (Bob Reilly, Reilly, and Reilly, 2003, 29–30). Standing Bear said that the Poncas were like a family trying to escape a river in flood, stumbling up a cliff, finding only one way out. Finally, he said, they spot a passage. "But a man bars that passage. He is a thousand times more powerful than I. Behind him I see soldiers as numerous as the leaves of the trees. They will obey that man's orders.... If he says I cannot pass, I cannot" (ibid., 30). Standing Bear turned to Dundy, and concluded: "You are that man" (ibid., 30). The judge wept, as did several other people in the courtroom. Dundy handed down his historic ruling a week later.

Further, Dundy ruled that the right of expatriation is "a natural and inherent right of all people, indispensable to the enjoyment of the rights of life, liberty, and the pursuit of happiness. An Indian," wrote Judge Dundy, "is a person within the meaning of the law, and there is no law giving the Army authority to forcibly remove Indians from their lands" (Johansen and Grinde, 1997, 367).

Shortly after Omaha federal Judge Dundy denied the Army's power to relocate Standing Bear and his party forcibly, his brother Big Snake tested the ruling by moving roughly 100 miles in Indian territory, from the Poncas' assigned reservation to one occupied by the Cheyennes. He was arrested by troops and returned. On October 31, 1879, Ponca Indian Agent William H. Whiteman called Big Snake a troublemaker and ordered a detail to imprison him. When Big Snake refused to surrender, contending he had committed no crime, he was shot to death. Later, the U.S. Senate called for an investigation of the shooting and other aspects of the Poncas' tragedy. Big Snake was unaware of the fact that Judge Dundy had limited his ruling to the Poncas who appeared before his court. In so doing, he did not deny the Army's power to relocate other Natives by force of arms.

In 1990, the Ponca tribe of Nebraska was restored to tribal status by an act of Congress, signed by President George H. W. Bush, following termination of its status in 1965. Across the United States, several dozen Native nations were following the same path. In 1992, the Poncas moved into new tribal offices at Niobrara, Nebraska.

THE ROAD TO WOUNDED KNEE

By 1890, the surviving Lakota people had been corralled into reservations on the plains. The Ghost Dance religion arrived at their lowest ebb. Originated by the prophet Wovoka, a Paiute, the Ghost Dance spread among the destitute Native peoples of the West, from Oregon to Nebraska, into the Dakotas, where Sitting Bull endorsed its vision of Native restoration. Wovoka's English name was Jack Wilson. Born a Paiute, he had spent his childhood, after age 14, with a white Christian family. Wovoka's father regularly read the Bible at meals. As Handsome Lake did before him, Wovoka combined Native and Christian symbols into a religion that evoked a messiah not in a person but in the promised delivery of Native people from misery that came with oppression by Euro-Americans. Wovoka's instructions to ghost dancers contained references to Christ as well as prophecies of native restoration: "Do not tell the white people about this. Jesus is now upon the earth. He appears like a cloud. The dead are all alive again. I do not know when they will be here; maybe this fall or in the spring. When the time comes there will be no more sickness and everyone will be young again" (Powers, 1973, 225).

The Lakota took to the Ghost Dance with a frenzy that Wovoka had not anticipated. Lakota medicine men also said that special "ghost shirts" would shield the Sioux from soldiers' bullets. Driven by hunger, desperation, and a determined desire to escape from their new, brutal reality, many Sioux ghost dancers worked themselves into a frenzy during which they said they had seen the return of the buffalo and spoken with dead relatives.

By late 1890, an estimated 3,500 people were gathered against their will in the hills near Wounded Knee Creek, which bisects the Pine Ridge Indian reservation. Many of them demanded the right to practice the Ghost Dance religion, which held that God would create a new world for them in which the buffalo would return, and white men would vanish. The rules of the reservation laid down by the Indian Bureau forbade practice of the religion.

Non-Indian immigrants demanded protection from what they regarded as an attempt to rally Native peoples against them. Several thousand U.S. Army troops converged on the area in anticipation of renewed conflict. "What treaty that the whites have kept has the red man broken?" Sitting Bull asked before his assassination, as his people were guarded by nervous soldiers. "Not one. What treaty that the whites ever made with us red men have they kept? Not one. When I was a boy, the Sioux owned the world. The sun rose and set in their lands. They sent 10,000 horsemen to battle. Where are the warriors today? Who slew them? Where are our lands? Who owns them?" (Johansen and Grinde, 1997, 355).

William Cody (1846–1917), the creator of Buffalo Bill's Wild West Show, figured into the last days of Sitting Bull's life as he tried to defuse tensions between Pine Ridge Indian agents and the aging chief. Cody had been born near Davenport, Iowa, but moved at the age of eight to Kansas, where his father became embroiled in antislavery politics. When he was eleven years of age, Cody's father died from an attack motivated by his politics. The younger Cody then moved to Colorado, where he tried panning for gold and spent some time as a rider on the Pony Express. During the early 1860s, Cody began serving as a scout for the U.S. Army. The name Buffalo Bill was given him by Union Pacific railway workers to whom he supplied buffalo meat under contract about 1866.

By 1868, Cody again was working as an Army scout; he may have killed the Cheyenne leader Tall Bull. In the meantime, Edward Zane Carroll Judson was beginning to glorify Buffalo Bill's real and imagined exploits in the earliest of 1,700 dime novels. By 1872, Cody had taken advantage of the publicity to become an entertainer, engaged in Wild West shows staged by a number of Army scouts who toured the eastern urban areas of the United States. Between show tours, Cody himself returned to work as an Army scout. On July 17, 1876, Cody reportedly killed and scalped the Cheyenne chief Yellow Hair. By the early 1880s, the Indian wars were winding down, and Cody became a full-time showman with his own Wild West Show that included Native Americans as a major attraction. Cody was known as a benevolent employer as he became friends with some of the same Native leaders he had once pursued as a scout. One of his closest friends was Sitting Bull. A publicity poster for the Wild West Show showed Sitting Bull and Cody clasping hands over the caption, "Foes in '76, Friends in '85."

Sitting Bull and Buffalo Bill Cody. (Courtesy of the Nebraska State Historical Society.)

As tensions mounted in South Dakota late in 1890, Cody was returning from a tour of Europe with forty-five Sioux, many of whom had been prominent leaders during the final years of the Plains Indian wars. In November 1890, trains pulled out of Omaha carrying troops bound for Pine Ridge Agency, newspaper reporters, and the Sioux from Buffalo Bill's troupe. The train carrying the forty-five Sioux arrived at Rushville, Nebraska, the train depot nearest the Pine Ridge Agency, on November 20. Cody had been asked for help in defusing tensions at Pine Ridge by General Nelson Miles, an adversary of Standing Rock Indian agent James McLaughlin. On his arrival at the agency, Cody was detained by associates of McLaughlin, who urged him to get drunk at the Fort Yates officers' mess. McLaughlin had Cody's authority rescinded as he pursued his own plans to arrest Sitting Bull.

Tension continued to intensify between McLaughlin, who was pressuring the Sioux to sign new treaties ceding more of their territory, and Sitting Bull, who had campaigned all his life against signing away Native homelands.

Sitting Bull was killed December 15, 1890, a few days before the massacre at Wounded Knee, as forty-three tribal police tried to arrest him. Accounts of Sitting Bull's assassination vary, but it appears that Bullhead, a police officer employed by the Indian agency, served a warrant on Sitting Bull as he protested that no reason existed for his arrest. Bullhead then shot him in the thigh, as his partner, Sargent Red Tomahawk, shot Sitting Bull in the head. A riot ensued, during which six policemen and eight of Sitting Bull's followers, including his son Crow Foot, also were killed.

L. Frank Baum, who later would author the *Oz* books, edited the Aberdeen, South Dakota, *Saturday Pioneer* from 1888 to 1891. During this time, he penned two vitriolic editorials that fanned racial hatred in the area. On December 20, 1890, days after the assassination of Sitting Bull and slightly more than a week before the Wounded Knee massacre, he wrote:

> The proud spirit of the original owners of these vast prairies...lingered last in the bosom of Sitting Bull. With his fall, the nobility of the Redskin is extinguished, and what few are left are a pack of whining curs who lick the hand that smites them. The Whites, by law of conquest, by justice of civilization, are masters of the American continent, and the best safety of the frontier settlements will be secured by the total annihilation of the few remaining Indians. Why not annihilation? Their glory has fled, their spirit broken, their manhood effaced; better that they should die than live [as] the miserable wretches that they are. (Stannard, 1992, 126)

A week after the massacre, the demand for annihilation was repeated in Baum's newspaper, with one difference. He misspelled "extermination" as "extirmination."

Baum was not alone. The Omaha *Bee* invoked the stereotype of Indian-as-devil to justify the assassination of Sitting Bull on December 10, 1890. Calling Sitting Bull "always hostile to the white man [and] ever the foe of civilization," the *Bee* said that Sitting Bull's demise should "give a sense of relief" to whites in South Dakota. "No sentiment should be wasted upon the death of Sitting Bull," wrote the *Bee,* echoing the opinion of L. Frank Baum in Aberdeen, South Dakota. "Whatever the circumstances...he deserved his fate as a rebellious and implacable enemy.... It cannot fail to have a salutary effect on his bloodthirsty followers" (Hugh Reilly, 1997, 201–202).

The Omaha *World-Herald,* influenced by Tibbles, reacted very differently from the *Bee* or Baum. It wrote of Sitting Bull's assassination: "The killing was only part of the unwarranted severity and oppression that the United States is now inflicting on the Indians.... There seems to be no end to the blunders, crimes, and atrocities into which the government is led in the treatment of the Indians. It is time for a change" (Hugh Reilly, 1997, 202–203).

According to Hugh Reilly's analysis of newspaper coverage of the Indian wars, unverified rumors regarding events at Wounded Knee were presented as reports from reliable sources, idle gossip became purported fact, and "a large number of the nation's newspapers indulged in a field day of exaggeration, distortion, and just plain faking" (1997, 183). In many ways, Wounded Knee was a journalistic training ground for sensational, mass-market newspaper provocation of the Spanish-American War eight years later.

While many newspapers stoked European American fears of Indian unrest in the months before the massacre at Wounded Knee, the Omaha *World-Herald,* influenced by Tibbles and Susette LaFlesche, struck a moderate tone. In an editorial November 8, 1890, the newspaper said the Ghost Dancers should be left alone. "The United States [government] takes this matter very stupidly—it always takes everything connected with the Indians stupidly," the newspaper said.

> All this is but a part of the general impression which the government and the people in it have always cherished, that the Indian has no right to any ideas of his own, or indeed to any nationality of his own. The Indian is not an idolater. He is distinctly religious. His ideas concerning the unknown are far from contemptible, yet they have never been respected." (Hugh Reilly, 1997, 183)

Among the reporters on the trains that departed from Omaha on November 18, 1890, bound for Pine Ridge country were Charles H. Cressey of the *Bee* and Carl Smith of the *World-Herald,* who covered the situation until he was replaced in late November by LaFlesche and Tibbles. LaFlesche thus became, according to Hugh Reilly (1997), one of the first female war correspondents to be officially employed by any American newspaper, and certainly America's first female, as a Native American war correspondent. While LaFlesche and Tibbles interviewed Native Americans, Cressey spun imaginative tales as he read conspiracies of intrigue and impending violence into expressions on the faces of Indians returning home after performing in Buffalo Bill Cody's Wild West Show. Cressey, for example, filed a report featuring an invented plot by Indians to attack a troop train at Valentine, Nebraska, just south of Pine Ridge. The attack never occurred.

The *Bee's* Cressey compared the Indians he saw at Pine Ridge to "cigar sign models" who replied to questions with "a grunt and a foolish look." Cressey

Susette LaFlesche. (Courtesy of Smithsonian
National Anthropological Archives.)

seemed to relish the stylistic turn of his stereotypes when, on December 8,
he further described the cigar sign models as "half-animated, long-haired,
blanket-swathed musk bags that make up nine-tenths of the inhabitants [who]
swim their tepees in tears and then go blind" (Hugh Reilly, 1997, 199).

The *World-Herald*, by contrast, reported that the fears of local ranchers and
farmers had no factual foundation, as the *Bee's* headlines, according to Reilly's
account, screamed "Fears of an Ambush" and "A Squaw's Warning." Cressey
reported that Sioux were dancing with rifles strapped to their backs, threat-
ening to "cut off soldiers' ears and otherwise maim them" (Hugh Reilly, 1997,
189–190). By Reilly's account, Cressey on November 21 quoted an unnamed
"prominent officer" as saying that "Nothing but a miracle could save us from
Custer's fate, and I hope to God that reinforcements will arrive before the
red devils make their break" (ibid., 190). Two days later, the *World-Herald*

published an editorial headlined "No Need for War" (ibid., 191), which compared the Ghost Dance to religious excitement experienced by the European Druids and the early Methodists. "And yet," said the *World-Herald*, "no arms were brought to bear on them. No retributions were prepared in the shape of a Hotchkiss gun or otherwise." On November 30, the newspaper quoted General Nelson A. Miles's opinion that the Ghost Dance troubles were more of a "correspondents' scare than an Indian scare" (ibid., 193).

In its editions of December 17, less than two weeks before the massacre, the *Bee* invented an entire battle under the headline, "Bloody Battle with Reds." The account said that the Indians had been routed by soldiers with "heavy losses" as the Army lost fifty men and two officers. In the midst of the story, the account was said to be "not authenticated" (Hugh Reilly, 1997, 205). After that statement, the *Bee* then continued to weave its fable in great detail. At the same time, Tibbles reported ten days before the massacre that events were coming to a head. He also worried (as reported later in his book *Buckskin and Blanket Days*, 1957) about complaints from his editors that his dispatches were not exciting enough.

The *World-Herald* often published LaFlesche's accounts under the headline "What Bright Eyes Thinks." Unlike most other correspondents, LaFlesche stressed the common humanity of the Ghost Dancers: "The causes that brought about the 'Messiah scare' may seem to be very simple if one stops to think, first of all, that the Sioux are human beings with the same feelings, desires, resentments, and aspirations as all other human beings" (Hugh Reilly, 1997, 198).

DEATH AT WOUNDED KNEE

During the days before the clash at Wounded Knee, roughly 120 men and 230 women and children led by Big Foot were intercepted and surrounded by General Whitside of the Seventh Cavalry, Custer's former unit, as they emerged from open country to surrender. Big Foot, weakened from pneumonia, could barely speak as Whitside's men herded the Indians into a circle and demanded their guns. Big Foot's band was surrounded by 500 cavalry and four Hotchkiss guns. When few firearms were forthcoming (most of which were broken), Whitside ordered a search of the camp. Tension mounted as Yellow Bird, a healer, began a Ghost Dance, throwing handfuls of dirt into the air, calling on warriors to be brave of heart and telling them that if they danced, their Ghost Shirts would protect them.

Hugh Reilly described the incident on December 29 that set off what the Army still maintains was a "battle."

The soldiers began to search the men for weapons [as] one young man leapt to his feet angrily, holding aloft his gun and saying he had paid good money for it and would not give it up. Some Indian witnesses said he was named Black Coyote, and others said it was a man named *Hosi Yanka*, which means "deaf."

Survivors of the Wounded Knee massacre, 1890. (Courtesy of
the Library of Congress.)

Two soldiers came behind the young man and tried to seize his weapon. In the
scuffle, it went off. (1997, 209)

At that point, by Hugh Reilly's account, "Several young warriors threw off
their blankets and fired a brief volley into the soldiers' ranks" (1997, 209).
The Seventh Cavalry answered these few shots with massive retaliation that
included not only bullets, but also devastating fire from Hotchkiss guns, a
turn-of-the-century combination of a small cannon with an early model of
machine gun. The withering fire quickly tore the Indian camp to shreds.

Many of the Indians sought refuge in a nearby ravine, which turned out
to be a trap as, according to Hugh Reilly, "the Hotchkiss guns on the ridge . . .
raked the camp," taking deadly aim at people hiding in the ravine (1997,
209). At least 170 Indians died (some of whom were tracked down and shot
miles from the scene of the original altercation). Most of them were women
and children. The Army lost twenty-nine killed and thirty-nine wounded.
Because much of the fire was delivered from a roughly circular position
around the Indian camp, an unknown number of the soldiers were killed or
wounded by their compatriots' own friendly fire.

Tibbles was on his way to the telegraph office at Pine Ridge to file a dispatch when he heard shooting and returned to the scene. Cressey saw at least some of the battle himself. His first dispatch was headlined: "Red Devils Bite the Dust" (Hugh Reilly, 1997, 210). Cressey's accounts during the ensuing two days called the incident "ghastly work of treacherous Reds" whom, wrote Cressey, fired at least 100 shots at the Seventh Cavalry before the soldiers, afraid of hitting their own men, replied. Cressey wrote that the men of the Seventh Cavalry had "once more shown themselves to be heroes in deeds of daring." Editorially, the *Bee* said that there should be no more "truckling in dealing with the murderous Sioux" (ibid., 211).

As the Indians took fire at point-blank range, some of them flew into desperate rages, fighting back with their hands or whatever they could find. Survivors were chased and gunned down by troops after the actual battle. After the shooting stopped, a blizzard swept the area, burying most of the Indian dead in drifts. The dead were later dragged out of the snow, heaped onto wagons, and buried in a common grave.

The *World-Herald* treated the conflict as a massacre rather than a battle, using headlines such as "All Murdered in a Mass." The newspaper's accounts emphasized the difference in the amount of firepower available to each side and the large number of women and children in the Native camp. Editorially, the *World-Herald* called what had happened at Wounded Knee "a crime against civilization." The paper asked: "What sentiment dignifies and raises it from the low estate of murder to that of war.... On a field on which there can be no honor" (Hugh Reilly, 1997, 211–212).

The *Bee's* reports emphasized the dying agonies "of...wounded and dying soldiers—gallant, utterly fearless, Seventh Cavalry boys, whose bravery in the discharge of their duties none...can ever fully appreciate" (Hugh Reilly, 1997, 213). The *Bee* created an illusion that the battle at Wounded Knee was only the precipitating spark of a far wider Indian war in which thousands would die.

While Cressey and the *Bee's* editorialists railed against "murderous Redskins," LaFlesche, under the headline "Horrors of War," described the sufferings of Indian women and children who had been seriously wounded in the shooting. This account, as compiled by Hugh Reilly, makes for wrenching reading. Susette LaFlesche was nearly alone in reporting the suffering of the Native people at Wounded Knee:

> There was a woman sitting on the floor with a wounded baby on her lap and four or five children around her, all her grandchildren. Their father and mother were killed. There was a young woman shot through both thighs and her wrist broken. Mr. Tibbles had to get a pair of pliers to get her rings off. There was a little boy with his throat apparently shot to pieces.... When we fed this little boy, we found that he could swallow. We gave him some gruel and he grabbed with both his little hands a dipper of water. When I saw him yesterday afternoon he looked worse than the day before, and when they fed him now, the food and water came out the side of his neck. (Hugh Reilly, 1997, 215)

Burial of the dead at Wounded Knee. (Courtesy of the Nebraska
State Historical Society.)

The anger of Bright Eyes was palpable. The Sioux believe that they have
been made to suffer because the whites want their land, she wrote. "If the
white people want their land and must have it, they can go about getting it
some other way than by forcing it from them by starving them or provoking
them to war and sacrificing the lives of innocent women and children" (Hugh
Reilly, 1997, 215).

Black Elk was one of the Lakota holy men who had performed the Ghost
Dance during the days before the massacre. In *Black Elk Speaks*, he recalled
how the Lakota's indignation had risen in 1874, when General Custer opened
the Black Hills, seeking "the yellow metal that drives white men crazy" (1972,
79). He remembered answering Crazy Horse's call to war at the Little Bighorn
and the brutal subjugation that followed. Black Elk visited Wounded Knee
a day or two after the blizzard and later told John G. Neihardt that his grief
was tempered by his belief that the Lakota who had died were now in a
better place.

Black Elk described the scene of the massacre as follows:

We followed down the dry gulch, and what we saw was terrible. Dead and
wounded women and children and little babies were scattered all along where

they had been trying to run away. The soldiers had followed along the gulch, as they ran, and murdered them in there. Sometimes they were in heaps because they had huddled together, and some were scattered all along. Sometimes bunches of them had been killed and torn to pieces where the wagon [Hotchkiss] guns hit them. I saw a little baby trying to suck its mother, but she was bloody and dead. (Collier, 1947, 104–105)

Eighteen U.S. Army troops received the Congressional Medal of Honor for actions at Wounded Knee Creek:

1st Sgt. William G. Austin	Pvt. George Hobday
Musician John E. Clancy	Sgt. George Loyd
Pvt. Mosheim Feaster	Sgt. Albert W. McMillan
1st Lt. Ernest A. Garland	Pvt. Thomas Sullivan
1st Lt. John C. Gresham	1st Sgt. Jacob Trautman
Pvt. Matthew B. Hamilton	1st Sgt. Frederick E. Toy
Pvt. Joshua B. Hartzog	Sgt. James Ward
2nd Lt. Harry L. Hathorne	Cpl. Paul H. Weinert
Pvt. Marvin C. Hillock	Pvt. Hermann Ziegner (Byrd, 2003, 1)

In addition, five other soldiers were awarded the Medal of Honor for participating in skirmishes along White Clay Creek as part of a search-and-destroy mission:

Sgt. Bernhard Jetter	1st Sgt. Theodore Ragner
Pvt. Adam Neder	Cpl. William O. Wilson (Byrd, 2003, 1)
Farrier Richard J. Nolan	

By awarding so many Medals of Honor, the Army supported its official version of events at Wounded Knee as a battle rather than a massacre. The Army also excused the murder of one of its officers, Lt. Edward W. Casey, by Plenty Horses, an Oglala Lakota, to maintain its version of events. When Plenty Horses was brought to trial in a civilian court, the Army refused to support the prosecution, maintaining that the murder, which had taken place in daylight under otherwise peaceful conditions, was an "act of war."

After five years at Carlisle Indian School, Plenty Horses returned to the Pine Ridge Indian reservation angry and alienated, just in time to witness the 1890 massacre at Wounded Knee. A few days after the massacre, on January 7, 1891, he shot Casey in the back, hoping to be hung for his bravery, to die as a man and a warrior in the Oglala Lakota tradition. Plenty Horses' wife, Roan Horse, also was killed in the ensuing melee.

After his arrest, Plenty Horses said that he killed Casey because

> I am an Indian. Five years I attended Carlisle and was educated in the ways of the white man. When I returned to my people, I was an outcast among them. I was no longer an Indian. I was not a white man. I was lonely. I shot the lieutenant so I might make a place for myself among my people. I am now one of them. I shall be hung, and the Indians will bury me as a warrior. They will be proud of me. I am satisfied. (Johansen and Grinde, 1997, 293)

Plenty Horses was imprisoned at Fort Meade and tried in Sioux Falls, South Dakota. Instead of convicting Plenty Horses and sentencing him to hang, a judge threw the case out because a state of war had existed on the Pine Ridge Reservation—the same state of war that the Army was using as a reason not to prosecute the soldiers who had taken part in the massacre. Plenty Horses was sent home to Rosebud, still very confused and alienated. He died at Pine Ridge during the 1930s.

Wovoka, who had initiated the Ghost Dance, was deeply saddened by the massacre at Wounded Knee. The massacre convinced Wovoka that the religion ought to be abandoned. Sadly, Wovoka told his followers that the path he had advised them to follow was now choked with sand and covered with grass. "My children," he preached, "I call upon you to travel a new trail, the only trail now open—the White Man's Road" (Tebbel and Jennison, 1960, 298).

After the Wounded Knee massacre, Black Elk watched his people, once the mounted lords of the plains, become hungry, impoverished prisoners, pent up on thirteen government reservations. Black Elk surveyed the scene with sadness: "The nation's hoop is broken and scattered. There is no center anymore, and the sacred tree is dead" (Johansen and Grinde, 1997, 36).

FURTHER READING

Ambrose, Stephen E. *Crazy Horse and Custer.* New York: New American Library, 1986.

Anderson, Terry L. *Sovereign Nations or Reservations: An Economic History of American Indians.* San Francisco: Pacific Research Institute for Public Policy, 1995.

Armstrong, Virginia Irving. *I Have Spoken: American History through the Voices of the Indians.* Chicago: Swallow Press, 1971.

Barrett, S. M. *Geronimo's Story of His Life.* New York: Duffield & Company, 1906.

Black Elk. *Black Elk Speaks, as told to John G. Neihardt.* New York: William Morrow, [1932] 1972.

Black Elk. *The Sacred Pipe: Black Elk's Account of the Seven Rites of the Oglala Sioux.* Edited by Joseph Epes Brown. New York: Penguin Books, 1973.

Branch, Douglas E. *The Hunting of the Buffalo.* Lincoln: University of Nebraska Press, 1973.

Brown, Dee. *Bury My Heart at Wounded Knee.* New York: Holt, Rinehart, Winston, 1970.

Byrd, Sydney. Wounded Knee: We Must Never Forget. *Lakota Journal*, January 3–10, 2003, 1. Available at http://www.lakotajournal.com/front.htm.

Calloway, Colin. *New Worlds for All: Indians, Europeans, and the Remaking of Early America*. Baltimore: Johns Hopkins University Press, 1997.

Clark, Robert A. *The Killing of Crazy Horse*. Lincoln: University of Nebraska Press, 1976.

Collier, John. *Indians of the Americas*. New York: New American Library, 1947.

Crosby, Alfred W. *The Columbian Voyages, the Columbian Exchange, and Their Historians*. Washington, DC: American Historical Association, 1987.

Custer, Elizabeth. *Boots and Saddles*. New York: Harper & Brothers, 1885.

Custer, George Armstrong. *My Life on the Plains*. Lincoln: University of Nebraska Press, 1966.

Darwin, Charles. *The Origin of Species by Means of Natural Selection, Or the Preservation of Favoured Races in the Struggle for Life*. London: John Murray, 1859.

Darwin, Charles. *The Voyage of the Beagle*. Garden City, NY: Doubleday, [1839] 1962.

Denhardt, Robert M. *The Horse of the Americas*. Norman: University of Oklahoma Press, 1975.

Drinnon, Richard. *Facing West: Indian Hating and Empire Building*. New York: Schoken Books, 1990.

Driver, Harold E. *Indians of North America*. Chicago: University of Chicago Press, 1969.

Dugan, Bill. *Sitting Bull*. San Francisco: HarperCollins, 1994.

Edmunds, R. David, ed. *American Indian Leaders: Studies in Diversity*. Lincoln: University of Nebraska Press, 1980.

Giago, Tim. Book Lacks Lakota View. *Indian Country Today*, August 4, 1993, n.p.

Gibson, Arrell Morgan. *The American Indian: Prehistory to Present*. Lexington, MA: Heath, 1980.

Graham, W. A. *The Custer Myth*. Lincoln: University of Nebraska Press, 1953.

Hamilton, Charles. *Cry of the Thunderbird*. Norman: University of Oklahoma Press, 1972.

Hodgson, Bryan. Buffalo: Back Home on the Range. *National Geographic* 186:5(November 1994):64–89.

Hoig, Stan. *The Sand Creek Massacre*. Norman: University of Oklahoma Press, 1961.

Holder, Preston. *The Hoe and the Horse on the Plains*. Lincoln: University of Nebraska Press, 1970.

Homaday, William T. *The Extermination of the American Bison*. Washington, DC: Annual Report of the U.S. National Museum, 1869.

Hoover, Dwight W. *Red and Black*. Chicago: Rand-McNally, 1976.

Hyde, George E. *A Sioux Chronicle*. Norman: University of Oklahoma Press, 1956.

Hyde, George E. *Red Cloud's Folk: A History of the Oglala Sioux Indians*. University of Oklahoma Press, 1967.

Jensen, Richard E., R. Eli Paul, and John E. Carter. *Eyewitness at Wounded Knee*. Lincoln: University of Nebraska Press, 1991.

Johansen, Bruce E., and Donald A. Grinde, Jr. *The Encyclopedia of Native American Biography*. New York: Henry Holt, 1997.

Johnson, Lowell. The Buffalo. In *The First Voices*, ed. Lowell Johnson. Lincoln, NE: Nebraska Game and Parks Commission, 1984: 60–61.

Josephy, Alvin, Jr. *The Patriot Chiefs*. New York: Viking, 1961.

Kay, Jeanne. The Fur Trade and Native American Population Growth. *Ethnohistory* 31:4(1984):265–287.

Massey, Rosemary, and the Omaha Indian Center. *Footprints in Blood: Standing Bear's Struggle for Freedom and Human Dignity.* Omaha, NE: American Indian Center of Omaha, 1979.

Mathes, Valerie Sherer. Helen Hunt Jackson and the Ponca Controversy. *Montana: The Magazine of Western History* 39:1(Winter 1989):42–53.

McLaughlin, James. *My Friend, the Indian.* Boston: Houghton Mifflin, 1910.

McNickle, D'Arcy. *They Came Here First: The Epic of the American Indian.* New York: Harper and Row Perennial Library, 1975: 177–178.

Milner, Richard. Red Cloud. In *The Encyclopedia of Evolution*, ed. Richard Milner. New York: Henry Holt, 1990: 387–388.

Monoghan, Jay. *Custer.* Lincoln: University of Nebraska Press, 1959.

Moore, John H. *The Cheyennes.* London: Blackwell, 1997.

Morgan, Lewis Henry. *League of the Iroquois.* Secaucus, NJ: Corinth Books, [1851] 1962.

Morris, Roy, Jr. *Sheridan: The Life and Wars of General Phil Sheridan.* New York: Crown, 1992.

Nabokov, Peter, ed. *Native American Testimony.* New York: Penguin Books, 1991.

Neihardt, Hilda. *Black Elk and Flaming Rainbow: Personal Memories of the Lakota Holy Man.* Lincoln: University of Nebraska Press, 1995.

Olson, James C. *Red Cloud and the Sioux Problem.* University of Nebraska Press, 1965.

Pascua, Maria Parker. Ozette: A Makah Village in 1491. *National Geographic*, October 1991, 38–53.

Powers, William K. *Indians of the Northern Plains.* New York: Capricorn Books, 1973.

Reilly, Bob, Hugh Reilly, and Pegeen Reilly. *Historic Omaha: An Illustrated History of Omaha and Douglas County.* San Antonio, TX: Historical Publishing Network, 2003.

Reilly, Hugh. Treatment of Native Americans by the Frontier Press: An Omaha, Nebraska Study, 1868–1891. Masters thesis, University of Nebraska at Omaha, 1997.

Rice, Julian. *Black Elk's Story.* Albuquerque: New Mexico University Press, 1991.

Roberts, David. Geronimo. *National Geographic*, October 1992, 46–71.

Roe, Frank Gilbert. *The Indian and the Horse.* Norman: University of Oklahoma Press, 1955.

Rosenberg, Bruce A. *Custer and the Epic of Defeat.* University Park: Pennsylvania State University Press, 1974.

Sandoz, Mari. *Crazy Horse: Strange Man of the Oglalas.* New York Knopf, 1942.

Schmitt, Martin F., and Dee Brown. *Fighting Indians of the West.* New York: Ballantine Books, 1948.

Snow, Dean. The First Americans and the Differentiation of Hunter-Gatherer Cultures. In Bruce G. Trigger and Wilcomb E. Washburn, eds., *The Cambridge History of the Native Peoples of the Americas.* Cambridge, England: Cambridge University Press, 1996, 125–199.

Stannard, David. *American Holocaust: Columbus and the Conquest of the New World.* New York: Oxford University Press, 1992.

Tebbel, John, and Keith Jennison. *The American Indian Wars.* New York: Bonanza Books, 1960.

Thomas, David Hurst. *Skull Wars: Kennewick Man, Archaeology, and the Battle for Native American Identity*. New York: Basic Books/Peter N. Nevraumont, 2000.

Tibbles, Thomas Henry. *Buckskin and Blanket Days; Memoirs of a Friend of the Indians Written in 1905*. Garden City, NY: Doubleday, 1957.

Tibbles, Thomas Henry. *The Ponca Chiefs: An Account of the Trial of Standing Bear*. Edited by Kay Graber. Lincoln: University of Nebraska Press, [1880] 1972.

Utley, Robert. *The Lance and the Shield: The Life and Times of Sitting Bull*. New York: Henry Holt, 1993.

Vestal, Stanley. *Sitting Bull: Champion of the Sioux*. Norman: University of Oklahoma Press, [1932] 1957.

Virtual Truth Commission. Telling the Truth for a Better America; Reports by Name: Col. John M. Chivington. June 22, 1998. Available at http://www.geocities.com/~virtualtruth/chiving.htm.

Walker, James R. *Lakota Society*. Edited by Raymond J. DeMallie. Lincoln: University of Nebraska Press, 1982.

Waters, Frank. *Brave Are My People*. Santa Fe: Clear Light, 1992.

Weeks, Philip. *Farewell, My Nation: The American Indian and the United States, 1820–1890*. Arlington Heights, IL: Harlan Davidson, 1990.

White, Richard. The Winning of the West: The Expansion of the Western Sioux in the Eighteenth and Nineteenth Centuries. *Journal of American History* 65:2(1978): 319–343.

Wissler, Clark. The Influence of the Horse in the Development of Plains Culture. *American Anthropologist* 16(1914):1–25.

CHAPTER 8

The Rise of the "Vanishing Race"

NATIVE AMERICAN ADAPTATIONS
TO ASSIMILATION

During the first half of the twentieth century, U.S. Indian policy vacillated between the two poles: aggressive assimilation and preservation of tribal identity to some degree. One can watch this cyclical evolution in the decisions of the courts, the acts of Congress, and the positions of various presidents, as well as in the responses of Native peoples themselves. The duality of conquest and curiosity about the cultures being crushed (and some evolving sense of respect for Native peoples' own desires) may be traced to the beginnings of colonization, to the 1630s, when Roger Williams rejected the idea that the Puritans had a divine right to the land they occupied. The somewhat tortured definition by the Marshall court (in *Worcester v. Georgia*, 31 U.S. [6 Pet.] 515 [1832]) that Native people comprised "dependent domestic nations" also illustrates this duality. Beginning in 1790, the federal government also passed a number of "nonintercourse acts" meant to restrain state and private taking of Native lands. Some of these laws have been used in recent years to support land claims, especially in the northeastern United States.

During the late nineteenth century, this duality was expressed in allotment legislation and the beginnings of the boarding schools, both undertaken expressly in what some European Americans took to be the Indians' best interests, as alternatives to extermination. By the first half of the twentieth century, European American responses to surviving Native presence varied from the progressivism of John Collier, under Franklin Roosevelt, to the renewed assimilationism of termination during the Eisenhower era.

Assimilation and alienation of land base usually was favored under business-oriented Republicans. Dissolution of the Indian estate and cultures was expressed legislatively in allotment and termination, the last great legal attempt at midcentury to eliminate the "vanishing race." The other pole of policy usually was implemented by Democratic presidents, such as Franklin Delano

Roosevelt, who brought John Collier into his administration to construct the Indian New Deal during the 1930s. This policy generally recognized Native peoples' right to exist in distinct groups on their own land but under governmental control. As a whole, however, the terms of debate on Native questions had changed little since the days when President Andrew Jackson squared off with Chief Justice John Marshall. Termination and programs urging Indians to move from reservations to urban areas were expressions of the same assumptions that produced removal policies during the 1830s and 1840s. The Indian New Deal (legislated as the Indian Reorganization Act in 1934) was an elaboration of Chief Justice Marshall's opinion that the Indians occupied "dependent domestic nations."

The twentieth century began with most Native Americans at their lowest point, considering population as well as social and economic organization and well-being, following three centuries of intensive subjugation by European American immigrants in North America. In less than one century, the United States had spread westward across most of North America's land mass. The removal of the Cherokees from their homelands near the Atlantic coast (1838) and the massacre at Wounded Knee (1890) occurred during the life spans of many individuals. The dominant national mindset at the turn of the century vis-à-vis Native Americans was still baldly imperialistic. President Theodore Roosevelt raised few white eyebrows when he said that the extermination of Indians and expropriation of their lands was "as ultimately beneficial as it was inevitable." Roosevelt believed that such a state of affairs was "sure to come when a masterful people, still in its raw barbarian prime, finds itself face to face with the weaker and wholly alien race which holds a coveted prize in its feeble grip." Roosevelt once quipped that "I don't go so far as to think that the only good Indians are dead Indians, but I believe that nine out of ten are, and I shouldn't like to inquire too closely about the case of the tenth" (Stannard, 1992, 245).

Among the self-professed non-Indian guardians of the Native body and soul, the alternatives seemed, late in the nineteenth century, to be assimilation or extinction. Remaking the Indian in a European American image was widely regarded as the more humane alternative. That Native Americans might be able to choose their own future seemed a precluded option outside Indian country itself. The government, under the influence of reformers, along with the customary cabal of special economic interests set about to solve the U.S. "Indian problem" by dissolving Native cultures and land bases into the great Anglo-American melting pot.

Beginning about 1960, Native Americans themselves took the debate outside the former ideological confines by advocating a much greater degree of self-determination. The phrase became a rallying cry throughout the 1960s and was officially embraced by President Nixon in the early 1970s, just as a new wave of Native self-assertion crested most visibly in the seizure of Alcatraz Island in 1969, followed by the occupation of the Washington, D.C., Bureau of Indian Affairs (BIA) offices in 1972 after a continent-spanning march called the Trail of Broken Treaties. The 71-day confrontation at Wounded Knee in 1973 was followed by a protracted, bloody battle at Pine Ridge in South Dakota between assimilationists (backed by the BIA and Federal Bureau of Investigation) and Native traditionalists allied with the urban, militant American Indian Movement.

By the end of the twentieth century, Native American peoples and nations were making measured, determined strides to reclaim their cultures, histories, and some measure of their treaty-guaranteed land bases. By the 1990 census, the number of people in the United States who identified themselves as Native American had grown to almost 2 million from about 250,000 at the turn of the century. The most interesting irony at the end of the twentieth century may have been the wave of popular interest in all things Native, in stark contrast to the assumptions of assimilation or annihilation that had opened it. A sizable number of people actually were faking being Native American. America's European immigrants were again discovering that their "errands in the wilderness" had shaped them as well as the continent's original inhabitants. One might imagine how the "reformers" of the late nineteenth century would regard the legions of plastic medicine men plying their wares a century later. These themes are developed in chapter 9.

ASSIMILATION

During much of its first century under the Constitution, the United States dealt with Indian nations as semisovereign political entities by treaty. The legal interpretation of this relationship was set down by Chief Justice John Marshall in his Marshall Trilogy. In 1871, however, Congress stopped treaty-making and embarked on a number of other measures aimed at assimilation.

Many Indians did not desire the future that was being constructed for them by powers beyond their control. General Philip Sheridan, one of the principal U.S. Army commanders during the Indian wars of the western plains, remarked in 1878, as the wars were ending: "We took away their [the Sioux's] country and their means of support, broke up their mode of living, their habits of life, introduced disease and decay among them, and it was for this and against this that they made war. Could anyone expect less?" (Morris, 1992, 376).

As early as 1819, the U.S. Congress passed an act to establish a "civilization fund" for Native Americans, notably the construction of schools. The act urged that the schools be used to introduce among the Indians "habits and arts of civilization," including "agriculture . . . and for teaching their children in reading, writing, and arithmetic." The act asserted that its provisions would be "for the purpose of providing against the further decline and final extinction of the Indian tribes" (Johansen, 1998, 22). Congress allotted $10,000 a year for the fund's first year.

In 1872, the commissioner of Indian affairs was quoted as saying that the reservation must become "a legalized reformatory" where Native Americans would adopt non-Indian ways "peaceably if they will, forcibly if they must." Some supporters of assimilation put the case for it in more ethnocentric terms, such as the Office of the Commissioner of Indian Affairs, in 1901: "Indian dances and so-called Indian feasts should be prohibited. In many cases these dances and feasts are simply subterfuges to cover degrading acts and disguise immoral purposes. You [Indian agents] are directed to use your best efforts in the suppression of these evils" (Johansen, 1998, 23).

The Rules for the Court of Indian Offenses on the Pine Ridge Reservation in 1908 included a ban on the Sun Dance, all other similar dances, as well as other religious ceremonies. An Indian convicted of dancing could, on the first offense, be deprived of rations (that is, semistarved) for as many as ten days. A second offense called for deprivation of rations for fifteen to thirty days or up to thirty days in the agency prison.

In 1875, Congress moved to make Indians on reservations subject to federally supervised policing. Family, religious, and economic affairs of Indians were strictly regulated by the BIA by 1882, and Congress established mechanisms to enforce an individualized property-holding ethic among Indians in the General Allotment Act of 1887.

From the points of view of many Native Americans, assimilation was the essence of political oppression on a very personal level. The Winnebago spiritual leader Reuben Snake (1991) recalled:

> The steam-rolling effort of the "civilized society" upon the Indian people has wreaked a havoc that extends far beyond that of loss of material possessions. The American Indian and Alaskan Native are caught in a world wherein they are trying to find out who they are, and where they are.... The land that was once their "mother," giving them food and clothing, was taken. Their spiritual strengths were decried as pagan and familial ties broken. Their own form of education, i.e. that of legends, how to live, how to respect themselves and others, were torn asunder by the White society's reading, writing, and arithmetic. No culture could, or can be, expected to be thrust into a world different from its own and adapt without problems of culture shock.

As assimilation was being legislated, the Supreme Court denied citizenship to Indians who wished to take the policy to its logical conclusion. In 1884, in *Elk v. Wilkins* (112 U.S. 94 [1884]), Indians were denied the right to vote despite the wording of the recently passed Fourteenth Amendment, which had extended the franchise to blacks.

THE GENESIS OF ALLOTMENT LEGISLATION

During the 1880s, plans were developed by the federal government to effectively nullify the several hundred treaties that had set aside land, much of

Henry Laurens Dawes. (Courtesy of the Library of Congress.)

which non-Indians deemed worthless at the time. Perhaps ironically in retrospect, the one legislative act most responsible for dismembering what remained of the Native land base evolved out of liberal concern for Indians' condition that developed after the Civil War.

As the Plains Indians were subjected to conditions like those of a concentration camp, a wave of compassion was stirred by publication of Helen Hunt Jackson's *Century of Dishonor* in 1881. Jackson (1830–1885) also wrote a novel, *Ramona*, which put the depredations she had described factually in *Century of Dishonor* into a novelistic format. The book went through about 300 printings and later inspired several movies. Jackson said at the time that she wanted Ramona to raise indignation regarding mistreatment of Indians to the degree that Harriet Beecher Stowe's *Uncle Tom's Cabin* had done regarding black slavery.

Despite her intentions as a reformer, Jackson's work often was used to support legislation, such as the Dawes (Allotment) Act, passed by Congress in 1887, that distributed many Native Americans' common landholdings among individuals in 80- or 160-acre parcels. Such allotments often were sold to non-Indians, eroding the Native American land base, cultures, and languages. "Surplus" lands, those remaining after assignment of individual plots, usually were sold to non-Natives. In some cases, these tracts comprised as much as 90 percent of some reservation land bases.

In the late 1800s, very few non-Indian reformers asserted a Native right to land, language, and culture. Instead, they sought, as General William Pratt, founder of the boarding school system, often said, to "kill the Indian and save the man" as an alternative to outright extermination. Jackson's work played into the plans of reformers who supported allotment. The Allotment Act evolved into yet another land grab by the Indian rings even though its expressed purpose was to turn surviving Indians into yeoman farmers in the Jeffersonian image.

The Dawes Severalty Act (1887) was sponsored primarily by Senator Henry Dawes of Massachusetts. Dawes was no expert in Indian Affairs but considered himself as such after a fact-finding mission that included a short tour of the Cherokee Nation of Oklahoma, which had been rebuilt largely along the lines of the prosperous republic that had been built in the Southeast before the Trail of Tears. In 1883, Dawes marveled at the prosperity that the Cherokees had hewn out of the land but then condemned Native peoples because they held their lands in common:

> There is not a pauper in that nation, and the nation does not owe a dollar. It built its own capitol...its schools and hospitals. Yet the defect of the system is apparent. They have got as far as they can go, because they hold their land in common.... There is no selfishness, which is at the bottom of civilization. (Hendrix, 1983, 32)

With allotment, selfishness definitely got the upper hand. Treaty-guaranteed land that was left over after allotment—often as much as 90 percent of native peoples' commonly held estate—was then sold to non-Indian immigrants.

The Dawes Act was designed to remedy this "defect," to "civilize" the Indians by breaking up their communal lands into individual farmsteads. Often, however, the family tracts (which were as small as ten acres each) were too small to sustain the people assigned to them, and farming was a highly uncertain business because of the variability of temperatures and precipitation across much of the northern and western high plains. More than 100 reservations were allotted, centering in the plains, where large tracts of several states had earlier been assigned to Native peoples by treaty. Most of these treaties had been signed within memory of a middle-aged person when allotment began to break up the Native peoples' communal estate.

The Allotment Act was passed by Congress at a time of growing non-Indian pressure to open remaining Native American lands for settlement. At the time, several Lakota, Natoka, and Dakota peoples still owned most of western South Dakota; the Flatheads and Blackfeet held title to much of western Montana, and a coalition of local Native nations, such as the Kiowa, and "removed" Indians, such as the Cheyennes and Apaches, occupied western Oklahoma. The Crow held a large area in southern Montana.

Allotment was only one way that land speculators used the government to seize ownership of Native American land. In 1857, for example, 127,000 acres in southeastern Nebraska were set aside for Indians of mixed blood who had no other reservation base. At a time when most other reservation land was held in common, the land of the Nemaha Half-Breed Reservation was individually allotted. Most of the land was quickly transferred to a number of land sharks, the majority from the eastern seaboard. This number included James W. Denver (after whom the city was named), who also was serving at the time as commissioner of Indian affairs, a fox in the henhouse.

According to research by Bill Moran, a middle school teacher in Auburn, Nebraska, Denver did not transfer the land directly to himself but through his father-in-law, Matthew Rombach. "Together, they acquired thousands of acres," said Moran. He traced the pattern of land purchases by checking records at local county courthouses. "Rombach's name [was] all over the place," said Moran (Associated Press, 1991, 16). Rombach and others were drawn to the land because they thought a railroad would be built through the area, raising the land's value. The speculation proved groundless because the Union Pacific eventually laid its tracks through Council Bluffs and Omaha. Denver served as a member of Congress from California, where he was privy to railroad planning; he later was appointed territorial governor of Kansas.

Although the introduction of private property was advanced ideologically as an aid in civilizing Native peoples, in reality allotment was a government-sponsored real estate agency that transferred land from Indians to European Americans. In 1880, before allotment became the law of the land, approximately 150 million acres were under Native title. Within two generations, two-thirds of that land, an area roughly the size of North and South Dakota combined, had been transferred to European Americans. The loss of this land sealed many Native people into poverty and dependence on promised government supplies and annuities.

The Allotment Act contributed importantly to the reduction of Native American population in the United States to about 250,000 between 1880 and about 1920. At the beginning of the twentieth century, even the friends of the Indian called them the vanishing Americans. This characterization was considered by some to be an act of compassion. Harold E. Driver, in *Indians of North America*, provides the following Native population figures for the continental United States (not including Alaska or Hawaii): about 250,000 in 1890; 271,000 in 1900; 336,000 in 1920 (1969, 527). D'Arcy McNickle, in *They*

Came Here First, asserted that the figure of 255,000 reported by the federal government in 1880 was the lowest population point for Native Americans in the United States (McNickle, 1975, 227–228).

As a mechanism for the transfer of land from one group of people to another, allotment worked hand in glove with the practice of homesteading, the granting of land to immigrating European Americans. The amount of land granted immigrants by homesteading peaked in 1884, three years before the passage of the Allotment Act.

Because allotment was based on the model of the Anglo-American nuclear family, many Native Americans who were subjected to its provisions were required to do more than change their property-holding customs. Indian extended families were devastated by the allotment system, in which close relatives who had lived together often were given distant parcels of land. Long-established ties between grandmothers and their children were severed, and a long-standing family structure destroyed. Native men who were married to more than one wife were told to divest all but one. Vine Deloria, Jr., recalled the tearful response of the Kiowa chief Quanah Parker, who, when told that he must give up his extra wives, "told the [Indian] agent that, if he must give them up, he could not choose which one to surrender and that the agent must do it for him" (Deloria and Lytle, 1983, 197).

The Allotment Act also authorized the Secretary of the Interior to sell timber from allotted land and strengthened existing powers authorizing the government to lease land for the supposed benefit of the allottees. Income from such activities was deposited in a BIA account, called Individual Indian Monies (IIM) to be paid to allottees only if the bureau deemed them "worthy." A scandal subsequently ensued in Oklahoma when full-blooded members of the Five Civilized Tribes in Oklahoma Territory died of starvation despite the fact that they had IIM accounts worth hundreds of thousands of dollars. The BIA had been diverting their income to pay for construction of schools and churches. During the late twentieth century, a number of IIM account holders asked for their money, only to be told that the BIA's records were so haphazard that the funds could not be located. A very large class action lawsuit followed.

According to legal scholar Charles F. Wilkinson: "Allotment and the other assimilationist programs that complemented it devastated Indian land base, weakened Indian culture, sapped the vitality of tribal legislative and judicial processes, and opened most Indian reservations for settlement by non-Indians" (1987, 19). The U.S. political leaders understood this to be the upshot of allotment at the time. President Theodore Roosevelt, for example, said: "The General Allotment Act is a mighty pulverizing engine to break up the tribal mass. It acts directly upon the family and the individual" (Johansen, 1997, 21). Over the generations, many individual allotments were subdivided into miniscule plots by inheritances, rendering many of them nearly useless for agriculture.

The breakdown of Native American estate, political traditions, and family relations was the stated aim of allotment legislation. BIA publications acknowledge that the trust of U.S. Indian policy in the 1870s and 1880s was to "further minimize the functions of tribal leaders and tribal institutions and to continually strengthen the position of the government representative and his subordinates, and to improve the effectiveness of their programs to break down traditional patterns within the Indian communities" (Johansen, 1997, 20–21).

A few non-Indians protested allotment and other forms of assimilation. Ethnologist Lewis Henry Morgan, known as the founder of American anthropology, predicted that a result of allotment for the Indian "would unquestionably be, that in a very short time he would divest himself of every foot of land and fall into poverty" (Johansen, 1998, 18). Morgan was echoing the minority opinion of the House Committee of Indian Affairs on the Allotment Act:

> The real purpose of this bill is to get at the Indian lands and open them up to [non-Indian] settlement. The provisions for the apparent benefit of the Indians are but the pretext to get his lands and occupy them.... If this were done in the name of greed, it would be bad enough; but to do it in the name of humanity, and under the cloak of an ardent desire to promote the Indian's welfare by making him like ourselves whether he will or not, is infinitely worse. (Johansen, 1997, 21)

The same minority report scoffed at the Allotment Act's professed humanitarianism. Representative Henry M. Teller of Colorado said that allotment was "a bill to despoil the Indians of their land and to make them vagabonds on the face of the earth." He said that the Indians would someday "curse the hand that was raised professedly in their defense" (Weeks, 1990, 220–221).

Although allotment impoverished many Indians as Morgan foresaw, the BIA prospered. In 1881, Native Americans owned 155.6 million acres of land; by 1890, their holdings had dropped to 104.3 million acres. By the turn of the century, the Native estate was 77.9 million acres. Between 1887 and 1934, as Native American estate was reduced to less than half what it had been before allotment had begun, the Indian Bureau increased its staff by 6,000 people and its budget 400 percent.

If the goal of allotment was to turn Native people into yeoman farmers in the Jeffersonian image, the experiment was an unmitigated failure. Many peoples who had practiced agriculture themselves preferred their own farming methods, especially in the West, where lands that often were wracked by drought were simply unsuited for agricultural methods developed in Europe and refined in humid eastern North America. In addition, for Native Americans, farming the staples of life (especially corn) often was closely associated with religious practices; among the Hopis and Pueblos, for example, the breaking of the ground with a plow was considered a sacrilege comparable to slashing the breast of Mother Earth. For peoples who had never farmed, the situation was often worse:

Chitto Harjo, or Crazy Snake. (Courtesy of the Library of Congress.)

Conversion of tribal land into individual allotments did not lead to family self-sufficiency. For the Cheyennes and Arapahoes, only 16 years had passed between their confinement on reservations in 1875 and allotment of their lands in 1891. Except for the most assimilated mixed-bloods, they had not made the transition from independent nomadism to settled commercial farming, nor had many of the men come to accept agricultural labor as anything more than complete humiliation. (Olson and Wilson, 1984, 88)

Native unwillingness to accept allotment occasionally erupted into violence. At the turn of the century, Chitto Harjo, a full-blooded Creek, established the

Snake Society, which formed a native-controlled tribal government. Harjo and his followers asserted that the United States could not annul legally signed treaties without the consent of native signers, despite legislation by Congress enacted in 1871, which had done that unilaterally. In 1901, the reorganized Creeks rejected allotment. Harjo's band assaulted some Creeks who had accepted individual parcels of land. The Snake Uprising was crushed quickly by federal troops as resistance to allotment began to spread to the Cherokees and Choctaws, who, like the Creeks, were descended from people who had been forced to march the trails of tears from the Southeast in the 1830s. For years after their turn-of-the-century uprising was crushed, many of the Snakes refused to live on their allotments. Instead, they camped on church, school, tribal, or government property. Their example was followed by some other members of the Five Civilized Tribes, some of whom even refused to cash royalty checks for oil found under the lands that had been assigned individually.

HOW THE OSAGES KEPT THEIR OIL

The Allotment Act occasionally was used in some novel ways to protect Native collective estate, quite opposite its original intention to "pulverize tribal mass." For example, the Osages, finding themselves exiled to Oklahoma atop a massive cache of oil, managed to write their version of the Allotment Act in 1906 to protect their collective ownership of natural resources, an arrangement that has been maintained since.

Thus, a law meant to convert Native Americans from collective property owners to individual Anglo-Saxon-style landholders was used at a key juncture to uphold collective Osage control of oil and other mineral rights. At every turn since 1906, the Osage tribal government has protected its rights to manage oil production for the common good of the nation, even as private interests have tried to assail it. Through several decades, the Osages have used legal resources to lobby Congress to use its plenary power to maintain its right to manage the nation's natural resources. Leases and royalties from oil and gas generated about $50 to $75 million annually during the 1990s.

The Osage reservation occupies nearly all of the roughly 1.5 million acres of Osage County in north central Oklahoma, adjacent to the Kansas border, a land that varies from woods to open plains and grasslands. Osage County, which is roughly the size of Delaware, is the largest county in Oklahoma and the only one created explicitly to accommodate an Indian reservation. The county was created because the Osages feared that Oklahoma statehood might crimp their ability to control their own affairs.

The Osage originally migrated from the banks of the Ohio River to present-day Missouri before contact with Europeans, which occurred in 1673 on the banks of the Osage River. The Osages were shuffled through several treaty councils, moved from their ancestral homelands, and deposited, during 1871, in Indian Territory, where nature had a surprise waiting for them. The lands assigned them contained some of the richest oil deposits in the United States. By 1906, smallpox and intermarriage had reduced the Osage population to about 2,200 people, about half of mixed blood. (In the mid-1990s, the tribal roll contained about 12,000 people.)

Oil was discovered under the Osages' land during 1896. Tribal records indicate that on March 16, 1896, the Osage Tribe executed an oil and gas lease to Edwin H. Foster for ten years, allowing him to explore anywhere on the 1.5 million acres of the reservation. The lease expired March 16, 1906, after which it was extended another ten years to March 1916, during which time Foster executed subleases to several other corporations.

During the Roaring Twenties, oil and gas royalties hit their height. Many white men married Osage women to tap into their headrights (individual shares of oil and gas royalties). Terry P. Wilson, in *The Underground Reservation: Osage Oil*, wrote that "It was commonly believed that in rural Osage County there were more Pierce Arrows [expensive automobiles] than in any other county in the United States" (1985, xi). During this time, Pawhuska, the major town on the reservation, had a population of roughly 8,000. The town supported the services of eighty attorneys and did so in style, according to Wilson (ibid., 140) Osage County also became the scene of several spectacular (and often unsolved) murders. Earnings per headright reached a height of $13,200 per year in 1925, then plummeted to $585 in 1932 with the onset of the Great Depression.

A letter from the Secretary of the Interior (July 16, 1917) contained regulations for the leasing of Osage lands for oil and gas mining. On April 28, 1922, House Resolution 10401 (66th Congress, First Session) contained an amendment adding a provision "preserving Osage tribal ownership of all oil, gas, coal, or other minerals." On February 26, 1921, House Report 1377 extended Osage Tribal mineral estate to April 7, 1946, at the same time allowing Oklahoma to collect a production tax "in lieu of all other State and county taxes." The same legislation also declared Osages to be U.S. citizens and allowed collection of an additional 1 percent gross production tax for roads and bridges in Osage County.

The Osages' collective exercise of leasing rights has been challenged by private interests. In 1931, 25 years after the 1906 Allotment Act, the Texas Company and the Indian Territory Illuminating Oil Company, holders of mineral leases from the Osage Tribal Council, made a case that they owned the land (and any oil, gas, etc. below its surface), having purchased it from individual Osage allottees. In *Adams et al. v. Osage Tribe of Indians et al.* (No. 642 District Court N. D. Oklahoma 50 F. 2d 918, 1931 U.S. Dist), a federal district judge found that "The contention of the complainants is untenable. A careful consideration of the various acts of Congress involved discloses that the complainants have never by reason of their purchase become vested with the title in and to the oil and gas and other minerals found under the lands involved in this action."

The court upheld the Osage Nation's right to control mineral rights. By act of Congress on March 3, 1921 (41 Stat. 1249), the Osage government's right to control mineral rights was extended to April 8, 1946; by act of Congress on March 2, 1929 (45 Stat. 1478), the "trust period over such mineral rights" was extended again, to 1959. In 1957, tribal control vis-à-vis the 1906 Allotment Act provision was extended from 1959 to 1984. The same right subsequently has been extended into our time.

The Osages' collective control of oil and gas leasing has been extended by Congress over the unsuccessful protests of the Osage County Homeowners' Association, a group of non-Indians who sought to control reservation oil and gas production for themselves. The right of Congress to extend the terms of the 1906 Allotment Act was justified as use of its plenary power in relationships with Indian nations, stemming from *Worcester v. Georgia* and several other federal cases.

The 1906 clause came up again in *United States v. Stanolind Crude Oil Purchasing Company; United States v. Gulf Oil Corporation; United States v. Sinclair Prairie Oil Company* (Numbers 1975–1977; 113 F. 2d 194 [10th Cir. 1940]). This case evolved from a dispute over royalty rates owed the Osages by companies producing oil from its leases, specifically the industry custom of deducting 3 percent from the volume of oil pumped to account for impurities, sediment, and shrinkage. The court found that the companies were entitled to the 3 percent deduction. This case, however, shows how aggressively the United States sometimes exercised its responsibility to act as the Osages' legal advocate in oil-related cases.

THE CURIOUS CONCEPT OF "WARDSHIP"

Assimilation was the basic rationale for a state of wardship, which has framed U.S. Indian policy from its beginnings. *Wardship* has come to refer to a legal doctrine, said to be based on opinions by U.S. Supreme Court Chief Justice John Marshall during the 1820s and 1830s, that Native Americans live in "dependent domestic nations" and are therefore wards of the federal government. The BIA was initially established to hold Indians' land and resources "in trust." Wardship status rationalized the establishment of Indian reservations and schools to assimilate Native Americans into mainstream U.S. culture.

The concept of wardship also lay behind the storage of thousands of Native skeletal remains and burial artifacts in many federal and state research institutions. The idea of Native sovereignty in modern times has been developed in large part in opposition to wardship doctrines. Indians reacted to a social control system that was so tight that in many cases (for example, if a will affected the status of allotted land) individual actions of Native American people were subject to approval by the Secretary of the Interior.

The assertion of states' rights over Native territory in the southeastern United States provided the legal grist for a 1832 Supreme Court decision written by Chief Justice John Marshall. In *Worcester v. Georgia*, Justice Marshall wrote that inhabitants of Native nations had assumed a relationship of "pupilege" in their relations with the United States. Using this doctrine, which has no constitutional basis, the executive branch of the U.S. government, principally through the BIA, created a superstructure of policies and programs that have had a vast impact on individual Native Americans and their governments. Through the use of the plenary power of Congress, such policies as allotment divested much of the Indian estate.

A concept of wardship also has been used since the mid-nineteenth century to construct for Native Americans a cradle-to-grave social control system that was described this way during the mid-twentieth century by legal scholar Felix Cohen:

> Under the reign of these magic words [wardship and trust] nothing Indian was safe. the Indian's hair was cut, his dances forbidden, his oil lands, timber lands, and grazing lands were disposed of by Indian agents and Indian commissioners for whom the magic word "wardship" always made up for lack of statutory authority. (Johansen, 1997, 19)

Although Chief Justice Marshall's opinions have been used as a legal rationale for government policies that have treated American Indians as wards, "There is nothing," according to Robert T. Coulter, executive director of the Indian Law Resource Center, "in the rulings of the Marshall Court [which] even remotely suggested that the United States could unilaterally impose a guardian-ward relationship on Indians, that it held trust title to Indian lands, or that, as trustee, it could dispose of lands without Indian consent" (Coulter and Tullberg, 1984, 199).

Wardship as historically practiced by the BIA differs markedly from the legal status of non-Indian wards. Under most conditions, wardship is usually taken to be a temporary condition with established standards for cession. Civil guardianship and custody law must allow people who have been deprived of their civil rights means of regaining them in accordance with the Due Process Clause. As developed by the BIA, however, Indian wardship has no standard for cession and no ending date. An Indian is defined as a ward regardless of his or her accomplishments or other actions, as the object of a policy that may have misinterpreted Marshall's intent.

REMAKING THE MIND: INDIAN EDUCATION

Assimilation was the goal of a paternalistic educational system established for Indian young people late in the 1870s by General Richard Henry Pratt (1840–1924), a reformer who coined the assimilationist slogan "Kill the Indian, save the man." The phrase was designed initially as an advertising

Classroom at Indian Industrial School, Carlisle, Pennsylvania.
(Courtesy of the Library of Congress.)

slogan in Congress to request appropriations for Indian education for a nationwide complex of schools around 1900.

Pratt's Indian schools were run with Army-style boot camp discipline, the idea being to make the Indian children anew in the image of small farmers and urban workers with the rudiments of Anglo-American cultural heritage. The Carlisle Indian Industrial School, Pratt's first, was run on an Army model. Students were strictly regimented and forced to divest themselves of all vestiges of Indian identity. They wore uniforms, and their hair was cut. Missionaries also were brought in to teach them Christianity. Runaways were punished severely. Discipline was sometimes personal and petty. Albert White Hat, an instructor of Lakota at Sinte Gleska University on the Rosebud Reservation in South Dakota, recalled instances at St. Francis Indian School in which he and his classmates had their mouths washed out with soap for speaking their Native languages.

Pratt described his philosophy in a book, *Battlefield and Classroom: Four Decades with the American Indian, 1867–1904* ([1964] 1987). His educational experiment began in the 1870s with seventy-two Native men, most of them Cheyenne, who were imprisoned in an old Spanish fort at St. Augustine,

Florida. In 1878, this class "graduated," and Pratt approached Congress for an appropriation to begin an Indian industrial school on an abandoned army post at Carlisle, Pennsylvania. To recruit students for his new school, Pratt visited the Sioux of the high plains. One hundred and sixty-nine students traveled eastward in 1879 to form Carlisle's first class. Included was Luther Standing Bear, who later became a well-known author. Standing Bear recalled his days at Carlisle in *My Indian Boyhood* ([1931] 1988).

The schools were established at a time when industrial enterprises were expanding rapidly in the United States; at the same time, the European American settlement frontier was crossing the western half of the present continental United States. The curriculum of the schools was intensely vocational. "This is to be an industrial school to teach young Indians how to make a living among civilized people by practicing agricultural and mechanical pursuits and the usual industries of civilized life," Pratt wrote in his book, *Battlefield and Classroom* ([1964] 1987, 235). Pratt approached Congress for money to buy a long list of items to further Indians' induction into what he regarded as civilized industrial society: carpenter's tools, blacksmith's forges and anvils, sewing machines, paint brushes, tools for making shoes and harnessing horses, printing presses and type.

Pratt ran the boarding schools on a model that was appropriate for training a factory workforce during the late nineteenth century. Thus, the communal lifeways of many American Indians were to be replaced by an emphasis on individual labor regarded as a commodity in the capitalistic marketplace. Pratt continuously stressed the value of boarding school education and the white man's world of work as two stops on the same avenue of assimilation for Native Americans.

By the 1880s, as the Anglo-American settlement frontier closed in the middle of the continent, government policy toward Indian education was marked by debate. One faction wanted to remove Native children from their homes under governmental or religious sponsorship and remake the Indians into English-speaking, God-fearing participants in an agricultural and industrial economy, person by person, within one generation. The other faction advocated establishment of reservation-based schools and a slower path to assimilation.

Even as many boarding school students were stunted by oppression and hundreds died in influenza and tuberculosis epidemics, other students overcame all obstacles to shine in Anglo-American culture. Jim Thorpe, a graduate of Carlisle Indian School, was named the greatest American athlete in America during the first half of the twentieth century by the Associated Press. Luther Standing Bear, a Lakota author, is another prominent example. Thus, mixed with memories of pain, isolation, and despair, the boarding schools produced occasional testaments to their value as havens from an aggressive European American world that could be very hostile to the few hundred thousand Native American peoples who survived the Indian wars.

Luther Standing Bear. (Courtesy of the Nebraska State Historical Society.)

Jim Thorpe with his family. (Courtesy of the Library of Congress.)

Born near Prague, Oklahoma, during 1888 of Irish, French, and Fox/
Potawatomi descent, Jim Thorpe (Wathohuck, the Bright Path) was an outstanding college and professional football player and a gold medal Olympic
athlete. Some sports historians have called him one of the greatest all-around
athletes of any era. Thorpe's mother was a granddaughter of the Sauk leader
Black Hawk.

Thorpe was an all-American college football player in 1911 and 1912, as
Coach Glenn S. (Pop) Warner turned the Carlisle Indian School into a national football power. Thorpe also won letters in ten sports besides football

while at Carlisle: baseball, track, boxing, wrestling, lacrosse, gymnastics, swimming, hockey, handball, and basketball. He also was a prize-winning marksman and excelled at golf. Thorpe represented the United States at the 1912 Olympics in Stockholm, where he won both the decathlon and the pentathlon, the first time the same person had ever won both events in the same Olympic games. King Gustav of Sweden called him the greatest athlete in the world. His gold medals were taken from Thorpe later when it was discovered that he had played professional baseball for a short time in 1911, violating Olympic rules.

Thorpe played professional baseball between 1913 and 1919 for the New York Giants and Boston Braves. During the 1920s, he began another professional sports career in football with the Chicago Cardinals and other teams. Thorpe also recruited an all-Native American team (the Oorang Indians) for the fledgling National Football League. The team played two seasons. In 1921, the team won two games and lost six; in 1922, before the team was disbanded, the Oorang Indians won one game and lost ten.

During the 1930s, Thorpe's sports career declined. He made celebrity appearances, played bit parts in a few movies, and returned to Oklahoma for a time to delve into tribal politics. During World War II, Thorpe joined the Merchant Marine, and after that, in 1950 and 1951, he took part in the filming of the movie *Jim Thorpe—All-American*. Thorpe died in Lomita, California, in 1953. The next year, two villages in Pennsylvania, Mauch Chunk and East Mauch Chunk, merged and named themselves for him.

In 1982, the Jim Thorpe Foundation was established to work for restoration of his Olympic medals. Replicas of the medals were presented to Thorpe's family in 1983. A year later, Dennis Banks and other members of the American Indian Movement helped organize the Longest Run, during which Indian runners saluted Thorpe with a relay across North America. The run began at Onondaga, New York, and ended at the site of the 1984 Summer Olympics in Los Angeles, where the return of his medals was celebrated.

Unlike Jim Thorpe, another Native American athlete, Big Hawk Chief (Kootahwecoosoolelehoolashar, Pawnee, born ca. 1850) is virtually unknown today. He probably ran a mile in less than four minutes nearly three-quarters of a century before anyone else. Big Hawk Chief joined the U.S. Army scout corps under Captain Luther North in 1876; he fought the Sioux and their allies in the final years of the Plains Indian wars. As he was waiting for orders to muster out of the Army, Big Hawk Chief twice ran a mile in under four minutes at Fort Sidney, Nebraska.

Captain North set up a mile-long course and put two stopwatches on Big Hawk Chief, who was reputed to be the fastest of a number of outstanding Pawnee runners. Big Hawk Chief was reported to have run the first half of the course in two minutes and the second half in one minute fifty-eight seconds at a time when the fastest recorded mile run by any other human being was 4:49. Captain North remeasured the course, and Big Hawk Chief duplicated the effort in the same time to the astonishment of nearly everyone at the fort. The next sub-four-minute mile would be run by Roger Bannister, an Englishman, in 1954, three-quarters of a century later.

Thorpe was probably the most notable single alumnus of Pratt's boarding school system. Unlike Thorpe, most students were being prepared for anonymous lives in an industrializing country. Boarding schools were usually purposefully located far from children's homes to break down ties to their families and cultures. During their scholastic careers, many native children were "outed" to European American families for as many as three years. Students who were outed often performed domestic labor (for women) and farm or urban wage labor (for men). Young men were trained in agriculture, carpentry, blacksmithing, harness and shoe-making, printing, tailoring, and baking. Young women were trained in cooking, sewing, and laundry.

The outing policy was based on an assumption that Native American children were less intelligent than European Americans. During the 1940s, the BIA and University of Chicago researchers set out to test this assumption. They compared Indian children's intelligence with that of non-Indians in a rural Midwestern area. They used performance tests in which comprehension of English was not the main factor in defining intelligence, testing Hopi, Navajo, Sioux, Papago, and Zuni children. A group of Hopis averaged a score of 111 to 117 on a battery of tests. A comparison group of European American children scored 101 to 103 on the same tests. Pine Ridge children averaged 101 to 114 on the tests, and the other Indian groups scored in similar ranges (Havighurst and Hilkevitch, 1944).

Native peoples also displayed an intense attachment to their traditions that the government did not expect. Sometimes, the curriculum of the boarding schools so profoundly rejected Native values and self-worth that they were self-defeating, propelling students to suicide or alcoholism (also eventually a form of suicide). Some rebelled outright at the contradictions they were being taught compared to the lives they knew and the traditions they were taught at home. The boarding school system had a curious effect on some of its best students. It turned some of them into the Indian militants of the 1960s. Even such a transformation is not totally unique to the twentieth century, however. Wovoka, who initiated the Ghost Dance, was raised in a Christian settler family during the early years of the boarding schools.

The boarding school system was based on an assumption that making students accept the degradation of their traditions as an objective fact would cause them to accept acculturation. The Carlisle School published one essay that its teachers regarded as "excellent":

Question: To what race do you belong?
Answer: The human race.
Question: How many classes belong to this race?

Answer: There are five classes belonging to the human race.
Question: Which was the first?
Answer: The white people are the strongest.
Question: Which are the next?
Answer: The Mongolian or yellows.
Question: The next?
Answer: The Ethiopians or blacks.
Question: Next?
Answer: The American or reds.
Question: Tell me something of the white people.
Answer: The Caucasian is way ahead of all the other races. He thought more than
any other race, he thought that somebody must [have] made the earth, and if
the white people did not find that out, nobody would ever know it—it is God
who made the world. (Weeks, 1990, 224–225)

The world into which many Native Americans were born during the early
twentieth century brings to mind George Orwell's novel *1984*. The influence
of the BIA pervaded every aspect of its wards' lives, from cradle to grave, in
the image of Big Brother. The minions of government usually thought they
were doing the Indians a favor, shaping them into melting pot Americans.
They were imposing a way of life that many Native people did not want and
often did their best, under difficult circumstances, to avoid.

If the BIA forbade traditional ceremonies such as the Sun Dance and the
rituals of the kiva, Native people took them underground. The same was true
of shamanistic practices, which survived stringent attacks in which they
were called "paganism." The off-reservation boarding schools were designed
to immerse Native students in anglicized culture and to strip them of their
own, beginning with language. English was taught and enforced as the *lingua
franca*. The speaking of Native languages often was punished, sometimes vi-
olently. Even under such pressure, many Native languages, the vessels of many
hundreds of cultures, survived.

By the time that treaty-making ended in 1871, the smothering bureaucratic arms of the BIA were reaching into the lives of most surviving Native
Americans. According to the "reformers" of the post–Civil War era, this nul-
lification of tribal sovereignty—by which Native peoples often had to go to
court to fight to regain what had been guaranteed them, often in eternal terms,
by treaties signed only a few years earlier—served the same purpose as Indian
boarding school education.

As allotment reduced the Native land base, enrollment in BIA-sponsored
schools increased. Between 1895 and 1905, the number of off-reservation
boarding schools designed on the Carlisle model rose from 19 to 25, and their
enrollment doubled to 9,736. The number of boarding schools on reservations increased from 75 to 93, with enrollment rising from 8,068 to 11,402
(Olson and Wilson, 1984, 90–100).

RE-LIVING THE BOARDING SCHOOL
EXPERIENCE IN CANADA

The paternalistic assumptions of Pratt's schools also informed Canadian educational policies. The Canadian minister of Indian affairs, Frank Oliver, forecast in 1908 that the residential school system would "elevate the Indian from his condition of savagery" and "make him a self-supporting member of the state, and eventually a citizen in good standing" (Johansen, 2000, 12). Canadian officials sent delegations south of the border to study boarding schools in the United States before establishing their own system. By the early twenty-first century, hundreds of Canadian Native Americans were suing churches and the federal government there because of maltreatment at these schools.

Even after decades, the memories of Native Americans who were forced to attend Canadian boarding schools have a searing quality. "It was like jail," Warner Scout, who was 54 years of age in 1999, told the *Calgary Herald*. "The scar will be there for the rest of our lives" (Lowey, 1999, A-1). Scout, who is one of 2,000 Canadian natives seeking legal redress for boarding school abuse, recalled regular beatings and taunts that he was "an ugly savage."

More than 100,000 Native American students attended residential schools across Canada until the 1980s. Most of these schools were funded by the Canadian federal government and operated by employees of the Catholic, Anglican, Presbyterian, and United churches. During the past few years, hundreds of men and women have filed lawsuits outlining the physical and sexual abuse they said they were forced to endure in these schools as children. Eventually, settlements could reach billions of Canadian dollars, possibly devastating the financial resources of the churches that had maintained the schools.

Scout was taken from his adopted family to attend the St. Paul residential school, operated by the Anglican Church of Canada on the Blood Reserve near Lethbridge, in southern Alberta. There, he said, "Teaching . . . was beaten into us" (Lowey, 1999, A-1). Scout watched as one Indian student was forced to eat his own vomit after he threw up into a bowl of porridge. Students who wet their beds had urine rubbed in their faces, and those who spoke the Blackfoot language had their heads shaven.

Jackie Blackface, who was 52 in 1999, recalled being beaten with a tractor's fan belt at an Anglican school on the Siksika First Nation Reserve east of Calgary. Federal Canadian law at the time gave the Indian agent on each Native reserve authority to invade homes and order children aged seven or older into residential schools. Parents who did not cooperate were threatened with time in jail.

Why has a drive to apologize and compensate for the abuses of boarding schools developed in Canada while the issue has been virtually untouched in the United States? The seeds were sown almost a decade ago with the summer of fire and iron at Oka, Quebec, on and near the Kanesatake Mohawk Reserve. That confrontation over a long-ignored land claim reverberated across Canada during and after 1990, causing intense soul-searching by many non-Native Canadians. This wave of questioning expressed itself in the appointment of the Royal Commission on Aboriginal Peoples, which in 1996 published a massive, multivolume study of the many ways in which Native Americans had been abused of their lands and rights during Canadian history.

Part of the report (volume 1, chapter 10) by the Royal Commission documented the abuses of the boarding schools, providing a basis for establishment of a $350 million "healing fund" by Canada's federal government as well as a tidal wave of lawsuits. The healing fund is reserved for community projects, not for individual compensation. Individual compensation must be sought through the Canadian court system or by negotiation with agencies of the federal government.

The graphic sexual nature of boarding school abuses shocked many Canadians. Their sense of disgust was not alleviated by the fact that many of the abuses took place at the hands of priests, nuns, and other clerics. The scope of the abuse also has shocked Canadians. The Royal Commission found that abuse was systemic, not occasional or accidental. Thousands of Native young people are said to have died in the schools, and thousands more were scarred for life by physical and sexual abuse.

Aboriginal people often realized the purpose of the schools at the beginning, according to the report of the Royal Commission:

> The Aboriginal leader George Manuel, a residential school graduate, was rather more blunt. The schools, he wrote, were the laboratory and production line of the colonial system...the colonial system that was designed to make room for European expansion into a vast empty wilderness needed an Indian population that it could describe as lazy and shiftless...the colonial system required such an Indian for casual labor. (Royal Commission, 1996)

The Royal Commission on Aboriginal Peoples found that the residential schools' concerted campaign to obliterate those habits and associations, Aboriginal languages, traditions, and beliefs and its vision of radical resocialization were compounded by mismanagement and underfunding, the provision of inferior educational services, and the woeful mistreatment, neglect, and abuse of many children—facts that were known to the department and the churches throughout the history of the school system.

The boarding school system was designed to transform Native children into Europeans from the ground up. In the words of the Royal Commission's report, their purpose was as follows:

> [To] release [the children] from the shackles that tied them to their parents, communities and cultures. The civilizers in the churches and the department understood this and, moreover, that it would not be accomplished simply by bringing the children into the school. Rather it required a concerted attack on the

ontology, on the basic cultural patterning of the children and on their world view. They had to be taught to see and understand the world as a European place within which only European values and beliefs had meaning; thus the wisdom of their cultures would seem to them only savage superstition. (Royal Commission, 1996)

The main enforcement mechanism in this transformation from "permissive" aboriginal life to white Canadian discipline was punishment, much of it violent. In 1943, the principal of St. George's School (located on the Fraser River, just north of Lyttons, BC) disclosed that a set of shackles had been used routinely "to chain runaways to the bed." Furthermore:

At the heart of the vision of residential education—of the school as home and sanctuary of motherly care—there was a stark contradiction, an inherent element of savagery in the mechanics of civilizing the children. The very language in which the vision was couched revealed what would have to be the essentially violent nature of the school system in its assault on child and culture. The basic premise of resocialization, of the great transformation from "savage" to "civilized", was violent. (Royal Commission, 1996)

In 1936, G. Barry, district inspector of schools in British Columbia, described the Alberni School on Vancouver Island, "where every member of staff carried a strap" and where "children have never learned to work without punishment" (Royal Commission, 1996). In 1896, according to the Royal Commission's report, Agent D. L. Clink refused to return a child to the Red Deer School because he feared "he would be abused." Without reprimand from the principal, a teacher had beaten children severely on several occasions, one of whom had to be hospitalized. "Such brutality," Clink concluded, "should not be tolerated for a moment" and "would not be tolerated in a white school for a single day in any part of Canada" (ibid.).

The Royal Commission also included a report by a senior official in western Canada, David Laird, on Norway House in 1907 detailing "frequent whippings" over an eight-year period of a young boy, Charlie Clines, for bedwetting. The severity of his punishment was not, Laird asserted, "in accordance with Christian methods." Clines hated the new Anglo world that was being thrust on him so much that he ran away from the school and slept in weather so severe that several toes froze and he lost them.

In 1902, Johnny Sticks found his son, Duncan, dead of exposure after he fled from the Williams Lake, British Columbia, industrial school. Nearly four decades later, in 1937 at the Lejac School, four boys ran away and were found frozen to death on the lake within sight of their community. They were wearing only summer clothes. In both cases, investigations uncovered a history of neglect and violence in evidence given by staff, children, and some graduates. Some students complained that they were given rotten, worm-ridden meat and punished if they did not eat it.

During 1921, a visiting nurse at Crowstand School discovered nine children "chained to the benches" in the dining room, one of them "marked badly by a strap" (Royal Commission, 1996). Children were frequently beaten severely with whips, rods, and fists; chained and shackled; bound hand and foot; and locked in closets, basements, and bathrooms.

The Royal Commission reported that, in 1919, a runaway student from the Anglican Old Sun's school was captured, then shackled to a bed, with his hands tied, and was "most brutally and unmercifully beaten with a horse quirt until his back was bleeding." The accused, P. H. Gentlemen, admitted to having used a whip and shackles. Canon S. Gould, the general secretary of the Missionary Society, mounted a curious defense: that such a beating was the norm "more or less, in every boarding school in the country." Gentlemen remained at the school.

Writing in 1991 of her experience in both Anglican and Catholic schools, Mary Carpenter (Johansen, 2000, 19) told an-all-too-familiar story: After a lifetime of beatings, going hungry, standing in a corridor on one leg, walking in the snow with no shoes for speaking Inuvialuktun, and having a heavy, stinging paste rubbed on her face (to stop her from expressing the Eskimo custom of raising eyebrows for "yes" and wrinkling noses for "no"), she lost the ability to speak her native language.

The Aboriginal Commission found the following:

> By the mid-1980s, it was widely and publicly recognized that the residential school experience . . . like smallpox and tuberculosis in earlier decades, had devastated and continued to devastate communities. The schools were, with the agents and instruments of economic and political marginalization, part of the contagion of colonization. In their direct attack on language, beliefs and spirituality, the schools had been a particularly virulent strain of that epidemic of empire, sapping the children's bodies and beings. In later life, many adult survivors, and the families and communities to which they returned, all manifested a tragic range of symptoms emblematic of "the silent tortures that continue in our communities." (Royal Commission, 1996)

Although school supervisors acknowledged and sometimes even took pride in stern discipline, including corporal punishment, they said very little about the deepest secret of the system: sexual abuse of the children. The official files ignore the issue almost completely. Any references were encoded in the language of repression that marked the Canadian discourse on sexual matters. One report at Red Deer School commented that "the moral aspect of affairs is deplorable." Others wrote of "questions of immorality" of "the breaking of the Seventh Commandment" (Royal Commission, 1996).

In 1990, the Toronto *Globe and Mail* (Johansen, 2000, 19) reported that Rix Rogers, special advisor to the minister of national health and welfare on child sexual abuse, had commented at a meeting of the Canadian Psychological Association that the abuse revealed to date was "just the tip of the iceberg" and that closer scrutiny of treatment of children at residential schools would show that all children at some schools were sexually abused. A 1989 study sponsored by the Native Women's Association of the Northwest Territories found that eight of ten girls under the age of eight had been victims of sexual abuse, and 50 percent of boys the same age had been sexually molested as well.

On January 7, 1998, Minister of Indian Affairs Jane Stewart read a Statement of Reconciliation into the record of Canada's federal Parliament at Ottawa that acknowledged the damage done to the Native population, including the hanging of Louis Riel after he led a rebellion of Indian and mixed-race people in western Canada in 1885. The government apology stopped short of pardoning Riel, a step that aboriginal leaders have demanded for decades. Stewart did, however, apologize for the government's assimilation policies, including the abuses of boarding schools.

"Attitudes of racial and cultural superiority led to a suppression of aboriginal culture and values," Stewart said. She continued:

> As a country, we are burdened by past actions that resulted in weakening the identity of aboriginal peoples, suppressing their languages and cultures, and outlawing spiritual practices. We must recognize the impact of these actions on the once self-sustaining nations that were disaggregated, disrupted, limited or even destroyed by the dispossession of traditional territory, by the relocation of aboriginal people, and by some provisions of the Indian Act. The time has come to state formally that the days of paternalism and disrespect are behind us and we are committed to changing the nature of the relationship between aboriginal and non-aboriginal people in Canada. (Bourrie, 1998)

Phil Fontaine, leader the Assembly of First Nations, a coalition of nationwide aboriginal groups, said that the apology paves the way for lasting peace between Native peoples and the Canadian government. "This celebrates the beginning of a new era," Fontaine told Interpress Service. "It is a major step forward in our quest to be recognized as a distinct order of government in Canada" (Bourrie, 1998).

Some aboriginal leaders were not happy with the reconciliation statement. Representatives of Inuit, Native women's groups, and Metis said they did not believe the apology was strong enough. They were critical because the statement did not refer in more detail to the wrongs done to their communities. The same groups also maintained that the money involved in recompense was too little, too late. Inuit and Metis leaders, who are not included in the Assembly of First Nations, also complained that Stewart's later statements did not mention specific programs for them.

Stewart's statement sparked a retort in the Canadian *Financial Post* from columnist David Frum, who wrote, in part:

> Let the groveling begin.... The descendants of the Europeans have had the good taste never to demand a thank-you from the descendants of the

aboriginals. . . . But at the very least they are entitled to refuse to bow and scrape and abase themselves for the sin of having tamed and civilized this inhospitable land. (Hipwell, 1998, 18)

Frum's column, published January 13, 1998, drew several indignant letters to the editor, one of which was from Bill Hipwell, a lecturer in political geography at Ottawa's Carlton University. Instead of apologizing, Hipwell suggested, Euro-Canadians should thank Native peoples for several things, among them democratic ideas: "The civilizations of the Mi'kmaq and the Haudenosaunee (Iroquois) Confederacy [which] taught Europeans such basic principles as human rights. . . . Jefferson borrowed liberally from the Haudenosaunee political system" (1998, 18).

Other non-Indian Canadians complained that the surge of lawsuits for residential school abuse would clog the court system, bankrupt some religious denominations, and strain the Canadian federal budget, requiring new taxes. By the end of the year 2002, according to the Canadian government, more than 19,000 Native persons had entered some form of claim, a number equal to roughly 15 to 20 percent of the boarding schools' living alumni. This legal backlog included four class action suits. Indian plaintiffs won all five boarding school abuse trials held during the late 1990s, two in Saskatchewan and three in British Columbia.

By early 1999, the Canadian federal government had paid out roughly $20 million worth of individual compensation, including awards to several victims of staff at the Gordon Reserve in Saskatchewan (which was run by the government without church affiliation). Late in 1998, the federal government and the Catholic Church also reached an out-of-court settlement with eleven men who were abused by Oblate priests while attending St. Joseph's residential school near Williams Lake, British Columbia, during the 1960s.

During late October 1998, the United Church of Canada, the country's largest Protestant body (including 3 million Presbyterians, Congregationalists, and Methodists) issued an apology for physical and sexual abuse meted out to Native students at boarding schools it had operated. The apology was made shortly after disclosure of evidence indicating that church officials knew of the abuse as early as 1960 and did nothing to stop it. Peter Grant, an attorney for former students at a British Columbia boarding school, had presented evidence indicating that the vice principal at the Port Alberni residential school was convicted of indecently assaulting male students between 1948 and 1968. Arthur Plint, who supervised the school's dormitories, pleaded guilty in 1995 to "dozens of sexual assaults," according to the Associated Press. He was sentenced to eleven years in prison. British Columbia Court Justice William Brenner ruled that both the federal government and the church were "vicariously responsible" for Plint's assaults on Native young people.

"I apologize for the pain and suffering that our church's involvement in the Indian residential school system has caused," the Rev. Bill Phipps, the church's chief executive (or moderator) told a news conference on October 27 (Associated Press, 1998). "We are aware of some of the damage that some of this cruel and ill-conceived system of assimilation has perpetuated on Canada's first nations," Phipps said. "We are truly and humbly sorry" (McIlroy, 1998, 5).

One of Grant's clients, Willy Blackwater, said that the church should be prepared to compensate abuse victims with money as well as words. Harry Daniels, president of the Congress of Aboriginal peoples, said "These things are nice to hear, but talk is cheap" (Associated Press, 1998). The Anglican and Roman Catholic churches of Canada expressed repentance for their role in boarding school abuses, but as of 2002 had not apologized, in part because they fear legal liability. The United Church seems to have decided that it will settle with litigants out of court.

The Royal Commission concluded the following:

> The terrible facts of the residential school system must be made a part of a new sense of what Canada has been and will continue to be for as long as that record is not officially recognized and repudiated. Only by such an act of recognition and repudiation can a start be made on a very different future. Canada and Canadians must realize that they need to consider changing their society so that they can discover ways of living in harmony with the original people of the land. (Royal Commission, 1996)

The Royal Commission called for a full investigation into Canada's residential school system "to bring to light and begin to heal the grievous harms suffered by countless Aboriginal children, families and communities as a result of the residential school system." Although not the forum the Royal Commission may have intended, such a public inquiry has begun to unfold, case by specific case, in many Canadian courtrooms. The economic stakes of boarding school compensation in Canada were reflected by the fact that, by late 2002, the Canadian federal government had reserved $1.7 billion to settle up to 18,000 native residential school lawsuits brought for physical and sexual abuse. The government was planning to require plaintiffs to waive rights to future litigation, including claims based on loss of language and culture.

The Anglican diocese of Caribou, British Columbia, during 2001 announced plans to close (to place its assets in trust) following a costly legal fight over compensation for victims of abuse at residential schools in which some of its ministers had a role. This is the first Canadian church to give up its corporate identity because of these claims. The churches in the small archdiocese will continue to operate, however. The diocese, which includes about 4,700 parishioners in British Columbia's interior, has legal bills totaling more than $350,000 from residential litigation according to the Canadian Broadcasting Corporation. After more than a decade of battling in court, it has paid out settlements to a small number of victims. All of the diocese's liquid assets have now been spent, according to officials.

ELK V. WILKINS *AS COUNTERPOINT TO ASSIMILATION*

During the same decade that the U.S. Congress sought to assimilate American Indians by requiring them to follow Anglo-American property-holding conventions and educational systems, the U.S. Supreme Court refused voting rights to a Native American who requested them. The Court held in *Elk v. Wilkins* that an American Indian is not a U.S. citizen under the Fourteenth Amendment to the U.S. Constitution. This position held even if the Indian is living apart from his nation or band.

At issue was the constitutional status of American Indians for purposes of citizenship and voting. The Fourteenth Amendment granted citizenship to "all persons born or naturalized in the United States, and subject to the jurisdiction of the United States." Did American Indians fall under this definition? A federal district court ruled that it did not apply to Indians who had not been "born subject to its jurisdiction—that is, in its power and obedience" (*McKay v. Campbell* 16 Fed. Cas. 161 [1871] [No. 8840]).

John Elk had been born outside U.S. jurisdiction but moved to Omaha as an adult and lived what the court described as a "civilized" life. He sought to become a citizen and to exercise the right to vote in Omaha elections during 1880. The Supreme Court ruled that the Fifteenth Amendment (which grants the right to vote to all persons regardless of race) did not apply in Elk's case because he was not born in an area under U.S. jurisdiction. Therefore, Elk was not a citizen within the meaning of the Fourteenth Amendment. The fact that Elk had abandoned his Indian relatives and style of life did not matter to the court. Elk's citizenship and voting rights were denied because the court held that an affirmative act was required of the United States before an Indian could become a citizen. The Supreme Court's opinion cited a dozen treaties, four court rulings, four laws, and eight opinions of the U.S. attorney general requiring "proof of fitness for civilization" as a precondition of granting Indians citizenship and voting rights.

Six years after John Elk's request for citizenship was denied, Congress passed the Indian Territory Naturalization Act (26 Stat. 81, 99–100), which allowed any Indian living in Indian Territory to apply for citizenship through the federal courts. The aim of this act was to break down communal loyalties among Native Americans in Indian Territory as it moved toward statehood as Oklahoma.

Thus, following the logic of *Elk v. Wilkins*, while federal courts were busy maintaining the plenary power of Congress over Indians, classifying Native Americans as wards of the federal government, and denying an international dimension to their political existence, individual Native Americans seeking to exercise constitutional rights were being told that they were, in effect, no more than the children of foreign subjects.

At a time when federal policy accentuated the dominance of European heritage, some Native Americans became well known for crossing cultural lines. Two examples were Arthur Parker, a Seneca who became notable in the world of museums, and the Kansa and Osage Charles Curtis, who served as a congressman and U.S. vice president in the administration of Herbert Hoover.

Arthur C. Parker: A Seneca Museum Curator

Some Native Americans adapted to the dominant society by becoming professionally proficient in lines of work, such as museum curating, that acted as gateways to the society's experience with indigenous peoples and cultures. One example was Arthur C. Parker (Gawasowaneh), a Seneca, who brought the word *museologist* into the English language. Joy Porter's *To Be Indian* (2001) was the first full-scale biography of Parker, long-time curator at the Rochester Municipal Museum, later known as the Rochester Museum and Science Center. Porter is a senior lecturer in American history at Anglia Polytechnic University in Cambridge, England.

Porter brings Parker to life:

> Although not tall, at perhaps five feet six inches, he cut a dignified figure in his smart clothes with his dark hair and hazel eyes winking out from under his trademark fedora. Some thought he looked quintessentially "Indian"; others thought of him as "white." However they encountered him, people seemed to have warmed to Parker because of his skill at putting them at ease. A lover of puns and word games, he was friendly, with a charming sense of humor. (2001, xvii)

Parker was best known as a museum director, but he also was a prolific writer, with roughly 500 pieces that ranged from books to journal and magazine articles (published and not), radio scripts, plays, and others. Porter's (2001) portrait of Parker is richly detailed, delineating a man walking the cusp of Indian and non-Indian worlds (he was one-fourth Seneca), a person always acutely aware of the interplay between the two. He was both a thirty-third degree Freemason as well as an adopted member of the Seneca Bear Clan.

Porter described a man who was intensely aware of prevailing ideological winds, with special attention throughout much of his life to a eugenic point of view that went severely out of intellectual fashion after Hitler's Nazis took its tenets to especially cruel extremes between 1933 and 1945. Before the Meriam Report (Meriam, 1928) and the Indian Reorganization Act (1934), Parker voiced doubts that Native Americans could maintain their cultural identity in the midst of popular demands for a breakdown of reservation land bases (through the Allotment Acts and other measures) and suffocating policies of assimilation.

As Parker sometimes favored restrictions on immigration to reduce the proportion of the "less fit," Porter wrote that he was "simply following a fashion" (2001, 30). After all, Porter wrote, Woodrow Wilson and George Eastman (of the Eastman-Kodak fortune) made similar statements. Later in the book, however, Porter raised doubts as to whether even the sterilization of 2 million defectives by the Nazis provoked Parker to "begin a fundamental reassessment of his deeply held assumptions about 'race' and human development" (ibid., 215). Until his retirement in 1946, after World War II had ended, Parker continued to "mull them over in print" (ibid., 215). At one point, Porter quoted Parker as having argued for "the preservation of racial type—that of the Aryan white man." He held forth against "indiscriminate blood-blending and inharmonious race contacts." At roughly the same time, circa 1920, Parker, according to Porter, "accepted a new imperative— white cultural and racial perpetuation" (ibid., 137).

Within a decade, however, the intellectual wind had begun to shift, and Parker started to shift with it. Native self-determination and preservation of identity became fashionable by the 1930s. Parker ended his professional life best known for popular innovation in museums, which he called "the university of the common man." On his death in 1955, Parker was recalled very warmly by Ray Fadden, who wrote to Martha Parker that "the Chief," as he often was called, "was a great person, desiring nothing for himself, and ever ready to do good for everyone, no matter who" (Porter, 2001, 241). Obscuring his earlier doubts about Native American cultural survival and his eugenic ruminations, Parker's affectionate personality won out in the end—a tribute to his essential humanity.

Charles Curtis: A Native American U.S. Vice President

At the same time that assimilation became the dominant ideology in Indian affairs, a Native American served as U.S. vice president. As a Republican politician, Charles Curtis (1860–1936), Kansa and Osage, also served as a member of the U.S. House of Representatives and as a U.S. senator. Curtis became a leading spokesperson for some assimilationist measures, including the General Allotment Act.

Born on Indian land that later was incorporated into North Topeka, Kansas, Curtis was the son of Oren A. Curtis (an abolitionist and Civil War Union cavalry officer) and Helen Pappan (Kaw/Osage). His mother died when he was three, and he was raised under the care of his maternal grandmother on the Kaw Reservation and in Topeka. Following an attack on Kaw Indians at Council Grove by Cheyenne militants, Curtis (who was one-eighth Indian) left the Indian mission school on the Kaw Reservation in 1868 and returned to Topeka, where he attended Topeka High School. For several years as a young man, he was a jockey and worked odd jobs until he met A. H. Case, a Topeka lawyer. Studying the law and working as a law clerk, Curtis was admitted to the Kansas bar in 1881.

Entering politics, Curtis was elected county prosecuting attorney in 1884 and 1886. From 1892 to 1906, he served eight terms in the U.S. House of Representatives. He authored the Curtis Act of 1898, which dissolved tribal governments and permitted the institution of civil government within the

Indian Territory, later Oklahoma. The Curtis Act, which attempted to force assimilation on American Indian peoples, brought the allotment policy to the Five Civilized Tribes of Oklahoma, who previously had been exempted from the initial Allotment Act. In essence, the Curtis Act paved the way for Oklahoma statehood in 1907 by destroying tribal land titles and governments.

Curtis served in the U.S. Senate from 1907 to 1913 (he was the first U.S. senator of American Indian ancestry) and 1915 to 1929. During his tenure in the Senate, Curtis was Republican party whip (1915–1924) and then majority leader (1924–1929). As chair of the Senate Committee on Indian Affairs in 1924, Curtis sponsored the Indian Citizenship Act. After an unsuccessful campaign for the presidential nomination, he ran as vice president with Herbert Hoover in 1928. He served as vice president from 1929 to 1933. Curtis was a deft politician who used his Indian background for personal advantage, even though his political adversaries called him "the Injun." Although a fiscal conservative, he supported veterans' benefits, farm relief, women's suffrage, and national prohibition.

The Hoover-Curtis ticket's bid for a second term was defeated in 1932 by Franklin Delano Roosevelt. On his retirement from politics in 1933, Curtis had served longer in the nation's Capitol than any active politician at that time. After leaving public office, Curtis headed the short-lived National Republican League and practiced law in Washington, D.C. He was also president of a gold mining company in New Mexico. In 1936, Curtis died of heart disease.

DESKAHEH OPPOSES ASSIMILATION

Assimilative policies were vigorously opposed by some important Native leaders. One example was Deskaheh (Levi General, Cayuga, 1873–1925), who was Tadadaho (speaker) of the Iroquois Grand Council at Grand River, Ontario, in the early 1920s, when Canadian authorities closed the traditional long-house, which had been asserting independence from Canadian jurisdiction. Canadian authorities proposed to set up a governmental structure that would answer to its Indian affairs bureaucracy. With Canadian police about to arrest him, Deskaheh traveled to the headquarters of the League of Nations in Geneva, Switzerland, with an appeal for support from the international community.

Several months of effort did not win Deskaheh a hearing before the inter-national body, in large part because of diplomatic manipulation by Great Britain and Canada, governments that were embarrassed by Deskaheh's mission. Lacking a forum at the League of Nations, Deskaheh and his supporters organized a privately organized meeting in Switzerland that drew several thousand people, who roared approval of Iroquois sovereignty.

In his last speech, March 10, 1925, Deskaheh had lost none of this distaste for forced acculturation. "Over in Ottawa, they call that policy 'Indian Advancement,'" he said. "Over in Washington, they call it 'Assimilation.' We who would be the helpless victims say it is tyranny.... If this must go on to

Deskaheh (Levi General). (Courtesy of John Kahionhes Fadden.)

the bitter end, we would rather that you come with your guns and poison gas and get rid of us that way. Do it openly and above board" (Johansen and Grinde, 1997, 111).

As he lay dying, relatives of Deskaheh who lived in the United States were refused entry into Canada to be at his bedside. Deskaheh died two-and-a-half months after his last defiant speech.

THE NATIVE AMERICAN CHURCH'S RESPONSE TO OPPRESSION

One of the most effective responses to the severe repression of Native peoples and cultures at the turn of the century was religious. After the Ghost

Dance played a role in the massacre at Wounded Knee, most practice of Native American religions went underground. There was no more showing of ghost shirts to be shot at by the cavalry. The Native American Church is historically important not only because it took native culture underground (and therefore revived forms of community that were being lost to assimilation), but also because it was an early example of a successful pan-Indian movement. Like the religion begun by the Iroquois Handsome Lake a century earlier, the Native American Church sought native members only and sometimes carried the air of a secret society, especially in the eyes on non-Indians. Both religions rejected aspects of European culture that had proved particularly harmful to American Native people, especially alcohol. Both religions mixed Native belief and custom with some aspects of Christianity. Both continue to attract adherents today.

The secrecy of the Native American Church (at least to European American eyes) caused some non-Indian observers to cry "paganism." The practice that brought down the wrath of non-Indians on the church's members was their use of peyote. Chewing peyote produces mild hallucinations; in the early years of the Native American Church, members took peyote to aid meditation. The so-called peyote cult arose in Mexico and spread among the Apaches and Comanches during the 1870s. After the decline of the Ghost Dance religion in the 1890s, peyotism swept over the plains and prairies in the central part of North America. The Native American Church itself was founded in 1918. By 1955, people associated with roughly eighty Native tribes and nations practiced some form of peyotism (Olson and Wilson, 1984, 90). Peyote was used as a religious sacrament and to blunt the pain and alienation of reservation life at its worst.

Some of the opposition to peyotism came from nonpracticing Native Americans. In 1940, the Navajo Tribal Council, dominated by Christians, outlawed the use of peyote. The Taos Pueblos, White Mountain Apaches, and several Sioux communities passed laws forbidding its use. Many of these were enacted at the behest of traditionalists, who saw the Native American Church as a threat to existing tribal religions. The territorial legislature of Oklahoma outlawed peyote's use outside Indian Territory in 1898. By 1923, fourteen states had banned use of peyote. Customs agents began seizing peyote crossing the border from Mexico. In 1940, Congress outlawed the shipment of peyote through the mail. The BIA tried, but failed, to enact laws to ban the use of peyote nationwide. Not enough non-Indians used peyote to fuel a good drug scare. By the 1990s, with legal protection of Native American religious practice in place, the use of peyote in religious ritual was legalized.

THE INDIAN CITIZENSHIP ACT (1924)

At the same time that Deskaheh was attempting to present the Iroquois case before the League of Nations, citizenship in the United States was extended to all Native Americans in the Citizenship Act of 1924. This was only four decades after the Supreme Court, in *Elk v. Wilkins* (1884), had denied the petition of an individual Indian for the same rights. Ironically, citizenship had been offered to some tribes as early as 1850, sometimes on condition that their lands be allotted to private ownership.

The granting of U.S. citizenship dovetailed with the abolition of Native national autonomy. Although citizenship for all Native Americans was not legislated until 1924, many Native people had been made citizens (often without their consent) decades earlier. By 1924, two-thirds of American Indians had been extended citizenship piecemeal. Citizenship was extended to individual Native persons when their land was allotted. In 1888, a year after passing the Allotment Act, Congress made Native people who married U.S. citizens eligible for citizenship. In 1890, as Oklahoma moved toward statehood, reservation residents in Indian Territory were offered citizenship if they applied to federal courts. In 1919, an act of Congress extended citizenship to Native American veterans of World War I. In 1901, Congress extended citizenship rights to all Native people living in what was then called Indian Territory.

Many Native people refused citizenship (or did their best to avoid it), especially after it was tied to the loss of communal land through allotment. Citizenship was to begin after the allotted land had been held in trust for 25 years. Some Native peoples have rejected citizenship, notably members of the Haudenosaunee (Iroquois) Confederacy and other Native people in New York State. During World War II, the Iroquois made a point of their sovereignty by declaring war on the Axis powers independent of the United States. Even today, many Iroquois abstain from voting in state and national elections, and a number have refused to pay income taxes. Some of the six Iroquois nations (Mohawk, Oneida, Onondaga, Tuscarora, Cayuga, and Seneca) issue their own vehicle license plates, as do several other Native American nations. The Iroquois Confederacy at Onondaga goes one step further: It sends diplomats to other countries with their own passports.

THE MERIAM REPORT (1928): A REPUDIATION OF ALLOTMENT

Shortly after 1920, a wave of sympathy emerged in response to the cruelties imposed on Native Americans during the nadir of the reservation era. This wave of political opinion produced the Meriam Report (Meriam, 1928), which documented the horrid condition of human health and welfare under the BIA's "wardship."

The Meriam Report also brought the argument on allotment full circle: from alleged harbinger of a new American Indian future, to the dismal, culturally destructive real estate agency it had become. The report laid the intellectual and political basis for the revolution that John Collier wrought in Indian Affairs during the early 1930s. The Meriam Report came to be widely regarded as the most important indictment of the BIA since Helen Hunt Jackson's *A Century of Dishonor* (1881). Although *A Century of Dishonor* was used to advance the merits of allotment, the Meriam Report became a political tool to repudiate it.

By 1923, an organized committee of influential Indians and non-Indians, the Committee of One Hundred, was lobbying for more respectful and humane treatment of Native Americans. Collier was an early member, with William Jennings Bryan, Clark Wissler, General John J. Pershing, Bernard Baruch, William Allen White, and the Seneca Arthur C. Parker. Parker was elected presiding officer at a convention in Washington, D.C., during December 1923. Under his aegis, in 1924 the group published its findings under the title *The Indian Problem* (Otis, 1924). This document formed the basis for the better-known Meriam Report four years later.

The Meriam Report was an exhaustive, 870-page narrative and statistical portrait of Native American life at a time sometimes called the era of the vanishing race. It covered health, education, economic conditions, legal aspects, and missionary activities, among others. The Meriam Report found generally that the government was failing miserably at its professed goal of protecting Indians, their land, and resources. Of the Allotment Act (1887), the report said the following:

> When the government adopted the policy of individual ownership of the land on the reservations, the expectation was that the Indians would become farmers. . . . It almost seems as if the government assumed that some magic in individual ownership of property would in itself prove an educational civilizing factor, but unfortunately this policy has for the most part operated in the opposite direction. (Meriam, 1928, 7)

The Meriam Report provided graphic evidence of just how badly the federal government's Indian wards were being treated. Infant mortality on Indian reservations, for example, was nearly three times that of European-descended Americans generally. Large numbers of Indians were dying from tuberculosis, trachoma, measles, and other diseases that had been largely eradicated in mainstream society. In this sea of disease, health services on reservations were ill-equipped and lacking sufficient trained staff. Diets heavy on cheap, government-issued carbohydrates were producing malnutrition in people who often were otherwise overweight. The government provided 11 cents a day to feed students at its boarding schools and skimped on equipment and salaries for teachers. Schools often were unsanitary. Per capita income for native reservation residents was less than $200 a year at a time when national average earnings were $1,350. All of this contributed to an average life span among Indians of 44 years.

According to the Meriam Report, the essential Indian problem was poverty caused by the fact that the U.S. government had done little to replace traditional Native economies with self-sustaining structures that could provide Indians a livelihood. The report found that forced assimilation did little to improve Indians' economic conditions; many of its recommendations, such as an end to allotment, were essentially rearguard actions meant to ameliorate problems caused by forced assimilation during the previous century.

Belief that government should address its mistakes regarding Indian affairs became a popular political theme after the release of the Meriam Report. Even before John Collier (who had been accused of communist tendencies during the "red scare" of the early 1920s) became Indian commissioner, a liberal tendency was evident under the otherwise conservative presidency of Herbert Hoover. Hoover brought Ray Lyman from the presidency of Stanford University to become secretary of interior. Hoover also chose Charles J. Rhoades, a devout Quaker, as commissioner of Indian Affairs. Rhoades enjoyed little success in his efforts to reform the federal bureaucracy to implement the Meriam Report. More fundamental reforms would have to wait until the presidency of Franklin D. Roosevelt and his appointment of John Collier as commissioner of Indian Affairs.

JOHN COLLIER'S BUREAU OF INDIAN AFFAIRS

John Collier filled the post of Indian commissioner for nearly the entire length of Franklin Roosevelt's presidency, twelve years, more time than any other person. His policies initiated a Native resurgence to some degree. Some land was added to the Native estate, reversing a U.S. trend of a century and a half. Although he was reviled frequently for favoring Native communalism over assimilation, Collier also encountered considerable criticism from Native people for ignoring their traditional systems of governance. He recognized that Native cultures and land bases should be maintained but thought that they ought to exist subject to the government's rules. The result of this synthesis was the Indian Reorganization Act (IRA), passed by Congress and signed into law by President Roosevelt during 1934. Mixing liberalism with bureaucratic prerogative, the IRA offered Native people a measure of self-government but demanded that those governments be created and conducted by its rules.

The IRA was the most fundamental and far-reaching piece of legislation relating to Native Americans passed by Congress during the first half of the twentieth century. The IRA eliminated the allotment system and established Native American governments for some reservations under systems that were partially self-governing. The IRA also established hiring preferences for Native Americans within the BIA. Although it was criticized by some Native American groups, some of the IRA's changes also were widely acclaimed at the time of its origins. For example, Native peoples were allowed by this act to resume their ceremonies openly, after a half-century of repression.

Before passage of the IRA, Native tribes and nations had been operated more or less as colonial enclaves by the United States. They were legally held to be subject to Congress and the president, delegated through the BIA. According to legal scholars Russel Barsh and James Henderson, "No local laws or assemblies were recognized, and a special police force was established to maintain federal supremacy. Traditional leadership was deposed, prosecuted, and sometimes killed when in conflict with federal Indian policy" (1980, 209). Under the IRA, colonialism was relaxed somewhat. Leaders were no longer appointed but were elected under constitutions that themselves were subject to U.S. government veto. In many cases, even individual ordinances passed by councils were subject to Interior Department review.

The IRA was introduced by Representative Edgar Howard of Nebraska and Senator Burton K. Wheeler of Montana and became known popularly as the Wheeler-Howard Act. The initial drafts of the fifty-page bill were the work mainly of John Collier, whom Roosevelt had appointed commissioner of Indian affairs. Before its provisions were modified during debates in the House and Senate, the IRA declared a federal policy that American Indians be encouraged to establish and control their own governments. Another part of Collier's draft required Indian schools to develop materials relevant to Native American histories and cultures. The third version of the original bill stopped allotment of Indian land and restored title to surplus lands still held by the government, as well as created reservations for Native American groups left without land by the usurpation of the previous century. Collier's bill also called for a Court of Indian Affairs. After compromise in the legislative process, many of Collier's ideas were discarded. Even so, the IRA established a new framework for Indian affairs, a hybrid of Collier's ideas and the older paternalistic system.

Native nations and tribes were given two years after the passage of the IRA to accept or reject its provisions. Within that period, 258 elections were held, with 181 Native groups accepting the terms of the IRA and 77 voting negatively. Some of those who rejected the IRA objected to its requirements that the federal government approve policies on land use, selection of legal counsel, and other matters (including constitutions). Although the act rhetorically upheld Native self-determination, it imposed a federal veto power over most major (and many minor) decisions that each Native government had proposed.

Frank Fools Crow, a Sioux, described the effects of the Indian New Deal in this way: "Being beaten in war was bad enough. Yet being defeated and placed in bondage by programs we could not understand . . . is worse, especially when it is done to one of the most powerful, independent, and proudest of the Indian nations of North America" (Mails, 1990, 146–147). Fools Crow believed that, for the Sioux people, the "years from 1930–1940 rank as the worst ten years I know of." Fools Crow stated that the traditional family structure was crumbling because of the following:

> Individual independence and . . . irresponsibility was being encouraged among the young people. Bootleggers were after the Indian's money, and were hauling

cheap wine and whiskey onto the reservation by the truckload....Even the young women were drinking now, and this assured a future tragedy of the worst possible proportions. (ibid., 146–147)

California was a major center of opposition to Collier's Indian New Deal. One of the principal leaders of this opposition was Rupert Costo, a young Cahuilla who had attended college and had the respect of his people. Costo believed that the Indian New Deal was a "great drive to assimilate the American Indian." Costo felt that the IRA was a program to colonize Indians because, in his view, genocide, treaty-making and treaty-breaking, substandard education, disruption of Indian culture and religion, and the Dawes Allotment Act had failed. Costo knew that partial assimilation already had taken place in native societies through the use of "certain technologies and techniques," but he knew that total assimilation which meant "fading into the general society with a complete loss of" culture and identity was another thing altogether. Costo called the IRA the Indian Raw Deal (Mails, 1990, 146).

By 1940, the IRA had come under enough criticism to prompt congressional hearings to consider its repeal. As of that date, according to Indian law scholar Lawrence C. Kelly, 252 Indian nations and bands had voted on the IRA as required by the act, including 99 small bands in California with a total population of less than 25,000. Seventy-eight groups had rejected it. Nationwide, 38,000 Indians voted in favor of IRA governments; 24,000 voted against. Another 35,000 eligible voters did not take part, most as a silent protest against the IRA.

THE INDIAN CLAIMS COMMISSION

The Meriam Report emphasized that no long-term solution of the Indian problem could occur without establishment of a commission to adjudicate compensation for outstanding land claims. Several legislative attempts to create such a body were made without success during the late 1920s and 1930s. After World War II, however, the United States was facing pressure regarding treatment of minorities at home after having criticized the human rights records of the Axis powers during the war. As a result, the Indian Claims Commission (ICC) was established by Congress in 1946.

By that time, much of the impetus of the Indian New Deal had ended, but the creation of the ICC in that year represented the final reform measure of the era. Before the enactment of the ICC, Native American nations were required to obtain the consent of Congress through special legislation to sue the federal government for violations of treaties and agreements. The Indian Claims Commission Act created a three-person commission to hear and determine claims existing prior to the bill's passage. The Congress felt that the ICC was to be part of a process that would enable to Native American groups to become autonomous.

A special tribunal was required to settle Indian claims because claims based on violation of Indian treaties had been barred from the jurisdiction of the general U.S. Court of Claims in 1863. Absent special congressional action, Indians in effect had no forum under U.S. law in which to present their claims until the Indian Claims Commission Act was passed in 1946. Under the act, suits were allowed by tribes, bands, or other "identifiable" groups of Native peoples. Appeals were permitted to the general Court of Claims and, via *certiorari*, to the U.S. Supreme Court. The Indian Claims Commission Act consolidated federal legal actions related to Indian claims for illegal taking of land, which heretofore had been dealt with through 142 different statutes. Congress created the ICC in an effort to extinguish all outstanding claims.

The ICC expired in 1978, at which time the 102 cases remaining on its docket were transferred to the U.S. Court of Claims. Between 1945 and 1975, the commission awarded $534 million to Indian claimants, $53 million of which was paid in attorney's fees. In all, the commission docketed 605 individual claims cases, nearly half of which resulted in monetary awards. The commission had originally been created for five years, but the volume of cases and the complexity of the commission's proceedings caused its bureaucratic life to be extended four times. Even so, when jurisdiction was transferred by Congress to the general Court of Claims, only 40 percent of the petitions filed had been adjudicated. The claims that were settled were paid conservatively, with land usually being valued at its cost when it was taken, usually in the late nineteenth century, without the benefit of several decades of increasing prices and land values. Many of the settlements amounted to less than $1 per acre.

THE 1950S: RELOCATION AND TERMINATION

By the 1950s, the economic rationale of allotment had become obsolete. The myth of the yeoman farmer had dissolved into the reality of large-scale, global agribusiness. Most Americans lived and worked in cities. Advocates of termination and relocation saw themselves generally as modernists and realists, promoting the eradication of Native land, identity, and lifeways for the Natives' own good to ease their transition into a modern industrial economy—the benign, all-knowing hand forever shaping the soft underside of conquest.

Between 1954 and 1966, Congress passed legislation terminating federal recognition and services to 109 Native American nations and bands. Some of them disappeared as organized communities. Their members moved to other places, particularly cities, where the BIA, through its "relocation" program, was busily shuttling Native Americans from reservations to cities. Some of the children of relocation would return to haunt the BIA as members of the self-determination generation of the 1960s and 1970s—a crisp contradiction of the belief that the hand of BIA paternalism would stir the last of Indian identity into the vast American urban melting pot.

Political momentum toward termination was accelerating as Dwight Eisenhower assumed the presidency in 1952. Eisenhower appointed Glenn L. Emmons, a supporter of Watkins's termination legislation, as commissioner of Indian affairs. Between 1953 and 1962, Congress passed legislation terminating federal recognition and services to 60 native nations and tribes.

Congress sometimes held up land claims payments until the Native tribe or nation in question also agreed to termination proceedings, thereby obliterating both past and present land bases. In 1963, for example, the Claims Commission awarded the Kalispels $3 million, an award that was held by Congress (under legislation passed at the behest of Idaho Senator Frank Church) until they agreed to termination. Sometimes, the pitch was different, but no less subtle. The Klamaths, holding title to a million acres of prime timber in Oregon, were enticed into terminating after BIA agents promised them per capita payments of $50,000. Only afterward did the Klamaths learn painfully that "going private" can be expensive. They found themselves paying rent, utilities, health care costs, and taxes they had never faced.

The Menominees of Wisconsin shared ownership of property valued at $34 million when their termination bill was enacted in 1953. By 1961, the federal government was out of Menominee Country, and each member of the former tribe had become the owner of 100 shares of stock and a negotiable bond valued at $3,000, issued in the name of Menominee Enterprises Incorporated (MEI), a private company that held the former tribe's land and businesses. Governmentally, the Menominee Nation had become Menominee County, the smallest (in terms of population) and poorest (in terms of cash income) in Wisconsin.

As a county, Menominee had to raise taxes to pay for its share of services, including welfare, health services, utilities, and the like. The only taxable property owner in the county was MEI, which was forced to raise the funds to pay its tax bill by restructuring so that stockholders had to buy their homes and the property on which they had been built. Most of the Menominees had little savings except for their $3,000 bonds, which were then sold to MEI to make the required residential purchases. Many Menominees faced private sector health costs, property taxes, and other expenses with no more money than they had possessed before termination. Unemployment rose to levels that most of the United States had known only during the Depression of the 1930s. By 1965, health indicators in Menominee County sounded like a reprint of the Meriam Report almost four decades earlier. Tuberculosis afflicted nearly 35 percent of the population, and infant mortality was three times the national average. Termination, like allotment, had been an abject failure at anything other than alienating Indian land.

One of the major opponents of relocation (and other assimilationist policies) was Felix Cohen (1907–1953), the author of *The Handbook of Indian Law* (1942), a basic reference book of the field for decades. He also was a student of Native American societies and a social critic, as well as a defender of Native

American estate as associate solicitor in the Interior Department. Cohen was a professor of law at the City University of New York and Yale.

Many of termination's opponents were Native American traditionalists, who believed that distinct cultures and land bases should be maintained. During the renaissance of native activism in the 1960s, they were joined in this effort by the young, urbanized children of an earlier generation that had made its own long marches, one by one or family by family, from their home-lands to the cities at the behest of the BIA. Between 1953 and 1972, more than 100,000 Native Americans moved to urban areas; by 1980, about half of the Native Americans in the United States lived in cities. Young Native Americans raised in urban areas in the 1960s began to reverse relocation's effects. By the 1970s, many young urban Indians, often veterans of the Vietnam War who had served terms in state and federal prisons, were returning to the reserva-tions.

FURTHER READING

Adams et al. v. Osage Tribe of Indians et al. No. 642 District Court N. D. Oklahoma 50 F. 2d 918, 1931 U.S. Dist.

Archuleta, Margaret L., Brenda J. Child, and K. Tsianina Lomawaima, eds. *Away from Home: American Indian Boarding School Experiences, 1879–2000.* Phoenix: Heard Museum, 2000.

Associated Press. *Omaha World-Herald*, December 9, 1991, 16.

Associated Press Canada. Canada's United Church Apologizes for Abuse at Indian Schools. October 28, 1998.

Barsh, Russel, and James Henderson. *The Road: Indian Tribes and Political Liberty.* Berkeley: University of California Press, 1980.

Bourrie, Mark. Canada Apologizes For Abuse of Native Peoples. Interpress Service, January 8, 1998. Available at http://www.oneworld.org/ips2/jan98/canada2.html.

British Columbia Anglican Diocese Set To Close over Lawsuit. Canadian Broadcasting Corporation News On-line, December 30, 2001. Available at http://cbc.ca/cgi-bin/view?/news/2001/12/30/anglican_011230.

Cohen, Felix. *The Handbook of Indian Law.* Washington, DC: U.S. Government Printing Office, 1942.

Cohen, Felix. *The Legal Conscience: The Selected Papers of Felix S. Cohen.* Edited by Lucy Kramer Cohen. New Haven, CT: Yale University Press, 1960.

Coulter, Robert T., and Steven M. Tullberg. Indian Land Rights, In Sandra L. Cad-wallader and Vine Deloria, Jr., eds., *The Aggressions of Civilization.* Philadelphia: Temple University Press, 1984: 185–214.

Deloria, Vine, Jr., and Clifford Lytle. *American Indians, American Justice.* Austin: University of Texas Press, 1983.

Deskaheh (Levi General) and Six Nations Council. *The Redman's Appeal for Justice.* Brantford, Ontario, Canada: Wilson Moore, 1924.

Driver, Harold E. *Indians of North America.* 2nd ed. Chicago: University of Chicago Press, 1969.

Elk v. Wilkins. 112 U.S. 94 (1884).

Fadden, Ray, and John Kahionhes Fadden. *Deskaheh: Iroquois Statesman and Patriot.* Six Nations Indian Museum Series. Akwesasne, NY: Akwesasne Notes, n.d.

Havighurst, Robert J., and Thea R. Hilkevitch. The Intelligence of Indian Children as Measured by a Performance Scale. *Journal of Abnormal and Social Psychology* 39(1944):419–433.

Hendrix, Janey B. Redbird Smith and the Nighthawk Keetoowahs. *Journal of Cherokee Studies* 8:1(1983):17–33.

Hipwell, Bill. Apology Should Have Been a Thank You. *The Financial Post* [Ottawa, Ontario], February 3, 1998, 18.

Jackson, Helen Hunt. *A Century of Dishonor: A Sketch of the United States Government's Dealings with Some of the Indian Tribes.* New York: Harper and Brothers, 1881.

Jackson, Helen Hunt. *Ramona.* Boston: Roberts Brothers, 1884.

Johansen, Bruce E. The BIA as Banker: Trust Is Hard when Billions Disappear. *Native Americas* 14:1(Spring 1997):14–23.

Johansen, Bruce E. *The Encyclopedia of Native American Legal Tradition.* Westport, CT: Greenwood Press, 1998.

Johansen, Bruce E. "Education—The Nightmare and the Dream: A Shared National Tragedy, a Shared National Disgrace." *Native Americas* 17:4(Winter 2000):10–19.

Johansen, Bruce E., and Donald A. Grinde, Jr. *The Encyclopedia of Native American Biography.* New York: Henry Holt, 1997.

Josephy, Alvin M., Jr. Modern America and the Indian. In Frederick E. Hoxie, ed., *Indians in American History: An Introduction.* Arlington Heights, IL: Harlan Davidson, 1988: 251–272.

Kelly, Lawrence C. The Indian Reorganization Act: The Dream and the Reality. *Pacific Historical Quarterly* 64(August 1975):291–312.

Kelly, Lawrence C. *The Assault on Assimilation: John Collier and the Origins of the Indian Reorganization Act.* Tucson: University of Arizona Press, 1983.

Levitan, Sar A. *Big Brother's Indian Programs—with Reservations.* New York: McGraw-Hill, 1971.

Lowey, Mark. Alberta Natives Sue Over Residential Schools. *Calgary Herald,* January 3, 1999, A-1.

Mails, Thomas E. *Fools Crow.* Lincoln: University of Nebraska Press, 1990.

McKay v. Campbell. 16 Fed. Cas. 161 (1871) (No. 8840).

McIlroy, Anne. Canadians Apologize for Abuse. *Manchester Guardian Weekly,* November 8, 1998, 5.

McLaughlin, Michael R. The Dawes Act, or Indian General Allotment Act of 1887: The Continuing Burden of Allotment. *American Indian Culture and Research Journal* 20:2(1996):59–105.

McNickle, D'Arcy. *They Came Here First: The Epic of the American Indian.* New York: Harper Perennial Library, 1975.

Meriam, Lewis. *The Problem of Indian Administration.* Baltimore: John Hopkins University Press, 1928.

Morgan, Lewis Henry. *League of the Iroquois.* Seacaucus, NJ: Citadel Press, [1851] 1962.

Morgan, Lewis Henry. *Houses and House-Life of the American Aborigines.* Edited by Paul Bohannon. Chicago: University of Chicago Press, 1965.

Morris, Roy, Jr. *Sheridan: The Life and Wars of General Phil Sheridan*. New York: Crown, 1992.

National Resources Board, Land Planning Committee. *Indian Land Tenure, Economic Status, and Population Trends*. Washington, DC: Government Printing Office, 1935.

O'Brien, Sharon. *American Indian Tribal Governments*. Norman: University of Oklahoma Press, 1989.

Olson, James S., and Raymond Wilson. *Native Americans in the Twentieth Century*. Urbana: University of Illinois Press, 1984.

Orwell, George. *1984*. London: Secker & Warburg, 1949.

Otis, Joseph E. *The Indian Problem: Resolution of the Committee of One Hundred Appointed by the Secretary of the Interior and a Review of the Indian Problem*. Washington, DC: U.S. Government Printing Office, 1924.

Parman, Donald L. *The Navajos and the New Deal*. New Haven, CT: Yale University Press, 1976.

Philip, Kenneth R. *John Collier's Crusade for Indian Reform, 1920–1954*. Tucson: University of Arizona Press, 1977.

Porter, Joy. *To Be Indian: The Life of Iroquois-Seneca Arthur Caswell Parker*. Norman: University of Oklahoma Press, 2001.

Pratt, William Henry. *Battlefield and Classroom: Four Decades with the American Indian, 1867–1904*. Edited by Robert M. Utley. Lincoln: University of Nebraska Press, [1964] 1987.

Prucha, Francis P. *Documents of United States Indian Policy*. Lincoln: University of Nebraska Press, 1975.

Resek, Carl. *Lewis Henry Morgan: American Scholar*. Chicago: University of Chicago Press, 1960.

Rostkowski, Joelle. The Redman's Appeal for Justice: Deskaheh and the League of Nations. In Christian F. Feest, ed., *Indians and Europe*. Aachen, Germany: Edition Herodot, 1987.

Royal Commission on Aboriginal Peoples. Vol. 1, chapter 10, 1996. Available at http://www.prsp.bc.ca/vol1ch10_files/Vol1%20Ch10.rtf. Accessed February 25, 2003.

Russell, Don. *The Lives and Legends of Buffalo Bill*. Norman: University of Oklahoma Press, 1960.

Sell, Henry B., and Victor Weybright. *Buffalo Bill and the Wild West*. New York: Oxford University Press, 1955.

Snake, Reuben. Personal interview with Bruce E. Johansen, in Seattle, WA, October 12, 1991.

Standing Bear, Luther. *My Indian Boyhood*. Lincoln: University of Nebraska Press, [1931] 1988.

Stannard, David. *American Holocaust: Columbus and the Conquest of the New World*. New York: Oxford University Press, 1992.

Thorpe, James, and Thomas F. Collinson. *Jim Thorpe's History of the Olympics*. Los Angeles, 1932.

Todd, Douglas. Natives' Abuse Suits Creating a Dilemma. *Vancouver Sun*, December 15, 1998, A-1.

Turtle Island Native Network. British Columbia Residential School Project. No date. Available at http://www.turtleisland.org/healing/infopack1a.htm.

United States v. Stanolind Crude Oil Purchasing Company; United States v. Gulf Oil Corporation; United States v. Sinclair Prairie Oil Company. 113 F. 2d 194 (10th Cir. 1940).

Waldman, Carl. *Who Was Who in Native American History.* New York: Facts on File, 1990.

Washburn, Wilcomb. *The Assault on Indian Tribalism: The General Allotment Law (Dawes Act) of 1887.* Philadelphia: J. B. Lippincott, 1975.

Weeks, Philip. *Farewell My Nation: The American Indian and the United States, 1820–1890.* Arlington Heights, IL: Harlan Davidson, 1990.

Wilkinson, Charles F. *American Indians, Time, and the Law: Native Societies in a Modern Constitutional Democracy.* New Haven, CT: Yale University Press, 1987.

Wilson, Terry P. *The Underground Reservation: Osage Oil.* Lincoln: University of Nebraska Press, 1985.

Worcester v. Georgia. 31 U.S. (6 Pet.) 515 (1832).

CHAPTER 9

A People's Revival—1961 to 1990

NATIVE SELF-DETERMINATION

In 1961, Native American voices of protest were raised at the American Indian Chicago Conference, which brought together more than 500 Native people from more than sixty groups. This conference was the opening salvo for a decade-plus wave of Native activism that would change the legal, social, and economic face of Native America. It was organized at the behest of President John F. Kennedy by Sol Tax, professor of anthropology at the University of Chicago, as a forum to enable Native peoples to express their views regarding their own futures. This gathering helped to ignite a social and political movement among many Native Americans that had an influence on later, better-known events. Also during 1961, a group of young, college-educated American Indians formed the National Indian Youth Council (NIYC). This organization had deep roots in impoverished, traditional Indian communities.

By 1964, the first modern civil disobedience by Native Americans was taking place on Puget Sound salmon streams as Indian "fish-ins" dramatized Native assertion of treaty rights to harvest fish that state authorities had long ignored. At roughly the same time, Native American militant organizations also were springing up in other cities as well. In 1968, the American Indian Movement (AIM) was formed in Minneapolis to resist selective law enforcement policies (and brutality toward American Indians) on the part of the Minneapolis police. Initially, an "Indian patrol" was established to follow police in Native American neighborhoods. Arrest rates of Native Americans declined to the general average in the city within nine months after the AIM patrols were introduced.

American Indian activism and nationalism was transformed by the occupation of the former Federal Penitentiary at Alcatraz Island by about 300 Native Americans and supporters on November 9, 1969. They were requesting title to the island under a federal law that gave Indians first refusal on federal "surplus" property. Activists executed a march across the United States during 1972 to protest broken treaties; this was followed, during the last week of the 1972 election, by an occupation of the Bureau of Indian Affairs (BIA) headquarters in Washington, D.C., followed by the occupation of Wounded Knee (1973).

Following the Wounded Knee occupation, more than sixty AIM members and supporters were killed on and near the Pine Ridge Reservation in South Dakota. Two Federal Bureau of Investigation (FBI) agents also lost their lives in the tense aftermath of Wounded Knee at Pine Ridge, deaths for which Leonard Peltier was convicted on what his defenders to this day contend was falsified evidence.

Copious media attention provided a national platform for discussion of American Indian issues relating to self-determination during this wave of activism. On December 16, 1969, the occupants of Alcatraz said the following:

> We are issuing this call in an attempt to unify our Indian brothers behind a common cause.... We are not getting anywhere fast by working alone as individual tribes. If we can get together as brothers and come to a common agreement, we feel that we can be much more effective, doing things for ourselves, instead of having someone else doing it, telling us what is good for us. So we must start somewhere. We feel that we are going to succeed, we must hold on to the old ways. This is the first and most important reason we went to Alcatraz Island. (Johansen, 1998, 13)

The occupants departed Alcatraz during 1971 without achieving their expressed goals of gaining title to the island and building an American Indian culture center there. The occupation did focus attention, as no one had done before, on the issues of American Indian identity, self-determination, and tribal lands.

Militant activities became more frequent in the early 1970s. During the spring of 1972, AIM leaders openly castigated the Chippewa tribal councils for allowing non-Indians to exploit reservation resources (especially fishing rights). For a few days at the Cass Lake Convention Center (Minnesota), AIM leaders blocked traffic and demanded that the tribal leadership reassert treaty fishing rights (the non-Indians, afraid of AIM's tactics, reluctantly accepted tribal control of resources as a result of this confrontation). At the same time, AIM led 1,000 American Indian people into Gordon, Nebraska, to protest the murder of Raymond Yellow Thunder by five European Americans. Protests over the death of Richard Oakes (a leader of the Alcatraz occupation) at the hands of a prison guard in California also flared up in 1972.

During the summer of 1972, Hank Adams (a leader of fish-ins in Washington) and Dennis Banks, a founder of AIM, met in Denver to plan a Trail of Broken Treaties caravan. Dennis Banks (Chippewa), who was born on the Leech Lake Reservation in northern Minnesota during 1932, became familiar to television news viewers along with Russell Means as the two most easily recognizable leaders of AIM.

Participants in the Trail of Broken Treaties aimed to marshal thousands of protesters across the United States to march on Washington, D.C., to dramatize issues related to American Indian self-determination. In Minneapolis, the group issued its Twenty Points, a document that sought to revive tribal sovereignty completely. Summarized, the Twenty Points advocated the following:

1. Repeal of the 1871 federal statute that ended treaty-making;
2. Restoration of treaty making status to native nations;
3. Establishment of a commission to review past treaty violations;
4. Resubmission of unratified treaties to the Senate;
5. That all Native Americans be governed by treaty relations;
6. Elimination all state jurisdiction over American Indian affairs. (Deloria, 1974a, 48–52)

Armed with their demands, the Trail of Broken Treaties caravan moved on to Washington, D.C. On their arrival on November 3, 1972, within days of a national election, the protesters learned that there was not enough lodging, so they elected to stay in the BIA building for several hours until security guards sought to forcibly remove them. At that point, events turned violent. The protesters seized the building for six days as they asserted their demands that Native sovereignty be restored and immunity be granted to all protesters. Files were seized, and damage was done to the BIA building (AIM leaders asserted that federal agents had infiltrated the movement and had done most of the damage). On November 8, 1972, federal officials offered immunity and transportation home to the protesters. The offer was accepted, and the crisis was resolved for the moment.

AMERICAN INDIAN MOVEMENT AT PINE RIDGE: THE OCCUPATION OF WOUNDED KNEE

Local issues at Pine Ridge laid the basis for the national attention given AIM as it occupied the small village of Wounded Knee early in 1973. Many traditional people on the Pine Ridge Reservation had rallied around AIM. Some people detested the brutality of the tribal police; others wanted help in settling fractionalized heirship problems that inhibited ranching and agriculture on the reservation.

The tiny hamlet of Wounded Knee, South Dakota, on the Pine Ridge Indian Reservation, the site at which more than 200 Sioux and others were massacred in 1890, became a symbolic site again as members of AIM were quickly surrounded by armored troops.

The seventy-one-day occupation of Wounded Knee began February 28, 1973. In early March, George McGovern and James Abourezk, U.S. senators from South Dakota, met with AIM leaders and the federal authorities to calm tempers. On March 11, 1973, AIM members declared their independence as the Oglala Sioux Nation, defining its boundaries according to the Treaty of Fort Laramie (1868). At one point, federal officials considered an armed attack on the camp at Wounded Knee, but the plan was ultimately discarded. Dennis Banks and Russell Means, AIM's best-known leaders, stated that they would hold out until the Senate Foreign Relations Committee had reviewed all broken treaties and the corruption of the BIA had been exposed to the world. After much gunfire and negotiation, AIM's occupation of Wounded Knee ended on May 7, 1973.

The occupation of Wounded Knee by Native American activists had a profound impact on non-Indians because news of the conflict was spread worldwide through the media. The occupation had a major effect on American culture: A book by Dee Brown, titled *Bury My Heart at Wounded Knee*, became an international best-seller. At the 1973 Academy Awards, held as Wounded Knee was being occupied, Marlon Brando, via his spokesperson Sacheen Littlefeather, refused to accept an Oscar to protest the treatment of American Indians.

Pine Ridge tribal police supported tribal chairman Richard Wilson (Oglala Lakota, 1936–1990). From the early 1970s until his defeat for the chairman's office by Al Trimble in 1976, Wilson outfitted a tribal police force that was often called the goon squad. This police force, which took goon to mean guardians of the Oglala Nation, was financed with money from the federal government. The local context of the occupation included an effort to confront Wilson's policies publicly, which often favored non-Indian ranchers, farmers, and corporations.

The struggle between AIM and Wilson also was taking place within the realm of tribal politics. When Wilson sought reelection in 1974, Russell Means, an Oglala who had helped found AIM, challenged him. In the primary, Wilson trailed Means, 667 votes to 511. Wilson won the final election over Means by fewer than 200 votes in balloting that the U.S. Commission on Civil Rights later found was permeated with fraud. The Civil Rights Commission recommended a new election, which was not held; Wilson answered his detractors by stepping up the terror, examples of which were described in a chronology kept by the Wounded Knee Legal Defense-Offense Committee. One of the goons' favorite weapons was the automobile. Officially, such deaths could be reported as traffic accidents.

Wilson had a formidable array of supporters on the reservation, and many criticized AIM for being urban based and insensitive to reservation residents' needs. Mona Wilson, one of Wilson's daughters, who was 17 years of age when Wounded Knee was occupied, recalled seeing him crying in his mother's arms at the time. Recalling the events two decades later, Wilson's wife, Yvonne, and two daughters recalled him as a kind and compassionate father who had the interests of his people at heart. They said that Wilson supported AIM when it protested the 1972 murder of Raymond Yellow Thunder in the reservation border town of Gordon, Nebraska. Only later, as events culminated in the siege of Wounded Knee, did Wilson and AIM leaders become deadly enemies.

Wilson was the first Oglala Lakota tribal chairman to serve two consecutive terms. He worked as a self-employed plumber, owner of a gas station, and on other short-term projects after his defeat by Trimble for the tribal chairmanship in 1976. Wilson's family recalled that he also had a traditional side. He was a pipe carrier, as well as a practicing Episcopalian. Wilson was known for feeding anyone who came to his door, and he had a major role in beginning a Lakota community college on the reservation, as well as a number of other tribal enterprises. Wilson died of a heart attack in 1990 as he was preparing to run for a third term as tribal chairman.

Following the occupation of Wounded Knee, Banks and Means were charged with three counts of assault on federal officers, one charge each of conspiracy, and one each of larceny. Banks and Means, facing five charges each, could have been sentenced to as many as eighty-five years in prison. For several months in 1974, a year after the occupation of Wounded Knee, the defense and prosecution presented their cases in a St. Paul, Minnesota, federal court. On September 16, Judge Fred J. Nichol dismissed all the charges. The judge said that the FBI's agents had lied repeatedly during the trial while under oath and had often furnished defense attorneys with altered documents. Judge Nichol said that R. D. Hurd, the federal prosecutor, had deliberately deceived the court. "The FBI," said Judge Nichol, "has stooped to a new low." To the chagrin of the judge and jurors, the Justice Department responded by presenting Hurd with an award for "superior performance" during the trial (Johansen and Maestas, 1979, 91).

THE FEDERAL BUREAU OF INVESTIGATION'S PURSUIT OF LEONARD PELTIER

An activist in the American Indian Movement during the 1973 confrontation at Wounded Knee, Leonard Peltier (Anishinabe, born 1944) was caught in a shootout with FBI agents and state police at the Jumping Bull Compound on the Pine Ridge Indian Reservation during June 1975. He was later convicted of killing two FBI agents, Jack Williams and Ronald Coler. The trial, which was held in Fargo, North Dakota, Federal District Court in 1977, has since become the focus of an international protest movement aimed at obtaining a retrial.

Before Peltier's trial opened in March 1977, the prosecution's case began to fall apart. Discovery proceedings produced an affidavit, signed by government witness Myrtle Poor Bear, dated February 19, 1976 (before two others known to the defense, dated February 23 and March 31), which said that the woman had not been on the scene of the June 25, 1975, gun battle in which the two FBI agents had been shot to death. This information, contained in an affidavit that had not been sent to Canada by the U.S. government during Peltier's extradition hearing, contradicted the other two statements attributed to Poor Bear.

Leonard Peltier. (Courtesy of the University of Washington *Daily*.)

More importantly, Poor Bear herself recanted. On April 13, out of earshot of the jury, Poor Bear told the court (having been called by the defense) that she had never seen Peltier before meeting him at the trial. Furthermore, Poor Bear said that she had not been allowed to read the three affidavits that bore her name and implicated Peltier in the murders, and that FBI agents David Price and Bill Wood had threatened physical harm to herself and her children if she did not sign them.

Judge Paul Benson refused to let the jury hear Poor Bear's testimony, ruling it "irrelevant" to the case. The next day, the judge changed his mind and ruled the testimony relevant but still would not let the jury hear it. He ruled this time that Poor Bear's testimony was prejudicial to the government's case and, if believed, could confuse the jury.

Prosecution testimony, which occupied the first five weeks of the trial, ranged far afield from what happened on the day of the shootings. The prosecution was allowed to bring up extraneous charges against Peltier on which he had not been tried, and testimony that ran counter to the federal rules of evidence. The defense's planned two weeks of testimony was reduced to two-and-a-half days by Judge Benson, who limited defense testimony to events directly connected with the shootings themselves.

The only evidence that directly linked Peltier to the killings of Coler and Williams (other than that fabricated in Poor Bear's name) came from Frederick Coward, an FBI agent, who said he had recognized Peltier from half a mile away through a seven-power rifle sight. The defense team replicated the sighting and found that the feat was impossible through such a sight at such a distance, even for a person with excellent vision. In court, defense attorneys offered to duplicate their experience for the jury so that its members could judge for themselves the veracity of the FBI agent's statement. Judge Benson refused the request. "Finally," said Bruce Ellison, a member of the defense team, "we brought in someone from a gun shop, who said that an idiot could tell you that it is impossible to recognize someone, even someone you know, from a half-mile away through a seven-power sight" (Johansen and Maestas, 1979, 114).

Three Native juveniles also testified that they had seen Peltier at the scene. Each of them also testified, under cross-examination, that their testimony had been coerced by the FBI. One of them, Mike Anderson, testified that he had been threatened with beating. Another, Wish Draper, said that he had been tied and handcuffed to a chair for three hours to elicit his statement. The third, Norman Brown, swore that he was told that if he did not cooperate he "would never walk the Earth again" (Johansen and Maestas, 1979, 115).

The prosecution, its eyewitness testimony in dispute, linked Peltier to the use of an AR-15, a semiautomatic rifle, which was not introduced as evidence because it had been blown apart during a Kansas freeway explosion on September 10, 1975. The prosecution also asserted that Peltier's thumbprint had been found on a bag containing a gun belonging to one of the dead agents. The bag and the gun were found on November 14, 1975, after the two men police described as Peltier and Dennis Banks had escaped their dragnet near Ontario, Oregon.

Following his conviction, Peltier became the object of a growing popular movement demanding a new trial. Peltier's request for a new trial was rejected by a U.S. Circuit Court (in St. Louis) during 1978; his appeal also was declined by the U.S. Supreme Court in 1978 and 1986. In the meantime, Peltier's support spread to the Soviet Union and Europe. In the Soviet Union, by 1986 an estimated 17 million people had signed petitions in his support. Peter Matthiessen's *In the Spirit of Crazy Horse* was readied for publication in the early 1980s and made a case for Peltier's innocence. The publisher, Viking, withdrew the book after former South Dakota Governor William Janklow threatened to sue for libel over passages in the book that linked him to the rape of a young Native American woman. Bootlegged copies of the book began to circulate, and it was published in 1991 after Janklow's case was dismissed by the South Dakota Supreme Court. *In the Spirit of Crazy Horse* presents, in an epilogue appended after the book had been suppressed for eight years, a case that Peltier was not the murderer of the two FBI agents. In an interview, a Native man known only as X confesses to the murders. In the meantime, the FBI had withheld from the public 6,000 pages of documents on the case for reasons the agency associated with national security.

Dennis Banks had eluded capture during the FBI dragnet that followed the shooting deaths of two agents at Pine Ridge for which Peltier was convicted. Banks went underground before receiving amnesty from Jerry Brown, governor of California. Banks earned an associate of arts degree at the University of California (Davis campus) and during the late 1970s helped found and direct Deganawidah-Quetzecoatl University, a Native-controlled college. After Jerry Brown's term as California governor ended, Banks in 1984 was sheltered by the Onondagas on their reservation near Syracuse, New York.

In 1984, Banks surrendered to face charges stemming from the 1970s in South Dakota. He later served 18 months in prison, after which he worked as a drug and alcohol counselor on the Pine Ridge Reservation. During the late 1980s, Banks's energies were concentrated on measures to protect Native American graves and human remains. He organized a campaign in Kentucky, where he lived as a single parent; the campaign resulted in statewide legal protections after robbers desecrated Native graves in Uniontown. Banks also organized several more ceremonial runs in the United States and Japan. His autobiography, *Sacred Soul*, was published in Japan during 1988.

Banks remained active in Native American politics throughout the 1990s, although he was not as often in the national spotlight. He had acting roles in several films, including *War Party*, *The Last of the Mohicans*, and *Thunderheart*. During the first half of 1994, Banks helped organize a five-month Walk for Justice across the United States on behalf of Peltier. About 400 people took part in the march, and 28 walked the entire 3,000 miles. The Walk for Justice ended in Washington, D.C., July 15 at a rally calling on President Bill Clinton to pardon Peltier. Clinton refused repeated pardon appeals throughout his presidency.

During the 1980s and 1990s, Peltier's appeals for a new trial were denied several times by U.S. federal courts. He was serving two life terms at Marion Federal Penitentiary, Illinois, and at Leavenworth Federal Penitentiary in Kansas, developing his talents as an artist, creating posters, paintings, and designs for a line of greeting cards that were sold nationwide. Peltier's case also became the focus of the feature film *Thunderheart* and a documentary, *Incident at Oglala*.

Peltier's case came to the attention of Amnesty International and the government of Canada, from which Peltier was extradited to face trial on the basis of the Poor Bear affidavits. Peltier's appeals were directed by several well-known legal personalities, including former U.S. Attorney General Ramsey Clark and attorney William Kunstler. His third appeal for a new trial was turned down by the Eighth Circuit Court of Appeals (St. Paul, MN) in 1993, exhausting his remedies within the U.S. court system.

THE DEATH OF ANNA MAE AQUASH (MICMAC), 1945–1976

Anna Mae Aquash (MicMac, 1945–1976) was one of the most note-worthy of more than sixty people who were killed for political reasons on the Pine Ridge Reservation during the three years following the Wounded Knee occupation. Aquash, from Nova Scotia, Canada, became involved in AIM during its peak of activity shortly after 1970; she was a close friend of Peltier, Banks, Means, and others who were arrested and charged in connection with the Wounded Knee occupation in 1973 and other events. Following the shooting deaths of FBI agents Ronald Coler and Jack Williams at the Jumping Bull Compound on the Pine Ridge Indian Reservation in June 1975, Aquash was pursued and arrested by the FBI as a possible material witness to the crime.

On February 24, 1976, Roger Amiott, a rancher, found Aquash's body near Wanblee, in the northeastern section of the Pine Ridge Indian Reservation. Dr. W. O. Brown, a pathologist who performed autopsies under contract with the BIA, arrived the following day. After examining the body, Brown announced that the woman, who still had not been officially identified, had died of exposure to the brutal South Dakota winter.

The FBI decided that the only way to identify the woman was to sever her hands and send them to the FBI's crime laboratories in the Washington, D.C., area. Agents on the scene reasoned that the body was too badly decomposed to take fingerprints at Pine Ridge. Ken Sayres, BIA police chief at Pine Ridge, would say later that no one had been called to the morgue to attempt identification of the body before the hands were severed.

A week after the body was found, Aquash—now missing her hands as well as her identity—was buried at Holy Rosary Catholic Cemetery, Pine Ridge. On March 3, the FBI announced Aquash's identity.

Aquash's family was notified of the death March 5. They did not believe that she had died of natural causes. At 32 years of age, Aquash had been in good health and was trained to survive in cold weather. She did not drink alcohol or smoke tobacco. Her friends remembered that she had smuggled food past federal government roadblocks into Wounded Knee during another brutal South Dakota winter, almost three years to the day before her body had been found. A new autopsy was demanded.

In the midst of the controversy, Aquash's body was exhumed. Her family retained an independent pathologist, Dr. Gary Peterson, of St. Paul, Minnesota. Dr. Peterson reopened the skull and found a .32-caliber bullet, which he said had been fired from a gun placed at the base of Aquash's neck. The bullet was not difficult to find: "It should have been discovered the first time,"

Peterson said (Johansen and Maestas, 1979, 106). Asked about the bullet he had not found, Dr. W. O. Brown, the BIA coroner, replied, according to an account in the Washington *Star* May 24, 1976, "A little bullet isn't hard to overlook" (ibid., 106).

Following identification of Aquash's decomposed body, the Canadian government and the U.S. Commission on Civil Rights demanded an investigation. The U.S. Justice Department announced that it would look into the case, but the "investigation" languished in bureaucratic limbo. Aquash's friends refused to let her spirit pass away. On March 14, Aquash's body was wrapped in a traditional star quilt as several women from Oglala Village mourned her passing for two days and two nights.

Twenty-seven years after Aquash's murder, federal agents on April 2, 2003, arrested a man and charged him with the death. Arlo Looking Cloud, 49, was arrested in Denver and pleaded innocent to a charge of first-degree murder. Looking Cloud worked as a security guard for AIM, checking people at the gates of events and patrolling the grounds, said Paul DeMain, editor of the bimonthly newspaper *News from Indian Country*. AIM was beset by internal disputes (and was infiltrated by FBI informers) at the time, DeMain said (Walker, 2003). On February 6, 2004, Looking Cloud was convicted of the murder.

BATTLES OVER FISHING RIGHTS IN WASHINGTON STATE

One of the most notable Native rights issues beginning during the 1960s was the right to fish in Pacific Northwest waters in accordance with treaties signed during the 1850s—a right that had been routinely denied by state authorities to that time.

To the Northwest Indian nations, the salmon was as central to economic life as the buffalo on the plains; 80 to 90 percent of the traditional Puyallup diet, for example, was fish. The salmon was more than food; it was the center of a way of life. A cultural festival accompanied the first salmon caught in the yearly run. The fish was barbecued over an open fire and bits of its flesh parceled out to all. The bones were saved intact, to be carried by a torch-bearing, singing, dancing, and chanting procession back to the river, where they were placed into the water, the head pointed upstream, symbolic of the spawning fish, so the run would return in later years.

Washington became a territory of the United States on March 2, 1853, with no consent from the Indians who occupied most of the land. Isaac Stevens was appointed governor and superintendent of Indian affairs for the territory. As governor, Stevens wished to build the economic base of the territory; this required the attraction of a proposed transcontinental railroad, which in turn required peace with the Indians. Stevens worked with remarkable speed; in 1854 and 1855 alone, he negotiated five treaties with 6,000 Indian people

Indians fishing for salmon at Celilo Falls, Oregon.
(Courtesy of the Library of Congress.)

west of the Cascades. By signing the treaties, the Indians ceded to the United States 2,240,000 acres of land, an immense sacrifice for the right to fish.

In 1914, about 16 million fish were caught annually; by the 1920s, annual catches had declined to an average of 6 million. In the late 1930s, following construction of several large hydroelectric dams on the Columbia River and its tributaries, the annual catch had fallen as low as 3 million, about one-sixth of what Native peoples alone had been harvesting a century earlier. By the 1970s, with more aggressive conservation measures in place, including construction of fish ladders at most major dams, the annual catch rose to 4 to 6 million, just short of a third of the precontact harvest.

Native American peoples who had signed the Medicine Creek Treaty and others were having a more difficult time harvesting enough fish to survive. By the early 1960s, state fisheries police were conducting wholesale arrests of Indians, confiscating their boats and nets. Denied justice in the state courts, the tribes pursued their claim at the federal level. During the 1960s and early 1970s, they also militantly protected their rights in the face of raids by state fisheries authorities. A nucleus of fishing rights activists from Franks Landing, living only a few miles from the site at which the Medicine Creek Treaty had

Spearing salmon. (Courtesy of the Library of Congress.)

been signed, continued to fish on the basis of the treaty, which gave them the right to fish as long as the rivers run.

The fish-ins continued for years, attracting multiethnic support from many places including, most notably, El Centro de la Raza of Seattle. Celebrities, including Marlon Brando, made a point of stopping by to pull a few nets. On February 12, 1974, U.S. District Court Judge George Boldt ruled that Indians were entitled to an opportunity to catch as many as half the fish returning to off-reservation sites that had been the "usual and accustomed places" when the treaties were signed. Boldt had put three years into the case; he used 200 pages to interpret one sentence of the treaty in an opinion that some legal scholars say is the most carefully researched and thoroughly analyzed ever handed down in an Indian fishing rights case. The nucleus of Boldt's decision had to do with nineteenth century dictionaries' definitions of "in common with." Boldt said the words meant to be shared equally. During the next three years, the Ninth Circuit Court of Appeals upheld Boldt's ruling, and the U.S. Supreme Court twice let it stand by refusing to hear an appeal by the state of Washington.

State officials and the fishermen whose interests they represented were furious at Boldt. Rumors circulated about the sanity of the 75-year-old judge. It was said that he had taken bribes of free fish and had an Indian mistress, neither of which was true. Judge Boldt was hung in effigy by angry non-Indian fishermen, who on other occasions formed "convoys" with their boats and rammed Coast Guard vessels that had been dispatched to enforce the court's orders. At least one with the Coast Guard was shot.

Among state officials during the middle and late 1970s, a backlash to Indian rights formed, which would become the nucleus for a nationwide non-Indian campaign to abrogate the treaties. Washington State Attorney General (later U.S. Senator) Slade Gorton called Indians supercitizens with special rights and proposed that constitutional equilibrium be reestablished not by open state violation of the treaties (Boldt had outlawed that) but by purchasing the Indians' fishing rights and abrogating the treaties on which they were based. The tribes, which had been listening to offers of money for Indian resources for a century, flatly refused Gorton's offer. To them, the selling of fishing rights would have been tantamount to termination.

FISHING RIGHTS IN EASTERN WASHINGTON

The 1974 Boldt decision restored recognition of treaty rights regarding salmon fishing west of the Cascades. East of the Cascades, during the 1980s, the fishing rights battle continued in a form that reminded many people of the Frank's Landing fish-ins of the 1960s. Many Native people along the Columbia River and its tributaries also fished for a livelihood long before European Americans migrated to their land, but they had no treaties protecting their right to do so. For years, David Sohappy (Wanapam, 1925–1991), his wife Myra, and their sons erected a riverbank shelter and fished in the traditional manner.

The Sohappys' name came from the Wanapam word *souiehappie*, meaning shoving something under a ledge. David Sohappy's ancestors had traded salmon with members of the Lewis and Clark expedition. The Wanapams never signed a treaty, wishing only to be left in peace to live as they had for hundreds, if not thousands, of years. By the early 1940s, Sohappy's family was pushed off its ancestral homeland at Priest Rapids and White Bluffs, which became part of the Hanford Nuclear Reservation. Hanford was located in the middle of a desert that Lewis and Clark characterized as the most barren piece of land that they saw between St. Louis and the Pacific Ocean. Still, David Sohappy fished, even as his father, Jim Sohappy, warned him that if he continued to live in the old ways, "The white man is going to put you in jail someday" (Johansen and Grinde, 1997, 363).

During the 1950s, development devastated the Celilo Falls, once one of the richest Indian fishing grounds in North America. Most of the people who had fished there gave up their traditional livelihood and moved to the nearby Yakima reservation or into urban areas. David Sohappy and his wife, Myra, moved to a sliver of federal land called Cook's Landing, just above the first of several dams along the Columbia and its tributaries. They built a small longhouse with a dirt floor. Sohappy built fishing traps from driftwood. As the fish-ins of the 1960s attracted nationwide publicity, Sohappy fished in silence until state game and fishing officials raided his camp, beat family members, and in 1968, put Sohappy in jail on charges of illegal fishing. He then brought legal action, and the case *Sohappy v. Smith* (302 F. Supp. 899 [D. Oregon, 1969]), produced a landmark federal ruling that was supposed to prevent the states of Washington and Oregon from interfering with Indian fishing except for conservation purposes.

The state ignored the ruling and continued to harass Sohappy and his family. Under cover of darkness, state agents sunk their boats and slashed their nets. In 1981 and 1982, the states of Washington and Oregon successfully (but quietly) lobbied into law a federal provision that made the interstate sale of fish taken in violation of state law a felony—an act aimed squarely at Sohappy. Eight months before the law was signed by President Reagan, the state enlisted federal undercover agents in a fish-buying sting that the press called Salmonscam to entrap Sohappy. He was later convicted in Los Angeles (the trial had been moved from the local jurisdiction because of racial prejudice against Indians) of taking 317 fish and sentenced to five years in prison. During the trial, testimony about the Sohappy's religion and the practice of conservation was not allowed.

Sohappy became a symbol of Native American rights across the United States. Myra Sohappy sought support from the United Nations Commission on Human Rights to have her husband tried by a jury of his peers in the Yakama Nation's Tribal Court. The new trial was arranged with the help of Senator Daniel Inouye, chair of the Senate Select Committee on Indian Affairs. The Yakama court found that the federal prosecution had interfered with Sohappy's practice of his Seven Drum religion.

Released after 20 months in prison, Sohappy had aged rapidly. Confinement and the prison diet had sapped his strength. Sohappy suffered several strokes during the months in prison, when he was even denied the use of an eagle prayer feather for comfort (it was rejected as contraband by prison officials). Back at Cook's Landing, Sohappy found that vindictive federal officials had tacked an eviction notice to his small house. Sohappy took the eviction notice to court and beat the government for what turned out to be his last time. He died in a nursing home in Hood River, Oregon, on May 6, 1991.

A few days later Sohappy was buried, his Wanapam relatives gathered in an old graveyard. They sang old songs as they lowered his body into the earth, having wrapped the body in a Pendleton blanket. He was placed so that the early morning sun would warm his head, facing west toward Mount Adams. Tom Keefe, Jr., an attorney who had been instrumental in securing Sohappy's release from prison, stood by the grave and remembered:

And while the sun chased a crescent moon across the Yakima Valley, I thanked David Sohappy for the time we had spent together, and I wondered how the salmon he had fought to protect would fare in his absence. Now he is gone, and the natural runs of Chinook that fed his family since time immemorial are headed for the Endangered Species Act list. "Be glad for my dad," David Sohappy, Jr. told the mourners. "He is free now, he doesn't need any tears." (Keefe, 1991, 6)

FURTHER READING

American Friends Service Committee. *Uncommon Controversy: Fishing Rights of the Muckleshoot, Puyallup, and Nisqually Indians.* Seattle: University of Washington Press, 1970.

Ball, Milnar. Constitution, Court, Indian Tribes. *American Bar Foundation Research Journal* 1(1987):1–140.

Barsh, Russel L. *The Washington Fishing Rights Controversy: An Economic Critique.* Seattle: University of Washington School of Business Administration, 1977.

Bates, Tom. The Government's Secret War on the Indian. *Oregon Times,* February–March 1976, 14.

Bluecloud, Peter. *Alcatraz Is Not an Island.* Berkeley, CA: Wingbow Press, 1972.

Brack, Fred. Fishing Rights: Who Is Entitled to Northwest Salmon? *Seattle Post-Intelligencer Northwest Magazine,* January 16, 1977, 8–10.

Brand, Johanna. *The Life and Death of Anna Mae Aquash.* Toronto: Lorimer, 1978.

Brown, Bruce. *Mountain in the Clouds: The Search for the Wild Salmon.* New York: Simon and Schuster, 1982.

Brown, Dee. *Bury My Heart at Wounded Knee: An Indian History of the American West.* New York: Holt, Rinehart and Winston, 1970.

Canby, William C., Jr. *American Indian Law.* St. Paul, MN: West, 1981.

Churchill, Ward. *Struggles for the Land.* Monroe, ME: Common Courage Press, 1993.

Churchill, Ward, and Jim Vander Wall. *Agents of Repression: The FBI's Secret War Against the Black Panther Party and the American Indian Movement.* Boston: South End Press, 1990a.

Churchill, Ward, and Jim Vander Wall. *The Cointelpro Papers.* Boston: South End Press, 1990b.

Deloria, Vine, Jr. *Behind the Trail of Broken Treaties.* New York: Delacorte, 1974a.

Deloria, Vine, Jr. *The Indian Affair.* New York: Friendship Press, 1974b.

Deloria, Vine, Jr. *The Nations Within.* New York: Pantheon, 1984.

Deloria, Vine, Jr. *American Indian Policy in the Twentieth Century.* Norman: University of Oklahoma Press, 1985.

Deloria, Vine, Jr. *Custer Died for Your Sins: An Indian Manifesto.* Norman: University of Oklahoma Press, 1988.

Deloria, Vine, Jr. *Behind the Trail of Broken Treaties.* Austin: University of Texas Press, 1990.

Deloria, Vine, Jr., and Clifford Lytle. *American Indians: American Justice.* Austin: University of Texas Press, 1984.

Gates, Paul W., ed. *The Rape of Indian Lands.* New York: Arno Press, 1979.

Hertzberg, Hazel W. *The Search for an American Indian Identity: Modern Pan-Indian Movements.* Syracuse: Syracuse University Press, 1971.

Jaimes, M. Annette, ed. *The State of Native America: Genocide, Colonization and Resistance.* Boston: South End Press, 1992.

Johansen, Bruce E. Peltier and the Posse. *The Nation,* October 1, 1977, 304–307.

Johansen, Bruce E. The Reservation Offensive. *The Nation,* February 25, 1978, 204–207.

Johansen, Bruce E., ed. *The Encyclopedia of Native American Legal Tradition.* Westport, CT: Greenwood Press, 1998.

Johansen, Bruce E., and Donald A. Grinde, Jr. *The Encyclopedia of Native American Biography.* New York: Henry Holt, 1997.

Johansen, Bruce E., and Roberto F. Maestas. *Wasi'chu: The Continuing Indian Wars.* New York: Monthly Review Press, 1979.

Josephy, Alvin, Jr. *Red Power.* New York: McGraw-Hill, 1971.

Keefe, Tom, Jr. A Tribute to David Sohappy. *Native Nations,* June/July 1991, 4–6.

Kickingbird, Kirke. *Indian Sovereignty.* Washington, DC: Institute for the Development of Indian Law, 1983.

Kilborn, Peter. Pine Ridge, A Different Kind of Poverty. *Omaha World-Herald,* September 30, 1992, 9.

LaMay, Konnie. 20 Years of Anguish. *Indian Country Today,* February 25, 1993, n.p.

Matthiessen, Peter. *In the Spirit of Crazy Horse.* New York: Viking, 1991.

Miller, Bruce J. The Press, the Boldt Decision, and Indian-White Relations. *American Indian Culture and Research Journal* 17:2(1993):75–98.

O'Brien, Sharon. *American Indian Tribal Governments.* Norman: University of Oklahoma Press, 1989.

Sohappy v. Smith. 302 F. Supp. 899 (D. Oregon, 1969).

U.S. Commission on Civil Rights. Report of Investigation: Oglala Sioux Tribe, General Election, 1974. Washington, DC: Civil Rights Commission, October 1974. Mimeographed.

United States v. Washington 384 F. Supp. 312 (1974).

Walker, Carson. Man Is Arrested in Activist's Death. April 2, 2003. Available at IndigenousNewsNetwork@topica.com.

Weir, David, and Lowell Bergman. The Killing of Anna Mae Aquash. *Rolling Stone*, April 7, 1977, 51–55.

Weisman, Joel. About That "Ambush" at Wounded Knee. *Columbia Journalism Review*, September/October 1975, 28–31.

CHAPTER 10

Majority Culture Borrowings from Native American Peoples and Cultures

For many years, European American immigrants to the continent they came to call North America studied history as if they had shaped its first peoples—it was *their* westward movement, *their* religion, *their* civilization, *their* conquest. Often left unexamined until recent years are the many ways in which the more recent immigrants absorbed Native foods, sports, social and political ideas.

As they acquired new foods and tools from Native Americans, early European American colonists also adopted Native American place names. Twenty-six of the states in the United States of America today bear names first spoken (at least in part) before Europeans immigrated here in large numbers. Thousands of words have entered English and other European languages from American Indian sources; they are too numerous even to survey in this brief overview. Assertions also have been made that Indian contributions helped shape Euro-American folk songs, locations for railroads and highways, ways of dying cloth, and even bathing habits (Frachtenberg, 1915, 64–69; Edwards, 1934, 255–272).

The U.S. Army did more than subjugate the Plains Indians. As troops chased the Lakota, they also learned from them. Many Plains people used sign language. Their smoke signals could be seen for many miles in open country. The Sioux later devised a system of signaling by mirrors. The U.S. Army adopted some of these signaling systems (in some cases, symbol-bearing blankets became flags), and they became the basis of the techniques used in the modern U.S. Army Signal Corps.

Even after more than five centuries in America, Europeans are still discovering the lands and inhabitants of a place their ancestors called the New World. Felix Cohen, author of the *Handbook of Federal Indian Law*, a basic reference in that field, compared Native American influence on immigrants from Europe to the ways in which the Greeks shaped Roman culture:

> When the Roman legions conquered Greece, Roman historians wrote with as little imagination as did the European historians who have written of the white man's conquest of America. What the Roman historians did not see was that captive Greece would take captive conquering Rome [with] Greek science [and] Greek philosophy. (1952, 180)

Cohen wrote that American historians had too often paid attention to military victories and changing land boundaries while failing to see that "in agriculture, in government, in sport, in education, and in our views of nature and our fellow men, it is the first Americans who have taken captive their battlefield conquerors" (1952, 180). American historians "have seen America only as an imitation of Europe," Cohen asserted. In his view, "the real epic of America is the yet unfinished story of the Americanization of the white man" (ibid., 180).

Many borrowings are indirect and so deeply ingrained in present-day culture that we have forgotten for the most part where they came from. The word *tuxedo*, for example, is anglicized from the Delaware (Lenni Lenape) word for wolf, *p'tuksit*. Neither wolves nor most American Indians wore tuxedos when this borrowing took place during the 1880s, of course. The tuxedo was first worn in a New York village by the name of Tuxedo, however. In our time a "Tux" is taken to be very conventional dress, but in the 1880s, young men wore it as an alternative to the older fashion of jackets with tails.

By 2002, however, the study of ways in which Native American ways of life shaped the rest of the world had become deep enough to sustain a 384-page reference book, Emory Dean Keoke and Kay Marie Porterfield's *Encyclopedia of American Indian Contributions to the World: 15,000 Years of Inventions and Innovations*. This book contains some surprises even for the avid student of cross-cultural communication. As its title suggests, the *Encyclopedia of American Indian Contributions to the World* is the first attempt to compile a comprehensive array of such material and intellectual influences under one cover. It is a wide-ranging effort, and one that may surprise even the most diligent student of ways in which Native American cultures have shaped others worldwide.

This encyclopedia merits reading cover to cover. It is a groundbreaking compilation of Native American contributions to sciences, technology, foods, lifeways, government, and other aspects of history and modern life. It is also, at the same time, a reminder of cultural amalgamation, that everything ultimately finds itself mixed with everything else. This was as true 500 years ago as today, with accelerated communication and transportation. Consider "Indian" (that is, Indian subcontinental) curry. The spices that comprise it actually began as a chili in what is now Brazil. They were transported to India by Portuguese seamen, then mixed with Asian spices to produce the mixture we know today (Keoke and Porterfield, 2002, 9, 78). One wonders what the Italians ate before tomato sauce, what the Irish consumed before potatoes, and what Jewish celebrants of Hanukkah used in lieu of potatoes for their latkes.

The idea of playing a game with a bouncing ball is indigenous to the Americas, particularly to Mesoamerica, where the Aztecs and Mayas played a game that had attributes of basketball, American football, and soccer. Europeans had no rubber before Columbus and thus no rubber balls. The Olmec, who lived in the Yucatan Peninsula, invented a way to treat raw latex to make usable items from rubber as early as 1700 B.C.E. They used it to make balls, soles for sandals, hollow bulbs for syringes, and waterproofed ponchos. This process was similar to vulcanization, which was patented by Charles Goodyear in 1844. Baseball shares attributes of English cricket and a Choctaw ballgame.

Numerous Native American contributions have become so familiar for so long that many of us have forgotten their origins. When we "sleep on it," for example, we forget that we are invoking an Iroquois custom, in which chiefs in council are implored to let at least one night intervene before making important decisions. The passage of time was said to allow the various members of a Haudenosaunee council to attain unanimity—"one mind"—necessary for consensual solution of a problem. The Grand Council also prohibited carrying debate after sunset to avoid hasty decision making caused by stress. Similarly, to "bury the hatchet" refers to the Iroquois practice of sequestering weapons under the Great Tree of Peace.

Pre-Columbian American Indian astronomers (notably the Maya) used a sophisticated system that could calculate celestial events such as solar eclipses. The Maya also created calendar systems, complete with corrections that were based on detailed observations of the sun and moon. Mayan astronomers' observations were so accurate that by the fifth century B.C. they had calculated a year's length to within a few minutes of today's calendars.

Keoke and Porterfield asserted that indigenous Americans employed technology that was in some respects more advanced than European techniques. They wrote, for example, that American Indian metallurgists invented electroplating of metals hundreds of years before its discovery in Europe. The Moche, who lived on the coast of northern Peru, utilized electroplating between 200 B.C.E. and 600 C.E. Europeans did not discover the process of electroplating until Sir Humphrey Davy's experiments during the late 1700s (2002, 98).

Keoke and Porterfield also weighed into the debate regarding who invented scalping. Their verdict: Native Americans did not do it. Keoke and Porterfield relied on precontact records indicating that Europeans took scalps, often buying them, centuries before the practice was utilized in North America. The practice was a well-established tradition for Europeans as early as 440 years before the common era, when the Greek historian Herodotus noted the practice. Much later, the English paid bounties for Irish scalps because they were easier to transport and store than entire heads. Keoke and Porterfield displayed records indicating that the English Earl of Wessex scalped enemies during the 11th century (Keoke and Porterfield, 2002).

Something else that Native Americans did not introduce to the world was syphilis, according to Keoke and Porterfield. They pointed to archeological evidence that they say provides strong evidence that syphilis was present in Europe before Columbus (2002, xi). Excavations at a friary in Hull, England, have revealed at least a dozen skulls carbon dated to between 1300 and 1450 C.E. that display evidence of third-stage syphilis. Pre-Columbian skeletons with syphilis also have been found elsewhere in Europe, including Ireland, Naples, and Pompeii, as well as in Israel (Porterfield, 2002).

NATIVE MEDICINES IN THE PHARMACOPOEIA OF THE UNITED STATES

Several American Indian medicines have come into use among European Americans. By the late twentieth century, more than 200 drugs first used by American Indians were listed in the United States *Pharmacopoeia* (*The Pharmacopoeia of the United States of America*, 1863), an official listing of all effective medicines and their uses. These include quinine, laxatives, muscle relaxants, and nasal remedies, as well as several dozen drugs and herbal medicines. To this day, scientists are discovering more beneficial drugs in plants once known only to Native Americans. One reason that many people are concerned at the demise of the Amazon rain forests is that such destruction could keep us from learning more about the Native American uses of plants there.

Some Native Americans used foxglove (*Digitalis purpurea*) to treat heart problems. They administered it with extreme care because high doses are required, and the plant is extremely toxic. American Indian healers developed a sophisticated system of medical treatment compared to European healers of the time, who relied on bloodletting, blistering, religious penance, and concoctions of lead, arsenic, and cow dung to treat disease. In addition to performing surgery, American Indians from several areas understood the importance of keeping wounds sterile as they used botanical antiseptics. They made syringes from bird bones and animal bladders to administer plant medicines.

Native peoples in the Americas had developed so many botanical medications by the time of contact that the Spanish King Philip II sent physician Francisco Hernando to the Americas in 1570 to record Aztec medical knowledge and bring it back to Europe. As early as 1635, after less than a generation in America, English colonists were using herbal medicines introduced to them by the native peoples. "A Relation of Maryland," written to give prospective immigrants information on the new colony, included this passage:

> This Countrey affords naturally, many excellent things for Physicke and Surgery, the perfect use of which, the English cannot yet learne from the Natives: They have a roote which is an excellent preservative against Pyson, called by the English the Snake roote. Other herbes and rootes they have wherewith they cure all manners of wounds; also Saxafras, Gummes, and Balsum. An Indian seeing one of the English, much troubled with the tooth-ake, fetched of the roote of a tree, and gave the party some of it to hold in his mouth, and it eased the pain presently. (Birchfield, 1997, 5:705–706)

By the eighteenth century, European American observers, many of them missionaries, were compiling lists of Native herbal remedies; some of these lists were published in several European languages. One carried to Europe the knowledge that the bark of a particular tree that grows in North America could alleviate toothache. The Canada shrubby elder could be used to combat agues and inflammations. The jalap root could be used as a laxative and to relieve the pain of rheumatism; the ipecacaunha also functioned as an emetic as well as an antidote to snakebite. Peter Kalm, the Swedish botanist, visited the Middle Atlantic states between 1748 and 1750 to catalogue Native medicinal herbs.

Captain John Smith learned through Pocahantas that her people applied a root that she called *wighsacan* to wounds for its healing power. John Lawson, visiting the Carolinas about 1700, observed that Natives there chewed a root (which he did not name) to soothe stomach ailments. European observers also wrote of Indians who committed suicide by eating certain roots and mushrooms. William Penn wrote that a Delaware woman who had been betrayed by her husband "went out, plunk't a Root out of the Ground, and ate it, upon which she immediately died" (Birchfield, 1997, 5:706). Native peoples often warned Europeans which plants, if eaten, could make them ill, produce skin rashes, or kill them. In some cases, Native peoples also provided antidotes. The Delaware, for example, dealt with the rash produced by contact with poison sumac by preparing a tea from the inner bark of the sour gum tree, which gave off a distinctive odor that caused native peoples to compare it to raw fish.

Some Native plant remedies became popular among Europeans based on their biological record; others took Europe by storm on the basis of unsupported health claims. Use of sassafras root (the "saxafras" in the "Relation of Maryland" above) was noted as early as Shakespeare's time. The use of sassafras tea spread throughout Europe as a general health tonic, and a trading network grew up across the Atlantic specializing in its harvest, sale, and transport. At about the same time, all sorts of extravagant claims were being made for the tonic effects of tobacco that do not stand up to scientific scrutiny. Tobacco was said to aid digestion, cure toothaches, kill nits and lice, and even stop coughing. The advocates of tobacco seemed to draw their advice from Native peoples, who often used tobacco as a ceremonial herb and who only very rarely became addicted to nicotine.

Tobacco was one of many herbal weapons in the arsenal of Native medicine men, or shamans, across the continent. The role of the medicine man had no direct counterpart in Europe. The various Native names for the persons who performed these functions can be translated as shaman, juggler, conjurer, sorcerer, priest, and physician, as well as medicine man. Even the translation of Native words that correspond to medicine in English can be tricky because Western culture has no single term that incorporates all the aspects of the shaman's work. Whereas medicine in English connotes treatment of a disease with a drug or other specific remedy, a medicine man was a spiritualist as well as a person who had learned the basics of physical medicine and herbal cures. Native shamans combined the art of mental suggestion with physical cures as well; the mental attitude of the patient was often considered as important as any physical cure. The casting of spells (and other practice of sorcery) had as much to do with a person's state of mind as with physical and biological reactions.

Most Native American peoples used the by-products of animals, as well as plants, for medicinal and cosmetic purposes. English immigrants in Virginia and Massachusetts learned early that an emollient of bear grease allowed Native people to range in the woods wearing a minimum of clothing on hot summer days without being bitten by mosquitoes and other stinging insects. Goose grease and bear fat were widely used as hair dressings, and skunk oil was sometimes applied to the chest and throat to relieve the symptoms of colds, including chest congestion. The Delawares sometimes slowed the flow of blood from a cut by inserting spider webs, which probably helped with blood clotting.

Witch hazel is a commonly used Native botanical remedy that has been adopted generally by Euro-American society. Used as a first aid treatment for insect bites and cuts, witch hazel is the distilled extract of the witch hazel bush combined with alcohol. The shrub grows commonly in the eastern United States; its leaves were boiled and applied to bites and cuts by many Native peoples in that area. The root and leaves of the wintergreen contain methyl salicylate, which is used today in creams and other forms to treat rheumatic pain, muscular aches, and similar ailments. Salicylic acid is the main active ingredient of aspirin, probably the most widely used relief for minor pain in the late twentieth century. The inner bark of the white pine (the national symbol of the Iroquois Confederacy) today is used in cough syrups. Terpin hydrate, a prescription drug used to treat coughs and colds, is derived from the sap of pine trees (turpentine). The Indians also were the first people to utilize caffeine as a stimulant.

Native American Vegetal Remedies

Balm-of-gilead: Mixed with cream to form a balm for sores.

Blackberry: Root as tea; said to cure dysentery.

Black haw: Liquid boiled from bark; relieves stomach and menstrual cramps.

Black walnut: Tea boiled from bark relieves severe colds.

Catnip: Tea from the leaves may quiet a restless baby.

Corn silk: As tea, combats pain caused by kidney trouble.

Dogwood: Tea from the roots serves as a general tonic.

Elder: Tea made from flowers relieves colic in children.

Elm (American or white): Liquid from steeping the inner bark in water relieves symptoms of flu, such as coughs and chills. Elm is also a poultice for gunshot wounds. (General Washington's Army used it during the Revolutionary War.)

Fishweed (Jerusalem artichoke): A tea made from its leaves may rid children of worms.

Flannel mullein: Heated leaves in a compress provide relief from rheumatic pains.

Hog weed (ragweed): The root is a strong laxative.

Hops: Leaves serve (in a tea) to relieve symptoms of a cold or (as a compress) to relieve pain.

Jimson weed: Heated leaves relieve pain of burns; not to be taken internally.

Morning glory: A tea of the leaves relieves some types of stomach pain.

Peach: Crushed leaves used as a compress reduce swelling.

Peppermint: Boiled leaves sometimes relieve stomach pains.

Prickly ash: Tea made from the bark relieves symptoms of colds; the bark and root can be used to relieve toothache pain.

Sassafras: A tea may reduce high blood pressure.

Tobacco: A soft wad of chewed tobacco will reduce the pain of a bee sting.

Watermelon: Tea from boiled seeds may relieve pain of kidney trouble.

Wild grape: Juice conditions hair and scalp.

Wild strawberry: Crushed fruit applied to face may improve complexion.

Yarrow: Crushed roots boiled as tea reduce excessive menstrual flow.

White oak: Liquid steeped from bark helps heal cuts and scratches.

THE ORIGINS OF THANKSGIVING

Ceremonies of thanksgiving for the bounty of nature are a common element in many Native American cultures. Feasts of gratitude and giving thanks have been a part of these cultures for several thousand years. In Lakota culture, a feast of thanksgiving is called a *Wopila*; in Navajo, it is *Hozhoni*; in Cherokee, it is *Selu i-tse-i*; and in Ho Chunk (Winnebago), it is *Wicawas warocu sto waroc*.

Thanksgiving in many cases is a yearlong event, celebrated, for example, after the safe birth of a baby, a safe journey, or construction of a new home.

Native peoples introduced their thanksgiving celebrations to English colonists near Plymouth Rock in 1621. A fall thanksgiving holiday, usually accompanied by feasting on traditional Native American foods (turkey, corn, yams, squashes, cranberry sauce, etc.) has been widely practiced since about 1800 by most non-Native people in the United States and Canada. Thanksgiving was declared a national holiday in 1863 by President Abraham Lincoln in the midst of the Civil War. Canada declared an official Thanksgiving holiday in 1879; this day is celebrated six weeks before its counterpart in the United States.

Thanksgiving is part of an annual cycle. Many Native American peoples celebrate a number of seasonal thanksgivings each year, of which general American culture has adopted only one. At each season, thanks is given for nature's provision of an economic base, whether it be corn, buffalo, or salmon. According to José Barreiro, editor of *Native Americas*:

> The Thanksgiving tradition requires that human beings place themselves in a humble position relative to the natural, plant, and animal elements and to consider, in one mind, the contributions of these other species to our well-being and survival.... Among the Iroquois and other traditionalists, the "wish to be appreciated" is the fundamental shared perception—the first principle—of existence. (1992, 28)

Mohawk Nation Council subchief Tom Porter offered a traditional thanksgiving prayer, "words before all else," that is used for all of the Iroquois' nine thanksgiving celebrations:

> [Before] our great-great grandfathers were first born and given the breath of life, our Creator at that time said the Earth will be your mother. And the Creator said to the deer, and the animals and the birds, the Earth will be your mother, too. And I have instructed the earth to give food and nourishment and medicine and quenching of thirst to all life.... We, the people, humbly thank you today, mother earth.
>
> Our Creator spoke to the rivers and our creator made the rivers not just as water, but he made the rivers a living entity.... You must have a reverence and great respect for your mother the earth.... You must each day say "thank you" [for] every gift that contributes to your life. If you follow this pattern, it will be like a circle with no end. Your life will be as everlasting as your children will carry on your flesh, your blood, and your heartbeat. (Grinde and Johansen, 1995, 34–35)

A tribute to the creator and a reverence for the natural world is reflected in many Native greetings the span of the North American continent. More than 2,500 miles from the homeland of the Mohawks, the Lummis of the Pacific

A Hopi cornfield. (Courtesy of the Library of Congress.)

Northwest coast begin public meetings this way: "To the Creator, Great Spirit, Holy Father: may the words that we share here today give the people and [generations] to come the understanding of the sacredness of all life and creation" (Grinde and Johansen, 1995, 34–35).

The domesticated fowl that would come to be called turkey in English was first eaten by Native Americans in the Valley of Mexico, including the Aztecs, who introduced it to invading Spaniards. By the time the Pilgrims reached Plymouth Rock, Massachusetts, in 1620, turkey had been bred in Spain and exported to England for almost a century. The passengers of the Mayflower had some turkeys on board their ship, so when they prepared for the first Thanksgiving, the English immigrants were familiar with the wild turkeys that were hunted by Native American peoples in eastern North America. Wild American turkeys seemed larger and better tasting to many colonists than their European-bred brethren. They also were easy to hunt. Thomas Morton said that a hunter in early seventeenth century New England could shoot one turkey while others nearby looked on, "The one being killed, the other sit fast everthelesse" (Cronon, 1983, 23). By the late twentieth century, wild turkeys were scarce in much of New England.

Native Americans gathered the seeds of corn when it was a wild grass and selected for the most productive, hardiest varieties. By the time European immigrants made landfall in North America, corn was more productive per acre than any cereal crop in the Old World. Corn, along with squashes, beans, fish, venison (deer meat), and various "fowls" (probably turkeys, ducks, and geese) were consumed during the first Anglo-American thanksgiving. The abundance was welcomed by the Pilgrims, who had arrived in the New World with English seeds, most of which did not sprout in American soil. They nearly starved during their first winter. William Bradford, governor of the small colony, wrote in his diary that Squanto, who was able to teach the immigrants how to survive in their own language, was "a special instrument sent of God for [our] good" (Case, 2002).

AMERICAN GOLD AND EUROPEAN CAPITALISM

Jack Weatherford's *Indian Givers* (1988) takes the influence of Native American contributions to European capitalism beyond individual products. It begins with the birth of money capitalism, fueled by Indian gold and silver, which provided the necessary capital for the rise of industrial capitalism. Spain, England, and France did not set out to America as empires. Each acquired much of its riches in America and elsewhere around the world.

England's industrial revolution provoked urbanization, which also created a need for an agricultural revolution to feed the populations of burgeoning cities. Weatherford argues that without Native American corn, potatoes, and other crops, many increasingly urbanized Europeans could have starved to death. Some scholars may argue that Weatherford has something of an intellectual love affair with the potato. How greatly any one contribution shaped history as a whole is always a dandy point of departure for debate. Regardless of possible differences regarding emphasis, Weatherford makes his point for appreciation of native precedents.

In Weatherford's *Native Roots* (1991), ancient Native ingenuity is described in ways that bear on present-day problems. Read, for example, how the Anasazi fashioned their dwellings to take advantage of passive solar energy, as well as the shading of overhanging cliffs, blunting the seasonal extremes of the Southwest and reducing the amount of precious firewood they had to burn. Weatherford also describes how the Inuit created a kayak that fits its occupant like a wetsuit, a boat so watertight that its occupant can turn upside down, then right side up again, without getting wet.

The idea of personal equality in the societies of many Native peoples pervades both of Weatherford's books, especially as he contrasts Native concepts of liberty with European notions of hierarchy. Weatherford sometimes describes architecture to make his point: Nowhere did native peoples of the Americas create the cathedrals or palaces commissioned by European elites. Instead, the Anasazis (for example) built relatively comfortable housing for the average person that European peasants might have envied. In the world of ideas, liberty and equality have a long American lineage: Over time and space, the spacious homes of the Anasazi could be imagined as the precursor of Jefferson's freehold farmer in his snug log cabin and the tract housing suburbs of modern-day American urban areas. Could it be argued that the Anasazis helped create the type of housing that characterizes the American dream?

Europeans did not bring liberty and prosperity to America; they sought it here, meanwhile forcing on Native people its antithesis—slavery and indentured servitude. Weatherford, in *Native Roots*, reveals that Native Americans were forced into slavery in large numbers. The Spanish, French, and English all enslaved native peoples; the name of Labrador, for example, may have been handed down to us from a Portuguese term for slave coast, Weatherford wrote (1991, 138).

NATIVE LINGUISTIC TRACKS IN ENGLISH AND SPANISH

The communication of names between cultures goes both ways, of course, and often involves some semantic confusion. The names that we most often use to describe various Native tribes and nations are a linguistic mishmash. One could generally tell whose enemy was whose. *Iroquois* is French for people who called themselves "Haudenosaunee," meaning People of the Longhouse. The Algonquians called the Iroquois the Nation of Snakes. It has been said that *Mohawk* is an Algonquian derivation for "man-eater." *Sioux* is an archaic French derivation for "snake" or "enemy." *Huron* is French for "lout" or "ruffian," used to describe people who called themselves Wendat (also Wyandot), meaning "dwellers on a peninsula." Huron is a once-removed phrase from archaic French that describes the bristles on the snout of a wild boar, not the type of image that most peoples would cultivate for themselves.

Native American languages have left their linguistic tracks all over English and not just in thousands of geographical place names. Many of the following words come from the Algonquian languages spoken over much of what is now the eastern United States: hickory, hominy, moose, succotash, terrapin, tomahawk, totem, woodchuck. *Blizzard* is a Native American word, although we do not know which language it came from. The first published reference to a blizzard was handed down to us by Davy Crockett, who according to Weatherford, used it in 1834. Crockett himself was a walking cultural amalgamation, of course, from his coonskin hat to his leggings and moccasins. He was not, however, in the habit of giving credit to Native peoples for much of what he borrowed from them.

European Americans also adapted to their own needs many Indian articles of clothing and other artifacts, including hammocks, kayaks, canoes, moccasins, smoking pipes, dog sleds, and parkas, a type of hooded jacket they invented. Most European and American arctic explorers borrowed extensively from the clothing of the Inuit, whose sleds often were pulled by the husky, also an Inuit word. *Muckamuck* (applied in derision to someone in authority) comes from trading jargon Chinook, as does the slang term *hootch* for alcoholic beverages. Other Native words now used in English include cigar (Mayan), tobacco (Arawakan), potato (Taino), and tomato (Nahuatl).

～

State Names, Native American Derivations

Roughly half the states in the United States of America have names that derive, in some way, from Native American languages. Most are English or French adaptations of the original Native American words. Sometimes, more than one meaning has been attributed to a name, in which case both are listed.

Alabama: From *alipama*, or *alibamu*, a Muskogee tribal name meaning "those who clear the land."

Alaska: From the Aleut word for their homeland on the Alaska peninsula, *Alakhskhakh*; also Aleut for "great land."

Arizona: Pagago, airzonac, probably meaning "small springs."

Arkansas: From the Illinois name for the Quapaw, *akansea*. The same word has been said to mean "downstream people."

Connecticut: Mohegan or Pequot for "long tidal river" or "wind-driven river."

Dakota (North and South): A Dakota Sioux term for themselves (*dahkota*), meaning "friends" or "allies." It is interesting that the immigrants expropriated the Sioux's own name for themselves, with its friendly connotations, meanwhile assigning the Dakota a corruption of an old French word, *Sioux*," meaning "snake" or "enemy."

Idaho: The Native language from which this state name is derived is unknown; it is said to have meant "gem of the mountains"; some say it means "The sun is coming up."

Illinois: The name of an Algonquian confederation, meaning "original people" or "superior men," after a term that the Illinois Indians used for themselves. The name originated with the Algonquian *iliniwak*, modified by French traders as Illinois.

Iowa: For the Ioway Indians, modified through French, from the Fox language, as *aayahooweewa* (possibly from the Sioux *ayuhba*). Both words mean "sleepy ones."

Kansas: Kansa for "people of the south wind."

Kentucky: From *Kenta*, possibly an Iroquois word for "planted field." Some say the word is Cherokee for "meadowland."

Massachusetts: Meaning "people of the big hill," this name was used to describe an Algonquian people who lived near a steep hill near Boston.

Michigan: Meaning "great water" (*michigamea*) or "big lake," the name is probably derived from the Algonquian or Ottawa language.

Minnesota: From *minisota*, a Dakota word meaning "sky-tinted water."

Mississippi: A combination of two Algonquian or Ojibway words: *misi*, meaning "great" or "large," and *sipi*, meaning "water," usually taken to mean "big river."

Missouri: A French adaptation of an Illinois (*Iliniwak*) word meaning "people with dugout canoes." Missouri is also the name of a tribe that lived near the river; Missouri also may also be taken to mean "big muddy river," after the Missouri Indians' name for it, *Pokitanou*, which carries that meaning. To this day, inhabitants of cities along the river customarily call it "the Big Muddy."

Nebraska: From the Omaha name *Nibdhathka*, meaning "flat river" or "flat water"; named for the shallow but wide Platte River. Some sources say the word is from the Oto language; it may be from both.

New Mexico: As a province of New Spain, New Mexico's name was derived from *Mexica*, the Aztecs' name for themselves.

Ohio: Derived from a Seneca word meaning "beautiful river."

Oklahoma: "Red men" in Choctaw, a translation of "Indian Territory" into the Choctaw language.

Tennessee: From *Tanasi*, a Cherokee name for the Little Tennessee River, as well as a principal Cherokee town by the same name. It is said to mean "area of traveling waters."

Texas: First a Spanish (*Tejas*), then also an English derivation from *taysa*, a word used among members of the Caddo tribal confederacy meaning (like Dakota) "friends or allies."

Utah: From the tribal name Ute, anglicized from *yuuttaa*, the Utes' name for their homeland, "the land of the sun."

Wisconsin: The name of a tribal confederacy living near the Wisconsin River, "Wisconsin" is probably derived from the Ojibway *Wees-kon-san*, "gathering of the waters" and "grassy place."

Wyoming: This name, meaning "big meadows" or "big river flats," originated with the Delaware (Lenni Lenape) of present-day Pennsylvania and New Jersey and was carried by non-Indian migrants to the state that now bears the name. "Wyoming" is anglicized rather liberally from the Lenni Lenape *maughwauwame*, a name given first to the Wyoming Valley of Pennsylvania.

◦◦◦

Examples of Foods Native to the Americas

Asparagus
Avocados
Blueberries
Cassava (tapioca)
Chewing gum (chicle)
Chocolate (cacao)
Corn

Corn products such as hominy, corn-
    starch, and cornmeal
Cranberries
Cucumbers
Currants
Green and yellow beans
Maple sugar and syrup

Mint and mint flavorings	Squashes, including pumpkins,
Peanuts and peanut products	watermelon, yams, and cantaloupe
Green and red peppers	Sunflower seeds
Pecans	Turkey
Popcorn	Vanilla
Potatoes and potato products	Venison
Sassafras tea	Wild rice

CRISPUS ATTUCKS: FIRST CASUALTY OF THE BOSTON MASSACRE

Crispus Attucks, son of an African American father and a Massachuset Indian mother, was the first casualty of the Boston Massacre of March 5, 1770, the first death in the cause of the American Revolution. Attucks's father was a black slave in a Framington, Massachusetts, household until about 1750, when he escaped and became a sailor. Crispus's mother lived in an Indian mission at Natick.

Serious tension had begun to build in the late summer and fall of 1769 when Bostonians believed that the British Redcoats were becoming permanent residents. The soldiers were subjected to every form of legal harassment by local magistrates, to say nothing of mounting acts of violence against the men in uniform. The redcoats in the ranks, like all European soldiers of their day, were hardly of the highest character, often recruited from the slums and the gin mills, and stories of theft, assault, and rape by the regulars were not without considerable foundation.

On the night of March 5, 1770, a small crowd gathered around a soldier at the guard post in front of the Customs House at Boston, accusing him of striking a boy who had made disparaging remarks about a British officer. John Adams depicted the hecklers as "a motley rabble of saucy boys, Negroes and mulattoes, Irish teagues and outlandish Jack tars" ("Africans in America," 2003). The sentinel's call for aid brought a file of eight men from the 29th Regiment and Captain Thomas Preston, officer of the day. The crowd grew, especially after someone rang the bell in the old Brick Meeting House; men and boys hurled snowballs and pieces of ice at the crimson-coated regulars and taunted them to retaliate with cries of "lobster," "bloody-back," and "coward."

Attucks was known around Boston as one of the Sons of Liberty's most aggressive agitators. When the British claimed that he had provoked their soldiers, they may have been right. Attucks and Paul Revere were among the earliest Sons of Liberty, a clandestine society that agitated against the British by engaging in acts of agitation, propaganda, and creative political mischief. The Sons of Liberty tormented Tories and their supporters, often stripping,

The bloody massacre perpetrated in King Street, Boston, on March 5, 1770. (Courtesy of the Library of Congress.)

tarring, and feathering tax collectors, then walking free at the hands of sympathetic colonial juries. They later would form the nucleus of a revolutionary armed force, but in the early years their main business was guerilla theater.

The Boston Massacre was the first shedding of colonial blood during the American Revolution. "Massacre Day," as it was called, later was commemorated in Boston by the tolling of bells and speeches. In 1888, a monument to Attucks was erected at the Boston Common.

THE NATIVE AMERICAN IMPACT ON MODERN FEMINISM

The role of women in Native American life alternately intrigued, perplexed, and sometimes alarmed European and European American observers (nearly all of whom were male) during the seventeenth and eighteenth centuries. In many cases, women held pivotal positions in Native political systems. Iroquois women, for example, nominated men to positions of leadership and could "dehorn," or impeach, them for misconduct. Women usually approved men's plans for war. In a matrilineal society (nearly all the confederacies that bordered the colonies were matrilineal), women owned all household goods except the men's clothes, weapons, and hunting implements. They also were the primary conduits of culture from generation to generation.

Among the Cherokees (as with the Iroquois), women never held the office of *Uku* (civil chief) or Raven (war chief), but they often attended council meetings and acted as advisors behind the scenes. More than once, treaty council business stalled after English delegates objected to the fact that Cherokee women were doing what the English regarded as "men's business." After one such objection, the Cherokee chief Little Carpenter curtly informed the English that all men present had been born of women. He then diplomatically told the English delegates to sit down, shut up, and get on with business (Corkran, 1962, 110).

In the Cherokee home, the woman was supreme. An eighteenth century observer reported: "The women rule the rost [sic], and weres the britches and sometimes will beat thire husbands within an inch of thire life" (Corkran, 1962, 110). Father Joseph Frances Lafitau made a similar statement in a more elegant tone: "It is she who maintains the tribe, the nobility of the blood, the genealogical tree, the order of generations, and the conservation of the families. They are the souls of the council" (Exhibit, 1983). Women also were the souls of the Iroquois Grand Council; they were often so influential that the men have been characterized as political representatives of them (Carr, 1884, 217, 218). The Iroquois system has been styled a "gynocracy" (Axtell, 1981, 150–153).

The Iroquois have an elaborate description of the duties and rights of women in their confederacy. The Iroquois also recognized by law that the earth belonged to women. In Charles Abram's "Iroquois Law of the Woman Chief," an unpaginated manuscript held in the Smithsonian Institution, women's roles in governmental processes are described clearly:

> We shall make the rule that, in the place where the Federal titles are placed, among all our tribes, also among the clans—the several clans which exist—the several women who control the official titles, it shall then be that the Eldest woman, upon whom the eyes of her entire uterine family shall rest, shall be charged with all these duties. (1923, n.p.).

During the American Revolution, General Philip Schuyler of New York paid attention to the wishes of Iroquois women regarding diplomacy. On January 16, 1776, Schuyler met with a delegation of Mohawks near Schenectady, New York. Urging neutrality on the Mohawks and Abraham, their leader, Schuyler asserted that "Your women have sent us a belt. We beg you to assure them of our regard, and intreat [sic] them to prevent your warriors from doing anything that would have the least tendency to incur our resentment or interrupt that harmony which we wish to subsist to the end of time" (*Pennsylvania Magazine*, 1776, 96). After this admonition, a Mohawk chief replied that "You may depend on it that we will use our utmost influence with our warriors, to claim their minds. You may depend on it likewise that our sisters will use their utmost influence for the same purpose" (*American Monthly Museum*, 1776, 97).

At an early nineteenth century treaty conference, another Iroquois sachem said the following:

> Our ancestors considered it a great offence to reject the counsel of women, particularly the female governesses [clan mothers]. They were esteemed the mistresses of the soil. Who, said our forefathers, bring us into being? Who cultivates our lands, kindles our fires, and boils our pots, but the women? . . . They entreat that the veneration of our ancestors in favor of the women not be disregarded, and that they may not be despised. . . . The female governesses beg leave to speak with the freedom allowed to women and agreeable to the spirit of our ancestors. They entreat the Great Chief to . . . preserve them in peace, for they are the life of the nation. ("Substance," 1814, 2:115)

The character of women's influence in traditional Iroquois society has been maintained for centuries since Europeans first encountered it. John Kahionhes Fadden, a Mohawk teacher and artist, related the following story, which he said occurred during the mid-1960s, in the Akwesasne Mohawk Longhouse:

> There was a fellow who had been "de-horned." He was an eloquent speaker, and in a charismatic manner was able to hold people spellbound. During one summer there was a conference of traditional people that traveled from reserve to reserve, meeting with like-minded people. They finally came to Akwesasne and the event went on for the good part of a week. . . . There were Creeks and Cherokees from Oklahoma, Utes from Utah, Malecites from New Brunswick, Manawaki Algonquians from north of Ottawa, plus a good representation of the nations of the Haudenosaunee and others, such as Hopis. . . .
>
> At one point, when all of these people were gathered in the Longhouse many benches deep, with a lot of people standing in the doorways, and some outside craning their necks and cocking their ears to listen to what was going on, the "de-horned" former chief couldn't resist the temptation of that audience. He stood to talk to the gathered people, and, as you know, a "de-horned" chief isn't supposed to talk, and for sure no one is supposed to hear his words. He was able to get out about two or three brief sentences before he was abruptly interrupted by a slicing

voice from the women's end of the Longhouse. She was a clan mother, and standing less than five feet tall, she made it quickly and abundantly clear that this man could not speak anymore. He had lost that right by abusing his former position. The six-foot, two-hundred-plus pound "chief" snapped his mouth shut, sat down, waited about a minute or so, then quietly, with his head kind of low, left the Longhouse. Now, as I see it, that's feminism. (Grinde and Johansen, 1991, 224)

Marriage customs among American Indians elicited descriptions from eighteenth century European and Euro-American observers that strike a surprisingly modern tone. Robert Rogers noted that in many American Indian nations, vows of marriage were voluntary: "They take companions for a shorter or longer time, as they please" (1966, 232–233). Rogers wrote that children of such arrangements were fully accepted in Native societies at a time when such children would have been stigmatized as "born out of wedlock" in European cultures. Thomas Paine pointed to the hypocrisy of European customs in a supposed conversation with "an American savage." According to the savage:

Either the Christian God was not as good and wise as he is represented, or he never meddled in the marriages of his people; since not one in a hundred of any of them had anything to do with either happiness or common sense. Hence, as soon as ever you meet, you long to part, and not having this relief in your power, by way of revenge, you double each others' misery. (Foner, 1945, 2:119–120)

Reverend Peters wrote that Indian women were better off as pagans than under Christian customs of his time, by which the woman was regarded as the husband's property. Before the arrival of Europeans in Connecticut during 1634, Indian women, according to Reverend Peters, had been "the most chaste set of people in the world. Concubinage and fornication are vices none of them are addicted to, except such as forsake the laws of Hobbomockow [the Great Spirit] and turn Christian" (Cameron, 1967, 158).

WOMEN'S RIGHTS AND NATIVE EXAMPLES

Pressure to broaden the ambit of natural and civil rights to women increased early in the nineteenth century at roughly the same time as the abolitionist movement against slavery. Although the landmark Seneca Falls conference, usually credited today with beginning the modern feminist movement in the United States, was not held until 1848, the ideological basis for the movement was set down by Lydia Maria Child in her *History of the Condition of Women, in Various Ages and Nations*, published in 1835. Child's book used the Iroquois and Wyandot cultures to counterpoise notions of European patriarchy, illustrating the importance of the woman's role in political decision making.

Matilda Joslyn Gage. (Courtesy of Sally Roesch Wagner.)

The Iroquois example also figured importantly in another important book in what feminist scholar Sally R. Wagner called "the first wave of feminism," Matilda Joslyn Gage's *Woman, Church and State* ([1893] 1980). In that book, Gage acknowledged, according to Wagner's research, that "the modern world [is] indebted for its first conception of inherent rights, natural equality of condition, and the establishment of a civilized government upon this basis," to the Iroquois (ibid., 10).

Gage was probably one of the three most influential feminist architects of the nineteenth century women's movement, with Elizabeth Cady Stanton and Susan B. Anthony, according to Wagner, whose research was among the first to provide a scholarly basis for a resurgent feminist movement in the late twentieth century. Gage was later "read out" of the movement and its history because of her radical views, especially regarding oppression of women

Elizabeth Cady Stanton, seated, and Susan B. Anthony. (Courtesy of the Library of Congress.)

by organized religion. Knowledge of the Iroquois' matrilineal system of society and government was widespread among early feminists, many of whom lived in upstate New York. The early feminists learned of the Iroquois not only through reading the works of Morgan, Schoolcraft, and others, but also through personal experience. Gage herself was admitted to the Iroquois Council of Matrons and was adopted into the Wolf Clan, with the name Karonienhawi, "she who holds the sky."

According to Gail Landsman, "Child's work was mined extensively by later suffragists, including Gage, who furthered Child's concept of Indian culture as a matriarchal alternative to American white patriarchy through her contact with the Iroquois" (1988, 8). With Stanton and Anthony, Gage coauthored the landmark *History of Woman Suffrage* ([1880] 1985). In her last book, *Women, Church, and State* ([1893] 1980), Gage opened with a chapter on "the matriarchate," a form of society she believed existed in a number of early societies, specifically the Iroquois. Gage discussed several Iroquois traditions that tended to create checks and balances between the sexes, including descent through the female line, the ability of women to nominate male leaders, the fact that women had a veto power over men's decisions to go to war, and the woman's supreme authority in the household. Gage also noted that Iroquois women had rights to their property and children after divorce (Landsman, 1988, 9).

The early suffragists developed their work about the same time as Lewis Henry Morgan, the pioneer anthropologist, whose descriptions of Iroquois society provided the groundwork for modern anthropology in the United States. According to Wagner, Stanton specifically referred to Morgan's work in her address (titled "The Matriarchate or Mother-Age") to the National Council of Women in 1891. Stanton referred to the influence of Iroquois women in national councils, to the fact that their society was descended through the female line, and to the irony that "our barbarian ancestors seem to have had a higher degree of justice to women than American men in the 19th century, professing to believe, as they do, in our republican principles of government" (1891, 2).

Wagner asserted that "Nineteenth century radical feminist theoreticians, such as Elizabeth Cady Stanton and Matilda Joslyn Gage, looked to the Iroquois for their vision of a transformed world" (1988, 32–33). Wagner also used the work of male students of the Iroquois who wrote at roughly the same time as Stanton, Gage, and other early feminists to illustrate just how appealing the Iroquois example must have been to women locked in a culture that considered them their husbands' property. She quoted Henry Schoolcraft, writing in 1846, two years before the Seneca Falls conference. "Marriage, among the Iroquois," wrote Schoolcraft, "appears to be a verbal contract between the parties, which does not affect the rights of property. Goods, personal effects, or valuables of any kind personal or real, which were the wife's before, remain so after marriage" (ibid., 32–33). Schoolcraft characterized marriage among the Iroquois as "a personal agreement, requiring neither civil nor ecclesiastical sanction, but not a union of the rights of property" (ibid., 32–33).

Stanton quoted the memoirs of the Reverend Asher Wright, who wrote that usually Seneca women "ruled the house." The stores were in common, "but woe to the luckless husband or lover who was too shiftless to do his share of the providing." No matter how many children, or whatever goods he might have in the house, he might at any time be ordered to pick up his blanket and move out; and after such an order, it would not be healthy for him to attempt to disobey. "The house would be too hot for him," wrote Wright, "and unless saved by the intercession of some aunt or grandmother he must retreat to his own clan, or go and start a new matrimonial alliance with some other" (1891, 4).

According to Stanton, Wright also noted that Iroquois women alone could "knock off the horns" of a sachem who had abused his office, as well as make the original nominations for sachemships. In early treaty negotiations, representatives of the United States, all male, often found themselves face-to-face with Iroquois women. Many of the treaties negotiated before 1800 are signed by both male sachems and their female advisors (1891, 4).

Paula Gunn Allen contrasted the woman's role in Native American societies with mass media portrayals of them: "I am intensely conscious of popular notions of Indian women as beasts of burden, squaws, traitors, or, at best, vanished denizens of a long-lost wilderness," she wrote. "How odd, then, must my contention seem that the gynocratic tribes of the American continent provided the basis for all the dreams of liberation that characterize the modern world. . . . Beliefs, attitudes and laws such as these became part of the vision of other human-liberation movements around the world." Allen continued: "Yet feminists too often believe that no one has ever experienced the kind of society that empowered women and made that empowerment the basis of its rules and civilization" (1986, 213–214). Even the history of feminism is too often overly Eurocentric. To Allen, lack of such knowledge robs feminists of their own history.

Realization of the Iroquois role in the history of feminism came to Wagner after seventeen years of studying feminism's European roots. Once she turned her attention to native inspirations, Wagner found them running throughout the primary sources of the period that she studied. Frances Wright, the first non-Quaker woman to speak publicly before audiences of both men and women in the United States, edited the pro-Indian *Free Enquirer* with Robert Dale Owen in the 1820s. Owen, like Child, inquired into the relative absence of rape by Indian men of Native women, wondering how their social structure influenced their behavior. To cite another example, Lucretia Mott, who called the Seneca Falls conference, met with the people of the Cattaraugus Seneca reservation just days before she met, during 1848, with Stanton and a group of Quaker friends to plan the Seneca Falls event, which became known as the world's first conference explicitly dedicated to women's rights.

FREDERICK ENGELS AND THE "MOTHER-RIGHT GENS"

Across the Atlantic, aging Karl Marx discovered the work of Lewis Henry Morgan during the late 1870s. After Marx's death, his copious notes on American indigenous societies were passed to Frederick Engels, who used them, with his own research, in preparing *The Origin of the Family, Private Property and the State* (1883). Engels picked up Morgan's refrain (which had also been a popular notion among many of the founders of the United States) that one could discern aspects of the political and economic future by using Native

American models as a window on the ancient past. Having discovered the "mother-right gens" (as he called the matriarchal society of the Iroquois) Engels could scarcely contain himself. "It has the same significance for the history of primitive society as Darwin's theory of evolution has for biology, and Marx's theory of surplus value for political economy," Engels enthused. "The mother-right gens," he wrote, "has become the pivot around which this entire science turns" (ibid., 3:201).

As contemporaries of Morgan, Engels, and Marx, the founding mothers of modern feminism in the United States shared their enthusiasm at finding functioning societies that incorporated notions of sexual equality. All seemed to believe that the Native model held promise for the future. Gage and Stanton looked to the Native model for a design of a "regenerated world" (Gage, [1893] 1980, 9). "Never was justice more perfect, never civilization higher than under the Matriarchate," Gage wrote (Wagner, 1989, 11; Gage, [1893] 1980, 246). She continued: "Under [Iroquois] women, the science of government reached the highest form known to the world" (Gage, [1893] 1980, 10.) Writing in the *New York Evening Post*, Gage contended that "division of power between the sexes in this Indian republic was nearly equal" (1875, 12).

In her 1891 speech before the National Council of Women, Stanton surveyed the research of Morgan and others indicating to her that, "Among the greater number of the American aborigines, the descent of property and children were in the female line. Women sat in the councils of war and peace and their opinions had equal weight on all questions" (Stanton, 1891, 1). In this regard, she mentioned the Iroquois' councils specifically. After surveying indigenous societies in other parts of the world as well, Stanton closed her speech with a case for sexual equality:

> In closing, I would say that every woman present must have a new sense of dignity and self respect, feeling that our mothers, during long periods in the long past, have been the ruling power and that they used that power for the best interests of humanity. As history is said to repeat itself, we have every reason to believe that our turn will come again. It may not be for woman's supremacy, but for, the as yet untried experiment of complete equality, when the united thought of man and woman will inaugurate a just government, a pure religion, a happy home, a civilization at last in which ignorance, poverty and crime will exist no more. Those who watch already behold the dawn of the new day. (Stanton, 1891, 7)

FURTHER READING

Abram, Charles. Law of the Woman Chief, May 21, 1923. Hewitt Collection, BAE Manuscript No. 1636, NAA, Smithsonian Institution. Cited in Grinde and Johansen, 1991, 259.

Africans in America: Revolution, Resource Bank, Part 2: 1750–1805: Crispus Attucks. Public Broadcasting Service. No date. Available at http://www.pbs.org/wgbh/aia/part2/2p24.html. Accessed February 20, 2003.

Allen, Paula Gunn. *The Sacred Hoop: Recovering the Feminine in American Indian Traditions.* Boston: Beacon Press, 1986.

American Monthly Museum [magazine], 2(February 1776), 96.

Anthony, Susan B., Elizabeth Cady Stanton, and Matilda Joslyn Gage, eds. *History of Woman Suffrage.* Salem, NH: Ayer, [1880] 1985.

Axtell, James. *The Indian Peoples of Eastern America: A Documentary History of the Sexes.* New York: Oxford University Press, 1981.

Barreiro, José. The Search for Lessons. In José Barreiro, ed., *Indigenous Economics: Toward A Natural World Order. Akwe:kon Journal* 9:2(Summer 1992):18–39.

Birchfield, D. L. *The Encyclopedia of North American Indians.* Vol. 5. New York: Marshall Cavendish, 1997.

Brown, Judith K. Economic Organization and the Position of Women Among the Iroquois. *Ethnohistory* 17:3–4(Summer-Fall 1970):151–167.

Cameron, Kenneth W., ed. *The Works of Samuel Peters.* Hartford, CT: Transcendental Books, 1967.

Carr, Lucien. *The Social and Political Position of Women Among the Huron-Iroquois Tribes.* Salem, MA: Salem Press, 1884.

Case, Nancy Humphrey. Gifts from the Indians: Native Americans Not Only Provided New Kinds of Food and Recreation; They May Have Given the Founding Fathers Ideas on How to Form a Government. *The Christian Science Monitor,* November 26, 2002. Available at http://www.csmonitor.com.

Child, Lydia Maria. *The History of the Condition of Women, in Various Ages and Nations.* 2 vols. Boston: J. Allen and Co., 1835.

Cohen, Felix. Americanizing the White Man. *American Scholar* 21:2(1952):177–191.

Cohen, Felix. *The Legal Conscience: Selected Papers of Felix S. Cohen.* Edited by Lucy Kramer Cohen. New Haven, CT: Yale University Press, 1960.

Corkran, David H. *The Cherokee Frontier: Conflict and Survival, 1740–62.* Norman: University of Oklahoma Press, 1962.

Cronon, William. *Changes in the Land: Indians, Colonists, and the Ecology of New England.* New York: Hill and Wang, 1983.

Crosby, Alfred W. *The Columbian Exchange: Biological and Cultural Consequences of 1492.* New York: Greenwood Press, 1972.

Edwards, Everett E. The Contributions of American Indians to Civilization. *Minnesota History* 15:3(1934):255–272.

Engels, Frederick. *The Origin of the Family, Private Property and the State.* 1883. Reprinted in *Karl Marx and Frederick Engles, Selected Works in One Volume.* New York: International Publishers, 1968.

"Exhibit on the Iroquois League," Yager Museum, Hartwick College, Oneonta, NY, June 1983.

Fenton, W. N. *Contacts Between Iroquois Herbalism and Colonial Medicine.* Washington, DC: Smithsonian Institution, 1941.

Foner, Philip S., ed. *Complete Writings of Thomas Paine.* New York: Citadel Press, 1945.

Forbes, Jack. *The Indian in America's Past.* New York: Prentice-Hall, 1964.

Frachtenberg, Leo J. Our Indebtedness to the American Indian. *Wisconsin Archeologist* 14:2(1915):64–69.

Gage, Matilda Joslyn. *Woman, Church and State.* Watertown, MA: Peresphone Press, [1893] 1980.

Gipson, Arrell Morgan. *The American Indian: Prehistory to Present*. Lexington, MA: D. C. Heath, 1980.

Grinde, Donald A., Jr., and Bruce E. Johansen. *Exemplar of Liberty: Native America and the Evolution of Democracy*. Los Angeles: UCLA American Indian Studies Center, 1991.

Grinde, Donald A., Jr., and Bruce E. Johansen. *Ecocide of Native America: Environmental Destruction of Indian Lands and Peoples*. Santa Fe, NM: Clear Light, 1995.

Keoke, Emory Dean, and Kay Marie Porterfield. *Encyclopedia of American Indian Contributions to the World*. New York: Facts on File, 2002.

Kraus, Michael. *The Atlantic Civilization: Eighteenth Century Origins*. New York: Russell and Russell, 1949.

Landsman, Gail. Portrayals of the Iroquois in the Woman Suffrage Movement. Paper presented at the Annual Conference on Iroquois Research, Rensselaerville, NY, October 8, 1988.

Myers, Albert Cook. *Narratives of Early Pennsylvania, West New Jersey and Delaware, 1630–1702*. New York: Charles Scribner's Sons, 1912.

New York Evening Post, September 24, 1875. Cited in Wagner, 1989, 12.

The Pharmacopoeia of the United States of America: by authority of the National Convention for Revising the Pharmacopoeia, held at Washington, A.D. 1860. 4th decennial rev. Philadelphia: Lippincott, 1863.

Porterfield, Kay Marie. Ten Lies about Indigenous Science—How to Talk Back. October 10, 2002. Available at http://www.kporterfield.com/aicttw/articles/lies.html.

Rogers, Robert. *Concise Account of North America*. New Haven, CT: Johnson Reprint, 1966.

Selsam, Millicent. *Plants that Heal*. New York: William Morrow, 1959.

Stanton, Elizabeth Cady. The Matriarchate or Mother-Age [address before the National Council of Women, February 1891]. *The National Bulletin* 1:5(February 1891):1–7.

Substance of the Speech of Good Peter to Governor Clinton and the Commissioners of Indian Affairs at Albany. Collections of the New York Historical Society, 1st Series (1814):2:115.

Wagner, Sally Roesch. The Iroquois Confederacy: A Native American Model for Non-Sexist Men. *Changing Men*, Spring-Summer 1988, 32–33.

Wagner, Sally Roesch. The Root of Oppression Is the Loss of Memory: The Iroquois and the Early Feminist Vision. *Akwesasne* Notes, Late Winter, 1989, 11.

Weatherford, Jack. *Indian Givers: How the Indians of the Americas Transformed the World*. New York: Fawcett Columbine, 1988.

Weatherford, Jack. *Native Roots: How the Indians Enriched America*. New York: Crown, 1991.

CHAPTER 11

Contemporary Issues in Native America

Native America today presents a varied mosaic of life, death, and pervasive struggle. Many issues are economic in nature, but others have to do with cultural respect, as well as for the earth we all share. This chapter is an attempt to sketch a sampling of contemporary issues—a few of many.

A survey of contemporary reservation economic conditions in South Dakota will be a corrective for anyone who thinks that modern-day gambling has made all Native Americans rich. Aside from some of the poorest counties in the United States (in and around reservations in South Dakota), Native peoples also occupy some of Canada's most desolate real estate, as characterized by the village of Pikangikum, Ontario, where major activities for young people are sniffling gasoline and suicide. Alcoholism is still a plague in the cities as well as on rural reservations. Readers will become acquainted with the hamlet of Whiteclay, Nebraska, where the major business is selling beer and other alcoholic beverages to Indians of the neighboring Pine Ridge Reservation, where such sales are illegal.

Is gambling the answer—the "new buffalo" as some Native Americans have called it? In some places, such as the Pequots' Foxwoods, in Connecticut, and some other locales, it has been, as small tribes' members have been enriched. In other places, such as the New York Oneidas' lands in upstate New York, gambling has provided an enriched upper class the means to hire police to force dissident antigambling traditionalists from their homes. Among the Mohawks at Akwesasne, people have died over the issue. Akwesasne's position on the border of the United States with Canada has made smuggling of cigarettes, liquor, other drugs, weapons, and human beings a major industry.

Environmental issues are very important in the contemporary Native American political equation. In this chapter, readers will come to know Navajos who mined some of the uranium that powered the nation's nuclear arsenal and have recently been dying of lung cancer. The U.S. fledgling Green Party is informed by Native American voices, including the naming of Winona LaDuke, an Anishinabe, as a candidate for vice president of the United States on its national ticket with Ralph Nader.

Today, Native activists campaign against the use of American Indian symbols as sports mascots, something that often has been handled with deft humor, as in the case of the "Fighting Whities," an intramural basketball team in Colorado, which stirred a national debate by adopting an upper middle class white mascot. Others struggle to remove the word *squaw* (often taken as a reference to Native women's vaginas) from place-names. Struggles are ongoing to return Native bones and burial artifacts to the earth and to revive Native languages that are on the verge of disappearing.

CONTEMPORARY RESERVATION ECONOMIC CONDITIONS

In some ways, life for Native people living on reservations was becoming more difficult as the twentieth century ended. By 1990, the Pine Ridge Oglala Lakota (Sioux) Reservation in southwest South Dakota, with people descended from Crazy Horse and Red Cloud and the site of the 1890 massacre at Wounded Knee and the 1973 confrontation there, had become the poorest area in the United States.

In the 2000 census, the rankings were little changed. In the 2000 census, Buffalo County, home of the Lower Brule Indian Reservation, had the lowest per capita income in the United States. Second-lowest ranking was Shannon County, home of the Pine Ridge Reservation. In Buffalo County, 61.8 percent of the children lived in poverty, the highest rate in the United States, followed by Zieback County (61.2 percent) and Shannon County (61 percent). These rates were much higher than those in any urban area.

The 2000 census indicated that South Dakota as a whole had the largest percentage increase in the United States for household median income between 1990 and 2000. At the same time, Buffalo County, home of the 3,500-member Crow Creek Sioux, exchanged places with Shannon County among the two poorest in the United States. In Buffalo County, the largest and most successful business during the 1990s was the Lode Star Casino. Shannon County has benefited somewhat from federal empowerment zone status that brought the county millions in federal dollars for economic development and a visit from President Bill Clinton.

In 1989, nearly seven of every ten people in Shannon County were unemployed, and virtually the only work, except for a few private businesses, came from government agencies and the underground economy. Pine Ridge village, the largest town on the reservation, had no railroad or bus connections and no bank, theater, clothing store, or barbershop. Big Bat's, the one major Native-owned business in Pine Ridge, was taken to court thirteen times by white land and business owners who tried to prevent its opening. Meanwhile, the pervasiveness of poverty shatters families and causes people to turn to alcohol and other drugs. Infant mortality at Pine Ridge was 29 per 1,000 children, three times the national average. The death rate from homicide was also three times the national average. People at Pine Ridge died from alcoholism at ten times the national rate (not taking into account damage caused by fetal alcohol syndrome). The death rate from adult diabetes was four times the national average. The tribal housing authority had a waiting list of 2,000 families for subsidized lodging, at least a quarter of the people on the reservation.

John Yellow Bird Steele, chair of the Oglala Sioux Tribal Council in 1992, advocated construction of three casinos to alleviate unemployment and provide private industry on the reservation. The Wounded Knee chapter of the American Indian Movement (AIM) believes that gambling will drive poor people on the reservation further into alcoholism and debt, a modern form of genocide. In the midst of deepening poverty and divisiveness, however, a tribal consensus to upgrade education produced improved schools and a number of well-kept school buildings. Since 1970, the tribe has gradually taken over administration of most reservation schools from the Bureau of Indian Affairs (BIA).

The indications of poverty in South Dakota were nearly duplicated in neighboring states. In Nebraska, unemployment on the Omaha reservation stood at 71 percent in the late 1980s; among the Santee Sioux, unemployment was 55 percent, compared to 65 percent among the Winnebago (Suzuki, 1991, 27–28). Nationwide, the civilian unemployment rate among Native Americans on reservations was about 30 percent in 1990. Unemployment on the Navajo reservation, with its workforce of 87,000 people (the largest in the United States) was 29.5 percent.

Nationwide, Native Americans' income level was falling in 1990 as measured against all other ethnic groups in the United States. According to the Census Bureau, the median household income for Native Americans (inflation adjusted) fell from $20,541 in 1980 to $20,025 in 1990; the same figure for citizens of European heritage rose from $29,632 to $31,435. The percentage of Native Americans defined as living below the "poverty line" increased from 27.5 percent in 1980 to 30.9 percent in 1990; the percentage for European Americans rose from 9.4 percent to 9.8 percent. In 1990, the Census Bureau found that 29.5 percent of blacks, 14.1 percent of Asians, and 25.3 percent of Hispanics lived in poverty. In 1989, the Children's Defense Fund found that 66 percent of Native American children in Minneapolis, Minnesota, were living in families with incomes below the poverty line.

Although many statistics indicate that Native Americans often were experiencing intensifying poverty at the end of the twentieth century, some indicators reveal improvement in some areas of health and welfare. For example, the Indian Health Service (IHS) reported that the homicide rate for Native

Americans (per 100,000 people) declined from 23.8 in 1955 to 14.1 in 1988, as the rate for all ethnic groups in the United States increased from 4.8 to 9.0 per 100,000. Although 57 percent of blacks and 47 percent of whites who died were killed with guns between 1966 and 1988, according to the Federal Bureau of Investigation (FBI), only 29 percent of Indians were murdered with firearms. Thirty-two percent were killed with knives. Deaths from alcoholism among Native Americans declined from 56.6 per 100,000 in 1969 to 33.9 in 1988; the rate for all races in the United States declined only slightly, from 7.7 to 6.3 per 100,000. Put another way, in 1969, the alcoholism death rate for Native Americans and Alaska Natives was 7.4 times that of the general population. In two decades, that figure fell to 5.4 times according to the IHS.

According to Jeffrey Wollock, writing in *Native Americas* (2003), from 1996 to 2001, crime rates on reservations rose while they fell elsewhere, Indians twelve to twenty years old are 58 percent more likely to be crime victims than whites and blacks. Indians under age fifteen years are murdered at twice the rate of whites.

The contemporary murder rate on Indian reservations is five times the average in the United States as a whole: 29,000 per 100,000 people compared to 5.6. The average in U.S. urban areas is 7 per 100,000 ("Crime Rate," 2003, 11). An Indian Country Crime Report, compiled from 1,072 cases prosecuted in U.S. District Courts, did not include felonies committed by non-Indians on reservations. Some small reservations have very high murder rates, according to this report. The Salt River Pima Maricopa Community in Arizona, for example, had 6 murders among 6,405 people, a murder rate 17 times the national average. The Gila River Reservation, with 11,257 enrollee members, suffered 11 murders, a similar rate (ibid., 11). According to Mac Rominger, an FBI agent on the Hopi and Navajo reservations, often-blamed problems such as alcoholism and poverty were being compounded by isolation. "Ninety-five per cent of the violent crime out there is directed towards family and friends," he said (ibid., 11).

Youth suicide among Native Americans is twice the rate of non-Indians. The American Medical Association reports that one in five Indian girls attempts suicide before leaving high school. The alcoholism death rate is four times the national average (Wollock, 2003, 30). In addition, more than 40 percent of Native Americans in the United States live in substandard housing compared with an average of 6 percent for the rest of the population. The crisis for Native American young people is closely tied to loss of culture, with youth "stuck between two worlds". Many more Native youths than in earlier times cannot speak their own languages and have little grasp of their traditional culture and history.

Similar statistics can assume a terrifying profile when they are described in personal context of a small village. Take, for example, the Ojibway-Cree village of Pikangikum, about 200 miles northeast of Winnipeg.

PIKANGIKUM'S CONTINUING DESOLATION ESCAPES
CANADA'S MINISTRY OF INDIAN AFFAIRS

The Ojibway-Cree village of Pikangikum, about 200 miles northeast of Winnipeg, has the highest documented suicide rate in the world. It is a place where the main recreational pastime for young people is glue sniffing. The reserve's only school was closed for more than a year because of a fuel leak. Pikangikum's water treatment plant was closed nearly as long, also because of an accidental fuel leak.

Of the adults in Pikangikum, 80 to 90 percent are unemployed. The village is so overcrowded, with 400 homes for 2,100 people, that some people sleep in shifts to make beds available for others. All food is flown in, so prices are about five times the average for the rest of Canada.

What did Canada's Ministry of Indian Affairs do about all of this? It suspended the fiscal authority of the village band council, provoking anger at Pikangikum. On May 17, 2001, Indian Affairs Minister Robert Nault took control of the Pikangikum first nation's $9 million (Canadian) annual budget and then gave control to a private consulting firm, A. D. Morrison and Associates Limited, of London, Ontario, a situation known within the Canadian Indian bureaucracy as "third-party management."

Chief Louis Quill, a spokesman for the Pikangikum council, said the community was shocked to learn that A. D. Morrison and Associates was a first nations-operated company. "I don't think that's the way to treat other Natives," said Quill. "We shouldn't be going after our own people on behalf of Indian Affairs" ("Pikangikum Update," *Canadian Aboriginal*, n.d.). The local council called Indian Affairs' actions paternalistic. The band council was not running a deficit when its fiscal powers were removed; it had passed previous financial audits. Quill said the third-party managers "are not welcome in our community" ("Pikangikum Update," *Canadian Aboriginal*, n.d.).

When the residents of Pikangikum refused to cooperate with Nault and the third-party managers, Nault, whose jurisdiction in Canada's Parliament includes Pikangikum, suspended federal transfer payments to its council, meaning that most of the 10 percent of the town's adults who had jobs stopped receiving paychecks.

More than forty young people killed themselves in Pikangikum during the ten years ending in 2002. The same rate would have yielded 70,500 suicides in a city of 3 million people. During 2000, the community's rate of suicide was 380 per 100,000 population. The national average suicide rate in Canada is 13 per 100,000. "If [third-party management] is being forced on the community [Pikangikum] from the outside . . . that just increases the sense of not having control, and that increases the distress," said David Masecar, president of the Canadian Association of Suicide Prevention (Elliott, June 7, 2001).

Most of the suicides were women who hung themselves (Elliott, June 7, 2001). During 2000 alone, nine Ojibway girls aged five to thirteen killed themselves in Pikangikum. Those suicides sent the year's suicide rate up to 470 deaths per 100,000, thirty-six times the Canadian national average. Three more young women killed themselves between mid-May and mid-June 2001. "When young women who are the bearers of life start to kill themselves, it's a real reflection on the health of the community," said Arnold Devlin, of Dilico Child and Family Services in Thunder Bay (Elliott, November 30, 2000).

Since 1995, the Pikangikum Youth Patrol, a team of young volunteers, has scoured Pikangikum almost every night looking for huddles of gas sniffers "whose spine-chilling howls permeate the community at night, but the young addicts often scatter into the darkness before patrollers can reach them. At peak suicide times like ... summer and fall, there's an attempt or two every night" (Elliott, November 30, 2000).

Louise Elliott wrote for Canadian Press (November 30, 2000):

> The [suicide] problem, while worst in Pikangikum, is region-wide. On Monday, another 13-year-old girl took her life in Summer Beaver, a reserve 300 kilometers east of Pikangikum, bringing the total suicides on northern Ontario reserves this year [2000] to 25. "This is the worst year on record [for suicide]," said Arnold Devlin, of Dilico Child and Family Services in Thunder Bay."

"It's very, very difficult," said band councilor Sam Quill, 62, his eyes welling with tears. Quill, who recalled Pikangikum's first rash of youth hangings in 1993 and 1994 saw his daughter and granddaughter take their own lives (Elliott, November 30, 2000). "There are no resources here, whatsoever," said Bonnie-Jean Muir, of Pokangikum. "There's nothing for kids and because there's no place else to go when they're not sleeping, they're out roaming and sniffing. It's a community out of control" (Gamble, n.d.).

A Grand River Mohawk who is also a medical doctor, Michael Monture, 42, became lost in the bush while serving a rotation on the reserve (five doctors rotate; the reserve has no other medical services). Reports say the entire community joined in a search for Monture because he is so well loved. He was found after losing his way in the bush for two-and-a-half days.

The previous week, according to a report in the Brantford (Ontario) *Expositor*, during his second visit to Pikangikum, "Monture tallied up some of the dire social ills that plague the 2,100-member community and was angry," said Bonnie-Jean Muir, who had shared a dinner with Monture the evening before he went into the bush, beginning a two-day ordeal (Gamble, n.d.). "He joined us until 10 P.M. and about 12:30 A.M. he went out for a long walk, intending to spend the night in the bush," Muir told the *Expositor* from Pikangikum. "He found the state of the Pikangikum people absolutely deplorable" (Gamble, n.d.). Monture was known as a skilled hunter who is at home in the back country.

Each visiting physician is given a large box of food for his rotation in Pikangikum. Monture gave most of his food away. "The most common concern was the lack of food. What am I supposed to do? Write a prescription for food for these people?" Monture told Canadian Press (Gamble, n.d.). Recently, Monture had decided to dedicate a good part his medical practice to the people of Pikangikum. He moved to Sioux Lookout, near Pikangikum, so that he could fly in to offer medical treatment to the community once or twice a month.

With little food and dwindling gasoline supplies, town residents used their own all-terrain vehicles and boats to comb the area. They set out each morning of the search from a base camp north of Pikangikum. Spotted by an Ontario Provincial Police helicopter, Monture emerged from the bush seven miles from Pikangikum after two-and-a-half cold, wet days. According to one news account, Monture said that "The suffering and desperation . . . on the remote reserve of Pikangikum . . . prompted him to set out on a spiritual quest for help" (Elliott, June 18, 2001, A-14).

"I was concerned and frustrated at the lack of resources," Monture said after he was rescued (Elliott, June 18, 2001, A-14). "What galvanized me was how people were lacking in basic food and necessities," he said. "It's not a question of *what* you're going to eat, it's *whether* you're going to eat" (ibid., A-14). Monture described seeing young children huddled near a burning pile of refuse at Pikangikum. "They have a fire going in the garbage dump to keep warm while looking for things to eat," he says. "It's very upsetting to think that this is Canada" (ibid., A-14).

Chief Quill said that Monture's actions had raised the community's profile and its spirits, according to Canadian Press reports, which noted: "Residents, apparently overwhelmed by the doctor's actions, circled around him as he prepared to fly off the reserve Saturday night, reaching out to touch him as though he were a hero" (Elliott, June 18, 2001, A-14).

"It was a political stance he was taking," said Muir. "He could not believe what he saw" (Elliott, June 16, 2001, A-16). Stan Beardy, the grand chief of Nishnawbe-Aski Nation, the political organization that represents northern Ontario reserves, says he believed that fury over the government's appointment of an Indian agent to take control of Pikangikum's finances also played a role in Monture's sojourn into the bush.

About 200 students lost access to education when Pikangikum's only school closed for about a year after 24,000 liters of diesel oil were accidentally pumped into the crawl space under the school building. In addition, on October 2, 2000, the Pikangikum water treatment plant flooded, leaking more than 250 gallons of fuel oil into the town's reservoir. According to a report in a local newspaper, the *Anishinabek News*, "Health Canada closed down the water system and closed the hotel. The workers working on the school had to leave as well. . . . Chief Peter Quill has stated that unless the water situation is dealt with immediately, the impact on the community will be devastating— both in terms of water-related medical problems and youth suicide" (Goulais, 2000, n.p.). Many Pikangikum residents were forced to buy water at the local store for $5.99 (Canadian) per four-liter jug. Residents who could not buy drinking water used bottled water that is (occasionally, owing to weather conditions) flown in by Indian Affairs. Otherwise, they boiled lake water.

Canadian Indian Affairs provided $1.3 million in repairs to the water plant, which were completed January 22, 2001. "At no time," said an Indian Affairs press release, "was any resident of Pikangikum without clean water. In addition, the department also flew in a portable Zenon water plant at a cost of $4,500 per month. The community continues to use this portable plant."

A local news account said: "The water situation is no stranger to the communities of the Anishinabek Nation. In August, Gull Bay First Nation tested positive for *e-coli* contamination in their water supply. According to Chief Oliver Poile of Gull Bay, somebody may have died as a result of that contamination" (Goulais, 2000, n.p.).

In addition to the suicides, Pikangikum has been grappling with $10 million in failed infrastructure projects. In March 1999, workers were putting finishing touches on a business center in Pikangikum that community leaders had hoped would foster new ventures. *Northern Ontario Business* described "a 1,080-square-meter business center [which] will house a hotel, full-service restaurant, offices, rental space and classroom facilities. The project is expected to create 15 permanent jobs in Pikangikum" (Lynch, 1999). Two years later, Indian Affairs' embargo on funds closed the hotel.

The list of woes afflicting Pikangikum included construction delays and legal disputes with contractors over an all-weather road and a power line intended to connect the community to the provincial power grid—two necessary steps toward building the kind of infrastructure community members say is necessary.

Meanwhile, at Pikangikum, according to Louise Elliott of the Canadian Press:

> On the roads . . . young children play on makeshift sleds—sharp-edged fragments of wainscotting they've pulled from stalled construction projects. Band leaders say the community doesn't have enough electricity right now to fix its water treatment plant, or to keep up with the need for new houses. A grid line to pipe in electricity from Balmertown, 100 kilometers south, is only half-finished—it stalled when the contractor walked off the job last summer. (December 3, 2000)

Elliott continued:

> Outside the graffiti-scrawled homes with no indoor plumbing, crosses marking the graves of old and young are lined up seven or eight meters from the front doors, in a unique Pikangikum custom. No one seems to know where this tradition began—some say it happened when people left their traditional church for another, and could no longer use the church graveyard. (December 3, 2000)

As Indian Affairs and the Pikangikum Council remained in stalemate, the number of suicides continued to rise among First Nations youths across

Ontario's north country. As of the end of July, sixteen young people had killed themselves on forty-nine northern reserves during 2001, compared to twenty-six during all of 2001, with fall ("suicide season") still to come. Seven of those suicides had occurred in Pikangikum, compared to eight during all of 2000 (Elliott, July 31, 2001, A-6).

Nault had his own take on the rising suicide rate across Ontario's north country. In a letter, he said that Pikangikum band leaders had "perpetuated" the community's suicide crisis by talking to the media. "I'm very concerned that the decision to pursue a media approach may in fact perpetuate the suicide crisis," Nault wrote, adding that a 1996 report by the Royal Commission on Aboriginal Peoples "suggests the more publicity given to suicides, the more suicides that follow in their wake" (Elliott, June 22, 2001).

Joseph Magnet, a University of Ottawa law professor who undertook a constitutional challenge to Nault's decision to take over the band's finances, said the letter unfairly blames the community's interviews with media in recent weeks for the suicide epidemic. "It's a weird thing to say—'we shouldn't bring our lawyers in, we shouldn't call the press, we should let our kids die in private.'" Magnet said of the letter. "It's ridiculous" (Elliott, June 22, 2001).

ALCOHOLISM: THE CONTINUING TOLL

Second only to the ravages of smallpox and other diseases, alcoholism has been the major cause of early death and other forms of misery for Native Americans since the "discovery" of the Americas by Columbus. Scarrooyady, an Iroquois sachem, told Pennsylvania treaty commissioners in 1750: "Your traders now bring us scarce anything but rum and flour. The rum ruins us. . . . Those wicked whiskey sellers, when they have got the Indians in liquor, make them sell the very clothes from their backs!" (Johansen, 1982, 68). In 1832, the sale of alcoholic beverages to Indians was made illegal, an act that was not repealed until the early 1950s, when it became evident that prohibition produced a bootlegging industry little different from that which flourished nationwide during the 1920s and early 1930s.

Alcoholism continues to be a major problem today. The disease of alcoholism continues to be the leading single cause of death in many Native American communities. Today, the sharpest increases in alcoholism are being suffered in faraway places such as Alaska and the Canadian North, where Native peoples have only recently been deprived of their traditional ways of life. In Manitoba, for example, several hundred Native people whose lands were flooded have been moved to settlements where they are no longer allowed (or able) to wrest a living from the land. Alcoholism and other forms of social disorientation have followed suit. As many as 90 percent of adults have abused alcohol and other drugs, and juveniles frequently engage in fights. In a settlement of fewer than 1,000 people, suicide attempts averaged fifteen per month in the 1980s. At nearby Cross Lake, another small village, suicide attempts averaged twenty a month, ten times the provincial average.

In 1960, before widespread energy development on Alaska's North Slope, the suicide rate among Native people there was 13 per 100,000, comparable to averages in the United States as a whole. By 1970, the suicide rate had risen to 25 per 100,000; by 1986, it was 67.6 per 100,000. Homicide rates by the mid-1980s were three times the average in the United States as a whole, between 22.9 and 26.6 per 100,000 people, depending on which study was used. Death rates from homicide and suicide were related to rising alcoholism. In the mid-1980s, 79 percent of Native suicide victims had some alcohol in their blood at the time of death. Slightly more than half (54 percent) were legally intoxicated.

In 1969, the IHS appointed a Task Force on Alcoholism that a year later concluded that alcoholism was one of the most significant health problems facing American Indians and Alaska Natives. Seven years later, the American Indian Policy Review Commission, established by the U.S. Congress, found alcoholism and its medical consequences were the most serious and widespread health problem among American Indians. According to the IHS, alcoholism has an insidious multiplier effect. It contributes not only to elevated rates of traffic deaths, but also to the majority of Indian homicides, other assaults, suicides, and other mental health problems.

Even today, among Plains Indians, 80 to 90 percent of Native American men drink alcohol, as do 50 to 60 percent of Indian women. By age 17, a majority of Indian boys and a large minority of Indian girls are steady drinkers. Drinking among Indian young people has been related directly to the highest suicide rate in the United States for any age group. Alcohol abuse also relates to low educational achievement, poor health, high rates of unemployment, and crime among Indian youths.

Nationwide, Indians have for several years averaged twelve times the number of arrests per capita compared to the general population. Three-quarters of these arrests were alcohol related, almost twice the national average. In 1973, the General Accounting Office surveyed six IHS hospitals and found that 60 percent of the caseload could be directly or indirectly attributed to alcohol use. Cirrhosis of the liver was a frequent cause of hospitalization and eventual death. According to the IHS, cirrhosis of the liver occurs in American Indians at five times the rate of the general population. The IHS also reports that many child-battering cases are alcohol related.

A major cause of Indian alcoholism is deprivation and poverty, rejection by European Americans as inferiors, deterioration of traditional cultures, and a generally high level of anxiety that attends day-to-day reservation life. The Klamaths, who were dispersed by federal government termination policies during the early 1950s, had a high rate of arrests for alcohol-related crime, even when compared to the averages for Indians, which are a dozen times those for non-Indians. By contrast, the Pueblo Indians of New Mexico, who have maintained most of their traditional way of life through 150 years of U.S.

domination (and two centuries under Spain and Mexico before that) have relatively low rates of alcohol-related arrests.

Given the history of Indian alcoholism, treatment for it is a relatively recent development. As late as the mid-1960s, intoxicated Indians arrested in Gallup, New Mexico, were simply put in jail until it filled. On winter nights, those who were not arrested ran a risk of freezing to death. In a routine winter, many Indians froze to death on the streets of Gallup.

For a number of reasons, most of them cultural, traditional non-Indian treatments, from hospitalization to non-Indian chapters of Alcoholics Anonymous, had very little success dealing with Indian alcoholism. In the late 1960s, along with a general thrust of Indian self-determination, Native treatment programs began to open. The idea of Indians treating Indians was hailed as revolutionary in some quarters, but it is not really new. Since at least the days of the Iroquois spiritual leader Handsome Lake in the early 19th century, Indian religious figures have opposed the use of alcohol and achieved moderate success in sobering their followers.

THE POLITICS OF MALT LIQUOR

During the 1990s, protests from Native groups arose in several states regarding the sale of Crazy Horse malt liquor. The beverage was being sold by Hornell Brewing Company of New York in forty-ounce bottles bearing a likeness of Crazy Horse, the nineteenth century Lakota leader. The brew was being manufactured by G. Heileman Brewing Company.

In Congressional hearings, U.S. Surgeon General Antonia Novello and representatives of Native American groups contended that Crazy Horse malt liquor was specifically aimed at underage Native American drinkers. The surgeon general also was attacking other brands of alcohol, as well as cigarettes, which appeared to be aimed at minorities, women, and teenagers. The campaign already had resulted in the removal from shelves of PowerMaster, also a malt liquor, after complaints that it was targeted at young blacks.

Crazy Horse malt liquor was not the first marketing attempt aimed specifically at Indians, of course; traders have been getting them addicted to liquor since the earliest days of contact. It also is not the first alcoholic product to enter into contemporary Native politics. In the late 1980s, Native groups across the northern tier of states (roughly from Wisconsin to Washington) protested the marketing of "treaty beer" by sportsmen's rights groups raising funds to annul Native agreements with the federal government. At the time, the fund-raising brew was called "the Klan in a can" by Indians in Washington State (Johansen, 1988, 13).

WHITECLAY: THE BUSINESS IS BEER

On June 26, 1999, which was 123 years and one day after their ancestors had removed George Armstrong Custer's scalp, Lakotas gathered in

Whiteclay, Nebraska, to demand details describing how Wilson "Wally" Black Elk, 40, and Ronald Hard Heart, 39, had died. Their partially decomposed bodies had been found June 8. Many people at Pine Ridge believed that the way in which Black Elk and Hard Heart died was similar to how two other Lakota, Wesley Bad Heart Bull and Raymond Yellow Thunder, were killed in 1972—beaten to death by white toughs having what they regarded as a sporting time with inebriated Oglala Lakotas.

A month and more after the killings of Black Elk and Hard Heart, the men's reservation relatives knew little or nothing officially of how they died. Law enforcement officials in Nebraska and FBI agents talked vaguely of "foul play" and "following leads" while anger spread at Pine Ridge. Pine Ridge tribal police chief Stan Star Comes Out told the *Omaha World-Herald* that the remains of the two men had been wounded and bloody. He also said the two men had been bludgeoned to death. The bodies were found on the Pine Ridge (South Dakota) side of the line, but many Lakota believed the men were murdered in Nebraska, closer to Whiteclay, after which their bodies were dragged across the border.

Lakota community responses to the deaths of Yellow Thunder and Bad Heart Bull defined the AIM during 1972, becoming a provocation for the occupation of Wounded Knee the next year. Yellow Thunder was kidnapped and beaten to death during the middle of February, 1972, in Gorton, Nebraska (about twenty-five miles southeast of Whiteclay and thirteen miles south of Pine Ridge) by several white toughs. Four young men were charged with manslaughter (not murder), and two of them were convicted. By March, Gordon was the scene of rallies of more than 1,000 Lakota and allies demanding justice for Yellow Thunder. Two brothers who were convicted of manslaughter served ten months (of a two-year sentence) and two years (of a six-year sentence), respectively.

Shortly after the murder of Yellow Thunder in 1972, Lakota Wesley Bad Heart Bull was stabbed to death by a young white man near Custer, South Dakota (in the Black Hills southwest of Rapid City). The assailant was charged with second-degree manslaughter, provoking demonstrations organized by AIM, some of which turned violent, at the courthouse in Custer.

In 1999, some of the major organizers were the same as they had been in Gordon and Custer—AIMsters with many more lines on their faces. They listened to speeches by Russell Means, Clyde Bellecourt, and Dennis Banks, among others, protesting basic injustices, such as young white men's penchant for taking out their aggressions (sometimes with fatal results) on drunken Indians near the dusty streets of Whiteclay, population twenty-four, where the main business was selling $3 million a year worth of beer to the people of Pine Ridge (Johansen, 1998, 5).

In reaction to the murders of Hard Heart and Black Elk, a Rally for Justice— 250 people walking accompanied by about 150 automobiles—traversed the two-lane blacktop to "take Whiteclay back" on June 26. As the larger rally was breaking up in Whiteclay, about twenty-five to thirty people trashed a grocery store, V. J.'s Market, in Whiteclay. It was said that V. J.'s owner, Vic Clarke, had treated Lakota in a demeaning manner. The store's freezer cases were destroyed and its cash registers doused with lighter fluid. Groceries were strewn through the store.

Claims of Lakota control of the ground on which Whiteclay sits are based on surveys taken for the Fort Laramie Treaty of 1868, which place Whiteclay within reservation borders. Documents related to the Dawes (Allotment) Act, notably legislation passed by Congress in 1889 to break up what was then called "the Great Sioux Nation," also support this assertion. An executive order issued in 1882 by President Chester Arthur created a 50-square-mile "buffer zone" (which includes the site of Whiteclay) south of the Pine Ridge reservation expressly to curtail the liquor trade. This order was rescinded on January 25, 1904, by President Theodore Roosevelt with the rationale that non-Indians needed the land.

For years, Nebraska officials had been warned by activist Frank LaMere and others that the situation in Whiteclay could explode. One day during the summer of 1997, LaMere, a Winnebago who was executive director of the Nebraska Inter-Tribal Development Corporation, visited Whiteclay. He counted thirty-two intoxicated Indians on the town's streets at 5:15 in the morning and forty-seven drunks on the streets during the afternoon, some of whom were fighting with each other. Several other Indians were passed out at the intersection of Nebraska Highway 87 with the road that leads to the reservation. A few of them were urinating on the street (Johansen, 1998, 5).

Shortly after he visited Whiteclay, LaMere asked the Nebraska Liquor Control Commission to shut Whiteclay down. "I don't know what constitutes infractions of liquor laws in Whiteclay, but my good sense tells me there is something terribly wrong" LaMere told Toni Heinzl of the *Omaha World-Herald*. "What I saw . . . in Whiteclay would not be acceptable in Omaha or Lincoln," LaMere continued (Johansen, 1998, 5).

The Pine Ridge Reservation in 1996 had an alcoholism-related death rate of 61.9 per 100,000 people, twice the average for Native American reservations and nine times the national average of 7.1. On the two-mile highway between Pine Ridge village and Whiteclay, tribal police issued at least 1,000 driving while intoxicated citations per year. Despite the police presence, residents who live along the road were constantly pestered by drunks. Several family dogs had been shot to death along the road as well.

On Saturday, July 3, 1999, about 100 sheriff's deputies and state patrol officers, many of them in riot gear, barricaded Whiteclay's business district. Ironically, the Nebraska State Patrol had met one of the protesters' demands: For Friday and Saturday at least, the beer stores of Whiteclay would be closed on one of their busiest weekends of the year. During Friday afternoon, caravans of cars from Pine Ridge circled Whiteclay and its barricades in an air of ghostly quiet, using several back roads.

Aside from a few rocks thrown and nine brief arrests (one of them of Russell Means), the July 3 march came and went without notable physical contact between the Lakota Sioux and the hundred SWAT-suited police officers barricading Whiteclay. Many participants in the march stressed the spiritual nature of their actions. Marchers stopped four times to pray (and to give elderly marchers some rest) during the hour and a half it took the group of several hundred people to move from Pine Ridge to Whiteclay on a hot and unusually humid day.

As they approached Whiteclay, marchers debated whether to cross a line of yellow plastic tape that police had strung across the road into the village. Most urged restraint, but Russell Means urged the group on. One man on a pinto pony tried to run the line but was stopped by police. Means and the eight others who were arrested also stepped over the line briefly, as they were cited for failure to obey a lawful order, to establish a basis for a later court case (the activists contended that their arrests were illegal). They were released an hour later. Other marchers threw mud at the helmeted troopers. A few spit on them and cursed. One protester plastered a bumper sticker reading "You Are on Indian Land" across one officer's helmet.

As the dust settled in Whiteclay following the second rally, the beer stores opened briefly Monday morning, but closed once again after Clyde Bellecourt told Stuart Kozel, owner of the Jumping Eagle Inn, that opening his store would provoke another confrontation with AIM. Another beer outlet with a distinctly Indian-sounding name, the Arrowhead Inn, also remained closed for an extra day.

On Saturday, July 10, a smaller rally was held, followed by another march and motorcade from Pine Ridge to Whiteclay. Roughly 100 people on foot and in cars sang and drummed as they paraded up and down Whiteclay streets unimpeded by police this time. AIM members posted "eviction notices" on the four beer stores, then withdrew to tipis and tents erected on the site where the bodies of Black Elk and Hard Heart had been found June 8. The people in the camp pledged to maintain it (along with weekly demonstrations in Whiteclay) until the border town went "dry."

In the meantime, LaMere, one of nine people who had been arrested at the initial rally, appealed again to the Nebraska Liquor Control Commission to shut down Whiteclay's beer businesses permanently. Again, the board did not act; within days, the activists were gone, and most of the Indians on the streets of Whiteclay were falling-down drunk.

President Bill Clinton visited Pine Ridge later the same summer. The White House called the tour (which included communities in Appalachia, the Mississippi Delta, South Phoenix, and the Watts area of Los Angeles as well as Pine Ridge) the New Markets Initiative. The main purpose of the four-day tour was to lobby for business development of impoverished areas; some White House planners had suggested that the federal government match certain forms of private investment in such areas.

When President Clinton arrived at Pine Ridge July 7, he found a page out of the Meriam Report (Lewis, 1928), a state of reservation life in many cases little changed from the days of Franklin Roosevelt or Dwight Eisenhower. The Pine Ridge and its neighboring Rosebud Sioux reservations are among the poorest ten counties in the United States. Clinton arrived at Ellsworth Air Force Base, near Rapid City, early Wednesday morning and after a lengthy drive arrived at Pine Ridge village by midmorning. The president ceremonially signed documents creating an empowerment zone at Pine Ridge (the first such zone on an Indian reservation), toured a few housing areas, gave a speech at Pine Ridge High School, and was on his way back to Ellsworth after lunch.

Clinton thus completed a three-hour visit to Pine Ridge that made him the first sitting U.S. president to visit an Indian reservation since Franklin Delano Roosevelt, as well as the first to visit Pine Ridge since Calvin Coolidge (in 1927). During his 20-minute speech at Pine Ridge High School, Clinton greeted the 4,500 people in Lakota and promised such things as a doubling of the number of federal-backed mortgages at Pine Ridge, a move meant to add 1,000 homes to the reservation within a few years. As Clinton spoke, the waiting list for housing there stood at 4,000 units.

GAMBLING: THE NEW BUFFALO?

During the late twentieth century, commercial gambling became a major source of income on some Indian reservations across the United States. Although many Native American cultures traditionally practiced forms of gambling as a type of sport (such as the Iroquois peachstone game), no Native American historical precedent exists for large-scale experience with gambling as a commercial enterprise. The arrival of gaming has brought dividends to some Native American peoples and controversy culminating in firefights and death for others.

The history of reservation-based commercial gambling began during 1979, when the Seminoles became the first Native nation to enter the bingo industry. By early 1985, 75 to 80 of the 300 recognized Indian tribes in the United States were conducting some sort of game of chance. By the fall of 1988, the Congressional Research Service estimated that more than 100 Indian nations and tribes participated in some form of gambling, which grossed about $255 million a year. By 1991, 278 Native reservations recognized by non-Indian governmental bodies, 150 had some form of gambling. According to the Interior Department, gross revenue from such operations passed $1 billion that year.

Individual prizes in some reservation bingo games were reported to be as high as $100,000; bingo stakes in surrounding areas under state jurisdiction were sometimes limited to $100. The reasons for growth in gambling on Indian land were readily apparent. Native governments sensed an opportunity for income that could make a substantial improvement in their economic conditions. A lack of state or federal regulations provided them a competitive advantage over off-reservation gambling regulated by the states. These advantages included a lack of state-imposed limits on the size of pots or prizes, no restrictions by the states on days or hours of operations, no costs for licenses or compliance with state regulations, and (unless they were negotiated) no state taxes on gambling operations.

By the 1990s, gambling was providing a small galaxy of material benefits for some formerly impoverished Native peoples. A half-hour's drive from the Twin Cities, blackjack players crowded forty-one tables, while 450 other players stared into video slot machines inside the tipi-shaped Little Six Casino, operated by the 103 members of the Shakopee Mdewakanton Sioux tribe. By 1991, each member of the tribe was getting a monthly dividend check averaging $2,000 as a shareholder in the casino. In addition to monthly dividends, members became eligible for homes (if they lacked them), guaranteed jobs (if they were unemployed), and full college scholarships. The tribal government took out health insurance policies for everyone on the reservation and established day care for children of working parents.

The largest casino to open by mid-1991 was the $3 million Sycuan Gaming Center on the Sycuan Indian Reservation, near El Cajon, a suburb of San Diego, California. The casino's rakish neon sign flashed against a rocky patch of land onto which the government forced the tribe to move more than a century ago. The sign was visible miles away over scrub-covered hills.

Native American gaming revenue grew to $10.6 billion during 2000, representing 16 percent of the $64.9 billion generated by gaming in the United States as a whole (Wanamaker, May 13, 2002). By 2002, Indian gaming revenue had grown to $14.5 billion, but according to the National Indian Gaming Commission, 65 percent of the cash was flowing into only 7 percent of the gaming tribes (Fialka, 2004). By 2003, Native American casinos in the United States took in $16.2 billion annually, a 12 percent increase from the prior year according to a study by Alan Meister, an economist with the Analysis Group of Los Angeles. Indian casinos' revenue was about 35 percent of the U.S. total. Native American casinos paid $5.3 in taxes and $16.3 billion in wages, providing 460,000 jobs ("Fast Growing," 2004).

Also according to the National Indian Gaming Association, Indian gaming by 2002 contributed approximately $120 million in state and local tax receipts annually. Gaming patrons spent an estimated $237 million in local communities around Indian casinos (Marquez, 2002). Of the 562 federally recognized Native American governmental entities in the United States at that time, 201 participated in class II or III gaming by 2001. Class II includes such games as bingo, pull tabs, lotto, punchboards, and certain card games permissible under individual state laws. Class III includes everything else, such as casino-style table games like roulette and craps and card games such as poker and blackjack. Indian casinos operated in 29 states under a total of 249 separate gaming compacts (Wanamaker, April 5, 2002).

The Oneidas of New York: A Business Called a Nation

Thirty years ago, the New York Oneidas' landholdings were down to thirty-two acres east of Syracuse, with almost no economic infrastructure. Three decades later, the New York Oneidas owned a large casino, the Turning Stone, which had incubated a number of other business ventures. Many of the roughly 1,000 Oneidas who resided in the area were receiving substantial material benefits.

The Turning Stone earns an estimated net profit of $70 million a year on $230 million gross income. Roughly 4.2 million visitors passed through the casino's doors per year (many of these were repeat visits). The casino's influence on the tax base of nearby small towns was enormous. James Chapell, mayor of the town of Oneida, for example, said that the Oneidas had taken so much land off the tax rolls that the town's tax revenues fell from $700,000 to $139,000 in one year. The town of Oneida has resisted requesting financial help from the Oneida Nation, but nearby Verona, which faced similar declines in tax revenue, negotiated funding for a water project as well as $800,000 for local services (Randolph, 2003).

A substantial dissident movement has grown among Oneidas, who assert that Raymond Halbritter, "nation representative" of the New York Oneidas, was never voted into such an office. This group is centered in the Shenandoah family, which includes the notable singer Joanne Shenandoah and her husband, activist Doug George-Kanentiio. They believe that the New York Oneidas under Halbritter have established a business, called it a nation, and acquired the requisite approvals from New York State and the U.S. federal government to use this status to open the Turning Stone. The dissidents' benefits as Oneidas were eliminated after they took part, during 1995, in a "march for democracy" to make these points (Johansen, 2002).

The New York Oneidas under Halbritter's aegis appointed a men's council (a body unheard of in traditional matrilineal Iroquois law or tradition), which issued a zoning code to "beautify" the Oneida Nation. This code enabled his fifty-four-member police force (patrolling a thirty-two-acre reservation) to "legally" evict from their homes Oneidas who opposed his role as leader of the New York Oneidas. Halbritter's control also was supported by the acquisition of a number of other businesses, a phalanx of public relations spin doctors, several lawyers, and ownership of *Indian Country Today*, a national Native American newspaper.

The story of the New York Oneidas is a particularly raw example of conflicts that beset many Native American nations that have attempted to address problems of persistent poverty and economic marginalization by opening casinos. Supporters of the casinos see them as the new buffalo; opponents look at them as a form of internal colonization, an imposition of European-descended economic institutions and values on Native American peoples.

In few areas is the conflict as sharp as among the Haudenosaunee, or Iroquois Confederacy, where New York State governor George Pataki promoted plans to

Shenandoah
OPENS WOODSTOCK 1994

J oanne Shenandoah opened Woodstock '95 with an original song entitled "America". The award winning artist has achieved national acclaim for her conscientious and original compositions. From traditional chants to contemporary ballads, her music has been described as a "powerful, emotional experience" and a "Native American Trance". From love songs to melodies which reach deep into the soul, her stellar performances and music recordings have astounded and electrified audiences around the world. Her songs have been heard on many television productions such as PBS, Discovery and the popular CBS series "Northern Exposure". Her albums include: Joanne Shenandoah, Loving Ways (with A. Paul Ortega), Once in a Red Moon and Life Blood (with Peter Kater).

For further information and booking contact:
Joanne Shenandoah
Oneida Indian Territory, Box Ten, Oneida, NY 13421
Tel & Fax (315) 363-1655

Joanne Shenandoah at Woodstock II. (Photo credit: Henry Diorio.
Courtesy of Joanne Shenandoah.)

open as many as six new Native-controlled casinos in an attempt to jump-start a state economy that was badly damaged by the attacks of September 11, 2001. On various Internet sites and chat rooms, supporters of Halbritter accused the Shenandoah family of supporting antitreaty groups, and opponents of the Oneidas' corporate structure routinely called Halbritter "the king" and "the despot."

The recent experience of the Oneidas of New York raised several significant questions for Indian Country as a whole. Is the Oneida model of an economic powerhouse key to defining the future of Native American sovereignty in the opening years of the twenty-first century, as many of its supporters believe? Materially, the New York Oneidas have gained a great deal in a quarter century, including repurchase of 14,000 acres of land. Have these gains been offset by an atmosphere of stifling totalitarianism and a devastating loss of traditional bearings, as many Oneida dissidents attest?

The Foxwoods Money Machine

Mashantucket means "the much-wooded land." The word *Foxwoods* is a combination of the notion of forest with the Pequots' reputation as "the fox people." Foxwoods started as a very small bingo parlor after roughly forty banks refused to loan money to the Pequots. The bingo parlor began operating in 1986 and became wildly successful, drawing its clientele mainly from the urban corridor that stretches from Boston to New York City. Having obtained backing from outside the United States, the Pequots opened their full-scale casino in 1992. At the time, Foxwoods was the only gaming establishment on the East Coast offering poker, which was banned at the time in Atlantic City.

The first day Foxwoods opened, February 14, 1992, its 1,700-car parking lot was full by 10:30 A.M. Roughly 75,000 people passed through the casino's doors there during that first day, and 2,000 of them were still present at the casino's 4 A.M. closing time. During the ensuing decade, Foxwoods expanded and became one of the most notable examples anywhere of Native American economic development.

By the year 2000, the Foxwoods complex was drawing about 50,000 people on an average day. By that time, the Foxwoods Resort Casino complex included five casinos housing more than 300,000 square feet of gaming space, 5,842 slot machines, 370 gaming tables, a 3,000-seat high-stakes bingo parlor with $1 million jackpots, a 200-seat Sportsbook, and a Keno lounge. Table games included baccarat, minibaccarat, big six wheels, blackjack, Caribbean stud poker, craps, pai gow, pai gow tiles, red dog, roulette, and a number of other games. The Foxwoods casino complex also included four hotels, ranging in size from 280 to 800 rooms each. In addition to gaming space and its four hotels, Foxwoods also offered twenty-three shopping areas, twenty-four food-and-beverage outlets, and a movie theater complex, as well as the

Mashantucket Pequot museum and a Fox Grand Theater featuring Las Vegas-style entertainment.

Foxwoods quickly became a very large financial success for its sponsors, as well as the state government of Connecticut, to which the casino's management pledged a quarter of its profits. During the fiscal year beginning July 1, 1999, and ending June 30, 2000, Foxwoods' gross revenues on its slot and video machines alone totaled more than $9 billion. Foxwoods quickly became an integral pillar of Connecticut's economy and a multimillion-dollar contributor to the state's charities. The Pequots' casino even put up cash one year to help the state balance its budget.

By 2000, the Foxwoods casino complex was paying the state of Connecticut more than $189 million a year in taxes. The Foxwoods and a second, more recently constructed, casino, the Mohegan Sun, paid the state of Connecticut more than $318 million during the 1999–2000 fiscal year. The Mashantucket Pequots became the state of Connecticut's largest single taxpayer and, with 13,000 jobs, one of its larger employers. The casino complex employed a staff of lawyers and maintained its own permanent lobbying office in Washington, D.C.

At the same time, the Pequots also became a significant contributor to the Smithsonian's new National Museum of the American Indian at $10 million. That amount was soon matched by the New York Oneidas, drawing from its own casino profits. The Mashantucket Pequots also gave $2 million to the Special Olympics and $500,000 to the Hartford Ballet, as well as $5 million to the Mystic, Connecticut, aquarium. During June 2001, the Mohegans, owners of the neighboring Mohegan Sun casino, made an equal pledge.

To illustrate the volume of money changing hands in these casinos, consider that Mohegan Sun casino investors included Trading Cove Associates, headed by Sol Kerzner, creator of the Sun City casino and resort in South Africa. By 2000, this firm had received more than $800 million in fees, a sum the company argued was fair compensation for services rendered.

Death at Akwesasne

Although gambling has brought benefits to some Native American communities, it brought violence to the Akwesasne Mohawks of St. Regis in upstate New York. The violence erupted in part over the issue of gambling. As many as seven casinos had opened illegally along the reservation's main highway as the area became a crossroads for illicit smuggling of drugs, including cocaine and tax-free liquor and cigarettes.

Tension escalated after early protests of gambling in the late 1980s (including the trashing of one casino and the burning of another, to attempts by gambling supporters to brutally repress this resistance). Residents blockaded the reservation to keep the casinos' customers out, prompting the violent destruction of the same blockades by gambling supporters in late April 1990.

By that time, violence had spiraled into brutal beatings of antigambling activists, drive-by shootings, and firefights that culminated in two Mohawk deaths during the early morning of May 1. Intervention of several police agencies from the United States and Canada followed the two deaths; outside police presence continued for years afterward (Johansen, 1993).

Everyone who is familiar with Akwesasne Mohawk Territory knows it has been the scene of considerable smuggling between the United States and Canada, but no one knew the extent of the traffic until its volume drew the attention of prosecutors and police in both countries. By late 1999, with several convicted smugglers awaiting sentencing, the size of the smuggling "industry" outlined in court records was astounding even veteran observers. The evidence presented by prosecutors is outlining the largest smuggling operation since the border between the United States and Canada was established.

Akwesasne is the only Native American reservation that straddles the U.S.-Canadian border and as such has long provided a smuggling route for anything illegal that may be in demand across either border. This cargo varies from cigarettes and hard liquor (which are taxed much more heavily in Canada than in the United States), to several varieties of illegal narcotics, automatic weapons, and even human beings. Immigration authorities at one point broke a smuggling ring that was ferrying people (most of them illegal immigrants from Asia) across the border at a cost of $45,000 to $50,000 each.

The right of Mohawks to cross the border unimpeded is recognized by the Jay Treaty (1794), which Canadian authorities have occasionally contested. Various enterprising Akwesasne residents have become adept at selling their connections as border middlemen, the central link in the smuggling chain. A few years ago, a story floated around the reservation that a local "kingpin" was negotiating to buy a small island in the St. Lawrence River for about $225,000 for use as a smuggling base. After the two parties agreed on the price, the new owner walked to a closet in his home, which was stacked floor to ceiling with cash in large denominations. He peeled an inch or two off the top of the stack to pay for the island.

The Canadian federal government has asserted that taxing authorities in that country lost $750 million in potential revenue because of smuggling through Akwesasne between 1991 and 1997, when the biggest smuggling ring was busted. Nearly as much money was laundered through an armored car business in Massena, New York. Prosecutors requested that U.S. District Court Judge Thomas McAvoy sentence John "Chick" Fountain of Massena to seven years in prison and forfeiture of an unspecified amount worth of personal property for his role in laundering $557 million through his armored car and currency exchange business. Before he started this business, Fountain had lived much more modestly as a New York State trooper.

Fountain, convicted November 3, 1998, was one of twenty-seven people prosecutors alleged had important roles in a smuggling ring that at its height operated large warehouses and squads of motorboats which were used to ferry goods and people across the St. Lawrence River. When the river was frozen, smuggling often took place in automobiles. The smuggling ring drew some well-known names at Akwesasne into its ambit, including long-time gambling developer Tony Laughing and former St. Regis Tribal Chief Leo David Jacobs, who was convicted of taking $32,000 in kickbacks paid to link Miller with a number of Akwesasne businessmen. One of these businessmen was Loran Thompson, owner of a marina, a restaurant, and what New York radio reporter Neil Drew of Malone, New York, called "a very busy cigarette warehouse along the St. Lawrence River . . . where millions of cartons were purchased for smuggling into Canada" (2001).

The alleged kingpin of the smuggling cartel was Larry Miller of Massena, who traveled the world in a Lear Jet and owned five houses in Las Vegas as well as an estate not far from the source of his income: the porous international border through Akwesasne. According to court records, Miller made as much as $35 million a year at the height of the operation. Prosecutors suggested that Judge McAvoy fine Miller $160 million in cash and personal assets in addition to asking that he be sentenced to 17 to 22 years in prison.

INDIVIDUAL INDIAN TRUST ASSETS: WHERE HAS ALL THE MONEY GONE?

The Individual Indian Monies (IIM) mess has become the stuff of political and legal legend since the *Cobell v. Norton* (240 F.3rd 1081 [DC Cir. 2001]) class action was first filed in 1996. With 500,000 plaintiffs for whom the BIA played banker for a century or more, the case has grown to be the largest class action ever filed against the U.S. federal government. Employing more than 100 lawyers on the payrolls of the Interior and Treasury Departments, *Cobell v. Norton* (after Elouise Cobell, lead plaintiff, and Gale Norton, Secretary of the Interior) has become the largest single employer of federal legal talent in the history of the republic.

How much money is at stake? In 1997 (Johansen, 1997, 14–23), the commonly accepted figure was between $2 and $3 billion. By late 2002, lead prosecutor Dennis Gingold placed the figure at "far north of $10 billion" (Kennedy, 2002). A report prepared for the Interior Department suggested that the federal government's total liability might reach $40 billion. Tack on a few billion more, and you have Uncle Sam's annual bill for the Iraq war.

On December 21, 1999, Judge Royce C. Lamberth, who is overseeing the case in the Washington, D.C., federal district court, issued his first (Phase One) opinion (the case is divided into two phases). The 126-page opinion stated that the government had baldly violated its trust responsibilities to Native Americans. He called the IIM mess the "most egregious misconduct by the federal government." Although *Cobell v. Norton* is certainly a big-stakes case, such a superlative overstated its historical scope. Perhaps it is the most egregious example of *financial* misconduct in a trust relationship by the U.S.

government, which in its two-plus centuries has done worse to Native Americans than lose several billion dollars.

Judge Lamberth later ordered the government to file reports quarterly describing in detail its efforts to account for the monies. The judge also ordered the Interior and Treasury Departments to compile an audit of the IIM trust fund system reaching to its origins in 1887. At present, the Bush Administration's unwillingness to follow Lamberth's order comprises the legal line of scrimmage in what may turn out to be a decades-long battle.

Judge Lamberth is a Republican appointee, a Texan with a taste for fancy boots and large cars who seemed, on the surface, unlikely to take a serious interest in a Native American class action suit. However, he possessed a keen knowledge of bureaucratic politics and an ability to read and comprehend vast amounts of information. Like fishing rights judge George Hugo Boldt (also a Republican appointee), Lamberth has a sharp sense of justice, regardless of vested interests. He is, in other words (also like Boldt), hard working and ruthlessly honest.

During its eight-year run to 2004, the IIM case has produced evidence of what must have been the world's sloppiest banking record keeping. Even Elouise Cobell, who initiated the suit, has been amazed at the sorry state of the BIA's banking system, if it could be called that. Cobell, a member of the Blackfeet Tribe and a banker by profession, filed the suit in 1996. Cobell, of Browning, Montana, founded (and still has a hand in operating) the first Native American–owned bank in the United States. She also served as treasurer of the Blackfeet from 1970 through 1983.

Cobell's education in the BIA's ways of banking began with a detailed examination of the Blackfeet's trust accounts. After Cobell discovered a number of problematic transactions, she began asking questions. Her initial inquiries were rebuffed by the BIA. "They said, 'Oh! you don't know how to read the reports,'" Cobell recalled. "I think they were trying to embarrass me, but it did the opposite—it made me mad" (Awehali, 2003).

Cobell has spent much of her life in and near the reservation town of Browning, Montana. She was one of eight children in a house with no electricity or running water. The major form of entertainment was old fashioned: oral history, sometimes describing Baker's Massacre, during which U.S. soldiers killed about 200 Blackfeet, a majority of them women and children, following an ambush near the Marias River. She also sometimes heard stories from her parents and their neighbors about small government checks that bore no relationship to reality.

Today, Cobell spends much of her time tutoring Blackfeet and other Native peoples in ways to start their own businesses. She also helps with chores on a ranch that she co-owns with her husband, Alvin. During a sojourn off the reservation in her twenties (she is now nearly fifty), Elouise met Alvin, who is also Blackfoot, in Seattle. He was fishing off the Alaska coast, and she held a job as an accountant with a Seattle television station.

At the age of thirty, Cobell returned to Browning with Alvin to resume a life on the family ranch. She also was offered a job as the reservation government's accountant. At the time, Browning had practically no Native-owned businesses; unemployment rose to more than 70 percent in winter (which can last into May), when construction employment ceased. She found the Blackfeet accounting system "in total chaos." Some trust accounts were being charged negative interest. Checks were being posted against accounts without her knowledge, even though she was supposed to be the only valid signatory. In 1987, Cobell moved on to start the first Native-owned bank in the United States, mainly to help finance local business ventures. In a few years, she could point to several businesses that she had helped to finance: the Glacier Restaurant, Browning Video, the Dollar Store (Kennedy, 2002).

Years before the class action suit was filed, Cobell asked questions within the system. As she began to delve into the trust issue on a national basis, in Washington, D.C., Cobell was introduced to Dennis A. Gingold, who is now the lead prosecuting attorney for the case, who was quoted in the *Los Angeles Times* as saying of his first meeting with her: "From my experience, American Indians were not involved in banking. I was looking for a bunch of people with turbans" (Kennedy, 2003). Gingold admitted that he had a great deal to learn about how the government had separated Native Americans from their trust assets.

Cobell did not decide to file suit lightly, but only after several rebuffs by the government that displayed an unwillingness to take the trust accounts problem seriously. She realized that large legal actions were massively expensive. Her years of activism and her experience as the Blackfeet's accountant had suggested some sources of support, however. She contacted the Arthur Bremer Foundation of St. Paul, Minnesota, and won a $75,000 grant and a $600,000 loan. In 1997, a year after she filed the class action suit, Cobell also received, quite unexpectedly, a $300,000 "genius" grant from the John D. MacArthur Foundation, most of which went into the case. Shortly after that, J. Patrick Lannan of the Lannan Foundation read about Cobell's MacArthur grant and traveled to Browning to meet with her. Lannan eventually donated $4 million to the cause. By mid-2002, the cost of the legal action had reached $8 million, still barely a drop in the proverbial bucket next to the hundreds of millions of dollars in tax money that the federal government has spent to defend itself.

Some in the government saw the problem coming before Cobell filed suit. During 1992, the House of Representatives Committee on Government Operations issued a report, "Misplaced Trust: The Bureau of Indian Affairs' Mismanagement of the Indian Trust Fund." During 1994, Congress passed the Indian Trust Fund Management Reform Act, with the stated aim of cleaning up the mess. As part of this law's implementation, Paul Homan, an expert at cleaning up failing private financial institutions, was hired. Homan, having taken stock of the situation, later quit in disgust as he described a banker's nightmare.

The BIA, for example, did not establish an accounts receivable system, so it never knew how much money it was handling at any given time. Partial records indicated that more than $50 million was never paid because the BIA had lost track of account holders. About 21,000 accounts were listed in the names of people who were dead. Large numbers of records had been stored in cardboard boxes, left to soak (and smear) in leaky warehouses. About $695 million had been paid, but to the wrong people or Native governmental entities. One property record valued chain saws at $99 million each. Some of the records were contaminated with asbestos, and others had been paved over by a parking lot. As he resigned, Homan said he had never seen anything like this in his 30 years as a banker.

Before he quit, Homan reported that no one knew just how many people were owed money. Of the 238,000 individual trusts that Homan's staff located, 118,000 were missing crucial papers, 50,000 had no addresses, and 16,000 accounts had no documents at all. Homan further reported that one could assume money had been skimmed extensively from the trust: "It's akin to leaving the vault door open," he said (Awehali, 2003).

In the meantime, before a dime has been paid to any of the 500,000 Native people who are part of the class action, the Bush administration seems to have established some sort of perpetual motion lawyer employment fund. It requested $554 million in the 2004 budget to "reform" the trust fund, an increase of $183.3 million over $370.2 million budgeted in 2003. Reform in this case means, to a large degree, paying legal talent to protect Uncle Sam against the class action suit; as with John Ashcroft's Patriot Act, the terminology here is highly Orwellian. In a January 2001 interview with Harlan McKosato on the national radio show *Native America Calling*, Cobell noted that "just by not settling the case, it's costing the government and taxpayers $160,000 an hour, $7 million a day, $2.5 billion a year" (Awehali, 2003).

Pen-and-Ink Witchcraft

With the government's mismanagement now so widely known, a sensible person might conclude that the time has come to find a way to reimburse the many Native people who have been cheated. If you are one of the 500,000 Native Americans who unwillingly did your banking with the BIA, when might you expect a corrective check in the mail? Don't hold your breath. If the Bush administration has its way, you could turn very blue before the guarantor of your trust makes you, as they say in financial litigation circles, "whole."

The spin doctors in the White House probably do not realize that their designs resemble some treaty negotiations for their Alice-in-Wonderland quality (things are never what they seem). In 1791, the famed Ottawa speaker Egushawa, observing treaty negotiations, called such machinations pen-and-ink witchcraft.

What Egushawa witnessed had nothing on the trust money mess. After eight years of legal shuck and jive by the federal government, the central fact of the case is this: The BIA and Treasury Department never built a record-keeping system capable of tracking the money owed to Native Americans based on income from its supervision of their resources.

As time passed (the system, in its modern incantation, began with the advent of the Allotment Act in 1887), the lack of a functioning banking system made record keeping worse; the sloppiness of errant (or nonexistent) record keeping was compounded, for example, because of divisions of estate required by generations of fractional Native inheritances. By the time Cobell and a few other banking-minded Native Americans began asking seriously what had become of their IIM, the Interior Department by and large did not have a clue.

In an average year, $500 million or more was deposited into the Individual Indian Trust from companies leasing Native American land for grazing, oil drilling, timber, coal, and other natural resources. According to law and financial theory, the money is collected by the Interior and sent to the Treasury, which is supposed to place it into individual trust accounts. Problems began with the roughly 50,000 accounts that lacked names or correct addresses. One such account contained $1 million (Awehali, 2003). Along the way, it also was learned that some people simply neglected to pay as expected; they soon learned that, much of the time, no one seemed to be watching.

As early as 1999, the plaintiffs' legal team discovered that the Departments of Interior and Treasury had "inadvertently" destroyed 162 boxes of vital trust records during the course of the trial, then waited months to notify the court of the "accident." "You tell me if that's fair," Cobell told Mike Wallace in a *60 Minutes* interview shortly after the discovery. "When they have to manage other people's money according to standards, why aren't they managing our money to standards? Is it because you manage brown people's money differently?" (Awehali, 2003).

Judge Lamberth was shocked when he discovered, in the course of the lawsuit, that the Interior and Treasury Departments had, as a matter of course, destroyed accounting documents and filed false reports with the court. In the course of the litigation, thirty-seven past and present government officials, including Bush's Secretary of the Interior Gale Norton and Clinton's Interior Secretary Bruce Babbitt, have been held in contempt of court. On August 10, 1999, Lamberth ordered the Treasury Department to pay $600,000 in fines for misconduct.

As he delved into the trust account debacle, Lamberth found that some records were stored in rat-infested New Mexico warehouses. Others were dispersed haphazardly on several remote reservations. When the Interior Department kept computerized records at all, they were so inadequate and insecure that hackers could set up their own accounts (and presumably draw money from them).

During the first phase of the case, many experts testified that the Interior and Treasury Departments lack the records to render any semblance of true accounting for the monies that the government was supposed to be managing. Instead, the plaintiffs have suggested various methods of estimating what is owed. For example, the Geographic Information System (GIS) might use satellite mapping technology to estimate the amount of oil produced by wells on Native lands and thereby derive an idea of royalties owed.

Land of the Midnight Rider

During September 2003, Judge Lamberth ordered the Interior Department to conduct a thorough investigation into money that was supposed to be paid to Indians for oil, gas, timber, and grazing activities on their land dating back to 1887. He said that the accounting must be completed by 2007.

Responding to Lamberth's first-phase opinion and this directive, Cobell was enthusiastic at the time. "This is a landmark victory," she said. "It is now clear that trust law and trust standards fully govern the management of the Individual Indian Trust and that Secretary Norton can no longer ignore the trust duties that she owes to 500,000 individual Indian trust beneficiaries" (Awehali, 2003).

The idea of a complete accounting, which sounded so simple, suddenly became very problematic in the land of pen-and-ink witchcraft. Interior and Treasury Departments, with their allies on Capitol Hill and in the Bush White House, prepared a hastily inserted "midnight rider" to a federal spending bill that forbade spending that would have implemented Lamberth's directive. Funding, according to the rider, was to be frozen for a year or until an accounting methodology could be agreed on by the Interior and Treasury Departments and Congress.

In the meantime, the Interior Department was reported by several news organizations as complaining that the type of historical accounting required by Judge Lamberth's ruling would take ten years and cost $6 to $12 billion. Some feat of accounting that would be—the accounting equivalent, perhaps, of building the Panama Canal or putting many men on the moon, a rubber figure with an odor of obstructionist politics. (To illustrate just how rubbery this estimate is, let us crunch a few round numbers. At $100,000 each per year, very good pay for an accountant, $10 billion would hire 100,000 accountants. Even if they worked ten years each, $10 billion would still pay 10,000 number crunchers. Add a few zeroes here and there, and soon we are talking about some very serious money. Bear in mind that the folks who came up with these quick estimates work at the same agencies that lost track of all that Native American money in the beginning.)

With a federal budget deficit approaching $400 billion a year (including Iraq and Afghanistan wars and reconstruction liabilities running at least $87 billion a year), the Bush Administration and Republican-controlled Congress seemed unwilling to seriously consider paying a century-plus of Indian trust money bills that could cost as much as $40 billion—the bill that could come out of the second phase of the case, once Interior and Treasury Departments assessed the due bills as ordered by Judge Lamberth. The midnight rider was sponsored in large part by a Republican-controlled executive branch and Congress that added 721,000 federal jobs to the payroll since George W. Bush assumed office almost four years prior.

About fifty Republicans voted against the appropriations bill containing the rider, however, led by Representative Richard Pombo (R-Calif.), chair of the House Resources Committee, with Representative J. D. Hayworth (R-Ariz.), co-chair of the bipartisan House Native American Caucus. Pombo, who favored a legislative solution to the court case, called the rider a "poison pill that was added to the legislation in blatant violation of House rules and protocol" (Reynolds, 2003). The rider passed narrowly, 216–205, October 30.

The Senate passed the spending bill (with the midnight rider) 87–2 November 4 and sent it to Bush for his signature November 10. Cobell sharply criticized President Bush's administration, including Interior Secretary Norton, for sponsoring the rider. Said Cobell: "What this vote shows is the length that the Interior Secretary and the Bush administration will go to in their efforts to deny Indians the accounting for funds that belong to Indians—not the federal government. Now American Indians are being victimized once again by politicians in Washington" (Reynolds, 2002). Cobell said that she expected the courts to strike down the rider as an illegal interference with the judicial process, a violation of the Constitution's separation of powers.

"It's a clear act of bad faith to seek a stay based on an unconstitutional statute," said Gingold ("Appeals Court," 2003). The Senate's legal counsel and House members from both parties said the provision is probably unconstitutional because the administration cannot dictate to courts how to interpret the law.

Whither the Trust Fund Billions?

So, wither the trust fund case? When all is said and done, will the plaintiffs in *Cobell v. Norton* ever get anything close to what they are owed? Although optimism is always in season and justice sometimes does actually prevail, there is ample precedent in U.S. legal history vis-à-vis Native Americans to create doubts that right and reasonable outcomes follow the opinions of courts presided over by hard-working, honest judges, even after the government has copiously admitted its errors.

Some historical parallels present themselves: John Marshall, chief justice of the U.S. Supreme Court, found in favor of the Cherokees' sovereignty; President Andrew Jackson ignored him and his Court, leading to the Trail of Tears (Jackson's action was an impeachable offense, contempt of the Supreme Court, a violation of his oath of office. It was never prosecuted because

Georgia made a states' rights case that could have started the Civil War 30 years before it actually began.)

More recently, during the mid-1970s, the courts found in favor of a 250,000-acre land claim for the Oneidas. Thirty years later, they have yet to receive any land from this legal proceeding.

Might *Cobell v. Norton* end up being another perpetual motion employment engine for lawyers and another reminder that sometimes the legal system talks the talk as the executive branch fails to walk the walk of justice? Or might the contending parties, with Judge Lamberth's prodding, find a way at least to estimate what is owed the plaintiffs—and take the necessary steps to pay them? The next few years may provide an answer after the second phase of *Cobell v. Norton* is adjudicated and a final ruling is issued by Judge Lamberth.

Senator Ben Nighthorse Campbell, who is Cheyenne, has insisted that all parties to the Cobell litigation must work together to resolve the case; he believes, otherwise, that it may not be resolved. "We have one year to reach settlement on this issue," he said during a hearing of the Senate Committee on Indian Affairs as it considered his bill, S. 1770, to encourage individual beneficiary settlements in the lawsuit (Reynolds, 2003).

Native-owned companies could benefit from the requirement that the Interior Department compile an accounting for the 117-year record of Indian trust fund mismanagement. Earnings for such work may reach $50 million by some estimates. Tlingit and Haida Technology Industries has applied to do some of the court-ordered accounting work, according to Dan DuBray, an Interior Department spokesperson quoted in the *Fairbanks Daily News-Miner* and the *Juneau Empire*, both on November 5, 2003.

Blackfeet History at Ghost Ridge

"I've heard from friends that the government thinks I'm tired and that they'll wear me down, so that I'll just go away," says Cobell (Awehali, 2003). Near Cobell's hometown, a marker describes the winter of 1884, when 500 Blackfeet died of starvation and exposure while awaiting supplies promised them by the federal government. The dead were buried in a mass grave that is now called Ghost Ridge. During the more difficult stages of the lawsuit, Cobell said she has visited Ghost Ridge, thinking of her ancestors who perished in the cold 120 years ago while waiting for the government to fulfill its promises.

The Blackfeet starved as U.S. Indian Agent John Young hoarded food that would have allowed them to survive. From Ghost Ridge, it is not difficult to draw parallels to the entire course of Indian–European American relations, most notably to the case at hand. Again, Native land and fiscal resources were taken and hoarded in faraway places as the promises of the "trust" relationship between the United States and Native peoples were massively abused.

REPATRIATION: "WHOSE BONES ARE THEY, ANYWAY?"

Controversy regarding return and reburial of American Indian human remains and funerary objects has become a volatile issue in the United States. When the United States enacted legal measures requiring their return in 1990, the remains or burial offerings of 2 million American Indians were being stored in museums, state historical societies, universities, the National Park Service offices, private warehouses, and curio shops.

Many Native Americans resent retention of such human remains on religious, humanitarian, ethical, and legal grounds. American Indians have requested return of human skeletal remains and related funerary objects to the earth for several reasons. A large majority of American Indian religions believe that the souls of the deceased will not find rest unless the remains are properly interred. Decent and timely reburial of remains also has become a matter of religious freedom. These points of view were incorporated in U.S. national law, established in 1990, as the Native American Graves Protection and Repatriation Act (NAGPRA).

On the past practices of academic archeology, David Hurst Thomas, writing in *Skull Wars: Kennewick Man, Archaeology, and the Battle for Native American Identity* (2000), quotes Walter L. Echo-Hawk and Roger C. Echo-Hawk (Pawnee attorney and historian, respectively): "If you desecrate a white grave, you end up sitting in prison. But desecrate an Indian grave, [and] you get a Ph.D. The time has come for people to decide: Are we Indians part of this country's living culture, or are we just here to supply museums with dead bodies?" (p. 210).

It has been argued that the private market for human remains and funerary objects reflects a non-Indian belief that Native Americans are not fully human, that all aspects of American Indian culture were not accorded respect and equality under the law, and that traders in human remains and burial artifacts envisage Native peoples as brutal savages who lack essential qualities for civilization. As with non-Indians who support the use of Native sports mascots, traders in Native bones and burial artifacts often state openly that they are supporting and appreciating Native American peoples and their cultures.

Many American Indians have argued that civil rights laws and the U.S. Constitution (Thirteenth, Fourteenth, and Fifteenth amendments) render such points of view as legally as well as culturally obsolete. The same goes, by this line of reasoning, for the rationale that large numbers of Native American remains are being stored purportedly for future scientific use. The Native American Rights Fund contends that retention of American Indian human remains violates the Fourteenth Amendment (equal protection) and constitutional guarantees of religious freedom.

Native American historian Donald A. Grinde, Jr., made the following comparison (personal interview, October 22, 1991): When the remains of members of the armed forces who have died while missing in action and of pilots and other Vietnam veterans were returned to the United States, no one stated that these bones should be studied to give us some answers about the dangers and treatment of Agent Orange and other perils of war. Instead, the remains were respectfully reinterred with appropriate dignity and ceremony.

Many anthropologists, archeologists, state historical society personnel, and others oppose return and reburial of Native American remains for a number of reasons. Many of these arguments are based on the assumed need to hold Native American remains for the future use of scientists exercising their academic freedom. Opponents of reburial also believe that scholars or granting agencies that excavate Indian human remains "own" them and thus giving them back to Indians raises serious "property" questions.

The Case of Kennewick Man

The case of Kennewick Man became the first broad legal test of NAGPRA's provisions. A lawsuit was filed against the Corps of Engineers regarding Kennewick Man, a nearly complete, 9,200-year-old skeleton found in eastern Washington during 1996. The eight anthropologists who filed the suit represented the first major legal challenge to NAGPRA. The basic legal question became: How far into the past do Native American claims to remains extend? A federal judge in this case held during 2002 that, at 9,000-plus years, the age of Kennewick Man's remains exceeded the scope of the law.

Writing to the Corps of Engineers, physical anthropologists Douglas W. Owsley of the Smithsonian Institution and Richard L. Jantz of the University of Tennessee (Knoxville) warned: "If a pattern of returning [such] remains without study develops, the loss to science will be incalculable and we will never have the data required to understand the earliest populations in America" (Slayman, 1997, 19). In a letter to the editor in the *New York Times*, William D. Lipe, president of the Society for American Archaeology, asked that the "tribe that has claimed the ancient Washington skeleton . . . reconsider and permit additional studies to be conducted" (ibid., 19).

U.S. Representative Doc Hastings of Washington wrote to Lieutenant General Joe Ballard, commander of the Army Corps of Engineers, expressing alarm that the corps planned to give up the skeleton before it could be studied. He urged Ballard to "postpone action until the [skeleton's] origins are determined conclusively or until Congress has the opportunity to review this important issue" (Slayman, 1997, 19). In the meantime, Representative Hastings requested that the Corps allow scientists access to the bones.

The eight scientists filed their suit against the Corps of Engineers in Federal District Court, Portland, Oregon. They sought access to the skeleton and an indefinite delay of its repatriation. The scientists are Robson Bonnichsen, director of the Center for the Study of the First Americans at Oregon State University; C. Loring Brace, curator of biological anthropology at the University of Michigan's Museum of Anthropology; Dennis J. Stanford, chairman of the Smithsonian's anthropology department; Richard Jantz; Douglas Owsley; and anthropologists George W. Gill of the University of Wyoming, C. Vance Haynes, Jr., of the University of Arizona, and D. Gentry Steele of Texas A&M University.

During August 2002, after more than a year of deliberation (much of it spent reading several thousand pages of documentation) U.S. District court Judge John Jelderks found for the scientists, denying Native Americans possession of Kennewick man's remains under NAGPRA. "Allowing study is fully consistent with applicable statutes and regulations, which are clearly intended to make archaeological information available to the public through scientific research," Jelderks wrote ("Judge," 2002, 10). Jelderks' ruling was affirmed by the Ninth District Court of Appeals in San Francisco; Northwest Native groups that had been seeking repatriation then declined further appeal to the U.S. Supreme Court.

James C. Chatters, the first forensic specialist to handle the remains, supported the scientists. Chatters said that he could support the provisions of NAGPRA and oppose returning Kennewick Man to the tribes for reburial. "I have conducted repatriations for some of the same tribes who claimed this skeleton," Chatters wrote in the *Wall Street Journal*. "I support the purpose of the law" (2002, D-10). Chatters maintained that Kennewick Man's remains were outside the scope of NAGPRA. "The act," he wrote, "was not intended to turn over all ancient skeletons to some Indian tribe, regardless of relationship. . . . The past is not a possession" (ibid., D-10). To the Native nations seeking to rebury the remains, Chatters's statement was something of a simplification. They asserted that under NAGPRA, when it concerns human remains, the past is indeed a possession. The question was—and remains—how far back in time the legality of possession reaches.

Native American historian Donald A Grinde, Jr., believes the following (1993):

> While the reburial debate manifests itself in a freedom for scientific inquiry versus American Indian religious freedom, the real issue for the dominant society is control. For generations, American Indians have been decapitated and their skulls sent to the Smithsonian under the ruse of "science." In reality, the purpose was to demonstrate the utter subjugation of Native American people by the Euro-American community.

The subsidiary status of Native Americans was enshrined in U.S. law by court decisions, of which *Worcester v. Georgia* (31 U.S. [6 Pet.] 515 [1832]) is the best known. Legal doctrine established during the nineteenth century held Native Americans to be in state of wardship vis-à-vis the federal government and living in domestic dependent nations. The reclamation of remains and burial artifacts late in the twentieth century is in a way an extension of step-by-step liberation from these doctrines. Following passage of NAGPRA, the

Smithsonian Institution decided in 1991 that, because of the new federal law, it would offer to return almost 20,000 American Indian human remains from its collections.

The passage of NAGPRA at the federal level was pre-dated by similar laws in some states. In Nebraska, for example, Jim Hanson, then executive director of the Nebraska State Historical Society, responded to a state law mandating return of Native American skeletons and burial artifacts by calling it "censorship". "The work of a generation of scholars will be lost," Hanson, who often decked himself in nineteenth century cowboy gear, told an annual meeting of the historical society in Kearney, Nebraska. "For the first time in my professional career, a state government has decided to dictate" (Johansen, 1989, 15).

The "dictator," to Hanson, was Nebraska State Senator Ernie Chambers, who sponsored the act mandating return of remains and burial objects that had passed the state's Unicameral 30–16 in May 1989. Within three months, agreements along similar lines opened much larger collections to Indian tribes at Stanford University, the University of Minnesota, the Peabody Museum of Harvard, and the Smithsonian Institution.

Chambers, a Black Muslim who routinely wears a muscle shirt on the Unicameral floor, was no novice to initiating nationwide controversy. Chambers, who represents North Omaha, Nebraska's only sizable black community, sponsored legislation that made Nebraska the first state government to divest its financial interests in South Africa during the mid-1980s. Chambers's major ally in the effort to return remains and artifacts was the Pawnee Indian Nation, which had carried on a three-year campaign against the State Historical Society. The measure was drafted with the aid of the Native American Rights Fund of Boulder, Colorado.

Until passage of the Nebraska law and NAGPRA, most governmental bodies and academic institutions released skeletons and artifacts only to Native peoples who could prove familial relations to the deceased. Such relationships are usually nearly impossible to prove because very few of the remains have names or family lineages attached to them. The Nebraska measure (and others negotiated later) allowed claims of remains on a collective basis, a link that is much easier to document than familial association.

Like Hanson, the American Anthropological Association asserted that return of bones and artifacts to Indian tribes would infringe on the rights of scholars. The subject was a focus of intense controversy at an annual meeting of the association in Washington, D.C., during which Vine Deloria, Jr. (whose books, such as *Custer Died for Your Sins* (1969) and *God is Red* (1994) helped initiate Indian self-determination efforts), leveled a stinging address at the anthropologists. He said, in part, that even today many anthropologists regard Indians more as artifacts than as living human beings.

The repatriation debate ranged beyond bones and burial artifacts to such things as the wampum belts used to preserve memories of the Iroquois Great Law of Peace. Until late in the twentieth century, many of the Iroquois' wampum belts had been held by New York State. Three months after Nebraska passed its repatriation law, New York State agreed to return twelve of the belts to the Onondagas, who tend the central council fire of the Haudenosaunee Confederacy. "These belts are our archives. That's why we have been trying to get them back," said Raymond Gonyea, an Onondaga who specializes in Native American affairs at the New York State Museum (Johansen, 1989, 15).

During fall 1990, the Nebraska State Historical Society prepared, reluctantly, to return about 37,000 artifacts to the Pawnees. These included not only items manufactured by members of the tribe, but also spurs, bits, and buckles worn by Spanish conquistadors, a French medal, thousands of trade beads, and the bones of now-extinct animals such as the Great Plains grizzly bear and the ivory-billed woodpecker. The Nebraska Historical Society also returned the remains of 398 human beings to the Pawnees. More than 100 of the skeletons were taken from a village site near present-day Genoa, Nebraska, after a Pawnee village was devastated by disease about 1750. Some of the remains dated to about 1600, when the Pawnees moved into Nebraska from Kansas.

The changes in repatriation policy also benefited the Omaha Indian Tribe. About 280 artifacts were returned to the Omahas in late August 1990 from Harvard's Peabody Museum. The Peabody had held them for more than 100 years. The Smithsonian Institution returned an albino buffalo hide and a ceremonial pipe to the Omahas in 1991 after having held them since 1898. The two objects, believed to be at least 300 years old, were housed at the University of Nebraska's Lincoln campus until the Omahas completed a historical and cultural museum at Macy, the largest town on their present-day reservation. Near Macy, the Omahas also buried the remains of 92 tribal members whose skeletons were returned to them by the University of Nebraska. Although the skeletons were reburied, tribal members elected to keep artifacts above ground for exhibit and further study. The Omahas also planned to send their artifacts on tour around Nebraska on the theory that they belong to everyone.

The artifacts returned to the Omahas from the Peabody Museum included the tribe's cottonwood-and-ash sacred pole (Umon'hon'ti, the Venerable Man, the personification of the U'ma'ha Nation; Kehoe, 2002, 236), which was used for centuries to signify the life force that unified and renewed the Omahas.

"Basically, we want dead Indians out, and live Indians in," Susan Shown Harjo, executive director of the National Congress of American Indians, told the *Washington Post*. "It's a victory for America to solve a disgraceful situation where Indians are an archaeological resource, [and] our relatives are U.S. property—not quite human" (Johansen, 1989, 15).

THE INTERCOURSE ACTS: THE HISTORICAL BASIS OF MANY CONTEMPORARY LAND CLAIMS

In 1789, in one of his first acts as president, George Washington asked Secretary of War Henry Knox to prepare a report on the status of Indian affairs. Knox prepared a lengthy report on Native Americans' rights and mechanisms for dealing with them under the new U.S. Constitution. His conclusions closely resembled Spanish and English interpretations of the Doctrine of Discovery since the time of Francisco de Vitoria during the early sixteenth century. Knox found that the Indians had a right to their lands, and that land could not be taken except by mutual consent (as in agreement to a treaty) or in a "just" war as defined by the European powers of the day. Knox determined that that non-Indian squatters must be kept off Indian lands to keep the peace on the frontier.

From Knox's report emerged the first of several Trade and Intercourse Acts passed by Congress between 1790 and 1834. Congress, convening under the Constitution, passed the first such act in 1790 (25 U.S.C. paragraph 177), which said that no sale of Indian lands was valid without the authority of the United States. This initial act was extended and amended several times, in 1793, 1796, 1802, 1817, 1822, and 1834. In addition to extending federal authority to land sales, many of the Trade and Intercourse Acts forbade European American entry into Indian lands, regulated trade, and prohibited the sale of liquor.

Some of the Trade and Intercourse Acts made depredations by non-Indians against Native persons a federal crime in protected areas and promised monetary compensation to injured Natives who did not seek revenge by other means. The acts also set uniform standards for punishment of crimes by non-Indians against Indians (and vice versa) and enunciated a goal of "civilization and education" for U.S. Indian policy. Trade with Indians also came under federal regulation via the Trade and Intercourse Acts.

In a legal sense, the Trade and Intercourse Acts were a double-edged sword for Indian sovereignty. On one hand, they were passed to protect Indians from land fraud; on the other, they were an extension of federal law over Indian Country. The later intercourse acts were drafted under the theory that tribes should be considered foreign nations and that tribal lands protected by treaty, even though situated within the boundaries of a state, should be considered outside the limits of state jurisdictions (act of June 30, 1834, 4 Stat. 729, 733).

Federal jurisdiction over trade and land sales concerning Native nations had been an issue at least since the Albany Plan of Union (1754), when Iroquois delegates led by Tiyanoga (Hendrick) advised Benjamin Franklin and other colonial delegates to develop a single system for trade, land dealings, and diplomacy. The Albany Plan was rejected by the individual colonies, but the idea that the federal government retains authority over the states for dealing with Indians was written into the Constitution and has been central to American Indian law in the United States for more than two centuries.

The Trade and Intercourse Act of 1817 (3 Stat. 383) attempted the first systematic regulation of criminal jurisdiction in Indian Country. The act held that anyone, Indian or not, who committed an offense in Indian Country would be subject to the same punishment as if the offense had occurred in the United States, except for offenses defined as domestic. This exception became an important influence on subsequent court decisions delimiting jurisdiction. This law became the source of opinions that defined the powers of Indian courts; generally, a non-Indian accused of a crime on Indian land has been held to be under the jurisdiction of the United States, while an Indian charged with an offense against another Indian is tried in a Native American court.

The Intercourse Acts are important today because violations of them form the legal basis for several large-scale land claims by Native Americans, especially in the northeastern United States. The Penobscot and Passamaquoddy mounted a claim to two-thirds of the state of Maine during the 1970s based on violations of the Intercourse Acts. The long-standing claims by the Oneidas and other Iroquois Nation Indians also are based on similar grounds.

In *County of Oneida v. Oneida Indian Nation* (470 U.S. 226 [1985]) the Oneida people won rights to 100,000 acres of land transferred to New York State in 1795. The case was filed in 1970 and was originally dismissed in federal courts for lack of jurisdiction. The case was contested in the courts until the Supreme Court reversed the lower court decisions during its 1985 session. The court held that the Oneidas had a right to sue under common law, and that the right had not been diminished by the passage of time because it was not limited by a statute of limitations or any other form of abatement. The court also said that the Oneidas had an "unquestioned right" to their lands, and that the Indians' right of occupancy was "as sacred as the fee simple of the whites." The court's decision was split five to four, and the case was bitterly contested because it denied the property rights of some owners who had held title for as long as 175 years. As of 2003, the specifics of the settlement remained to be worked out between the Oneida Indian Nation and the state of New York. A key impediment to settlement had become the state and New York Oneidas' insistence on excluding Oneidas residing in Wisconsin and Ontario from any prospective settlement.

LEGAL STATUS OF NATIVE CLAIMS TO HAWAI'I

The 1893 overthrow of the Hawai'ian monarchy by the United States was invalid under international law. Native Hawai'ians have secured an apology from the U.S. House of Representatives for the overthrow and have been pressing a land claim that would return 1.8 million acres (of Hawai'i's 4.2-million-acre land area) to the jurisdiction of a government to be elected at a Native Hawai'ian constitutional convention. During the summer of 1996, about 30,000 Native Hawai'ians voted by a margin of three to one to establish such a government. Roughly 40 percent of Native Hawai'ians who were eligible to vote took part. The land claim includes all state and federal lands on the islands but leaves private owners untouched. The 200,000 acres presently occupied by U.S. military bases would be leased to the Department of Defense at market value for a fixed period of time.

This sovereignty movement had gained a large amount of support among the 200,000 members of Native Hawai'ian society by the 1990s, 100 years after the United States colonized the islands. During 1995 and 1996, Native Hawai'ians registered to vote in a referendum that will decide whether to initiate a Native legislature to press the land claim and other issues. On September 9, 1996, an overwhelming majority of Native Hawai'ians voted to elect delegates to a constitutional convention. This effort was being headed by the state government's Office of Hawaiian Affairs. In the 1990s, for the first time since 1893, the chief executive of Hawai'i was an ethnic Hawai'ian.

A modern "Hawai'ian renaissance" began in the 1970s. The Native language, which had nearly died, began to flourish again; Hawai'ians, who had once thought themselves homeless in their own land, began to recapture their heritage. Teams of seafarers built canoes capable of traveling to Tahiti to renew ties with indigenous people there. They sailed and practiced ancient navigational skills that tied together the people of widely dispersed islands centuries ago (Weinberg, 1996).

REQUEST AT WOUNDED KNEE: REVOKE THE ARMY'S MEDALS

During 1990, a century after the massacre at Wounded Knee, South Dakota's governor declared a "year of reconciliation" between Euro-Americans and Native peoples in that state. Even as South Dakota Governor George Mickelson smoked a ceremonial peace pipe with representatives of South Dakota's nine Indian tribes in the rotunda of the state capitol at Pierre as part of a year of reconciliation a century after the Wounded Knee massacre, he refused to advocate the revocation by the federal government of two dozen Medals of Honor awarded to members of the U.S. Army for their roles in the massacre.

About 9 percent of South Dakota's residents were of Indian descent in 1990, exactly one century after the territory became a state. "Should the American soldiers involved in My Lai in Vietnam have been awarded Medals of Honor for their actions?" asked Tim Giago, publisher and editor of the *Lakota Times* (Hill, 1999). The government should "stand tall, admit it was wrong, and atone for that massacre," said Mario Gonzalez, an attorney for the Wounded Knee Survivors' Association, which wants Congress to erect a national monument to the victims of Wounded Knee along with restitution (plus interest) for property taken from them. "We hurt and cry deep in our souls as we remember the stories told to us by our families," said Claudia Iron Hawk Sully, whose grandmother died at Wounded Knee in 1890. "Each of us here knows more about the truth of the blackest day than any historian or Indian expert, or classroom book will ever know" (ibid.). The Lakota say that more than 400 people died at Wounded Knee, while the Interior Department says that 153 Indians were killed and 44 wounded.

THE HIGH PRICE OF URANIUM MINING
AMONG THE NAVAJOS

About half the recoverable uranium on private land within the United States lies within New Mexico, and about half of that is beneath the Navajo Nation. Uranium has been mined on Navajo land since the late 1940s; the Indians dug the ore that started the U.S. stockpile of nuclear weapons mostly from 1,100 uranium mines on the Navajo Nation. The Grants Uranium Belt near the Four Corners, mainly on Navajo land, has been responsible for at least 80 percent of the U.S. production of uranium since it became a profitable commodity about 1950.

For thirty years after the first atomic explosions in New Mexico, uranium was mined much like any other mineral. More than 99 percent of the product of the mines was waste, cast aside near mine sites after the uranium had been extracted. One of the mesalike waste piles grew to a mile long and 70 feet high. On windy days, dust from the tailings blew into local communities, filling the air and settling on water supplies. The Atomic Energy Commission assured worried local residents that the dust was harmless.

The first uranium miners in the area, almost all of them Navajos, remember being sent into shallow tunnels within minutes after blasting. They loaded the radioactive ore into wheelbarrows and emerged from the mines spitting black mucus from the dust, coughing so hard they had headaches. Such mining practices exposed the Navajos to between 100 and 1,000 times the amount of radon gas later considered safe.

During the late 1940s and 1950s, Navajo uranium miners hauled radioactive ore out of the earth as if it were coal. Some of the miners ate their lunches in the mine and slaked their thirst with radioactive water. Some of their hogans were built of radioactive earth. Many sheep watered in small ponds that formed at the mouths of abandoned uranium mines that were called "dog holes" because of their small size. On dry, windy days, the gritty dust from uranium waste tailing piles covered everything in sight. The Navajo language has no word for radioactivity, and no one told the miners that within a few decades, many of them would die.

In their rush to profit from uranium mining, very few companies provided ventilation in the early years. Some miners worked as many as twenty hours a day, entering their dog holes just after blasting of local sandstone had filled the mines with silica dust. The dust produced silicosis in the miners' lungs in addition to lung cancer and other problems associated with exposure to radioactivity. As early as 1950, government workers were monitoring radiation levels in the mines, and the levels were as much as 750 times limits deemed acceptable at that time according to Peter Eichstaedt's account in *If You Poison Us: Uranium and American Indians* (1995). By 1970, nearly 200 of the miners already had died of uranium-related causes. Roughly one in four of the miners

INDIAN AWARENESS WEEK

CO-AUTHORS OF"WASI-CHU"
MAY 23   FRIDAY   7P.M.

LOCATION
the New Life Baptist Church   Reverend Pitford
618 North Puget, Olympia, Washington
7–9 P.M.
Speakers: BRUCE JOHANSEN and ROBERTO MAESTAS
Co-Authors of "Wasi-Chu (Continuing Indian Wars)"
9 P.M.
Speaker: Dr. Naciyana followed by
MOVIE: "Six Days of Soweto"
FREE ADMISSION

THE NATIVE AMERICAN STUDENT ASSOCIATION

Indian Awareness Week, stressing opposition to nuclear power and
uranium mining, Evergreen State College, Olympia, Washington.

had died, most of them from lung cancer, in an area where the disease had been nearly unknown before uranium mining began.

Some miners were put to work packing 1,000-pound barrels of "yellowcake," ore rich in uranium. These workers carried radioactive dust home on their clothes. Some of the miners ingested so much of the dust that it was "making the workers radioactive from the inside out" (Eichstaedt, 1995, 62). Downwind of uranium processing mills, the dust from yellowcake sometimes was so thick that it stained the landscape a half-mile away.

With the end of the Cold War and the cloud of controversy cast over civilian uses of nuclear power, the uranium boom, and most of the mining, had ended by the 1980s. With the boom over, the mining town of Grants, New Mexico, tried to sell itself as a tourist destination with the slogan "Grants Enchants." In the meantime, many of the miners had been condemned to slow deaths by lung cancer. The U.S. government (particularly the Atomic Energy Commission) knew that uranium mining was poisoning the Navajos almost from the beginning. The government and the mining companies kept medical knowledge from the miners out of concern for national security and profits.

"We used to play in it," said Terry Yazzie of an enormous tailings pile behind his house. "We would dig holes and bury ourselves in it" (Eichstaedt, 1995, 140). The neighbors of this particular tailings pile were not told it was dangerous until 1990, twenty-two years after the mill that produced the tailings pile closed and twelve years after Congress authorized the cleanup of uranium mill tailings in Navajo country. Abandoned mines also were used as shelter by animals, who inhaled radon and drank contaminated water. Local people milked the animals and ate their contaminated meat.

Harris Charley, who worked in the mines for fifteen years, told a U.S. Senate hearing in 1979: "We were treated like dogs. There was no ventilation in the mines" (Grinde and Johansen, 1995, 214). Pearl Nakai, daughter of a deceased miner, told the same hearing that "No one ever told us about the dangers of uranium" (ibid., 214).

The Senate hearings were convened by Senator Pete Domenici, New Mexico Republican, who was seeking compensation for disabled uranium miners and for the families of the deceased. "The miners who extracted uranium from the Colorado Plateau are paying the price today for the inadequate health and safety standards that were then in force," Domenici told the hearing, held at a Holiday Inn near the uranium boomtown of Grants (Grinde and Johansen, 1995, 214).

Bills to compensate the miners were introduced, discussed, and died in Congress for a dozen years. By 1990, the death toll among former miners had risen to 450 and was still rising, even as (by 1997) more than 1,000 mines on the reservation had been closed. Compensation was finally approved by Congress and signed into law by President Clinton during the early 1990s. A small number of disabled miners and families collected $100,000, but many were screened out by stringent bureaucratic requirements of proof.

NAVAJO-KVINNE I KULLBRUDD (FOTO: BRUCE JOHANSEN)

Emma Yazzie at bottom of coal strip mine, Four Corners, 1976; inset of table of contents, exhibition program, University of Oslo Ethnology Museum, 1993. (Courtesy of Bruce Johansen.)

Part of uranium mining's legacy on the Navajo Nation was the biggest expulsion of radioactive material in the United States, which occurred July 16, 1978, at 5 A.M. On that morning, more than 1,100 tons of uranium mining wastes—tailings—gushed through a packed-mud dam near Church Rock, New Mexico. With the tailings, 100 million gallons of radioactive water gushed through the dam before the crack was repaired.

By 8 A.M., radioactivity was monitored in Gallup, New Mexico, nearly fifty miles away. According to the Nuclear Regulatory Commission, the contaminated river, the Rio Puerco, showed 6,000 times the allowable standard of radioactivity below the broken dam shortly after the breach was repaired.

A month after the spill occurred, United Nuclear Corporation, which owned the dam, had cleaned up only 50 of the 1,100 tons of spilled waste. Workers were using pails and shovels because heavy machinery could not negotiate the steep terrain near the Rio Puerco. Along the river, officials issued press releases telling people not to drink the water. They had a few problems; many of the Navajo residents could not read English and had no electricity to power television sets and radios. Another consumer of the water, cattle, also did not read the press releases.

Uranium was but one form of energy exploitation on the Navajo Nation; during the 1970s, coal strip mining (for electric power generation) was protested by Navajos in the Four Corners area. One of their leaders was an elderly sheep herder, Emma Yazzie, who took her protests into the mines, obstructing the draglines at risk of her life, because pollution from coal-fired electric plants was making her sheep sick.

GROWING NUMBERS OF NATIVE AMERICANS IN THE UNITED STATES

In 1900, anthropologists and government officials called Native Americans the vanishing race. By 1990, however, American Indians had become the fastest-growing ethnic group in the United States. The 1990 census reported that 1.8 million people classified themselves as Native American, more than three times as many as the 523,600 reported thirty years earlier. The 1890 U.S. Census reported 228,000 American Indians.

The same trend continued in the 2000 census, in which more than 4.1 million people said they were at least partially Native American, an increase of more than 100 percent in ten years and thirteen times the official figure of about 300,000 a century earlier. Part of the increase was caused by an excess of births over deaths among Native Americans. The census figures must be qualified for several reasons, however: First, they are based on self-identification. A century ago, asserting Native American roots could be harmful to one's physical health. Today, many people have become fond of claiming a Cherokee princess or two on the family tree, even if no blood links can be established. Second, in the 2000 census for the first time, people were allowed to claim more than one ethnic background. Of the 4.1 million people who selected "American Indian or Alaska Native," 40 percent checked more than one category. Of the 4.1 million counted, 2.5 million said they were solely American Indian or Alaska Native. This reflects a 26 percent increase between 1990 and 2000.

One in four of the 4.1 million American Indians and Alaska Natives counted in the 2000 census hailed from California or Oklahoma. California had the largest presence, 628,000 people. Aside from these two states, the other top ten states with Native population were Arizona, Texas, New Mexico, New York, Washington, North Carolina, Michigan, and Alaska.

Most American Indians and Alaska Natives live in the West, and a majority live in urban areas, most notably New York City (87,241 people) and Los Angeles (53,092). Other cities with large American Indian and Alaska Native communities were Chicago, Houston, Philadelphia, Phoenix, San Diego, Dallas, San Antonio, and Detroit.

Roughly 74 percent of those counted indicated a Native national identity. Aside from Cherokee and Navajo, the largest American Indian tribal groupings were Cherokee, Navajo, Latin American Indian (a census category comprising 181,000 people but not a single tribe), Choctaw, Sioux, Chippewa, Apache, Blackfoot, Iroquois, and Pueblo (Table 11.1).

TABLE 11.1
Largest American Indian Tribal Groupings, Year 2000

	American Indian Tribal Grouping Alone or in Combination with One or More Races	American Indian Tribal Grouping Alone
Cherokee	729,533	281,069
Navajo	298,197	281,069
Latin American Indian	180,940	104,354
Choctaw	158,774	87,349
Sioux	153,360	108,272
Chippewa	149,669	105,907
Apache	96,833	57,060
Blackfoot	85,750	27,104
Iroquois	80,822	45,212
Pueblo	74,085	59,533

Source: U.S. Census Bureau. Available at
http://www.census.gov/mso/www/pres_lib/c2k_aian/c2k_aian.ppt

THE DRIVE TO RETIRE INDIAN MASCOTS ACCELERATES

The mascot issue became active during the 1960s with the founding of AIM in Minneapolis. Because of AIM, some of the first Indian stereotypes were contested in the Midwest. At the University of Nebraska at Omaha, for example, a chapter of AIM spearheaded a change of mascot from Indians to Mavericks, a beef animal with an attitude, in 1971. The change was popular on campus in part because the visual depiction of Owumpie, the "Omaha Indian" was so tacky by comparison that he made the Cleveland Indians' Chief Wahoo look like a real gentleman. The student body of the university eventually voted to give Owumpie the boot. Stanford University (Stanford, CA) changed its Indian mascot to a cardinal at about the same time. During the late 1960s, the National Congress of American Indians launched a campaign to bring an end to the use of Indian sports mascots and other media stereotypes.

During the early 1980s, Choctaw filmmaker Phil Lucas addressed the mascot question on the pages of *Four Winds*, a short-lived glossy magazine devoted to Native American art, history, and culture, by asking how whites would react if a sports team was named the "Cleveland Caucasians." What would European Americans think, Lucas asked, if Indians adopted racial names (such as the Window Rock Negroes or the Tahlequah White Boys) for their sports teams (1980, 69)?

Since the early 1970s, about half of the 3,000 elementary schools, high schools, and colleges in the United States that once used American Indian nicknames and mascots have dropped them according to Susan Shown Harjo, president of the Morningstar Institute in Washington, D.C. Marquette University (Milwaukee, WI) has replaced Warriors in favor of Golden Eagles. Dartmouth (Hanover, NH) changed its Indians to Big Green, and Miami of Ohio (Oxford) changed Redskins to the RedHawks. At Seattle University in Washington, the Chieftains have become the Redhawks. In the meantime, producers of Crayola crayons have done away with the color Indian red (Babwin, 2000).

In 1994, Wisconsin's education department issued a directive urging school districts in that state to drop Indian mascots. Los Angeles schools have done the same (Gormley, 2000). Ten public schools in Dallas shed their Indian mascots during 1998, at a time when roughly fifty U.S. public high schools, thirteen U.S. colleges, and three colleges in Texas still used Indian mascots (Doclar, 1998).

Washington's Redskins

Susan Harjo, president of the Morningstar Institute, has sued the Washington Redskins over their use of Indian imagery. The Redskin lawsuit (*Harjo v. Pro-Football, Inc.*, 1999) was heard before a three-judge panel of trademark

Chief Owumpie, University of Omaha, ca. 1968, book cover.

judges of the Trademark Trial and Appeals Board (TTAB). In a case heard May 27, 1998, and decided April 2, 1999, the board found the following:

> Although the marks (Redskin logos) were not scandalous, they were disparaging to the relevant segment of the population (i.e., Native Americans) at the time of their registration. As a consequence, the marks had a tendency to bring Native Americans into contempt or disrepute. These findings were based primarily on a survey provided by the Petitioners, and the TTAB decided to cancel the registration of the word marks at issue, finding that the Petitioners' survey met their burden of proof by preponderance of the evidence. (*Harjo*, 1999)

The survey in question found that 46.2 percent of Native Americans questioned found the term *Redskin* offensive. The trademark board ruling against the Washington Redskins is under appeal, a legal process that could last for years. Washington Redskin imagery is, of course, still very visible. In 2003, a U.S. District Court judge, Colleen Kolar-Kotelly, denied the action on procedural grounds. That finding was appealed to circuit court, which agreed.

Cleveland's Indians

Cleveland entered professional baseball more than a century ago with a team named the Spiders; in the team's first year, the Spiders lost 134 games. Later, the team was called the Naps. The Cleveland Indian name was adopted by a vote of the fans during 1914. Chief Wahoo was created by a *Cleveland Plain Dealer* columnist during the 1940s and first sewn into Cleveland Indian uniforms in 1947.

Until the year 2000, the Cleveland Indians' official media guide maintained that the name was adopted in honor of Louis Sockalexis, a Penobscot who played for the Spiders between 1897 and 1899. Therefore, many Indians fans boasted that the name was an honor, not an insult. The media guide first mentioned the Sockalexis story in 1968 (just as early protests began to roll in from the new AIM).

Sockalexis was said to have been the first Native American to play in baseball's major leagues. It is unknown whether this is true or spin control meant to turn a slur into a belated act of affirmative action. In 1999, the media guide devoted an entire page to the Sockalexis "story," which was coyly declared bogus a year later. In January 2000, the wording of the guide was changed, with the reference to Sockalexis taken as "legend." The old version was proved factually inaccurate by Ellen Staurowsky, a professor at Ithaca College, New York, who maintained that the team should drop its Indian moniker. Any change could cost the baseball club a pretty penny because Chief Wahoo is among the best-selling sports images on clothing, caps, and other merchandise.

Sockalexis began playing baseball at Holy Cross College, Worcester, Massachusetts, less than five years after the massacre at Wounded Knee. He was raised on the Indian Island Reservation in Old Town, Maine. By 1897, he was playing baseball at Notre Dame in Ohio, a school from which he was expelled after only a month because of public drunkenness. The Cleveland Spiders then signed him to a professional contract for $1,500. At first, Sockalexis experienced something of a hitting streak. By the middle of his first season with the Spiders, he was hitting .335. It has been said that some fans "took to wearing Indian headdresses and screaming war whoops every time Sockalexis came to bat" (Nevard, n.d.). During July 1897, Sockalexis got drunk and injured himself. He spent most of the rest of his baseball career on the bench before being released in 1899. For a decade after that, Sockalexis performed manual labor in Cleveland as he continued to suffer from alcoholism. He died in 1913. A novel based on his life (*The Cleveland Indian: The Legend of King Saturday*) was written by Luke Salisbury (1992).

Atlanta's Braves

The Atlanta Braves moved to Georgia from Boston. Before the team adopted Braves in 1912, it was known as the Boston Beaneaters, the Boston Rustlers, and the Boston Doves. During October 1991, when the Atlanta Braves arrived in Minneapolis for the World Series, they found more than 200 protestors arrayed at the stadium's gates with placards reading (among other things), "500 Years of Oppression Is Enough." Minneapolis is AIM's hometown, and even the mayor had made a statement calling on the Braves to sack their Indian imagery. When the Twins management asked the police to move the demonstrators further from the Metrodome, they refused, citing the protestors' freedom of speech and assembly.

The Atlanta Braves' emphasis on Indian imagery has spawned a number of mascot wannabes, the best known of whom is Tomahawk Tom, also known as Tom Sullivan. According to the *Atlanta Journal-Constitution*, Tomahawk Tom arrives at the ballpark "in an Indian headdress, a catcher's mask, and a cape" (Pomerantz, 1995). Tomahawk Tom is not officially sanctioned by the Braves, but he leads fans in tomahawk chop cheers, signs autographs, and passes out free baseball cards to children. Sullivan also regards himself as an inventor. One of his inventions is an ice cream treat called the Tomahawk Chop Pop.

Tomahawk Tom has learned to walk gingerly during the last few years as protests against the Braves' logo and the tomahawk chop have intensified. During early October 1995, before a Braves playoff game, a Native protester named Aaron Two Elk took a swing at Tomahawk Tom, knocking his catcher's mask askew, as he told Tom that he was desecrating Native American cultures. Two Elk, a Cherokee, earlier had become well known at the Braves' ballpark for his handwritten placards in a free speech area near Hank Aaron's statue at the stadium's entrance. A week later, Sullivan called on Atlanta police for an escort into the ballpark. Sullivan later walked into the stadium in street clothes, changing into his buckskins in a restroom, to avoid several dozen protestors who gathered in the free speech area, carefully watched by a dozen Atlanta police.

Indian Mascot Controversies: A National Sampler

The struggle over sports mascots can evoke anger and even violence. In the otherwise peaceful town of West Hurley, New York, in the Catskills, a mascot struggle also sparked a contest for control of a local school board. A ban on use of racial images was enacted during April 2000 by the board governing the 2,300-student Onteora school board. The mascot then became a heated issue in a campaign for control of the school board. During May, supporters of the Indian image won a majority of board seats. In June, the school district's Indian imagery was reinstated.

During the fall of 2000, opponents of the Indian mascot found their cars vandalized, with nails and screws driven into tires and paint splattered, usually while the cars were parked at school board meetings. Tobe Carey, an opponent of the Indian mascot whose car was damaged, told *Indian Time* (a newspaper based at Akwesasne) that "A climate of intimidation makes it impossible to speak at public meetings. Citizens working to remove racial stereotypes in our public schools have endured criminal incidents for ten months" (Johansen, 2001, 59–60).

Supporters of Onteora's Indian imagery (which includes a tomahawk chop, totem poles in the school cafeteria, and various pseudo-Indian songs and dances) have been known to bristle at any suggestion that their images degrade Native Americans in any way. Joseph Doan, a member of the school board that voted to reinstate the Indian imagery, said that many white citizens see the Indian image as a symbol of honor and environmental protection. "Our Indian has nothing to do with degrading Indians. It's our symbol and we're proud of it," said Doan (Gormley, 2000). In West Hurley, the proms are called tomahawk dances. Onteora has used Indian images since the 1950s. Until 1997, no one had formally complained when a student in buckskins led cheers at football games or when songs and dances mimicked Native American religious rituals.

Regarding Chief Illiniwek, a mascot at the University of Illinois, a decades-old struggle continues. "The chief is a religious figure for Native American people and he doesn't belong as entertainment for drunk football fans at halftime," said Monica Garreton, a University of Illinois senior and anti-chief activist. "It's comparable to Little Black Sambo and *Amos 'n Andy*" (Babwin, 2000). Every Columbus Day since 1992, opponents of the Illiniwek imagery have held demonstrations on the University of Illinois campus.

In a paper titled, "Chief Illiniwek: Dignified or Damaging?" Joseph P. Gone, a Gros Ventre, wrote:

> One primary obstacle to political and economic renewal and self-determination in Indian communities around the country is the appalling ignorance of most

American citizens, including policymakers at local, state and federal levels of government, regarding Native American histories and cultures. As multidimensional peoples engaged in complex struggles for autonomy and equality. . . . Indians are virtually invisible to the American consciousness, which gleans any awareness of Natives from caricatured Hollywood portrayals, tourist excursions and, yes, popular symbols like Chief Illiniwek. Thus, the continued prevalence of Indian stereotypes fortifies a wall of misunderstanding between our peoples. ("Indian Mascots," 2000)

The faculty of Blacksburg High School in Roanoka, Virginia, voted late in 2000 to retire the school's Indian mascot. Other schools in the Roanoke area also have changed their mascots. The Shawsville High Shawnees became the Colts, for example. A citizens' coalition raised the issue in 1999, saying that the names "objectify Indians, teach negative stereotypes and abuse spiritual symbols such as eagle feathers" (Calnan, 2000). The University of California at San Diego retired its Aztec during the fall of 2000. At about the same time (in late September), Maine's Scarborough School Board voted to drop its Redskins nickname.

Most of the faculty in the University of North Dakota's Teaching and Learning Department in Grand Forks have petitioned the university's president to change its Fighting Sioux nickname because, they contend, "it dehumanizes Indian people" (Benedict, 2000). On October 6, 2000, three of the university's students were arrested for blocking traffic in protest of the Fighting Sioux nickname. The local newspaper, the *Grand Forks Herald*, reported that these were the first arrests of students engaging in protest at the university since the days of the Vietnam War.

Tim Giago, editor of the *Lakota Times*, commented: "Would you paint your face black, wear an Afro wig, and prance around a football field trying to imitate your perceptions of black people? Of course not! That would be insulting to Blacks. So why is it OK to do it to Indians" (Nevard, n.d.)? Still, after all this, Chief Wahoo endures. The tomahawk chop seems to have assumed the kind of historical inevitability that a quarter century ago was assigned to the Berlin Wall and the federal budget deficit—a rock-solid artifact of imperial popular culture. Ted Turner, who organized the Goodwill Games and gave $1 billion to the United Nations, has been unable, or unwilling, as owner of the Atlanta Braves, to touch the tomahawk chop.

Go Get 'em Fighting Whities!

During February 2002, an intramural basketball team composed of Native American, Latino, and European American students at Greeley's University of Northern Colorado decided to change its name from Native Pride to the Fighting Whites, a purposeful parody of North America's many Native mascots, most notably nearby Eaton High School's Fighting Reds.

The team printed a few T-shirts (their uniform of choice) with the team's new name; the computer clip art with a suited, clean-cut white man; and the slogan "Everythang's Gonna Be All White." There ensued a wave of nearly instant, continentwide publicity that stood the long-standing debate over the decency of Native sports team mascots on its head. The Fighting Whites set thousands of virtual tongues wagging. Everyone had an opinion, from AIM to affiliates of the Ku Klux Klan. The reactions provided a flash-frozen ideoscape of racial humor in an age of political correctness.

Within weeks, the Fighting Whites (or, as they soon became known in many circles, the Fighting Whities) had become nearly as well known as established professional monikers such as the Washington Redskins and the Cleveland Indians. A cursory Internet search under "Fighting Whities" (on Google.com) turned up 4,700 "hits"; "Fighting Whites" provided 2,930 Web page mentions, something of a media feeding frenzy for a mascot that had not existed three months earlier. The publicity helped to sell thousands of T-shirts and other items for a hastily endowed scholarship fund to aid Native American students. Within nine months, more than 15,000 articles of Whities team gear had been sold, raising roughly $100,000 for student scholarships (Cornelius, 2002).

As the official home page of the Fighting Whites explained, in a statement written by Ryan White (who is Mohawk), John Messner, and Charles Cuny:

> We came up with the "Fighting Whites" logo and slogan to have a little satirical fun and to deliver a simple, sincere, message about ethnic stereotyping. Since March 6, when our campus newspaper first reported on the Fighting Whites, we have been launched into the national spotlight, propelled by a national debate over stereotyping American Indians in sports symbolism. (Page, 2002)

The Fighting Whites' parody very quickly sprang from the sports pages to the front pages. From the student newspaper, the story spread to the *Greeley Tribune*, then over the state, regional, and national Associated Press wire services. Some of the stories popped up as far away as London's *Guardian*. The Whities also were contacted by Fox Sports Net and NBC News, among many other electronic media. Soon, the Fighting Whites had developed at least nine T-shirt designs for sale on an Internet Site, with receipts fueled by publicity in many major daily newspapers, electronic news outlets, and such other large-audience venues as the *Jay Leno Show*. The effect on sales was downright salubrious. Soon the merchandise was available not only on T-shirts, but also on sweatshirts, tank tops, baseball jerseys, several styles of caps, a coffee mug, boxer shorts, and mouse pads.

On the court, the Whities confessed that they were hardly championship caliber, but soon their prowess at basketball did not matter. Their reputation soon had very little to do with dribbling, jumping, or shooting and more to do with the incendiary nature of the ongoing debate regarding Native American names for sports teams. Brooks Wade, 23, a member of the Fighting Whites who is a Choctaw and an employee at the University of Northern Colorado Native American Student Services, told the *Rocky Mountain News* March 15, 2002: "It's a huge media rush. It kind of snowballed out of control, really. We started it as more of a protest so we could change things in our little world, and suddenly it's worldwide" (BeDan, 2002, 12-A).

The original protest had been aimed at Eaton (Colorado) High School's Indian mascot, the Fightin' Reds, after the wife of one of the Fighting Whites resigned a job there in anger over the issue. Solomon Little Owl, a Crow, whose wife resigned at Eaton, was director of the university's Native American Student Services when he joined the team. Little Owl's wife, Kacy Little Owl (who is European American), taught special education at the high school seven miles north of Greeley for two years before leaving at the end of the previous school year (Garner, 2002).

"The message is, let's do something that will let people see the other side of what it's like to be a mascot," said Little Owl ("Fighting Whities," March 12, 2002). The Whities had reason to agree with a comment on the *Wampum Chronicles* message board, a Native American Web site: "They'll swamp the country with publicity which has everyone laughing at their opponents, all the while our boys will be laughing all the way to the bank. Way to go, Fighting Whities. Give 'em hell" (*Wampum Chronicles*, n.d.).

WINONA LADUKE: VICE PRESIDENTIAL CANDIDATE FOR THE GREEN PARTY

Winona LaDuke (Anishinabe, born 1959) became one of the foremost environmental advocates in Native America during the last quarter of the twentieth century. She lectured, wrote, and pressed authorities for answers for issues ranging from the Navajo uranium mines, to Hydro-Quebec's construction sites at James Bay, to toxic waste sites on Native Alaskan and Canadian land along the Arctic Ocean. Twice during that period, she ran as Ralph Nader's vice presidential candidate on the Green Party ticket.

LaDuke was a daughter of Vincent LaDuke, who was an Indian activist in the 1950s, and Betty LaDuke, a painter. She was educated at Harvard University in the late 1970s, and in the early 1980s moved to the White Earth Ojibwa Reservation in Minnesota at Round Lake. LaDuke became involved in protests of environmental racism and in recovery of Native American land base. With the $20,000 Reebok Human Rights Award, she founded the White Earth Land Recovery Program, which took action to regain land base on her 36-square-mile home reservation, which by the early 1990s was 92 percent owned by non-Indians.

For much of the late twentieth century, LaDuke publicized her findings in numerous newspaper and magazine articles and as a founder of the Indigenous Women's Network, director of the White Earth Recovery Project, and board member of Greenpeace. In 1996 and 2000, LaDuke ran for vice president of the United States on the Green Party ticket with Ralph Nader, as she emphasized that the United States needs the following:

> [A] new model of electoral politics [regarding] . . . the distribution of power and wealth, the abuse of power, the rights of the natural world, the environment, and the need to consider an amendment to the U.S. Constitution in which all decisions made today would be considered in light of the impact on the seventh generation from now. (Johansen, 1996a, 3)

NATIVE AMERICAN LANGUAGE REVIVAL

At least 300 distinct Native American languages were spoken in North America at the time of Columbus's first landfall in 1492. Today, 190 languages remain, but a great many of them are in imminent danger of being lost. Michael Kraus, former president of the Society for the Study of Indigenous Languages, wrote, in his book *Stabilizing Indigenous Languages*, that only 20 of 175 surviving Native American languages in the United States are still being learned by children from their parents as a first language (Johansen, 2000, 57). The emphasis on language revival is arriving barely in time for some Native American languages, those that have reached stage eight of Joshua A. Fishman's eight stages of language loss (1996), when only a few elders speak the tongue which once served an entire people at home and in their working lives.

The people of the Cochiti Pueblo were moved to revitalize their language after they conducted a survey that disclosed that all of its fluent speakers were 35 years of age or older. The few speakers under age thirty-five were semiliterate, said Mary Eunice Romero. Romero then asked: "What is going to happen to our language in 20 years when those [who are] 35 years old become 55? In 20 more years, when they're 75?" (Johansen, 2000, 56). The Cochiti immersion program began in 1996 with a summer program for thirty children, under instruction from the Tribal Council that all instruction be carried out orally with no written texts. After that, according to Romero, the program grew quickly. "When the kids went home," she said, "They spread the news that, 'Wow, they're not using any English. They're not writing. It's just totally in Cochiti.' We started out with four teachers. The next day, we got 60 kids. By the third week, we had 90 kids. By the end of the summer, the kids were starting to speak" (ibid., 56).

Romero also watched the mode of instruction change the behavior of the children. "The behavior change was a major miracle," she continued. "These kids came in rowdy as can be. By the time they left, knew the appropriate protocol of how you enter a house, greet your elder, say good-bye. The fact that they could use verbal communication for the most important piece of culture, values, and love started a chain reaction in the community" (Johansen, 2000, 56).

Experiences at the Cochiti Pueblo illustrate a trend across North America. Native American languages, many of which are nearly extinct, have enjoyed a revival during the 1990s, largely because many Native nations adopted "immersion" programs, which teach a language as the major part of many tribal school curricula. Such programs are the historical opposite of the government's traditional emphasis on assimilation into English-speaking mainstream culture that was encapsulated in a slogan ("Kill the Indian, save the man") used by Richard Henry Pratt, who founded the Carlisle Indian Industrial School in 1879. The revival of Native languages has been a grassroots affair in many Native American communities, as immersion programs have spread across Turtle Island, from the Akwesasne Mohawk territory (which straddles the borders of New York State and Ontario and Quebec in Canada), to the Cochiti Pueblo of New Mexico and the Native peoples of Hawai'i.

Why teach language? Richard Little Bear said that, "Language is the basis of sovereignty" as well as the vessel of culture. During the nineteenth century, said Little Bear, the United States showed its respect for Native American languages' essential role in culture by trying to eliminate them.

> We have all those attributes that comprise sovereign nations: a governance structure, law and order, jurisprudence, a literature, a land base, spiritual and sacred practice, and that one attribute that holds all of these...together: our languages. So once our languages disappear, each one of these attributes begins to fall apart until they are all gone. (Johansen, 2000, 56)

Little Bear said that, for the Cheyennes, the transition to a written language occurred about a century ago. As more and more communication took place in English, "Those in my generation who speak the Cheyenne language are quite possibly the last generation able to joke in our own language" (ibid., 56).

Many immersion programs were started after parents became concerned about (in the words of author Joshua Fishman) "what you lose when you lose your language." Fishman wrote the following:

> The most important relationship between language and culture...is that most of the culture is expressed in the language. Take language away from the culture and you take away its greetings, its curses, its praises, its laws, its literature, its songs, riddles, proverbs, and prayers. The culture could not be expressed and handled in any other way. You are losing all those things that essentially are the way of life, the way of thought, the way of valuing the land upon which you live and the human reality that you're talking about. (Johansen, 2000, 57)

Darryl Kipp, codirector of the Piegen Institute, a language immersion program on Montana's Blackfoot Reservation, asserted that without programs to make young people fluent in Native languages, 70 percent of the Native languages spoken today in North America will die within the next few generations with the passing of the last elders speaking them. As on many other reservations, the Blackfoot Confederacy (totaling about 40,000 people) started language immersion as a response to the failure of education provided them by outside governments and agencies: "Out of the 17,000 that belong to my band, less than one per cent have a college education. Sixty-five per cent of the students in our schools never finish the tenth grade" (Johansen, 2000, 57).

A group of Blackfoot, including Kipp, spent five years developing ways to teach the language. They ran into some opposition from tribal members, who asserted that knowledge of the language was not of practical use. One woman asked him, "Can you make soup with your language?" Kipp replied, "I struggled and had a hard time with that one. While I can't necessarily make soup, we can make healthy children, and healthy children can make all kinds of soups" (Johansen, 2000, 57).

Julia Kushner, describing language-revival work among the Arikara) cited studies that indicate that 90 percent of the 175 Native languages that survived General Platt's educational gauntlet have no child speakers (Reyhner et al., 1999, 81). That figure dates from the mid-1990s. Elsewhere in the book, speakers mourn the continuing loss of several languages, more than a dozen of which lost their last living speakers during the first half of the 1990s alone. Revived Native languages become living tools of culture in daily life, not museum pieces of a presumably also-dead culture.

The reach of language revivals is worldwide; lessons and examples are freely borrowed from the Maori of New Zealand, who have conducted an active language-revival program for several decades. The New Zealand government has maintained a Maori Language Commission since 1987.

"Repatriated Bones, Unrepatriated Spirits," a poem by Little Bear that appears at the beginning of *Revitalizing Native Languages* (Reyhner et al., 1999), reveals a sense that revival of Native American languages close a historical and cultural circle:

> We were brought back here
> to a place we don't know.
>
> We were brought back here
> and yet we are lost.
>
> But now we are starting to sing our songs.
> We are singing our songs
> that will help us find our way.
>
> We came back to a people who
> look like us but whose language
> we do not understand anymore.
> Yet we know in our hearts
> they are feeling good too, to have
> us back here among them.
> —Reyhner et al., 1999, frontispiece

In *Revitalizing Indigenous Languages*, editor Jon Reyhner stresses the need to use a revitalized language as a living tool to teach academic subjects, not as a "second language." The language must be restored to its place in everyday life of a people, he believes.

One subject that provokes controversy in Native language revitalization studies is whether the revived language should be written or solely oral. Some language activists point out that many Native languages were first committed to writing by missionaries seeking, as Reyhner writes, "to translate their *Bible* and convert Natives from their traditional religions" (Reyhner, 1999, xiii). A wide range of programs have evolved locally, some in opposition to earlier efforts at written languages by church-affiliated programs, and others have grown from the same type of programs. Although some of the programs strive to maintain an emphasis on spoken language to the exclusion of written communication, others emphasize production of written bilingual sources in the Native language to be revived as well as in English. Some of the programs use computers extensively; others avoid them as a culturally inappropriate intrusion.

Fishman himself comes down squarely on the side of literacy: "Unless they are entirely withdrawn from the modern world, minority ethno-linguistic groups need to be literate in their mother tongue (as well as in some language of wider communication)" (Reyhner et al., 1999, 38).

The often-disputed distinction between oral and literate language may be culturally artificial because many Native American cultures possessed forms of written communication, even if many European immigrants did not recognize them as such. From the wampum belts of the Haudenosaunee, to the illustrated codices of the Aztecs and Maya, to the winter counts of the Plains, written communication was used in America long before Columbus. Reyhner et al. cited H. Russell Bernard, as he urged Native Americans to establish publishing houses (1999, xiii).

Language revival also is being used in some cases to encourage the expression of Native oral histories in both written and spoken forms as well as in musical composition. Some teachers of language are finding that music is an amazingly effective way to introduce young students to languages and cultural heritage. "Why music?" asks Amar Almasude, who writes about language revival in Northern Africa:

> It is perhaps the best vehicle for becoming acquainted with humans. It is the expression that is the most pervasive. In songs, human society is portrayed and every-day experiences are reflected. Their themes are usually social issues and historical events, including national and religious feasts and holidays.... Thus, music is a fundamental element in human life. (Reyhner et al., 1999, 121)

Two books edited by Jon Reyhner (1997; Reyhner et al., 1999) present precise descriptions and examples from teachers who have been involved in a wide variety of language-revival programs, from several Native bands in British Columbia, to the Cheyenne, Yaqui, Arapaho, and Navajo. While describing individual programs, these books also sketch the common pedagogical essentials basic to all language-revitalization efforts. Reyhner suggests use of the "3 M's" of language revitalization: methods, materials, and motivation.

> Methods deal with what teaching techniques will be used at what age levels and stages of language loss. Materials deal with what things will be available for teachers and learners to use, including audiotapes, videotapes, storybooks, dictionaries, grammars, textbooks, and computer software. Motivation deals with increasing the prestige (including giving recognition and awards to individuals and groups who make special efforts) and usefulness of the indigenous language in the community, and using teaching methods that learners enjoy, so they will come back for more indigenous language instruction. (Reyhner et al., 1999, xviii)

Language must become a familiar part of a student's life; immersion specialists believe that 600 to 700 hours of such contact is necessary to acquire the kind of fluency that allows for transmission of culture from generation to generation.

Language revitalization efforts across America now share a treasure trove of linguistic innovation describing how Native languages are being revived in some ways that are very old and in others use modern technology to extend the reach of oral cultures. In Mexico, traditional Aztec *Danza* (dance) is being used to teach classical Nahuatl. The dances are part of an eighteen-ceremony ecological calendar, so while learning the language, students also absorb some knowledge of Aztec history and culture. These ceremonies deal with rain, germination, ripening of corn, war victory, hunting, and [the] tribal dead, comment authors of a study on "revenacularizing" classical Nahuatl through Aztec dance. The authors listed the intertwined benefits of this approach, by which students acquire not only knowledge of language, but also "Nahua [Mexica, or Aztec] history from an indigenous perspective, a deeper understanding of Danza steps, creation myths, [and the] making and playing of indigenous [musical] instruments" (Reyhner, 1997, 71).

In Alaska, a number of Deg Hit'an (Ingalik Athabasken) people have been teaching each other their language, Deg Xinag, over the telephone, using conference calls. Telephone technology allows widely dispersed speakers of the language to create a space to practice their skills and to teach each other new phrases and words. Phone conferences are hardly immersive (because the calls last only an hour a week), but language still is being taught. Callers have joined the conversations from as far away as Seattle.

In a similar vein, KTNN AM 660, the Navajo Nation's official radio station, has been making plans to offer instruction in the Navajo language over the air in an attempt to follow Joshua Fishman's advice that revitalized languages, to be successful, must be shared by a people via the communications media of their communities. "The Voice of the Navajo Nation," as KTNN is called, has a signal that reaches from Albuquerque to Phoenix.

"SQUAWBLES"

The state of Minnesota has enacted a legal ban on the use of the word *squaw* in geographic place-names for lakes, streams, and points, agreeing with two Chippewa high school students on the Leech Lake Reservation that the word is degrading to Native American women. The state law was overwhelmingly approved by the state legislature and signed by Governor Arne Carlson. A debate has since developed that the Associated Press, with a straight journalistic face, called "a squawble" (Johansen, 1996b, 4). The law affected nineteen place-names in Minnesota. One Squaw Lake became Nature Lake, and another Squaw Lake became Wahbegon. Squaw Point became Oak Point, and Squaw Creek became Fond-du-Lac. Squaw Pond became Scout Camp Pond.

In Minnesota's Lake County, a swatch of forest, streams, and lakes with 10,000 residents that reaches the shores of western lake Superior near the Canadian border, non-Indian residents suggested that their Squaw Creek and Squaw Bay be changed to Politically Correct Creek and Politically Correct Bay, respectively. The state rejected Lake County's proposal, which arrived with a letter from Sharon Hahn, head of the Lake County Board of Commissioners: "The term 'squaw' is in common use throughout North America, far beyond its Algonquian origin," she wrote. "We find nothing derogatory in continued use of this term" (Johansen, 1996b, 4).

County officials in Lake County refused to change names as required by the state, citing standard dictionary definitions that define "squaw" as an Indian woman (generically). They also protested the expense of making the changes on signs and maps. Indeed, the 1983 edition of Webster's *New Universal Unabridged Dictionary* defined *squaw* as (1) an American Indian woman or wife; (2) any woman, chiefly humorous. Some dictionaries attribute the word to "squáas," in an Algonquian language (Massachuset, Natick, or Narraganset), and add that it is a derogatory word for women of any race or ethnic group. Unabridged dictionaries also sometimes list several derivations, such as "squaw winter," said to be a spell of unusually cold and stormy weather before Indian summer.

In *Literature of the American Indian* (1973), edited by Thomas E. Sanders and Walter W. Peek, however, squaw is said to be a French corruption of an "Iroquois" word, *otiska*, referring to female private parts. Which Iroquois language is involved here is not addressed. The phrase was probably carried into the north woods of Minnesota (and the rest of Anglo-American culture) by French fur trappers, with the word later anglicized by English-speaking colonists. According to the *Thesaurus of American Slang*, edited by Ester and Albert A. Lewis, the word *squaw* is used as a synonym for "prostitute" (Johansen, 1996b, 4).

The town of Squaw Lake, Minnesota, with 140 permanent residents and surrounded by the Leech Lake Indian Reservation, kept its name because non-Indian residents also grumbled about overindulgence in political correctness. Names of towns with the "S" word were omitted from the original law, but a movement is now afoot to include them as well. Muriel Charwood Litzau, a Native American who is a resident of Squaw Lake as well as the Leech Lake Reservation, loathes the "S" word so much that she does not want to tell people where she lives. She said that squaw is a French corruption of an Iroquois (possibly Mohawk) word for "vagina" (Johansen, 1996b, 4). Her daughter, Dawn Litzau and another student, Angelene Losh, began the campaign to eliminate squaw as a geographic place-name in Minnesota as part of a Native American studies class at Cass Lake-Bena High School, a public school within the Leech Lake Reservation. Students of the school's Name Change Committee also met with students at the Pequot Lakes High School in northern Minnesota and persuaded the student body to change its Indian mascot.

According to the U.S. Geological Survey's Board on Geographic Names, the word *squaw* has been affixed to 1,050 geographic names in the United States, most of them in the West and Midwest (Johansen, 1996b, 4). In California, for example, a request has been filed with the Survey Board to change the name Squaw Gulch, in Siskiyou County, to Taritsi Gulch. Also in California, questions are being raised about the name of the Squaw Valley ski resort. Activists in Arizona and Oregon (with 161 place-names that include "squaw") were taking up the refrain, advocating state laws similar to Minnesota's.

The Board on Geographic Names has exercised a role in "political correctness" debates before. In 1967, it directed that 143 places using the place-name *nigger* be changed to "Negro." The same year, the board ordered that *Jap* be changed to "Japanese" in 26 place-names across the United States.

FURTHER READING

Appeals Court Halts Indian Trust Accounting. *Billings Gazette*, November 14, 2003. Available at http://www.billingsgazette.com/index.php?id=1&display=rednews/2003/11/14/build/nation/42-indiantrust.inc.

Awehali, Brian. Fighting Long Odds: Government Continues to Shred, Evade, Obstruct, Lie, and Conspire in Indian Trust Case. *LiP Magazine*, December 15, 2003. Available at http://www.lipmagazine.org.

Babwin, Don. Opposition to Indian Mascots Mounts. Associated Press, November 6, 2000. Available at http://www.copleynewspapers.com/couriernews/top/e06mascots.htm.

BeDan, M. International Eye Drawn to "Fightin' Whities"; Protest of Mascot for Eaton High School "Has Kind of Snowballed." *Rocky Mountain News*, March 15, 2002, 12-A.

Benedict, Michael. UND: Another Voice; Faculty Group Gives Kupchella Petition Urging Nickname Change. *Grand Forks* [North Dakota] *Herald*, November 9, 2000. Available at http://web.northscape.com/content/gfherald/2000/11/09/local/MB1109UND.htm.

Brandon, William. *The Last Americans*. New York: McGraw-Hill, 1974.

Calnan, Christopher. Faculty Votes to Retire Mascot. *Roanoke Times*, November 8, 2000. Available at http://www.roanoke.com/roatimes/news/story102344.html.

Chatters, James C. Politics Aside, These Bones Belong to Everybody. *Wall Street Journal*, September 5, 2002, D-10.

Cobell v. Norton. 240 F3rd 1081 (DC Cir. 2001).

Committee on Government Operations, U.S. House of Representatives. "Misplaced Trust: The Bureau of Indian Affairs' Mismanagement of the Indian Trust Fund." April 1, 1992. Washington, D.C.: U.S. Government Printing Office, 1992.

Cornelius, Coleman. Fightin' Whites Fund Scholarships: T-Shirt Sales Reap $100,000 for Indians. *Denver Post*, December 1, 2002. Available at http://www.denverpost./com/Stories/0,1413,36%7E53%7E1021717%7E,00.html.

County of Oneida v. Oneida Indian Nation. 470 U.S. 226 (1985).

Crime Rate on Indian Reservations Much Higher than U.S. *Indian Time* [Akwesasne Mohawk Reservation, New York], October 9, 2003, 11.

Crisis at Akwesasne [transcript]. Hearings of the New York Assembly, July–August 1990. Albany and Fort Covington, NY: State of New York.

Deloria, Vine, Jr. *Custer Died for Your Sins: An Indian Manifesto*. New York: Avon Books, 1969.

Deloria, Vine, Jr. *God is Red*. Golden, CO: Fulcrum, 1994.

Department of Indian Affairs and Northern Development. Press release, June 20, 2001. Available at http://www1.newswire.ca/releases/June2001/20/c6060.html.

Diebel, Linda. $12 Billion Lawsuit Seeks Redress For Abuse In Residential Schools. *Toronto Star*, December 8, 2002. Available at http://www.thestar.ca/NASApp/cs/ContentServer?pagename=thestar/Layout/Article_Type1&c=Article&cid=1035775341135&call_page=TS_GTA&call_pageid=968350130169&call_pagepath=GTA/News&pubid=968163964505&StarSource=email.

Doclar, Mary. Protests Cause Reassessment of Dallas Schools' Indian Mascots. *Fort Worth Star-Telegram*, December 5, 1998. Available at http://www.startext.net/news/doc/1047/1:arl71/1:arl71120598.html.

Drew, Neil. Personal e-mail communication, July 1, 2001.

Eichstaedt, Peter. *If You Poison Us: Uranium and American Indians*. Santa Fe, NM: Red Crane Books, 1995.

Elliott, Louise. Ontario Native Suicide Rate One of Highest in World, Expert Says. *Vancouver Sun*, November 30, 2000. Available at http://www.vancouversun.com.

Elliott, Louise. Aboriginal Girls Taking Their Lives in Record Numbers Across Ontario's North. *Canadian Aboriginal*, December 3, 2000. Available at http://www.canadianaboriginal.com/health/health15b.htm.

Elliott, Louise. Hunger and Suicide Stalk Reserve after Feds Cut Funds. *Montreal Gazette*, June 7, 2001, A-15.

Elliott, Louise. Native Community Searches for Doctor. *Toronto Star*, June 16, 2001, A-16.3.

Elliott, Louise. Reserve's Doctor Safe After Two-Day Walk in Wilderness. *Montreal Gazette*, June 18, 2001, A-14.

Elliott, Louise. Band Talking to Media May Perpetuate Suicide Crisis, Says Nault. Canadian Press, June 22, 2001. Available at http://ca.news.yahoo.com/010622/6/6ei2.html.

Elliott, Louise. Native Groups Warn of Suicide Crisis. *Toronto Star*, July 31, 2001, A-6.

Fast Growing Indian Gambling Drew $16.2 Billion. *Omaha World-Herald*, July 8, 2004, A-5.

Federal Bureau of Investigation. *Crime in the United States: Annual Report, 1989.* Washington, DC: FBI, 1989.

Federal Paternalism Angers Pikangikum. *Canadian Aboriginal*. No date. Available at http://www.canadianaboriginal.com/news/news131a.htm.

Fialka, John J. Tribe Gets Private-Sector Jobs; Winnebagos Build Profitable Businesses with Casino Seed Money. *Wall Street Journal*, February 18, 2004, A-4.

"'Fighting Whities' Make a Statement; American Indian Students Try to Raise Awareness of Stereotypes." Associated Press, in *Philadelphia Daily News,* March 12, 2002. Available at www.philly.com/mld/dailynews/sports/2841746.htm.

Fishman, Joshua F. "Maintaining Languages: What Works, What Doesn't?" In G. Cantoni, ed. *Stabilizing Indigenous Languages.* Flagstaff, AZ: Northern Arizona University, 1996, 186-198.

Gamble, Susan. M.D. Shocked at Conditions on Reserve. *Brantford Expositor*, n.d., n.p. Available at http://www.southam.com/brantfordexpositor.

Garner, J. "Whities' Mascot about Education, Not Retaliation; Intramural Basketball Team Takes Shot at Indian Caricature Used by Eaton High School. *Rocky Mountain News*, March 12, 2002. Available at http://www.rockymountainnews.com/drmn/state/article/0,1299,DRMN_21_1026337,00.html.

Gormley, Michael [Associated Press]. State Commissioner to Take a Stand on Indian Mascots, Names. *Boston Globe On-line*, 11:42 A.M. October 28, 2000. Available at http://www.boston.com/dailynews/302/region/state_commissioner_to_take_a_s:.html.

Goulais, Bob. Water Crisis Latest Plague to Visit Pikangikum. *Anishinabek News*, November 2000. Available at http://www.anishinabek.ca/news/Past%20issues/2000/November%20issue/Nov00watercrisis.htm.

Grinde, Donald A., Jr. Personal interview, March 23. 1993.

Grinde, Donald A., Jr., and Bruce E. Johansen. *Ecocide of Native America: Environmental Destruction of Indian Lands and Peoples.* Santa Fe, NM: Clear Light, 1995.

Harjo v. Pro-Football, Inc. 1999 WL 329721 (P.T.O., April 2, 1999). The Trademark Trial and Appeals Board, Patent and Trademark Office. Available at http://www.kentlaw.edu/student_orgs/jip/trade/skins.htm.

Hill, Richard W., Sr. Wounded Knee, a Wound that Won't Heal. Did the Army Attempt to Cover Up the Massacre of Prisoners of War? October 7, 1999. Available at http://www.dickshovel.com/hill.html. Accessed February 13, 2003.

Hornung, Rick. *One Nation Under the Gun: Inside the Mohawk Civil War.* New York: Pantheon, 1991.

Indian Mascots: An Idea Whose Time Has Passed [editorial]. *Asheville, NC, Citizen-Times*, September 30, 2000. Available at http://www.main.nc.us/wncceib/PeweAC-T9300editorial.htm.

Johansen, Bruce E. *Forgotten Founders: Benjamin Franklin, the Iroquois, and the Rationale for the American Revolution.* Ipswich, MA: Gambit, 1982.

Johansen, Bruce E. The Klan in a Can. *The Progressive*, July 1988, 13.

Johansen, Bruce E. Dead Indians Out, Live Indians In. *The Progressive*, December 1989, 15–16.

Johansen, Bruce E. *Life and Death in Mohawk Country*. Golden, CO: North American Press/Fulcrum, 1993.

Johansen, Bruce E. Running for Office: LaDuke and the Green Party. *Native Americas* 13:4(Winter 1996a):3–4.

Johansen, Bruce E. "Squawbles" in Minnesota. *Native Americas* 13:4(Winter 1996b):4.

Johansen, Bruce E. The BIA as Banker: "Trust" Is Hard When Billions Disappear. *Native Americas* 14:1(Spring 1997):14–23.

Johansen, Bruce. Whiteclay, Nebraska: The Town that Booze Built. *Native Americas* 15:1(Spring 1998):5.

Johansen, Bruce E. Living and Breathing: Native Languages Come Alive. *Native Americas* 17:1(Spring 2000):56–59.

Johansen, Bruce E. Mascots: Honor Be Thy Name. *Native Americas* 18:1(Spring 2001): 58–61.

Johansen, Bruce E. The New York Oneidas: A Case Study in the Mismatch of Cultural Tradition and Economic Development. *American Indian Culture and Research Journal* 26:3(2002):25–46.

Johansen, Bruce E., and Donald A. Grinde, Jr. *The Encyclopedia of Native American Biography*. New York: Henry Holt, 1997.

Judge: Scientists Can Study Ancient Bones of Man Indian Tribes Claim as Ancestor. *Indian Time* 20:35(September 5, 2002):10.

Kehoe, Alice Beck. *America Before the European Invasions*. London: Longman, 2002.

Kennedy, J. Michael. Truth and Consequences on the Reservation. *Los Angeles Times Sunday Magazine*, July 7, 2002, cover story. Available at LATimes.com.

Kilborn, Peter. Pine Ridge: A Different Kind of Poverty. *New York Times*, in *Omaha World-Herald*, September 30, 1992, p. A-1.

King, C. Richard, and Charles Frueling Springwood. *Team Spirits: The Native American Mascots Controversy*. Lincoln: University of Nebraska Press, 2001.

Meriam, Lewis. *The Problem of Indian Administration*. Baltimore: Johns Hopkins University Press, 1928.

Lucas, Phil. Images of Indians. *Four Winds: The International Forum for Native American Art, Literature, and History*, Autumn 1980, 69–77.

Lynch, John. Pikangikum First Nation Looks Beyond "Opening a Store." It Wants to Create Private-Sector Partnerships. *Northern Ontario Business*, March 1999. Available at http://www.nob.on.ca/archives/mar99story/step.html.

Marquez, Deron. Indian Gaming Is Different from Other Forms of Gambling. *Indian Country Today*, February 12, 2002, n.p., in LEXIS.

Murphy, Maureen. Gambling on Indian Reservations. Congressional Research Service, Library of Congress, April 26, 1985.

Nevard, David. Wahooism in the USA. A Red Socks Journal. No date. Available at http://www.ultranet.com/~kuras/bhxi3d.htm.

Page, Charles. The "Fighting Whites" Offer Lesson in Cultural Diversity. *Newsday*, March 19, 2002, A-32.

Pomerantz, Gary. Atlanta Fan's Headdress Ruffles Indian Feathers. *Atlanta Journal-Constitution*, October 21, 1995. Available at http://www.fastball.com/braves/archives/stories/1995/66ws1021.html.

Randolph, Eleanor. New York's Native American Casino Contributes, But Not to Tax Rolls. *New York Times*, October 18, 2003, n.p.

Reyhner, Jon, ed. *Teaching Indigenous Languages*. Flagstaff: Center for Excellence in Education, Northern Arizona University, 1997.

Reyhner, Jon, Gina Cantoni, Robert N. St. Clair, and Evangeline Parsons Yazzie. *Revitalizing Native Languages*. Flagstaff: Center for Excellence in Education, Northern Arizona University, 1999.

Reynolds, Jerry. Bush Administration Likely Behind Cobell Appropriations Rider. *Indian Country Today*, November 1, 2003. Available at http://www.indiancountry.com/?1067709828.

Salisbury, L. *The Cleveland Indian: The Legend of King Saturday*. Brooklyn, NY: The Smith Publishers, 1992.

Sanders, Thomas E., and Walter W. Peek, eds. *Literature of the American Indian*. Beverly Hills, CA: Glencoe, 1976.

Seminole Tribe of Florida v. Butterworth. 658 F. 2d 310 (5th Cir., 1980).

Slayman, Andrew L. A Battle over Bones. *Archaeology* 50:1(January/February 1997): 16–23.

Smith, Dean Howard. *Modern Tribal Development: Paths to Self-Sufficiency and Cultural Integrity in Indian Country*. Walnut Creek, CA: AltaMira Press, 2000.

Spindel, Carol. *Dancing at Halftime: Sports and the Controversy over American Indian Mascots*. New York: New York University Press, 2001.

Suzuki, Peter T. Housing on the Nebraska Indian Reservations: Federal Policies and Practices. *Habitat International* 15:4(1991):27–32.

Thomas, David Hurst. *Skull Wars: Kennewick Man, Archaeology, and the Battle for Native American Identity*. New York: Basic Books/Peter N. Nevraumont, 2000.

U.S. Department of Health and Human Services. *Trends in Indian Health*. Washington, D.C.: Government Printing Office, 1991.

Walke, Roger. Gambling on Indian Reservations: Updated October 17, 1988. Congressional Research Service, Library of Congress, Washington, DC.

Wampum Chronicles message board. No date. Available at http://pub11.ezboard.com/fwampumchroniclescurrentevents.showMessage?topicID=265.topic.

Wanamaker, Tom. Indian Gaming Column. *Indian Country Today*, April 5, 2002, n.p., in LEXIS.

Wanamaker, Tom. Debunking the Myth of Unregulated Indian Gaming. *Indian Country Today*, May 13, 2002, n.p., in LEXIS.

Weinberg, Bill. Land and Sovereignty in Hawai'i: A Native Nation Re-emerges. *Native Americas* 13:2(Summer 1996):30–41.

Wollock, Jeffrey. On the Wings of History: American Indians in the 20th Century. *Native Americas* 20:1(Spring 2003):14–31.

Selected Bibliography

Abram, Charles. Law of the Woman Chief, May 21, 1923. Hewitt Collection, BAE Manuscript No. 1636, NAA, Smithsonian Institution. Cited in Grinde and Johansen, 1991, 259.

Adair, James. *History of the American Indians*. Edited by Samuel Cole Williams. Johnson City, TN: Watauga Press, [1775] 1930.

Adams, Charles F. *Works of John Adams*. Boston: Little-Brown, 1851.

Adams, John. *Defence of the Constitutions . . . of the United States*. Philadelphia: Hall and Sellers, 1787.

Africans in America: Revolution, Resource Bank, Part 2: 1750–1805: Crispus Attucks. Public Broadcasting Service. No date.

Available at http://www.pbs.org/wgbh/aia/part2/2p24.html. Accessed February 20, 2003.

Allen, Paula Gunn. *The Sacred Hoop: Recovering the Feminine in American Indian Traditions*. Boston: Beacon Press, 1986.

Ambrose, Stephen E. *Crazy Horse and Custer*. New York: New American Library, 1986.

American Monthly Museum [magazine], 2(February 1776):96.

American Friends Service Committee. *Uncommon Controversy: Fishing Rights of the Muckleshoot, Puyallup, and Nisqually Indians*. Seattle: University of Washington Press, 1970.

Anthony, Susan B., Elizabeth Cady Stanton, and Matilda Joslyn Gage, eds. *History of Woman Suffrage*. Salem, NH: Ayer Company, 1985.

Anderson, Eva Greenslit. *The Life Story of Chief Seattle*. Caldwell, OH: Caxton, 1950.

Anderson, Terry L. *Sovereign Nations or Reservations?: An Economic History of American Indians*. San Francisco: Pacific Research Institute for Public Policy, 1995.

Appeals Court Halts Indian Trust Accounting. *Billings Gazette*, November 14, 2003. Available at http://www.billingsgazette.com/index.php?id=1&display=rednews/2003/11/14/build/nation/42-indiantrust.inc.

Aquila, Richard. *The Iroquois Restoration: Iroquois Diplomacy on the Colonial Frontier, 1701–1754*. Detroit: Wayne State University Press, 1983.

Archuleta, Margaret L., Brenda J. Child, and K. Tsianina Lomawaima, eds. *Away from Home: American Indian Boarding School Experiences, 1879–2000*. Phoenix: Heard Museum, 2000.

Arden, Harvey. The Fire that Never Dies. *National Geographic,* September 1987, 374–403.

Armstrong, Virginia Irving. *I Have Spoken: American History through the Voices of the Indians.* Athens, OH: Swallow Press, 1984.

Associated Press. *Omaha World-Herald,* December 9, 1991, 16.

Associated Press. Canada's United Church Apologizes for Abuse at Indian Schools. *Associated Press Canada,* October 28, 1998.

Awehali, Brian. Fighting Long Odds: Government Continues to Shred, Evade, Obstruct, Lie, and Conspire in Indian Trust Case. *LiP Magazine.* December 15, 2003. Available at http://www.lipmagazine.org.

Axtell, James. *The Indian Peoples of Eastern America: A Documentary History of the Sexes.* New York: Oxford University Press, 1981.

Babwin, Don. Opposition to Indian Mascots Mounts. Associated Press, November 6, 2000. Available at http://www.copleynewspapers.com/couriernews/top/e06mascots.htm.

Baily, L. R. *Indian Slave Trade in the Southwest.* Los Angeles: Westernlore Press, 1973.

Baker, Leonard. *John Marshall: A Life in Law.* New York: Macmillan, 1974.

Ball, Milnar. Constitution, Court, Indian Tribes. *American Bar Foundation Research Journal* 1(1987):1–140.

Ballantine, Betty, and Ian Ballantine. *The Native Americans: An Illustrated History.* Atlanta: Turner, 1994.

Barbeau, C. M. *Huron and Wyandot Mythology with an Appendix Containing Earlier Published Records.* No. 11, Anthropological Series, Memoir 80. Ottawa: Government Printing Bureau, 1915:35–51.

Barreiro, José. The Search for Lessons. In José Barreiro, ed., *Indigenous Economics: Toward A Natural World Order. Akwe:kon Journal* 9:2(Summer 1992):18–39.

Barsh, Russel L. *The Washington Fishing Rights Controversy: An Economic Critique.* Seattle: University of Washington School of Business Administration, 1977.

Barsh, Russel, and James Henderson. *The Road: Indian Tribes and Political Liberty.* Berkeley: University of California Press, 1980.

Bates, Tom. The Government's Secret War on the Indian. *Oregon Times,* February–March 1976, 14.

Beal, Merrill D. *I Will Fight No More Forever.* Seattle: University of Washington Press, 1963.

Beals, Ralph L., and Harry Hoijer. *An Introduction to Anthropology.* New York, 1965.

Beckhard, Arthur J., *Black Hawk.* New York: Julian Messner, 1957.

BeDan, M. International Eye Drawn to "Fightin' Whities"; Protest of Mascot for Eaton High School "Has Kind of Snowballed." *Rocky Mountain News,* March 15, 2002, 12-A.

Benedict, Michael. UND: Another Voice; Faculty Group Gives Kupchella Petition Urging Nickname Change. *Grand Forks* [North Dakota] *Herald,* November 9, 2000. Available at http://web.northscape.com/content/gfherald/2000/11/09/local/MB1109UND.htm.

Bergh, Albert E., ed. *The Writings of Thomas Jefferson.* Washington: Jefferson Memorial Association, 1903–1904: vol. 11.

Bigelow, John, ed. *Autobiography of Benjamin Franklin.* Philadelphia: J. B. Lippincott, 1868.

Birchfield, D. L. *The Encyclopedia of North American Indians.* New York: Marshall Cavendish, 1997: vol. 5.

Blackbird, Andrew J. *Complete Both Early and Late History of the Ottawa and the Cheppewa Indians of Michigan: A Grammar of Their Language, Personal and Family History of the Author.* Harbor Springs, Michigan: Babcock and Darling, 1897.

Black Elk. *Black Elk Speaks, as Told to John G. Neihardt.* New York: William Morrow, [1932] 1972.

Black Elk. *The Sacred Pipe: Black Elk's Account of the Seven Rites of the Oglala Sioux.* Edited by Joseph Epes Brown. New York: Penguin Books, 1973.

Black Hawk. *Life of Ma-ka-tai-me-she-kia-kiak, or Black Hawk, Dictated by Himself.* Boston, 1834.

Bluecloud, Peter. *Alcatraz Is Not an Island.* Berkeley, CA: Wingbow Press, 1972.

Bolton, Herbet Eugene, ed. *Spanish Exploration in the Southwest, 1542–1706.* New York: Charles Scribner's Sons, 1916.

Bolton, Herbet Eugene. *Coronado on the Turquoise Trail.* Albuquerque: University of New Mexico Press, 1949.

Bone Shirt, Alfred. Via Internet to Marcel Guay. Canadian Aboriginal News/First Nations Skyvillage. Available at http://www.canadianaboriginal.com/.

Boorstin, Daniel J. *The Lost World of Thomas Jefferson.* New York: Henry Holt, 1948.

Borah, Woodrow. The Historical Demography of Aboriginal and Colonial America: An Attempt at Perspective. In William M. Denevan, ed., *The Native American Population of the Americas in 1492.* Madison: University of Wisconsin Press, 1976: 13–34.

Borah, Woodrow, and Sherburne Cook. *The Aboriginal Population of Mexico on the Eve of the Spanish Conquest.* Ibero-Americana No. 45. Berkeley: University of California Press, 1963.

Bourrie, Mark. Canada Apologizes for Abuse of Native Peoples. Interpress Service, January 8, 1998. Available at http://www.oneworld.org/ips2/jan98/canada2.html.

Boyd, Julian P., ed. *Indian Treaties Printed by Benjamin Franklin, 1736–1762.* Philadelphia: Historical Society of Pennsylvania, 1938.

Boyd, Julian P., ed. *The Papers of Thomas Jefferson.* Princeton, NJ: Princeton University Press, 1950 to date.

Boyd, Julian P. Dr. Franklin, Friend of the Indian. In Ray Lokken, Jr., ed., *Meet Dr. Franklin.* Philadelphia: Franklin Institute, 1981: 237–245.

Boyd, Robert. *The Coming of the Spirit of Pestilence: Introduced Infectious Diseases and Population Decline Among Northwest Coast Indians, 1774–1874.* Vancouver, BC: University of British Columbia Press, 1999.

Brack, Fred. Fishing Rights: Who Is Entitled to Northwest Salmon?" *Seattle Post-Intelligencer Northwest Magazine,* January 16, 1977, 8–10.

Bradford, William. *History of Plymouth Plantation.* Edited by Charles Deane. Boston: Private printing, 1856.

Bradford, William. *History of Plymouth Plantation.* Edited by Samuel Eliot Morison. New York: Modern Library, 1967.

Branch, Douglas E. *The Hunting of the Buffalo.* Lincoln: University of Nebraska Press, 1973.

Brand, Johanna. *The Life and Death of Anna Mae Aquash.* Toronto: Lorimer, 1978.

Brandon, William. *The American Heritage Book of Indians.* New York: Dell, 1961.

Brandon, William. *The Last Americans.* New York: McGraw-Hill, 1974.

Brandon, William. *The Rise and Fall of North American Indians from Prehistory through Geronimo.* Lanham, MD: Taylor Trade, 2003.

Bricker, Victoria R. *The Indian Christ, the Indian King.* Austin: University of Texas Press, 1981.

A Brief Notice of the Recent Outrages Committed by Isaac Stevens... May 17, 1856. In W. H. Wallace, *Martial Law in the Washington Territory*, *The Annals of America*, 1856, 384–389.

British Columbia Anglican Diocese Set to Close over Lawsuit. Canadian Broadcasting Corporation News On-line, December 30, 2001. Available at http://cbc.ca/cgi-bin/view?/news/2001/12/30/anglican_011230.

Brockunier, Samuel H. *The Irrepressible Democrat: Roger Williams*. New York: Ronald Press, 1940.

Brown, Bruce. *Mountain in the Clouds: The Search for the Wild Salmon*. New York: Simon and Schuster, 1982.

Brown, Dee. *Bury My Heart at Wounded Knee*. New York: Holt, Rinehart, Winston, 1970.

Brown, Jennifer S. H. *Strangers in Blood: Fur Trade Families in Indian Country*. Vancouver, BC: University of British Columbia Press, 1981.

Brown, Judith K. Economic Organization and the Position of Women among the Iroquois. *Ethnohistory* 17:3–4(Summer–Fall 1970):151–167.

Bryant, Martha F. *Sacajawea: A Native American Heroine*. New York: Council for Indian Education, 1989.

Burnham, Philip. Review *Seven Myths of the Spanish Conquest*, by Matthew Restall. *Indian Country Today*, August 5, 2004. Available at http://www.indiancountry.com/?1091714398.

Butterfield, Consul Wilshire. *History of the Girtys, Being a Concise Account of the Girty Brothers—Thomas, Simon, James and George, and of Their Half-Brother, John Turner—Also of the Part Taken by Them in Lord Dunmore's War, in the Western Border War of the Revolution, and in the Indian War of 1790–1795*. Cincinnati: Robert Clark, 1890.

Butterfield, Lyman H., ed. *The Diary and Autobiography of John Adams*. Cambridge, MA: Harvard University Press, 1961.

Byrd, Sydney. Wounded Knee: We Must Never Forget. *Lakota Journal*, January 3–10, 2003, 1. Available at http://www.lakotajournal.com/front.htm.

Caduto, Michael J., and Joseph Brudhac. *Keepers of the Earth: Native American Stories and Environmental Activities for Children*. Golden, CO: Fulcrum, 1988.

Calamai, Peter. Demise of Maya Tied to Droughts: Study Points to Climate Change Culture Depended on Growing Maize. *Toronto Star*, March 14, 2003. Available at http://www.thestar.ca/NASApp/cs/ContentServer?pagename=thestar/Layout/Article_Type1&c=Article&cid=1035779188042&call_page=TS_Canada&call_pageid=968332188774&call_pagepath=News/Canada&pubid=968163964505&StarSource=email.

Calloway, Colin. *The Western Abenakis of Vermont, 1600–1800: War, Migration, and the Survival of an Indian People*. Norman: University of Oklahoma Press, 1990.

Calloway, Colin. *New Worlds for All: Indians, Europeans, and the Remaking of Early America*. Baltimore: Johns Hopkins University Press, 1997.

Calnan, Christopher. Faculty Votes to Retire Mascot. *Roanoke Times*, November 8, 2000. Available at http://www.roanoke.com/roatimes/news/story102344.html.

Cameron, Kenneth W., ed. *The Works of Samuel Peters*. Hartford, CT: Transcendental Books, 1967.

Canby, Thomas Y. The Anasazi: Riddles in the Ruins. *National Geographic*, November 1982, 554–592.

Canby, William C., Jr. *American Indian Law*. St. Paul, MN: West, 1981.

Carr, Lucien. *The Social and Political Position of Women among the Huron-Iroquois Tribes*. Salem, MA: Salem Press, 1884.

Carter, Harvey Lewis. *The Life and Times of Little Turtle: First Sagamore of the Wabash*. Urbana: University of Illinois Press, 1987.

Carver, Jonathan. *Travels through the Interior Parts of North America*. London: C. Dilly, 1778.

Case, Nancy Humphrey. Gifts from the Indians: Native Americans Not Only Provided New Kinds of Food and Recreation; They May Have Given the Founding Fathers Ideas on How to Form a Government. *Christian Science Monitor*, November 26, 2002. Available at http://www.csmonitor.com.

Castillo, Bernal Diaz del. *Historia Verdadera de la Conquista de la Nueva Espana*. Edited by Joaquin Ramirez Cabanas. Mexico City: Editorial Purrua, 1968.

Castillo, Bernardino Diaz del. *Conquest of Mexico*. New York, 1958.

Chalmers, Harvey. *The Last Stand of the Nez Perce*. New York: Twayne, 1962.

Champagne, Duane. *American Indian Societies: Strategies and Conditions of Political and Cultural Survival*. Cambridge, MA: Cultural Survival, 1989.

Chapin, Howard H. *Sachems of the Narragansetts*. Providence: Rhode Island Historical Society, 1931.

Chatters, James C. Politics Aside, These Bones Belong to Everybody. *Wall Street Journal*, September 5, 2002, D-10.

Cherokee Nation v. Georgia (5 Peters 1, 1831).

Chittenden, Hiram M. *The American Fur Trade of the Far West*. New York: Press of the Pioneers, 1935.

Church, Thomas. *Diary of King Philip's War, 1676–77*. Edited by Alan and Mary Simpson. Chester, CT: Pequot Press, 1975.

Churchill, Ward. *Struggles for the Land*. Monroe, ME: Common Courage Press, 1993.

Churchill, Ward, and Jim Vander Wall. *Agents of Repression: The FBI's Secret War Against the Black Panther Party and the American Indian Movement*. Boston: South End Press, 1990a.

Churchill, Ward, and Jim Vander Wall. *The Cointelpro Papers*. Boston: South End Press, 1990b.

Chupack, Henry. *Roger Williams*. New York: Twayne, 1969.

Clark, Robert A. *The Killing of Crazy Horse*. Lincoln: University of Nebraska Press, 1976.

Coe, Michael D. *America's First Civilization*. New York: American Heritage, 1968.

Coe, William R. Resurrecting the Grandeur of Tikal. *National Geographic*, December 1975, 792–799.

Cohen, Felix. Americanizing the White Man. *American Scholar* 21:2(1952):177–191.

Cohen, Felix. *The Legal Conscience: The Selected Papers of Felix S. Cohen*. Edited by Lucy Kramer Cohen. New Haven, CT: Yale University Press, 1960.

Colden, Cadwallader. *The History of the Five Nations of Canada*. New York: Amsterdam, [1765] 1902.

Colden, Cadwallader. *The History of the Five Nations Depending on the Province of New York in America*. Ithaca, NY: Cornell University Press, [1727, 1747] 1958.

Cole, Donald B. *Presidency of Andrew Jackson*. Lawrence: University Press of Kansas, 1993.

Collier, John. *Indians of the Americas*. New York: New American Library, 1947.

Commager, Henry Steele. *Jefferson, Nationalism and the Enlightenment*. New York: George Braziller, 1975.

Cook, Sherburne F. Interracial Warfare and Population Decline among the New England Indians. *Ethnohistory* 20:1(Winter 1973):1–24.

Cook, Sherburne F., and Woodrow Borah, *The Indian Population of Central Mexico, 1521-1610.* Ibero-Americana No. 44. Berkeley: University of California Press, 1960.

Cook, Sherburne F., and Leslie B. Simpson. The Population of Central Mexico in the Sixteenth Century. *Ibero-Americana* 31. Berkeley and Los Angeles: University of California Press, 1948.

Converse, Harriet Maxwell [Ya-ie-wa-noh]. *Myths and Legends of the New York State Iroquois.* Edited by Arthur Caswell Parker. New York State Museum Bulletin 125. Education Department Bulletin No. 437. Albany: University of the State of New York, 1908: 31–36.

Copway, George [Kah-ge-ga-gah-bowh]. *The Life, Letters, and Speeches.* New York: S. W. Benedict, 1850.

Corkran, David H. *The Cherokee Frontier: Conflict and Survival,* 1740–62. Norman: University of Oklahoma Press, 1962.

Cornelius, Coleman. Fightin' Whites Fund Scholarships: T-shirt Sales Reap $100,000 for Indians. *Denver Post,* December 1, 2002. Available at http://www.denverpost.com/Stories/0,1413,36%7E53%7E1021717%7E,00.html.

Cornplanter, Jesse J. *Legends of the Longhouse.* Edited by William G. Spittal. Illustrated by J. J. Cornplanter. Ohsweken, Ontario, Canada: Iroqrafts, [1938] 1992.

Coulter, Robert T., and Steven M. Tullberg. Indian Land Rights. In Sandra L. Cadwallader and Vine Deloria, Jr., eds., *The Aggressions of Civilization.* Philadelphia: Temple University Press, 1984: 185–214.

Covey, Cyclone. *The Gentle Radical: A Biography of Roger Williams.* New York: Macmillan, 1966.

Cramblit, Andre. Survivor (Humor). October 25, 2002.

Cramblit, Andre. Item via IndigenousNewsNetwork@topica.com, March 31, 2003.

Cramblit, Andre. Item via IndigenousNewsNetwork@topica.com. May 17, 2003.

Cramblit, Andre. Item via IndigenousNewsNetwork@topica.com. June 1, 2003.

Cramblit, Andre. Reservations for Whites. E-mail newsletter item via Digest for IndigenousNewsNetwork@topica.com, issue 114, June 19, 2003.

Crevecouer, Hector Saint John de. *Journey into Northern Pennsylvania and the State of New York* [in French]. Ann Arbor: University of Michigan Press, [1801] 1964.

Crevecoeur, St. Jean de. *Letters from an American Farmer.* New York: Dutton, 1926.

Crime Rate on Indian Reservations Much Higher than U.S. *Indian Time* (Akwesasne Mohawk Reservation, New York), October 9, 2003, 11.

Crisis at Akwesasne [transcript]. Hearings of the New York Assembly, July–August, 1990. Albany and Fort Covington, NY: State of New York.

Cronon, William. *Changes in the Land: Indians, Colonists, and the Ecology of New England.* New York: Hill and Wang, 1983.

Crosby, Alfred W. *The Columbian Exchange: Biological and Cultural Consequences of 1492.* New York: Greenwood Press, 1972.

Crosby, Alfred W. *The Columbian Voyages, the Columbian Exchange, and Their Historians.* Washington, DC: American Historical Association, 1987.

Custer, Elizabeth. *Boots and Saddles.* New York, 1885.

Custer, George Armstrong. *My Life on the Plains.* Lincoln: University of Nebraska Press, 1966.

Darwin, Charles. *The Voyage of the Beagle.* Garden City, NY: Doubleday, 1962, 433–434.

Davis, Russell, and Brant Ashabranner. *Chief Joseph: War Chief of the Nez Perce.* New York: McGraw-Hill, 1962.

Deardorff, Merle H. *The Religion of Handsome Lake: Its Origins and Development.* American Bureau of Ethnology Bulletin No. 149. Washington, DC: BAE, 1951.

Deloria, Vine, Jr. *Behind the Trail of Broken Treaties.* New York: Delacorte, 1974a.

Deloria, Vine, Jr. *The Indian Affair.* New York: Friendship Press, 1974b.

Deloria, Vine, Jr. *The Nations Within.* New York: Pantheon, 1984.

Deloria, Vine, Jr. *American Indian Policy in the Twentieth Century.* Norman: University of Oklahoma Press, 1985.

Deloria, Vine, Jr. *Custer Died for Your Sins: An Indian Manifesto.* Norman: University of Oklahoma Press, 1988.

Deloria, Vine, Jr. *Behind the Trail of Broken Treaties.* Austin: University of Texas Press, 1990.

Deloria, Vine, Jr. *God Is Red.* Golden, CO: North American Press, 1992.

Deloria, Vine, Jr., and Clifford Lytle. *American Indians: American Justice.* Austin: University of Texas Press, 1984.

Demarest, Arthur A. The Violent Saga of a Mayan Kingdom. *National Geographic*, February 1993, 95–111.

Demarest, Arthur A., Prudence M. Rice, and Don S. Rice, eds. *The Terminal Classic in the Maya Lowlands: Collapse, Transition, and Transformation.* Boulder, CO: University Press of Colorado, 2003.

Denhardt, Robert M. *The Horse of the Americas.* Norman: University of Oklahoma Press, 1975.

Dennis, Matthew. *Cultivating a Landscape of Peace.* Ithaca, NY: Cornell University Press, 1993.

Department of Indian Affairs and Northern Development. Press release. June 20, 2001. Available at http://www1.newswire.ca/releases/June2001/20/c6060.html.

Deskaheh: Iroquois Statesman and Patriot. Onchiota, NY: Six Nations Indian Museum Series, n.d.

Deskaheh (Levi General) and Six Nations Council. *The Redman's Appeal for Justice.* Brantford, Ontario, Canada: Wilson Moore, 1924.

DeVoto, Bernard. *Across the Wide Missouri.* Cambridge, MA: Harvard University Press, 1947.

DeVoto, Bernard. *The Course of Empire.* Boston: Houghton-Mifflin, 1952.

Diamond, Jared. The Last Americans: Environmental Collapse and the End of Civilization. *Harper's*, June 2003, 43–51.

Diebel, Linda. $12 Billion Lawsuit Seeks Redress for Abuse in Residential Schools. *Toronto Star*, December 8, 2002. Available at http://www.thestar.ca/NASApp/cs/ContentServer? pagename=thestar/Layout/Article_Type1&c=Article&cid=1035775341135&call_ page=TS_GTA&call_pageid=968350130169&call_pagepath=GTA/News&pubid= 968163964505&StarSource=email.

Diehl, Richard A. *Tula: The Toltec Capital of Ancient Mexico.* London: Thames and Hudson, 1981.

Dillehay, Thomas D. *The Settlement of the Americas: A New Prehistory.* New York: Basic Books, 2000.

Dillehay, Tom D. Palaeoanthropology: Tracking the First Americans. *Nature* 425 (September 4, 2003):23–24.

Dittert, Alfred E., Jr. The Archaeology of Cebolleta Mesa and Acoma Pueblo: A Preliminary Report Based on Further Investigation. *El Palacio* 59(1952):191–217.

Dobyns, Henry F. Estimating Aboriginal American Population. *Current Anthropology* 7(October 1966):395–412.

Dobyns, Henry F. *Their Number Became Thinned.* Knoxville: University of Tennessee Press, 1983.

Dobyns, Henry F. More Methodological Perspectives on Historical Demography. *Ethnohistory* 36:3(Summer 1989):286–289.

Doclar, Mary. Protests Cause Reassessment of Dallas Schools' Indian Mascots. *Fort Worth Star-Telegram*, December 5, 1998. Available at http://www.startext.net/news/doc/1047/1:arl71/1:arl71120598.html.

Dozier, Edward P. *The Pueblo Indians of North America.* New York: Holt, Rinehart, and Winston, 1970.

Drew, Neil. Personal e-mail communication, July 1, 2001.

Drinnon, Richard. *Facing West: Indian Hating and Empire Building.* New York: Schoken Books, 1990.

Driver, Harold E. *Indians of North America.* 2nd ed., rev. Chicago: University of Chicago Press, 1969.

Drucker, Philip. *Indians of the Northwest Coast.* New York: McGraw-Hill, 1955.

Duby, Gertrude and Frans Blom. The Lacandon. In Robert Wauchope, ed. *Handbook of Middle-American Indians.* Vol. 7. Austin: University of Texas Press, 1969: 276–297.

Dugan, Bill. *Sitting Bull.* San Francisco: HarperCollins, 1994.

Eckert, Allan W. *A Sorrow in Our Heart: The Life of Tecumseh.* New York: Bantam, 1992.

Edmonds, Della and Margot. *Sacajawea of the Lewis and Clark Expedition.* Berkeley: University of California Press, 1979.

Edmunds, R. David., ed., *American Indian Leaders: Studies in Diversity.* Lincoln: University of Nebraska Press, 1980.

Edmunds, R. David. *The Shawnee Prophet.* Lincoln: University of Nebraska Press, 1983.

Edmunds, R. David. *Tecumseh and the Quest for Indian Leadership.* Boston: Little-Brown, 1984.

Edwards, Everett E. The Contributions of American Indians to Civilization. *Minnesota History* 15:3(1934):255–272.

Eggleston, Edward and Lillie Eggleston-Seelye. *Tecumseh and the Shawnee Prophet.* New York, 1878.

Eichstaedt, Peter. *If You Poison Us: Uranium and American Indians.* Santa Fe, NM: Red Crane Books, 1995.

Elliott, Louise. Ontario Native Suicide Rate One of Highest in World, Expert Says. *Vancouver Sun*, November 30, 2000. Available at http://www.vancouversun.com.

Elliott, Louise. Aboriginal Girls Taking Their Lives in Record Numbers Across Ontario's North. *Canadian Aboriginal*, December 3, 2000. Available at http://www.canadianaboriginal.com/health/health15b.htm.

Elliott, Louise. Hunger and Suicide Stalk Reserve after Feds Cut Funds. *Montreal Gazette*, June 7, 2001, A-15.

Elliott, Louise. Native Community Searches for Doctor. *Toronto Star*, June 16, 2001, A-16.

Elliott, Louise. Reserve's Doctor Safe After Two-Day Walk in Wilderness. *Montreal Gazette*, June 18, 2001, A-14

Elliott, Louise. Band Talking to Media May Perpetuate Suicide Crisis, Says Nault. Canadian Press, June 22, 2001. Available at http://ca.news.yahoo.com/010622/6/6ei2.html.

Elliott, Louise. Native Groups Warn of Suicide Crisis. *Toronto Star*, July 31, 2001, A-6.

Ellis, George W., and John E. Morris. *King Philip's War*. New York: The Grafton Press, 1906.

Emily of Kanesatake. Personal e-mail communication via John Kahionhes Fadden, March 21, 2003.

Engels, Frederick. *Origin of the Family, Private Property, and the State*. In *Karl Marx and Frederick Engels: Selected Works in One Volume*. New York: International Publishers, 1968.

Ernst, James. *Roger Williams: New England Firebrand*. New York: Macmillan, 1932.

Exhibit on the Iroquois Confereracy, Yager Museum, Hartwick College, Oneonta, NY, June 1983.

Fadden, John Kahionhes. Personal communication, June 14, 1989.

Fadden, John Kahionhes. Personal communication, March 20, 2001.

Fadden, John Kahionhes. Personal communication, February 22, 2003.

Fagan, Brian. *Before California: An Archaeologist Looks at Our Earliest Inhabitants*. Lanham, MD: Rowman and Littlefield, 2003.

Fahey, John. *The Flathead Indians*. Norman: University of Oklahoma Press, 1974.

Fahey, John. *The Kalispel Indians*. Norman: University of Oklahoma Press, 1986.

Fash, William L., Jr., and Barbara W. Fash. Scribes, Warriors and Kings: The Lives of the Copan Maya. *Archaeology*, May–June 1990, 28.

Fast Growing Indian Gambling Drew $16.2 Billion. *Omaha World-Herald*, July 8, 2004, A-5.

Federal Paternalism Angers Pikangikum. *Canadian Aboriginal*. No date. Available at http://www.canadianaboriginal.com/news/news131a.htm.

Fee, Chester. *Chief Joseph: The Biography of a Great Indian*. New York: Wilson Erickson, 1936.

Fenn, Elizabeth. *Pox Americana: The Great Smallpox Epidemic of 1775–82*. New York: Hill & Wang, 2001.

Fenton, W. N. *Contacts Between Iroquois Herbalism and Colonial Medicine*. Washington, DC: Smithsonian Institution, 1941.

Fenton, William N. *Roll Call of the Iroquois Chiefs*. Washington, DC: Smithsonian Institution, 1950.

Fenton, William N., ed. *Symposium on Cherokee and Iroquois Culture*. Smithsonian Institution Bureau of Ethnology Bulletin 180. Washington, DC: Government Printing Office, 1961.

Fenton, William N., ed. *Parker on the Iroquois*. Syracuse, NY: Syracuse University Press, 1968.

Fialka, John J. Tribe Gets Private-Sector Jobs; Winnebagos Build Profitable Businesses with Casino Seed Money. *Wall Street Journal*, February 18, 2004, A-4.

Fiscus, Carolyn. Personal communication, June 17, 2003.

Foner, Philip S., ed. *Complete Writings of Thomas Paine*. New York: Citadel Press, 1945.

Forbes, Jack. *The Indian in America's Past*. New York: Prentice-Hall, 1964.

Ford, Paul L., ed. *The Writings of Thomas Jefferson*. Vol. 3. New York: J. P. Putnam's Sons, 1892–1899.

Frachtenberg, Leo J. Our Indebtedness to the American Indian. *Wisconsin Archeologist* 14:2(1915):64–69.

Frazier, Joseph B. Humans in Oregon 10,000 Years Ago? Associated Press. November 25, 2002. Available at senior-staff@nativenewsonline.org.

Frazier, Neta L. *Sacajawea: The Girl Nobody Knows*. New York: McKay, 1967.

Furtwangler, Albert. *Answering Chief Seattle*. Seattle: University of Washington Press, 1997.

Gage, Matilda Joslyn. *Woman, Church and State*. Watertown, MA: Peresphone Press, [1893] 1980.

Gallay, Alan. Indian Slave Trade Thrived in Early America. *Daytona Beach News-Journal*, August 3, 2003, 3-B.

Gamble, Susan. M.D. Shocked at Conditions on Reserve. *Brantford (Ontario) Expositor*, n.d., n.p. Available at http://www.southam.com/brantfordexpositor.

Garner, J. Whities' Mascot about Education, Not Retaliation; Intramural Basketball Team Takes Shot at Indian Caricature Used by Eaton High School. *Rocky Mountain News*, March 12, 2002. Available at http://www.rockymountainnews.com/drmn/state/article/0,1299,DRMN_21_1026337,00.html.

Gates, Paul W., ed. *The Rape of Indian Lands*. New York: Arno Press, 1979.

Gerhard, Peter. *A Guide to the Historical Geography of New Spain*. Princeton, NJ: Princeton University Press, 1972.

Gerhard, Peter. *The North Frontier of New Spain*. Princeton, NJ: Princeton University Press, 1982.

Giago, Tim. Book Lacks Lakota View. *Indian Country Today*, August 4, 1993, n.p.

Gibson, Arrell M. *The American Indian: Prehistory to Present*. Lexington, KY: Heath, 1980.

Gibson, Charles. *The Aztecs Under Spanish Rule: A History of the Indians of the Valley of Mexico, 1519–1810*. Palo Alto, CA: Stanford University Press, 1964.

Giddings, James L. Roger Williams and the Indians [typescript]. Providence: Rhode Island Historical Society, 1957.

Gill, Richardson. *The Great Maya Droughts*. Albuquerque: University of New Mexico Press, 2000.

Gill, Sam. *Mother Earth: An American Story*. Chicago: University of Chicago Press, 1987.

Goebel, Ted, Michael R. Waters, and Margarita Dikova. The Archaeology of Ushki Lake, Kamchatka, and the Pleistocene Peopling of the Americas. *Science* 301(July 25, 2003):501–505.

Gonzalez-José, Rolando, Antonio Gonzalez-Martin, Miquel Hernandez, Hector M. Pucciarelli, Marina Sardi, Alfonso Rosales, and Silvina Van der Molen. Craniometric Evidence for Palaeoamerican Survival in Baja California. *Nature* 425(September 4, 2003):62–66.

Gormley, Michael [Associated Press]. State Commissioner to Take a Stand on Indian Mascots, Names. *Boston Globe On-line*, 11:42 A.M. October 28, 2000. Available at http://www.boston.com/dailynews/302/region/state_commissioner_to_take_a_s:.html.

Goss, Eldridge Henry. *The Life of Colonel Paul Revere*. Boston: G. K. Hall and Co./Gregg Press, 1972.

Goulais, Bob. Water Crisis Latest Plague to Visit Pikangikum. *Anishinabek News*, November 2000. Available at http://www.anishinabek.ca/news/Past%20issues/2000/November%20issue/Nov00watercrisis.htm.

Graham, W. A. *The Custer Myth*. Lincoln: University of Nebraska Press, 1953.

Green, Michael D. The Expansion of European Colonization to the Mississippi Valley, 1780–1880. In Bruce G. Trigger and Wilcomb E. Washburn, eds., *The Cambridge*

History of the Native Peoples of the Americas. Cambridge, England: Cambridge University Press, 1996: 461–538.

Green, Rayna. The Museum of the Plains White Person. In Arlene Hirschfelder, ed., *Native Heritage: Personal Accounts by American Indians, 1790 to the Present.* New York: Macmillan, 1995: 184–185.

Griffith, Benjamin W., Jr. *McIntosh and Weatherford: Creek Indian Leaders.* Tuscaloosa: University of Alabama Press, 1988.

Grinde, Donald A., Jr. The Reburial of American Indian Remains and Funerary Objects. *Northeast Indian Quarterly,* Summer 1991, 35–38.

Grinde, Donald A., Jr. Personal communication, March 23, 1993.

Grinde, Donald A., Jr., and Bruce E. Johansen. *Exemplar of Liberty: Native America and the Evolution of Democracy.* Los Angeles: UCLA American Indian Studies Center, 1991.

Grinde, Donald A., Jr., and Bruce E. Johansen. *Ecocide of Native America: Environmental Destruction of Indian Lands and Peoples.* Santa Fe, NM: Clear Light, 1995.

Guay, Marcel. Canadian Aboriginal. News. November 12, 2002. Available at http://www.canadianaboriginal.com.

Guild, Reuben Aldridge. *Footprints of Roger Williams.* Providence, RI: Tibbetts and Preston, 1886.

Gunther, Erna. *Indian Life on the Northwest Coast of North America.* Chicago: University of Chicago Press, 1972.

Hagan, William T. *The Sac and Fox Indians.* Norman: University of Oklahoma Press, 1958.

Hale, Horatio. *The Iroquois Book of Rites.* Philadelphia, 1883.

Hamilton, Charles. *Cry of the Thunderbird.* Norman: University of Oklahoma Press, 1972.

Harjo v. Pro-Football, Inc. 1999 WL 329721 (P.T.O., April 2, 1999). The Trademark Trial and Appeals Board, Patent and Trademark Office. Available at http://www.kentlaw.edu/student_orgs/jip/trade/skins.htm.

Harold, Howard. *Sacajawea.* Norman: University of Oklahoma Press, 1971.

Hassler, Peter. Cutting through the Myth of Human Sacrifice: The Lies of the Conquistadors. *World Press Review,* December 1992, 28–29. Reprinted from *Die Zeit,* Hamburg, Germany.

Haug, Gerald H., Detlef Gunter, Larry C. Peterson, Daniel M. Sigman, Konrad A. Hughen, and Beat Aeschlimann. Climate and the Collapse of Maya Civilization. *Science* 299(March 14, 2003):1731–1735.

Havighurst, Robert J., and Thea R. Hilkevitch. The Intelligence of Indian Children as Measured by a Performance Scale. *Journal of Abnormal and Social Psychology* 39(1944):419–433.

Haynes, Gary. *The Early Settlement of North America: The Clovis Era.* Cambridge, England: Cambridge University Press, 2002.

Hays, Wilma P. *Pontiac: Lion in the Forest.* Boston: Houghton-Mifflin, 1965.

Heckenberger, Michael J., Afukaka Kuikuro, Urissap Tabata Kuikuro, J. Christian Russell, Morgan Schmidt, Carlos Fausto, and Bruna Franchetto. Amazonia 1492: Pristine Forest or Cultural Parkland? *Science* 301(September 19, 2003):1710–1714.

Heckewelder, John. *History, Manners, and Customs of the Indian Nations Who Once Inhabited Pennsylvania and the Neighboring States.* The First American Frontier Series. New York: Arno Press and the *New York Times,* [1820, 1876] 1971.

Heckewelder, John. *Narrative of the Mission of the United Brethren among the Delaware and Mohegan Indians from Its Commencement, in the Year 1740, to the Close of the Year 1808.* New York: Arno Press, [1818] 1971.

Henderson, John F. *The World of the Ancient Maya.* Ithaca, NY: Cornell University Press, 1981.

Hendrix, Janey B. Redbird Smith and the Nighthawk Keetoowahs. *Journal of Cherokee Studies* 8:1(1983):17–33.

Henige, David. *Numbers from Nowhere: The American Indian Contact Population Debate.* Norman: University of Oklahoma Press, 1998.

Henige, David. Can a Myth be Astronomically Dated? *American Indian Culture and Research Journal* 23:4(1999):127–157.

Hertzberg, Hazel W. *The Search for an American Indian Identity: Modern Pan-Indian Movements.* Syracuse, NY: Syracuse University Press, 1971.

Hewitt, J. N. B. *Legend of the Founding of the Iroquois League.* Washington, DC: Smithsonian Institution, 1892.

Hewitt, J. N. B. Iroquoian Cosmology, First Part. In *Twenty-First Annual Report of the Bureau of American Ethnology to the Secretary of the Smithsonian Institution, 1899–1900.* Washington, DC: Government Printing Office, 1903: 127–339.

Hewitt, J. N. B. *A Constitutional League of Peace in the Stone Age of America.* Washington, DC: Smithsonian Institution, 1918.

Hewitt, J. N. B. Iroquoian Cosmology, Second Part. In *Forty-third Annual Report of the Bureau of American Ethnology to the Secretary of the Smithsonian Institution, 1925–1926.* Washington, DC: Government Printing Office, 1928: 453–819.

Hewitt, J. N. B. Notes on the Creek Indians. In J. R. Swanton, ed., *Bureau of American Ethnology Bulletin No. 123.* Washington, DC: U.S. Government Printing Office, 1939: 124–133.

Hill, Richard. Continuity of Haudenosaunee Government: Political Reality of the Grand Council. *Northeast Indian Quarterly* 4:3(Autumn 1987):10–14.

Hill, Richard W., Sr. Wounded Knee, A Wound that Won't Heal. Did the Army Attempt to Cover Up the Massacre of Prisoners of War? October 7, 1999. Available at http://www.dickshovel.com/hill.html. Accessed February 13, 2003.

Hipwell, Bill. Apology Should Have Been a Thank You. *Financial Post (Ottawa, Ontario),* February 3, 1998, 18.

Hobson, Charles F. *The Great Chief Justice: John Marshall and the Rule of Law.* Lawrence: University Press of Kansas, 1996.

Hodgson, Bryan. Buffalo: Back Home on the Range. *National Geographic* 186:5(November 1994):64–89.

Hoig, Stan. *The Sand Creek Massacre.* Norman: University of Oklahoma Press, 1961.

Holder, Preston. *The Hoe and the Horse on the Plains.* Lincoln: University of Nebraska Press, 1970.

Homaday, William T. *The Extermination of the American Bison.* Washington, DC: Annual Report of the U.S. National Museum, 1869.

Hornung, Rick. *One Nation Under the Gun: Inside the Mohawk Civil War.* New York: Pantheon, 1991.

Hoover, Dwight W. *The Red and the Black.* Chicago: Rand McNally, 1976.

Howard, Helen A. Hiawatha: Co-founder of an Indian United Nations. *Journal of the West* 10:3(1971):428–438.

Howard, Helen A., and Dan L. McGrath. *War Chief Joseph*. Caldwell, ID: Caxton, 1952.

Howard, Oliver O. *Nez Perce Joseph*. Boston: Lee & Shepherd, 1881.

Hughes, J. Donald. *American Indian Ecology*. El Paso: Texas Western Press, 1983.

Humor Can be Good Medicine. November 10, 2002. Available at nativeculture@ yahoo.com.

Hyde, George E. *A Sioux Chronicle*. Norman: University of Oklahoma Press, 1956.

Hyde, George E. *Red Cloud's Folk: A History of the Oglala Sioux Indians*. Norman: University of Oklahoma Press, 1967.

Indian Mascots: An Idea Whose Time Has Passed [editorial]. *Asheville, NC, Citizen-Times*, September 30, 2000. Available at http://www.main.nc.us/wncceib/PeweAC T9300editorial.htm.

Iverson, Peter. Taking Care of the Earth and Sky. In Alvin Josephy, ed., *America in 1492: The World of the Indian Peoples Before the Arrival of Columbus*. New York: Knopf, 1992: 85–118.

Jackson, Donald, ed. *Black Hawk: An Autobiography*. Urbana: University of Illinois Press, 1964.

Jackson, Helen Hunt. *A Century of Dishonor: A Sketch of the United States Government's Dealings with Some of the Indian Tribes*. New York: Harper and Brothers, 1881.

Jacobs, Wilbur. *Diplomacy and Indian Gifts: Anglo-French Rivalry among the Ohio and Northwest Frontiers, 1748–1763*. Stanford, CA: Stanford University Press, 1950.

Jacobs, Wilbur R. *Wilderness Politics and Indian Gifts*. Lincoln: University of Nebraska Press, 1966.

Jaimes, M. Annette, ed. *The State of Native America: Genocide, Colonization and Resistance*. Boston: South End Press, 1992.

Jefferson, Thomas. *Notes on the State of Virginia*. Edited by Willam Peden. Chapel Hill: University of North Carolina Press, [1784] 1955.

Jensen, Richard E., R. Eli Paul, and John E. Carter. *Eyewitness at Wounded Knee*. Lincoln: University of Nebraska Press, 1991.

Johansen, Bruce E. Peltier and the Posse. *The Nation*, October 1, 1977, 304–307.

Johansen, Bruce E. The Reservation Offensive. *The Nation*, February 25, 1978, 204–207.

Johansen, Bruce E. *The Forgotten Founders: Benjamin Franklin, the Iroquois, and the Rationale for the American Revolution*. Ipswich, MA: Gambit, 1982.

Johansen, Bruce E. The Klan in a Can. *The Progressive*, July 1988, 13.

Johansen, Bruce E. Dead Indians Out, Live Indians In. *The Progressive*, December 1989, 15–16.

Johansen, Bruce E. *Life and Death in Mohawk Country*. Golden, CO: Fulcrum/North American Press, 1993.

Johansen, Bruce E. Dating the Iroquois Confederacy. *Akwesasne Notes New Series* 1:3/ 4(Fall 1995):62–63.

Johansen, Bruce E. Running for Office: LaDuke and the Green Party. *Native Americas* 13:4(Winter 1996):3–4.

Johansen, Bruce E. "Squawbles" in Minnesota. *Native Americas* 13:4(Winter 1996):4.

Johansen, Bruce E. Wampum. In D. L. Birchfield, ed., *The Encyclopedia of North American Indians*. Vol. 10. New York: Marshall Cavendish, 1997: 1352–1353.

Johansen, Bruce E. The BIA as Banker: Trust Is Hard When Billions Disappear. *Native Americas* 14:1(Spring 1997):14–23.

Johansen, Bruce E. *The Encyclopedia of Native American Legal Tradition.* Westport, CT: Greenwood Press, 1998a.

Johansen, Bruce. Whiteclay, Nebraska: The Town that Booze Built. *Native Americas* 15:1(Spring 1998b):5.

Johansen, Bruce E. Living and Breathing: Native Languages Come Alive. *Native Americas* 17:1(Spring 2000a):56–59.

Johansen, Bruce E. Education—The Nightmare and the Dream: A Shared National Tragedy, a Shared National Disgrace. *Native Americas* 12:4(Winter 2000b):10–19.

Johansen, Bruce E. Native Languages: The New Phoenix. *Native Americas* 17:1(Spring 2000c):60–61.

Johansen, Bruce E. *Shapers of the Great Debate on Native Americans: Land, Spirit, and Power.* Westport, CT: Greenwood Press, 2000.

Johansen, Bruce E. Mascots: Honor Be Thy Name. *Native Americas* 18:1(Spring 2001):58–61.

Johansen, Bruce E., and Donald A. Grinde, Jr. *The Encyclopedia of Native American Biography.* New York: Henry Holt, 1997.

Johansen, Bruce E., and Roberto F. Maestas. *Wasi'chu: The Continuing Indian Wars.* New York: Monthly Review Press, 1979.

Johansen, Bruce E., and Barbara Alice Mann, eds. *Encyclopedia of the Haudenosaunee (Iroquois Confederacy).* Westport, CT: Greenwood Press, 2000.

Johnson, Lowell, ed. The Buffalo. In *The First Voices.* Lincoln, NE: Nebraska Game and Parks Commission, 1984: 60–61.

Johnson v. MacIntosh (8 Wheaton 543, 1823).

Jones, Louis Thomas. *Aboriginal American Oratory.* Los Angeles: Southwest Museum, 1965.

Joseph, Chief [In-mut-too-yah-lat-lat]. An Indian's View of Indian Affairs. *North American Review* 128(April 1879):415–433.

Josephy, Alvin, Jr. *The Patriot Chiefs.* New York: Viking, 1961.

Josephy, Alvin, Jr. *Red Power.* New York: McGraw-Hill, 1971.

Josephy, Alvin M. *The Nez Perce Indians and the Opening of the Northwest.* New Haven, CT: Yale University Press, 1965.

Josephy, Alvin M., Jr. Modern America and the Indian. In Frederick E. Hoxie, ed., *Indians in American History: An Introduction.* Arlington Heights, IL: Harlan Davidson, 1988: 251–272.

Journals of Captain John Montresor, 1757–1778. Vol. 14. April 4, 1766. Collections of the New York Historical Society. New York: Printed for the Society, 1868–1949, 2nd Set, 357, 367–368.

Judge: Scientists Can Study Ancient Bones of Man Indian Tribes Claim as Ancestor. *Indian Time* 20:35(September 5, 2002):10.

Kay, Jeanne. The Fur Trade and Native American Population Growth, *Ethnohistory* 31:4(1984):265–287.

Keefe, Tom, Jr. A Tribute to David Sohappy. *Native Nations*, June/July 1991, 4–6.

Kehoe, Alice Beck. *North American Indians: A Comprehensive Account.* Englewood Cliffs, NJ: Prentice-Hall, 1981.

Kehoe, Alice Beck. *America before the European Invasions.* London: Longman, 2002.

Kelley, David H. *Deciphering the Maya Script.* Austin: University of Texas Press, 1976.

Kelly, Lawrence C. The Indian Reorganization Act: The Dream and the Reality. *Pacific Historical Quarterly* 64(August 1975):291–312.

Kelly, Lawrence C. *The Assault on Assimilation: John Collier and the Origins of the Indian Reorganization Act.* Tucson: University of Arizona Press, 1983.

Kennedy, J. Michael. Truth and Consequences on the Reservation. *Los Angeles Times Sunday Magazine*, July 7, 2002, cover story. Available at LATimes.com.

Kennedy, John Hopkins. *Jesuit and Savage in New France.* New Haven, CT: Yale University Press, 1950.

Keoke, Emory Dean, and Kay Marie Porterfield. *Encyclopedia of American Indian Contributions to the World.* New York: Facts on File, 2002.

Kickingbird, Kirke. *Indian Sovereignty.* Washington, DC: Institute for the Development of Indian Law, 1983.

Kilborn, Peter. Pine Ridge, a Different Kind of Poverty. *New York Times* in *Omaha World-Herald*, September 30, 1992, 9.

King, C. Richard, and Charles Frueling Springwood. *Team Spirits: The Native American Mascots Controversy.* Lincoln: University of Nebraska Press, 2001.

Kraus, Michael. *The Atlantic Civilization: Eighteenth Century Origins.* New York: Russell and Russell, 1949.

Kroeber, A. L. *Cultural and Natural Areas of Native North America.* University of California Publications in American Archeology and Ethnology 38. Berkeley: University of California, 1939.

Labaree, Benjamin L. *America's Nation-Time: 1607–1789.* Boston: Allyn and Bacon, 1972.

Labaree, Leonard, ed. *The Papers of Benjamin Franklin.* Vol. 21. New Haven, CT: Yale University Press, 1950 to date.

La Fay, Howard. The Maya, the Children of Time. *National Geographic*, December 1975, 729–766.

LaMay, Konnie. Twenty Years of Anguish. *Indian Country Today*, February 25, 1993, n.p.

Landsman, Gail. Portrayals of the Iroquois in the Woman Suffrage Movement. Paper presented at the Annual Conference on Iroquois Research, Rensselaerville, NY, October 8, 1988.

Lara, Jesus. *La Poesia Quechua.* Cochabamba, Bolivia: Imprenta Universitaria, n.d., 193–194. Cited in Wright, 1992, 31.

La Republica, Lima, Peru. Reprinted in *World Press Review*, September, 1991, 50.

Las Casas, Bartolome de. *History of the Indies.* Translated and edited by Andree Collard. New York: Harper and Row, 1971.

Las Casas, Bartolome de. *The Devastation of the Indies.* New York: Seabury Press, [1542] 1974.

Lavender, David. *Let Me Be Free.* San Francisco: HarperCollins, 1992.

Leon-Portilla, M. *Los Antiguos Mexicanos a Traves de sus* Cronicas y Cantares. Mexico City: Fondo de Cultura Economica, 1972.

Leon-Portilla, Miguel. *The Broken Spears: The Aztec Account of the Conquest of Mexico.* Boston: Beacon Press, 1962.

Leon-Portilla, Miguel. *Pre-Columbian Literature of Mexico.* Norman: University of Oklahoma Press, 1969.

Leon-Portilla, Miguel. *The Aztec Image of Self and Society: An Introduction to Nahua Culture.* Salt Lake City: University of Utah Press, 1992.

Levitan, Sar A. *Big Brother's Indian Programs—With Reservations.* New York: McGraw-Hill, 1971.

Licon, Ernesto Gonzalez. *Vanished Mesoamerican Civilizations: The History and Cultures of the Zapotecs and Mixtecs.* Armonk, NY: Sharpe, 2001.

Linné, Sigvald. *Archaeological Researches at Teotihuacan, Mexico.* Tuscaloosa: University of Alabama Press, 2003

Lovell, W. George. *Conquest and Survival in Colonial Guatemala: A Historical Geography of the Cuchumatan Highlands, 1500–1821.* Montreal: McGill-Queen's University Press, 1985.

Lowey, Mark. Alberta Natives Sue over Residential Schools. *Calgary Herald,* January 3, 1999, A-1.

Lucas, Phil. Images of Indians. *Four Winds: The International Forum for Native American Art, Literature, and History,* Autumn 1980, 69–77.

Lynch, John. Pikangikum First Nation Looks Beyond "Opening a Store." It Wants to Create Private-Sector Partnerships. *Northern Ontario Business,* March 1999. Available at http://www.nob.on.ca/archives/mar99story/step.html.

Mails, Thomas E. *Fools Crow.* Lincoln: University of Nebraska Press, 1990.

Mann, Barbara A. The Fire at Onondaga: Wampum as Proto-writing. *Akwesasne Notes New Series* 1:1(Spring 1995):40–48.

Mann, Barbara A. *The Last of the Mohicans* and *The Indian-haters*; Forbidden Ground: Racial Politics and Hidden Identity in James Fenimore Cooper's Leather-Stocking Tales. Ph.D. dissertation, University of Toledo, 1997.

Mann, Barbara A., and Jerry L. Fields. A Sign in the Sky: Dating the League of the Haudenosaunee. *American Indian Culture and Research Journal* 21:2(1997):105–163.

Mann, Charles C. 1491: America before Columbus Was More Sophisticated and More Populous than We Have Ever Thought—And a More Livable Place than Europe. *The Atlantic Monthly,* March 2002, 41–53.

Marquez, Deron. Indian Gaming Is Different from Other Forms of Gambling. *Indian Country Today,* February 12, 2002, n.p., in LEXIS.

Marsh, Thelma R. *Lest We Forget: A Brief Sketch of Wyandot County's History.* Upper Sandusky, OH: Wyandot County Historical Society, 1967.

Martin, Calvin. *Keepers of the Game.* Berkeley: University of California Press, 1979.

Massey, Rosemary. *Footprints in Blood: Standing Bear's Struggle for Freedom and Human Dignity.* Omaha, NE: American Indian Center of Omaha, 1979, unpaginated.

Mather, Increase. *A Brief History of the War with the Indians in New England.* London: Richard Chiswell, 1676.

Mathes, Valerie Sherer. Helen Hunt Jackson and the Ponca Controversy. *Montana: The Magazine of Western History* 39:1(Winter 1989):42–53.

Matthiessen, Peter. *In the Spirit of Crazy Horse.* New York: Viking, 1991.

Maxwell, James A., ed. *America's Fascinating Indian Heritage.* Pleasantville, NY: Reader's Digest, 1978.

McDowell, Bart. The Aztecs. *National Geographic,* December 1980, 704–752.

McKee, Jesse O., and Jon A. Schlenker. *The Choctaws: Cultural Evolution of a Native American Tribe.* Jackson: University Press of Mississippi, 1980.

McIlroy, Anne. Canadians Apologize for Abuse. *Manchester Guardian Weekly,* November 8, 1998, 5.

McLaughlin, James. *My Friend, the Indian.* Boston: Houghton Mifflin, 1910.

McLaughlin, Michael R. The Dawes Act, or Indian General Allotment Act of 1887: The Continuing Burden of Allotment. *American Indian Culture and Research Journal* 20:2(1996):59–105.

McManus, John C. An Economic Analysis of Indian Behavior in the North American Fur Trade. *Journal of Economic History* 32(1972):36–53.

McNickle, D'Arcy. *They Came Here First: The Epic of the American Indian.* Philadelphia: Lippincott, 1949.

McNickle, D'Arcy. *Native American Tribalism.* New York: Oxford University Press, 1973.

McNickle, D'Arcy. *They Came Here First: The Epic of the American Indian.* New York: Harper and Row Perennial Library, 1975.

Meggers, Betty J., Eduardo S. Brondizio, Michael J. Heckenberger, Carlos Fausto, and Bruna Franchetto. Revisiting Amazonia Circa 1492 [letter to the editor]. *Science* 302(December 19, 2003):2067.

Meriam, Lewis. *The Problem of Indian Administration.* Baltimore: John Hopkins University Press, 1928.

Mexican Skull May Explain Indigenous Origins. Reuters, December 5, 2002. Available at http://story.news.yahoo.com/news?tmpl=story&u=/nm/20021205/sc_nm/science_mexico_skull_dc_1.

Miller, Bruce J. The Press, the Boldt Decision, and Indian-White Relations. *American Indian Culture and Research Journal* 17:2(1993):75–98.

Miller, Perry. *Roger Williams: His Contribution to the American Tradition.* Indianapolis, IN: Bobbs-Merrill, 1953.

Milner, Richard. Red Cloud. In Richard Milner, ed. *The Encyclopedia of Evolution.* New York: Henry Holt, 1990: 387–388.

Minge, Ward Alan. *Acoma: Pueblo in the Sky.* Albuquerque: University of New Mexico Press, 1991.

Mochtezuma, Eduardo Matos. Templo Mayor: History and Interpretation. In Johanna Broda, David Carrasco, and Mochtezuma, eds., *The Great Temple of Tenochtitlan: Center and Periphery in the Aztec World.* Berkeley: University of California Press, 1988: 15–60.

The Mohawk Creation Story. *Akwesasne Notes* 21.5(Spring 1989):32–29.

Molina Montes, Augusto F. The Building of Tenochtitlan. *National Geographic,* December 1980, 753–766.

Monoghan, Jay. *Custer.* Lincoln: University of Nebraska Press, 1959.

Mooney, James, Population. In F. W. Hodge, ed., *Handbook of American Indians North of Mexico. Bureau of American Ethnology Bulletin* 30(part 2):28–87. Washington, DC: Smithsonian Institution, 1910.

Mooney, James. *The Aboriginal Population of North America North of Mexico.* Smithsonian Miscellaneous Collections 80(7). Washington, DC: Smithsonian Institution, 1928.

Moore, John H. How Giveaways and Pow-wows Redistribute the Means of Subsistence. In John H. Moore, ed., *The Political Economy of North American Indians.* Norman: University of Oklahoma Press, 1993: 240–269.

Moore, John H. *The Cheyennes.* Oxford, England: Blackwell, 1997.

Moore, Oliver. Pre-Mayan Written Language Found in Mexico. *Toronto Globe and Mail,* December 5, 2002. Available at http://www.globeandmail.com/servlet/ArticleNews/front/RTGAM/20021205/wlang1205/Front/homeBN/breakingnews.

Moquin, Wayne. *Great Documents in American Indian History.* New York: Praeger, 1973.

Morgan, Lewis Henry. *League of the Ho-de-no-sau-nee, or Iroquois.* New York: Corinth Books, [1851] 1962.

Morgan, Lewis Henry. *Houses and House-Life of the American Aborigines.* Edited by Paul Bohannon. Chicago: University of Chicago Press, 1965.

Morison, Patricia. Wisdom of the Aztecs. *London Financial Times.* Reprinted in Notes on the Arts, *World Press Review,* January 1993, 54.

Morris, Roy, Jr. *Sheridan: The Life and Wars of General Phil Sheridan.* New York: Crown, 1992.

Moulton, Gary. *John Ross: Cherokee Chief.* Athens: University of Georgia Press, 1978.

Moulton, Gary, ed. *The Journals of the Lewis and Clark Expedition.* Lincoln: University of Nebraska Press, 2001.

Mr. Penn's Plan for a Union of the Colonies in America, February 8, 1697. In E. B. O'Callaghan, ed., *Documents Relative to the Colonial History of New York.* Vol. 4. Albany, NY: Weed, Parsons, 1853–1887: 296–297.

Murphy, Maureen. Gambling on Indian Reservations. Washington DC: Congressional Research Service, Library of Congress, April 26, 1985.

Myers, Albert Cook. *Narratives of Early Pennsylvania, West New Jersey and Delaware, 1630–1702.* New York: Charles Scribner's Sons, 1912.

Nabokov, Peter, ed. *Native American Testimony.* New York: Viking, 1991.

National Resources Board, Land Planning Committee. *Indian Land Tenure, Economic Status, and Population Trends.* Washington, DC: U.S. Government Printing Office, 1935.

Nebard, Grace R. *Sacajawea.* Glendale, CA: Arthur H. Clark, 1932.

Neihardt, Hilda. *Black Elk and Flaming Rainbow: Personal Memories of the Lakota Holy Man.* Lincoln: University of Nebraska Press, 1995.

Nevard, David. Wahooism in the USA: A Red Socks Journal. No date. Available at http://www.ultranet.com/~kuras/bhxi3d.htm.

Notice. *Philadelphia Gazette.* 2705(April 17, 1782):2.

Oberg, Kalervo. *The Social Economy of the Tlinget Indians.* Seattle: University of Washington Press, 1973.

O'Brien, Sharon. *American Indian Tribal Governments.* Norman: University of Oklahoma Press, 1989.

O'Callagahan, E. B., ed. *Documentary History of the State of New York.* Vol. 1. Albany, NY: Weed, Parsons, 1849.

O'Callaghan, E. B., ed., *Documents Relative to the Colonial History of New York.* Vol. 6. Albany, NY: Weed, Parsons, 1853–1887.

Olexer, Barbara. *The Enslavement of the American Indian.* Monroe, NY: Library Research Associates, 1982.

Olson, James, and Raymond Wilson. *Native Americans in the Twentieth Century.* Urbana: University of Illinois Press, 1984.

Olson, James C. *Red Cloud and the Sioux Problem.* Lincoln: University of Nebraska Press, 1965.

Oskinson, John M. *Tecumseh and His Times.* New York: J. P. Putnam, 1938.

Oswalt, Wendell H. *This Land Was Theirs: A Study of North American Indians.* 7th ed. Boston: McGraw-Hill, 2002.

Page, Charles. The "Fighting Whites" Offer Lesson in Cultural Diversity. *Newsday,* March 19, 2002, A-32.

Page, Jake. *In the Hands of the Great Spirit: The 20,000 Year History of the American Indian.* New York: Free Press, 2003.

Paine, Thomas. *The Political Writings of Thomas Paine.* New York: Peter Eckler, 1892.

Parker, Arthur. *Parker on the Iroquois.* Edited by William Fenton. Syracuse, NY: Syracuse University Press, 1968.

Parker, Arthur C. *The Code of Handsome Lake, the Seneca Prophet.* New York State Museum Bulletin 163, November 1, 1912. Albany: University of the State of New York, 1913.

Parkman, Francis. *History of the Conspiracy of Pontiac.* Boston: Little, Brown, 1868.

Parman, Donald L. *The Navajos and the New Deal.* New Haven, CT: Yale University Press, 1976.

Parrington, Vernon Louis. *Main Currents in American Thought.* New York: Harcourt, Brace, 1927.

Pascua, Maria Parker. Ozette: A Makah Village in 1491. *National Geographic,* October 1991, 38–53.

Peckham, Howard H. *Pontiac and the Indian Uprising.* Chicago: University of Chicago Press, 1947.

Peopling the Americas: A New Site to Debate. *National Geographic (Geographica),* September 1992, n.p.

Perdue, Theda. Indians in Southern History. In Frederick E. Hoxie, ed., *Indians in American History: An Introduction.* Arlington Heights, IL: Harlan Davidson, 1988.

Phillips, Kate. *Helen Hunt Jackson: A Literary Life.* Berkeley: University of California Press, 2003.

Phillips, Paul C. *The Fur Trade.* 2 vols. Norman: University of Oklahoma Press, 1961.

Philp, Kenneth R. *John Collier's Crusade for Indian Reform, 1920–1954.* Tucson: University of Arizona Press, 1977.

Pitulko, V. V., P. A. Nikolsky, A. Yu. Girya, A. E. Basilyan, V. E. Tumskoy, S. A. Koulakov, S. N. Astakhov, E. Yu. Pavlova, and M. A. Anisimov. The Yana RHS Site: Humans in the Arctic Before the Last Glacial Maximum. *Science* 303(January 2, 2004):52–56.

Pohl, Frederick Julius. *The Viking Settlements of North America.* New York: Potter, 1972.

Pohl, Mary E. D., Kevin O. Pope, and Christopher von Nagy. Olmec Origins of Mesoamerican Writing. *Science* 298(December 6, 2002):1984–1987.

Pomerantz, Gary. Atlanta Fan's Headdress Ruffles Indian Feathers. *Atlanta Journal-Constitution,* October 21, 1995. Available at http://www.fastball.com/braves/archives/stories/1995/66ws1021.html.

Porter, C. Fayne. *Our Indian Heritage: Profiles of Twelve Great Leaders.* Philadelphia: Chilton, 1964.

Porter, Joy. *To Be Indian: The Life of Iroquois-Seneca Arthur Caswell Parker.* Norman: University of Oklahoma Press, 2001.

Porterfield, Kay Marie. Ten Lies about Indigenous Science—How to Talk Back. October 10, 2002. Available at http://www.kporterfield.com/aicttw/articles/lies.html.

Powers, William K. *Indians of the Northern Plains.* New York: Capricorn Books, 1973.

Pratt, William Henry. *Battlefield and Classroom: Four Decades with the American Indian, 1867–1904.* Edited by Robert M. Utley. Lincoln: University of Nebraska Press, 1987.

Proceedings of the Commissioners Appointed by the Continental Congress to Negotiate a Treaty with the Six Nations, 1775. Papers of the Continental Congress, 1774–89, National Archives (M247, Roll 144, Item No. 134). See Treaty Council at German Flats, New York, August 15, 1775, unpaginated.

Prucha, Francis P. *Documents of United States Indian Policy.* Lincoln: University of Nebraska Press, 1975.

Radell, Davis R. The Indian Slave Trade and Population of Nicaragua During the Sixteenth Century. In William E. Denevan, ed., *The Native Population of the Americas.* Madison: University of Wisconsin Press, 1976: 67–76.

Ramenofsky, Ann F. *Vectors of Death: The Archeology of European Contact.* Albuquerque: University of New Mexico Press, 1987.

Randolph, Eleanor. New York's Native American Casino Contributes, But Not to Tax Rolls. *New York Times,* October 18, 2003, n.p.

Reaman, G. Elmore. *The Trail of the Iroquois Indians: How the Iroquois Nation Saved Canada for the British Empire.* London: Frederick Muller, 1967.

Recer, Paul. Researchers Find Evidence of Sophisticated, Pre-Columbian Civilization in the Amazon Basin. Associated Press, September 19, 2003, in LEXIS.

Recer, Paul. Evidence Found of Arctic Hunters Living in Siberia Near New World 30,000 Years Ago. Associated Press, January 2, 2004, in LEXIS.

Recinos, Adrian, and Delia Goetz, trans. *The Annals of the Cakchiquels.* Norman: University of Oklahoma Press, 1953.

Reilly, Bob, Hugh Reilly, and Pegeen Reilly. *Historic Omaha: An Illustrated History of Omaha and Douglas County.* San Antonio, TX: Historical Publishing Network, 2003.

Reilly, Hugh. Treatment of Native Americans by the Frontier Press: An Omaha, Nebraska Study, 1868–1891. Masters thesis, University of Nebraska at Omaha, 1997.

Resek, Carl. *Lewis Henry Morgan: American Scholar.* Chicago: University of Chicago Press, 1960.

Restall, Matthew. *Seven Myths of the Spanish Conquest.* New York: Oxford University Press, 2004.

Reyhner, Jon, ed. *Teaching Indigenous Languages.* Flagstaff: Center for Excellence in Education, Northern Arizona University, 1997.

Reyhner, Jon, Gina Cantoni, Robert N. St. Clair, and Evangeline Parsons Yazzie. *Revitalizing Native Languages.* Flagstaff: Center for Excellence in Education, Northern Arizona University, 1999.

Reynolds, Jerry. Bush Administration Likely Behind Cobell Appropriations Rider. *Indian Country Today,* November 1, 2003. Available at http://www.indiancountry.com/?1067709828.

Rice, Julian. *Black Elk's Story.* Albuquerque: New Mexico University Press, 1991.

Richter, Daniel K. *The Ordeal of the Longhouse: The Peoples of the Iroquois League in the Era of European Colonization.* Chapel Hill: University of North Carolina Press, 1992.

Rider, Sidney S. *The Lands of Rhode Island as They Were Known to Caunonicus and Miantunnomu When Roger Williams Came in 1636.* Providence, RI: Sidney S. Rider, 1904.

Roberts, David. Geronimo. *National Geographic,* October 1992, 46–71.

Roe, Frank Gilbert. *The Indian and the Horse.* Norman: University of Oklahoma Press, 1955.

Rogers, Robert. *Concise Account of North America.* New Haven, CT: Johnson Reprint, [1765] 1966.

Rogin, Michael Paul. *Fathers and Children: Andrew Jackson and the Subjugation of the American Indian.* New York: Alfred A. Knopf, 1975.

Rosenberg, Bruce A. *Custer and the Epic of Defeat.* University Park: Pennsylvania State University Press, 1974.

Rosenstiel, Annette. *Red and White: Indian Views of the White Man, 1492–1982*. New York: Universe Books, 1983.

Rostkowski, Joelle. The Redman's Appeal for Justice: Deskaheh and the League of Nations. In Christian F. Feest, ed., *Indians and Europe*. Aachen, Germany: Edition Herodot, 1987.

Royal Commission on Aboriginal Peoples. Vol. 1, chapter 10. No date. Available at http://www.prsp.bc.ca/vol1ch10_files/Vol1%20Ch10.rtf. Accessed February 25, 2003.

Roys, Ralph L. *The Book of Chilam Balam of Chumayel*. Norman: University of Oklahoma Press, 1967.

Rozema, Vicki, ed. *Voices from the Trail of Tears*. Winston-Salem, NC: John F. Blair, 2003.

Ruby, Robert H., and John A Brown. *Indian Slavery in the Pacific Northwest*. Spokane, WA: Arthur H. Clark, 1993.

Russell, Don. *The Lives and Legends of Buffalo Bill*. Norman: University of Oklahoma Press, 1960.

Sahagún, Bernardino de. *General History of the Things of New Spain: Florentine Codex*. Translated by A. J. O. Anderson and C. E. Dibble. Salt Lake City: University of Utah Press, and Santa Fe, NM: School of American Research, 1950.

Sahagún, Bernardino de. *Historia General de las Cosas de Nueva Espana*. 4 vols. Edited and translated by Angel Maria Garibay. Mexico, D.F.: Porrua, [ca. 1555] 1956.

Sahagún, Bernardino de. *Historia de las Cosas de la Nueva Espana*. 1905–1907. Cited in Portilla, 1992.

Sahagún, Fray Bernardino de. In Arthur J. O. Anderson and Charles E. Dibble, eds. *Florentine Codex: General History of the Things of New Spain*. 12 vols. Salt Lake City: University of Utah Press: 1950–1982.

Sando, Joe S. *The Pueblo Indians*. San Francisco: Indian Historian Press, 1976.

Sandoz, Mari. *Crazy Horse: Strange Man of the Oglalas*. New York: Alfred A. Knopf, 1942.

Satz, Ronald N. *American Indian Policy in the Jacksonian Era*. Lincoln: University of Nebraska Press, 1975.

Saum, Lewis. *The Fur Trader and the Indian*. Seattle: University of Washington Press, 1965.

Schele, Linda. The Owl, Shield, and Flint Blade. *Natural History*, November, 1991, 7–11.

Schmitt, Martin F., and Dee Brown. *Fighting Indians of the West*. New York: Ballantine Books, 1948.

Scholars Rewrite Mayan History after Hieroglyphics Found. *Omaha World-Herald*, September 20, 2002, 12-A.

Segal, Charles M., and Stineback, David C. *Puritans, Indians, and Manifest Destiny*. New York: Putnam, 1977.

Sell, Henry B., and Victor Weybright. *Buffalo Bill and the Wild West*. New York: Oxford University Press, 1955.

Selsam, Millicent. *Plants that Heal*. New York: William Morrow, 1959.

Seminole Tribe of Florida v. Butterworth. 658 F. 2d 310 (5th Cir., 1980).

Seymour, Flora W. *Sacajawea: American Pathfinder*. New York: Macmillan, 1991.

Sherzer, Joel. A Richness of Voices. In Alvin Josephy, ed., *America in 1492: The World of the Indian Peoples Before the Arrival of Columbus*. New York: Knopf, 1992.

Siegel, Beatrice. *Fur Trappers and Traders*. New York: Walker, 1981.

Slayman, Andrew L. A Battle Over Bones. *Archaeology* 50:1 (January/February 1997):16–23.

Slotkin, Richard, and James K. Folsom, eds. *So Dreadful a Judgement: Puritan Responses to King Philip's War 1676–1677*. Middleton, CT: Wesleyan University Press, 1978.

Smith, Dean Howard. *Modern Tribal Development: Paths to Self-Sufficiency and Cultural Integrity in Indian Country*. Walnut Creek, CA: AltaMira Press, 2000.

Smith, Henry A. Early Reminiscences. Number Ten. Scraps from a Diary. Chief Seattle—A Gentleman by Instinct—His Native Eloquence, etc., etc. *Seattle Star*, October 29, 1887, n.p.

Smith, Jean Edward. *John Marshall: Definer of a Nation*. New York: Henry Holt, 1996.

Smith, Michael E. The Aztec Migrations of the Nahuatl Chronicles: Myth or History? *Ethnohistory* 31:3(1984):153–186.

Smyth, Albert H., ed. *The Writings of Benjamin Franklin*. Vol. 3. New York: Macmillan, 1905–1907.

Snake, Reuben. Personal communication to Bruce E. Johansen, in Seattle, October 12, 1991.

Snell, William Robert. Indian Slavery in Colonial South Carolina, 1671–1795. Ph.D. dissertation, University of Alabama, Tuscaloosa, 1972.

Snow, Dean. *The Iroquois*. London: Blackwell, 1994.

Snow, Dean. The First Americans and the Differentiation of Hunter-Gatherer Cultures. In Bruce G. Trigger and Wilcomb E. Washburn, eds. *The Cambridge History of the Native Peoples of the Americas*. Cambridge, England: Cambridge University Press, 1996: 125–199.

Snow, Dean R., and Kim M. Lanphear. European Contact and Indian Depopulation in the Northeast: The Timing of the First Epidemics. *Ethnohistory* 35:1(Winter 1988):16–24.

Snow, Dean R., and Kim M. Lanphear. "More Methodological Perspectives:" A Rejoinder to Dobyns. *Ethnohistory* 36:3(Summer 1989):299–300.

Soustelle, Jacques. *Daily Life of the Aztecs on the Eve of the Spanish Conquest*. Translated by Patrick O'Brian. Palo Alto, CA: Stanford University Press, 1961.

Spicer, Edward H. *Cycles of Conquest*. Tucson: University of Arizona Press, 1962.

Spindel, Carol. *Dancing at Halftime: Sports and the Controversy over American Indian Mascots*. New York: New York University Press, 2001.

Stannard, David E. *American Holocaust: The Conquest of the New World*. New York: Oxford University Press, 1992.

Stanton, Elizabeth Cady. The Matriarchate or Mother-Age [address before the National Council of Women, February, 1891]. *The National Bulletin* 1:5(February 1891):1–7.

Stevens, William K. Andean Culture Found to be as Old as the Great Pyramids. *New York Times*, October 3, 1989, C-1.

Stokstad, Erik. Oldest New World Writing Suggests Olmec Innovation. *Science* 298 (December 6, 2002):1872–1874.

Stokstad, Erik. Amazon Archaeology: "Pristine" Forest Teemed With People. *Science* 301(September 19, 2003):1645–1646.

Stone, Richard. Late Date for Siberian Site Challenges Bering Pathway. *Science* 301 (July 25, 2003):450–451.

Stone, Richard. A Surprising Survival Story in the Siberian Arctic. *Science* 303(January 2, 2004):33.

Straus, Oscar S. *Roger Williams: Pioneer of Religious Liberty*. New York: Century, 1894.

Stuart, George E. Riddle of the Glyphs. *National Geographic*, December 1975, 768–791.

Stuart, George E. Etowah: A Southeast Village in 1491. *National Geographic*, October 1991, 54–67.

Stuart, George E. Mural Masterpieces of Ancient Cacaxtla. *National Geographic*, September 1992, 120–136.

Stubben, Jerry. Iowa State University. Personal communication, October 30, 2002.

Substance of the Speech of Good Peter to Governor Clinton and the Commissioners of Indian Affairs at Albany. *Collections of the New York Historical Society, 1st Series* 2:(1814):115.

Suzuki, Peter T. Housing on the Nebraska Indian Reservations: Federal Policies and Practices. *Habitat International* 15:4(1991):27–32.

Swan, Bradford F. New Light on Roger Williams and the Indians. *Providence Sunday Journal Magazine*, November 23, 1969, 14.

Swanton, J. R. The Social Significance of the Creek Confederacy. *Proceedings of the International Congress of Americanists* 19:(1915):327–334.

Talbot, Steve. *Contemporary Indian Nations of North America: An Indigenist Perspective.* New York: Prentice-Hall, 2004.

Tebbel, John, and Keith Jennison. *The American Indian Wars.* New York: Bonanza Books, 1960.

Tehanetorens [Ray Fadden]. *Tales of the Iroquois.* Rooseveltown, NY: *Akwesasne Notes,* 1976.

Tehanetorens [Ray Fadden]. *Basic Call to Consciousness.* Rooseveltown, NY: *Akwesasne Notes,* 1986.

Tehanetorens [Ray Fadden]. *Wampum Belts.* Onchiota, NY: Six Nations Museum, n.d.

Thomas, David Hurst. *Skull Wars: Kennewick Man, Archaeology, and the Battle for Native American Identity.* New York: Basic Books/Peter N. Nevraumont, 2000.

Thornton, Russell. Cherokee Population Losses during the Trail of Tears: A New Perspective and a New Estimate. *Ethnohistory* 31(1984):4.

Thorpe, James, and Thomas F. Collinson. *Jim Thorpe's History of the Olympics.* Los Angeles: Wetzel Publishing Co., 1932.

Thwaites, Reuben Gold. *The Original Journals of Lewis and Clark.* New York: Dodd, Mead & Co., 1904–1905.

Tibbles, Thomas Henry. *The Ponca Chiefs: An Account of the Trial of Standing Bear* (1880) Edited by Kay Graber. Lincoln: University of Nebraska Press, 1972.

Tocqueville, Alexis de. *Democracy in America.* Translated by Henry Reeve. New York: Century, 1898.

Todd, Douglas. Natives' Abuse Suits Creating a Dilemma. *Vancouver Sun*, December 15, 1998, A-1.

Townsend, Camilla. Burying the White Gods: New Perspectives on the Conquest of Mexico. *American Historical Review* 108(June 2003):659–687.

Trelease, Allen W. *Indian Affairs in Colonial New York: The Seventeenth Century.* Ithaca, NY: Cornell University Press, 1960.

Trigger, Bruce G. *Children of the Aataentsic: A History of the Huron People.* Montreal: McGill-Queen's University Press, 1976.

Tucker, Glenn. *Tecumseh: Vision of Glory.* Indianapolis: Bobbs-Merrill, 1956.

Turtle Island Native Network. British Columbia Residential School Project. No date. Available at http://www.turtleisland.org/healing/infopack1a.htm.

Young, Calvin M. *Little Turtle.* Fort Wayne, IN: Public Library of Fort Wayne and Allen County, 1956.

U.S. Commission on Civil Rights, Report of Investigation: Oglala Sioux Tribe, General Election, 1974. Mimeograph. Washington, DC: Civil Rights Commission, October 1974.

U.S. Department of Health and Human Services. *Trends in Indian Health*. Washington, DC: U.S. Government Printing Office, 1991.

United States v. Washington 384 F. Supp. 312 (1974).

Utley, Robert. *The Lance and the Shield: The Life and Times of Sitting Bull*. New York: Henry Holt, 1993.

Vanderwerth, W. C., ed. *Indian Oratory: Famous Speeches by Noted Indian Chieftains*. Norman: University of Oklahoma Press, 1971.

Van Doren, Carl, and Julian P. Boyd, eds. *Indian Treaties Printed by Benjamin Franklin 1736–1762*. Philadelphia: Historical Society of Pennsylvania, 1938.

Van Every, Dale. *Disinherited: The Lost Birthright of the American Indian*. New York: William Morrow, 1966.

Van Kirk, Sylvia. *Many Tender Ties: Women in Fur Trade Society, 1670–1870*. Norman: University of Oklahoma Press, 1983.

Vaughan, Alden T. *New England Frontier: Puritans and Indians, 1620–1675*. Boston: Little, Brown, 1965.

Vestal, Stanley. *Sitting Bull: Champion of the Sioux*. Norman: University of Oklahoma Press, [1932] 1957.

Virtual Truth Commission. Telling the Truth for a Better America; Reports by Name: Col. John M. Chivington. June 22, 1998. Available at www.geocities.com/~virtual-truth/chiving.htm. Accessed February 24, 2003.

Wagner, Sally Roesch. The Iroquois Confederacy: A Native American Model for Non-sexist Men. *Changing Men* (Spring–Summer 1988):32–33.

Wagner, Sally Roesch. The Root of Oppression Is the Loss of Memory: The Iroquois and the Early Feminist Vision, *Akwesasne Notes*, Late Winter, 1989, 11.

Waldman, Carl. *Who Was Who in Native American History*. New York: Facts on File, 1990.

Walke, Roger. Gambling on Indian Reservations: Updated October 17, 1988. Washington, DC: Congressional Research Service, Library of Congress.

Walker, Carson. Man Is Arrested in Activist's Death. Associated Press item in IndigenousNewsNetwork@topica.com, e-mail newsletter, April 2, 2003.

Walker, James R. *Lakota Society*. Edited by Raymond J. DeMallie. Lincoln: University of Nebraska Press, 1982.

Wallace, Anthony F. C. *The Death and Rebirth of the Seneca*. New York: Random House, 1969.

Wallace, Paul A. W. Captivity and Murder. In Paul A. W. Wallace, ed. *Thirty Thousand Miles with John Heckewelder*. Pittsburgh: University of Pittsburgh Press, 1958: 170–207.

Wallace, Paul A. W. *The White Roots of Peace*. Santa Fe, N.M.: Clear Light Publishers, 1994. (Originally published in 1946 by University of Pennsylvania Press)

Walton, Marsha, and Michael Coren. Archaeologists Put Humans in North America 50,000 Years Ago. Cable News Network, November 17, 2004. Available at http://www.cnn.com/2004/TECH/science/11/17/carolina.dig/index.html.

Wampum Chronicles message board. No date. Available at http://publ1.ezboard.com/fwampumchroniclescurrentevents.showMessage?topicID=265.topic.

Wanamaker, Tom. Indian Gaming Column. *Indian Country Today*, April 5, 2002, n.p., in LEXIS.

Wanamaker, Tom. Debunking the Myth of Unregulated Indian Gaming. *Indian Country Today*, May 13, 2002, n.p., in LEXIS.

Washburn, Wilcomb E., ed. *The American Indian and the United States: A Documentary History.* New York: Random House, 1973.

Washburn, Wilcomb E. *The Assault on Indian Tribalism: The General Allotment Law (Dawes Act) of 1887.* Philadelphia: Lippincott, 1975.

Waters, Frank. *Brave Are My People: Indian Heroes Not Forgotten.* Santa Fe, NM: Clear Light, 1993.

Weatherford, Jack. *Indian Givers: How the Indians of the Americas Transformed the World.* New York: Fawcett Columbine, 1988.

Weatherford, Jack. *Native Roots: How the Indians Enriched America.* New York: Crown, 1991.

Webster, David. *The Fall of the Ancient Maya.* London: Thames and Hudson, 2002.

Weeks, Philip. *Farewell, My Nation: The American Indian and the United States, 1820–1890.* Arlington Heights, IL: Harlan Davidson, 1990.

Weinberg, Bill. Land and Sovereignty in Hawai'i: A Native Nation Re-emerges. *Native Americas* 13:2(Summer 1996):30–41.

Weir, David, and Lowell Bergman. The Killing of Anna Mae Aquash. *Rolling Stone*, April 7, 1977, 51–55.

Weisman, Joel. About That "Ambush" at Wounded Knee. *Columbia Journalism Review*, September/October 1975, 28–51.

Wheaton, Henry. *Elements of International Law.* Boston: Dana, 1866.

Wilson, James. *The Earth Shall Weep: A History of Native America.* Boston: Atlantic Monthly Press, 1998.

Wissler, Clark. The Influence of the Horse in the Development of Plains Culture. *American Anthropologist* 16(1914):1–25.

White, Richard. The Winning of the West: The Expansion of the Western Sioux in the Eighteenth and Nineteenth Centuries, *Journal of American History* 65:2(1978):319–343.

White Roots of Peace. *The Great Law of Peace of the Longhouse People.* Rooseveltown, NY: White Roots of Peace, 1971.

Wilford, John Noble. Did Warfare Doom the Mayas' Ecology? *New York Times* in *Miami Herald*, December 22, 1991, 7-L.

Wilkerson, Jeffery K. Following the Route of Cortes. *National Geographic*, October 1984, 420–459.

Wilkinson, Charles F. *American Indians, Time, and the Law: Native Societies in a Modern Constitutional Democracy.* New Haven, CT: Yale University Press, 1987.

William Penn to the Society of Free Traders, August 16, 1683. In Richard S. and Mary M. Dunn, eds., *The Papers of William Penn.* Vol. 2. Philadelphia: University of Pennsylvania Press, 1982.

Williams, Richard B. The True Story of Thanksgiving. November 19, 2002. Available at IndigenousNewsNetwork@topica.com.

Williams, Roger. *A Key into the Languages of America.* Providence, RI: Tercentenary Committee, [1643] 1936.

Williams, Roger. *The Complete Writings of Roger Williams.* Vol. 1. New York: Russell and Russell, 1963.

Williams, Stephen. *Fantastic Archaeology: The Wild Side of North American Prehistory.* Philadelphia: University of Pennsylvania Press, 1991.

Wilson, Edmund. *Apologies to the Iroquois.* New York: Farrar, Strauss, and Cudahy, 1960.

Wilson, Terry P. *The Underground Reservation: Osage Oil.* Lincoln: University of Nebraska Press, 1985.

Winslow, Elizabeth Ola. *Master Roger Williams*. New York: Macmillan, 1957.

Wishart, David J. *The Fur Trade and the American West, 1807–1840*. Lincoln: University of Nebraska Press, 1979.

Wishart, David J. *An Unspeakable Sadness: The Dispossession of the Nebraska Indians*. Lincoln: University of Nebraska Press, 1994.

Wollock, Jeffrey. On the Wings of History: American Indians in the 20th Century. *Native Americas* 20:1(Spring 2003):14–31.

Wood, Gordon S. *The Creation of the American Republic*. Chapel Hill: University of North Carolina, 1969.

Wood, H. Clay. *The Status of Young Joseph and His Band of Nez Perce Indians*. Portland, OR: Assistant Adjutant General's Office, Department of the Columbia, 1876.

Wood, William. *New England's Prospect*. Amherst: University of Massachusetts Press, 1977.

Woodbury, Hanni, Reg Henry, and Harry Webster, comps. *Concerning the League: The Iroquois League Tradition as Dictated in Onondaga by John Arthur Gibson*. Algonquian and Iroquoian Linguistics Memoir No. 9. Winnipeg, Manitoba, Canada: University of Manitoba Press, 1992.

Worcester, Donald, ed. *Forked Tongues and Broken Treaties*. Caldwell, ID: Caxton, 1975.

Worcester v. Georgia 31 U.S. (6 Pet.) 515(1832).

Wright, Ronald. *Stolen Continents: The Americas through Indian Eyes since 1492*. Boston: Houghton-Mifflin, 1992.

Zorita, Alonso de. *Life and Labor in Ancient Mexico*. Translated by Benjamin Keen. New Brunswick, NJ: Rutgers University Press, 1963.

Index